Concrete Abstractions

Concrete Abstractions
An Introduction to Computer Science Using Scheme

Max Hailperin
Gustavus Adolphus College

Barbara Kaiser
Gustavus Adolphus College

Karl Knight
Gustavus Adolphus College

An Imprint of Brooks/Cole Publishing Company

I(T)P® An International Thomson Publishing Company

Pacific Grove • Albany • Belmont • Bonn • Boston • Cincinnati • Detroit
Johannesburg • London • Madrid • Melbourne • Mexico City • New York
Paris • Singapore • Tokyo • Toronto • Washington

Sponsoring Editor: *Suzanne Jeans*
Marketing Team: *Nathan Wilbur, Michele Mootz*
Editorial Assistant: *Kathryn Schooling*
Production Manager: *Marlene Thom*
Manuscript Editor: *Linda Thompson*
Interior Design: *Merry Obrecht Sawdey*

Cover Design: *Vernon T. Boes*
Cover Photo: *Craig Cowan. Courtesy of Couturier Gallery, Los Angeles, CA*
Project Management and Typesetting: *Integre Technical Publishing Co., Inc.*
Printing and Binding: *Webcom, Ltd.*

For more information, contact:

BROOKS/COLE PUBLISHING COMPANY
511 Forest Lodge Road
Pacific Grove, CA 93950
USA

International Thomson Publishing Europe
Berkshire House 168–173
High Holborn
London WC1V 7AA
England

Thomas Nelson Australia
102 Dodds Street
South Melbourne, 3205
Victoria, Australia

Nelson Canada
1120 Birchmount Road
Scarborough, Ontario
Canada M1K 5G4

International Thomson Editores
Seneca 53
Col. Polanco
11560 México, D.F., México

International Thomson Publishing GmbH
Königswinterer Strasse 418
53227 Bonn
Germany

International Thomson Publishing Asia
221 Henderson Road
#05–10 Henderson Building
Singapore 0315

International Thomson Publishing Japan
Hirakawacho Kyowa Building, 3F
2-2-1 Hirakawacho
Chiyoda-ku, Tokyo 102
Japan

Printed in Canada

10 9 8 7 6 5 4 3 2 1

Library of Congress Cataloging in Publication Data
Hailperin, Max.
      Concrete abstractions : an introduction to computer science using
   Scheme / Max Hailperin, Barbara Kaiser, Karl Knight.
         p.   cm.
      ISBN 0-534-95211-9 (alk. paper)
      1. Computer science.   2. Abstract data types (Computer science)
   I. Kaiser, Barbara (Barbara K.).   II. Knight, Karl (Karl
   W.).   III. Title.
   QA76.H296   1997
   005.13′3—dc21   98-34080
                                              CIP

Contents

Preface   ix

PART I   Procedural Abstraction

CHAPTER 1
Computer Science and Programming   3

   1.1   What's It All About? / 3
       Sidebar: Responsible Computer Use / 5
   1.2   Programming in Scheme / 5
   1.3   An Application: Quilting / 15

CHAPTER 2
Recursion and Induction   22

   2.1   Recursion / 22
       Sidebar: Exponents / 28
   2.2   Induction / 28
   2.3   Further Examples / 34
   2.4   An Application: Custom-Sized Quilts / 40

CHAPTER 3
Iteration and Invariants   48

   3.1   Iteration / 48
   3.2   Using Invariants / 54
   3.3   Perfect Numbers, Internal Definitions, and Let / 58
   3.4   Iterative Improvement: Approximating the Golden Ratio / 61
   3.5   An Application: The Josephus Problem / 65

CHAPTER 4
Orders of Growth and Tree Recursion 75

4.1 Orders of Growth / 75
   Sidebar: Selection Sort / 77
   Sidebar: Merge Sort / 78
   Sidebar: Merging / 79
   Sidebar: Logarithms / 82
4.2 Tree Recursion and Digital Signatures / 83
   Sidebar: Modular Arithmetic / 87
4.3 An Application: Fractal Curves / 95

CHAPTER 5
Higher-Order Procedures 109

5.1 Procedural Parameters / 109
5.2 Uncomputability / 113
   Sidebar: Alan Turing / 116
5.3 Procedures That Make Procedures / 118
5.4 An Application: Verifying ID Numbers / 120

PART II Data Abstraction

CHAPTER 6
Compound Data and Data Abstraction 133

6.1 Introduction / 133
6.2 Nim / 135
6.3 Representations and Implementations / 143
   Sidebar: Nim Program / 144
   Sidebar: Game State ADT Implementation / 152
6.4 Three-Pile Nim / 153
6.5 An Application: Adding Strategies to Nim / 156
   Sidebar: Type Checking / 157

CHAPTER 7
Lists 167

7.1 The Definition of a List / 167
7.2 Constructing Lists / 169
7.3 Basic List Processing Techniques / 172
7.4 List Processing and Iteration / 179
7.5 Tree Recursion and Lists / 182

7.6   An Application: A Movie Query System / 187
Sidebar: Is There More to Intelligence Than the Appearance of Intelligence? / 202

CHAPTER 8
Trees   212

8.1   Binary Search Trees / 212
8.2   Efficiency Issues with Binary Search Trees / 220
Sidebar: Privacy Issues / 225
8.3   Expression Trees / 226
8.4   An Application: Automated Phone Books / 229

CHAPTER 9
Generic Operations   243

9.1   Introduction / 243
9.2   Multiple Representations / 244
9.3   Exploiting Commonality / 253
9.4   An Application: Computer Graphics / 262

CHAPTER 10
Implementing Programming Languages   278

10.1   Introduction / 278
10.2   Syntax / 279
Sidebar: The Expressiveness of EBNF / 285
10.3   Micro-Scheme / 289
10.4   Global Definitions: Mini-Scheme / 303
10.5   An Application: Adding Explanatory Output / 311

PART III   Abstractions of State

CHAPTER 11
Computers with Memory   333

11.1   Introduction / 333
11.2   An Example Computer Architecture / 333
11.3   Programming the SLIM / 340
Sidebar: What Can Be Stored in a Location? / 342
Sidebar: SLIM's Instruction Set / 348
11.4   Iteration in Assembly Language / 349
11.5   Recursion in Assembly Language / 357
11.6   Memory in Scheme: Vectors / 361
11.7   An Application: A Simulator for SLIM / 367

CHAPTER 12
Dynamic Programming 379

12.1 Introduction / 379
12.2 Revisiting Tree Recursion / 380
12.3 Memoization / 388
12.4 Dynamic Programming / 398
12.5 Comparing Memoization and Dynamic Programming / 406
12.6 An Application: Formatting Paragraphs / 406

CHAPTER 13
Object-based Abstractions 420

13.1 Introduction / 420
13.2 Arithmetic Expressions Revisited / 421
13.3 RA-Stack Implementations and Representation Invariants / 432
    Sidebar: Strings and Characters / 433
13.4 Queues / 446
13.5 Binary Search Trees Revisited / 453
13.6 Dictionaries / 472

CHAPTER 14
Object-oriented Programming 486

14.1 Introduction / 486
14.2 An Object-oriented Program / 487
14.3 Extensions and Variations / 511
14.4 Implementing an Object-oriented Prog. System / 517
14.5 An Application: Adventures in the Land of Gack / 543

CHAPTER 15
Java, Applets, and Concurrency 577

15.1 Introduction / 577
15.2 Java / 578
15.3 Event-Driven Graphical User Interfaces in Applets / 599
15.4 Concurrency / 616
    Sidebar: Nested Calls to Synchronized Methods and Deadlock / 625
15.5 An Application: Simulating Compound Interest / 632

APPENDIX Nonstandard Extensions to Scheme 645

Bibliography 649

Index 653

Preface

At first glance, the title of this book is an oxymoron. After all, the term *abstraction* refers to an idea or general description, divorced from physical objects. On the other hand, something is concrete when it is a particular object, perhaps something that you can manipulate with your hands and look at with your eyes. Yet you often deal with concrete abstractions. Consider, for example, a word processor. When you use a word processor, you probably think that you have really entered a document into the computer and that the computer is a machine which physically manipulates the words in the document. But in actuality, when you "enter" the document, there is nothing new inside the computer—there are just different patterns of activity of electrical charges bouncing back and forth. Moreover, when the word processor "manipulates" the words in the document, those manipulations are really just more patterns of electrical activity. Even the program that you call a "word processor" is an abstraction—it's the way we humans choose to talk about what is, in reality, yet more electrical charges. Still, although these abstractions such as "word processors" and "documents" are merely convenient ways of describing patterns of electrical activity, they are also *things* that we can buy, sell, copy, and use.

As you read through this book, we will introduce several abstract ideas in as concrete a way as possible. As you become familiar and comfortable with these ideas, you will begin to think of the abstractions as actual concrete objects. Having already gone through this process ourselves, we've chosen to call computer science "the discipline of concrete abstractions"; if that seems too peculiar to fathom, we invite you to read the book and then reconsider the notion.

This book is divided into three parts, dealing with procedural abstractions, data abstractions, and abstractions of state. A *procedure* is a way of abstracting what's called a computational process. Roughly speaking, a process is a dynamic succession of events—a happening. When your computer is busy doing something, a process is going on inside it. When we call a process a *computational* process, we mean that we are ignoring the physical nature of the process and instead focusing on the information content. For example, consider the problem of conveying some information to a bunch of other people. If you think about writing the message on paper airplanes and tossing it at the other people, and find yourself considering whether the airplanes have enough lift to fly far enough, then you are considering a mechanical process rather than a computational one. Similarly, if you think about using the phone, and find yourself worrying about the current carrying capacity of the copper wire, you are considering an electrical process rather than a computational one. On the other hand, if you find yourself considering the alternative of sending your message (whether by phone or paper airplane) to two people, each of whom send it to two more, each of whom send it to two more, and so forth, rather than directly sending the message to all the recipients, then you are thinking about a computational process.

What do computer scientists do with processes? First of all, they write descriptions of them. Such descriptions are often written in a particular programming language and are called procedures. These procedures can then be used to make the processes happen. Procedures can also be analyzed to see if they have been correctly written or to predict how long the corresponding processes will take. This analysis can then be used to improve the performance or accuracy of the procedures.

In the second part of the book, we look at various types of data. *Data* is the information processed by computational processes, not only the externally visible information, but also the internal information structures used within the processes. First, we explore exactly what we mean by the term data, concentrating on how we use data and what we can do with it. Then we consider various ways of gluing small pieces of atomic data (such as words) into larger, compound pieces of data (such as sentences). Because of our computational viewpoint, we write procedures to manipulate our data, and so we analyze how the structure of the data affects the processes that manipulate it. We describe some common data structures that are used in the discipline, and show how to allow disparate structures to be operated on uniformly in a mix-and-match fashion. We end this part of the book by looking at programs in a programming language as data structures. That way, carrying out the computational processes that a program describes is itself a process operating on a data structure, namely the program.

We start the third part of the book by looking at computational processes from the perspective of the computer performing the computation. This shows how procedurally described computations actually come to life, and it also naturally calls attention to the computer's memory, and hence to the main topic of this part, state. *State* is anything that can be changed by one part of a computation in order to have an effect on a later part of the computation. We show several important uses for state: making processes model real-world phenomena more naturally, making processes that are more efficient than without state, and making certain programs divide into modules focused on separate concerns more cleanly. We combine the new material on state with the prior material on procedural and data abstraction to present *object-oriented programming,* an approach to constructing highly modular programs with state. Finally, we use the objects' state to mediate interactions between concurrently active subprocesses.

In summary, this book is designed to introduce you to how computer scientists think and work. We assume that as a reader, you become actively involved in reading and that you like to play with things. We have provided a variety of activities that involve hands-on manipulation of concrete objects such as paper chains, numbered cards, and chocolate candy bars. The many programming exercises encourage you to experiment with the procedures and data structures we describe. And we have posed a number of problems that allow you to play with the abstract ideas we introduce.

Our major emphasis is on *how* computer scientists think, as opposed to *what* they think about. Our applications and examples are chosen to illustrate various problem-solving strategies, to introduce some of the major themes in the discipline, and to give you a good feel for the subject. We use sidebars to expand on various topics in computer science, to give some historical background, and to describe some of the ethical issues that arise.

Audience

This book is primarily intended as the text for a first (and possibly only) undergraduate course in computer science. We believe that every college student should have a trial experience of what it's like to think abstractly, the way mathematicians and computer scientists think. We hope that the tangible nature of the computer scientist's abstractions will attract some of the students who choose to avoid math courses. Because of this, we don't require that our readers have taken a college-level math course. On the other hand, mathematics is used in computer science in much the same way it is used in biology, chemistry, and physics. Thus we do assume that our readers have a knowledge of high school algebra.

Although we've tried to reach a broad audience, this is *not* a watered-down text unsuitable for serious students planning to major in computer science. We reject the notion than an introduction for majors should be different from an introduction for non-majors. Beyond the obvious difficulty that most students will not have any reasonable basis for categorizing themselves without having taken even a single course, we feel strongly that the most important need of a prospective major is the same as that of a non-major: a representative trial experience of what it is like to think the computer science way. Those who part company with us after this book will have an appreciation for what we do; those who stay with us will know what lies ahead for them.

Like most introductory college-level books, we make some assumptions about the readers' backgrounds. As we have said before, we assume that the readers understand the material that is typically taught in a high school algebra course. We also make some assumptions about the readers' attitudes towards mathematics; in short, they should be willing to use mathematics as a tool for analyzing and solving problems. We occasionally use some mathematical tools that aren't typically taught in high school. When we do this, we present the relevant material in the text and the students need to be willing to learn this material on the fly.

Similarly, we also assume that our readers may not have had much computing or programming experience, beyond playing an occasional computer game or using a word processor. However, we do not describe how to start a computer, how to use a Scheme programming environment, or similar mechanics. This kind of information varies greatly from machine to machine and is best taught by a person rather than a book. Again, keeping an open mind about learning is probably more important than any prior experience.

Additionally, we assume that students have had some experience in writing. When we teach a course based on this book, we rely heavily on writing assignments. Students are expected to be able to write descriptions of what their procedures do and need to be able to articulate clearly the problems they may have in order to get help in solving them. Most of our students find that their writing skill improves considerably over the semester.

Finally, although we attempt to be reasonably gentle toward those with little prior mathematical or computer programming experience, in our experience even those students who think of themselves as experts find much here that is not only unfamiliar, but also challenging and interesting.

In short: this is an introduction for everyone.

Technical Assumptions

To make full use of this book, you will need access to a computer with an implementation of the Scheme programming language; for the final chapter, you will also need an implementation of the Java™ programming language, version 1.1 or later. Most of our examples should work on essentially any modern Scheme, since we have used constructs identified in the so-called "R⁴RS" standard for Scheme—the *Revised⁴ Report on the Algorithmic Language Scheme*, which is available on the web site for this book, located at http://www.pws.com/compsci/authors/hailperin. The following materials are available:

- all code shown in this text, together with some additional supporting code;
- information on obtaining various Scheme implementations and using them with this text;
- Java applets that provide instructional support, such as simulations;
- manipulatives (i.e., physical materials to experiment with);
- the Scheme language specification;

- bug-reporting forms and author contact information;
- a list of errata; and
- tips for instructors.

One notable exception is that we use graphics, even though there are no graphics operations defined in R⁴RS. Nearly every modern Scheme will have some form of graphics, but the details vary considerably. We have provided "library" files on our web site for each of several popular Scheme systems, so that if you load the library in before you begin work, the graphics operations we presume in this book will be available to you. The nonstandard Scheme features, such as graphics, that we use in the book are explained in the Appendix, as well as being identified where they are first used.

Teaching with This Book

Enough material is here to cover somewhere in the range from two quarters to two semesters, depending on your pace. If you want to cut material to fit a shorter format, the dependencies among the chapters allow for a number of possibilities beyond simply truncating at some point:

- Chapter 10 has only weak ties to the later chapters, so it can be omitted easily.
- Chapter 11 is primarily concerned with computer organization and assembly language programming; however, there is also a section introducing Scheme's vectors. It would be possible to skip the machine-level material and cover just the vectors with only minor adverse impact.
- Chapter 12 can be omitted without serious impact on the later chapters.
- Chapter 13 divides roughly into two halves: elementary data structures (stacks and queues) and an advanced data structure (red-black trees). You can stop after the queues section if you don't want the more advanced material.
- Chapter 14 has a large section on how object-oriented programming is implemented, which can be omitted without loss of continuity.
- You can skip straight from Chapter 7 to the vector material in Chapter 11, provided you stop after the queues section in Chapter 13. (Chapter 8 is crucial for the red-black tree material in Chapter 13, and Chapter 9 is crucial for Chapter 14.)

All exercises, other than those in the separate "review problems" section at the end of each chapter, are an integral part of the text. In many cases skipping over them will cause loss of continuity, or omission of some idea or language feature introduced in the exercise. Thus as a general rule, even when you don't assign the exercises, you should consider them part of the reading.

Acknowledgments

Because the project of writing this book has extended over several years, many extremely helpful people have had the opportunity to give us a hand, and three slightly disorganized people (the authors) have had the opportunity to lose track of a few of them. So, before we get to all the people we managed to keep track of, we'd like to thank and apologize to the anonymous others who have slipped through the cracks. Also, we'd like to make the standard disclaimer: the people listed here deserve much of the credit, but absolutely none of the blame. If nothing else, we chose to ignore some of the good advice they offered.

This text has benefited from repeated class testing by Tim Colburn and Keith Pierce at the University of Minnesota at Duluth, and by Mike Hvidsten, Charley Sheaffer, and David Wolfe at Gustavus Adolphus College.

The ever-patient students at these two institutions also provided many valuable bug reports and suggestions. We'd particularly like to mention Rebekah Bloemker, Kristina Bovee, Gene Boyer, Jr., Brian Choc, Blaine Conklin, Scott Davis, Steve Davis, DeAnn DeLoach, John Engebretson, Lars Ericson, Melissa Evans, Bryan Kaehler, Andrew Kay, Tim Larson, Milo Martin, Jason Molesky, Oskar Norlander, Angela Peck, Ted Rice, Antony Sargent, Robert Shueey, Henrik Thorsell, Mark Tomforde, Dan Vanorny, and Cory Weinrich.

We received lots of valuable feedback from reviewers retained by the publishers. In addition to some who remained anonymous, these include Tim Colburn of the University of Minnesota at Duluth, Timothy Fossum of the University of Wisconsin at Parkside, Chris Haynes of Indiana University, Tim Hickey of Brandeis University, Rhys Price Jones of Oberlin College, Roger Kirchner of Carleton College, Stuart A. Kurtz of the University of Chicago, Keith Pierce of the University of Minnesota at Duluth, and John David Stone of Grinnell College.

Finally, a miscellaneous category of people made helpful suggestions without falling into any of the earlier categories: Hal Abelson and Bob Givan of MIT, Theodore Hailperin, and Carol Mohr.

We would like to extend a great big "Thanks!" to all the above people who contributed directly to the book, and also to the family members and colleagues who contributed indirectly through their support and encouragement.

Finally, we should mention some of the giants on whose shoulders we are standing. We all learned a great deal from Hal Abelson and Gerry Sussman of MIT—one of us as a student of theirs, all of us as students of their textbook [2]. Anyone familiar with their book will see plenty of echos in ours. The most significant new ingredient we added to their recipe is the interplay of proving with programming—which we learned from Bob Floyd and John McCarthy at Stanford.

Max Hailperin
Barbara Kaiser
Karl Knight

Procedural Abstraction

Computer scientists study the processing of information. In this first part of the book, we will focus our attention on specifying the nature of that processing, rather than on the nature of the information being processed. (The latter is the focus of Parts II and III.) For this part of the book, we will look at procedures for processing only a few simple kinds of data, such as numbers and images; in the final chapter of Part I, we will look at procedures for processing other procedures.

We'll examine procedures from several different viewpoints, focusing on the connection between the form of the procedure and the form of the process that results from carrying it out. We'll see how to design procedures so that they have a desired effect and how to prove that they indeed have that effect. We'll see various ways to make procedures generate "expansible" processes that can grow to accommodate arbitrarily large instances of a general problem and see how the form of the procedure and process influences the efficiency of this growth. We'll look at techniques for capturing common processing strategies in general form, for example, by writing procedures that can write any of a family of similar procedures for us.

CHAPTER ONE

Computer Science and Programming

1.1   What's It All About?

Computer science revolves around *computational processes*, which are also called *information processes* or simply *processes*. A process is a dynamic succession of events—a happening. When your computer is busy doing something, a process is going on inside it. What differentiates a computational process from some other kind of process (e.g., a chemical process)? Although computing originally referred to doing arithmetic, that isn't the essence of a computational process: For our purposes, a word, for example, enjoys the same status as a number, and looking up the word in a dictionary is as much a computational process as adding numbers. Nor does the process need to go on inside a computer for it to be a computational process—it could go on in an old-fashioned library, where a patron turns the pages of a dictionary by hand.

What makes the process a computational process is that we study it in ways that ignore its physical nature. If we chose to study how the library patron turns the pages, perhaps by bending them to a certain point and then letting gravity flop them down, we would be looking at a mechanical process rather than a computational one. Here, on the other hand, is a *computational* description of the library patron's actions in looking up *fiduciary*:

1. Because *fiduciary* starts with an *f*, she uses the dictionary's index tabs to locate the *f* section.
2. Next, because the second letter (*i*) is about a third of the way through the alphabet, she opens to a point roughly a third of the way into the *f* section.
3. Finding herself slightly later in the alphabet (*fjord*), she then scans backward in a straightforward way, without any jumping about, until she finds *fiduciary*.

Notice that although there are some apparently physical terms in this description (*index tab* and *section*), the interesting thing about index tabs for the purposes of this process description is not that they are tabs but that they allow one to zoom in on those entries of the dictionary that have a particular initial letter. If the dictionary were stored in a computer, it could still have index tabs in the sense of some structure that allowed this operation, and essentially the same process could be used.

There are lots of questions one can ask about computational processes, such as

1. How do we describe one or specify which one we want carried out?
2. How do we prove that a process has a particular effect?
3. How do we choose a process from among several that achieve the same effect?
4. Are there effects we can't achieve no matter what process we specify?
5. How do we build a machine that automatically carries out a process we've specified?
6. What processes in the natural world are fruitfully analyzed in computational terms?

We'll touch on all these questions in this book, although the level of detail varies from several chapters down to a sentence or two. Our main goal, however, is not so much to answer the questions computer scientists face as to give a feel for the manner in which they formulate and approach those questions.

Because we'll be talking about processes so much, we'll need a notation for describing them. We call our descriptions *programs*, and the notation a *programming language*. For most of this book we'll be using a programming language called *Scheme*. (Two chapters near the end of the book use other programming languages for specialized purposes: assembly language, to illustrate at a detailed level how computers actually carry out computations, and Java, to illustrate how computational processes can interact with other, concurrently active processes.) One advantage of Scheme is that its structure is easy to learn; we will describe its basic structure in Section 1.2. As your understanding of computational processes and the data on which they operate grows, so too will your understanding of how those processes and data can be notated in Scheme.

An added benefit of Scheme (as with most useful programming languages) is that it allows us to make processes happen, because there are machines that can read our notation and carry out the processes they describe. The fact that our descriptions of abstract processes can result in their being concretely realized is a gratifying aspect of computer science and reflects one side of this book's title. It also means that computer science is to some extent an experimental science.

However, computer science is not purely experimental, because we can apply mathematical tools to analyze computational processes. Fundamental to this analysis is a way of modeling these evolving processes; we describe the so-called substitution

> ### ▶ Responsible Computer Use
>
> If you are using a shared computer system, there are some issues you should think about regarding the social acceptability of your behavior.
>
> The most important point to keep in mind is that the feasibility of an action and its acceptability are quite different matters. You may well be technically capable of rummaging through other people's computer files without their approval. However, this act is generally considered to be like going down the street turning doorknobs and going inside if you find one unlocked.
>
> Sometimes you won't know what is acceptable. If you have any doubts about whether a particular course of action is legal, ethical, and socially acceptable, err on the side of caution. Ask a responsible system administrator or faculty member first.

model in Section 1.2. This abstract model of a concrete process reflects another side of the book's title as it bears on the computational process itself.

As was mentioned above, computational processes do not only deal with numbers. The final section of this chapter applies the concepts of this chapter to an example involving building quilt-cover patterns out of more basic images. We will continue this convention of having the last section of each chapter be an application of that chapter's concepts. Following this application section, each chapter concludes with a collection of review problems, an inventory of the material introduced in the chapter, and notes on reference sources.

1.2 Programming in Scheme

The simplest possible Scheme program is a single number. If you ask the Scheme system to process such a program, it will simply return the number to you as its answer. We call what the Scheme system does finding the *value* of the *expression* you provide, or more simply *evaluation*. Exactly how this looks will vary from one version of Scheme to another; in our book, we'll show it as follows, with **dark, upright type** for your input and *light, slanted type* for the computer's output:

```
12
12
```

The first line here was typed by a human, whereas the second line was the computer's response. Other kinds of numbers also work: negative numbers, fractions, and decimals:

```
-7
-7
```

```
1/3
```
1/3

```
3.1415927
```
3.1415927

In Scheme, decimals are used for inexact approximations (as in the above approximation to π), and fractions are used for exact rational numbers.

Other kinds of expressions are less boring to evaluate. For example, the value of a *name* is whatever it is a name for. In a moment we'll see how we can name things ourselves, but there are many names already in place when we start up Scheme. Most are names for *procedures*; for example, the name **sqrt** names a procedure, as does the name **+**. If we evaluate either of them, we'll see a printed representation of the corresponding procedure:

```
sqrt
```
#<procedure>

```
+
```
#<procedure>

The appearance of procedures varies from one version of Scheme to another; in this book, we'll show them as **#<procedure>**, but you may see something different on your computer. However, this difference generally doesn't matter because procedures aren't meant to be looked at; they're meant to be used.

The way we use a procedure is to *apply* it to some values. For example, the procedure named **sqrt** can be applied to a single number to take its square root, and the procedure named **+** can be applied to two numbers to add them. The way we apply a procedure to values is as follows:

```
(sqrt 9)
```
3

```
(+ 3 6)
```
9

In every case, an application consists of a parenthesized list of expressions, separated by spaces. The first expression's value is the procedure to apply; the values of the remaining expressions are what the procedure should be applied to. Applications are themselves expressions, so they can be nested:

```
(sqrt (+ 3 6))
```
3

Here the value of the expression (+ 3 6) is 9, and that is the value to which the procedure named `sqrt` is applied. (More succinctly, we say that 9 is the *argument* to the `sqrt` procedure.)

There are any number of other useful procedures that already have names, such as * for multiplying, - for subtracting, and / for dividing.

▶ Exercise 1.1

What is the value of each of the following expressions? You should be able to do them in your head, but checking your answers using a Scheme system will be a good way to get comfortable with the mechanics of using your particular system.

a. (* 3 4)

b. (* (+ 5 3) (- 5 3))

c. (/ (+ (* (- 17 14) 5) 6) 7)

It is customary to break complex expressions, such as in Exercise 1.1c, into several lines with indentation that clarifies the structure, as follows:

```
(/ (+ (* (- 17 14)
         5)
      6)
   7)
```

This arrangement helps make clear what's being multiplied, what's being added, and what's being divided.

Now that we've gained some experience using those things for which we already have names, we should learn how to name things ourselves. In Scheme, we do this with a *definition*, such as the following:

```
(define ark-volume (* (* 300 50) 30))
```

Scheme first evaluates the expression (* (* 300 50) 30) and gets 450000; it then remembers that **ark-volume** is henceforth to be a name for that value. You may get a response from the computer indicating that the definition has been performed; whether you do and what it is varies from system to system. In this book, we'll show no response. The name you defined can now be used as an expression, either on its own or in a larger expression:

```
ark-volume
```
450000

```
(/ ark-volume 8)
56250
```

Although naming allows us to capture and reuse the results of computations, it isn't sufficient for capturing reusable *methods* of computation. Suppose, for example, we want to compute the total cost, including a 5 percent sales tax, of several different items. We could take the price of each item, compute the sales tax, and add that tax to the original price:

```
(+ 1.29 (* 5/100 1.29))
1.3545
(+ 2.40 (* 5/100 2.40))
2.52
  ⋮
```

Alternatively, we could define a *procedure* that takes the price of an item (such as $1.29 or $2.40) and returns the total cost of that item, much as **sqrt** takes a number and returns its square root. To define such a total cost procedure we need to specify how the computation is done and give it a name.

We can specify a method of computation by using a *lambda expression*. In our sales tax example, the lambda expression would be as follows:

```
(lambda (x) (+ x (* 5/100 x)))
```

Other than the identifying keyword **lambda**, a lambda expression has two parts: a parameter list and a body. The parameter list in the example is **(x)** and the body is **(+ x (* 5/100 x))**. The value of a lambda expression is a procedure:

```
(lambda (x) (+ x (* 5/100 x)))
#<procedure>
```

Normally, however, we don't evaluate lambda expressions in isolation. Instead, we apply the resulting procedure to one or more argument values:

```
((lambda (x) (+ x (* 5/100 x))) 1.29)
1.3545
((lambda (x) (+ x (* 5/100 x))) 2.40)
2.52
```

When the procedure is applied to a value (such as 1.29), the body is evaluated, but with the parameter (x in this example) replaced by the argument value (1.29). In our example, when we apply (lambda (x) (+ x (* 5/100 x))) to 1.29, the computation done is (+ 1.29 (* 5/100 1.29)). When we apply the same procedure to 2.40, the computation done is (+ 2.40 (* 5/100 2.40)), and so on.

Including the lambda expression explicitly each time it is applied is unwieldy, so we usually use a lambda expression as part of a definition. The lambda expression produces a procedure, and **define** simply associates a name with that procedure. This process is similar to what mathematicians do when they say "let $f(x) = x \times x$". In this case, the parameter is x, the body is $x \times x$, and the name is f. In Scheme we would write

```
(define f (lambda (x) (* x x)))
```

or more descriptively

```
(define square
  (lambda (x) (* x x)))
```

Now, whenever we need to square a number, we could just use **square**:

```
(square 3)
9

(square -10)
100
```

> **Exercise 1.2**

a. Create a name for the tax example by using **define** to name the procedure (lambda (x) (+ x (* 5/100 x))).

b. Use your named procedure to calculate the total price with tax of items costing $1.29 and $2.40.

> **Exercise 1.3**

a. In the text example, we defined **f** and **square** in exactly the same way. What happens if we redefine **f**? Does the procedure associated with **square** change also?

b. Suppose we wrote:

```
(define f (lambda (x) (* x x)))
(define square f)
```

Fill in the missing values:

```
(f 7)
```

_____

```
(square 7)
```

_____

```
(define f (lambda (x) (+ x 2)))
(f 7)
```

_____

```
(square 7)
```

_____

Here is another example of defining and using a procedure. Its parameter list is `(radius height)`, which means it is intended to be applied to two values. The first should be substituted where `radius` appears in the body, and the second where `height` appears:

```
(define cylinder-volume
  (lambda (radius height)
    (* (* 3.1415927 (square radius))
       height)))
(cylinder-volume 5 4)
314.15927
```

Notice that because we had already given the name `square` to our procedure for squaring a number, we were then able to simply use it by name in defining another procedure. In fact, it doesn't matter which order the two definitions are done in as long as both are in place before an attempt is made to apply the `cylinder-volume` procedure.

We can model how the computer produced the result `314.15927` by consulting Figure 1.1. In this diagram, the vertical arrows represent the conversion of a problem to an equivalent one, that is, one with the same answer. Alternatively, the same process can be more compactly represented by the following list of steps leading from the original expression to its value:

```
(cylinder-volume 5 4)
(* (* 3.1415927 (square 5)) 4)
(* (* 3.1415927 (* 5 5)) 4)
(* (* 3.1415927 25) 4)
(* 78.5398175 4)
314.15927
```

Whether we depict the evaluation process using a diagram or a sequence of expressions, we say we're using the *substitution model* of evaluation. We use this name because of the way we handle procedure application: The argument values are sub-

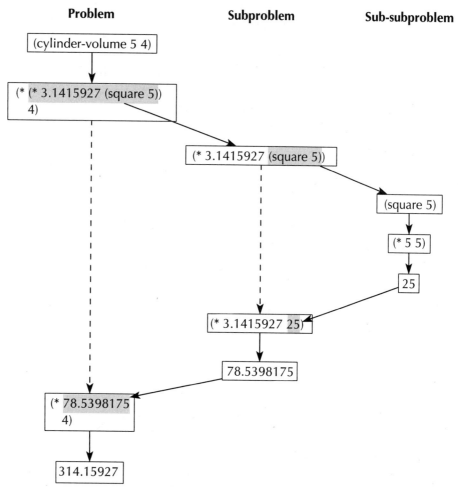

Figure 1.1   The process of evaluating (`cylinder-volume 5 4`)

stituted into the procedure body in place of the parameter names and then the resulting expression is evaluated.

▶ **Exercise 1.4**

According to the *Joy of Cooking*, candy syrups should be cooked 1 degree cooler than listed in the recipe for each 500 feet of elevation above sea level.

a. Define `candy-temperature` to be a procedure that takes two arguments: the recipe's temperature in degrees and the elevation in feet. It should calculate the temperature to use at that elevation. The recipe for Chocolate Caramels calls for a temperature of 244 degrees; suppose you wanted to make them in Denver, the "mile high city." (One mile equals 5280 feet.) Use your procedure to find the temperature for making the syrup.

b. Candy thermometers are usually calibrated only in integer degrees, so it would be handy if the `candy-temperature` procedure would give an answer rounded to the nearest degree. Rounding can be done using the predefined procedure called `round`. For example, (round 7/3) and (round 5/3) both evaluate to 2. Insert an application of `round` at the appropriate place in your procedure definition and test it again.

Procedures give us a way of doing the same computation to different values. Sometimes, however, we have a computation we want to do to different values, but not exactly in the same way with each. Instead, we want to choose a particular computation based on the circumstances. For example, consider a simplified income tax, which is a flat 20 percent of income; however, those earning under $10,000 don't have to pay any tax at all. We can write a procedure for calculating this tax as follows:

```
(define tax
  (lambda (income)
    (if (< income 10000)
        0
        (* 20/100 income)))))
```

Two things are new in this example. The first is the procedure named `<`. Unlike the procedures we've seen so far, it doesn't calculate a number. Instead it calculates a *boolean* or *truth value*—i.e., either true or false. It's what we call a *test* or *predicate*: a procedure that determines whether some fact is true or not. (In this case, it determines whether the income is less than $10,000.) The other new thing is the `if` expression, which uses the truth value to decide which of the remaining two expressions to evaluate. (As you may have guessed, there are other predefined predicates, including

>, =, <=, >=, even?, odd?, and many others. Of those we mentioned, only <= and >= are perhaps not self-explanatory; they correspond to the mathematical symbols ≤ and ≥ respectively.)

We can trace through the steps the computer would take in evaluating (tax 30000) as follows:

```
(tax 30000)
(if (< 30000 10000) 0 (* 20/100 30000))
(if #f 0 (* 20/100 30000))
(* 20/100 30000)
6000
```

In going from the second to the third line, the expression (< 30000 10000) is evaluated to the false value, which is written #f. (Correspondingly, the true value is written #t.) Because the if's test evaluated to false, the second subexpression (the 0) is ignored and the third subexpression (the (* 20/100 30000)) is evaluated. We can again show the computational process in a diagram, as in Figure 1.2.

Exercise 1.5

The preceding tax example has (at least) one undesirable property, illustrated by the following: if you earn $9999, you pay no taxes, so your net income is also $9999. However, if you earn $10,000, you pay $2000 in taxes, resulting in a net income of $8000. Thus, earning $1 more results in a net loss of $1999!

The U.S. tax code deals with this potential inequity by using what is called a *marginal tax rate*. This policy means roughly that each additional dollar of income is taxed at a given percentage rate, but that rate varies according to what income level the dollar represents. In the case of our simple tax, this would mean that the first $10,000 of a person's income is not taxed at all, but the amount above $10,000 is taxed at 20 percent. For example, if you earned $12,500, the first $10,000 would be untaxed, but the amount over $10,000 would be taxed at 20 percent, yielding a tax bill of $20\% \times (\$12,500 - \$10,000) = \$500$. Rewrite the procedure tax to reflect this better strategy.

Exercise 1.6

The *Joy of Cooking* suggests that to figure out how many people a turkey will serve, you should allow 3/4 of a pound per person for turkeys up to 12 pounds in weight, but only 1/2 pound per person for larger turkeys. Write a procedure, turkey-servings, that when given a turkey weight in pounds will calculate the number of people it serves.

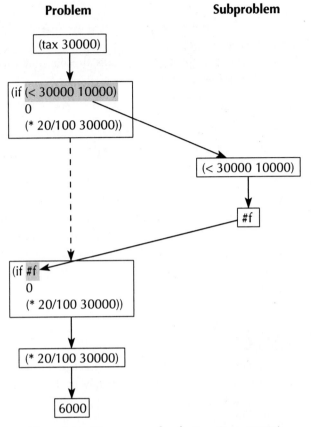

Figure 1.2   The process of evaluating (tax 30000)

 Exercise 1.7

Write a succinct English description of the effect of each of the following procedures. Try to express *what* each calculates, not *how* it calculates that.

a. (define puzzle1
      (lambda (a b c)
        (+ a (if (> b c)
                 b
                 c))))
b. (define puzzle2
      (lambda (x)
        ((if (< x 0)
             -
             +)
         0 x)))

Figure 1.3   A sample of the *Repeating Crosses* quilt

1.3   An Application: Quilting

Now we turn our attention to building procedures that operate on rectangular images, rather than numbers. Using these procedures we can produce geometric quilt patterns, such as the *Repeating Crosses* pattern shown in Figure 1.3.

In doing numeric computations, the raw materials are numbers you type in and some primitive numeric procedures, such as +. (By *primitive procedures*, we mean the fundamental predefined procedures that are built into the Scheme system.) The situation here is similar. We will build our images out of smaller images, and we will build our image procedures out of a few primitive image procedures that are built into our Scheme system. Unfortunately, image procedures are not as standardized as numeric procedures, so you can't count on these procedures to work in all versions of Scheme; any Scheme used with this book, however, should have the procedures we use here. There is also the problem of how to input the basic building-block images that are to be manipulated. Graphic input varies a great deal from computer to computer, so rather than tell you how to do it, we've provided a file on the web site for this book that you can load into Scheme to define some sample images. Loading that file defines each of the names shown in Figure 1.4 as a name for the corresponding image. (Exercise 1.11 at the end of this section explains how these blocks are produced.)

We'll build our quilts by piecing together small square images called *basic blocks*. The four examples in Figure 1.4 are all basic blocks; the one called `rcross-bb` was used to make the Repeating Crosses quilt. The quilt was made by piecing together copies of the basic block, with some of them turned.

To make the Repeating Crosses quilt, we need at least two primitive procedures: one that will produce an image by piecing together two smaller images and one

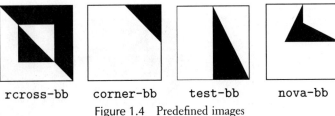

rcross-bb   corner-bb   test-bb   nova-bb

Figure 1.4   Predefined images

that will turn an image a quarter turn to the right. These procedures, which are built into the Scheme systems recommended for this book, are called `stack` and `quarter-turn-right`.

Exercise 1.8

Try evaluating the following expressions:

```
(stack rcross-bb corner-bb)
(quarter-turn-right test-bb)
```

What happens if you nest several expressions, such as in the following:

```
(stack (stack rcross-bb corner-bb) test-bb)
(stack (stack rcross-bb corner-bb)
       (stack (quarter-turn-right test-bb) test-bb))
```

Can you describe the effect of each primitive?

Exercise 1.9

Before undertaking anything so ambitious as making an actual quilt, it may pay to have a few more tools in our kit. For example, it would be nice if we could turn an image to the left, or half way around, as well as to the right. Similarly, it would be desirable to be able to join two images side by side as well as stacking them on top of one another.

a. Define procedures `half-turn` and `quarter-turn-left` that do as their names suggest. Both procedures take a single argument, namely, the image to turn. You will naturally need to use the built-in procedure `quarter-turn-right`.

b. Define a procedure `side-by-side` that takes two images as arguments and creates a composite image having the first image on the left and the second image on the right.

If you don't see how to build the three additional procedures out of `quarter-turn-right` and `stack`, you may want to play more with combinations of those two. Alternatively, try playing with paper squares with basic blocks drawn on them. (The web site for this book has some basic blocks you can print out, but hand-drawn ones work just as well.)

Exercise 1.10

Each dark cross in the repeating crosses pattern is formed by joining together four copies of the basic block, each facing a different way. We can call this operation *pinwheeling* the basic block; here is an example of the same operation performed on the image `test-bb`:

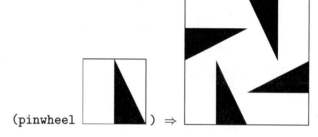

(pinwheel [ ]) ⇒

Define the `pinwheel` procedure and show how you can use it to make a cross out of the basic block.

Now try pinwheeling the cross—you should get a sample of the quilt, with four dark crosses, as shown at the beginning of the section. If you pinwheel that, how big is the quilt you get?

Try making other pinwheeled quilts in the same way, but using the other basic blocks. What do the designs look like?

Although you have succeeded (through the exercises) in making the Repeating Crosses quilt described at the beginning of this section, there are at least two questions you may have. First, how are the basic blocks constructed in the first place? And second, how could we create quilts that aren't pinwheels of pinwheels? This latter question will be dealt with in the next two chapters, which introduce new programming techniques called *recursion* and *iteration*. The former question is addressed in the following exercise.

Exercise 1.11

All four basic blocks shown previously can be produced using two primitive graphics procedures supported by all the Scheme systems recommended for this book. The first of these procedures, `filled-triangle`, takes six arguments, which are the *x* and *y* coordinates of the corners of the triangle that is to be filled in. The coordinate system runs from −1 to 1 in both dimensions. For example, here is the definition of `test-bb`:

```
(define test-bb
  (filled-triangle 0 1 0 -1 1 -1))
```

The second of these procedures, `overlay`, combines images. To understand how it works, imagine having two images on sheets of transparent plastic laid one on top of the other so that you see the two images together. For example, here is the definition of `nova-bb`, which is made out of two triangles:

```
(define nova-bb
  (overlay (filled-triangle 0 1 0 0 -1/2 0)
           (filled-triangle 0 0 0 1/2 1 0)))
```

a. Use these primitive graphics procedures to define the other two basic blocks from Figure 1.4.

b. Now that you know how it is done, be inventive. Come up with some basic blocks of your own and make pinwheeled quilts out of them. Of course, if your system supports direct graphical input, you can also experiment with freehand images, or images from nature. You might find it interesting to try experiments such as overlaying rotated versions of an image on one another.

Review Problems

▷ **Exercise 1.12**

Find two integers such that applying `f` to them will produce 16 as the value, given that `f` is defined as follows:

```
(define f
  (lambda (x y)
    (if (even? x)
        7
        (* x y))))
```

▷ **Exercise 1.13**

Write a Scheme expression with no multidigit numbers in it that has 173 as its value.

▷ **Exercise 1.14**

Write a procedure that takes two arguments and computes their average.

▷ **Exercise 1.15**

What could be filled into the blank in the following procedure to ensure that no division by zero occurs when the procedure is applied? Give several different answers.

```
(define foo
  (lambda (x y)
    (if _____
        (+ x y)
        (/ x y))))
```

▷ **Exercise 1.16**

A 10-foot-long ladder leans against a wall, with its base 6 feet away from the bottom of the wall. How high on the wall does it reach? This question can be answered by evaluating (`ladder-height 10 6`) after entering the following definition. Make a diagram such as the one in Figure 1.1 showing the evaluation of (`ladder-height 10 6`) in the context of this definition:

```
(define ladder-height
  (lambda (ladder-length base-distance)
    (sqrt (- (square ladder-length)
             (square base-distance)))))
```

Chapter Inventory

Vocabulary

computer science
computational process
information process
process
program
programming language
Scheme
value
expression
evaluation

procedure
apply
argument
parameter
substitution model
boolean
truth value
test
predicate
primitive procedure

New Predefined Scheme Names

The dagger symbol (†) indicates a name that is not part of the R⁴RS standard for
Scheme.

sqrt	<=
+	>=
*	even?
-	odd?
/	stack†
round	quarter-turn-right†
<	filled-triangle†
>	overlay†
=	

New Scheme Syntax

number	parameter list
name	body
application	if expression
definition	#f
lambda expression	#t

Scheme Names Defined in This Chapter

ark-volume	corner-bb
square	test-bb
cylinder-volume	nova-bb
candy-temperature	half-turn
tax	quarter-turn-left
turkey-servings	side-by-side
puzzle1	pinwheel
puzzle2	ladder-height
rcross-bb	

Sidebars

Responsible Computer Use

Notes

The identifying keyword `lambda`, which indicates that a procedure should be created,
has a singularly twisted history. This keyword originated in the late 1950s in a
programming language (an early version of Lisp) that was a direct predecessor to
Scheme. Why? Because it was the name of the Greek letter λ, which Church
had used in the 1930s to abstract mathematical functions from formulas [12]. For

example, where we write (lambda (x) (* x x)), Church might have written $\lambda x.x \times x$. Because the computers of the 1950s had no Greek letters, the λ needed to be spelled out as lambda. This development wasn't the first time that typographic considerations played a part in the history of lambda. Barendregt [6] tells "what seems to be the story" of how Church came to use the letter λ. Apparently Church had originally intended to write $\hat{x}.x \times x$, with a circumflex or "hat" over the x. (This notation was inspired by a similar one that Whitehead and Russell used in their *Principia Mathematica* [53].) However, the typesetter of Church's work was unable to center the hat over the top of the x and so placed it before the x, resulting in $\char`^x.x \times x$ instead of $\hat{x}.x \times x$; a later typesetter then turned that hat with nothing under it into a λ, presumably based on the visual resemblance.

The formula for candy-making temperatures at higher elevations, the recipe for chocolate caramels, and the formula for turkey servings are all from the *Joy of Cooking* [42]. The actual suggested formula for turkey servings gives a range of serving sizes for each class of turkeys; we've chosen to use the low end of each range, because we've never had a shortage of turkey.

The quilting application is rather similar to the "Little Quilt" language of Sethi [49]. The Repeating Crosses pattern is by Helen Whitson Rose [43].

CHAPTER TWO

Recursion and Induction

2.1 Recursion

We have used Scheme to write procedures that describe how certain computational processes can be carried out. All the procedures we've discussed so far generate processes of a fixed size. For example, the process generated by the procedure `square` always does exactly one multiplication no matter how big or how small the number we're squaring is. Similarly, the procedure `pinwheel` generates a process that will do exactly the same number of `stack` and `turn` operations when we use it on a basic block as it will when we use it on a huge quilt that's 128 basic blocks long and 128 basic blocks wide. Furthermore, the size of the procedure (that is, the size of the procedure's text) is a good indicator of the size of the processes it generates: Small procedures generate small processes and large procedures generate large processes.

On the other hand, there are procedures of a fixed size that generate computational processes of varying sizes, depending on the values of their parameters, using a technique called *recursion*. To illustrate this, the following is a small, fixed-size procedure for making paper chains that can still make chains of arbitrary length— it has a parameter *n* for the desired length. You'll need a bunch of long, thin strips of paper and some way of joining the ends of a strip to make a loop. You can use tape, a stapler, or if you use slitted strips of cardstock that look like this ⌐￣￣￣￣￣￣￣￣￣￣⌐, you can just slip the slits together. You'll need some classmates, friends, or helpful strangers to do this with, all of whom have to be willing to follow the same procedure as you. You will need to stand in a line.

To make a chain of length n:

1. If $n = 1$,
    (a) Bend a strip around to bring the two ends together, and join them.
    (b) Proudly deliver to your customer a chain of length 1.
2. Otherwise,
    (a) Pick up a strip.
    (b) Ask the person next in line to please make you a chain of length $n - 1$.
    (c) Slip your strip through one of the end links of that chain, bend it around, and join the ends together.
    (d) Proudly deliver to your customer a chain of length n.

Now you know all there is to know about recursion, you have met a bunch of new people, and if you were ambitious enough to make a long chain, you even have a nice decoration to drape around your room. Despite all these advantages, it is generally preferable to program a computer rather than a person. In particular, using this same recursive technique with a computer comes in very handy if you have a long, tedious calculation to do that you'd rather not do by hand or even ask your friends to do.

For example, imagine that you want to compute how many different outcomes there are of shuffling a deck of cards. In other words, how many different orderings (or *permutations*) of the 52 cards are there? Well, 52 possibilities exist for which card is on top, and for each of those 51 possibilities exist for which card is next, or 52×51 total possibilities for what the top two cards are. This pattern continues similarly on down the deck, leading to a total number of possibilities of $52 \times 51 \times 50 \times \cdots \times 3 \times 2 \times 1$, which is the number that is conventionally called 52 *factorial* and written 52!. To compute 52! we could do a lot of tedious typing, spelling out the 51 multiplications of the numbers from 52 down to 1. Alternatively, we could write a general procedure for computing any factorial, which uses its argument to determine which multiplications to do, and then apply this procedure to 52.

To write this procedure, we can reuse the ideas behind the paper chain procedure. One of these is the following very important general strategy:

The recursion strategy: Do nearly all the work first; then there will only be a little left to do.

Although it sounds silly, it describes perfectly what happened with the paper chain: You (or rather your friends) did most of the work first (making a chain of length $n - 1$), which left only one link for you to do.

Here we're faced with the problem of multiplying 52 numbers together, which will take 51 multiplications. One way to apply the recursion principle is this: Once 50 of the multiplications have been done, only 1 is left to do.

We have many possible choices for which 50 multiplications to do first versus which one to save for last. Almost any choice can be made to work, but some may make us work a bit harder than others. One choice would be to initially multiply together the 51 largest numbers and then be left with multiplying the result by the smallest number. Another possibility would be to initially multiply together the 51 smallest numbers, which would just leave the largest number to multiply in. Which approach will make our life easier? Stop and think about this for a while.

We start out with the problem of multiplying together the numbers from 52 down to 1. To do this, we're going to write a general factorial procedure, which can multiply together the numbers from anything down to 1. Fifty-two down to 1 is just one special case; the procedure will be equally capable of multiplying 105 down to 1, or 73 down to 1, *or 51 down to 1.*

This observation is important; if we make the choice to leave the largest number as the one left to multiply in at the end, the "nearly all the work" that we need to do first is itself a factorial problem, and so we can use the same procedure. To compute 52!, we first compute 51!, and then we multiply by 52. In general, to compute $n!$, for any number n, we'll compute $(n-1)!$ and then multiply by n. Writing this in Scheme, we get:

```
(define factorial
  (lambda (n)
    (* (factorial (- n 1))
       n)))
```

The strategy of choosing the subproblem to be of the same form as the main problem is probably worth having a name for:

The self-similarity strategy: Rather than breaking off some arbitrary big chunk of a problem to do as a subproblem, break off a chunk that is of the same form as the original.

Will this procedure for computing factorials work? No. It computes the factorial of any number by first computing the factorial of the previous number. That works up to a point; 52! can be computed by first computing 51!, and 51! can be computed by first computing 50!. But, if we keep going like that, we'll never stop. Every factorial will be computed by first computing a smaller one. Therefore 1! will be computed in terms of 0!, which will be computed in terms of $(-1)!$, which will be computed in terms of $(-2)!$, and so on.

When we have a lot of multiplications to do, it makes sense to do all but one and then the one that's left. Even if we only have one multiplication to do, we could do all but one (none) and then the one that's left. But what if we don't have any multiplications at all to do? Then we *can't* do all but one and then the one that's left—there isn't one to leave for last. The fundamental problem with this procedure is, it tries to always leave one multiplication for last, even when there are none to be done.

Computing 1! doesn't require any multiplications; the answer is simply 1. What we can do is treat this *base case* specially, using if, just like in the human program for making chains:

```
(define factorial
  (lambda (n)
    (if (= n 1)
        1
        (* (factorial (- n 1))
           n))))
```

```
(factorial 52)
80658175170943878857166063685640376697528950544088327782400000000000
000
```

Thus, base cases are treated separately in recursive procedures. In particular, they result in no further recursive calls. But we also need to guarantee that the recursion will always eventually end in a base case. This is so important that we give it the following name:

The base case imperative: In a recursive procedure, all roads must lead to a base case.

This procedure generates what is called a *recursive process*; a similar but smaller computation is done as a subgoal of solving the main problem. In particular, cases like this with a single subproblem that is smaller by a fixed amount, are called *linear recursions* because the total number of computational steps is a linear function of the problem size. We can see the recursive nature of the process clearly in Figure 2.1, which shows how the evaluation of (factorial 3) involves as a subproblem computing (factorial 2), which in turn involves computing (factorial 1) as a sub-subproblem. If the original problem had been (factorial 52), the diagram would be 52 columns wide instead of only 3.

This diagram isn't complete—the evaluation of the if expression with its equality test isn't explicitly shown and neither is the subtraction of one. These omissions were made to simplify the diagram, leaving the essential information more apparent. If we included all the details, the first three steps (leading from the problem (factorial 3) to the subproblem (factorial 2)) would expand into the ten steps shown in Figure 2.2.

Problem　　**Subproblem**　　**Sub-subproblem**

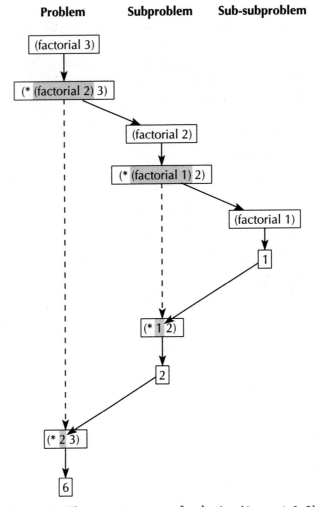

Figure 2.1　The recursive process of evaluating (`factorial 3`).

Although the recursive nature of the process is most evident in the original diagram, we can as usual save space by instead listing the evaluation steps. If we do this with the same details omitted, we get

```
(factorial 3)
(* (factorial 2) 3)
(* (* (factorial 1) 2) 3)
(* (* 1 2) 3)
(* 2 3)
6
```

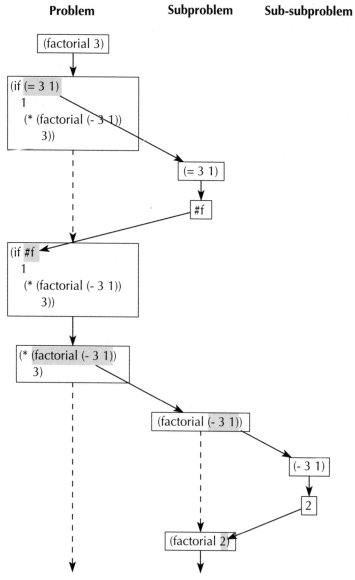

Figure 2.2   Details of the recursive process of evaluating (`factorial 3`).

Let's sum up what we've done in both the paper chain example and the factorial example. In both, we had to solve a problem by doing something repeatedly, either assembling links or multiplying numbers. We broke off a big chunk of each problem (the recursion principle) that was just like the original problem (the self-similarity principle) except that it was smaller. After that chunk was finished, we only had a little work left to do, either by putting in one more link or multiplying by one more

> ### ▶ Exponents
>
> In this book, when we use an exponent, such as the k in x^k, it will almost always be either a positive integer or zero. When k is a positive integer, x^k just means k copies of x multiplied together. That is, $x^k = x \times x \times \cdots \times x$, with k of the x's. What about when the exponent is zero? We could equally well have said that $x^k = 1 \times x \times x \times \cdots \times x$ with k of the x's. For example, $x^3 = 1 \times x \times x \times x$, $x^2 = 1 \times x \times x$, and $x^1 = 1 \times x$. If we continue this progression with one fewer x, we see that $x^0 = 1$.

number. In each case, the smaller subproblems must invariably lead to a problem so small that it could be made no smaller (the base case imperative), that is, when we needed to make a chain of length 1 or when we had to compute 1!, which is handled separately.

▶ Exercise 2.1

Write a procedure called **power** such that (**power** *base exponent*) raises *base* to the *exponent* power, where *exponent* is a nonnegative integer. As explained in the sidebar on exponents, you can do this by multiplying together *exponent* copies of *base*. (You can compare results with Scheme's built-in procedure called **expt**. However, do not use **expt** in **power**. **Expt** computes the same values as **power**, except that it also works for exponents that are negative or not integers.)

2.2 Induction

Do you believe us that the **factorial** procedure really computes factorials? Probably. That's because once we explained the reasoning behind it, there isn't much to it. (Of course, you may also have tried it out on a Scheme system—but that doesn't explain why you believe it works in the cases you didn't try.)

Sometimes, however, it is a bit trickier to convince someone that a procedure generates the right answer. For example, here's another procedure for squaring a number that is rather different from the first one:

```
(define square
  (lambda (n)
    (if (= n 0)
        0
        (+ (square (- n 1))
           (- (+ n n) 1))))))
```

Just because it is called **square** doesn't necessarily mean that it actually squares its argument; we might be trying to trick you. After all, we can give any name we want to anything. Why should you believe us? The answer is: You shouldn't, yet, because we haven't explained our reasoning to you. It is not your job as the reader of a procedure to figure it out; it is the job of the writer of a procedure to accompany it with adequate explanation. Right now, that means that we have our work cut out for us. But it also means that when it becomes your turn to write procedures, you are going to have to similarly justify your reasoning.

Earlier we said that the procedure was "for squaring a number." Now that we're trying to back up that claim, we discover we need to be a bit more precise: This procedure squares any *nonnegative integer*. Certainly it correctly squares 0, because it immediately yields 0 as the answer in that case, and $0^2 = 0$. The real issue is with the positive integers.

We're assuming that – subtracts and + adds, so (- n 1) evaluates to $n - 1$, and (- (+ n n) 1) evaluates to $(n + n) - 1$ or $2n - 1$. What if we went one step further and assumed that where **square** is applied to $n - 1$, it squares it, resulting in the value $(n - 1)^2$? In that case, the overall value computed by the procedure is $(n-1)^2 + 2n - 1$. With a little bit of algebra, we can show that $(n-1)^2 + 2n - 1 = n^2$, and so in fact the end result is n^2, just like we said it was.

But wait, not so fast: To show that **square** actually squares n, we had to assume that it actually squares $n - 1$; we seem to need to know that the procedure works in order to show that it works. This apparently circular reasoning isn't, however, truly circular: it is more like a spiral. To show that **square** correctly squares some particular positive integer, we need to assume that it correctly squares some *smaller* particular integer. For example, to show that it squares 10, we need to assume that it can square 9. If we wanted to, though, we could show that it correctly squares 9, based on the assumption that it correctly squares 8. Where does this chain of reasoning end? It ends when we show that (**square** 1) really computes 1^2, based on the fact that (**square** 0) really computes 0^2. At that point, the spiraling stops, because we've known since the very beginning that **square** could square 0.

The key point that makes this spiral reasoning work is that the chain of reasoning leads inexorably down to the base case of zero. We only defined **square** in terms of *smaller* squares, so there is a steady progression toward the base case. By contrast, even though it is equally true that $n^2 = (n + 1)^2 - (2n + 1)$, the following procedure does *not* correctly compute the square of any positive integer:

```
(define square        ; This version doesn't work.
  (lambda (n)
    (if (= n 0)
        0
        (- (square (+ n 1))
           (+ (+ n n) 1)))))
```

The reason why this procedure doesn't correctly compute the square of any positive integer isn't that it computes some incorrect answer instead. Rather, it computes no answer at all, because it works its way further and further from the base case, stopping only when the computer runs out of memory and reports failure. We say that the computational process doesn't *terminate*.

We've also used this procedure to introduce another feature of the Scheme programming language: *comments*. Any text from a semicolon to the end of the line is ignored by the Scheme system and instead is for use by human readers.

The reasoning technique we've been using is so generally useful that it has a name: *mathematical induction*. Some standard terminology is also used to make arguments of this form more brief. The justification that the base case of the procedure works is called the *base case* of the proof. The assumption that the procedure works correctly for smaller argument values is called the *induction hypothesis*. The reasoning that leads from the induction hypothesis to the conclusion of correct operation is called the *inductive step*. Note that the inductive step only applies to those cases where the base case doesn't apply. For `square`, we only reasoned from $n - 1$ to n in the case where n was positive, not in the case where it was zero.

Putting this all together, we can write an inductive proof of `square`'s correctness in a reasonably conventional format:

Base case: (`square` 0) terminates with the value 0 because of the evaluation rule for `if`. Because $0 = 0^2$, (`square` 0) computes the correct value.

Induction hypothesis: Assume that (`square` k) terminates with the value k^2 for all k in the range $0 \leq k < n$.

Inductive step: Consider evaluating (`square` n), with $n > 0$. This will terminate if the evaluation of (`square` (- n 1)) does and will have the same value as (+ (`square` (- n 1)) (- (+ n n) 1)). Because (- n 1) evaluates to $n - 1$ and $0 \leq n - 1 < n$, we can therefore assume by our induction hypothesis that (`square` (- n 1)) does terminate, with the value $(n - 1)^2$. Therefore (+ (`square` (- n 1)) (- (+ n n) 1)) evaluates to $(n - 1)^2 + 2n - 1$. Because $(n - 1)^2 + 2n - 1 = n^2$, we see that (`square` n) does terminate with the correct value for any arbitrary positive n, under the inductive hypothesis of correct operation for smaller arguments.

Conclusion: Therefore, by mathematical induction on n, (`square` n) terminates with the value n^2 for any nonnegative integer n.

If you have trouble understanding this, one useful trick is to think of proving one special case of the theorem each day. The first day you prove the base case. On any subsequent day, you prove the next case, making use only of results you've *previously* proven. There is no particular case that you won't eventually show to be true—so the theorem must hold in general.

We wish to point out two things about this proof. First, the proof is relative in the sense that it assumes that other operations (such as + and -) operate as advertised. But this is an assumption you must make, because you were not there when the people who implemented your Scheme system were doing their work. Second, an important part of verifying that a procedure computes the correct value is showing that it actually terminates for all permissible argument values. After all, if the computation doesn't terminate, it computes no value at all and hence certainly doesn't compute the correct value. This need for *termination* explains our enjoinder in the base case imperative given earlier.

▶ **Exercise 2.2**

Write a similarly detailed proof of the `factorial` procedure's correctness. What are the permissible argument values for which you should show that it works?

Proving is also useful when you are trying to *debug* a procedure that doesn't work correctly, that is, when you are trying to figure out what is wrong and how to fix it. For example, look at the incorrect version of `square` given earlier. If we were trying to prove that this works by induction, the base case and the inductive hypothesis would be exactly the same as in the proof above. But look at what happens in the inductive step:

Inductive step: Consider evaluating `(square n)`, with $n > 0$. This will terminate if the evaluation of `(square (+ n 1))` does and will have the same value as `(- (square (+ n 1)) (+ (+ n n) 1))`. Because `(+ n 1)` evaluates to $n + 1$ and $0 \leq n + 1 < n$ ... *Oops* ...

The next time you have a procedure that doesn't work, try proving that it does work. See where you run into trouble constructing the proof—that should point you toward the *bug* (error) in the procedure.

▶ **Exercise 2.3**

Here's an example of a procedure with a tricky bug you can find by trying to do an induction proof. Try to prove the following procedure also computes n^2 for any nonnegative integer n. Where does the proof run into trouble? What's the bug?

```
(define square   ; another version that doesn't work
  (lambda (n)
    (if (= n 0)
        0
        (+ (square (- n 2))
           (- (* 4 n) 4)))))
```

The most important thing to take away from this encounter with induction is a new way of thinking, which we can call *one-layer thinking*. To illustrate what we mean by this, contrast two ways of thinking about what the `square` procedure does in computing 4^2:

1. You can try thinking about all the layers upon layers of squares, with requests going down through the layers and results coming back up. On the way down, 4^2 requests 3^2 requests 2^2 requests 1^2 requests 0^2. On the way back up, 0 gets $1 + 1 - 1$ added to it yielding 1, which gets $2 + 2 - 1$ added to it yielding 4, which gets $3 + 3 - 1$ added to it yielding 9, which gets $4 + 4 - 1$ added to it yielding 16, which is the answer.
2. Alternatively, you can just stick with one layer. The computation of 4^2 requests 3^2 and presumably gets back 9, because that's what 3^2 is. The 9 then gets $4 + 4 - 1$ (or 7) added to it, yielding the answer 16.

This is really just an informal version of relying on an induction hypothesis—that's what we were doing when we said "... and presumably gets back 9, because that's what 3^2 is." It saves us having to worry about how the whole rest of the computation is done.

One-layer thinking is much better suited to the limited capacities of human brains. You only have to think about a little bit of the process, instead of the entire arbitrarily large process that you've really got. Plunging down through a whole bunch of layers and then trying to find your way back up through them is a good way to get hopelessly confused. We sum this up as follows:

The one-layer thinking maxim: Don't try to think recursively about a recursive process.

One-layer thinking is more than just a way to think about the process a procedure will generate; it is also the key to writing the procedure in the first place. For example, when we presented our recursive version of `square` at the beginning of this section, you may well have wondered where we got such a strange procedure. The answer is that we started with the idea of computing squares recursively, using smaller squares. We knew we would need to have a base case, which would probably be when $n = 0$. We also knew that we had to relate the square of n to the square of some smaller number. This led to the following template:

```
(define square
  (lambda (n)
    (if (= n 0)
        0
        (____ (square _____)
              _____)))))
```

We knew that the argument to **square** would have to be less than n for the induction hypothesis to apply; on the other hand, it would still need to be a nonnegative integer. The simplest way to arrange this is to use (- n 1); thus we have

```
(define square
  (lambda (n)
    (if (= n 0)
        0
        (____ (square (- n 1))
              _____))))
```

At this point, our one-layer thinking tells us not to worry about the specific computational process involved in evaluating (**square** (- n 1)). Instead, we assume that the value will be $(n - 1)^2$. Thus the only remaining question is, What do we need to do to $(n - 1)^2$ to get n^2? Because $(n - 1)^2 = n^2 - 2n + 1$, it becomes clear that we need to add $2n - 1$. This lets us fill in the remaining two blanks, arriving at our procedure:

```
(define square
  (lambda (n)
    (if (= n 0)
        0
        (+ (square (- n 1))
           (- (+ n n) 1))))))
```

▶ **Exercise 2.4**

Use one-layer thinking to help you correctly fill in the blanks in the following version of **square** so that it can square any nonnegative integer:

```
(define square
  (lambda (n)
    (if (= n 0)
        0
        (if (even? n)
            (____ (square (/ n 2))
                  _____)
            (+ (square (- n 1))
               (- (+ n n) 1))))))
```

2.3 Further Examples

Recursion adds great power to Scheme, and the recursion strategy will be fundamental to the remainder of the book. However, if this is your first encounter with recursion, you may find it confusing. Part of the confusion arises from the fact that recursion seems "circular." However, it really involves spiraling down to a firm foundation at the base case (or base cases). Another problem at this point is simply lack of familiarity. Therefore, we devote this section to various examples of numerical procedures involving recursion. And the next section applies recursion to quilting.

As our first example, consider the built-in Scheme procedure `quotient`, which computes how many times one integer divides another integer. For example,

```
(quotient 9 3)
```
3

```
(quotient 10 3)
```
3

```
(quotient 11 3)
```
3

```
(quotient 12 3)
```
4

Even though `quotient` is built into Scheme, it is instructive to see how it can be written in terms of a more "elementary" procedure, in this case subtraction. We'll write a procedure that does the same job as `quotient`, but we'll call it `quot` instead so that the built-in `quotient` will still be available. (Nothing stops you from redefining `quotient`, but then you lose the original until you restart Scheme.) In order to simplify the discussion, suppose we want to compute (`quot n d`), where $n \geq 0$ and $d > 0$. If $n < d$, d doesn't divide n at all, so the result would be 0. If, however, $n \geq d$, d will divide n one more time than it divides $n - d$. Writing this in Scheme, we have

```
(define quot
  (lambda (n d)
    (if (< n d)
        0
        (+ 1 (quot (- n d) d))))))
```

The built-in version of `quotient`, unlike the `quot` procedure just shown, allows either or both of the arguments to be negative. The value when one or both arguments are negative is defined by saying that negating either argument negates the quotient. For example, because the quotient of 13 and 3 is 4, it follows that the quotient of −13 and 3 is −4, and so is the quotient of 13 and −3. Because negating either argument negates the quotient, negating both of them negates the quotient twice, or in other words leaves it unchanged. For example, the quotient of −13 and −3 is 4.

In order to negate a number in Scheme, we could subtract it from zero; for example, to negate the value of n, we could write (- 0 n). However, it is more idiomatic to instead write (- n), taking advantage of a special feature of the predefined procedure named -, namely, that it performs negation if only given a single argument. Note that (- n) is quite different in form from -5: The former applies a procedure to an argument, whereas the latter is a single number. It is permissible to apply the procedure named - to a number, as in (- 5), but you can't put a negative sign on a name the way you would on a number: -n isn't legal Scheme.

We could build these ideas into our procedure as follows:

```scheme
(define quot
  (lambda (n d)
    (if (< d 0)
        (- (quot n (- d)))
        (if (< n 0)
            (- (quot (- n) d))
            (if (< n d)
                0
                (+ 1 (quot (- n d) d))))))))
```

Notice that our first version of quot corresponds to the innermost if; the outer two if's deal with negative values for *n* and *d*.

This new, more general, quot procedure is our first example of a procedure with ifs nested within one another so deeply that they jeopardize the readability of the procedure. Procedures like this can be clarified by using another form of conditional expression that Scheme offers as an alternative to if: cond. Here is how we can rewrite quot using cond:

```scheme
(define quot
  (lambda (n d)
    (cond ((< d 0) (- (quot n (- d))))
          ((< n 0) (- (quot (- n) d)))
          ((< n d) 0)
          (else    (+ 1 (quot (- n d) d)))))))
```

A cond consists of a sequence of parenthesized *clauses*, each providing one possible case for how the value might be calculated. Each clause starts with a test expression, except that the last clause can start with the keyword else. Scheme evaluates each test expression in turn until it finds one that evaluates to true, to decide which clause to use. Once a test evaluates to true, the remainder of that clause is evaluated to produce the value of the `cond` expression; the other clauses are ignored. If the `else` clause is reached without any true test having been found, the `else` clause's expression is evaluated. If, on the other hand, no test evaluates to true and there is no `else` clause, the result is not specified by the Scheme language standard, and each system is free to give you whatever result it pleases.

Exercise 2.5

Use addition to write a procedure `multiply` that calculates the product of two integers (i.e., write `*` for integers in terms of `+`).

Suppose we want to write a procedure that computes the sum of the first n integers, where n is itself a positive integer. This is a very similar problem to `factorial`; the difference is that we are adding up the numbers rather than multiplying them. Because the base case $n = 1$ should yield the value 1, we come up with a solution identical in form to `factorial`:

```
(define sum-of-first
  (lambda (n)
    (if (= n 1)
        1
        (+ (sum-of-first (- n 1))
           n))))
```

But why should $n = 1$ be the base case for `sum-of-first`? In fact, we could argue that the case $n = 0$ makes good sense: The sum of the first 0 integers is the "empty sum," which could reasonably be interpreted as 0. With this interpretation, we can extend the allowable argument values as follows:

```
(define sum-of-first
  (lambda (n)
    (if (= n 0)
        0
        (+ (sum-of-first (- n 1))
           n))))
```

This extension is reasonable because it computes the same values as the original version whenever $n \geq 1$. (Why?) A similar extension for `factorial` would be

```
(define factorial
  (lambda (n)
    (if (= n 0)
        1
        (* (factorial (- n 1))
           n)))))
```

It is not as clear that the "empty product" should be 1; however, we've seen empty products when we talked about exponents (see the sidebar, Exponents). The product of zero copies of *x* multiplied together is 1; similarly the product of the first zero positive integers is also 1. Not coincidentally, this agrees with the mathematical convention that $0! = 1$.

▶ **Exercise 2.6**

Let's consider some variants of the basic form common to `factorial` and `sum-of-first`.

a. Describe precisely what the following procedure computes in terms of *n*:

```
(define subtract-the-first
  (lambda (n)
    (if (= n 0)
        0
        (- (subtract-the-first (- n 1))
           n)))))
```

b. Consider what happens when you exchange the order of multiplication in `factorial`:

```
(define factorial2
  (lambda (n)
    (if (= n 0)
        1
        (* n
           (factorial2 (- n 1))))))
```

Experimentation with various values of *n* should persuade you that this version computes the same value as did the original `factorial`. Why is this so? Would the same be true if you switched the order of addition in `sum-of-first`?

c. If you reverse the order of subtraction in `subtract-the-first`, you will get a different value in general. Why is this so? How would you precisely describe the value returned by this new version?

One way to generalize `sum-of-first` is to sum up the integers between two specified integers (e.g., from 4 to 9). This would require two parameters and could be written as follows:

```
(define sum-integers-from-to
  (lambda (low high)
    (if (> low high)
        0
        (+ (sum-integers-from-to low (- high 1))
           high)))))
```

Note that this could also be accomplished by increasing `low` instead of decreasing `high`.

Exercise 2.7

Rewrite `sum-integers-from-to` in this alternative way.

Exercise 2.8

Another type of generalization of `sum-of-first` can be obtained by varying what is being summed, rather than just the range of summation:

a. Write a procedure `sum-of-squares` that computes the sum of the first n squares, where n is a nonnegative integer.

b. Write a procedure `sum-of-cubes` that computes the sum of the first n cubes, where n is a nonnegative integer.

c. Write a procedure `sum-of-powers` that has two parameters n and p, both nonnegative integers, such that (`sum-of-powers n p`) computes $1^p + 2^p + \cdots + n^p$.

In the factorial procedure, the argument decreases by 1 at each step. Sometimes, however, the argument needs to decrease in some other fashion. Consider, for example, the problem of finding the number of digits in the usual decimal way of writing an integer. How would we compute the number of digits in n, where n is a nonnegative integer? If $n < 10$, the problem is easy; the number of digits would be 1. On the other hand, if $n \geq 10$, the quotient when it is divided by 10 will be all but the last digit. For example, the quotient when 1234 is divided by 10 is 123. This lets us define the number of digits in *n* in terms of the number of digits in a smaller number, namely, (quotient n 10). Putting this together, we have

```
(define num-digits
  (lambda (n)
    (if (< n 10)
        1
        (+ 1 (num-digits (quotient n 10))))))
```

We could extend num-digits to negative integers using cond:

```
(define num-digits
  (lambda (n)
    (cond ((< n 0)  (num-digits (- n)))
          ((< n 10) 1)
          (else     (+ 1 (num-digits (quotient n 10)))))))
```

If we want to do more with the digits than count how many there are, we need to find out what each digit is. We can do this using the remainder from the division by 10; for example, when we divide 1234 by 10, the remainder is 4. A built-in procedure called remainder finds the remainder; for example, (remainder 1234 10) evaluates to 4.

▶ **Exercise 2.9**

Write a procedure that computes the number of 6s in the decimal representation of an integer. Generalize this to a procedure that computes the number of *d*'s, where *d* is another argument.

▶ **Exercise 2.10**

Write a procedure that calculates the number of odd digits in an integer. (Reminder: There is a built-in predicate called odd?.)

▶ **Exercise 2.11**

Write a procedure that computes the sum of the digits in an integer.

> ### Exercise 2.12

Any positive integer i can be expressed as $i = 2^n k$, where k is odd, that is, as a power of 2 times an odd number. We call n the exponent of 2 in i. For example, the exponent of 2 in 40 is 3 (because $40 = 2^3 5$) whereas the exponent of 2 in 42 is 1. If i itself is odd, then n is zero. If, on the other hand, i is even, that means it can be divided by 2. Write a procedure for finding the exponent of 2 in its argument.

2.4 An Application: Custom-Sized Quilts

At the end of the previous chapter we made some quilts by pinwheeling basic blocks. The only problem is that the quilts only come in certain sizes: You could make a single cross by pinwheeling `rcross-bb`, or a quilt that is two crosses wide and high by pinwheeling the cross, or four wide and high by pinwheeling that, or .... But we want a quilt that is four crosses wide and *three* high. We're not being stubborn; we have a paying customer whose bed isn't square. In fact, given that there are lots of different sizes of beds in the world, it would probably be best if we wrote a general purpose procedure that could make a quilt any number of crosses wide and any number high. We know how to make a cross; the challenge is how to replicate an image a desired number of times.

> ### Exercise 2.13

We can often simplify a problem by first considering a one-dimensional version of it. Here, this means we should look at the problem of stacking a specified number of copies of an image one on top of another in a vertical column. Write a procedure `stack-copies-of` so that, for example, (`stack-copies-of 5 rcross-bb`) produces a tall, thin stack of five basic blocks. By the way, the name `stack-copies-of` illustrates a useful trick for remembering the order of the arguments. We chose the name so that it effectively has blanks in it for the arguments to fill in: "stack _____ copies of _____."

> ### Exercise 2.14

Use your `stack-copies-of` from the previous exercise to define a procedure called `quilt` so that (`quilt (pinwheel rcross-bb) 4 3`) makes our desired quilt. In general, (`quilt image w h`) should make a quilt that is *w* images wide and *h* images high. Try this out.

Some quilts have more subtle patterns, such as checkerboard-style alternation of light and dark regions. Consider, for example, the *Blowing in the Wind* pattern,

Figure 2.3 The *Blowing in the Wind* quilt pattern.

shown in Figure 2.3. This is again made out of pinwheels of a basic block; the basic block, which we've defined as `bitw-bb`, is

and the result of pinwheeling it is

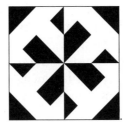

Five copies of this pinwheel appear as the white-on-black regions in the corners and the center of the quilt. The four black-on-white regions of the quilt are occupied by a black/white reversal of the pinwheel, namely,

This "inverted" version of the pinwheel can be produced using the primitive procedure `invert` as follows: `(invert (pinwheel bitw-bb))`.

The trick is to make a checkerboard out of alternating copies of `(pinwheel bitw-bb)` and `(invert (pinwheel bitw-bb))`. We can approach this in many different ways, because so many algebraic identities are satisfied by `invert`, `stack`, and `quarter-turn-right`. For example, inverting an inverted image gives you the original image back, and inversion "distributes" over stacking (inverting a stack gives the same result as stacking the inverses).

Before you write a procedure for alternating inverted and noninverted copies of an image, you should pin down exactly what *alternating* means. For example, you might specify that the image in the lower left corner is noninverted and that the images within each row and column alternate. Or, you could specify that the alternation begins with a noninverted image in the upper left, the upper right, or the lower right. For a three-by-three checkerboard such as is shown here, all of these are equivalent; only if the width or height is even will it make a difference. Nonetheless, it is important before you begin to program to be sure you know which version you are programming.

![Exercise 2.15]

One way or another, develop a procedure `checkerboard` for producing arbitrarily sized checker-boarded quilts of images. Making a call of the form `(checkerboard (pin-wheel bitw-bb) 3 3)` should result in the Blowing in the Wind pattern of Figure 2.3. The `checkerboard` procedure also produces an interesting "boxed crosses" pattern if you pinwheel `rcross-bb` instead of `bitw-bb` (check it out), although we hadn't intended it for that purpose, and it can be used with a black (or white) image to make a regular checkerboard. You might be interested to try it on some of your own basic blocks as well.

Review Problems

▷ **Exercise 2.16**

Consider the following procedure foo:

```
(define foo
  (lambda (x n)
    (if (= n 0)
        1
        (+ (expt x n) (foo x (- n 1)))))))
```

Use induction to prove that (foo x n) terminates with the value

$$\frac{x^{n+1} - 1}{x - 1}$$

for all values of $x \neq 1$ and for all integers $n \geq 0$. You may assume that expt works correctly, (i.e., (expt b m) returns b^m). *Hint:* The inductive step will involve some algebra.

▷ **Exercise 2.17**

Perhaps you have heard the following Christmas song:

> On the first day of Christmas
> My true love gave to me
> A partridge in a pear tree.

> On the second day of Christmas
> My true love gave to me
> Two turtle doves
> And a partridge in a pear tree.

> On the third day of Christmas
> My true love gave to me
> Three French hens,
> Two turtle doves,
> And a partridge in a pear tree.

And so on, through the twelfth day of Christmas. Note that on the first day, my true love gave me one present, on the second day three presents, on the third day six presents, and so on. The following procedure determines how many presents I received from my true love on the *n*th day of Christmas:

```
(define presents-on-day
  (lambda (n)
    (if (= n 1)
        1
        (+ n (presents-on-day (- n 1))))))
```

How many presents did I receive total over the 12 days of Christmas? This can be generalized by asking how many presents I received in total over the first n days. Write a procedure called **presents-through-day** (which may naturally use **presents-on-day**) that computes this as a function of n. Thus, (**presents-through-day** 1) should return 1, (**presents-through-day** 2) should return $1 + 3 = 4$, (**presents-through-day** 3) should return $1 + 3 + 6 = 10$, etc.

▷ **Exercise 2.18**

Prove by induction that for every nonnegative integer n the following procedure computes $2n$:

```
(define f
  (lambda (n)
    (if (= n 0)
        0
        (+ 2 (f (- n 1))))))
```

▷ **Exercise 2.19**

Prove that for all nonnegative integers n the following procedure computes the value $2^{(2^n)}$:

```
(define foo
  (lambda (n)
    (if (= n 0)
        2
        (expt (foo (- n 1)) 2))))
```

Hint: You will need to use certain laws of exponents, in particular that $(2^a)^b = 2^{ab}$ and $2^a 2^b = 2^{a+b}$.

▷ **Exercise 2.20**

Prove that the following procedure computes $n/(n+1)$ for any nonnegative integer n. That is, (**f** n) computes $n/(n + 1)$ for any integer $n \geq 0$.

```
(define f
  (lambda (n)
    (if (= n 0)
        0
        (+ (f (- n 1))
           (/ 1 (* n (+ n 1)))))))
```

▷ **Exercise 2.21**

a. Appendix A describes the predefined procedure `stack` by saying (among other things) that (`stack` *image₁ image₂*) produces an image, the height of which is the sum of the heights of *image₁* and *image₂*. How would you describe the height of the image that is the value of (`stack-on-itself` *image*), given the following definition of `stack-on-itself`?

```
(define stack-on-itself
  (lambda (image)
    (stack image image)))
```

b. Use induction to prove that given the definition in part **a** and the following definition of **f**, the value of (`f` *image n*) is an image 2^n times as high as *image*, provided *n* is a nonnegative integer.

```
(define f
  (lambda (image n)
    (if (= n 0)
        image
        (stack-on-itself (f image (- n 1))))))
```

▷ **Exercise 2.22**

Consider the following procedure:

```
(define foo
  (lambda (n)
    (if (= n 0)
        0
        (+ (foo (- n 1))
           (/ 1 (- (* 4 (square n)) 1))))))
```

a. What is the value of (foo 1)? Of (foo 2)? Of (foo 3)?

b. Prove by induction that for every nonnegative integer *n*, (foo n) computes $n/(2n + 1)$.

▷ **Exercise 2.23**

Suppose we have made images for each of the digits 0–9, which we name **zero-bb**, **one-bb**, ..., **nine-bb**. For example, if you evaluate **five-bb**, you get the following image:

a. Write a procedure **image-of-digit** that takes a single parameter *d* that is an integer satisfying $0 \le d \le 9$ and returns the image corresponding to *d*. You should definitely use a **cond**, because you would otherwise have to nest the **if**s ridiculously deep.

b. Using the procedure **image-of-digit**, write another procedure **image-of-number** that takes a single parameter *n* that is a nonnegative integer and returns the image corresponding to it. Thus, (**image-of-number 143**) would return the following image:

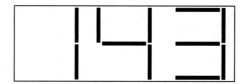

Hint: Use the Scheme procedures **quotient** and **remainder** to break *n* apart. Also, you may use the procedure **side-by-side** from Exercise 1.9b without redefining it here.

Chapter Inventory

Vocabulary

recursion
permutations
factorial
base case (of a procedure)

recursive process
linear recursion
mathematical induction
base case (of a proof)

induction hypothesis	debug
inductive step	bug
termination	one-layer thinking

Slogans

The recursion strategy	The base case imperative
The self-similarity strategy	One-layer thinking maxim

New Predefined Scheme Names

The dagger symbol (†) indicates a name that is not part of the R⁴RS standard for Scheme.

`expt`	`remainder`
`quotient`	`invert`†

New Scheme Syntax

comments	clauses (of a `cond`)
`cond`	`else`

Scheme Names Defined in This Chapter

`factorial`	`sum-of-powers`
`power`	`num-digits`
`square`	`stack-copies-of`
`quot`	`quilt`
`multiply`	`bitw-bb`
`sum-of-first`	`checkerboard`
`subtract-the-first`	`presents-on-day`
`factorial2`	`presents-through-day`
`sum-integers-from-to`	`image-of-digit`
`sum-of-squares`	`image-of-number`
`sum-of-cubes`	

Sidebars

Exponents

Notes

The Blowing in the Wind pattern is by Rose [43]. The image of mathematical induction in terms of successive days is used very powerfully by Knuth in his fascinating "mathematical novelette" *Surreal Numbers* [32].

CHAPTER THREE

Iteration and Invariants

3.1 Iteration

In the previous chapter, we used a general problem-solving strategy, namely, recursion: solve a smaller problem first, then do the little bit of work that's left. Now we'll turn to a somewhat different problem-solving strategy, known as *iteration*:

The iteration strategy: By doing a little bit of work first, transform your problem into a smaller one with the same solution. Then solve the resulting smaller problem.

Let's listen in on a hypothetical student thinking aloud as she uses this strategy to devise an alternative `factorial` procedure:

I've got a factorial problem, like $6 \times 5 \times 4 \times 3 \times 2 \times 1$.

Gee, I wonder if I can transform that into a simpler problem with the same answer? What would make it simpler? Well, the problem I've got is six numbers multiplied together. Five numbers multiplied together would be simpler. I wonder if I can find five numbers that when multiplied together give the same result?

$$6 \times 5 \times 4 \times 3 \times 2 \times 1 = \underline{\quad} \times \underline{\quad} \times \underline{\quad} \times \underline{\quad} \times \underline{\quad}$$

Well, I can't just put the numbers I've got into the blanks, because I've got more numbers than blanks. (That's the whole point.) Because I have one extra number, maybe I can put two numbers into one blank. I guess I can't really get something for nothing—if I only want to have four multiplications left to do, I better do one of my five now. If I multiply two of the numbers together now and put the product in one of the blanks, that would be a way to get two numbers into one blank. Maybe

I'll multiply the first two together, the 6 and the 5, to get 30. So I have

$$6 \times 5 \times 4 \times 3 \times 2 \times 1 = 30 \times 4 \times 3 \times 2 \times 1$$

That was great, I got the problem down from a five multiplication problem to a four multiplication problem. I bet I could transform it the same way into a three-multiplication problem:

$$\ldots = 120 \times 3 \times 2 \times 1$$

If I keep going like this, one multiplication at a time, eventually it will all boil down to a single number:

$$\ldots = 360 \times 2 \times 1$$
$$\ldots = 720 \times 1$$
$$\ldots = 720$$

I guess I could call that last step a "zero multiplication" problem. And that's the answer to the original problem, because it's equal to all the preceding problems, all the way back to the original factorial one.

Now I want to write a procedure that could solve any problem of this form. What specifics do I have to give it to tell it which problem of this form to solve? Well, I could give it the numbers to multiply together. .... No, that's silly, there could be lots of them. I wonder if there is some more concise description of these problems .... Oh, I see, the numbers after the first are always consecutive, down to 1. So I could describe the problems by saying "30 times 4 down to 1" or "120 times 3 down to 1" or that kind of thing. Oh, in fact the "down to 1" part just means it's a factorial, so I've got problems like "30 times 4!" or "120 times 3!." So what I want is a procedure to multiply some number times some factorial:

```
(define factorial-product
  (lambda (a b) ; compute a * b!
    ))
```

What I did with those products was transform them into smaller ones, like this:

```
(define factorial-product
  (lambda (a b) ; compute a * b! as (a*b) * (b-1)!
    (factorial-product (* a b) (- b 1))))
```

Of course, I have to stop making the factorial part smaller eventually, when it can't get any smaller—let's see, that's when there were zero multiplications left— right after multiplying 720 by 1. Because when I had 720 times 1 that was $720 \times 1!$,

I guess the next step is $720 \times 0!$. I never really thought about $0!$ before, but it would make sense; the factorial is just some consecutive numbers to multiply together, and here there aren't any, so that's $0!$. That means I stop when b is 0:

```scheme
(define factorial-product
  (lambda (a b) ; compute a * b!
    (if (= b 0)
        a
        (factorial-product (* a b) (- b 1)))))
```

Now I have a general way of solving problems of the form one number times the factorial of the other number. Wait a second, that wasn't what I really wanted: I really wanted just to do factorials. Hmmm ..., I could just trick my procedure into doing plain factorials by telling it to multiply by 1, because that doesn't change anything:

```scheme
(define factorial
  (lambda (n)
    (factorial-product 1 n)))
```

A couple things are worth noticing here. One is that the student changed our original problem of finding a factorial to the more general problem of finding the product of a factorial and another number. Our original problem is then just a special case of this latter problem. This is a good example of what Polya calls "the inventor's paradox" in his excellent book on problem solving, *How to Solve It*. Sometimes, trying to solve a more general or "harder" problem actually makes the original problem easier to solve.

Another point to notice is that the student made use of comments (starting with semicolons) to explain her Scheme program. Her comment identifies what `factorial-product` computes (namely, its first argument times the factorial of its second argument). We'll say more about this comment in a bit; it's an extremely important kind of comment that you should definitely make a habit of using.

▶ Exercise 3.1

At the very beginning of the above design of the iterative factorial, a choice needed to be made of which two numbers to multiply together, in order to fit the two of them into one blank. In the version shown above, the decision was made to multiply together the leftmost two numbers (the 6 and the 5). However, it would have been equally possible to make some other choice, such as multiplying together the rightmost two numbers. Redo the design, following this alternative path.

The iterative way of doing factorials may not seem very different from the recursive way. In both cases, the multiplications get done one at a time. In both cases, one multiplication is done explicitly, and the others are implicitly done by the procedure reinvoking itself. The only difference is whether all but one of the multiplications are done first and then the remaining one, or whether one multiplication is done first and then all the rest. However, this is actually an extremely important distinction. It is the difference between putting the main problem on hold while a subproblem is solved versus progressively reducing the problem.

The subproblem approach is less efficient because some of the computer's memory needs to be used to remember what the main problem was while it is doing the subproblem. Because the subproblem itself involves a subsubproblem, and so forth, the recursive approach actually uses more and more memory for remembering what it was doing at each level as it burrows deeper. This was illustrated by the diagram of the recursive factorial process shown in Figure 2.1 on page 26. That diagram had one column for the original problem of evaluating (`factorial 3`), one for the subproblem of evaluating (`factorial 2`), and one for the sub-subproblem of evaluating (`factorial 1`). We remarked that a diagram of the recursive evaluation of (`factorial 52`) would have had 52 columns. The number of columns in these diagrams corresponds to the amount of the computer's memory that is used in the evaluation process.

By contrast, the iterative approach is only ever solving a single problem—the problem just changes into an easier one with the same answer, which becomes the new single problem to solve. Thus, the amount of memory remains fixed, no matter how many reduction steps the iterative process goes through. If we look at the diagram in Figure 3.1 (on page 53) of the iterative process of evaluating (`factorial 3`), we can see that the computation stays in a single column. (As usual, we've been selective in showing details.) Even if we were to evaluate (`factorial 52`), we wouldn't need a wider sheet of paper, just a taller one. (The vertical dimension corresponds to time: It would take longer to compute (`factorial 52`).) The difference between the two types of processes is less clear if we simply list the computational steps than it is from the diagrams, but with a practiced eye you can also see the iterative nature of the process in this more compact form:

```
(factorial 3)
(factorial-product 1 3)
(if (= 3 0) 1 (factorial-product (* 1 3) (- 3 1)))
(factorial-product (* 1 3) (- 3 1))
(factorial-product 3 2)
(if (= 2 0) 3 (factorial-product (* 3 2) (- 2 1)))
(factorial-product (* 3 2) (- 2 1))
(factorial-product 6 1)
(if (= 1 0) 6 (factorial-product (* 6 1) (- 1 1)))
```

```
(factorial-product (* 6 1) (- 1 1))
(factorial-product 6 0)
(if (= 0 0) 6 (factorial-product (* 6 0) (- 0 1)))
6
```

If we work through the analogous computational steps for (`factorial 6`), but this time leave out some more steps, namely, those involving the `if`s and the arithmetic, the skeleton we're left with mirrors exactly the hypothetical student's calculation of 6! done at the beginning of this chapter:

`(factorial 6)`	6!
`(factorial-product 1 6)`	$= 1 \times 6!$
`(factorial-product 6 5)`	$= 6 \times 5!$
`(factorial-product 30 4)`	$= 30 \times 4!$
`(factorial-product 120 3)`	$= 120 \times 3!$
`(factorial-product 360 2)`	$= 360 \times 2!$
`(factorial-product 720 1)`	$= 720 \times 1!$
`(factorial-product 720 0)`	$= 720 \times 0!$
`720`	$= 720$

To dramatize the reduced memory consumption of iterative processes, take down the paper chain that is decorating your room, disassemble it, and reassemble it using this new process:

▪ To make a chain of length n,
   (a) Bend one strip around and join its ends together.
   (b) Ask yourself to link $n - 1$ more links onto it.
▪ To link k links onto a chain,
   (a) If $k = 0$, you are done. Hang the chain back up in your room.
   (b) Otherwise,
      i. Slip one strip through an end link of the chain, bend it around, and join the ends together.
      ii. Ask yourself to link $k - 1$ links onto the chain.

Notice the key difference: You are able to do this one alone, in the privacy of your own room, without having to invite a whole bunch of friends over to stand in line. The reason why the recursive process required one person per link is that you had to stand there with a link in your hand and wait for the rest of the crew

Problem

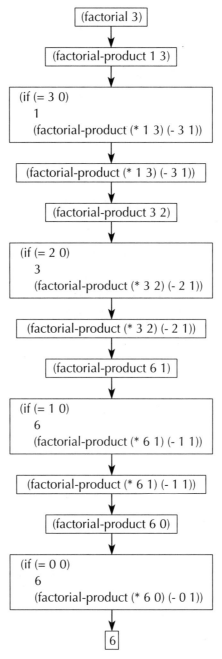

Figure 3.1 The iterative process of evaluating (`factorial 3`).

to build the chain of length $n - 1$ before you could put your link on. Because the process continued that way, each of your friends in turn wound up having to stand there waiting to put a link on. With the new iterative version, there's no waiting for a subtask to be completed before work can proceed on the main task, so it can all be done singlehandedly (which in a computer would mean with a fixed amount of memory).

Just to confuse everybody, procedures such as the ones we've looked at in this chapter are still called *recursive procedures*, because they invoke themselves. They simply don't generate *recursive processes*. A recursive procedure is any procedure that invokes itself (directly or indirectly). If the self-invocation is to solve a subproblem, where the solution to the subproblem is not the same as the solution to the main problem, the computational process is a recursive process, as in the prior chapter. If, on the other hand, the self-invocation is to solve a reduced version of the original problem (i.e., a simpler version of the problem but with the exact same answer as the original), the process is an iterative process, as in this chapter.

> ### Exercise 3.2

Write a new procedure for finding the exponent of 2 in a positive integer, as in Exercise 2.12 on page 40, but this time using an iterative process.

> ### Exercise 3.3

You have one last chance to quilt. (In the next chapter we'll do something different, but equally pretty.) Rewrite your procedure for making arbitrary sized quilts so that it generates an iterative process. Do the same for your procedure for checkerboard quilts. As before, it helps to start with the one-dimensional case, that is, an iterative version of `stack-copies-of`.

3.2 Using Invariants

Comments such as the one on the `factorial-product` procedure—the one that said what the procedure computed, as a function of the argument values—can be very handy. A comment such as this one is called an *invariant* because it describes a quantity that doesn't change. Every time around the `factorial-product` iteration, b decreases by 1, but a increases by a multiple of the old b, so the product $a \times b!$ remains constant. In fact, that's another good way to think about the design of such a procedure: Some parameter keeps moving toward the base case, and some other parameter changes in a compensatory fashion to keep the invariant quantity fixed. In this section, we'll show how invariants can be used to write iterative procedures and how they can be used to prove a procedure is correct.

Let's start with `factorial-product`. Because the procedure is already written, we'll prove that it is correct, that is, that it really does compute $a \times b!$, provided b is a nonnegative integer. (Notice how we're focusing on the invariant.)

Base case: If $b = 0$, it follows from the way `if` expressions work that the procedure terminates with a as its value. Because $a \times 0! = a \times 1 = a$, the theorem therefore holds in this base case.

Induction hypothesis: We will assume that (`factorial-product i k`) terminates with value $i \times k!$ provided that k is in the range $0 \le k < b$.

Inductive step: Consider the evaluation of (`factorial-product a b`), with $b > 0$. Clearly the procedure will terminate with the same value as the expression (`factorial-product (* a b) (- b 1)`), provided that this recursive call terminates. However, because $0 \le b - 1 < b$, the induction hypothesis allows us to assume that this call will indeed terminate, with $(a \times b) \times (b - 1)!$ as its value. Because $(a \times b) \times (b - 1)! = a \times (b \times (b - 1)!) = a \times b!$, we see that the procedure does indeed terminate with the correct answer in this case, assuming the induction hypothesis.

Conclusion: Therefore, by mathematical induction, the evaluation of (`factorial-product a b`) will terminate with the value $a \times b!$ for any nonnegative integer b (and any number a).

Having shown this formal proof by induction, it's illuminating to look back at the comments the hypothetical student included in the `factorial-product` definition. We already identified the primary comment, that the procedure computes $a \times b!$, as the invariant, which is what the proof is proving. However, note that at a critical moment in designing the procedure the student amplified it to say that the procedure "computes $a \times b!$ as $(a \times b) \times (b - 1)!$." This can now be recognized as a simplified version of the inductive step. Proof by induction should be used this way: first as comments written while you are designing the procedure, that give a bare outline of the most important ingredients of the proof. Later, if you need to, you can flesh out the full proof. Of course, leaving the comments in can be helpful to a reader who needs the same points made explicit as you did.

Next we'll look at writing an iterative version of the **power** procedure from Exercise 2.1 on page 28. Finding a power involves doing many multiplications, so it is somewhat similar to **factorial**. For that reason, we'll define **power** and **power-product** analogously to the way we did with **factorial** and we'll use a similar invariant:

```
(define power-product
  (lambda (a b e)     ; returns a times b to the e power
    (if (= e 0)

        _____

        (power-product _____  _____  _____)))))
```

```
(define power
  (lambda (b e)
    (power-product 1 b e)))
```

If we imagine trying to prove this is correct using induction, filling in the first blank is connected with the base case of the induction proof. Because we're trying to prove that $a \times b^0$ is returned in this case, and because $b^0 = 1$, we should fill in that first blank with **a**.

How should we fill in the remaining three blanks? Think about an induction proof. In order for the induction hypothesis to apply, we've got to fill in the last blank with something that is a nonnegative integer and is strictly less than e. We know that e is a positive integer (it was originally only guaranteed to be nonnegative, but we just handled the case of $e = 0$). This means that $e - 1$ is a nonnegative integer, and it is of course less than e. Therefore, we should probably put $e - 1$ in the last blank. The base goes in the next to last blank. Because we're trying to multiply e copies of b together, the base should probably remain unchanged as b. Thus we are left with what to fill in as the first parameter of the recursive call to **power-product**. Our invariant comes in handy here. Suppose we put in some expression, say x, here. According to our invariant (and our induction hypothesis), this call to **power-product** will return $x \cdot b^{e-1}$. On the other hand, this is also the value that gets returned from the whole procedure when $e > 0$. But the invariant says that this value should be $a \cdot b^e$. Thus, we can set up an equation and solve it for x:

$$x \cdot b^{e-1} = a \cdot b^e$$
$$x = \frac{a \cdot b^e}{b^{e-1}}$$
$$x = a \cdot b$$

Putting this all together gives us:

```
(define power-product
  (lambda (a b e)     ; returns a times b to the e power
    (if (= e 0)
        a
        (power-product (* a b) b (- e 1)))))))
```

▶ **Exercise 3.4**

Give a formal induction proof that `power-product` is correct.

▶ **Exercise 3.5**

If when you did Exercise 3.2, you didn't write down the invariant for your iterating procedure, do so now. Next, use induction to prove that your procedure does in fact compute this invariant quantity.

In our final example, we'll write a procedure that a sixteenth-century mathematician, Pierre Fermat, thought would produce prime numbers. A *prime number* is a positive integer with exactly two positive divisors, 1 and itself. Fermat thought that all numbers produced by squaring 2 any number of times and then adding 1 would be prime. Certainly, the numbers $2 + 1 = 3$ (in which 2 isn't squared at all), $2^2 + 1 = 5$, $(2^2)^2 + 1 = 17$, $((2^2)^2)^2 + 1 = 257$, and $(((2^2)^2)^2)^2 + 1 = 65{,}537$ are prime numbers (although checking 65,537 does take some effort). We call these the zeroth through fourth *Fermat numbers*, corresponding to zero through four squarings. Unfortunately, the fifth Fermat number, 4,294,967,297, is not a prime, because it equals $641 \times 6{,}700{,}417$. In fact, the only Fermat numbers known to be prime are the zeroth through fourth. Many Fermat numbers are known to be composite (i.e., not prime); the largest of these is the 23,471st Fermat number. On the other hand, no one knows whether the twenty-fourth Fermat number is prime or composite. (This is the smallest Fermat number for which the primality is unknown.)

We can translate our definition of Fermat numbers into Scheme:

```
(define fermat-number        ; computes the nth Fermat number
  (lambda (n)
    (+ (repeatedly-square 2 n) 1)))
```

Most of the work is done in `repeatedly-square`, which we can outline as follows:

```
(define repeatedly-square  ; computes b squared n times, where
  (lambda (b n)            ;   n is a nonnegative integer
    (if (= n 0)
        b      ;not squared at all
        (repeatedly-square _____  _____))))
```

How do we fill in the blanks? Again, to be able to apply the induction hypothesis, we've got to fill in the second blank with something that is a nonnegative integer and is strictly less than *n*. As before, we'll try $n - 1$. This brings us to

```
(define repeatedly-square   ; computes b squared n times, where
  (lambda (b n)             ;   n is a nonnegative integer
    (if (= n 0)
        b     ; not squared at all
        (repeatedly-square _____ (- n 1)))))
```

Now, whatever we fill in the remaining blank, we know from the induction hypothesis that it will be squared $n-1$ times. We don't need to think about *how* it will be squared $n-1$ times; that's what makes this one-layer thinking. Now the question is, What should be squared $n-1$ times to produce the desired result, b squared n times? The answer is b^2; that is, if we square b once and then $n-1$ more times, it will have been squared n times in all. This leads to

```
(define repeatedly-square   ; computes b squared n times, where
  (lambda (b n)             ;   n is a nonnegative integer
    (if (= n 0)
        b     ;not squared at all
        (repeatedly-square (square b) (- n 1)))))
```

We explicitly concern ourselves only with squaring b the first time and trust based on the induction hypothesis that it will be squared the remaining $n-1$ times.

3.3   Perfect Numbers, Internal Definitions, and Let

Having seen how iteration works, let's work through an extended example using iteration, both to solidify our understanding and also to provide opportunity for learning a few more helpful features of Scheme.

A number is called *perfect* if the sum of its divisors is twice the number. (Equivalently, a number is perfect if it is equal to the sum of its divisors other than itself.) Although this is a simple definition, lots of interesting questions concerning perfect numbers remain unanswered to date; for example, no one knows whether there are any odd perfect numbers. In this section, we'll use the computer to search for perfect numbers.

A good starting point might be to write a simple `perfect?` predicate, leaving all the hard part for `sum-of-divisors`:

```
(define perfect?
  (lambda (n)
    (= (sum-of-divisors n) (* 2 n))))
```

The simplest way to compute the sum of the divisors of n would be to check each number from 1 to n, adding it into a running sum if it divides n. This computation sounds like an iterative process; as we check each number, the range left to check gets smaller, and thus transforms the problem into a smaller one. The running sum changes in a compensatory fashion: Any divisor no longer included in the range to check is instead included in the running sum. The invariant quantity is the sum of the divisors still in the range plus the running sum. The following definition is based on these ideas. Note that `divides?` needs to be written.

```
(define sum-of-divisors
  (lambda (n)
    (define sum-from-plus ; sum of all divisors of n which are
      (lambda (low addend) ; >= low, plus addend
        (if (> low n)
            addend      ; no divisors of n are greater than n
            (sum-from-plus (+ low 1)
                           (if (divides? low n)
                               (+ addend low)
                               addend)))))
    (sum-from-plus 1 0)))
```

The preceding definition illustrates a useful feature of Scheme: It is possible to nest a definition inside a lambda expression, at the beginning of the body. This nesting achieves two results:

▪ The internally defined name is private to the body in which it appears. This means that we can't invoke `sum-from-plus` directly but rather only by using `sum-of-divisors`. It also means that we're able to use a relatively nondescriptive name (it doesn't specify what it is summing) without fear that we might accidentally give two procedures the same name. As long as the two definitions in question are internal to separate bodies, the same name can be used without problem.

▪ The `sum-from-plus` procedure is able to make use of n, without needing to have it passed as a third argument. This is because a nested procedure can make use of names from the procedure it is nested inside of (or from yet further out, in the case of repeated nesting).

Why didn't we nest `sum-of-divisors` itself inside of the `perfect?` procedure? Although we wrote `sum-of-divisors` for the sake of `perfect?`, it could very well be useful on its own, for other purposes. This is in contrast to `sum-from-plus`, which is hard to imagine as a generally useful procedure rather than merely a means to implement `sum-of-divisors`.

The only detail remaining before we have a working `perfect?` test is the predicate `divides?`. We can implement it using the primitive procedure `remainder`:

```
(define divides?
  (lambda (a b)
    (= (remainder b a) 0)))
```

> **Exercise 3.6**

Although the method we use for computing the sum of the divisors is straightforward, it isn't particularly efficient. Any time we find a divisor d of n, we can infer that n/d is also a divisor. In particular, all the divisors greater than the square root of n can be inferred from the divisors less than the square root. Make use of this observation to write a more efficient version of **sum-of-divisors** that stops once $low^2 \geq n$. Remember that if $low^2 = n$, low and n/low are the same divisor, not two different ones.

If you start testing numbers for perfectness by trying them out one by one with **perfect?**, you'll quickly grow bored: It seems almost nothing is perfect. Because perfect numbers are so few and far between, we should probably automate the search. The following procedure finds the first perfect number after its argument value:

```
(define first-perfect-after
  (lambda (n)
    (if (perfect? (+ n 1))
        (+ n 1)
        (first-perfect-after (+ n 1)))))
```

Having this start searching with the first number *after* its argument is convenient for using it to search for consecutive perfect numbers, like this:

```
(first-perfect-after 0)
```
6

```
(first-perfect-after 6)
```
28

```
(first-perfect-after 28)
```
496

Because the search starts after the number we specify, we can specify each time the perfect number we just found, and it will find the next. Unfortunately, starting with the next number causes us to use three copies of the expression (+ n 1), which is a bit ugly.

Rather than put up with this, or changing how the procedure is used, we can make use of another handy Scheme feature, namely, `let`:

```
(define first-perfect-after
  (lambda (n)
    (let ((next (+ n 1)))
      (if (perfect? next)
          next
          (first-perfect-after next)))))
```

What this means is to first evaluate `(+ n 1)` and then locally let `next` be a name for that value while evaluating the body of the `let`. Not only does this make the code easier to read, it also means that `(+ n 1)` only gets evaluated once. There are two sets of parentheses around `next` and `(+ n 1)` because you can have multiple name/expression pairs. One set of parentheses goes around each name and its corresponding value expression, and another set of parentheses goes around the whole list of pairs. For example,

```
(define distance
  (lambda (x0 y0 x1 y1)
    (let ((xdiff (- x0 x1))
          (ydiff (- y0 y1)))
      (sqrt (+ (* xdiff xdiff)
               (* ydiff ydiff))))))
```

All the value expressions are evaluated before any of the new names are put into place. Those new names may then be used only in the body of the let. Note that a let expression is just like any other expression; in particular, you can use it anywhere you'd use an expression, not just as the body of a lambda expression.

3.4   Iterative Improvement: Approximating the Golden Ratio

One important kind of iterative process is the *iterative improvement* of an approximation to some quantity. We start with a crude approximation, successively improve it to better and better approximations, and stop when we have found one that is good enough. Recall that our general definition of an iterative process is that it works by successively transforming the problem into a simpler problem with the same answer. Here the original problem is to get from a crude approximation to one that is good enough. This problem is transformed into the simpler problem of getting from a somewhat less crude approximation to one that is good enough. In other words, our goal is still to get to the good enough approximation, but we move the starting point one improvement step closer to that goal. Our general outline, then, is

```
(define find-approximation-from
  (lambda (starting-point)
    (if (good-enough? starting-point)
        starting-point
        (find-approximation-from (improve starting-point)))))))
```

In this section, we'll follow this general outline in order to develop one specific example of an iterative improvement procedure.

Since ancient times, many artists have considered that the most aesthetically pleasing proportion for a work of art has a ratio of the long side to the short side that is the same as the ratio of the sum of the sides to the long side, as illustrated in Figure 3.2. This ratio is called the *golden ratio.*

Among its many interesting properties (which range from pure mathematics to aesthetics and biology), the golden ratio is irrational, that is, it is not equal to any ratio of integers. Real artists, however, are generally satisfied with close approximations. For example, when we drew the illustration in Figure 3.2, we made it 377 points wide and 233 points high. (The point is a traditional printer's unit of distance.) The ratio 377/233 isn't exactly the golden ratio, but it is a quite good approximation: It's off by less than 1/50,000. How do we know that? Or more to the point, how did we

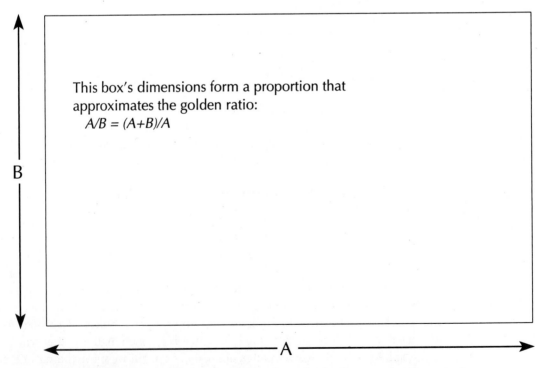

Figure 3.2   An illustration of the golden ratio, said to be the most pleasing proportion.

set about finding a ratio of integers that was that close? That's what we're about to embark on. Our goal is to write a procedure that, given a maximum tolerable error, will produce a rational approximation that is at least that close to the golden ratio. In other words, by the time we're done, you'll be able to get the above answer in the following way:

```
(approximate-golden-ratio 1/50000)
```
377/233

Recall that the definition of the golden ratio is that it is the ratio A/B such that $A/B = (A + B)/A$. Doing a little algebra, it follows that $A/B = 1 + B/A = 1 + 1/(A/B)$. In other words, if we take the golden ratio, divide it into 1, and then add 1, we'll get the golden ratio back again. For brevity, let's start calling the golden ratio not A/B but instead ϕ, the Greek letter phi, which is in honor of the sculptor Phidias, who is known to have consciously used the golden ratio in his work. This makes our equation

$$\phi = 1 + \frac{1}{\phi}$$

Because this is an equation, we can substitute the right-hand side for ϕ anywhere it occurs. In particular, we can substitute it for the ϕ on the right-hand side of the same equation:

$$\phi = 1 + \frac{1}{1 + \frac{1}{\phi}}$$

We could keep doing this over and over again, and we would get the infinite *continued fraction* for ϕ:

$$\phi = 1 + \frac{1}{1 + \frac{1}{1 + \frac{1}{\ddots}}}$$

It turns out that this continued fraction is the key to finding rational approximations to ϕ. All we have to do is calculate some finite part of that infinite tower. In particular, the following are better and better approximations of ϕ:

$$\phi_0 = 1$$

$$\phi_1 = 1 + \frac{1}{\phi_0}$$

$$\phi_2 = 1 + \frac{1}{\phi_1}$$

$$\phi_3 = 1 + \frac{1}{\phi_2}$$

$$\vdots$$

Using this technique, write a procedure, `improve`, that takes one of the approximations of ϕ and returns then next one. For example, given ϕ_2, it would return ϕ_3.

The only remaining problem is to figure out how good each of these approximations is, so we know when we've got a good enough one and can stop. Using some number theory, it is possible to show that the error of each approximation is less than 1 over the square of its denominator. So, for example, it follows that 377/233 is within $1/233^2$ of ϕ. We can stop when this is less than our acceptable error, or *tolerance* as it is called. We'll do this by setting up the overall `approximate-golden-ratio` procedure as follows:

```
(define approximate-golden-ratio
  (lambda (tolerance)
    (define find-approximation-from
      (lambda (starting-point)
        (if (good-enough? starting-point)
            starting-point
            (find-approximation-from (improve starting-point)))))
    (define good-enough?
      (lambda (approximation)
        (< (/ 1 (square (denominator approximation)))
           tolerance)))
    (find-approximation-from 1)))
```

The Scheme procedure `denominator` is used here, which returns the denominator of a rational number. (To be precise, it computes the denominator the number has when written in lowest terms; the denominator is always positive, even when the rational number is negative.)

Presumably any art work needs to be made out of something, and there are only about 10^{79} electrons, neutrons, and protons in the universe. Therefore, we can conservatively assume that no artist will ever need to know ϕ to better than one part in 10^{79}. Calculate an approximation that is within a tolerance of $1/10^{79}$, which can also be expressed as 10^{-79}. (To calculate this tolerance in Scheme, you could use the `expt` procedure, as in `(/ 1 (expt 10 79))` or `(expt 10 -79)`.)

An Application: The Josephus Problem

In the fast-paced world of computing, about the most damning comment you can make regarding the relevance of a technique is to say that it is of purely historical interest. At the other extreme of the relevance spectrum, you could say that something is a matter of life or death. In this section, we'll see an application of iterative processes that is quite literally both a matter of life or death *and* of purely historical interest—because we'll be deciding the life or death fate of people who lived in Galilee nearly 2000 years ago. Our real goal is to provide you with a memorable illustration that iterative processes operate by progressively reducing a problem to a smaller problem with the same answer: in this case, the problem will be made smaller by the drastic means of killing someone.

Josephus was a Jewish general who was in the city of Jotapata, in Galilee, when it fell after a brutal 47-day siege by the Roman army under Vespasian, in 67 CE. The Romans massacred the inhabitants of Jotapata, but Josephus initially evaded capture by hiding (by day) in a cavern. Forty other "persons of distinction" were already hiding in that cavern. One of these nameless other people was captured while out and about and revealed the location where Josephus and the others still hid. The Romans sent word that Josephus was to be captured alive, rather than killed. Josephus himself was all for this and ready to go over to the Romans. However, the others with him advocated mass suicide as preferable to enslavement by the Romans. They were sufficiently angered by Josephus's preference for surrender that he was barely able to keep them from killing him themselves. In order to satisfy them, Josephus orchestrated a scheme whereby they all drew lots (Josephus among them) to determine their order of death and then proceeded to kill themselves, with the second killing the first, the third the second, etc. However, Josephus managed to be one of the last two left and convinced the other who was left with him that they should surrender together.

How did Josephus wind up being one of the two who survived? The Greek version of Josephus's account attributes it to fortune or the providence of God. However, the Slavonic version (which shows some signs of originating from an earlier manuscript than the Greek) has a more interesting story: "He counted the numbers cunningly, and so deceived them all." The Slavonic version also doesn't specifically mention the drawing of lots, instead leaving it open exactly how the order was determined in which the cornered Jews killed one another. Thus, we have a tantalizing suggestion that Josephus used his mathematical ability to arrange what appeared to be a chance ordering, but in fact was rigged so that he would be one of the last two.

Out of this historical enigma has come a well-known mathematical puzzle. Suppose this is how Josephus's group did their self-killing: They stood in a circle and killed every third person, going around the circle. It is fairly clear who will get killed early on: the third, sixth, ninth, etc. However, once the process wraps around the circle, the situation is much less clear, because it will be every third still-surviving person who will be killed, skipping over those who are already dead from the previous round. Can you determine which people will live and which will die?

Our goal is to write a procedure that will determine the fate of a person, given his or her position in the circle and the total number of people in the circle. Rather than using any advanced mathematical ideas, we'll simply simulate the killing process, stopping when the position we are interested in is either killed or is one of the last two who are left.

Let's call the number of people in the circle n and number the positions from 1 to n. We'll assume that the killing of every third person starts with killing the person in position number 3. That is, we start by skipping over 1 and 2 and killing 3. We want to write a procedure, `survives?`, that takes as its arguments the position number and n and returns `#t` if the person in that position is one of the last two survivors; otherwise it returns `#f`. For example, we've already figured out that position 3 doesn't survive:

```
(survives? 3 40)
#f
```

Recall that Josephus called the killing off when he was left with only one other; thus we will say that if there are fewer than three people left, everybody remaining is a survivor:

```
(define survives?
  (lambda (position n)
    (if (< n 3)
        #t
        we still need to write this part)))
```

On the other hand, if there are three or more people left, we still have some killing left to do. As we saw above, if the person we care about is in position 3, that person is the one killed and hence definitely not a survivor:

```
(define survives?
  (lambda (position n)
    (if (< n 3)
        #t
        (if (= position 3)
            #f
            we still need to write this part))))
```

Suppose we aren't interested in the person in position number 3 but rather in some other person—let's say J. Doe. The person in position number 3 got killed, so

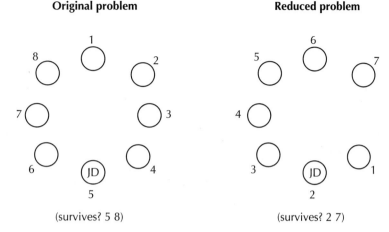

Figure 3.3   Determining the fate of J. Doe, who is initially in position 5 out of 8, can be reduced to finding the fate of position 2 out of 7.

now we only have $n - 1$ people left. Of that smaller group of $n - 1$, there will still be two survivors, and we still want to know if J. Doe is one of them. In other words, we have reduced our original problem (Is J. Doe among the survivors from this group of n?) to a smaller problem (Is J. Doe among the survivors from this group of $n - 1$?).

We can solve this smaller problem by using `survives?` again. However, the `survives?` procedure assumes that the positions are numbered so that we start by skipping over positions 1 and 2 and killing the person in position 3. Yet we don't really want to start back at position 1—we want to keep going from where we left off, skipping over 4 and 5 and killing 6. To solve this problem, we can renumber all the survivors' positions. The survivor who was in position 4 (just after the first victim) will get renumbered to be in position 1, because he is now the first to be skipped over. The survivor who was in position 5 gets renumbered to position 2, etc. For example, suppose we are interested in the fate of a specific person, let's say J. Doe, who is in position 5 out of a group of 40 people. Then we are initially interested in (`survives? 5 40`). Neither of the base cases applies, because $40 \geq 3$ and $5 \neq 3$. Therefore, we reduce the problem size by 1 (by killing off one of J. Doe's companions) and ask (`survives? 2 39`). The answer to this question will be the same as the answer to our original question (`survives? 5 40`), because J. Doe is now in position number 2 in our new renumbered circle of 39 people. Figure 3.3 illustrates this, but rather than going from 40 to 39 people, it goes from 8 to 7.

▶ **Exercise 3.9**

How about the people who were in positions 1 and 2; what position numbers are they in after the renumbering?

Exercise 3.10

Write a procedure for doing the renumbering. It should take two arguments: the old position number and the old number of people (*n*). (It can assume that the old position number won't ever be 3, because that person is killed and hence doesn't get renumbered.) It should return the new position number.

Exercise 3.11

Finish writing the `survives?` procedure, and carefully test it with a number of cases that are small enough for you to check by hand but that still cover an interesting range of situations.

Exercise 3.12

Write a procedure, analogous to `first-perfect-after`, that can be used to systematically search for surviving positions. What are the two surviving positions starting from a circle of 40 people? (Presumably Josephus chose one of these two positions.)

Now that you have settled the urgent question of where Josephus should stand, we can take some time to point out additional features of the Scheme programming language that would have simplified the procedure a little bit. You may recall that the overall form of the procedure involved two `if` expressions. The outer one checked to see if the killing was over; if it was, then the person we cared about was definitely a survivor, so the answer was `#t`. The inner `if` took care of the case where more killing was still needed. If our person of interest was in position number 3, and so was the next to go, the answer was `#f`. This succession of tests can be reformulated in a different way. Our person of interest is a survivor if the killing is over (i.e., $n < 3$) *or* we are *not* interested in position number 3 *and* the person survives in the reduced circle of $n - 1$ people. Writing this in Scheme, we get

```
(define survives?
  (lambda (position n)
    (or (< n 3)
        (and (not (= position 3))
             your part with n − 1 people goes here))))
```

This procedure illustrates three new features of Scheme: `or`, `and`, and `not`. Of these, `not` is just an ordinary procedure, which we could write ourselves, although it happens to be predefined. If its argument is `#f`, it returns `#t`; otherwise it returns `#f`. That way, it returns the true/false opposite of its argument. The other two logical operations, or and and, are not procedures. They are special language constructs like if. In fact, you can see their close relationship to if by comparing our new version of survives? with our old one. In particular, if $n < 3$, the computation is immediately over, with the answer of #t; the second part of the or is not evaluated. Similarly, if we don't have $n < 3$, but the position is equal to 3, the computation is immediately over with the answer of #f; the second part of the and is not evaluated.

The official definitions of or and and are made a bit more complicated by two factors:

- There needn't be just two expressions in an or or and. There can be more than two or even none or one.

- Any value other than #f counts as true in Scheme, not just #t. Thus we need to be careful about which true value gets returned.

The resolution to these issues is as follows. The expressions listed inside an or get evaluated one by one in order. As soon as one that produces a true value is found, that specific true value is returned as the value of the or expression. If none is found, the false value produced by the last expression is returned. If there are no expressions at all, #f is immediately returned. Similarly for and, the expressions are evaluated one by one in order. As soon as one that produces a false value is found, that false value is returned as the value of the and expression. If none is found, the specific true value produced by the last expression is returned. If there are no expressions in the and, #t is returned as the value.

Review Problems

▷ **Exercise 3.13**

In Exercises 2.12 and 3.2 you saw that any positive integer n can be expressed as $2^j k$ where k is odd, and you wrote a procedure to compute j, the exponent of 2. The following procedure instead computes k, the odd factor (which is the largest odd divisor of n). Does it generate a recursive process or an iterative process? Justify your answer.

```
(define largest-odd-divisor
  (lambda (n)
    (if (odd? n)
        n
        (largest-odd-divisor (/ n 2)))))
```

▷ **Exercise 3.14**

Here is a procedure that finds the largest number k such that $b^k \leq n$, assuming that n and b are integers such that $n \geq 1$ and $b \geq 2$. For example, (closest-power 2 23) returns 4:

```
(define closest-power
  (lambda (b n)
    (if (< n b)
        0
        (+ 1 (closest-power b (quotient n b))))))
```

a. Explain why this procedure generates a recursive process.

b. Write a version of closest-power that generates an iterative process.

▷ **Exercise 3.15**

Consider the following two procedures:

```
(define f
  (lambda (n)
    (if (= n 0)
        0
        (g (- n 1)))))

(define g
  (lambda (n)
    (if (= n 0)
        1
        (f (- n 1)))))
```

a. Use the substitution model to evaluate each of (f 1), (f 2), and (f 3).

b. Can you predict (f 4)? (f 5)? In general, which arguments cause f to return 0 and which cause it to return 1? (You need only consider nonnegative integers.)

c. Is the process generated by f iterative or recursive? Explain.

▷ **Exercise 3.16**

Consider the following two procedures:

```
(define f
  (lambda (n)
    (if (= n 0)
        0
        (+ 1 (g (- n 1))))))

(define g
  (lambda (n)
    (if (= n 0)
        1
        (+ 1 (f (- n 1))))))
```

a. Use the substitution model to illustrate the evaluation of (f 2), (f 3), and (f 4).

b. Is the process generated by f iterative or recursive? Explain.

c. Predict the values of (f 5) and (f 6).

▷ **Exercise 3.17**

Falling factorial powers are similar to normal powers and also similar to factorials. We write them as $n^{\underline{k}}$ and say "n to the k falling." This means that k consecutive numbers should be multiplied together, starting with n and working downward. For example, $7^{\underline{3}} = 7 \times 6 \times 5$ (i.e., three consecutive numbers from 7 downward multiplied together).

Write a procedure for calculating falling factorial powers that generates an iterative process.

▷ **Exercise 3.18**

We've already seen how to raise a number to an integer power, provided that the exponent isn't negative. We could extend this to allow negative exponents as well by using the following definition:

$$b^n = \begin{cases} 1 & \text{if } n = 0 \\ b^{n-1} \times b & \text{if } n > 0 \\ b^{n+1}/b & \text{if } n < 0 \end{cases}$$

a. Using this idea, write a procedure power such that (power b n) raises b to the n power for any integer n.

b. Use the substitution model to show how (power 2 -3) would be evaluated. (You can leave out steps that just determine which branch of a cond or if should be taken.) Does your procedure generate a recursive process or an iterative one?

▷ **Exercise 3.19**

Prove that, for all nonnegative integers n and numbers a, the following procedure computes the value $2^n \times a$:

```
(define foo
  (lambda (n a)
    (if (= n 0)
        a
        (foo (- n 1) (+ a a)))))
```

▷ **Exercise 3.20**

Consider the following two procedures:

```
(define factorial
  (lambda (n)
    (product 1 n)))

(define product
  (lambda (low high)
    (if (> low high)
        1
        (* low
           (product (+ low 1) high)))))
```

a. Use the substitution model to illustrate the evaluation of (factorial 4).

b. Is the process generated by factorial iterative or recursive? Explain.

c. Describe exactly what product computes in terms of its parameters.

Chapter Inventory

Vocabulary

iteration

the inventor's paradox

recursive procedure

invariant

prime number

Fermat number

perfect number

iterative improvement

golden ratio

continued fraction

tolerance

falling factorial powers

Slogans

The iteration strategy

New Predefined Scheme Names

```
denominator
not
```

New Scheme Syntax

nested (or internal) definitions   or
```
let
```
                                    and

Scheme Names Defined in This Chapter

```
factorial                  divides?
factorial-product          first-perfect-after
stack-copies-of            distance
power                      approximate-golden-ratio
power-product              improve
fermat-number              survives?
repeatedly-square          largest-odd-divisor
perfect?                   closest-power
sum-of-divisors            product
```

Notes

The way we have used the term *invariant* is superficially different from the way most other authors use it, but the notions are closely related. Most authors use *invariant assertions* rather than *invariant quantities*. That is, they focus not on a numerical quantity that remains constant but rather on a logical assertion such as $a = (b + 1) \times (b + 2) \times \cdots \times n$, the truth of which remains unchanged from one iteration to the next. The other difference is that most authors focus on what the computation has already accomplished rather than on what it is going to compute. So, although we say that `factorial-product` will compute $a \times b!$, others say that when `factorial-product` is entered, it is already the case that $a = (b + 1) \times (b + 2) \times \cdots \times n$. The relationship between these two becomes clear when we recognize that `factorial-product` is ultimately being used to compute $n!$. This gives the equation $n! = a \times b!$, which is equivalent to $a = (b + 1) \times (b + 2) \times \cdots \times n$.

Polya's *How to Solve It* introduced the phrase "inventor's paradox" for the idea that some problems can be made easier to solve by generalizing them [40]. Our information regarding which Fermat numbers are known to be prime or composite is from Ribenboim's *The New Book of Prime Number Records* [41]. For information on Fermat numbers, perfect numbers, continued fractions, and rational approximations, any good textbook on number theory should do. The classic is Hardy and Wright [25]. Perhaps the most accessible source of golden-ratio trivia is in Martin Gardner's second collection of mathematical recreations [22]. Our source for the number of subatomic particles in the universe is Davis's *The Lore of Large Numbers* [15]. For the story of Josephus, see his *Jewish Wars*, Book III, for example in the translation of H. St. J. Thackeray [28] or G. A. Williamson [29]; both these translations have appendixes pointing out the relevant deviation in the Slavonic version.

CHAPTER FOUR

Orders of Growth and Tree Recursion

4.1 Orders of Growth

In the previous chapters we've concerned ourselves with one aspect of how to design procedures: making sure that the generated process calculates the desired result. Although this is clearly important, there are other design considerations as well. If we compare our work to that of an aspiring automotive designer, we've learned how to make cars that get from here to there. That's important, but customers expect more. In this chapter we'll focus on considerations more akin to speed and gas mileage. Along the way we'll also add another style of process to our repertoire, alongside linear recursion and iteration.

At first glance, comparing the speed of two alternative procedures for solving the same problem should be easy. Pull out your stopwatch, time how long one takes, and then time how long the other takes. Nothing to it: one wins, the other loses. This approach has three primary weaknesses:

1. It can't be used to decide which procedure to run, because it requires running both. Similarly, you can't tell in advance that one process is going to take a billion years, and hence isn't worth waiting for, whereas the other one will be done tomorrow if you'll just be patient and wait that long.

2. It doesn't tell you how long other instances of the same general problem are going to take or even which procedure will be faster for them. Maybe method A calculates 52! in 1 millisecond, whereas procedure B takes 5 milliseconds. Now you want to compute 100!. Which method should you use? Maybe A, maybe B; sometimes the method that is faster on small problems is slower on large problems, like a sprinter doing poorly on long-distance races.

3. It doesn't distinguish performance differences that are flukes of the particular hardware, Scheme implementation, or programming details from those that are deeply rooted in the two problem-solving strategies and will persist even if the details are changed.

Computer scientists use several different techniques to cope with these difficulties, but the primary one is this:

The asymptotic outlook: Ask not which takes longer, but rather which is more rapidly taking longer as the problem size increases.

This idea is exceptionally hard to grasp. We are all much more experienced with feeling what it's like for something to be slow than we are with feeling something quickly growing slower. Luckily we have developed a foolproof experiment you can use to get a gut feeling of a process quickly growing slow.

The idea of this experiment is to compare the speeds of two different methods for sorting a deck of numbered cards. To get a feeling for which method becomes slow more rapidly, you will sort decks of different sizes and time yourself. Before you begin, you'll need to get a deck of 32 numbered cards; the web site for this book has sheets of cards that you can print out and cut up, or you could just make your own by writing numbers on index cards. Ask a classmate, friend, or helpful stranger to work with you, because timing your sorting is much easier with a partner. One of you does the actual sorting of the cards. The other keeps track of the rules of the sorting method, provides any necessary prompting, and points out erroneous moves. This kibitzer is also in charge of measuring and recording the time each sort takes (a stopwatch is really helpful for this).

The two sorting methods, or sorting *algorithms*, are described in sidebars that follow. (The word *algorithm* is essentially synonymous with *procedure* or *method*, with the main technical distinction being that only a procedure that is guaranteed to terminate may be called an algorithm. The connotation, as with method, is that one is referring to a general procedure independent of any particular embodiment in a programming language. This distinguishes algorithms from programs.) Before you begin, make sure that both you and your partner understand these two algorithms. You might want to try a practice run using a deck of four cards for selection sorting and a deck of eight cards for merge sorting, because the pattern of that sort isn't so discernible with only four cards.

Now that you're ready to begin, make a deck of four cards by shuffling all the cards well and then taking the top four as the deck to sort. Sort them using selection sort, keeping track of how long the sorting took. Do this again using a deck of 8 cards, then a deck of 16 cards, and finally all 32. Be sure to shuffle all the cards each time. Finally, try sorting decks of 4, 8, 16, and 32 cards using the merge sort algorithm.

Selection Sort

You will use three positions for stacks of cards:

destination

source   discard

Initially you should put all the cards, face down, on the source stack, with the other two positions empty. Now do the following steps repeatedly:

1. Take the top card off the source stack and put it face-up on the destination stack.
2. If that makes the source stack empty, you are done. The destination stack is in numerical order.
3. Otherwise, do the following steps repeatedly until the source stack is empty:
   (a) Take the top card off the source stack and compare it with the top of the destination stack.
   (b) If the source card has a larger number,
      i. Take the card on top of the destination stack and put it face down on the discard stack.
      ii. Put the card you took from the source stack face up on the destination stack.

      Otherwise, put the card from the source stack face down on the discard stack.
4. Slide the discard stack over into the source position, and start again with step 1.

► Merge Sort

You will need lots of space for this sorting procedure—enough to spread out all the cards—so it might be best done on the floor. (There are ways to do merge sort with less space, but they are harder to explain.) The basic skill you will need for merge sorting is merging two stacks of cards together, so first refer to the sidebar titled "Merging" (on the following page) for instructions on how to merge. Once you know how to merge, the actual merge sorting process is comparatively easy.

To do the actual merge sort, lay out the cards face down in a row. We will consider these to be the initial source "stacks" of cards, even though there is only one card per stack. The merge sort works by progressively merging pairs of stacks so that there are fewer stacks but each is larger; at the end, there will be a single large stack of cards.

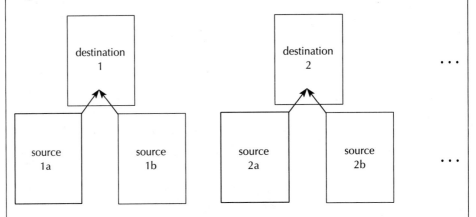

Repeat the following steps until there is a single stack of cards:

1. Merge the first two face-down stacks of cards.
2. As long as there are at least two face-down stacks, repeat the merging with the next two stacks.
3. Flip each face-up stack over.

The key question is: Suppose we now asked you to sort sixty-four cards. How would you feel about doing it using selection sort? We allowed some space there for you to groan. That's the feel of a process that is quickly becoming slow.

Although the most important point was that gut feeling of how quickly selection sort was becoming a stupid way to sort, we can try extracting some more value from

▶ Merging

You will have the two sorted stacks of cards to merge side by side, face down. You will be producing the result stack above the other two, face up:

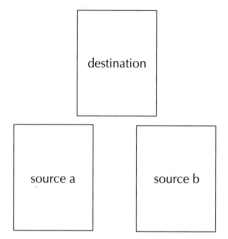

Take the top card off of each source stack—source *a* in your left hand, source *b* in your right hand. Now do the following repeatedly, until all the cards are on the destination stack:

1. Compare the two cards you are holding.
2. Place the one with the larger number on it onto the destination stack, face-up.
3. With the hand you just emptied, pick up the next card from the corresponding source stack and go back to step 1. If there is no next card in the empty hand's stack because that stack is empty, put the other card you are holding on the destination stack face-up and continue flipping the rest of the cards over onto the destination stack.

all your labor. Make a table showing your timings, or better yet graph them, or best yet pool them together with timings from everyone else you know and make a graph that shows the average and range for each time. Figure 4.1 is a graph like that for ten pairs of our students; the horizontal ticks are the averages, and the vertical bars represent the range.

If you look very closely at Figure 4.1, you'll notice that the fastest selection sorters can sort four cards faster than the slowest merge sorters. Therefore, if you only have four cards to sort, neither method is intrinsically superior: Either method might turn out faster, depending on the particular skills of the person doing the sorting. On

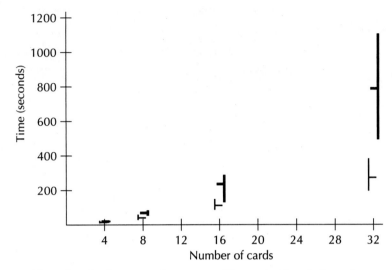

Figure 4.1　Times for selection sort and merge sort. The vertical bars indicate the range of times observed, and the horizontal marks are the averages. The lighter lines with the ranges shown on the left side are for merge sort, and the darker ones with the ranges shown on the right are for selection sort.

the other hand, for 32 cards even the clumsiest merge sorter can outdo even the most nimble-fingered selection sorter. This general phenomenon occurs whenever two methods get slow at different rates. Any initial disparity in speed, no matter how great, will always be eventually overcome by the difference in the intrinsic merits of the algorithms, provided you scale the problem size up far enough. If you were to race, using your bare hands, against a blazingly fast electronic computer programmed to use selection sort, you could beat it by using merge sort, provided the contest involved sorting a large enough data set. (Actually, the necessary data set would be so large that you would be dead before you won the race. Imagine passing the race on to a child, grandchild, etc.)

Another thing we can see by looking at the graph is that if we were to fit a curve through each algorithm's average times, the shapes would be quite different. Of course, it's hard to be very precise, because four points aren't much to go on, but the qualitative difference in shape is rather striking. The merge sort numbers seem to be on a curve that has only a very slight upward bend—almost a straight line. By contrast, no one could mistake the selection sort numbers for falling on a line; they clearly are on a curve with a substantial upward curvature. This corresponds to your gut feeling that doubling the number of cards was going to mean a lot more work—much more than twice as much.

Gathering any more empirical data would strain the patience of even the most patient students, so we use another way to describe the shape of these curves. We will find a function for each method that describes the relationship between deck size and the number of steps performed. We concentrate on the number of steps rather than how long the sorting takes because we don't know how long each step takes. Indeed, some may take longer than others, and the length may vary from person to person. However, doing the steps faster (or slower) simply results in a rescaled curve and does not change the basic shape of it.

First consider what you did in selection sorting n cards. On the first pass through the deck, you handled all n cards, once or twice each. On the second pass you handled only $n - 1$ of them, on the third pass $n - 2$ of them, and so forth. So, the total number of times you handled a card is somewhere between $n + (n - 1) + (n - 2) + \cdots + 1$ and twice that number. How big is $n + (n-1) + (n-2) + \cdots + 1$? It's easy to see that it is no bigger than n^2, because n numbers are being added and the largest of them is n. We can also see that it is at least $n^2/4$, because there are $n/2$ of the numbers that are $n/2$ or larger. Thus we can immediately see that the total number of times you handled a card is bounded between $n^2/4$ and $2n^2$. Because both of these are multiples of n^2, it follows that the basic shape of the touches versus n curve for selection sort must be roughly parabolic. In symbols we say that the number of times you handle a card is $\Theta(n^2)$. (The conventional pronunciation is "big theta of en squared.") This means that for all but perhaps finitely many exceptions it is known to lie between two multiples of n^2. (More particularly, between two *positive* multiples of n^2, or the lower bound would be too easy.)

With a bit more work, we could produce a simple exact formula for the sum $n + (n - 1) + \cdots + 1$. However, this wouldn't really help any, because we don't know how often you only touch a card once in a pass versus twice, and we don't know how long each touch takes. Therefore, we need to be satisfied with a somewhat imprecise answer. On the other hand, we can confidently say that you take at least one hundredth of a second to touch each card, so you take at least $n^2/400$ seconds to sort n cards, and similarly we can confidently say that you take at most 1000 seconds to touch each card, so you take at most $2000n^2$ seconds. Thus, the imprecision that the Θ notation gives us is exactly the kind we need; we're able to say that not only is the number of touches $\Theta(n^2)$ but also the time you take is $\Theta(n^2)$. Our answer, though imprecise, tells the general shape or *order of growth* of the function. Presuming that we do wind up showing merge sort to have a slower order of growth, as the empirical evidence suggests, the difference in orders of growth would be enough to tell us which method must be faster for large enough decks of cards.

▶ **Exercise 4.1**

Go ahead and figure out exactly what $n + (n - 1) + \cdots + 2 + 1$ is. Do this by adding the first term to the last, the second to the second from last, and so forth. What does each pair add up to? How many pairs are there? What does that make the sum?

Moving on to merge sort, we can similarly analyze how many times you handled the cards by breaking it down into successive passes. In the first pass you merged the n initial stacks down to $n/2$; this involved handling every card. How about the second pass, where you merged $n/2$ stacks down to $n/4$; how many cards did you handle in that pass? Stop and think about this.

If you've thought about it, you've realized that you handled all n cards in every pass. This just leaves the question of how many passes there were. The number of stacks was cut in half each pass, whereas the number of cards per stack doubled. Initially each card was in a separate stack, but at the end all n were in one stack. So, the question can be paraphrased as "How many times does 1 need to be doubled to reach n?" or equivalently as "How many times does n need to be halved to reach 1?" As the sidebar on logarithms explains, the answer is the logarithm to the base 2 of n, written $\log_2 n$, or sometimes just $\lg n$. Putting this together with the fact that you handled all cards in each round, we discover that you did $n \log_2 n$ card handlings. This doesn't account for the steps flipping the stacks over between each pass, and of course there is still the issue of how much time each step takes. Therefore, we're best off again being intentionally imprecise and saying that the time taken to merge sort n cards is $\Theta(n \log n)$.

One interesting point here is that we left the base off of the logarithm. This is because inside a Θ, the base of the logarithm is irrelevant, because changing from one base to another is equivalent to multiplying by a constant factor, as the sidebar explains. Remember, saying that the time is big theta of some function simply means it is between two multiples of that function, without specifying which particular multiples. The time would be between two multiples of $2n^2$ if and only if

► Logarithms

If $x^k = y$, we say that k is the logarithm to the base x of y. That is, k is the exponent to which x needs to be raised to produce y. For example, 3 is the logarithm to the base 2 of 8, because you need to multiply three 2s together to produce 8. In symbols, we would write this as $\log_2 8 = 3$. That is, $\log_x y$ is the symbol for the logarithm to the base x of y. The formal definition of logarithm specifies its value even for cases like $\log_2 9$, which clearly isn't an integer, because no number of 2s multiplied together will yield 9. For our purposes, all that you need to know is that $\log_2 9$ is somewhere between 3 and 4, because 9 is between 2^3 and 2^4.

Because we know that three 2s multiplied together produce 8, and two 8s multiplied together produce 64, it follows that six 2s multiplied together will produce 64. In other words, $\log_2 64 = \log_2 8 \times \log_8 64 = 3 \times 2 = 6$. This illustrates a general property of logarithms, namely, $\log_b x = \log_b c \times \log_c x$. So, no matter what x is, its logarithms to the bases b and c differ by the factor $\log_b c$.

it were between two multiples of n^2, so we never say $\Theta(2n^2)$, only the simpler $\Theta(n^2)$. This reason is the same as that for leaving the base of the logarithm unspecified.

In conclusion, note that our analytical results are consistent with our empirical observations. The function $n \log n$ grows just a bit faster than linearly, whereas quadratics are noticeably more upturned. This difference makes merge sort a decidedly superior sorting algorithm; we'll return to it in Chapter 7, when we have the apparatus needed to program it in Scheme.

4.2   Tree Recursion and Digital Signatures

If you watch someone merge sort cards as described in the previous section, you will see that the left-hand and the right-hand halves of the cards don't interact at all until the very last merge step. At that point, each half of the cards is already sorted, and all that is needed is to merge the two sorted halves together. Thus, the merge sort algorithm can be restructured in the following way.

To merge sort a deck of n cards:

1. If $n = 1$, it must already be in order, so you're done.
2. Otherwise:
   a. Merge sort the first $n/2$ cards.
   b. Merge sort the other $n/2$ cards.
   c. Merge together the two sorted halves.

When formulated this way, it is clear that the algorithm is recursive; however, it is not the normal kind of linear recursion we are used to. Rather than first solving a slightly smaller version of the problem and then doing the little bit of work that is left, merge sort first solves *two* much smaller versions of the problem (half the size) and then finishes up by combining their results. This strategy of dividing the work into two (or equally well into three or four) subproblems and then combining the results into the overall solution is known as *tree recursion*. The reason for this name is that the main problem branches into subproblems, each of which branches into sub-subproblems, and so forth, much like the successive branching of the limbs of a tree.

Sometimes this tree-recursive way of thinking can lead you to an algorithm with a lower order of growth than you would otherwise have come up with. This reduced order of growth can be extremely important if you are writing a program designed to be used on very large inputs. To give an example of this, we are going to consider the problem of *digital signatures*.

If you receive a paper document with a signature on it, you can be reasonably sure it was written (or at least agreed to) by the person whose signature it bears. You can also be sure no one has reattached the signature to a different document, at least as long as each page is individually signed. Finally, you can convince an impartial third party, such as a judge, of these facts, because you are in no better position to falsify the signature than anyone else.

Now consider what happens when you get a digital document, such as an electronic mail message or a file on a disk. How do you know it is authentic? And even if it is authentic, how do you prevent the writer from reneging on anything he agreed to, because he can always claim you forged the agreement? Digital signatures are designed to solve these problems. As such, they are going to be of utmost importance as we convert to doing business in a comparatively paperless manner.

Digital signature systems have three components: a way to reduce an entire message down to a single identifying number, a way to sign these numbers, and a way to verify that any particular signed message is valid. The identifying numbers are called *message digests*; they are derived from the messages by a publicly available *digest function*. The message digests are of some agreed-upon limited size, perhaps 40 digits long. Although a lot of 40 digit numbers exist, far more possible messages do; therefore the digest function is necessarily many to one. However, the digest function must be carefully designed so that it is not feasible to find a message that will have a particular digest or to find two messages that share the same digest. So the validity of a message is effectively equivalent to the validity of its digest. Thus, we have reduced the task of signing messages to the easier mathematical task of signing 40-digit numbers. Although digest functions are interesting in their own right, we'll simplify matters by assuming that the messages we're trying to send are themselves numbers of limited size, so we can skip the digesting step and just sign the message itself. In other words, our messages will be their own digests.

The second part of a digital signature system is the way to sign messages. Each person using the system has a private signature function. If you are sending a message, you can sign it by applying your signature function to the message. Each signature function is designed so that different messages have different signatures and so that computing the signature for a particular message is virtually impossible without knowing the signature function. Because only you, the sender, know the signature function, no one else could forge your signature. When you send a message, you also send along the signature for that message. This pair of numbers is called a *signed message*.

What happens when you receive a signed message? This is the third part of the digital signature system. As receiver, you want to verify that the signature is the right one. To do this you look up the sender's verification function in a public directory and apply it to the signature. This will give you a 40-digit number, which should be equal to the message. Because no one other than the sender can compute the signature for a particular message, you can be reasonably sure that you received a valid signed message. Note that the signature and verification functions are closely related to each other; mathematically speaking, they are inverses. Figure 4.2 shows a

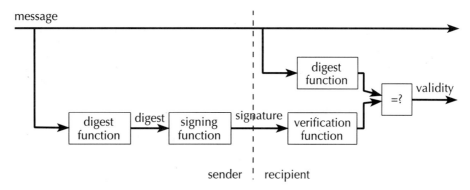

Figure 4.2   The full digital signature system, including the digest function

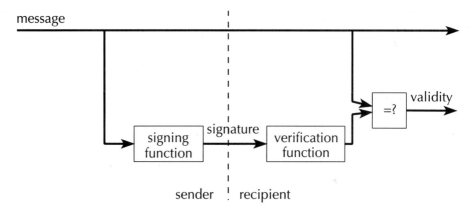

Figure 4.3   Our simplified digital signature system, without a digest function

block diagram of the full version of the digital signature system, including the digest function, and Figure 4.3 similarly depicts the simplified version we're using.

One popular signature and verification strategy is based on an idea known as *modular arithmetic*, which is explained in the accompanying sidebar. In this system, each person has a large number called the *modulus* listed in a public directory under his or her name. The verification function for that person consists of computing the remainder when the cube of the signature is divided by that person's modulus. The `verify` procedure below does this in a straightforward way, using the built-in procedures `remainder` and `expt`. `Expt` raises its first argument to the power specified by its second argument, just like the `power` procedure you wrote in Exercise 2.1.

```
(define verify
  (lambda (signature modulus)
    (remainder (expt signature 3)
               modulus)))
```

Note that we have not yet given the signature function that is the inverse of the verification function above. Before doing that, let us consider an example illustrating how a given signed message is verified.

Suppose that you get a message purporting to come from the authors of this book and containing a partial solution to Exercise 3.8 on page 64. You suspect that the message is actually from a friend playing a prank on you, so you want to check it. The message says that the numerator of the result of (`approximate-golden-ratio` (`expt 10 -79`)) and its signature are as follows:

```
(define gold-num 59723042738777441355693383976920205353504)
(define signature 14367622178330772814011855673053282570996235969
51473988726330337289482255409401120915769529658684452651613736161
53020167902900930324840824269164789456142215776895016041636987254
84811944994040885630)
```

What you need to do is feed that second number into our verification function and see if you get back the first number. If so, you can be sure the message was genuine, because nobody but us knows how to arrange for this to be the case (yet; we're going to give the secret away in a bit). Suppose you looked us up in a directory and found that our modulus is:

```
(define modulus 67162948804860340061536525817498565549007659719419
61654084419360475089601218289012435425548442232148763481664098799
231759689309995696195638345433333958485027650558453766363029391294
0840460009374858969)
```

At this point, you would do the following to find out that we really did send you a personal hint (only the second expression need be evaluated; we evaluate both so that you can see the number returned by the verification function):

```
(verify signature modulus)
59723042738777441355693383976920205353504

(= gold-num
   (verify signature modulus))
#t
```

Having seen how to verify signed messages, we're ready to consider how to generate the signatures. Recall that the signature and verification functions are inverses of each other. So the signature of a given message is an integer s such that the remainder you get when you divide s^3 by the modulus is the original message. In some sense, the signature function might be called the "modular cube root." You should keep in mind, however, that this is quite different from the ordinary cube root. For example,

▶ Modular Arithmetic

The basic operations of arithmetic are $+$, $-$, $*$, and $/$. These are ordinarily considered as operating on integers, or more generally, real numbers. There are, of course, restrictions as to their applicability; for example, the quotient of two integers is not in general an integer, and division by 0 is not allowed. On the other hand, these operations satisfy a number of formal properties. For example, we say that addition and multiplication are *commutative*, meaning that for all numbers x and y,

$$x + y = y + x$$

$$x * y = y * x$$

Other formal properties are *associativity*:

$$(x + y) + z = x + (y + z)$$

$$(x * y) * z = x * (y * z)$$

and *distributivity*:

$$x * (y + z) = x * y + x * z$$

Are there other types of number systems whose arithmetic operations satisfy the properties given above? One such example is *modular arithmetic*, which might also be called *remainder* or *clock arithmetic*. In modular arithmetic, a specific positive integer m called the *modulus* is chosen. For each nonnegative integer x, we let $x \bmod m$ denote the remainder of x when divided by m; this is just (`remainder x m`) in Scheme. Note that $x \bmod m$ is the unique integer r satisfying $0 \leq r < m$ and for which there is another integer q such that $x = qm + r$. The integer q is the integer quotient of x by m (i.e., (`quotient x m`) in Scheme).

If two integers differ by a multiple of m, they have the same remainder mod m. We can use this fact to show that for all integers x and y,

$$xy \bmod m = (x \bmod m)(y \bmod m) \bmod m$$

$$(x + y) \bmod m = ((x \bmod m) + (y \bmod m)) \bmod m$$

To show that these equalities hold, let $x = q_1 m + r_1$ and $y = q_2 m + r_2$. Then $xy = (q_1 r_2 + q_2 r_1 + q_1 q_2 m)m + r_1 r_2$ and $x + y = (q_1 + q_2)m + (r_1 + r_2)$.

The set of all possible remainders mod m is $\{0, 1, \ldots, m - 1\}$. We can define $+_m$ and $*_m$ on this set by

(Continued)

$$x +_m y \overset{\text{def}}{=} (x + y) \bmod m$$

$$x *_m y \overset{\text{def}}{=} (x * y) \bmod m$$

(The symbol $\overset{\text{def}}{=}$ denotes "is defined as.") In Scheme they would be defined as follows:

```
(define mod+
  (lambda (x y)
    (remainder (+ x y) modulus)))

(define mod*
  (lambda (x y)
    (remainder (* x y) modulus)))
```

(We assume `modulus` has been defined.) It is not hard to show that $+_m$ and $*_m$ satisfy commutativity, associativity, and distributivity.

Other operations, such as modular subtraction, division, and exponentiation can be defined in terms of $+_m$ and $*_m$. We'll only consider modular subtraction here, because exponentiation is investigated in the text and division poses theoretical difficulties (namely, it can't always be done).

How should we define modular subtraction? Formally, we would want

$$x - y = x + (-y)$$

where $-y$ is the additive inverse of y (i.e., the number z such that $y + z = 0$). Does such a number exist in modular arithmetic? And if so, is it uniquely determined for each y? The answer to both of these questions is Yes: The (modular) additive inverse of y is $(m - y) \bmod m$, because that is the unique number in $\{0, 1, \ldots, m - 1\}$ whose modular sum with y is 0. For example, if $m = 17$ and $y = 5$, then $-y = 12$ because $(5 + 12) \bmod 17 = 0$. This allows us to define modular subtraction as follows:

```
(define mod-
  (lambda (x y)
    (remainder (+ x (- modulus y)) modulus)))
```

if the modulus were a smaller number such as 17, the modular cube root of 10 would be 3. (Why?) In particular, the signature must be an integer.

Signature functions use the same mathematical process as verification functions. The underlying mathematics is somewhat deeper than you have probably encountered and is partly explained in the notes at the end of this chapter. Briefly, for the types of moduli used in this strategy, there is an exponent called the *signing exponent*, depending on the modulus, that is used to calculate the signature. The signature of a number is calculated by raising the number to the signing exponent and then finding the remainder when the result is divided by the modulus. Mathematically, this means that if m is the modulus, e is the signing exponent, x is the message, and s is its signature,

$$s = x^e \bmod m$$

$$x = s^3 \bmod m$$

The fact that this works follows from the fact that for all choices of nonnegative integers $x < m$,

$$x = (x^e \bmod m)^3 \bmod m$$

Thus, the only difference between signing and verifying is the exponent—that's our secret. Only we (so far) know what exponent to use in the signing so that an exponent of 3 will undo it. In fact, for a 198-digit modulus like ours, no one knows how to find the signing exponent in any reasonable amount of time, without knowing something special about how the modulus was chosen.

What is our secret signing exponent? It is

```
(define signing-exponent 4477529920324022670769101721166571032671
77314627974436056129069833930674788593416236170322948214322483305
17527801279310239221589593147057716354461360014347167979987666468
6423606429437389098641670667)
```

That's a big number, in case you didn't notice (again, 198 digits long). This poses a bit of a problem. From a strictly mathematical standpoint, all we would have to do to sign the numerator is

```
(remainder (expt gold-num signing-exponent) modulus)
```

However, this isn't practical, because the result of the exponentiation would be an extremely large number. We don't even want to tell you how large it would be by telling how many digits are in it, because even the number of digits is itself a 200-digit number. This means that if the computer were to evaluate the expression above, it couldn't possibly have enough memory to store the intermediate result produced by the exponentiation. Keep in mind that there are only about 10^{79} subatomic particles in the universe. This means that if each one of those particles was replaced by a whole universe, complete with 10^{79} particles of its own, and the computer were to store a trillion trillion trillion digits of the intermediate result on each of the particles in this universe of universes, it wouldn't have enough memory.

Luckily there is an out, based on a property noted in the sidebar on modular arithmetic. Namely,

$$xy \bmod m = (x \bmod m)(y \bmod m) \bmod m$$

In other words, we are allowed to do the mod operation before the multiplication as well as after without changing the answer. This is important, because taking a number mod m reduces it to a number less than m. For exponentiation, the important point is this: Rather than multiplying together lots of copies of the base and then taking the result mod m, we can do the mod operation after each step along the way, so the numbers involved never grow very big. Here is a Scheme procedure that does this, based on the observations that $b^0 = 1$ and $b^e = b^{e-1}b$:

```
(define mod-expt
  (lambda (base exponent modulus)
    (define mod*
      (lambda (x y)
        (remainder (* x y) modulus)))
    (if (= exponent 0)
        1
        (mod* (mod-expt base (- exponent 1) modulus)
              base)))))
```

We can try this out by using it to reverify the original signature:

```
(mod-expt signature 3 modulus)
```
597230427387774413556933839769202053504

It works. So now we're all set to use it to sign a new message. Let's sign a nice small number, like 7:

```
(mod-expt 7 signing-exponent modulus)
```

What happens if you try this?

If you tried the above experiment, you probably waited for a while and then got a message like we did:

;Aborting!: out of memory

The problem is that the definition given above for `mod-expt` does one recursive step for each reduction of the exponent by 1. Because each step takes some amount of memory to hold the main problem while working on the subproblem, this means that the total memory consumption is $\Theta(e)$, where e is the exponent. Given that our signing exponent is nearly 200 digits long, it is hardly surprising that the computer ran out of memory (again, even all the particles in a universe of universes wouldn't be enough). We could fix this problem by switching to a linear iterative version of the procedure, much as in Section 3.2 where we wrote an iterative version of the `power` procedure from Exercise 2.1. This procedure would just keep a running product as it modularly multiplied the numbers one by one. This would reduce the memory consumption to $\Theta(1)$ (i.e., constant).

Unfortunately, the time it would take to do the exponentiation would still be $\Theta(e)$, so even though there would be ample memory, it would all have crumbled to dust before the computation was over. (In fact, there wouldn't even be dust left. The fastest computers that even wild-eyed fanatics dream of would take about 10^{-12} seconds to do a multiplication; there are about 10^7 seconds in a year. Therefore, even such an incredibly fast machine would take something like 10^{180} years to do the calculation. For comparison, the earth itself is only around 10^9 years old, so the incredibly fast computer would require roughly a trillion earth-lifetimes for each particle in our hypothetical universe of universes.)

So, because chipping away at this huge signing exponent isn't going anywhere near fast enough, we are motivated to try something drastic, something that will in one fell swoop dramatically decrease it. Let's cut it in half, using a tree recursive strategy. Keep in mind that b^e means e b's multiplied together. Provided that e is even, we could break that string of multiplications right down the middle into two, each of which is only half as big:

```
(define mod-expt
  (lambda (base exponent modulus)
    (define mod*
      (lambda (x y)
        (remainder (* x y) modulus)))
    (if (= exponent 0)
        1
        (if (even? exponent)
            (mod* (mod-expt base (/ exponent 2) modulus)
                  (mod-expt base (/ exponent 2) modulus))
            (mod* (mod-expt base (- exponent 1) modulus)
                  base)))))
```

Does this help any? Unfortunately not—although at least this version won't run out of memory, because the recursion depth is only $\Theta(\log e)$. Consider what would

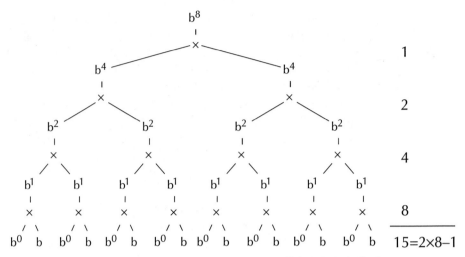

Figure 4.4   A tree recursive exponentiation still does $\Theta(e)$ multiplications.

happen in the simplest possible case, which is when the exponent is a power of 2, so it is not only initially even but in fact stays even after each successive division by 2 until reaching 1. The multiplications form a tree, with one multiplication at the root, two at the next level, four at the next, eight at the next, and so on down to e at the leaves of the tree. This totals $2e - 1$ multiplications when all the levels are added up; Figure 4.4 illustrates this for $e = 8$. The details would be slightly different for an exponent that wasn't a power of 2, but in any case the number of multiplications is still $\Theta(e)$.

Exercise 4.2

In this exercise you will show that this version of `mod-expt` does $\Theta(e)$ multiplications, as we claimed.

a. Use induction to prove each of the following about this latest version of `mod-expt`:
   (1) e is a nonnegative integer, (`mod-expt` b e m) does at least e multiplications.
   (2) When e is a positive integer, (`mod-expt` b e m) does at most $2e - 1$ multiplications.
b. To show that the number of multiplications is $\Theta(e)$, it would have sufficed to show that it lies between e and $2e$. However, rather than having you prove that the number of multiplications was at most $2e$, we asked you prove more, namely, that the number of multiplications is at most $2e - 1$. Try using induction to prove that when e is a positive integer, at most $2e$ multiplications are done. What goes wrong? Why is it easier to prove more than you need to, when you're using induction?

You may be wondering why we went down this blind alley. The reason is that although the tree-recursive version is not itself an improvement, it serves as a stepping stone to a better version. You may have already noticed that we compute (`mod-expt base (/ exponent 2) modulus`) twice, yet clearly the result is going to be the same both times. We could instead calculate the result once and use it in both places. By doing this, we'll only need to do one computation for each level in the tree, eliminating all the redundancy. We can make use of `let` to allow us to easily reuse the value:

```
(define mod-expt
  (lambda (base exponent modulus)
    (define mod*
      (lambda (x y)
        (remainder (* x y) modulus)))
    (if (= exponent 0)
        1
        (if (even? exponent)
            (let ((x (mod-expt base (/ exponent 2) modulus)))
              (mod* x x))
            (mod* (mod-expt base (- exponent 1) modulus)
                  base)))))
```

Although this is only a small change from our original tree-recursive idea, it has a dramatic impact on the order of growth of the time the algorithm takes, as illustrated in Figure 4.5. The exponent is cut in half at worst every other step, because 1 less

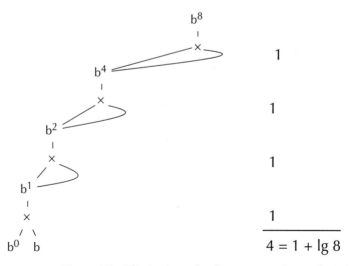

Figure 4.5 Eliminating redundant computations makes a big difference.

than an odd number is an even number. Therefore, the number of steps (and time taken) is $\Theta(\log e)$. Because a logarithmic function grows *much* more slowly than a linear one, the computation of (mod-expt 7 signing-exponent modulus) can now be done in about 7 seconds on our own modest computer, as opposed to 10^{180} years on an amazingly fast one. To give you some appreciation for the immense factor by which the computation has been speeded up, consider that the speed of a ... no, even *we* are at a loss for a physical analogy this time.

▷ **Exercise 4.3**

Write a procedure that, given the exponent, will compute how many multiplications this latest version of mod-expt does.

Although we now have a version of mod-expt that takes $\Theta(\log e)$ time and uses $\Theta(\log e)$ memory, both of which are quite reasonable, we could actually do one better and reduce the memory consumption to $\Theta(1)$ by developing an iterative version of the procedure that *still* cuts the problem size in half. In doing so, we'll be straying even one step further from the original tree-recursive version, which is now serving as only the most vague source of motivation for the algorithm. To cut the problem size in half with a recursive process, we observed that when e was even, $b^e = (b^{e/2})^2$. To cut the problem size in half but generate an iterative process, we can instead observe that when e is even, $b^e = (b^2)^{e/2}$. This is the same as recognizing that when e is even, the string of e b's multiplied together can be divided into $e/2$ pairs of b's multiplied together, rather than two groups containing $e/2$ each.

▷ **Exercise 4.4**

Develop a logarithmic time iterative version of mod-expt based on this concept.

At this point you have seen how an important practical application that involves very large problem sizes can be turned from impossible to possible by devising an algorithm with a lower order of growth. In particular, we successively went through algorithms with the following growth rates:

- $\Theta(e)$ space and time (linear recursion)
- $\Theta(1)$ space and $\Theta(e)$ time (linear iteration)
- $\Theta(\log e)$ space and $\Theta(e)$ time (tree recursion)
- $\Theta(\log e)$ space and time (logarithmic recursion)
- $\Theta(1)$ space and $\Theta(\log e)$ time (logarithmic iteration)

An Application: Fractal Curves

The tree-recursive `mod-expt` turned out not to be such a good idea because the two half-sized problems were identical to one another, so it was redundant to solve each of them separately. By contrast, the tree-recursive merge sort makes sense, because the two half-sized problems are distinct, although similar. Both are problems of the form "sort these $n/2$ cards," but the specific cards to sort are different. This typifies the situation in which tree recursion is natural: when the problem can be broken into two (or more) equal-sized subproblems that are all of the same general form as the original but are distinct from one another.

Fractal curves are geometric figures that fit this description; we say that they possess *self-similarity*. Each fractal curve can be subdivided into a certain number of subcurves, each of which is a smaller version of the given curve. Mathematicians are interested in the case where this subdividing process continues forever so that the subcurves are quite literally identical to the original except in size and position. Because we can't draw an infinitely detailed picture on the computer screen, we'll stop the subdivision at some point and use a simple geometric figure, such as a line or triangle, as the basis for the curve. We call that basis the *level* 0 curve; a level 1 curve is composed out of level 0 curves, a level 2 curve is composed out of level 1 curves, and so forth.

As a first example, consider the fractal curve in Figure 4.6, known as *Sierpinski's gasket*. As indicated in Figure 4.7, the gasket contains three equally sized subgaskets, each of which is a smaller version of the larger gasket. Figure 4.8 shows Sierpinski's gaskets of levels 0, 1, and 2.

A level n Sierpinski's gasket is composed of three smaller Sierpinski's gaskets of level $n - 1$, arranged in a triangular fashion. Furthermore, the level 0 Sierpinski's gasket is itself a triangle. Therefore, triangles play two different roles in Sierpinski's

Figure 4.6   An example of Sierpinski's gasket.

Figure 4.7   An example of Sierpinski's gasket, with the three subgaskets circled.

gasket: the *self-similarity* (i.e., the composition out of lower-level components) is triangular, and the *basis* (i.e., level 0 curve) is also triangular.

In some fractals the self-similarity may differ from the basis. As an example, consider the so-called *c-curve*, which is displayed in Figure 4.9 at levels 6 and 10. The basis of a c-curve is just a straight line. A level n curve is made up of two level $n - 1$ c-curves, but the self-similarity is somewhat difficult to detect. We will describe this self-similarity by writing a procedure that produces c-curves. To write this procedure, we'll need to write a procedure that takes five arguments. The first four are the x and y coordinates of the starting and ending points, the fifth is the level of the curve. A level 0 c-curve is simply a line from the starting point, say $(x0, y0)$, to

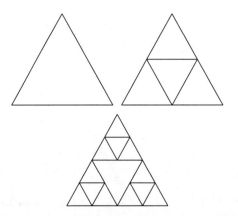

Figure 4.8   Sierpinski's gaskets of levels 0, 1, and 2.

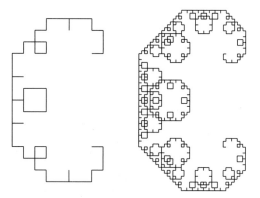

Figure 4.9 C-curves of levels 6 and 10.

the ending point, say $(x1, y1)$. This is what the built-in procedure `line` will produce. For higher level c-curves, we need to join two subcurves together at a point that we'll call (xa, ya). Figure 4.10 illustrates the relationship between the three points; the two subcurves go from point 0 to point a and then from point a to point 1.

```
(define c-curve
  (lambda (x0 y0 x1 y1 level)
    (if (= level 0)
        (line x0 y0 x1 y1)
        (let ((xmid (/ (+ x0 x1) 2))
              (ymid (/ (+ y0 y1) 2))
              (dx (- x1 x0))
              (dy (- y1 y0)))
          (let ((xa (- xmid (/ dy 2)))
                (ya (+ ymid (/ dx 2))))
            (overlay (c-curve x0 y0 xa ya (- level 1))
                     (c-curve xa ya x1 y1 (- level 1)))))))))
```

Try out the `c-curve` procedure with various values for the parameters in order to gain an understanding of their meaning and the visual effect resulting from changing their values. Overlaying two or more c-curves can help you understand what is going on. For example, you might try any (or all) of the following:

```
(c-curve 0 -1/2 0 1/2 0)
(c-curve 0 -1/2 0 1/2 1)
(c-curve 0 -1/2 0 1/2 2)
(c-curve 0 -1/2 0 1/2 3)
(c-curve 0 -1/2 0 1/2 4)
```

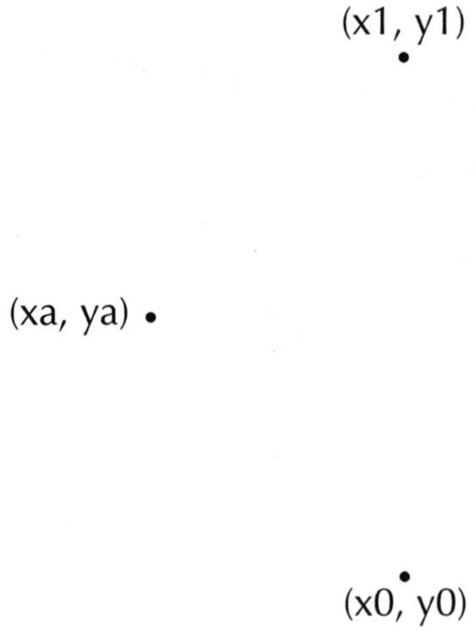

(x1, y1)
•

(xa, ya) •

•
(x0, y0)

Figure 4.10   The three key points in a c-curve of level greater than zero.

```
(c-curve -1/2 0 0 1/2 3)
(c-curve 0 -1/2 -1/2 0 3)
(overlay (c-curve -1/2 0 0 1/2 3)
         (c-curve 0 -1/2 -1/2 0 3))

(c-curve 0 -1/2 0 1/2 6)
(c-curve 0 -1/2 0 1/2 10)

(c-curve 0 0 1/2 1/2 0)
(c-curve 0 0 1/2 1/2 4)
(c-curve 1/2 1/2 0 0 4)
```

▶ **Exercise 4.5**

A c-curve from point 0 to point 1 is composed of c-curves from point 0 to point *a* and from point *a* to point 1. What happens if you define a d-curve similarly but with the direction of the second half reversed, so the second half is a d-curve from point 1 to point *a* instead?

▶ **Exercise 4.6**

Using the procedure `c-curve` as a model, define a procedure called `length-of-c-curve` that, when given the same arguments as `c-curve`, returns the length of the path that would be traversed by a pen drawing the c-curve specified.

> **Exercise 4.7**

See what numbers arise when you evaluate the following:

```
(length-of-c-curve 0 -1/2 0 1/2 0)
(length-of-c-curve 0 -1/2 0 1/2 1)
(length-of-c-curve 0 -1/2 0 1/2 2)
(length-of-c-curve 0 -1/2 0 1/2 3)
(length-of-c-curve 0 -1/2 0 1/2 4)
```

Do you see a pattern? Can you mathematically show that this pattern holds?

> **Exercise 4.8**

C-curves can be seen as more and more convoluted paths between the two points, with increasing levels of detours on top of detours. The net effect of any c-curve of any level still is to connect the two endpoints. Design a new fractal that shares this property. That is, a level 0 curve should again be a straight line, but a level 1 curve should be some different shape of detour path of your own choosing that connects up the two endpoints. What does your curve look like at higher levels?

> **Exercise 4.9**

We will now turn to Sierpinski's gasket. To get this started, write a procedure called `triangle` that takes six arguments, namely the x and y coordinates of the triangle's three vertices. It should produce an image of the triangle. Test it with various argument values; (`triangle -1 -.75 1 -.75 0 1`) should give you a large and nearly equilateral triangle.

> **Exercise 4.10**

Use `triangle` to write a procedure called `sierpinskis-gasket` that again takes six arguments for the vertex coordinates but also takes a seventh argument for the level of curve.

Review Problems

> **Exercise 4.11**

Consider the following procedures:

```
(define factorial
  (lambda (n)
    (if (= n 0)
        1
        (* n (factorial (- n 1))))))

(define factorial-sum1 ; returns 1! + 2! + ... + n!
  (lambda (n)
    (if (= n 0)
        0
        (+ (factorial n)
           (factorial-sum1 (- n 1))))))

(define factorial-sum2 ; also returns 1! + 2! + ... + n!
  (lambda (n)
    (define loop
      (lambda (k fact-k addend)
        (if (> k n)
            addend
            (loop (+ k 1)
                  (* fact-k (+ k 1))
                  (+ addend fact-k)))))
    (loop 1 1 0)))
```

In answering the following, assume that *n* is a nonnegative integer. Also, justify your answers.

a. Give a formula for how many multiplications the procedure `factorial` does as a function of its argument *n*.

b. Give a formula for how many multiplications the procedure `factorial-sum1` does (implicitly through `factorial`) as a function of its argument *n*.

c. Give a formula for how many multiplications the procedure `factorial-sum2` does as a function of its argument *n*.

▷ **Exercise 4.12**

How many ways are there to factor *n* into two or more numbers (each of which must be no smaller than 2)? We could generalize this to the problem of finding how many ways there are to factor *n* into two or more numbers, each of which is no smaller than *m*. That is, we write

```
(define ways-to-factor
  (lambda (n)
    (ways-to-factor-using-no-smaller-than n 2)))
```

Your job is to write `ways-to-factor-using-no-smaller-than`. Here are some questions you can use to guide you:

- If $m^2 > n$, how many ways are there to factor n into two or more numbers each no smaller than m?
- Otherwise, consider the case that n is not divisible by m. Compare how many ways are there to factor n into two or more numbers no smaller than m with how many ways there are to factor n into two or more numbers no smaller than $m + 1$. What is the relationship?
- The only remaining case is that $m^2 \leq n$ and n is divisible by m. In this case, there is at least one way to factor n into numbers no smaller than m. (It can be factored into m and n/m.) There may, however, be other ways as well. The ways of factoring n divide into two categories: those using at least one factor of m and those containing no factor of m. How many factorizations are there in each category?

▷ **Exercise 4.13**

Consider the following procedure:

```
(define bar
  (lambda (n)
    (cond ((= n 0) 5)
          ((= n 1) 7)
          (else (* n (bar (- n 2)))))))
```

How many multiplications (expressed in Θ notation) will the computation of `(bar n)` do? Justify your answer. You may assume that n is a nonnegative integer.

▷ **Exercise 4.14**

Consider the following procedures:

```
(define foo
  (lambda (n)              ; computes n! + (n!)^n
    (+ (factorial n)       ; that is, (n! plus n! to the nth power)
       (bar n n))))
```

```
(define bar
  (lambda (i j)     ; computes (i!)^j (i! to the jth power)
    (if (= j 0)
        1
        (* (factorial i)
           (bar i (- j 1))))))

(define factorial
  (lambda (n)
    (if (= n 0)
        1
        (* n (factorial (- n 1))))))
```

How many multiplications (expressed in Θ notation) will the computation of (foo n) do? Justify your answer.

▷ **Exercise 4.15**

Suppose that you have been given n coins that look and feel identical and you've been told that exactly one of them is fake. The fake coin weighs slightly less than a real coin. You happen to have a balance scale handy, so you can figure out which is the fake coin by comparing the weights of various piles of coins. One strategy for doing this is as follows:

- If you only have 1 coin, it must be fake.
- If you have an even number of coins, you divide the coins into two piles (same number of coins in each pile), compare the weights of the two piles, discard the heavier pile, and look for the fake coin in the remaining pile.
- If you have an odd number of coins, you pick one coin out, divide the remaining coins into two piles, and compare the weights of those two piles. If you're lucky, the piles weigh the same and the coin you picked out is the fake one. If not, throw away the heavier pile and the extra coin, and look for the fake coin in the remaining pile.

Note that if you have one coin, you don't need to do any weighings. If you have an even number of coins, the maximum number of weighings is one more than the maximum number of weighings you'd need to do for half as many coins. If you have an odd number of coins, the maximum number of weighings is the same as the maximum number of weighings you'd need for one fewer coins.

a. Write a procedure that will determine the maximum number of weighings you need to do to find the fake coin out of *n* coins using the above strategy.

b. Come up with a fancier (but more efficient) strategy based on dividing the pile of coins in thirds, rather than in half. (Hint: If you compare two of the thirds, what are the possible outcomes? What does each signify?)

c. Write a procedure to determine the maximum number of weighings using the strategy based on dividing the pile in thirds.

▷ **Exercise 4.16**

Perhaps you noticed in Section 4.3 that as you increase the value of the *level* parameter in `c-curve` (while keeping the starting and ending points fixed), the c-curve gets larger. Not only is the path larger, but the curve extends further to the left, further to the right, and extends higher and lower. One way to measure this growth would be to ask how far left it extends (i.e., what its minimum *x*-value is). This could be done by defining a procedure called `min-x-of-c-curve`, taking exactly the same arguments as `c-curve`, which returns the minimum *x*-value of the given c-curve. One strategy for implementing `min-x-of-c-curve` is as follows:

■ If *level* = 0, the c-curve is just a line from $(x0, y0)$ to $(x1, y1)$, so return the smaller of $x0$ and $x1$.

■ If *level* ≥ 1, the given c-curve is built from two c-curves, each of which has *level* − 1 as its level. One goes from $(x0, y0)$ to (xa, ya), and the other from (xa, ya) to $(x1, y1)$. Therefore, you should return the smaller of the min-*x*-values of these two sub-c-curves.

Write the procedure `min-x-of-c-curve`. As an aid in writing it, note that there is a built-in procedure `min` that returns the smaller of its arguments. So we would have

```
(min 1 3)        (min 2 -3)        (min 4 4)
1                -3                 4
```

As a hint, note that `min-x-of-c-curve` can be structured in a manner very similar to both `c-curve` and `length-of-c-curve`.

▷ **Exercise 4.17**

Consider the following enumeration problem: How many ways can you choose *k* objects from *n* distinct objects, assuming of course that $0 \le k \le n$? For example, how many different three-topping pizzas can be made if you have six toppings to choose from?

The number that is the answer to the problem is commonly written as $C(n, k)$. Here is an algorithm for computing $C(n, k)$:

- As noted above, you may assume that $0 \le k \le n$, because other values don't make sense for the problem.

- The base cases are $k = 0$ and $k = n$. It should not be too hard to convince yourself that $C(n, n)$ should equal 1, and similar reasoning can be used to show that $C(n, 0) = 1$ is also the reasonable choice.

- The general case is $0 < k < n$. Here you might argue as follows: Consider one of the objects. Either you select it as one of the k objects, or you don't. If you do select it, then you must select $k - 1$ more objects from the remaining $n - 1$, presumably a simpler problem that you assume you can do recursively. If on the other hand you don't select the first object, you must select k objects from the remaining $n - 1$, which is also a simpler problem whose value is computed recursively. Then the total number of ways to select k objects from these n objects is the sum of the numbers you get from these two subproblems.

Using this algorithm, write a tree-recursive procedure that calculates the numbers $C(n, k)$ described above.

▷ **Exercise 4.18**

One way to sum the integers from a up to b is to divide the interval in half, recursively sum the two halves, and then add the two sums together. Of course, it may not be possible to divide the interval exactly in half if there are an odd number of integers in the interval. In this case, the interval can be divided as nearly in half as possible.

a. Write a procedure implementing this idea.

b. Let's use n as a name for the number of integers in the range from a up to b. What is the order of growth (in Θ notation) of the number of additions your procedure does, as a function of n? Justify your answer.

▷ **Exercise 4.19**

The following illustration shows a new kind of image, which we call a *tri-block*:

What kind of process do you think was used to generate this image (i.e., was it linear recursive, iterative, or tree recursive)? Write a paragraph carefully explaining *why* you think this.

▷ **Exercise 4.20**

Consider the following procedure:

```
(define foo
  (lambda (low high level)
    (let ((mid (/ (+ low high) 2)))
      (let ((mid-line (line mid 0 mid (* level .1))))
        (if (= level 1)
            mid-line
            (overlay mid-line
                     (overlay (foo low mid (- level 1))
                              (foo mid high (- level 1)))))))))
```

Examples of the images produced by this procedure are given below:

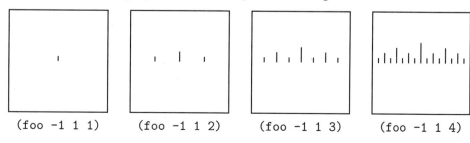

| (foo -1 1 1) | (foo -1 1 2) | (foo -1 1 3) | (foo -1 1 4) |

a. What kind of process does `foo` generate (i.e., linear recursive, iterative, or tree recursive)? Justify your answer.

b. Let's call the number of lines in the image `foo` produces $l(n)$, where n is the level. Make a table showing $l(n)$ versus n for $n = 1, 2, 3, 4$. Write a mathematical equation showing how $l(n)$ can be computed from $l(n-1)$ when n is greater than 1. Explain how each part of your equation relates to the procedure. What is $l(5)$?

Chapter Inventory

Vocabulary

algorithm

selection sort

merge sort

Θ (big theta)

order of growth

logarithm

tree recursion

digital signature

message digest

digest function

modular arithmetic

modulus

commutative

associativity

distributivity

number system

fractal curve

self-similarity

basis (of a fractal)

Sierpinski's gasket

c-curve

Slogans

The asymptotic outlook

New Predefined Scheme Names

The dagger symbol (†) indicates a name that is not part of the R⁴RS standard for Scheme.

```
line†
min
```

Scheme Names Defined in This Chapter

```
verify
mod+
mod*
mod-
gold-num
signature
modulus
```

```
signing-exponent
mod-expt
c-curve
length-of-c-curve
triangle
sierpinskis-gasket
factorial-sum1
```

`factorial-sum2`
`ways-to-factor`

`ways-to-factor-using-no-`
    `smaller-than`
`min-x-of-c-curve`

Sidebars

Selection Sort
Merge Sort
Merging

Logarithms
Modular Arithmetic

Notes

The definitive work on sorting algorithms is by Knuth [31]. Knuth reports that merge sort is apparently the first program written for a stored program computer, in 1945.

Our definition of Θ allowed "finitely many exceptions." Other books normally specify that any number of exceptions are allowed, provided that they are all less than some cutoff point. The two definitions are equivalent given our assumption that n is restricted to be a nonnegative integer. If that restriction is lifted, the more conventional definition is needed. In any case, the reason for allowing exceptions to the bounds is to permit the use of bounding functions that are ill-defined for small n. For example, we showed that merge sort was $\Theta(n \log n)$. When $n = 0$, the logarithm is undefined, so we can't make a claim that the time to sort 0 cards is bounded between two positive constant multiples of $0 \log 0$.

The digital signature method we've described is known as the *RSA cryptosystem*, named after the initials of its developers: Ron Rivest, Adi Shamir, and Leonard Adleman. The way we were able to produce our public modulus and secret signing key is as follows. We randomly chose two 100-digit primes, which we've kept secret; call them p and q. We made sure $(p-1)(q-1)$ wasn't divisible by 3. Our modulus is simply the product pq. This means that in principle anyone could discover p and q by factoring our published modulus. However, no one knows how to factor a 200-digit number in any reasonable amount of time. Our secret signing exponent is calculated using p and q. It is the multiplicative inverse of 3 (the verification exponent), mod $(p-1)(q-1)$. That is, it is the number that when multiplied by 3 and then divided by $(p-1)(q-1)$ leaves a remainder of 1. For an explanation of why this works, how the inverse is quickly calculated, and how to find large primes, consult Cormen, Leiserson, and Rivest's superb *Introduction to Algorithms* [14]. For general information on the RSA system, there is a useful publication from RSA Laboratories by Paul Fahn [16]. We should point out that the use of the RSA system for digital signatures is probably covered by several patents; however, the relevant patent holders have indicated that they won't prosecute anyone using the system as an educational exercise. Also, it is worth mentioning that the export from the United

States of any product employing the RSA system is regulated by the International Traffic in Arms Regulation.

There has been a recent explosion of books on fractals, aimed at all levels of audience. Two classics by Mandelbrot, who coined the word *fractal*, are [36] and [37].

Some aspects of our treatment of fractals, such as the c-curve example and the `length-of-c-curve` exercise, are inspired by a programming assignment developed by Abelson, Sussman, and friends at MIT [1].

CHAPTER FIVE

Higher-Order Procedures

Procedural Parameters

In the earlier chapters, we twice learned how to stop writing lots of specific expressions that differed only in details and instead to write one general expression that captured the commonality:

- In Chapter 1, we learned how to define procedures. That way when we had several expressions that differed only in the specific values being operated on, such as (* 3 3), (* 4 4), and (* 5 5), we could instead define a general procedure:

```
(define square
  (lambda (x)
    (* x x)))
```

This one procedure can be used to do all of the specific calculations just listed; the procedure specifies what operations to do, and the parameter allows us to vary which value is being operated on.

- In Chapter 2, we learned how to generate variable-size computational processes. That way if we had several procedures that generated processes of the same form, but differing in size, such as (define square (lambda (x) (* x x))) and (define cube (lambda (x) (* (* x x) x))), we could instead define a general procedure:

```
(define power
  (lambda (b e)
    (if (= e 1)
        b
        (* (power b (- e 1)) b))))
```

This one procedure can be used in place of the more specific procedures listed previously; the procedure still specifies what operations to do, but the parameters now specify how many of these operations to do as well as what values to do them to.

Since learning about these two kinds of variability—variability of values and of computation size—we've concentrated on other issues, such as the amount of time and memory that a process consumes. In this chapter, we will learn about a third kind of variability, which, once again, will allow us to replace multiple specific definitions with a single more general one.

Suppose that you replace the operation name * with `stack` in the previous definition of `power`. By making this one change, you'll have a procedure for stacking multiple copies of an image instead of doing exponentiation. That is, the general structure of the two procedures is the same; the only difference is the specific operation being used. (Of course, it would make the procedure easier to understand if you also made some cosmetic changes, such as changing the name from `power` to `stack-copies-of` and changing the name and order of the parameters. If you do this, you'll probably wind up with the exact same procedure you wrote for Exercise 2.13 on page 40.)

This commonality of structure raises an interesting question: Can we write one general purpose procedure for all computations of this kind and then tell it not only how many copies we want of what but also how they should be combined? If so, we could ask it to stack together 3 copies of rcross-bb, to multiply together 5 copies of 2, or .... We might use it like this:

```
(together-copies-of stack 3 rcross-bb)  ⇒
```

```
(together-copies-of * 5 2)
32
```

The first argument is a procedure, which is how we specify the kind of combining we want done. The names `stack` and * are evaluated, just like the name `rcross-bb` is or any other expression would be. Therefore, the actual argument value is the procedure itself, not the name.

To start writing the procedure `together-copies-of`, we give a name for its procedural parameter in the parameter list, along with the other parameters:

```
(define together-copies-of
  (lambda (combine quantity thing)
```

Here we have three parameters, called `combine`, `quantity`, and `thing`, filling in the blanks in "combine together quantity copies of thing." We chose to use a verb for the procedural parameter and nouns for the other parameters to remind ourselves how they are used. Now we can finish writing the procedure, using the parameter names in the body wherever we want to have the specifics substituted in. For example, when we want to check whether the specific quantity requested is 1, we write (= quantity 1). Similarly, when we want to use the specific combining operation that was requested, we write (combine ... ...). Here is the resulting procedure:

```
(define together-copies-of
  (lambda (combine quantity thing)
    (if (= quantity 1)
        thing
        (combine (together-copies-of combine
                                     (- quantity 1)
                                     thing)
                 thing))))
```

Once we've got this general purpose procedure, we can use it to simplify the definition of other procedures:

```
(define stack-copies-of
  (lambda (quantity image)
    (together-copies-of stack quantity image)))

(define power
  (lambda (base exponent)
    (together-copies-of * exponent base)))

(define mod-expt
  (lambda (base exponent modulus)
    (together-copies-of (lambda (x y)
                          (remainder (* x y) modulus))
                        exponent base)))
```

(Notice that we didn't bother giving a name, such as mod*, to the combining procedure used in mod-expt. Typically, using a lambda expression to supply the procedural argument directly is easier than stopping to give it a name with **define** and then referring to it by name.)

Together-copies-of is an example of a *higher-order* procedure. Such procedures have procedural parameters or (as we'll see later) return procedural values. One great benefit of building a higher-order procedure is that the client procedures such as stack-copies-of and mod-expt are now completely independent of the process used for combining copies. All they say is that so many copies of such and such should be combined with this combiner, without saying how that combining should be organized. This means that we can improve the technique used by `together-copies-of` and in one fell swoop the performance of `stack-copies-of`, `mod-expt`, and any other client procedures will all be improved.

> **Exercise 5.1**

Write a linear iterative version of `together-copies-of`.

> **Exercise 5.2**

Write a logarithmic-time version of `together-copies-of`. You may assume that the combiner is associative.

> **Exercise 5.3**

What does the following procedure compute? Also, compare its performance with each of the three versions of `together-copies-of` installed, using relatively large values for the first argument, perhaps in the ten thousand to a million range.

```
(define mystery
  (lambda (a b)
    (together-copies-of + a b)))
```

For our second example, note that counting the number of times that 6 is a digit in a number (Exercise 2.9 on page 39) is very similar to counting the number of odd digits in a number (Exercise 2.10 on page 39). In the former case, you're testing to see if each digit is equal to 6 and in the latter you're testing to see if each digit is odd. Thus we can write a general procedure, `num-digits-in-satisfying`, that we can use to define both of these procedures. Its second parameter is the particular test predicate to use on each digit.

```
(define num-digits-in-satisfying
  (lambda (n test?)
    (cond ((< n 0)
           (num-digits-in-satisfying (- n) test?))
          ((< n 10)
           (if (test? n) 1 0))
          ((test? (remainder n 10))
           (+ (num-digits-in-satisfying (quotient n 10) test?)
              1))
          (else
           (num-digits-in-satisfying (quotient n 10) test?)))))
```

We can then define the procedures asked for in Exercises 2.9 and 2.10 as special cases of the more general procedure `num-digits-in-satisfying`:

```
(define num-odd-digits
  (lambda (n)
    (num-digits-in-satisfying n odd?)))

(define num-6s
  (lambda (n)
    (num-digits-in-satisfying n (lambda (n) (= n 6)))))
```

Exercise 5.4

Use `num-digits-in-satisfying` to define the procedure `num-digits`, which was defined "from scratch" in Section 2.3.

Exercise 5.5

Rewrite `num-digits-in-satisfying` so that it generates an iterative process.

Another computational pattern that occurs very frequently involves summing the values of a function over a given range of integers.

Exercise 5.6

Write a general purpose procedure, that when given two integers, *low* and *high*, and a procedure for computing a function f, will compute $f(low) + f(low + 1) + f(low + 2) + \cdots + f(high)$. Show how it can be used to sum the squares of the integers from 5 to 10 and to sum the square roots of the integers from 10 to 100.

5.2 Uncomputability

Designing general purpose procedures with procedural parameters is an extremely practical skill. It can save considerable programming, because a procedure can be written a single time but reused in many contexts. However, despite this practicality, the single most interesting use of a procedure with a procedural parameter is in a theoretical proof. In this section we'll take a look at the history and importance of this proof.

By now we've seen that procedures are quite powerful. They can be used for doing arithmetic on 200-digit numbers in order to produce digital signatures, for making a variety of complex images, and for looking words up in dictionaries. You probably know of lots of other things procedures can be used for. There seems to be no limit to what we can do with them. At the beginning of the twentieth century, mathematicians addressed exactly that question: whether a procedure could be found to compute any function that could be precisely mathematically specified. That question was settled in the 1930s by the discovery of several *uncomputable functions* (one of which we'll examine in this section).

The specific function we'll prove uncomputable is a higher-order one and is often called the *halting problem*. It takes a procedure as an argument and returns a true/false value telling whether the given procedure generates a terminating process, as opposed to going into an infinite loop. Now imagine that one of your brilliant friends gives you a procedure, called `halts?`, that supposedly computes this function. You could then use this procedure on the simple procedures `return-seven` and `loop-forever` defined below. Evaluating `(halts? return-seven)` should result in `#t`, whereas `(halts? loop-forever)` should evaluate to `#f`.

```
(define return-seven
  (lambda ()
    7))

(define loop-forever
  (lambda ()
    (loop-forever)))
```

(`Return-seven` and `loop-forever` happen to be our first examples of procedures with no parameters. This is indicated by the empty parentheses.)

Clearly `halts?` would be a handy procedure to have, if it really worked. To start with, it could be used to test for a common kind of bug. Never again would you have to guess whether you'd goofed and accidentally written a nonterminating procedure. You could tell the difference between a computation that was taking a long time and one that would never finish.

Above and beyond this, you could answer all sorts of open mathematical questions. For example, we mentioned earlier that no one knows whether there are any odd perfect numbers. It would be easy enough to write a procedure that tested all the odd numbers, one by one, stopping when and if it found one that was perfect. Then all we'd have to do is apply `halts?` to it, and we'd have the answer—if we're told that our search procedure halts, there are odd perfect numbers; otherwise, there aren't. This suggests that such a procedure might be a bit too wonderful to exist—it would make obsolete centuries of mathematicians' hard work. However, this is far from a proof that it doesn't exist.

Another related sense in which `halts?` is a bit too good to be true forms a suitable basis for a proof that it can't be a sure-fire way to determine whether a given procedure generates a halting process. (In other words, there must be procedures for which it either gives the wrong answer or fails to give an answer.) `Halts?` in effect claims to predict the future: It can tell you now whether a process will terminate or not at some point arbitrarily far into the future. The way to debunk such a fortune-teller is to do the exact opposite of what the fortune-teller foretells (provided that the fortune-teller is willing to give unambiguous answers to any question and that you believe in free will). This will be the essence of our proof that `halts?` can't work as claimed.

What we want is a procedure that asks `halts?` whether it is going to stop and then does the opposite:

```
(define debunk-halts?
  (lambda ()
    (if (halts? debunk-halts?)
        (loop-forever)
        666)))
```

Debunk-halts? halts if and only if `debunk-halts?` doesn't halt—provided the procedure `halts?` that it calls upon performs as advertised. But nothing can both halt and not halt, so there is only one possible conclusion: our assumption that such a `halts?` procedure exists must be wrong—there can be no procedure that provides that functionality.

The way we proved that the halting problem is uncomputable is called a *proof by contradiction*. What we did was to assume that it was computable, that is, that a procedure (`halts?`) exists that computes it. We then used this procedure to come up with `debunk-halts?`, which halts if and only if it doesn't halt. In other words, whether we assume that `debunk-halts?` halts or that it doesn't halt, we can infer the opposite; we are stuck with a contradiction either way. Because we arrived at this self-contradictory situation by assuming that we had a `halts?` procedure that correctly solved the halting problem, that assumption must be false; in other words, the halting problem is uncomputable.

This version of proof by contradiction, where the contradiction is arrived at by using an alleged universal object to produce the counterexample to its own universality, is known as a *diagonalization* proof. Another variation on the theme can be used to show that most functions can't even be specified, let alone implemented by a procedure.

We should point out that we've only given what most mathematicians would call a "sketch" of the actual proof that the halting problem is uncomputable. In a formal proof, the notions of what a procedure is, what process that procedure generates, and whether that process terminates need to be very carefully specified in formal mathematical terms. This ensures that the function mapping each procedure to a truth value based on whether or not it generates a terminating process is a well-defined mathematical function. The mathematician Alan Turing spent considerable effort on these careful specifications when he originated the proof that `halts?` can't exist.

The discovery that there are mathematical functions that can be specified but not computed is one of the wedges that served to split computer science off from mathematics in the middle of the twentieth century. Of course, this was the same period when programmable electronic computers were first being designed and built (by Turing himself, among others). However, we can now see that the fundamental subject matter of mathematics and computer science are distinct: Mathematicians study any abstraction that can be formally specified, whereas computer scientists confine their attention to the smaller realm of the computable. Mathematicians sometimes are satisfied with an answer to the question "is there a ...," whereas computer scientists ask "How do I find it?"

▶ Alan Turing

One of the surest signs of genius in a computer scientist is the ability to excel in both the theoretical and the practical sides of the discipline. All the greatest computer scientists have had this quality, and most have even gone far beyond the borders of computer science in their breadth. Given the youth of the discipline, most of these greats are still alive, still alternating between theory and application, the computer and the pipe organ. Alan Turing, however, has the dual distinction of having been one of these greats who passed into legend.

Turing developed one of the first careful theoretical models of the notions of algorithm and process in the 1930s, basing it on a bare-bones computing machine that is still an important theoretical model—the *Turing machine*, as it is called. He did this as the basis of his careful proof of the uncomputability of the halting problem, sketched in this section. In so doing he made a contribution of the first magnitude to the deepest theoretical side of computer science.

During World War II, Turing worked in the British code-breaking effort and successfully designed real-life computing machines dedicated to this purpose. He is given a considerable portion of the credit for the Allied forces' decisive cryptographic edge and in particular for the breaking of the German "Enigma" ciphers.

After the war Turing led the design of the National Physical Laboratory's ACE computer, which was one of the first digital electronic stored-program computers designed anywhere and the first such project started in England.

During this same post-war period of the late forties Turing returned more seriously to a question he had dabbled with for years, the question of *artificial*

Continued

■▶ **Alan Turing (Continued)**

intelligence: whether intelligence is successfully describable as a computational process, such that a computing machine could be programmed to be intelligent. He made a lasting contribution to this area of thought by formulating the question in *operational* terms. In other words, he made the significant choice not to ask "is the machine *really* intelligent inside or just faking" but rather "can the machine be distinguished from a human, simply by looking at its outward behavior." He formulated this in a very specific way: Can a computer be as successful as a man at convincing an interrogator that it is a woman? He also stipulated that the computer and the man should both be communicated with only through a textual computer terminal (or teletype). In the decades since Turing published this idea in 1950, it has been generalized such that any operational test of intelligence is today referred to as a "Turing test." Theoretical foundations, applications to code breaking, computer design, and questions of artificial intelligence weren't all that concerned Turing, however. He also made an important contribution to theoretical biology. His famous 1952 paper "The Chemical Basis of Morphogenesis" showed how chemical reactions in an initially homogeneous substance can give rise to large-scale orderly forms such as are characteristic of life.

Turing's work on morphogenesis (the origins of form) never reached completion, however, because he tragically took his own life in 1954, at the age of 42. There is considerable uncertainty about exactly why he did this, or more generally about his state of mind. It is documented that he had gone through periods of depression, as well as considerable trauma connected with his sexual orientation. Turing was rather openly homosexual, at a time when sex between men was a crime in England, even if in private and with consent. In 1952 Turing was convicted of such behavior, based on his own frank admission. His lawyer asked the court to put him on probation, rather than sentence him to prison, on the condition that he undergo experimental medical treatment for his homosexuality—paradoxically it was considered an illness as well as a crime. The treatment consisted of large doses of estrogen (female hormones), which caused impotence, depression, and further stigmatization in the form of enlarged breasts. The treatment ended in 1953, but there is circumstantial evidence suggesting that British intelligence agencies kept close tabs on Turing thereafter, including detaining a foreign lover to prevent a rendezvous. (Apparently they were concerned that Turing might divulge his secret information regarding cryptography and related fields.) Although there is no clear evidence, this sequence of events probably played a role in the overall emotional progression leading to Turing's suicide, cutting off what could have been the entire second half of his career.

Since the 1930s, when Turing showed that there could be no procedure that solves this halting problem, many other functions have been shown to be uncomputable. Many of these proofs have the form: "If I had this procedure, I could use it in this clever way to implement **halts?**. But **halts?** can't exist, so this procedure must not either." This is known as a *proof by reduction*.

5.3 Procedures That Make Procedures

Now we can return to the more practical question of what programming techniques are made possible by procedures that operate on procedures. (Recall that this is what *higher-order* means.) So far we have seen procedures that take other procedures as parameters, just as they might take numbers or images. However, procedures don't just take values in: They also return values as the result of their computations. This carries over to procedural values as well; higher-order procedures can be used to compute procedural results. In other words, we can build procedures that will build procedures. Clearly this could be a very labor-saving device.

How do we get a procedure to return a new procedure? We do it in the same way that we get a procedure to return a number. Recall that in order to ensure that a procedure returns a number when it is applied, its body must be an expression that evaluates to a number. Similarly, for a procedure to create a new procedure when it is applied, its body must be an expression that evaluates to a procedure. At this point, we know of only one kind of expression that can evaluate to a new procedure—a lambda expression. For example, here is a simple "procedure factory" with examples of its use:

```
(define make-multiplier
  (lambda (scaling-factor)
    (lambda (x)
      (* x scaling-factor))))

(define double (make-multiplier 2))

(define triple (make-multiplier 3))

(double 7)
14

(triple 12)
36
```

When we evaluate the definition of **make-multiplier**, the outer lambda expression is evaluated immediately and has as its value the procedure named **make-multiplier**. That procedure is waiting to be told what the scaling factor is. When we evaluate

```
(define double (make-multiplier 2))
```

the body of the procedure named `make-multiplier` is evaluated, with the value 2 substituted for `scaling-factor`. In other words, the expression `(lambda (x) (* x scaling-factor))` is evaluated with 2 substituted for `scaling-factor`. The result of this evaluation is the procedure that is named `double`, just as though the definition had been `(define double (lambda (x) (* x 2)))`. When we apply `double` to 7, the procedure `(lambda (x) (* x 2))` is applied to 7, and the result is, of course, 14.

> **Exercise 5.7**

Write a procedure `make-exponentiater` that is passed a single parameter *e* (an exponent) and returns a function that itself takes a single parameter, which it raises to the *e* power. You should use the built-in Scheme procedure `expt`. As examples, you could define `square` and `cube` as follows:

```
(define square (make-exponentiater 2))

(define cube (make-exponentiater 3))

(square 4)
16

(cube 4)
64
```

For another example of a procedure factory, suppose that we want to automate the production of procedures like `repeatedly-square`, from Section 3.2. That procedure took two arguments, the number to square and how many times it should be squared. We could make a procedure factory called `make-repeated-version-of` that would be able to make `repeatedly-square` out of `square`:

```
(define make-repeated-version-of
  (lambda (f)   ; make a repeated version of f
    (define the-repeated-version
      (lambda (b n)   ; which does f n times to b
        (if (= n 0)
            b
            (the-repeated-version (f b) (- n 1)))))
    the-repeated-version))

(define square (lambda (x) (* x x)))
```

```
(define repeatedly-square
  (make-repeated-version-of square))

(repeatedly-square 2 3)   ; 2 squared squared squared
256
```

One thing worth noticing in this example is that we used an internal definition of the-repeated-version to provide a name for the generated procedure. That way we can refer to it by name where it reinvokes itself to do the $n - 1$ remaining repetitions. Having internally defined this name, we then return the procedure it is a name for.

> ## Exercise 5.8

Define a procedure that can be used to produce factorial (Section 2.1) or sum-of-first (Section 2.3). Show how it can be used to define those two procedures.

> ## Exercise 5.9

Generalize your solution to the previous exercise so it can also be used to produce sum-of-squares and sum-of-cubes from Exercise 2.8 on page 38.

5.4   An Application: Verifying ID Numbers

Does this scenario sound familiar?

May I have your credit card number please?
Yes, it's 6011302631452178.
I'm sorry, I must have typed that wrong. Could you please say it again?

How did the sales representative know the number was wrong?

Credit card numbers are one of the most common examples of *self-verifying numbers*. Other examples include the ISBN numbers on books, the UPC (Universal Product Code) numbers on groceries, the bank numbers on checks, the serial numbers on postal money orders, the membership numbers in many organizations, and the student ID numbers at many universities.

Self-verifying numbers are designed in such a way that any valid number will have some specific numerical property and so that most simple errors (such as getting two digits backward or changing the value of one of the digits) result in numbers that don't have the property. That way a legitimate number can be distinguished from one that is in error, even without taking the time to search through the entire list of valid numbers.

What interests us about self-verifying numbers is that there are many different systems in use, but they are almost all of the same general form. Therefore, although we will need separate procedures for checking the validity of each kind of number, we can make good use of a higher-order procedure to build all of the verifiers for us.

Suppose we call the rightmost digit of a number d_1, the second digit from the right d_2, etc. All of the kinds of identifying numbers listed previously possess a property of the following kind:

$$f(1, d_1) + f(2, d_2) + f(3, d_3) + \cdots \text{ is divisible by } m$$

All that is different between a credit card and a grocery item, or between a book and a money order, is the specific function f and the divisor m.

How do we define a procedure factory that will construct verifiers for us? As we did in Section 5.3, we will first look at one of the procedures that this factory is supposed to produce. This verifier checks to see whether the sum of the digits is divisible by 17; in other words, the divisor is 17 and the function is just $f(i, d_i) = d_i$. To write the verifier, we'll first write a procedure to add the digits. Recall from Chapter 2 that we can get at the individual digits in a number by using division by 10. The remainder when we divide by 10 is the rightmost digit, d_1, and the quotient is the rest of the digits. For example, here is how we could compute the sum of the digits in a number (as in Exercise 2.11 on page 39) using an iterative process:

```
(define sum-of-digits
  (lambda (n)
    (define sum-plus ;(sum of n's digits) + addend
      (lambda (n addend)
        (if (= n 0)
            addend
            (sum-plus (quotient n 10)
                      (+ addend (remainder n 10))))))
    (sum-plus n 0)))
```

Exercise 5.10

Write a predicate that takes a number and determines whether the sum of its digits is divisible by 17.

Exercise 5.11

Write a procedure `make-verifier`, which takes f and m as its two arguments and returns a procedure capable of checking a number. The argument f is itself a procedure, of course. Here is a particularly simple example of a verifier being made and used:

```
(define check-isbn (make-verifier * 11))

(check-isbn 0262010771)
#t
```

The value **#t** is the "true" value; it indicates that the number is a valid ISBN.

As we just saw, for ISBN numbers the divisor is 11 and the function is simply $f(i, d_i) = i \times d_i$. Other kinds of numbers use slightly more complicated functions, but you will still be able to use **make-verifier** to make a verifier much more easily than if you had to start from scratch.

Exercise 5.12

For UPC codes (the barcodes on grocery items), the divisor is 10, and the function $f(i, d_i)$ is equal to d_i itself when i is odd, but to $3d_i$ when i is even. Build a verifier for UPC codes using **make-verifier**, and test it on some of your groceries. (The UPC number consists of all the digits: the one to the left of the bars, the ones underneath the bars, and the one on the right.) Try making some mistakes, like switching or changing digits. Does your verifier catch them?

Exercise 5.13

Credit card numbers also use a divisor of 10 and also use a function that yields d_i itself when i is odd. However, when i is even, the function is a bit fancier: It is $2d_i$ if $d_i < 5$, and $2d_i + 1$ if $d_i \geq 5$. Build a verifier for credit card numbers. In the dialog at the beginning of this section, did the order taker really mistype the number, or did the customer read it incorrectly?

Exercise 5.14

The serial number on U.S. postal money orders is self-verifying with a divisor of 9 and a very simple function: $f(i, d_i) = d_i$, with only one exception, namely, $f(1, d_1) = -d_1$. Build a verifier for these numbers, and find out which of these two money orders is mistyped: 48077469777 or 48077462766.

Actually, *both* of those money order numbers were mistyped. In one case the error was that a 0 was replaced by a 7, and in the other case two digits were reversed. Can you figure out which kind of error got caught and which didn't? Does this help explain why the other kinds of numbers use fancier functions?

Review Problems

▷ Exercise 5.15

Write a higher-order procedure called `make-function-with-exception` that takes two numbers and a procedure as parameters and returns a procedure that has the same behavior as the procedural argument except when given a special argument. The two numerical arguments to `make-function-with-exception` specify what that exceptional argument is and what the procedure made by `make-function-with-exception` should return in that case. For example, the `usually-sqrt` procedure that follows behaves like `sqrt`, except that when given the argument 7, it returns the result 2:

```
(define usually-sqrt
  (make-function-with-exception 7 2 sqrt))
```

```
(usually-sqrt 9)
3
```

```
(usually-sqrt 16)
4
```

```
(usually-sqrt 7)
2
```

▷ Exercise 5.16

If two procedures *f* and *g* are both procedures of a single argument such that the values produced by *g* are legal arguments to *f*, the *composition* of *f* and *g* is defined to be the procedure that first applies *g* to its argument and then applies *f* to the result. Write a procedure called `compose` that takes two one-argument procedures and returns the procedure that is their composition. For example, `((compose sqrt abs) -4)` should compute the square root of the absolute value of −4.

▷ Exercise 5.17

Suppose you have a function and you want to find at what integer point in a given range it has the smallest value. For example, looking at the following graph of the function $f(x) = x^2 - 2x$, you can see that in the range from 0 to 4, this function has the smallest value at 1.

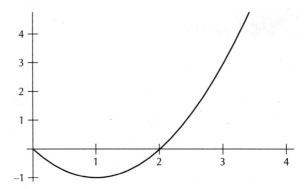

We could write a procedure for answering questions like this; it could be used as follows for this example:

```
(integer-in-range-where-smallest (lambda (x)
                                     (- (* x x) (* 2 x)))
                                  0 4)
```
1

Here is the procedure that does this; fill in the two blanks to complete it:

```
(define integer-in-range-where-smallest
  (lambda (f a b)
    (if (= a b)
        a
        (let ((smallest-place-after-a
               _____))
          (if _____
              a
              smallest-place-after-a)))))
```

 Exercise 5.18

Consider the following definitions:

```
(define make-scaled
  (lambda (scale f)
    (lambda (x)
      (* scale (f x)))))
```

```
(define add-one
  (lambda (x)
    (+ 1 x)))
```

```
(define mystery
  (make-scaled 3 add-one))
```

For the following questions, be sure to indicate how you arrived at your answer:

a. What is the value of (mystery 4)?

b. What is the value of the procedural call ((make-scaled 2 (make-scaled 3 add-one)) 4)?

▷ **Exercise 5.19**

If *l* and *h* are integers, with *l* < *h*, we say *f* is an increasing function on the integer range from *l* to *h* if $f(l) < f(l + 1) < f(l + 2) < \cdots < f(h)$. Write a procedure, increasing-on-integer-range?, that takes *f*, *l*, and *h* as its three arguments and returns true or false (that is, #t or #f) as appropriate.

▷ **Exercise 5.20**

Suppose the following have been defined:

```
(define f
  (lambda (m b)
    (lambda (x) (+ (* m x) b))))
```

```
(define g (f 3 2))
```

For each of the following expressions, indicate whether an error would be signaled, the value would be a procedure, or the value would be a number. If an error is signaled, explain briefly the nature of the error. If the value is a procedure, specify how many arguments the procedure expects. If the value is a number, specify which number.

a. f

b. g

c. (* (f 3 2) 7)

d. (g 6)

e. (f 6)

f. ((f 4 7) 5)

▷ **Exercise 5.21**

We saw in Section 5.3 the following procedure-generating procedure:

```
(define make-multiplier
  (lambda (scaling-factor)
    (lambda (x)
      (* x scaling-factor))))
```

You were also asked in Exercise 5.7 to write the procedure `make-exponentiater`.

Notice that these two procedures are quite similar. We could abstract out the commonality into an even more general procedure `make-generator` such that we could then just write:

```
(define make-multiplier (make-generator *))
```

```
(define make-exponentiater (make-generator expt))
```

Write `make-generator`.

▷ **Exercise 5.22**

The function `halts?` was defined as a test of whether a procedure with no parameters would generate a terminating process. That is, `(halts? f)` returns true if and only if the evaluation of `(f)` would terminate. What about procedures that take arguments? Suppose we had a procedure `halts-on?` that tests whether a one-argument procedure generates a terminating process when given some particular argument. That is, `(halts-on? f x)` returns true if and only if the evaluation of `(f x)` would terminate.

a. Use `halts-on?` in a definition of `halts?`.

b. What does this tell you about the possibility of `halts-on?`

▷ **Exercise 5.23**

Consider the following example:

```
(define double (lambda (x) (* x 2)))
(define square (lambda (x) (* x x)))
(define new-procedure
  (make-averaged-procedure double square))
```

```
(new-procedure 4)
```
12
```
(new-procedure 6)
```
24

In the first example, the `new-procedure` that was made by `make-averaged-procedure` returned 12 because 12 is the average of 8 (twice 4) and 16 (4 squared). In the second example, it returned 24 because 24 is the average of 12 (twice 6) and 36 (6 squared). In general, `new-procedure` will return the average of whatever `double` and `square` return because those two procedures were passed to `make-averaged-procedure` when `new-procedure` was made.

Write the higher-order procedure factory `make-averaged-procedure`.

▷ **Exercise 5.24**

Consider the following procedure:

```
(define positive-integer-upto-where-smallest
  (lambda (n f)  ; return an integer i such that
                 ; 1 <= i <= n and for all integers j
                 ; in that same range, f(i) <= f(j)
    (define loop
      (lambda (where-smallest-so-far next-to-try)
        (if (> next-to-try n)
            where-smallest-so-far
            (loop (if (< (f next-to-try)
                         (f where-smallest-so-far))
                      next-to-try
                      where-smallest-so-far)
                  (+ next-to-try 1)))))
    (loop 1 2)))
```

a. Write a mathematical formula involving n that tells how many times this procedure uses the procedure it is given as its second argument. Justify your answer.

b. Give a simple Θ order of growth for the quantity you determined in part **a**. Justify your answer.

c. Suppose you were to rewrite this procedure to make it more efficient. What (in terms of n) is the minimum number of times it can invoke `f` and still always determine the correct answer? Justify your answer. (You are *not* being asked to actually rewrite the procedure.)

Chapter Inventory

Vocabulary

procedural parameter

higher-order procedure

uncomputable function

halting problem

proof by contradiction

diagonalization proof

proof by reduction

Turing machine

artificial intelligence

operational test of intelligence

Turing test

self-verifying number

composition

Scheme Names Defined in This Chapter

```
together-copies-of
stack-copies-of
power
mod-expt
mystery
num-digits-in-satisfying
num-odd-digits
num-6s
num-digits
return-seven
loop-forever
debunk-halts?
make-multiplier
double
triple
make-exponentiater
square
cube
make-repeated-version-of
```

```
repeatedly-square
factorial
sum-of-first
sum-of-squares
sum-of-cubes
sum-of-digits
make-verifier
check-isbn
make-function-with-exception
compose
integer-in-range-where-smallest
make-scaled
add-one
increasing-on-integer-range?
make-generator
new-procedure
make-averaged-procedure
positive-integer-upto-
    where-smallest
```

Sidebars

Alan Turing

Notes

Turing's original proof that `halts?` can't exist is in [51]. The standard biography of Turing is Hodges's [26], and we heartily recommend it.

We remarked in passing that diagonalization can also be used to prove that most functions can't even be specified, let alone implemented by a procedure. To give some flavor for this, let's restrict ourselves to functions mapping positive integers to positive integers and show that any notational scheme must miss at least one of them. Consider an infinitely long list of all possible function specifications in the notational scheme under consideration, arranged in alphabetical order; call the first one f_1, the second one f_2, etc. Now consider the function f that has the property that for all n, $f(n) = f_n(n) + 1$. Clearly there is no n for which f is identical to f_n, because it differs from each of them in at least one place (namely, at n). Thus f is a function that is not on the list.

Our information about the various schemes used for self-verifying numbers is gleaned in small part from experimentation but primarily from two articles by Gallian, [20] and [19]. Those articles contain more of the mathematical underpinnings and citations for additional sources. We confess that the ISBN checker we defined as an example will only work for those ISBNs that consist purely of digits; one-eleventh of all ISBNs end with an X rather than a digit. This X is treated as though it were a digit with value 10.

PART II

Data Abstraction

In the previous part, we looked at how procedures describe computational processes. In this part, we will turn our attention to the data that is manipulated by those processes and how it can be structured. There are many qualitatively dissimilar ways of structuring data. For example, the list of stops for a bus route bears little resemblance to someone's family tree. In this part, we'll focus on a few representative data structures and the collection of operations that is appropriate to each one.

In Chapter 6, we'll work through the fundamentals of using and representing compound data in the relatively simple context of data types with a fixed number of components. Our focus is on the collection of operations that forms the interface between the uses of the data type and its representation. In Chapter 7, we'll show how two-component data structures can actually be used to represent lists of any length, by treating each nonempty list as having a first element and a list of the remaining elements. We'll extend this recursive approach to structuring data to hierarchical, tree-like structures in Chapter 8. Next we'll examine how a diverse collection of different data representations can present a single, uniform collection of interface operations. Finally, we'll look at programs as themselves being hierarchically composed data (expressions made of subexpressions) and see how to provide a uniform "evaluate" operation across the diversity of different expression types. By doing so, we'll show that implementing a programming language is really a specific application of the techniques introduced in this part of the book.

CHAPTER SIX

Compound Data and Data Abstraction

6.1 Introduction

Up until now, each value passed to one of our procedures as an argument or returned as a result was a single thing: a number, an image, a truth value, or a procedure. If we wanted to pass a procedure two numbers, we needed two separate arguments, because each argument value could only be a single thing. This kind of data is called *atomic* data. On the other hand, you can easily think of programs that use more complex data. For example, a program that plays poker would use hands of cards. There might be a `compare-hands` procedure that takes two arguments, namely, the two hands to compare, and reports which is better. Each argument to this procedure is a single thing, namely, a hand. Yet we can also select an individual card from a hand. So, at the same time as the hand is a single thing, it is also a collection of component cards. How about the cards themselves? Each card is clearly a single thing, yet we can also treat it as a combination of a suit and a rank. Data such as this, which we can interpret as both a single entity and also as a collection of parts, is called *compound data*.

In order to see how we can get a computer to navigate these strange waters between singular and plural, consider the following scenario. Suppose you run a mail-order company and want to start selling custom-knit "socks" for cats' tails—great for those cold nights. (You figure you'll have the market all to yourself.) The problem is, your order form only has space for a single model number, but the customer needs to specify both the length (to the nearest centimeter) and also whether or not they want the deluxe (mohair) version. In other words, they need to send you a combination of a number (the length) and a truth value (whether or not deluxe) but can only send in one thing—the model number. What do you do? You hire a consulting firm.

The consulting firm designs three calculator-like gizmos with keypads and displays. One of them, the *constructor*, is to be mailed out to your customers along with their catalogs. It *constructs* the model number from the length and the deluxeness choice. The other two gizmos, the *selectors*, are for use at your company. The deluxeness selector displays "yes" or "no" on its display when you enter a model number. The length selector displays the length in centimeters when you enter a model number.

You and your customers can use these devices without needing to know anything about how they work. In particular, you don't need to know how the two pieces of information are encoded into the model number. In contrast, the consultants who designed the gizmos (and who are likely to be the only ones who get rich on this whole harebrained scheme) need to decide on this encoding. They need to choose a particular *representation* of the two pieces of information, and this same representation needs to be embodied in both the constructor and the selectors.

This idea, that the representation of data can be exclusively the concern of a constructor and selectors, rather than of the ultimate creators and users of the data, is known as *data abstraction*. In slightly more general terms, data abstraction refers to separating the way a new type of data is used from the way it is represented. This means that when we add a new data type, we first decide what operations (procedures) are necessary to create and manipulate the data values. Then we figure out a good way of representing the data values using the types that are already part of our Scheme system. Finally, we find algorithms necessary for implementing the essential operations. Whenever we use the new data type in another program, we create and manipulate the data values *only* by using the essential operations, and not by accessing the underlying representation of the data.

The self-discipline of data abstraction brings three rewards. First of all, by specifying the basic operations that manipulate the new data type, the programmer needn't worry about how the data values are actually represented. This means that she can work with the abstract model of the data that she has in her head rather than constantly switching from the model to the underlying representation and back. (A programmer working in this representation-independent way is said to be using an *abstract data type*, or *ADT* .) Secondly, if we separate the way the data is used from how it is implemented, the implementation can be developed independently from the programs using the data. Because of this, we can often break down a large programming project into pieces that different teams of programmers can work on simultaneously. Finally, because the application programs access the data only through the basic operations, we can easily change the way the data is represented by simply changing these procedures. In particular, if we want to move a large software program (such as the Scheme system) from one type of computer to another (this process is called *porting*), a lot of the work is restricted to modifying the ADT implementations.

In the remainder of this chapter, we illustrate the technique of data abstraction by writing a program that plays the game of Nim. This is our first example of an interactive program, thereby introducing the reader to some simple input and output procedures in Scheme. For most of this chapter, our compound data will have only two components; however, we show how to create data types with three components in Section 6.4. This technique can be extended to any (fixed) number of components. Our application section considers how to use higher-order programming together with data abstraction to add strategies to the game of Nim.

In later chapters, we consider more complex data structures, such as lists and hierarchically structured data, that do not restrict the number of components in the data. We also consider complex "generic" operators that can be used on multiple data types. Finally, we apply these ideas to one very special kind of compound data, programs, and a particularly interesting operation, the running of those programs.

6.2 Nim

In this section we will start to write the procedures for playing a variation on the game of Nim. The first appearance of "official" rules for Nim is in a 1901 paper by Charles Bouton, in which he analyzed the game and presented a winning strategy. However, like many informal folk games, there are many different ways of playing Nim. All the variations start with objects of some sort arranged in some way. Two players alternate removing objects according to certain rules, and the player who takes the last object is the winner (or the loser, in some variations). We present three ways to play Nim:

1. The version we'll call three-pile Nim is presented in Bouton's paper. It is played using three piles of objects, say coins. When the game starts, the three piles have different numbers of coins. Two players take turns removing coins. Each player must take at least one coin each turn and may take more as long as they are all from the same pile. The winner is the player who takes the last coin (or coins). Because finding a winning strategy for this version is relatively easy, Bouton suggested the variation in which the player who takes the last coin loses the game.

2. Instead of three piles, some other number of piles can be used, each starting with some arbitrary number of coins in it. The game proceeds exactly as above, with the winner (or loser) being the last person to remove one or more coins. In particular, we'll work with the two-pile version in most of this chapter.

3. The final version is the tastiest one. The game wouldn't be conceptually any different if something else were progressively reduced other than the number of coins in piles. How about the number of rows and the number of columns in a chocolate bar? You start with the kind of chocolate candy bar that is scored into rows and columns so that you could break it into small squares. Pretend that the square in the bottom left-hand corner is poisoned. The players take turns breaking

the bar into two pieces by breaking along one of the horizontal grooves or one of the vertical grooves in the bar and then eating the section not containing the poisoned square. Eventually, one player will be left with just one square, which is poisoned. That player loses.

How is the last version related to the previous two? In fact it is equivalent to two-pile Nim. To see this, you need to realize that the candy bar is completely specified by the number of horizontal and vertical grooves (or scores). If we represent the bar by two piles, one with a coin for each horizontal score and the other with a coin for each vertical score, breaking the candy bar along a vertical or horizontal score corresponds to removing coins from one of the piles, and ending with the poisoned square corresponds to both piles being empty (because when the bar is down to a single square, there are no scores left). Breaking the chocolate at the last place it can be broken is like taking the last coin.

Before we write a program for the computer to play Nim with a human user, we must first decide which version we want to play. We've chosen to concentrate on the two-pile version, with the winner being the player who takes the last coin. As the above discussion suggests, it doesn't matter whether we actually play with two piles of coins or, instead, use a chocolate bar. When we play with the computer, we presumably won't use either physical piles or a chocolate bar, but rather some third option better suited to the computer's capabilities. To get a feel for how to play Nim, find a partner and play a few games. (We disclaim all responsibility if you choose the chocolate bar version.) As you play, think about how you might write a program that could play Nim with you.

What type of data will such a program need? If you think about how you played, you will see that you and your partner started with a particular configuration of coins and took turns transforming the current configuration into a new configuration by making legal moves. The configuration of the coins in the two piles described the state (or condition) of the game at a given time. For this reason, we will call the configurations *game states*; they are our new data type. That is, we will arrange things so that we can pass a game state into a procedure as an argument or return a game state as the result of a procedure, just as we can with any other type of value. That way, the transformation you do in making a move can be a procedure. Game states can be physically represented by two piles of coins, which we call the first pile and the second pile.

Next, find a third person to be a gamekeeper and play another game with your partner. This time, instead of physically removing coins from piles, have the gamekeeper do all the work. The gamekeeper should keep track of the individual game states; you and your partner will give him directions and ask him questions. As you play, concentrate on what directions you give the gamekeeper and what questions you ask. You should discover that you repeatedly ask how many coins there are in a particular pile of the current game state and that you tell the gamekeeper to change to a new game state by removing some number of coins from a particular pile. This tells us that there are at least two operations we need for our data structure. One tells us how many coins are in either one of the piles and the other allows us to "remove" a specified number of coins from a pile, by making a new state with fewer coins in that pile. In Scheme, we could specify these operations as follows:

```
(size-of-pile game-state p)
  ;returns an integer equal to the number of coins in the p-th
  ;pile of the game-state
```

```
(remove-coins-from-pile game-state n p)
  ;given a Nim game-state, returns a new game state with n
  ;fewer coins in pile p
```

We will also need an operation that creates a new game state with a specified number of coins in each pile. This operation is what is used to set up an initial game state:

```
(make-game-state n m)
  ;returns a game state with n coins in the first pile
  ;and m coins in the second pile
```

▶ Exercise 6.1

A fourth version of Nim uses two piles of coins but adds the restriction that a player can remove at most three coins in any one turn. To implement this version, we could use the three operations, `make-game-state`, `size-of-pile`, and `remove-coins-from-pile`, as before. In this case, whenever we use `remove-coins-from-pile`, the parameter indicating how many coins to remove should have a value of 1, 2, or 3.

Alternatively, we could replace `remove-coins-from-pile` with the three operations, `remove-one`, `remove-two`, and `remove-three`, where each of these operations would have just two parameters: the current game state and the pile to remove from. With this implementation, we would have five operations instead of three. Compare these two approaches to implementing this new version of Nim. What are the advantages and disadvantages of each one? Is one implementation better than the other?

Are these three operations (`make-game-state`, `size-of-pile`, and `remove-coins-from-pile`) enough? In other words, if someone else implemented the abstract data type of game states for us, could we then write the procedures we need to have the computer play Nim? Let's try to do this.

Recall that when you and your partner played Nim, you progressed through a succession of game states by alternately making moves and that you continued to do so until all the coins were gone. The game would eventually end, because every move reduces the total number of coins by at least one. In other words, each move transforms the game into a smaller game, if we measure the size of the game in terms of the total number of coins. Therefore, the main game-playing procedure, which we will call `play-with-turns`, should repeatedly reduce the game state by alternately having the computer and the human make a move. We will have two procedures, `human-move` and `computer-move`, to do these separate reductions. When the game is over (which will be determined by an as yet unwritten predicate `over?`,) the computer should announce the winner; we'll do that using the procedure `announce-winner`.

The procedure `play-with-turns` will use two new aspects of Scheme: quoted *symbols* and the equality predicate `equal?`. A symbol is a basic Scheme data type that is simply a name used as itself, rather than as the name of something. You specify a symbol by putting a single *quote mark* before it. To illustrate, here is some Scheme dialog:

```
'human
human

'x
x

(define x 'y)
x
y

(define z x)
z
y

(define w 'x)
w
x
```

The quote mark isn't part of the symbol itself; instead, the combination of the quote mark and the symbol is an expression, the value of which is the symbol. As this example shows, the value of the expression `'x` is the symbol x, whereas the value of the expression x is whatever x has been defined as a name for (here, the symbol y).

Because the equality predicate = only works for numbers, we need to use the more general equality predicate `equal?` for symbols. Putting this all together, we come up with the following version of `play-with-turns`:

```
(define play-with-turns    ;warning: this is not the final version
  (lambda (game-state player)
    (cond ((over? game-state)
           (announce-winner player))
          ((equal? player 'human)
           (play-with-turns (human-move game-state) 'computer))
          ((equal? player 'computer)
           (play-with-turns (computer-move game-state) 'human)))))
```

We would play a game by evaluating an expression such as

```
(play-with-turns (make-game-state 5 8) 'human)
```

There is one major problem with `play-with-turns`. Consider what would happen if we attempted to play a game by evaluating the expression (`play-with-turns (make-game-state 5 8) 'humman`). Because the symbol `humman` is neither `human` nor `computer`, and because the game is clearly not over, none of the conditions in the `cond` would be met. Thus, the game would not be played and an undefined value would be returned. Furthermore, the user would have no idea why nothing happened. One way to fix this is to use an `else` instead of (`equal? player 'computer`); however, this is still unsatisfactory because the game gets played with the computer having the first turn and the user has no idea why he didn't get to go first.

A better strategy is to use the procedure `error`, which, although not a part of R[4]RS Scheme, is predefined in the versions of Scheme that are recommended for this book. The procedure `error` stops the normal execution of the program and notifies the user that an error occurred. In order to tell the user the nature of the error, we give `error` a description of the error as an argument, as in

```
(error "player wasn't human or computer")
```

This descriptive argument is a *character string*, which is written as a sequence of characters enclosed in double quotes. In this book, we'll generally use character strings in cases like this, for output. We can also tell the user more about the error by passing additional arguments to `error`, which it will display. For example, we can use

```
(error "player wasn't human or computer:" player)
```

to let the user know what specific unexpected player argument was provided.

We can use `error` in `play-with-turns` by adding an `else` clause to the `cond`:

```
(define play-with-turns
  (lambda (game-state player)
    (cond ((over? game-state)
           (announce-winner player))
          ((equal? player 'human)
           (play-with-turns (human-move game-state) 'computer))
          ((equal? player 'computer)
           (play-with-turns (computer-move game-state) 'human))
          (else
           (error "player wasn't human or computer:" player)))))
```

Evaluating (play-with-turns (make-game-state 5 8) 'humman) still won't start the game. However, we'll see the message "player wasn't human or computer: humman," which will give us some explanation of what went wrong, unlike before.

We will write the procedure computer-move so that it uses the very simple strategy of removing one coin from the first pile. If the first pile is empty, the computer will remove one coin from the second pile. Note that if both piles are empty, the computer will still try to remove one coin from the second pile. However, this can never happen, because if both piles are empty, the game is over:

```
(define computer-move
  (lambda (game-state)
    (if (> (size-of-pile game-state 1) 0)
        (remove-coins-from-pile game-state 1 1)
        (remove-coins-from-pile game-state 1 2)))))
```

Unfortunately, the human player has no way of knowing what strategy the computer is using and so has no idea what the state of the game is after the computer has moved. We must therefore add some output statements to tell the human player what the computer is doing. We will use two built-in Scheme procedures, display and newline. These procedures are best described by example, but roughly speaking, display takes a single argument that it immediately prints out as output, and newline takes no arguments and causes the output to go to the next line.

For example, the following procedure takes a game state and displays it in a reasonable manner:

```
(define display-game-state
  (lambda (game-state)
    (newline)
    (newline)
    (display "    Pile 1: ")
    (display (size-of-pile game-state 1))
```

```
(newline)
(display "    Pile 2: ")
(display (size-of-pile game-state 2))
(newline)
(newline)))
```

Note that in two cases, we passed `display` a character string, because we wanted to control exactly what was output, as previously with `error`. Also, the definition of the Scheme programming language doesn't make any guarantees about the value (if any) returned by `display` and `newline`—they are only used for their effect.

How do we incorporate output into our program? Well, the game state should be displayed before each player makes a move, and the computer should inform the human player of its move. The first of these goals is most easily accomplished by adding one line to `play-with-turns`:

```
(define play-with-turns
  (lambda (game-state player)
    (display-game-state game-state)                    ;<-- output
    (cond ((over? game-state)
           (announce-winner player))
          ((equal? player 'human)
           (play-with-turns (human-move game-state) 'computer))
          ((equal? player 'computer)
           (play-with-turns (computer-move game-state) 'human))
          (else
           (error "player wasn't human or computer:" player)))))
```

In order to tell the human player what the computer is doing, we can add similar output statements. However, the output depends on which pile the computer uses. Because we also need to know which pile to use in the call to `remove-coins-from-pile`, we create a local variable by using a `let`:

```
(define computer-move
  (lambda (game-state)
    (let ((pile (if (> (size-of-pile game-state 1) 0)
                    1
                    2)))
      (display "I take 1 coin from pile ")
      (display pile)
      (newline)
      (remove-coins-from-pile game-state 1 pile))))
```

To write the procedure `human-move`, we need to get some input from the (human) player. We do this by first writing a procedure, `prompt`, which takes a "prompting string" and returns the number entered by the user:

```
(define prompt
  (lambda (prompt-string)
    (newline)
    (display prompt-string)
    (newline)
    (read)))
```

Here we used the basic Scheme input procedure `read`, which takes no arguments and returns whatever value the user enters. (The user's input must have the right form to be a Scheme value.) We are assuming that the user will type in an appropriate value, for example, when asked for the pile number, either 1 or 2.

We can use `prompt` in `human-move` to prompt for the pile number and the number of coins. Note that we use enclosing `let` statements in order to ensure that the user is always prompted for the pile first and the number of coins second. Depending on those answers, we remove the appropriate number of coins from the specified pile:

```
(define human-move
  (lambda (game-state)
    (let ((p (prompt "Which pile will you remove from?")))
      (let ((n (prompt "How many coins do you want to remove?")))
        (remove-coins-from-pile game-state n p)))))
```

▶ **Exercise 6.2**

When you played Nim with another person and a gamekeeper, what did the game-keeper do if you asked her to remove more coins from a pile than she could possibly remove? (For example, what if you asked her to remove six coins from a pile with only five coins in it?) If we want our computer version to work in a similar way, we need to build in some sort of error checking on the part of the input procedures. What would you modify in order to continue asking the user for another number if the number selected was illegal (both for coins and pile)? Is it better to do the error checking in `human-move` or `prompt`? Could you use a procedural parameter to good effect?

Finally, in order to finish the game, we need to be able to determine when the game is over and have the computer announce who the winner is. Note that we're assuming that the players play until the bitter end, so the game is over when both piles are empty:

```
(define total-size
  (lambda (game-state)
    (+ (size-of-pile game-state 1)
       (size-of-pile game-state 2))))

(define over?
  (lambda (game-state)
    (= (total-size game-state) 0)))

(define announce-winner
  (lambda (player)
    (if (equal? player 'human)
        (display "You lose. Better luck next time.")
        (display "You win. Congratulations."))))
```

There is the program. (For your convenience, we include the entire program in a sidebar. We don't include `display-game-state` and `total-size`, because we consider them to be part of the abstract data type game state.) Without having any idea of how we are going to represent our game states or implement the three operations `make-game-state`, `remove-coins-from-pile`, and `size-of-pile`, we've written all the procedures needed to play Nim. This illustrates one of the main advantages of data abstraction. We can develop the application of our data type independently of developing the implementation.

> ### Exercise 6.3

The version of Nim we have just written designates the winner as the one taking the last coin. What needs to be changed in order to reverse this, that is, to designate the one taking the last coin as the loser?

6.3   Representations and Implementations

In order to actually use the program in the previous section, we need to implement the ADT of game states. This means that we need to find some way of representing game states and we need to figure out the algorithms and write the procedures for the three operations. To do this, let's think about physical (as opposed to electronic) ways of constructing piles. First of all, the fact that we used coins was totally irrelevant to how we played the game. We could have used packets of sugar, vertical hatch

Nim Program

```scheme
(define play-with-turns
  (lambda (game-state player)
    (display-game-state game-state)
    (cond ((over? game-state)
           (announce-winner player))
          ((equal? player 'human)
           (play-with-turns (human-move game-state) 'computer))
          ((equal? player 'computer)
           (play-with-turns (computer-move game-state) 'human))
          (else
           (error "player wasn't human or computer:" player)))))

(define computer-move
  (lambda (game-state)
    (let ((pile (if (> (size-of-pile game-state 1) 0)
                    1
                    2)))
      (display "I take 1 coin from pile ")
      (display pile)
      (newline)
      (remove-coins-from-pile game-state 1 pile))))


(define prompt
  (lambda (prompt-string)
    (newline)
    (display prompt-string)
    (newline)
    (read)))

(define human-move
  (lambda (game-state)
    (let ((p (prompt "Which pile will you remove from?")))
      (let ((n (prompt "How many coins do you want to remove?")))
        (remove-coins-from-pile game-state n p)))))

(define over?
  (lambda (game-state)
    (= (total-size game-state) 0)))

(define announce-winner
  (lambda (player)
    (if (equal? player 'human)
        (display "You lose. Better luck next time.")
        (display "You win. Congratulations."))))
```

marks, or the horizontal and vertical score lines on a chocolate bar. Similarly, how we arranged our coins in two piles was also unimportant. We could have made two heaps, we could have made two neat lines, or we could have arranged the coins in two separate rectangular arrays. Some arrangements might make counting the number of coins in a pile easier, but as long as we can determine how many coins there were in each pile, how we arrange the piles doesn't matter. What really matters is the number of coins in each pile. Thus, in order to represent game states in Scheme, we can use two numbers that we glue together in some way. We consider four different ways to do so.

The first way of representing game states is based on the fact that, as humans, we can easily see the separate digits in a numeral. If we add the restriction that there can't be more than nine coins in each pile, we can use two-digit numbers to represent the two piles. The first digit will be the number of coins in the first pile and the second digit will be the number in the second pile. (For example, a game state of 58 would have five coins in the first pile and eight coins in the second pile.) To create a game state with n coins in the first pile and m coins in the second, we would just physically write those two digits together, nm. This number is $n \times 10 + m$. Therefore, we can implement the operations `make-game-state` and `size-of-pile` as follows:

```
(define make-game-state
  ;; assumes no more than 9 coins per pile
  (lambda (n m) (+ (* 10 n) m)))

(define size-of-pile
  (lambda (game-state pile-number)
    (if (= pile-number 1)
        (quotient game-state 10)
        (remainder game-state 10))))
```

Removing coins from a pile can be done in two different ways: either taking advantage of the particular representation we've chosen, or not. If we take advantage of our particular representation, in which pile 1 is represented by the tens place and pile 2 by the ones place, we can remove coins from a pile by subtracting the specified number of either tens or ones:

```
(define remove-coins-from-pile
  (lambda (game-state num-coins pile-number)
    (- game-state
       (if (= pile-number 1)
           (* 10 num-coins)
           num-coins))))
```

Alternatively, we can have `remove-coins-from-pile` first select the two pile numbers using `size-of-pile`, then subtract the number of coins from the appropriate one of them, and finally use `make-game-state` to glue them back together:

```
(define remove-coins-from-pile
  (lambda (game-state num-coins pile-number)
    (if (= pile-number 1)
        (make-game-state (- (size-of-pile game-state 1)
                            num-coins)
                         (size-of-pile game-state 2))
        (make-game-state (size-of-pile game-state 1)
                         (- (size-of-pile game-state 2)
                            num-coins)))))
```

This version of `remove-coins-from-pile` has the advantage that when we change representations, all we need to change are the algorithms for `make-game-state` and `size-of-pile`.

Exercise 6.4

The restriction that we can only use at most nine coins in each pile is somewhat unreasonable. A more reasonable one would be to limit the size of the piles to at most 99 coins. Change the implementation above so that it reflects this restriction.

Exercise 6.5

What happens if we try to remove more coins from a pile than are actually in the pile? For example, what would be the result of evaluating

```
(remove-coins-from-pile (make-game-state 3 2) 5 1)
```

Modify `remove-coins-from-pile` so that such a request would result in just removing all of the coins from the specified pile.

Exercise 6.6

What are some other ways of coping with errors?

The biggest problem with this way of gluing our two numbers together is that we must put some arbitrary restriction on the size of the numbers. This approach is fine when we can reasonably make this restriction, as in two-pile Nim. However, there are data types where we can't reasonably restrict the size of the components, for example, the budget of the U.S. government. Our second representation (theoretically) gets around this restriction.

In this representation we will use integers of the form $2^n \times 3^m$, where n is the number of coins in the first pile and m is the number of coins in the second. Constructing a game state is quite easy, using the built-in procedure `expt`:

```
(define make-game-state
  (lambda (n m) (* (expt 2 n) (expt 3 m))))
```

Getting at the component parts of a game state is not so bad either, using the procedure in the following exercise.

> **Exercise 6.7**

Look back at the procedures for calculating the exponent of 2 in a number that you wrote in Exercise 2.12 on page 40 and Exercise 3.2 on page 54. Generalize one of these to a procedure `exponent-of-in` such that (`exponent-of-in` n m) returns the exponent of the highest power of n that divides evenly into m.

With this procedure, we can easily write `size-of-pile`:

```
(define size-of-pile
  (lambda (game-state pile-number)
    (if (= pile-number 1)
        (exponent-of-in 2 game-state)
        (exponent-of-in 3 game-state))))
```

This implementation has two drawbacks. The first is that accessing the number of items in a pile does not take constant time. Instead, the time depends linearly on the size of the pile. The second drawback is that the integers representing the game states get very big very rapidly. This is not so important when we're implementing game states; however, when we implement a data structure where the component parts are often big numbers, this method would result in representations too large to fit in the computer's memory.

The first two implementations use integers to represent the values that a game state could have. Note that some integers, such as 36, could be used in either representation. That is, a game state represented by 36 could be either one where the first pile has three coins and the second has six (in the first representation) or one where each pile has two coins (in the second representation). In fact, the only way we know what game state is represented by a specific integer is by knowing which representation we're using. The three operations are what interpret the values for us. The need for a consistent interpretation is one of the reasons that we use *only* the specified operations to manipulate values in an abstract data type.

Our third representation for game states uses procedures instead of integers to represent the game states. So when we apply `make-game-state`, the result should be a procedure, because `make-game-state` creates game states. Now, a game state has two observable properties, the number of coins in each of the two piles. Because the only property that we can observe about a procedure is its return value, the procedure generated by `make-game-state` should have two different return values. Therefore, this procedure should have at least one argument so that we can have some way of controlling which of the two values should be returned. Because there is no need for more than one argument, we want `(make-game-state n m)` to produce a procedure with one argument that sometimes returns n and sometimes returns m. What should this procedure be? We have complete freedom to choose. It could return n when its argument is odd and m when its argument is even; it could return n for positive values of its argument and m for negative values, or whatever. For now, let's arbitrarily decide to use the first option:

```
(define make-game-state
  (lambda (n m)
    (lambda (x)
      (if (odd? x)
          n
          m))))
```

Now we need to write the procedure `size-of-pile`. If we think about how `make-game-state` and `size-of-pile` should work together, we can write two equations:

$$(\text{size-of-pile} \ (\text{make-game-state} \ n \ m) \ 1) = n$$

$$(\text{size-of-pile} \ (\text{make-game-state} \ n \ m) \ 2) = m$$

Because `make-game-state` produces a procedure that returns *n* when it gets an odd argument and *m* when it gets an even one, and 1 happens to be odd and 2 even, one way to write `size-of-pile` is to have it simply apply its game state argument (which is a procedure) to the pile number argument:

```
(define size-of-pile
  (lambda (game-state pile-number)
    (game-state pile-number)))
```

> **Exercise 6.8**

Verify that the two equations relating `make-game-state` and `size-of-pile` just given hold for the procedural representation.

This procedural representation of game states has the advantages of each of the previous ones, without the corresponding disadvantages. In other words, we don't need to restrict the size of the piles, and the procedure `size-of-pile` will still generate a constant-time process. We can do little to improve on this representation (but we still have a fourth representation to present anyway, for reasons that will become clear).

At this point, having seen two representations of game states as integers and one as procedures, you may be confused. You may be wondering just what *is* a game state? Surely there should be some definite thing that I can look at and say, *this* is a game state. There are two answers to this. The first answer is to say, Yes, at any time there is one kind of thing that is a game state, which depends on which matched set of constructor and selector definitions has been evaluated. If, for example, you've evaluated the most recent set, game states are procedures.

However, another, better answer to the question above is: Don't worry about what a game state is in that sense. Pretend a game state is a whole new kind of thing. This new kind of thing is produced by `make-game-state`, and you can find information out about it using `size-of-pile`.

In other words, instead of saying "a game state is an integer" or "a game state is a procedure," we'll say "a game state is what `make-game-state` creates (and `size-of-pile` expects)." If the procedures that operate on game states are happy with something, it is a game state. This is worth highlighting as a general principle:

> **The data-abstraction principle (or, the operational stance):** If it acts like an X (i.e., is suitable for operations that operate on X's), it *is* an X.

One related question that you may have is what if you do a game-state operation to something that isn't a game state? Or what if you do some other operation to a game state, other than those that make sense for game states? For example, what if you evaluate any of the following?

```
(size-of-pile (* 6 6) 1)

(size-of-pile sqrt 1)

(sqrt (make-game-state 3 6))

((make-game-state 3 6) 7)
```

Again, there are two answers: (1) That depends on the details of which representation was chosen and how the operations were implemented and (2) Don't do that. As unsatisfactory as this second answer may sound, it generally is the more useful one. We can sum this all up as follows:

> **The strong data-abstraction principle:** If it acts like an X, it *is* an X. Conversely, if it is an X, only expect it to act in X-like ways.

When we discussed our procedural representation of game states above, we mentioned that we'd be hard pressed to improve upon it. So, why then do we still have a fourth representation up our sleeves? The answer is that although we'd be hard pressed to do better, someone else might not be. In particular, whoever designed your Scheme system might have some slightly more efficient way of gluing two values together, using behind-the-scenes magic.

So, what we'll do for our final implementation of game states is turn data abstraction to our advantage and use a built-in data type in Scheme called *pairs*. Whoever built your Scheme system represented pairs as efficiently as they possibly could. Exactly how they did this might vary from one Scheme system to another. However, thanks to data abstraction, all we have to know about pairs is what operations produce them and answer questions about them. The basic operations that Scheme provides to deal with pairs include a procedure for making a pair, a procedure for determining what the first element in a pair is, and a procedure for determining what the second element is. These have extremely weird names:

- cons takes any two objects and glues them together into a pair.
- car takes a pair of objects and returns the first object.
- cdr (pronounced "could-er") takes a pair of objects and returns the second object.

The name cons is easy to understand: It is short for constructor, and sure enough, the procedure called cons is the constructor for pairs. But what about the names car and cdr, which are the names of the selectors for the pair type? These two names are reminders that even smart people sometimes make dumb mistakes. The people who developed an early predecessor of Scheme (at MIT, in the late 1950s) chose to represent pairs on the IBM 704 computer they were using in such a way that the selectors could be implemented using low-level features of the IBM 704 hardware that had the acronyms CAR and CDR (for contents of address part of register and contents of decrement part of register). So, rather than call the selectors first and second, left and right, or one and the-other, they named them car and cdr, after how they were implemented on the 704. (One of the implementers later wrote that "because of an unfortunate temporary lapse of inspiration, we couldn't think of any other names.") In so doing, they were violating the spirit of the strong data-abstraction principle, by basing the abstract interface to the data type on their particular representation. (Of course, in a certain sense, "left" and "right" are just as representation-specific, because they are based on the way we westerners write things down on a page.) A few months after the original naming, the perpetrators of car and cdr tried renaming the operations, but to no avail: Other users were already accustomed to car and cdr and unwilling to change. At any rate, car and cdr have survived for over three decades as the names for the two selector operations on pairs, and so they are likely to survive forever as permanent reminders of how *not* to name operations.

As we said before, cons takes two objects and glues them together in a pair. How do we know which order it uses? In other words, if we use cons to glue *a* and *b* together in a pair, which will be the first object of that pair and which will be the second? What we're really asking here is how cons, car, and cdr work together. The answer is best described by two equations:

$$(\text{car } (\text{cons } a \ b)) = a$$

$$(\text{cdr } (\text{cons } a \ b)) = b$$

These say that if you cons two objects together into a pair, the first object becomes the car of the pair and the second object becomes the cdr of the pair. (We've used this paragraph to introduce you to the way Schemers talk about pairs. We use cons as a verb, as in "cons two objects together," and we talk about the car and cdr of a pair, instead of the first and second components of it.)

Pairs of this sort are a natural way to implement game states, because a game state is most easily thought of as a pair of numbers. Thus, our two operations would be

```
(define make-game-state
  (lambda (n m) (cons n m)))

(define size-of-pile
  (lambda (game-state pile-number)
    (if (= pile-number 1)
        (car game-state)
        (cdr game-state))))
```

Note that in the definition of make-game-state, we simply apply cons to the two arguments. In other words, make-game-state does exactly the same thing as cons and hence can simply be the same procedure as cons:

```
(define make-game-state cons)
```

The way Scheme displays pairs if left to its own devices is in general quite confusing. Therefore, when you are using pairs to represent something else, like

▶ **Game State ADT Implementation**

```
(define make-game-state
  (lambda (n m) (cons n m)))

(define size-of-pile
  (lambda (game-state pile-number)
    (if (= pile-number 1)
        (car game-state)
        (cdr game-state))))

(define remove-coins-from-pile
  (lambda (game-state num-coins pile-number)
    (if (= pile-number 1)
        (make-game-state (- (size-of-pile game-state 1)
                            num-coins)
                         (size-of-pile game-state 2))
        (make-game-state (size-of-pile game-state 1)
                         (- (size-of-pile game-state 2)
                            num-coins)))))

(define display-game-state
  (lambda (game-state)
    (newline)
    (newline)
    (display "    Pile 1: ")
    (display (size-of-pile game-state 1))
    (newline)
    (display "    Pile 2: ")
    (display (size-of-pile game-state 2))
    (newline)
    (newline)))

(define total-size
  (lambda (game-state)
    (+ (size-of-pile game-state 1)
       (size-of-pile game-state 2))))
```

a game state, you should always look at them using an appropriate procedure like `display-game-state`.

Again for your convenience, we include all of the ADT procedures in a sidebar, using just the pair implementation. Together with the Nim program on page 144, this is a full, working program. In the next section we examine the changes needed for three-pile Nim; in the final section we extend the two-pile program so that the computer can use other strategies for selecting its moves.

6.4   Three-Pile Nim

Now suppose we want to write a program that plays Nim with three piles instead of two. We'll need to extend the game state ADT so that it uses three piles instead of two. This means that the procedure `make-game-state` will get three parameters instead of two and needs to glue all three together somehow, depending on which representation we use. If we use one of the numerical representations, the main change would be to use three-digit numbers instead of two or to use numbers of the form $2^n \times 3^m \times 5^k$ instead of $2^n \times 3^m$. The procedural representation is equally easy to change: The procedures created by `make-game-state` must be able to return any of three values instead of just two. But, at first glance, using pairs seems impossible. After all, a pair has only two "slots," whereas we have three numbers, and we can't put three things into two slots.

Wait a minute—of course we can put three things into two slots, as long as we put two of them in one slot and the third in the other slot. How do we put two things into one slot, though? Each slot is allowed to contain only one thing. But there are no restrictions on what that one thing could be; for example, *it could be another pair*. Thus, in order to make a three-pile game state, we'll cons together two of the numbers and cons that together with the remaining one.

Does it matter which order we cons things together? The answer to that is no, sort of. We can cons the three numbers together in any order we like as long as whenever we ask for the number of coins in a particular pile, we get back the correct number. In other words, the procedures `make-game-state` and `size-of-pile` need to work together correctly—the constructors and selectors must agree on the representation, as usual.

Exercise 6.9

Write the equations for three-pile game states that correspond to those given earlier for two-pile game states.

For example, suppose we cons the third pile onto the cons of the first and the second:

```
(define make-game-state
  (lambda (n m k) (cons k (cons n m))))
```

Then how do we pull a game state apart? If we want the size of the third pile, we just need the first element of the game state (i.e., `(car game-state)`). But getting the size of the first or second pile is somewhat trickier, because those two numbers are bundled together. We can get this pair of first and second piles by taking `(cdr game-state)`. Then, to get the size of the first pile, say, we need to take the car of that pair, or `(car (cdr game-state))`. Similarly, to get the size of the second pile, we'll need the cdr of that pair, or `(cdr (cdr game-state))`. Putting this all together gives

```
(define size-of-pile
  (lambda (game-state pile-number)
    (cond ((= pile-number 3)
           (car game-state))
          ((= pile-number 1)
           (car (cdr game-state)))
          (else ;pile-number must be 2
           (cdr (cdr game-state))))))
```

> **Exercise 6.10**

Check that this implementation actually works (i.e., that the constructor and selector actually do agree on the representation).

To help clarify how we get at the components of a three-pile game state, we can draw some pictures. Evaluating an expression such as `(cons 1 2)` results in a pair whose components are the numbers 1 and 2. If we think of that pair as having two slots that have been filled in with those numbers, the picture that comes to mind is `1 2`.

Similarly, when we evaluate `(define gs (cons 3 (cons 1 2)))`, we know that **gs** is a pair whose first component is the number 3 and whose second component is the pair containing the numbers 1 and 2. Thus our picture would look like this:

Now to get at that 2 in **gs**, we need to look at the second component of **gs**. This is itself the pair `1 2`, and so we need to get the second component of this pair. Therefore we must evaluate `(cdr (cdr gs))`.

Although these pictures are quite helpful for understanding data entities that have three components, they quickly become unwieldy to draw if we start building any bigger structures. We can solve this problem by drawing the boxes a standard, small size, putting the contents outside, and using arrows to point to the contents. For a simple pair such as the value of (cons 1 2), moving the contents out leads to

and a pair such as the value of (cons 3 (cons 1 2)) would look like

In addition to solving the problem of unwieldiness, moving the contents out of the boxes makes it easier to see what portion of a structure is reused or "shared." For example, if we evaluate the two definitions:

```
(define p1 (cons 1 2))
(define p2 (cons 3 p1))
```

and use our original style of drawing pairs, we get the picture

which seems to indicate that there are three pairs—at odds with the fact that cons was applied only twice. (We know that each time cons is applied, exactly one pair is created.) In contrast, with our new, improved style of diagram with the contents moved out of the boxes, we can draw

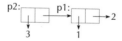

and now it is clear that only one new pair was produced by each of the two applications of cons.

Exercise 6.11

Now that we have the main constructor and selector for the three-pile game state ADT, we need to change the procedures remove-coins-from-pile, total-size, and display-game-state appropriately. Do so.

> **Exercise 6.12**

What will go wrong if we use the existing `computer-move` with three-pile game states? Change `computer-move` so that it works correctly with three-pile game states.

6.5 An Application: Adding Strategies to Nim

In this section, we return to the two-pile version of Nim for simplicity's sake. (Also, we like playing the chocolate bar version.) Much of what we do here easily extends to three-pile Nim. However, finding a winning strategy for three piles is more challenging.

The computer's strategy of removing one coin from the first nonempty pile is not very intelligent. Although we might initially enjoy always winning, eventually it gets rather boring. Is there some way of having the computer use a better strategy? Or perhaps, could we program several different strategies? In that case, what would a strategy be?

If you think about it, a strategy is essentially a procedure that, when given a particular game state, determines how many coins to remove from which pile. In other words, a strategy should return two numbers, one for the number of coins and one for the pile number. Because procedures can return just one thing, we have a real problem here. One way to solve it is to think of these two numbers as an instruction describing the appropriate move to make. We can create a new data type, called *move instruction*, that glues together the number of coins to remove and the pile number to remove them from. We can then view a strategy as a procedure that takes a game state and returns the instruction for the next move.

> **Exercise 6.13**

In this exercise, we will construct the move instruction data type and modify our program appropriately.

a. First, you need to decide what the basic operations for move instructions should be. There are several ways to do this. You can think about how move instructions are going to be used—in particular, what information other procedures need to know about a given move instruction. You can think how you would fully describe a move instruction to someone. You can model move instructions on game states. In any case, it should be clear that you will need one constructor and two selectors. Give a specification for move instructions similar to the one we gave the game state data type. That is, what is the name of each operation, what sort of parameters does it take, and what sort of result does it return? (We will call the move instruction constructor `make-move-instruction` in the following discussion and will assume it takes the number of coins as its first argument and the pile number as its second argument, so you might want to do the same.) Can you also write equations that describe how the operations are related?

b. Choose a representation and implement these procedures.

c. We have used the procedure `remove-coins-from-pile` to progress from one game state to the next, passing to it the current game state and the two integers that specify the move. But with our *move instruction* data type, it makes more sense to have a procedure that is passed the current game state and the move instruction and returns the next game state. We could call the procedure just `remove`; alternatively, we could call it `next-game-state`. The latter seems more descriptive.

Write the procedure `next-game-state`, which takes two parameters, a game state and a move instruction, and returns a game state. You will need to change `computer-move` and `human-move` so that they correctly call `next-game-state` instead of `remove-coins-from-pile`. Run your program to make sure everything works as before.

Type Checking

Both game states and move instructions are compound data types with exactly two components and integers as the values of these components. Let's suppose that we've decided to implement both of these types by using Scheme's pairs. In this case, the value of the expression (`cons 2 1`) could represent either a game state or a move instruction. This can create some havoc in our programs if we're not careful. For example, suppose you wanted to find the next game state after taking one coin from pile one, starting in a state with five and eight coins in the two piles. At first glance, the following looks reasonable:

```
(display-game-state
  (next-game-state (make-move-instruction 1 1)
                   (make-game-state 5 8)))
```

However, if you try this, you'll get output like the following:

```
Pile 1: 1
Pile 2: -4
```

What went wrong? We got the order of the parameters to `next-game-state` backward. Although the principle of data abstraction tells *us* to think of things

Continued

▶ **Type Checking (Continued)**

as move instructions or game states, rather than as pairs of integers, the Scheme system regrettably thinks of both as just pairs of integers. Therefore, although we can see that we got the move instruction and game state backward, the program got exactly what it expected: two pairs of integers. This kind of error is particularly hard to catch. One way to find such errors is by doing a process called *type checking*. The basic idea is that every piece of data has a particular type, such as integer, game state, move instruction, etc. The type of a procedure is described by saying that it is a procedure that takes certain types of arguments and returns a certain type of result. For example, `make-move-instruction` is a procedure that takes two integers and returns a move instruction, wheras `next-game-state` takes a game state and a move instruction and returns a game state. We can check that a procedure application is probably correct by checking that the types of the arguments are consistent with those expected by the procedure. For example, we know that (`make-move-instruction 1 1`) has probably been called correctly, because its two arguments are integers. Notice that its return value will be a move instruction. On the other hand, the call

```
(next-game-state (make-move-instruction 1 1)
                 (make-game-state 5 8))
```

is definitely incorrect because `next-game-state` gets a move instruction and a game state for arguments when it is supposed to get a game state and a move instruction. Note that type checking only catches errors that are caused by using arguments that are the wrong types. It won't catch the error in (`make-move-instruction 5 6`), where the pile number is too big, unless we use a more refined notion of type, where we can say that the second argument is "an integer in the range from 1 to 2" rather than just that it is an integer.

If we then view strategies as procedures that, when given a particular game state, return the instruction for the next move, we could write the simple strategy currently used by the computer as follows:

```
(define simple-strategy
  (lambda (game-state)
    (if (> (size-of-pile game-state 1) 0)
        (make-move-instruction 1 1)
        (make-move-instruction 1 2))))
```

But how do we need to change our program in order to incorporate various strategies into it? Certainly the procedure `computer-move` must be changed: In addition to the game state, it must be passed the strategy to be employed. But this means `play-with-turns` must also be changed, because it calls `computer-move`: It must have an additional argument that indicates the computer's strategy. If you do this correctly, an initial call of the form

```
(play-with-turns (make-game-state 5 8) 'human simple-strategy)
```

should play the game as before.

▶ Exercise 6.14

In this exercise, you will change the procedures `computer-move` and `play-with-turns` as indicated previously. After making these changes, test the program by making the previous initial call.

a. Modify the procedure `computer-move` so that it takes an additional parameter called `strategy` and uses it appropriately to make the computer's move. Remember that when the strategy is applied to a game state, a move instruction is returned. This can then be passed on to `next-game-state`.

b. Modify `play-with-turns` so that it also has a new parameter (the computer's strategy), modifying in particular the call to `computer-move` so that the strategy is employed. Note that you must make additional changes to `play-with-turns` in order that the strategy gets "passed along" to the next iteration.

Now we can add a variety of different strategies to our program. This amounts to writing the various strategies and then calling `play-with-turns` with the strategies we want. We ask you in the next few exercises to program various strategies.

▶ Exercise 6.15

Write a procedure `take-all-of-first-nonempty` that will return the instruction for taking all the coins from the first nonempty pile.

▶ Exercise 6.16

Write a procedure `take-one-from-random-pile` that implements the following "random" strategy: randomly select a nonempty pile and then remove one coin from it. Randomness can be simulated using the `random` procedure, which should be pre-defined in any Scheme used with this book (although it isn't specified by the R⁴RS standard for Scheme). If *n* is a positive integer, a call of the form (random n) will return a random integer between 0 and $n-1$, inclusive. (Actually, it returns a so-called *pseudo-random integer*; pseudo-random integers are produced systematically and hence are not random, but sequences of consecutive pseudo-random integers have many of the same statistical properties that sequences of random integers do.)

Exercise 6.17

Take the previous exercise one step further by writing a procedure that, when given a particular game state, will return a move instruction where both components are chosen at random. Remember to ensure that the move instruction returned is a valid one. In particular, it should not suggest a move that takes coins from an empty pile.

Exercise 6.18

If we consider the chocolate bar version of Nim, we can describe a strategy that allows you to win whenever possible. Remember that in this version, the players alternate breaking off pieces of the bar along a horizontal or a vertical line, and the person who gets the last square of chocolate loses (so the person who makes the last possible break wins, just as the person who takes the last coin wins). If it's your turn and the chocolate bar is not square, you can always break off a piece that makes the bar into a square. If you do so, your opponent must make it into a nonsquare. If you always hand your opponent a square, he will get smaller and smaller squares, leading eventually to the minimal square (i.e., the poisoned square). Write a procedure which implements this strategy in two-pile Nim. What action should it take if presented with (the equivalent of) a square chocolate bar?

Exercise 6.19

Suppose you want to randomly intermingle two different strategies. How can this be done? The answer is with higher-order programming. Write a procedure random-mix-of that takes two strategies as arguments and returns the strategy that randomly chooses between these two procedures each turn. Thus, a call of the form

```
(play-with-turns (make-game-state 5 8)
                 'human
                 (random-mix-of simple-strategy
                                take-all-of-first-nonempty))
```

would randomly choose at each turn between taking one coin or all the coins from the first nonempty pile.

> **Exercise 6.20**

Those of us with a perverse sense of humor enjoy the idea of the computer playing games with itself. How would you modify `play-with-turns` so that instead of having the computer play against a human, it plays against itself, using any combination of strategies?

> **Exercise 6.21**

By adding an "ask the human" strategy, the introverted version of `play-with-turns` from the preceding exercise can be made to be sociable again. In fact, it can even be turned into a gamekeeper for two human players. Demonstrate these possibilities.

Review Problems

▷ **Exercise 6.22**

Suppose we decide to implement an ADT called *Interval* that has one constructor `make-interval` and two selectors `upper-endpoint` and `lower-endpoint`. For example,

```
(define my-interval (make-interval 3 7))
(upper-endpoint my-interval)
7
```

defines `my-interval` to be the interval $[3, 7]$ and then returns the upper endpoint of `my-interval`.

Note that we are saying nothing about how *Interval* is implemented. Your work below should only use the constructor and selectors.

a. Write a procedure `mid-point` that gets an interval as an argument and returns the midpoint of that interval. For example, supposing that `my-interval` is as just defined:

```
(mid-point my-interval)
5
```

b. Write a procedure `right-half` that gets an interval as an argument and returns the right half of that interval. Again supposing that `my-interval` is as just defined:

```
(right-half my-interval)
```

returns the interval $[5, 7]$.

▷ **Exercise 6.23**

A three-dimensional (3D) vector has x, y, and z coordinates, which are numbers. 3D vectors can be constructed and accessed using the following abstract interface:

```
(make-3D-vector x y z)
(x-coord vector)
(y-coord vector)
(z-coord vector)
```

  a. Using this abstract interface, define procedures for adding two vectors, finding the dot-product of two vectors, and scaling a vector by a numerical scaling factor. (The sum of two vectors is computed by adding each coordinate independently. The dot-product of the vectors (x_1, y_1, z_1) and (x_2, y_2, z_2) is $x_1 x_2 + y_1 y_2 + z_1 z_2$. To scale a vector, you multiply each coordinate by the scaling factor.)
  b. Choose a representation for vectors and implement `make-3D-vector`, `x-coord`, `y-coord`, and `z-coord`.

▷ **Exercise 6.24**

Suppose we wished to keep track of which classrooms are being used at which hours for which classes. We would want to have a compound data structure consisting of three parts:

- A classroom designation (e.g. OH321)
- A course designation (e.g. MC27)
- A time (e.g. 1230)

Assume that rooms and courses are to be represented by symbols and the times are to be represented as numbers. The interface is to look like this:

```
(make-schedule-item 'OH321 'MC27 1230)
```

```
(room (make-schedule-item 'OH321 'MC27 1230))
OH321
```

```
(course (make-schedule-item 'OH321 'MC27 1230))
MC27
```

```
(time (make-schedule-item 'OH321 'MC27 1230))
1230
```

Use a procedural representation to write a constructor and three selectors for this schedule-item data type.

▷ **Exercise 6.25**

We previously said that each move in Nim "transforms the game into a smaller game, if we measure the size of the game in terms of the total number of coins." This raises the possibility that we could define a predicate `game-state-<` that would compare two game states and determine whether the first is smaller (in the sense of having a smaller total number of coins). Similarly, we could define `game-state->`, `game-state-=`, `game-state-<=`, etc. Define a general purpose procedure called `make-game-state-comparator` for making procedures like those just described, given the numerical comparison procedure (e.g., `<`) to use. Here are some examples of its use, together with examples using the comparators it makes:

```
(define game-state-< (make-game-state-comparator <))
```

```
(game-state-< (make-game-state 3 7) (make-game-state 1 12))
#t
```

```
(define game-state-> (make-game-state-comparator >))
```

```
(game-state-> (make-game-state 3 7) (make-game-state 1 12))
#f
```

```
(game-state-> (make-game-state 13 7) (make-game-state 1 12))
#t
```

▷ **Exercise 6.26**

Recall that when you worked with fractals in Section 4.3, many of the procedures required parameters that represented the x and y coordinates of points in an image; for example, the built-in procedure `line` required coordinates for the starting point and the ending point, and the procedure `triangle` required coordinates for the triangle's three vertices.

a. Use `cons`-pairs to implement a *point* ADT. You should write a constructor `make-point`, that takes two arguments representing the x and y coordinates and returns the corresponding point and two selectors `x-coord` and `y-coord` that take a point and return the corresponding coordinate.

b. Write a procedure `distance` that takes two points and returns the distance between them. Use the selectors `x-coord` and `y-coord` rather than relying on the specific representation from part a. For example, you should see the following interaction:

```
(define pt-1 (make-point -1 -1))

(define pt-2 (make-point -1 1))

(distance pt-1 pt-2)
2
```

Remember: The distance between the points with coordinates (x_1, y_1) and (x_2, y_2) is $\sqrt{(x_2 - x_1)^2 + (y_2 - y_1)^2}$.

Chapter Inventory

Vocabulary

atomic data
compound data
constructor
selector
representation
data abstraction

abstract data type (ADT)
porting
procedural representation
pseudo-random integer
type checking

Slogans

The data abstraction principle
   (or, the operational stance)
The strong data-abstraction principle

Abstract Data Types

game states
move instructions
pairs
intervals

3D vectors
schedule items
points

New Predefined Scheme Names

The dagger symbol (†) indicates a name that is not part of the R⁴RS standard for
Scheme.

equal?	cons
error†	car
display	cdr
newline	random†
read	

New Scheme Syntax

symbols
quote mark
character strings

Scheme Names Defined in This Chapter

size-of-pile	upper-endpoint
remove-coins-from-pile	lower-endpoint
make-game-state	mid-point
play-with-turns	right-half
computer-move	make-3D-vector
human-move	x-coord
over?	y-coord
announce-winner	z-coord
display-game-state	make-schedule-item
prompt	room
total-size	course
exponent-of-in	time
make-move-instruction	game-state-<
next-game-state	game-state->
simple-strategy	game-state-=
take-all-of-first-nonempty	game-state-<=
take-one-from-random-pile	make-game-state-comparator
random-mix-of	make-point
make-interval	distance

Sidebars

Nim Program
Game State ADT Implementation
Type Checking

Notes

Bouton's seminal article on Nim is [8]. The chocolate-bar version of the game was presented as a puzzle by Dr. Ian Stewart on the Canadian Broadcasting Company's program "Quirks and Quarks" [10].

The history of the names `car` and `cdr` is told by Steve Russell (one of the originators of those names) in [45].

The idea of augmenting a game with strategy procedures and higher-order strategies comes from a lunar lander programming assignment developed by Abelson, Sussman, and friends at MIT [1].

CHAPTER SEVEN

Lists

7.1   The Definition of a List

In Chapter 6, we learned how to construct abstract data types where any element of the type had the same number of components as any other. Sometimes, however, the individual data will have varying sizes. One example is lists. In this chapter, we first give a formal definition of lists. Then we show how this definition is used to construct lists, and we explore common list-processing idioms.

Exactly what is a list? We could start thinking of some concrete examples of lists by having everyone in our class make a list of the classes he or she attended yesterday. Some people may have relatively long lists, and others may have been to just one or two classes. Some people may have not have attended any classes at all. (If today is Monday, perhaps everyone is in this situation.) Lists can be written in a variety of ways as well. Some people might write lists in a column, others might use rows, and still others may come up with more creative ways of doing it. No matter how the lists are written, those lists that have at least one element have some inherent order (i.e., each list can be written to start with the first class of the day and work its way forward from there). Thus we could define a list as being a collection of 0 or more elements, written in some particular order.

Now imagine that we need to write a computer program to deal with lists of some sort of elements, say, integers for simplicity. Our first job is to decide what procedures we need to define the abstract data type of integer lists. The definition we gave in the foregoing is not much of a guide. Clearly, we are going to be implementing compound data, because some of our lists may have quite a few components. But how many components are we going to need? With the abstract data types that we considered in Chapter 6, each individual piece of data had exactly the same number of components as any other piece. Different lists, on the other hand, could have wildly different sizes. So what do we do?

Let's think about this question a little more. In Chapter 6 we learned how to construct abstract data types where all values belonging to a particular type had the same number of components as each other. Now we want to have values of varying sizes belong to a single type. This parallels what happened moving from Chapter 1 to Chapter 2. In Chapter 1 we wrote procedures where all processes generated by a particular procedure were of the same size as each other. In Chapter 2 we asked how to have a single procedure generate processes of varying size. There the answer was recursion.

We also learned in Chapter 6 that the best way to define an abstract data type is to first concentrate on how the type is used. We can illustrate how lists are used by looking at the example of grocery lists. One of the authors usually constructs grocery lists so that the items are ordered by their positions in the grocery store. The list is then used by finding the first thing on it, putting that item into the cart, and crossing it off the list. This gives us a new grocery list (with one less item) that is used to continue the grocery shopping. Eventually, there is only one item left on the list (the chocolate candy bar located just before the checkout counter). After putting this item into the cart and crossing it off the list, the grocery list is empty. This means that it is time to check out and pay for the groceries.

This grocery list example has a strong recursive flavor to it, and so we can use it as a model for a recursive definition of lists. We will need a "base case" that defines the smallest possible list, and we will need some way of defining larger lists in terms of smaller lists. The base case is easy—there is a special list, called the *empty list*, which has no elements in it. The general case is hinted at in the grocery list example above: a nonempty list has two parts, one of which is an element (the first item in the list), and the other is a list, namely, the list of all the other items in the whole list. We can put this more succinctly:

The two-part list viewpoint: A list is either empty or it consists of two parts: the first item in the list and the list of its remaining items.

The first element of a nonempty list is often called the *head* of the list, whereas the list of remaining elements is called the *tail*. The two-part list viewpoint is one of the things that distinguish a computer scientist from a normal person. Normal people think lists can have any number of components (the items on the list), whereas computer scientists think that all nonempty lists have two components (the head and the tail). The tail isn't one item that's on the list; it's a whole list of items itself.

How can we implement lists in Scheme? Given that most lists have two parts, it would be natural to use pairs: Let the car of the pair be the first element of the list, and let the cdr of the pair be the tail. However, because a list may be empty and would therefore not have two parts, we need to account for empty lists as well. Scheme does so by having a special type of value called the empty list, which we explain in the next section, and a predicate `null?` that tests whether a given list is empty. Using `null?` in conjunction with the pair operators `cons`, `car`, and `cdr`, we can implement the list ADT in Scheme by adopting the following conventions:

> (cons *elt lst*) Given an element *elt* and a list *lst*, `cons` returns the list whose head is *elt* and whose tail is *lst*.

> (car *lst*) If *lst* is a nonempty list, `car` returns its head.

> (cdr *lst*) If *lst* is a nonempty list, `cdr` returns its tail.

> (null? *lst*) `Null?` returns true if and only if *lst* is the empty list.

Of course, a better data-abstraction practice would be to define a separate set of procedures, perhaps called `make-list`, `head`, `tail`, and `empty-list?`, that would keep the separation between the list abstraction and the particular representation using pairs. However, because this particular representation of lists is such a long-established tradition, Scheme programmers normally just use the pair operations as though they were also list operations. For example, the `car` and `cdr` selectors of the pair data type are traditionally used as though they were also the head and tail selectors of the list data type. You can always define `head` and `tail` and use them in your programming, if you'd rather, but you'll be in a small minority.

Note that these procedures do what is described above only when all parameters that need to be lists have themselves been constructed using these conventions. Furthermore, one common mistake to avoid is applying `car` or `cdr` to the empty list.

A number of the procedures we will write are actually built into Scheme. We're going to write them anyway because they provide excellent examples of list processing techniques. Furthermore, by writing them, you should gain a better understanding of what the built-in procedures do.

7.2   Constructing Lists

How do we make lists in Scheme? Fundamentally, all nonempty lists are made by using the pair-constructor `cons`. However, rather than using `cons` directly, we can also use some other procedure that itself uses `cons`. For example, Scheme has a built-in procedure, `list`, that you can use to build a list if you know exactly what elements you want to be in your list. You pass the list elements into `list` as its arguments:

```
(list 1 2 3)
```
(1 2 3)

Note that we let Scheme display the resulting list value by itself and that the displayed value consisted of the elements of the list in order, separated by spaces and surrounded by a pair of parentheses. The fact that we allowed Scheme to display the list is one exception to the general rule stated in the preceding chapter, where we said that the way Scheme displays pairs is confusing, and therefore you should write special purpose display procedures, such as `display-game-state`. In the case where pairs are used to represent lists, the way Scheme displays them is simple and natural, so there is no need to write something like `display-list` ourselves.

Another thing to note is that the stuff that gets printed out when a list is displayed is not an expression that will evaluate to the list. Just as you can't make a game state by evaluating the output from `display-game-state`, namely, something like "Pile 1: 5 Pile 2: 8," so too you can't make a list by evaluating (1 2 3). If you were to evaluate that, it would try to apply 1 as a procedure to 2 and 3, which fails because 1 isn't a procedure. This particular list was displayed in a way that looked like an erroneous Scheme expression. Other lists are displayed in ways that look like valid Scheme expressions; for example, if the first element of the list were the symbol + rather than the number 1, the list would display as (+ 2 3). Even evaluating this expression won't produce the list (+ 2 3). (From this past sentence onward, we will take a shortcut and say things like "the list (+ 2 3)" when what we really mean is "the list that, when displayed, looks like (+ 2 3).")

▶ Exercise 7.1

You also can't get the list (+ 2 3) by evaluating (`list` + 2 3).

a. What *do* you get if you evaluate that expression? Explain why.
b. What expression can you evaluate that will produce the list (+ 2 3), which starts with the symbol +?

We've seen that when you want the list (+ 2 3), you can't just type in (+ 2 3). For example, you couldn't find the cdr of this list by evaluating (`cdr` (+ 2 3)), because that would try to find the cdr of 5. One option would be to get some procedure to build the list you want for you, instead of typing it in. For example, you could use `list`. There is one other option, however, that lets you type in a list as itself. You can use the same quoting mechanism that you use to type in symbols. For example,

```
(cdr '(1 2 3))
(2 3)
```

Lists and symbols both need quoting for the same reason: They look like expressions, but we want the name itself or the list itself, not the result of evaluating the name or list. Quote also gives us a way to get the empty list, namely, as the value of the expression '().

What if we want to construct a list that is too long to type? For example, suppose we needed the list of integers from 1 to 2000. Rather than tediously typing in the whole list, or typing in all 2000 arguments to the `list` procedure, we should automate the process by writing a procedure to do it for us. As in the factorial example in the second chapter, it makes sense to write a general purpose procedure that produces the list of integers from *low* to *high* and then use it on 1 and 2000. To see how to write such a procedure, let's first construct some fairly short lists, using `cons`. We'll also draw a box and pointer diagram of each of these lists, using the technique from Section 6.4, to illustrate the structure of lists:

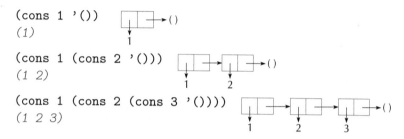

```
(cons 1 '())
(1)

(cons 1 (cons 2 '()))
(1 2)

(cons 1 (cons 2 (cons 3 '())))
(1 2 3)
```

Note that to get the list of integers from 1 to 3, we consed 1 to the list of integers from 2 to 3, which shows us how to write the general procedure:

```
(define integers-from-to
  (lambda (low high)
    (if (> low high)
        '()
        (cons low
              (integers-from-to (+ 1 low) high)))))
```

Such lists can then be created by making calls like the following one:

```
(integers-from-to 1 7)
(1 2 3 4 5 6 7)
```

This technique of using `cons` to recursively construct a list is often called *consing up a list.*

▶ **Exercise 7.2**

What do you get if you evaluate (`integers-from-to 7 1`)? Exactly which integers will be included in the list that is the value of (`integers-from-to` *low high*)? More precisely, describe exactly when a given integer k will be included in the list that is the value of (`integers-from-to` *low high*). (You can do so by describing how *k*, *low*, and *high* are related to each other.) Do you think the result of `integers-from-to` needs to be more carefully specified (for example, in a comment) than the implicit specification via the procedure's name? Or do you think the behavior of the procedure should be changed? Discuss.

> **Exercise 7.3**

Write a procedure that will generate the list of even integers from *a* to *b*.

> **Exercise 7.4**

We could rewrite `integers-from-to` so that it generates an iterative process. Consider the following attempt at this:

```
(define integers-from-to  ; faulty version
  (lambda (low high)
    (define iter
      (lambda (low lst)
        (if (> low high)
            lst
            (iter (+ 1 low)
                  (cons low lst)))))
    (iter low '())))
```

What happens when we evaluate (`integers-from-to` 2 7)? Why? Rewrite this procedure so that it generates the correct list.

7.3 Basic List Processing Techniques

Suppose we need to write a procedure that counts the number of elements in a list. We can use the recursive definition of lists to help us define exactly what we mean by the number of elements in a list. Recall that a list is either empty or it has two parts, a first element and the list of its remaining elements. When a list is empty, the number of elements in it is zero. When it isn't empty, the number of elements is one more than the number of elements in its tail. We can write this in Scheme as

```
(define length
  (lambda (lst)
    (if (null? lst)
        0
        (+ 1 (length (cdr lst))))))
```

Similarly, to write a procedure that finds the sum of a list of integers, we would do the following:

```
(define sum
  (lambda (lst)
    (if (null? lst)
        0
        (+ (car lst) (sum (cdr lst))))))
```

Notice how similar these procedures are to recursive procedures with integer parameters, such as `factorial`. The base case in `length` and `sum` occurs when the list is empty, just as the base case in `factorial` is when the integer is 0. In `factorial` we reduced our integer by subtracting 1, and in `length` and `sum`, we reduce our list by taking its cdr. Procedures that traverse a list by working on the cdr in this manner are said to *cdr down a list*.

Exercise 7.5

Generalize `sum` to a higher-order procedure that can accumulate together the elements of a list in an arbitrary fashion by using a combining procedure (such as `+`) specified by a procedural parameter. When the list is empty, `sum` returned 0, but this result isn't appropriate for other combining procedures. For example, if the combining procedure is `*`, 1 would be the appropriate value for an empty list. (Why?) Following are two possible approaches to this problem:

a. Write the higher-order procedure so that it only works for nonempty lists. That way, the base case can be for one-element lists, in which case the one element can be returned.

b. Write the higher-order procedure so that it takes an additional argument, beyond the list and the combining procedure, that specifies the value to return for an empty list.

Exercise 7.6

a. Write a procedure that will count the number of times a particular element occurs in a given list.

b. Generalize this procedure to one that will count the number of elements in a given list that satisfy a given predicate.

Exercise 7.7

In addition to the procedure `length`, Scheme has a built-in procedure `list-ref` that returns a specified element of a list. More precisely, a call of the form (`list-ref lst n`) will return the $(n + 1)$st element of *lst*, because by convention $n = 0$ returns the first element, $n = 1$ returns the second, etc. Try this procedure for various parameter values. Write this procedure yourself.

Exercise 7.8

Here are some more exercises in cdring down a list:

a. Write a predicate that will determine whether or not a particular element is in a list.

b. Generalize this to a predicate that will determine whether any element of a list satisfies a given predicate.

c. Write a procedure that will find and return the first element of a list that satisfies a given predicate.

d. Write a procedure that will determine whether all elements of a list satisfy a given predicate.

e. Write a procedure that will find the position of a particular element in a list. For example,

```
(position 50 '(10 20 30 40 50 3 2 1))
4
```

Notice that we are using the same convention for position as is used in `list-ref`, namely, the first position is 0, etc. What should be returned if the element is not in the list? What should be returned if the element appears more than once in the list?

f. Write a procedure that will find the largest element in a nonempty list.

g. Write a procedure that will find the position of the largest element in a nonempty list. Specify how you are breaking ties.

Exercise 7.9

This exercise involves cdring down two lists.

a. Write a procedure that gets two lists of integers of the same size and returns true when each element in the first list is less than the corresponding element in the second list. For example,

```
(list-< '(1 2 3 4) '(2 3 4 5))
#t
```

What should happen if the lists are not the same size?

b. Generalize this procedure to one called `lists-compare?`. This procedure should get three arguments; the first is a predicate that takes two arguments (such as `<`) and the other two are lists. It returns true if and only if the predicate always returns true on corresponding elements of the lists. We could redefine `list-<` in the following manner:

```
(define list-<
  (lambda (l1 l2)
    (lists-compare? < l1 l2)))
```

We frequently will use lists to build other lists, in which case we cdr down one list while consing up the other. To illustrate what we mean, here is a simple procedure that selects those elements of a given list that satisfy a given predicate:

```
(define filter
  (lambda (ok? lst)
    (cond ((null? lst)
           '())
          ((ok? (car lst))
           (cons (car lst) (filter ok? (cdr lst))))
          (else
           (filter ok? (cdr lst))))))
(filter odd? (integers-from-to 1 15))
(1 3 5 7 9 11 13 15)
```

At this point, we've seen enough isolated examples of list processing procedures. Let's embark on a larger-scale project that will naturally involve list-processing. Consider the following remarkable fact: After doing a certain small number of "perfect shuffles" on a 52 card deck, the deck always returns to its original order. (By a perfect shuffle, we mean that the deck is divided into two equal parts, which are then combined in a strictly alternating fashion starting with the first card in the first half.) How many perfect shuffles are required to return a 52 card deck to its original order?

We can represent our original deck as a list of the numbers 1 to 52 using the procedure `integers-from-to`. How do we divide the deck into two equal halves? We can write two general purpose procedures, one to get the first however many elements of a list and the other to get the remaining elements.

Let's first write the procedure that will construct a list of the first *n* elements of a given list. This procedure is very similar to the procedure `list-ref` in Exercise 7.7:

```
(define first-elements-of
  (lambda (n list)
    (if (= n 0)
        '()
        (cons (car list)
              (first-elements-of (- n 1)
                                 (cdr list))))))
```

Exercise 7.10

Write the procedure `list-tail`, that gets a list and an integer *n* and returns the list of all but the first *n* elements in the original list. (`List-tail` is actually already built into Scheme.)

For any given value of *n* in the range $0 \leq n \leq$ (`length lst`), the procedures `first-elements-of` and `list-tail` can be used to split `lst` into two parts.

Once we've cut our deck into two halves, we still need to combine those halves into the shuffled deck. We combine them by using the procedure `interleave`, which takes two lists and combines them into a single list in an alternating manner:

```
(define interleave     ; interleaves lst1 and lst2, starting with
  (lambda (lst1 lst2) ; the first element of lst1 (if any)
    (if (null? lst1)
        lst2
        (cons (car lst1)
              (interleave lst2 (cdr lst1))))))
```

To see why `interleave` works correctly, focus on the comment, which says that the first element in the result is going to be the first element from `lst1` (i.e., the first element of the first argument). What does the rest of the result look like, after that first element? If you interleave a stack of red cards with a stack of black cards, so that the top card is red, what does the rest of it look like? Well, the rest (under that top red card) will start with a black card and then will alternate colors. It will include all of the black cards and all the rest of the red cards. In other words, it is the result of interleaving the black cards with the rest of the red cards. This explains why in the recursive call to `interleave`, we pass in `lst2` as the first argument (so that the first element from `lst2` winds up right after the first element of `lst1` in the result) and then the cdr of `lst1`.

Combining `interleave`, `list-tail`, and `first-elements-of`, we can now define the procedure `shuffle`, which takes as arguments the deck as well as its size:

```
(define shuffle
  (lambda (deck size)
    (let ((half (quotient (+ size 1) 2)))
      (interleave (first-elements-of half deck)
                  (list-tail deck half)))))
```

The purpose of the parameter `size` is efficiency—otherwise we would need to use the procedure `length`. We write (quotient (+ size 1) 2) instead of the more natural (quotient size 2) in order to ensure that when *size* is odd, the first half of the deck has the extra card. Notice that when *size* = 52, (quotient (+ size 1) 2) = 26.

In order to find out how many shuffles are needed, we write the following procedure, which automates multiple shuffles:

```
(define multiple-shuffle
  (lambda (deck size times)
    (if (= times 0)
        deck
        (multiple-shuffle (shuffle deck size)
                          size (- times 1)))))
```

We can then find out how many shuffles are needed by making calls as follows:

```
(multiple-shuffle (integers-from-to 1 52) 52 1)
```
(1 27 2 28 3 29 4 30 5 31 6 32 7 33 8 34 9 35 10 36 11 37 12 38 13 39 14 40 15 41 16 42 17 43 18 44 19 45 20 46 21 47 22 48 23 49 24 50 25 51 26 52)

```
(multiple-shuffle (integers-from-to 1 52) 52 2)
```
(1 14 27 40 2 15 28 41 3 16 29 42 4 17 30 43 5 18 31 44 6 19 32 45 7 20 33 46 8 21 34 47 9 22 35 48 10 23 36 49 11 24 37 50 12 25 38 51 13 26 39 52)

$$\vdots$$

```
(multiple-shuffle (integers-from-to 1 52) 52 8)
```
(1 2 3 4 5 6 7 8 9 10 11 12 13 14 15 16 17 18 19 20 21 22 23 24 25 26 27 28 29 30 31 32 33 34 35 36 37 38 39 40 41 42 43 44 45 46 47 48 49 50 51 52)

Thus, eight perfect shuffles return the deck to its original order.

> ### Exercise 7.11

We have written `shuffle` so that it can operate on decks of any size. In fact, decks of all sizes have the property that after a certain number of perfect shuffles, the deck is returned to its original order. In this exercise you will write procedures that will automate the process of finding the number of shuffles, which we call the *shuffle-number*, required for a deck of a given size.

a. Given that you start with an ordered deck, the first thing you will need is a predicate, called `in-order?`, that determines whether a list of integers is in increasing order. Write this procedure.

b. Using `in-order?`, write a procedure `shuffle-number` that, when passed a positive integer n, returns the shuffle-number for n. You should start off with an ordered deck of size n and repeatedly shuffle until the deck is in order.

> ### Exercise 7.12

Throughout this section on perfect shuffles, we've been passing in the size of the deck as well as the list representing the deck itself in order to avoid computing the length of the list when we already knew it. Another approach would be to create a new compound data type for decks, with two selectors: one to get the list of elements and the other to get the length. That way we could pass in just a single thing, the deck, but could still find the length without counting. Flesh out the remaining details of this idea, implement it, and try it out.

We end this section with another example of using higher-order programming with lists. Suppose you wanted to find the shuffle-number for decks of size 1, 2, 3, . . . , 100 so that you could look at them all and see if there seemed to be any pattern. Rather than manually applying your `shuffle-number` procedure to each of the integers from 1 to 100, you could get a list of those integers, using `integers-from-to`, and then use some general purpose higher-order procedure to *map* each element of that list into its `shuffle-number`. A procedure called `map` that is built into Scheme does this mapping. Its first argument is the procedure to use for the mapping, and its second argument is the list of values that should be mapped. So in order to get the shuffle numbers for decks ranging in size from 1 to 100, we could do the following:

```
(map shuffle-number (integers-from-to 1 100))
```

Or, we could find the squares of 5, 12, and 13 by evaluating

```
(map (lambda (x) (* x x)) '(5 12 13))
(25 144 169)
```

▶ **Exercise 7.13**

The procedure **map** is extraordinarily handy for creating lists of all sorts. Each of the following problems can be solved by using **map**.

a. Write a procedure that, when given a positive integer *n*, returns a list of the first *n* perfect squares.

b. Write a procedure that, when given a positive integer *n*, returns a list of the first *n* even integers.

c. Write a procedure called **sevens** that, when given a positive integer *n*, returns a list of *n* sevens. For example:

```
(sevens 5)
(7 7 7 7 7)
```

d. Write a procedure that, when given a list of positive integers, returns a list of lists of integers. Each of these lists should be the positive integers from 1 to whatever was in the original list. For example,

```
(list-of-lists '(1 5 3))
((1) (1 2 3 4 5) (1 2 3))
```

▶ **Exercise 7.14**

Even though **map** is built into Scheme, it is a good exercise to write it yourself. Do so.

7.4   List Processing and Iteration

A palindrome is a word, such as *madam*, that stays unchanged when you write the letters in reverse order. Sometimes, entire sentences are palindromes, if you ignore spaces and punctuation; one of the classic examples is "Madam, I'm Adam." In this section, we'll test lists of symbols to see whether they are palindromes when viewed symbol by symbol rather than letter by letter. What we mean by this is that reversing the order of the elements of the list leaves it unchanged. For example, the list (m a d a m) is a palindrome and so is (record my record).

We can determine whether or not a list of symbols is a palindrome by reversing it and seeing if the result is equal to the original list. We can do the equality testing using **equal?** but need to figure out how to reverse the list. Actually, as so often, there is a procedure built into Scheme called **reverse** that does just what we need. But in the best of no-pain/no-gain tradition, we'll write it ourselves.

Reversing an empty list is quite easy. To reverse a nonempty list, one approach is to first reverse the cdr of the list and then to stick the car onto the end of this reversed cdr. The major obstacle is that we don't have any procedure currently in our toolbox for tacking an element onto the end of a list. What we want is a procedure **add-to-end** such that (add-to-end '(1 2 3) 4) would evaluate to the list (1 2 3 4). We can write this procedure in our usual recursive way, cdring down the list and consing up the result:

```
(define add-to-end
  (lambda (lst elt)
    (if (null? lst)      ; adding to an empty list
        (cons elt '()) ;  makes a one-element list
        (cons (car lst)
              (add-to-end (cdr lst)
                          elt)))))
```

Given this, we can write **reverse** as follows:

```
(define reverse
  (lambda (lst)
    (if (null? lst)
        '()
        (add-to-end (reverse (cdr lst))
                    (car lst)))))
```

This way of reversing a list is very time consuming because of the call to **add-to-end**. A good way to measure how much time it takes is to count up the number of times **cons** is called. Adding to the end of a k-element list will make $k + 1$ calls to **cons**. Suppose we use $R(n)$ to denote the number of **cons**es that **reverse** does (indirectly, by way of **add-to-end**) when reversing a list of size n. Then we know that $R(0) = 0$ because **reverse** simply returns the empty list when its argument is empty. When the argument to **reverse** is a nonempty list, the number of calls to **cons** will be however many are done by reversing the cdr of the list plus however many are done by adding to the end of this reversed cdr. Thus,

$$R(n) = R(n - 1) + ((n - 1) + 1) = R(n - 1) + n$$

But by the same argument

$$R(n - 1) = R(n - 2) + ((n - 2) + 1) = R(n - 2) + (n - 1)$$

so we get

$$R(n) = R(n - 1) + n$$
$$= R(n - 2) + (n - 1) + n$$
$$\vdots$$
$$= R(0) + 1 + 2 + 3 + \cdots + (n - 2) + (n - 1) + n$$
$$= 0 + 1 + 2 + 3 + \cdots + (n - 2) + (n - 1) + n$$
$$= \frac{n(n + 1)}{2}$$

Therefore the number of **cons**es done by this version of **reverse** is $\Theta(n^2)$. (The last equation, expressing the sum as $n(n + 1)/2$, is from the solution to Exercise 4.1 on page 81. Even without it you could figure out that the sum was $\Theta(n^2)$ using the reasoning given in Section 4.1.) We can expect the time taken to similarly be $\Theta(n^2)$, which implies that as lists get longer, reversing them will slow down more than proportionately quickly. A 200-element list is likely to take 4 times as long to reverse as a 100-element list, rather than only twice as long.

There must be a better way of reversing a list. In fact, if you remember Exercise 7.4, our initial attempt to write an iterative procedure that generates the list of integers from a to b produced a list with the right numbers but in reverse order. Although that was a mistake there, it suggests an iterative strategy for reversing a list.

Before trying to write an iterative **reverse**, a concrete example might be helpful. Put a stack of cards on the table face up in front of you and reverse the order of them, leaving them face up. Chances are you did it by taking the first card off of top of the stack and setting it down elsewhere on the table, then moving the next card from the top of the original stack to the top of the new stack, etc., until all the cards had been moved. If you interrupt this process somewhere in the middle and turn the rest of the job over to someone else, you might tell them to "reverse the rest of these cards onto this other stack."

In terms of our Scheme procedure, we can reduce the problem of reversing (1 2 3 4) to the smaller problem of putting the elements of (2 3 4) in reverse order onto the front of (1), which in turn reduces to putting the elements of (3 4) in reverse order onto the front of (2 1), etc.:

```
(define reverse
  (lambda (lst)
    (define reverse-onto    ; return a list of the elements of lst1
      (lambda (lst1 lst2)   ;   in reverse order followed by the
                            ;   elements of lst2
```

```
        (if (null? lst1)
            lst2
            (reverse-onto (cdr lst1)
                          (cons (car lst1)
                                lst2)))))
    (reverse-onto lst '())))
```

The internally defined procedure **reverse-onto** does one **cons** for each element in the list, as it moves it from the front of *lst1* to the front of *lst2*. Notice that the total number of **cons**es is equal to the total number of **cdr**s; if we use n to denote the size of the list *lst*, the number of **cons**es is n. Thus we have reduced a $\Theta(n^2)$ process to a $\Theta(n)$ one.

Now we have all the procedures that we need to determine whether or not a list is actually a palindrome:

```
(define palindrome?
  (lambda (lst)
    (equal? lst (reverse lst))))
```

```
(palindrome? '(m a d a m i m a d a m))
#t
```

7.5   Tree Recursion and Lists

In this section, we will look at two examples of using tree recursion with lists. The first example is a merge sort procedure roughly paralleling what you did by hand in Chapter 4. The basic approach to merge sorting a list is to separate the list into two smaller lists, merge sort each of them, and then merge the two sorted lists together. We can only separate a list into two shorter lists if it has at least two elements, but luckily all empty and one-element lists are already sorted. Thus our merge sort procedure would look something like the following:

```
(define merge-sort
  (lambda (lst)
    (cond ((null? lst)
           '())
          ((null? (cdr lst))
           lst)
          (else
           (merge (merge-sort (one-part lst))
                  (merge-sort (the-other-part lst)))))))
```

We still have to do most of the programming, namely, writing `merge` and figuring out some way to break the list into two parts, which for efficiency should be of equal size or at least as close to equal size as possible.

We start with the procedure `merge`. Here we have two lists of numbers, where each list is in order from the smallest to the largest. We want to produce a third list, that consists of all of the elements of both of the original lists and that is still in order. Notice that we have essentially two base cases, which occur when either one of the original lists is empty. In each case, the result that we want to return is the other (possibly nonempty) list. We additionally have three recursive cases, depending on how the first elements of the two lists compare to each other. We always want to cons the smaller number onto the result of merging the cdr of the list this number came from with the other list. What happens if both lists have the same number as their first element? The answer depends on why we're merging the two lists. There are some applications where we want to keep only one of the duplicated number, and some applications where we want to keep both duplicates. Here, we've arbitrarily decided to keep only one of the duplicated element. This will result in a `merge-sort` that eliminates duplicates as it sorts:

```
(define merge
  (lambda (lst1 lst2)
    (cond ((null? lst1) lst2)
          ((null? lst2) lst1)
          ((< (car lst1) (car lst2))
           (cons (car lst1) (merge (cdr lst1) lst2)))
          ((= (car lst1) (car lst2))
           (cons (car lst1) (merge (cdr lst1) (cdr lst2))))
          (else
           (cons (car lst2) (merge  lst1 (cdr lst2)))))))
```

What about breaking the list into two halves? One way of doing so would be to use the procedures `first-elements-of` and `list-tail` as we did in the perfect shuffle problem. The problem with this approach is that we would need to know how long the list is that we're trying to sort. True, we can use `length` to determine this. But instead we'll show off a different way of separating the list into parts, which is roughly the opposite of interleaving. In other words, if we think of our list as a deck of cards, we could separate it into halves by dealing the cards to two people. One person would get the first, third, fifth, ... cards, and the other would get the second, fourth, sixth, ... cards. We'll call the resulting two hands of cards the odd part and the even part.

To write the procedures `odd-part` and `even-part`, think about how you deal a deck of cards to two people, let us say Alice and Bob. You start out facing Alice and are going to give her the odd part and Bob the even part. In other words, you are going to give the odd-numbered cards to the person you are facing. You start by dealing Alice the first card. Now you turn and face Bob, holding the rest of the cards in your hand. At this moment, the situation is exactly as it was at the beginning, except that you are facing Bob and have one fewer card. You are about to give Bob the first, third, etc., of the remaining cards, and Alice the even-numbered ones. So, all in all, Alice's hand of cards (the odd part of the deck) consists of the first card and then the even part of the remaining cards. Meanwhile, Bob's hand of cards (the even part of the deck) consists of the odd part of what's left of the deck after dealing out the first card. The `odd-part` and `even-part` procedures therefore provide an interesting example of *mutual recursion*, because we can most easily define them in terms of each other:

```
(define odd-part
  (lambda (lst)
    (if (null? lst)
        '()
        (cons (car lst) (even-part (cdr lst))))))

(define even-part
  (lambda (lst)
    (if (null? lst)
        '()
        (odd-part (cdr lst)))))
```

Now all we need to do to make `merge-sort` work is

```
(define one-part odd-part)
(define the-other-part even-part)
```

Our second example of using tree recursion comes from a family outing. One day, we took our sons (aged 3 and 4) to the local video arcade to play a game called Whacky Gator. Each child won several tickets that could be exchanged for "prizes" at the main counter. Each kind of prize has a price attached. Some prizes are worth ten tickets, some are worth nine tickets, and so on down to the plastic bugs, which are only worth one ticket. The older child had won ten tickets and wanted to know what prizes he could get. Obviously, he could get only one of the ten ticket prizes. Alternatively, he could get one nine-ticket prize and one one-ticket prize or one eight-ticket prize and two one-ticket prizes or one eight-ticket prize and one two-ticket prize or …. As the child's mother started enumerating the different combinations that he could get, we whipped out our pocket Scheme systems and discovered that there are 1778 possible combinations of prizes that the child had to choose from, given the number of different prizes there were. (See Table 7.1.)

TABLE 7.1   The low-value prizes at our local video arcade

Value in tickets	Number of distinct prizes
10	9
9	3
8	2
7	4
6	3
5	4
4	3
3	3
2	4
1	2

How did we do that? First, we decided to write a general procedure for figuring out how many prize combinations there were. To see how we developed that procedure, let's consider a much smaller problem. Suppose that there are only two kinds of one-ticket prizes, plastic spiders and plastic beetles. Then there are plastic worms that are worth three tickets and little magnifying glasses that are worth five tickets. If the child has five tickets, he can either get a magnifying glass or not. If he doesn't get a magnifying glass, he needs to get some combination of the rest of the prizes that adds up to 5. If he does get the magnifying glass, he's used up all his tickets and there's only one combination of additional prizes worth the remaining 0 tickets, (i.e., the empty combination).

This approach gives us a way of reducing our problem to smaller problems. Suppose the prizes are represented by a list of their values. In our small example above, we would use the list (5 3 1 1) to represent the magnifying glasses, the worms, the beetles, and the spiders. In this case, if a child has a certain amount of tickets, she can get a combination of prizes that includes the first item in the list or one that doesn't include the first item. If she chooses the first item, we need to count the number of combinations that she can get for the amount of tickets minus the value of the first item. If she doesn't choose the first item, we need to count how many combinations of items she can get for the amount of tickets using only the rest of the list. Thus, our recursive call would look like

```
(define count-combos
  (lambda (prize-list amount)
    .
    .
    .

    (+ (count-combos prize-list (- amount (car prize-list)))
       (count-combos (cdr prize-list) amount))))
```

What are the base cases? To figure these out, note that our problem gets smaller in one of two ways: either the prize list gets smaller or the amount of tickets decreases, because all of the prizes have positive prices. Thus the process should halt when the amount is 0, when it is less than 0, or when the prize list is null.

▶ **Exercise 7.15**

What values should be returned in each of these cases? Using your answer, finish writing the procedure `count-combos`.

To check to see if there really were 1778 possible combinations worth 10 tickets, we need to enter a list of 37 numbers. Alternatively, we could write a procedure that will generate that list for us, given the data. What is the best way to give the data? One way would be to give it as a list of pairs, where the first number in each pair is the value and the second number is the number of distinct prizes worth that value. Another way would be to give the data by giving the value of the most expensive prize and then giving the list of numbers of different prizes, with the first number representing the number of different prizes for the most expensive prize, the second number representing the number of distinct prizes worth one ticket less than the most expensive prize, and so on.

▶ **Exercise 7.16**

Which representation is best? Why? Can you think of any other, better way of representing the data? Think about what the corresponding procedures would look like as well as entering the data.

▶ **Exercise 7.17**

Write the procedure that would generate the list needed for `count-combos` given the data in Table 7.1. Check to see that there really are 1778 possible combinations of prizes that are worth 10 tickets.

▶ **Exercise 7.18**

One of our children has learned that he doesn't need to spend all of his tickets because he can save them up for his next trip. Thus, instead of finding the number of combinations that he can get with one particular amount he would like to know the number of combinations that he can get for any amount that is less than or equal to the number of tickets he has. Write a procedure that is given a prize list and a maximum amount and returns the number of combinations of prizes that you can buy using no more than than the maximum amount of tickets.

▶ **Exercise 7.19**

When our children started bringing home dozens of cheap plastic spiders, we asked them to restrict themselves to getting only one of each kind of prize. Write a procedure that is given the prize list and amount and computes the number of prize combinations that you can buy using exactly that amount and assuming that you can't get more than one of any particular prize.

▶ **Exercise 7.20**

Write another procedure that will determine the number of combinations you can buy using no more than a maximum amount of tickets while still insisting that you can have at most one of each kind of prize.

▶ **Exercise 7.21**

A similar problem to this is to imagine that you have an unlimited amount of quarters, dimes, nickels, and pennies and that you need to come up with a combination of these coins to make a certain amount. How many different ways can you do this? Write a procedure that will count the number of ways to make change for a given amount using only quarters, dimes, nickels, and pennies.

7.6   An Application: A Movie Query System

Have you ever gone to a video store to rent a movie, only to be confronted with so many movies that you couldn't find one you wanted to see? Perhaps you were interested in seeing a movie by a given director, but you didn't know which ones they were, and the movies weren't organized by director anyway. Or perhaps you wanted to know which movies were directed by the person, whose name you forgot, who directed some favorite movie? What if you didn't know the name of the movie, but you knew that it was made in the mid to late 1980s and Dennis Quaid starred in it?

Being able to answer such questions would go a long ways toward finding a movie. One possibility would be to ask the store personnel, but perhaps they are busy or unfriendly or only like slasher movies. Another possibility would be to take some movie expert, say Roger Ebert, along with you to the store, but that is probably unrealistic. Wouldn't it be nice if the video store provided a computer that had a program you could ask such questions? Perhaps it could even tell you which movies were currently available at the store.

Let's imagine how this program might be structured. First, it must have access to the database of movies owned by the store. Second, it should have the ability to search through the database in various ways. Finally, the user should be able to use these search procedures flexibly and intuitively. Perhaps the user could carry on a dialog with the computer that looks much like an ordinary English conversation. Such a feature is called a *natural language query system*.

We will write a small version of such a program in this section. The database will simply be a list of movie records. Next we will write procedures to search through this list in various ways. Finally, we provide a query system for the program by using pattern-matching on the user's queries.

So let's first create the database. For the individual movies, we need to define a compound ADT with four components: the title of the movie, the name of its director, the year the movie was made, and a list of the actors in it. For simplicity's sake, we assume that the year is a number and that names (of movies and of people) are lists of symbols. We could construct movie records in a manner similar to how we constructed three-pile game states in Chapter 6; alternatively, we could simply put everything into a list. Because this alternative is easily done using the built-in procedure `list`, we'll represent movie records as lists:

```
(define make-movie
  (lambda (title director year-made actors)
    (list title director year-made actors)))

(define movie-title car)
(define movie-director cadr)
(define movie-year-made caddr)
(define movie-actors cadddr)
```

(These definitions take advantage of the fact that `cadr`, `caddr`, and `cadddr` are built into Scheme as procedures for selecting the second, third, and fourth element of a list. The names stand for "the car of the cdr," etc.) We can then define `our-movie-database` to be a list of such records as follows:

```
(define our-movie-database
  (list (make-movie '(amarcord)
                    '(federico fellini)
                    1974
                    '((magali noel) (bruno zanin)
                                    (pupella maggio)
                                    (armando drancia)))
```

```
(make-movie '(the big easy)
            '(jim mcbride)
            1987
            '((dennis quaid) (ellen barkin)
                             (ned beatty)
                             (lisa jane persky)
                             (john goodman)
                             (charles ludlam)))
 (make-movie '(the godfather)
             '(francis ford coppola)
             1972
             '((marlon brando) (al pacino)
                               (james caan)
                               (robert duvall)
                               (diane keaton)))
 (make-movie '(boyz n the hood)
             '(john singleton)
             1991
             '((cuba gooding jr.) (ice cube)
                                  (larry fishburne)
                                  (tyra ferrell)
                                  (morris chestnut)))))
```

This example is of course a very small database. In the software on the web site for
this book, we include a more extensive database, also called our-movie-database,
that you can use for experimentation.

What types of database search procedures will we want to implement? We might
want to find all the movies by a given director or all of the movies that were made
in a given year or all the movies that have a particular actor in them.

▶ **Exercise 7.22**

We can use the procedure `filter` defined in Section 7.3 to do any one of these
searches. For example, to find all the movies that were made in 1974, we would
evaluate

```
(filter (lambda (movie) (= (movie-year-made movie) 1974))
        our-movie-database)
```

a. Write a procedure called movies-made-in-year that takes two parameters, the
list of movies and a year, and finds all the movies that were made in that year.

b. Use the procedure `filter` to find all the movies that were directed by John Singleton.

c. Write a procedure called `movies-directed-by` that takes two parameters, the list of movies and the name of a director, and finds all of the movies that were directed by that director.

d. Write a procedure called `movies-with-actor` that takes two parameters, a list of the movies and the name of an actor, and finds all the movies that have that actor in them. You could use the Scheme predicate `member`, which tests to see whether its first argument is equal to any element of its second argument (which must be a list).

▶ Exercise 7.23

The biggest problem with the previous procedures is that they return a list of the actual movie records, when we often would prefer just a list of the titles of the movies. Write a procedure called `titles-of-movies-satisfying` that takes two arguments, a list of movies and a predicate, and returns a list of the titles of the movies satisfying the predicate argument. For example, evaluating the expression

```
(titles-of-movies-satisfying our-movie-database
                    (lambda (movie)
                      (= (movie-year-made movie)
                         1974)))
```

would give the list of titles of movies made in 1974. *Hint:* Use the procedure `map` described in Section 7.3.

▶ Exercise 7.24

Sometimes we want some attribute other than the title when we're searching for the movies that satisfy a given property. Generalize `titles-of-movies-satisfying` to a procedure `movies-satisfying` that takes three arguments: a list of movie records, a predicate, and a selector. Evaluating the expression

```
(movies-satisfying our-movie-database
            (lambda (movie)
              (= (movie-year-made movie) 1974))
            movie-title)
```

should have the same result as the previous exercise.

Now that we have procedures to search through our database, we need to consider the people who use the system. Typical video store patrons are not going to be willing to deal with the kind of Scheme expressions that we've been evaluating to find answers to their questions, and so we need to build a query system (i.e., an interface that allows them to ask questions more easily).

The goal of the query system is to handle the user's questions, causing the appropriate database searching procedures to be called and the results reported to the user. We will construct a query system that at least superficially simulates an English dialog between the program and the user; such an interface is often called a *natural language interface*. (*Natural* in this context refers to a naturally occurring human language like English as opposed to a computer language such as Scheme; *interface* refers to the fact that it is the point of contact between the user and the internals of the program.) Thus, the task of this query system will be to read the user's questions, interpret them as requesting specific actions, and perform and report the results of those actions.

Let's be as concrete as possible. Suppose that we have a procedure called `query-loop` that repeatedly reads and responds to the user's questions. We would like to have an interaction something like the following; the first line is a Scheme expression, which is evaluated to start the loop, and the remaining lines are the interaction with the loop:

```
(query-loop)

(who was the director of amarcord)
(federico fellini)

(who were the actors in the big easy)
((dennis quaid)
 (ellen barkin)
 (ned beatty)
 (lisa jane persky)
 (john goodman)
 (charles ludlam))

(what movies were made in 1991)
((boyz n the hood) (dead again))

(what movies were made between 1985 and 1990)
((the big easy))

(what movies were made in 1921)
(i do not know)

(why is the sky blue)
(i do not understand)
```

```
(so long)
```
(see you later)

Some observations are

- The user's questions are English sentences without punctuation and enclosed in parenthesis; our program views them as lists of symbols.
- The program displays the list of answers to the user's query. If no answer is found, it responds with (i do not know); if it can't interpret the question, it responds with (i do not understand).
- The movie database we used for this sample interaction is slightly larger than the one given above.

How can we program such an interaction? Remember the query loop repeatedly reads a question, interprets that question as a request for some specific action, performs that action, and reports the result. Not all questions can be interpreted. However, those that can be interpreted typically match one of a small set of patterns. For example, the questions (who was the director of amarcord) and (who was the director of the big easy) both have the form (who was the director of ...). The key idea to programming the query loop is to use an abstract data type called *pattern/action pairs*. Roughly speaking, a pattern specifies one possible form that questions can have, whereas the corresponding action is the procedure for answering questions of that form. The procedure query-loop will use a list of these pattern/action pairs to respond to the user and will terminate if the user's question appears in a list of the ways of quitting the program. (This test for quitting is done in the exit? procedure using the predefined procedure member, which tests whether its first argument is equal to any element of its second argument. We introduced member in Exercise 7.22d.)

```
(define query-loop
  (lambda ()
    (newline)
    (newline)
    (let ((query (read)))
      (cond ((exit? query) (display '(see you later)))
            ;; movie-p/a-list is the list of the
            ;;  pattern/action pairs
            (else (answer-by-pattern query movie-p/a-list)
                  (query-loop))))))

(define exit?
  (lambda (query)
    (member query '((bye)
```

```
(quit)
(exit)
(so long)
(farewell)))))
```

All of the real work in `query-loop` gets done by the procedure `answer-by-pattern`. How does this procedure work? The idea is that each of the questions that the program can answer must match one of the patterns in the pattern/action list. The action corresponding to the matching pattern is an actual Scheme procedure that does what needs to be done in order to answer the given question. In order to apply this action, we figure out what particular information must be substituted into the blanks in the general pattern to make it match the specific question. These substitutions are the arguments to the action procedure. Our `answer-by-pattern` procedure will use two (as yet unwritten) procedures: `matches?`, which determines if a question matches a given pattern, and `substitutions-in-to-match`, which determines the necessary substitutions.

What should `answer-by-pattern` display? By looking at `query-loop`, we know that the output should be a list that answers the user's question. Thus, if the question matched none of the patterns, the answer should be the list (i do not understand). On the other hand, if the user's question did match one of the patterns, `answer-by-pattern` applies an action procedure that causes our database to be searched. The value of this expression will be a list of answers. If that list of answers is nonempty, we can simply display it; if it is empty, no answers were found. In this case we should display the list (i do not know), indicating that we could not find the movie or movies the user was looking for.

```
(define answer-by-pattern
  (lambda (query p/a-list)
    (cond ((null? p/a-list)
           (display '(i do not understand)))
          ((matches? (pattern (car p/a-list)) query)
           (let ((subs (substitutions-in-to-match
                         (pattern (car p/a-list))
                         query)))
             (let ((result (apply (action (car p/a-list))
                                   subs)))
               (if (null? result)
                   (display '(i do not know))
                   (display result)))))
          (else
           (answer-by-pattern query
                              (cdr p/a-list))))))
```

This procedure cdrs down the list of pattern/action pairs until it finds a pattern matching the query. It then uses `substitutions-in-to-match` to get the substitutions from the query and applies the appropriate action to those substitutions. We are using the built-in Scheme procedure `apply` to apply the action procedure to its arguments. To illustrate how `apply` works, consider the following interaction:

```
(apply + '(1 4))
5

(apply * '(2 3))
6

(apply (lambda (x) (* x x)) '(3))
9

(apply movies-satisfying
       (list our-movie-database
             (lambda (movie) (= (movie-year-made movie) 1974))
             movie-title))
((amarcord))
```

Notice that the first argument to `apply` is a procedure and the second argument is the list of arguments to which the procedure is applied. Therefore, when we make the following call in `answer-by-pattern`,

```
(apply (action (car p/a-list))
       subs)
```

we are applying the action procedure in the first pattern/action pair to the list consisting of the substitutions we got from the pattern match.

To get our query system working, we need to do three things. We need to construct an ADT for pattern/action pairs, we need to start building the list of these pairs, and we need to write the procedures `matches?` and `substitutions-in-to-match`. Doing these things depends on understanding what patterns are. Consider the following possible questions:

```
(who is the director of amarcord)
(who is the director of the big easy)
(who is the director of boyz n the hood)
```

The common pattern of these three questions is clear. If we use ellipsis points (. . .) to represent the title, we can write this pattern as

```
(who is the director of ...)
```

The ellipsis points are sometimes called a *wild card*, because they can stand in for any title.

What action should correspond to this pattern? As we said before, an action is simply a procedure. After determining that (who is the director of the big easy) matches this pattern, we will need to apply our action to the title (the big easy), because we would substitute the title for the ... wild card to make the question match the pattern. Thus, this particular action should be a procedure that takes a title, finds the movie in our movie database that has this title, and returns the director of that movie:

```
(lambda (title)
  (movies-satisfying our-movie-database
             (lambda (movie)
               (equal? (movie-title movie) title))
             movie-director))
```

Constructing the pattern/action ADT and building a list of pattern/action pairs is straightforward. We define the pattern/action ADT much as we defined game states in Chapter 6:

```
(define make-pattern/action
  (lambda (pattern action)
    (cons pattern action)))

(define pattern car)
(define action cdr)
```

We start building our list of pattern/action pairs by constructing a list with just one pair:

```
(define movie-p/a-list
  (list (make-pattern/action
          '(who is the director of ...)
          (lambda (title)
            (movies-satisfying
             our-movie-database
             (lambda (movie) (equal? (movie-title movie) title))
             movie-director)))))
```

We will be extending this list throughout the rest of the section.

▶ **Exercise 7.25**

Add a pattern of the form (who acted in ...) to your program by adding the appropriate pattern/action pair to movie-p/a-list and reevaluating this definition. What other patterns can you add?

To make answer-by-pattern work, we still need to write the procedures matches? and substitutions-in-to-match. To begin with, suppose that all of our patterns have the same form as (who is the director of ...) or (who acted in ...). Therefore, a pattern would be a list of symbols; the last symbol (and only the last) could be the ... wild card. For a pattern to match a question, all non-wild card symbols in the pattern must be equal to the corresponding symbols in the question. Beyond these equal symbols, if the pattern ends with the ... wild card, there must be one or more additional symbols at the end of the question. Thus, to write matches?, we need to cdr down both the pattern and the question, checking that the cars are equal. We should stop if either of the two lists is empty, if the ... wild card is the car of the pattern list, or if the two cars are not equal:

```
(define matches?
  (lambda (pattern question)
    (cond ((null? pattern)  (null? question))
          ((null? question) #f)
          ((equal? (car pattern) '...) #t)
          ((equal? (car pattern) (car question))
           (matches? (cdr pattern)
                     (cdr question)))
          (else #f))))
```

The procedure substitutions-in-to-match will be very similar to matches? in that it will get two arguments, a pattern and a question. However, substitutions-in-to-match will be called only when these two lists match. It needs to return a *list* of the substitutions for the wild cards in the pattern that will make it match the question. Currently, we are assuming that there will only be one substitution, which is the list of symbols that are matched by the ... wild card. However, we will soon extend the definitions of both matches? and substitutions-in-to-match so that patterns can contain more than one wild card. Thus, your substitutions-in-to-match should return a one-element list, where the one element is the list of symbols that matches the ... wild card, as follows:

```
(substitutions-in-to-match '(foo ...)
                           '(foo bar baz))
```

((bar baz))

> **Exercise 7.26**

Write the procedure `substitutions-in-to-match`. Be sure to return a list containing the list of symbols that are matched by the `...` symbol. *Note:* You needn't use the whole query system to test whether `substitutions-in-to-match` works. Instead, you could check whether you have interactions like the preceding one. This note applies as well to later exercises that ask you to extend `matches?` and `substitutions-in-to-match`.

> **Exercise 7.27**

Test the whole query system by evaluating the expression (`query-loop`).

At this point, a typical question/answer might look like

```
(who is the director of amarcord)
((federico fellini))
```

Note that the answer is a list containing the director's name, which is itself a list. This is because `movies-satisfying` is finding the director of each of the movies called `amarcord`, even though there's only one. Asking for the actors in a particular movie is even uglier; you get a list containing the list of the actors' names, which are themselves lists.

We can get better looking output by writing a procedure called `the-only-element-in` and changing the action for finding the director of a movie to

```
(lambda (title)
  (the-only-element-in
   (movies-satisfying
    our-movie-database
    (lambda (movie) (equal? (movie-title movie) title))
    movie-director)))
```

The procedure `the-only-element-in` has a single parameter, which should be a list. If this list has only one element in it, `the-only-element-in` returns that element.

> **Exercise 7.28**

What should it return if there are no elements in the list? What if there are two or more? Write this procedure, and use it to modify the action for finding the actors of a particular movie.

Now that our program can recognize very simple patterns, we can start adding more complicated ones. The next pattern we add to our list is typified by the following sentences:

```
(what movies were made in 1955)
(what movie was made in 1964)
```

What is the common pattern for these two queries? By using an extended pattern language, we could write it as follows:

```
(what (movie movies) (was were) made in _)
```

We have extended our pattern language in two ways:

1. The symbol _ stands for a single-word wild card (as opposed to the multiword wild card ...). Note that we can have as many _'s as we want; each one matches a single word. Unlike with the ... wild card, the _ wild cards need not appear at the end of the pattern.
2. List wild cards such as (movie movies) and (was were) in the pattern are more restricted versions of the _ wild card. A wild card of either type must be matched by a single word. However, the _ wild card can be matched by any word at all, whereas a list wild card can be matched only by one of its elements. Thus, the wild card (movie movies) can only match movie or movies.

Here's how we can extend matches? to account for the second extension to our pattern language. We use the Scheme predicate list?, which returns true if the argument is a list, and also once again use member to test for list membership:

```
(define matches?
  (lambda (pattern question)
    (cond ((null? pattern)  (null? question))
          ((null? question) #f)
          ((list? (car pattern))
           (if (member (car question) (car pattern))
               (matches? (cdr pattern)
                         (cdr question))
               #f))
          ((equal? (car pattern) '...) #t)
          ((equal? (car pattern) (car question))
           (matches? (cdr pattern)
                     (cdr question)))
          (else #f))))
```

> **Exercise 7.29**

Extend `matches?` so that it also checks for the _ wild card. Remember that this is a wild card for a single word. Also, remember that there can be more than one _ in a single pattern and that they need not be at the end of the pattern.

> **Exercise 7.30**

Extend `substitutions-in-to-match` to account for both of these extensions. It should return the list of substitutions, one for each wild card.

Using these extended versions, we can redefine `movie-p/a-list` as follows:

```
(define movie-p/a-list
  (list (make-pattern/action
          '(who is the director of ...)
          (lambda (title)
            (the-only-element-in
             (movies-satisfying
              our-movie-database
              (lambda (movie) (equal? (movie-title movie) title))
              movie-director)))))
        (make-pattern/action
          '(what (movie movies) (was were) made in _)
          (lambda (noun verb year)
            (movies-satisfying
             our-movie-database
             (lambda (movie) (= (movie-year-made movie) year))
             movie-title)))))
```

Note that the action for this new pattern totally ignores the first two substitutions. The substitutions for the first two wild cards in (what (movie movies) (was were) made in _) are often called *noise words* because they are not used in the corresponding action. Not all list wild cards are used for noise words, however. Suppose that instead of the pattern (what (movie movies) (was were) made in _), we used (what (movie movies) (was were) made (in before after since) _). The corresponding action would still ignore those first two noise words, but it would need to know the substitution for the third wild card in order to know which comparison operator to use.

▶ **Exercise 7.31**

What would the action corresponding to (`what (movie movies) (was were) made (in before after since) _`) be? Remember, because the pattern contains four wild cards, the action procedure should get four arguments. It ignores the first two of these and uses the third and fourth to construct a predicate. Note that the third argument is a symbol; you will need to use that symbol to decide which comparison to do.

▶ **Exercise 7.32**

Add a pattern/action for the pattern

```
(what (movie movies) (was were) made between _ and _)
```

▶ **Exercise 7.33**

What if the user asks for the director of "Godfather," which is listed in our database as "The Godfather"? As it stands, the program will respond that it doesn't know, even though it really does have the movie in its database. The point is that the symbol **the** rarely contributes significant information as to the movie's title. Similarly the symbols **a** and **an** add little significant information.

Write a predicate that compares two titles but ignores any articles in either title. Where would you use this predicate in the interface?

▶ **Exercise 7.34**

It would be nice if we could add patterns of the form

```
(when was the godfather made)
(when was amarcord made)
```

The pattern could be (`when was ... made`), but unfortunately, `matches?` and `substitutions-in-to-match` require that the ... wild card occur at the end of the pattern, because as written, the ... absorbs the remainder of the sentence.

Extend `matches?` and `substitutions-in-to-match` to allow for patterns having only one occurrence of the ... wild card but where that occurrence need not be at the end of the pattern. *Hint:* If the pattern starts with ... and is of length n, and the sentence is of length m, and there can be no additional ... wild cards in the rest of the pattern, then how many words must the ... match up with?

Using these extended versions, add a pattern/action for the pattern

```
(when was ... made)
```

Exercise 7.35

If you allow more than one ... in the same pattern, there can be more than one set of substitutions that makes the pattern match a sentence. For example, if the pattern is (do you have ... in ...), and the sentence is (do you have boyz in the hood in the store), the pattern will match not only if you substitute "boyz in the hood" for the first wild card and "the store" for the second but also if you substitute "boyz" for the first wild card and "the hood in the store" for the second wild card.

Redesign `substitutions-in-to-match` so it returns a list of all the possible sets of substitutions that make the pattern match the sentence, rather than just one set. Allow multiple instances of ... in the same pattern. You'll need to make other changes in the way the program uses `substitutions-in-to-match`. You can also redesign the program to eliminate `matches?`, because a pattern matches if there are one or more sets of substitutions that make it match.

Exercise 7.36

Add pattern/action pairs that allow the user to ask other questions of your own choosing. Try to make the patterns as general as possible, for example, by allowing singular and plural as well as past and present tenses. Also allow for the various ways the user might pose the query.

Exercise 7.37

Earlier, we said that the query system reads the user's questions as lists of symbols. We were stretching the truth, as illustrated by the query:

```
(what movie was made in 1951)
```

The last element of that question is not a symbol; it's the number 1951. This raises an interesting point. Because it is a number, it can be compared to other numbers using the = operator. However, consider what would happen if we had the question

```
(what movie was made in Barcelona)
```

In this case, the action procedure attempts to compare the symbol `Barcelona` with the year each movie was made using the = operator, and because `Barcelona` isn't a number, an error is signaled. The whole problem here is that the _ is too general; it will match anything at all and not just a number. Change the pattern language (and the query system) to allow wild cards that are predicates such as **number?**.

▶ Exercise 7.38

The pattern (what (movie movies) (was were) made in _) would match questions such as (what movie were made in 1967). To enforce grammatical correctness, we would need to change our pattern language so that it would allow wild cards that provide a choice among alternative lists of words rather than simply among single words. One example of this would be the pattern

```
(what ((movie was) (movies were)) made in _)
```

Make the appropriate changes in the query system to allow for patterns of this type.

▶ Is There More to Intelligence Than the Appearance of Intelligence?

The natural language interface presented in this section is quite clearly unintelligent. It has no real understanding of the sentences it accepts as input or produces as output—it is just mechanically matching patterns and spitting out canned responses. Yet if you ignore little things like punctuation and capitalization (which are easy, but uninteresting, to fix), the dialog between the system and the user could easily be mistaken for one between two humans.

Of course, the illusion only holds up as long as the input sentences are well suited to the patterns and actions that are available. However, as we add more patterns, the range of coverage gets larger. What if we also added progressively more and more sophisticated kinds of pattern-matching, and stored data about more and more topics? Presumably it would get harder and harder to distinguish the system from an intelligent being—yet it would still be every bit as much a mechanical "symbol pusher" as the current system. What if this progression were taken to such extremes that no one could tell the difference between the system's behavior and that of a human? Even if no one ever achieves this feat of programming, the hypothetical question has already provoked much philosophical debate.

Some people, including most mainstream computer scientists, apply the operational stance to intelligence: If it acts intelligent, it *is* intelligent. The idea that an intelligent entity could be (at least hypothetically) the endpoint in a

(Continued)

Is There More to Intelligence Than the Appearance of Intelligence?

progression of progressively fancier mechanistic symbol pushers isn't bothersome to these people. There is no inherent contradiction between "mechanistic" and "intelligent" because one refers to how the behavior is produced, and the other refers to the nature of the behavior. Perhaps no mechanistic symbol-pushing system could ever produce behavior that matched that of humans—after all, not all kinds of mechanisms can be used to produce all kinds of results. But, these people argue, if such a system ever *did* produce behavior like that of humans, we would have no choice but to accept it as intelligent—after all, what else could "intelligent" mean other than "behaving intelligently"? This operational stance regarding intelligence was subscribed to by Alan Turing, among others, as described in the biographical sketch of him in Chapter 5, and is frequently referred to as the *Turing test* definition of intelligence.

On the other hand, some people (of whom the most well known is the philosopher John Searle) say that if every program in our progression is a mechanical symbol pusher, every one of them is operating on tokens that to us may bring real things like people and movies to mind, but to the program are completely content-free groupings of letters. The only sense in which the sentences can be said to be "about movies" is that we humans can successfully associate them with movies. To the computer, there is nothing but the words themselves. This is every bit as true for the hypothetical endpoint of our evolution, which is indistinguishable in its behavior from a human as it is for the crude version presented in this section. Even flawless conversation "about movies" is only truly "about movies" for us humans, this group of philosophers would argue—to the computer, even the hypothetical flawless conversation is just a string of words. Because Searle made this point using a story about being locked in a room following precise rules for processing things that were to him just squiggles, but to certain outsiders made sense as Chinese text, this argument against the Turing test definition of intelligence is frequently called the *Chinese room argument*.

A related point, which has also been persuasively argued by Searle, is that we humans can do things in our minds, such as liking a movie, whether or not we choose to utter the string of words that conventionally expresses this state, whereas there is no particular reason to assume that some mechanical system that utters "I like *Boyz N the Hood*" really does like the movie or even is the kind of thing that is capable of liking. When other people state their likes, we may or may not trust them to have honestly done so, but at least we accept that they can have likes because we have likes and the other people are similar to us. For a dissimilar thing, such as a computer program, we don't have any reason to believe there are truly any likes inside the shell of statements about likes. We have no reason to

(Continued)

> **Is there more to intelligence? (Continued)**
>
> suppose the program is the kind that could lie about its likes, any more than that it could tell the truth, because there is nothing we can presume the existence of that would form the standard against which a purported like would be judged. In a fellow human, on the other hand, we presume that there are "real likes" and other *mental states* inside because we feel them in ourselves.
>
> In short, Turing prefers to define *intelligence* in terms of behavior we can observe, whereas Searle would prefer to define it in terms of internal mental states. Searle presumes that a mute, paralyzed human being has such states and reserves judgment on flawlessly communicating computer programs.

Review Problems

Exercise 7.39

Prove using induction on *n* that the following procedure produces a list of length *n*.

```
(define sevens
   (lambda (n)
      (if (= n 0)
          '()
          (cons 7
                (sevens (- n 1))))))
```

Exercise 7.40

Suppose that $f_1, f_2, \ldots, f_n$ are all functions from real numbers to real numbers. The functional sum of $f_1, f_2, \ldots, f_n$ is the function that, when given a number x, returns the value $f_1(x) + f_2(x) + \cdots + f_n(x)$. Write a procedure **function-sum** that takes a list of functions and returns the functional sum of those functions. For example

```
(define square
   (lambda (x) (* x x)))
```

```
(define cube
   (lambda (x) (* x (* x x))))
```

```
((function-sum (list square cube)) 2)
12
```

▷ **Exercise 7.41**

Write an iterative version of the following procedure:

```
(define square-sum
  (lambda (lst)
    (if (null? lst)
        0
        (+ (square (car lst))
           (square-sum (cdr lst))))))
```

▷ **Exercise 7.42**

Write a procedure called `apply-all` that, when given a list of functions and a number, will produce the list of the values of the functions when applied to the number. For example,

```
(apply-all (list sqrt square cube) 4)
(2 16 64)
```

▷ **Exercise 7.43**

Prove by induction on n that the following procedure produces a list of $2n$ seventeens:

```
(define seventeens
  (lambda (n)
    (if (= n 0)
        '()
        (cons 17 (cons 17 (seventeens (- n 1)))))))
```

▷ **Exercise 7.44**

Consider the following two procedures. The procedure `last` selects the last element from a list, which must be nonempty. It uses `length` to find the length of the list.

```
(define last
  (lambda (lst)
    (if (= (length lst) 1)
        (car lst)
        (last (cdr lst)))))
```

```
(define length
  (lambda (lst)
    (if (null? lst)
        0
        (+ 1 (length (cdr lst))))))
```

a. How many cdrs does (length *lst*) do when *lst* has n elements?

b. How many calls to length does (last *lst*) make when *lst* has n elements?

c. Express in Θ notation the total number of cdrs done by (last *lst*), including cdrs done by length, again assuming that *lst* has n elements.

d. Give an exact formula for the total number of cdrs done by (last *lst*), including cdrs done by length, again assuming that *lst* has n elements.

▷ **Exercise 7.45**

Lists are collections of data accessible by *position*. That is, we can ask for the first element in a list, the second, ..., the last. Sometimes, however, we'd prefer to have a collection of data accessible by *size*. In other words, we'd like to be able to ask for the largest element, the second largest, ..., the smallest.

In this problem, we'll simplify this goal by restricting ourselves to collections containing exactly two real numbers. Thus the two selectors will select the **smaller** and **larger** of the two numbers. Here are some examples of this data abstraction in use; the constructor is called **make-couple**. Note that the order in which the argument values are given to the constructor is irrelevant, because selection is based on their relative size.

```
(define x (make-couple 2 7))
(define y (make-couple 5 3))
(define z (make-couple 4 4))
```

(smaller x)	(larger x)
2	7

(smaller y)	(larger y)
3	5

(smaller z)	(larger z)
4	4

Write two versions of **make-couple**, **smaller**, and **larger**. One version should have **make-couple** compare the two numbers, and the other version should leave that to **smaller** and **larger**.

▷ **Exercise 7.46**

Write a higher-order procedure `make-list-scaler` that takes a single number *scale* and returns a procedure that, when applied to a list *lst* of numbers, will return the list obtained by multiplying each element of *lst* by *scale*. Thus, you might have the following interaction:

```
(define scale-by-5 (make-list-scaler 5))

(scale-by-5 '(1 2 3 4))
(5 10 15 20)
```

▷ **Exercise 7.47**

Write a procedure `map-2` that takes a procedure and two lists as arguments and returns the list obtained by mapping the procedure over the two lists, drawing the two arguments from the two lists. For example, it would yield the following results:

```
(map-2 + '(1 2 3) '(2 0 -5))
(3 2 -2)

(map-2 * '(1 2 3) '(2 0 -5))
(2 0 -15)
```

Write this procedure `map-2`. You may assume that the lists have the same length.

▷ **Exercise 7.48**

Given the following procedure:

```
(define sub1-each
  (lambda (nums)
    (define help
      (lambda (nums results)
        (if (null? nums)
            (reverse results)
            (help (cdr nums)
                  (cons (- (car nums) 1) results)))))
    (help nums '())))
```

Evaluate the expression `(sub1-each '(5 4 3))` using the substitution model of evaluation. Assume `reverse` operates in a single "black-box" step, but otherwise show each step in the evolution of the process. What kind of process is generated by this procedure?

▷ **Exercise 7.49**

Given a predicate that tests a single item, such as `positive?`, we can construct an "all are" version of it for testing a list; an example is a predicate that tests whether all elements of a list are positive. Define a procedure `all-are` that does this; that is, it should be possible to use it in ways like the following:

```
((all-are positive?) '(1 2 3 4))
#t

((all-are even?) '(2 4 5 6 8))
#f
```

▷ **Exercise 7.50**

Consider the following procedure (together with two sample calls):

```
(define repeat
  (lambda (num times)
    (if (= times 0)
        '()
        (cons num (repeat num (- times 1))))))

(repeat 3 2)
(3 3)

(repeat 17 5)
(17 17 17 17 17)
```

a. Explain why `repeat` generates a recursive process.
b. Write an iterative version of `repeat`.

▷ **Exercise 7.51**

If a list contains multiple copies of the same element in succession, the list can be stored more compactly using *run length encoding*, in which the repeated element is given just once, preceded by the number of times it is repeated. The `expand` procedure given here is designed to decompress a run-length-encoded list; for example, it could be used as follows to expand to full size some 1950s lyrics we got from Abelson and Sussman's text:

```
(expand '(get a job sha 8 na get a job sha 8 na wah 8 yip sha
           boom))
```
(get a job sha na na na na na na na na get a job sha na na na na na na na na wah yip yip yip yip yip yip yip yip sha boom)

a. Given the following definition of the **expand** procedure, show the key steps in evaluating **(expand '(3 ho merry-xmas))** using the substitution model.

b. Does this procedure generate an iterative or recursive process? Justify your answer.

```
(define expand
  (lambda (lst)
    (cond ((null? lst) lst)
          ((number? (car lst))
           (cons (cadr lst)
                 (expand (if (= (car lst) 1)
                             (cddr lst)
                             (cons (- (car lst) 1)
                                   (cdr lst)))))))
          (else
           (cons (car lst)
                 (expand (cdr lst)))))))
```

▷ **Exercise 7.52**

Suppose you have a two-argument procedure, such as + or *, and you want to apply it elementwise to two lists. For example, the procedures **list+** and **list*** would apply + and *, respectively, to the corresponding elements of two lists as follows:

```
(list+ '(1 2 3) '(2 4 6))
(3 6 9)
```

```
(list* '(1 2 3) '(2 4 6))
(2 8 18)
```

Because the two procedures **list+** and **list*** are so similar in form, it makes sense to write the higher-order procedure "factory" **make-list-combiner** that generates the two procedures **list+** and **list*** as follows:

```
(define list+
  (make-list-combiner +))

(define list*
  (make-list-combiner *))
```

Write the procedure `make-list-combiner`. You may assume that the two list arguments have the same length.

Chapter Inventory

Vocabulary

empty list
head
tail
cons up
cdr down
mutual recursion
database

natural language query system
natural language interface
wild card
noise word
Chinese room argument
mental state
run length encoding

Slogans

The two-part list viewpoint

Abstract Data Types

lists
movies

pattern/action pairs
couples

New Predefined Scheme Names

null?
list
length
list-ref
list-tail
map
reverse

cadr
caddr
cadddr
member
apply
list?
number?

Scheme Names Defined in This Chapter

integers-from-to
length
sum

position
list-<
lists-compare?

filter   titles-of-movies-satisfying
first-elements-of   movies-satisfying
list-tail   query-loop
interleave   exit?
shuffle   answer-by-pattern
multiple-shuffle   matches?
in-order?   substitutions-in-to-match
shuffle-number   make-pattern/action
sevens   pattern
list-of-lists   action
add-to-end   movie-p/a-list
reverse   the-only-element-in
palindrome?   sevens
merge-sort   function-sum
merge   square-sum
odd-part   apply-all
even-part   last
count-combos   make-couple
make-movie   smaller
movie-title   larger
movie-director   make-list-scaler
movie-year-made   map-2
movie-actors   sub1-each
our-movie-database   all-are
movies-made-in-year   repeat
movies-directed-by   expand
movies-with-actor   make-list-combiner

Sidebars

Is there more to intelligence than the
appearance of intelligence?

Notes

For more information about perfect shuffles, including their applications in magic and computing, see Morris [38].

Turing's operational definition of intelligence is given in [52], and Searle's Chinese-room argument, in [47]. Searle has more recently (and more persuasively) made the case for mental states in his book *The Rediscovery of the Mind* [48].

CHAPTER EIGHT

Trees

8.1 Binary Search Trees

Joe S. Franksen, one of the co-owners of the video store that uses your query system, has been getting a lot of customer complaints that searching for a video by director takes too long. Now he's hired us to try to fix the problem. The problem doesn't appear to be in the query-matching part of our system. Therefore, we will need to look at the procedures we used for looking up a particular director or video.

Recall that we used a list of video records, and in Exercise 7.22c you wrote a procedure for searching for the ones by a given director. This procedure has to search through the entire list of movies, even if the ones by the specified director happen to be near the front, because it has no way of knowing that there aren't any more movies by the same director later in the list. When Franksen's video rental business was only a small part of his gas station/convenience store, this was no big deal because he only had about a hundred videos. But now that he's expanded his business and acquired 10,000 videos, the time it takes to find one becomes noticeably long.

Are there better ways to structure the list of videos so that finding those by a particular director won't take so long? One idea would be to sort the list, say, alphabetically by the director's name. When we search for a particular director, we can stop when we reach the first video by a director alphabetically "greater than" the one we're searching for.

Is this approach any better? A lot depends on the name of the director. If we're searching for videos directed by Alfred Hitchcock, the search will be relatively quick (because this name begins with an A), whereas if we're looking for videos directed by Woody Allen, we will still need to search through essentially the entire list to get to W. We can show that, on the average, using a sorted list will take about half the time that using an unsorted one would. From an asymptotic point of view, this is not a significant improvement.

We can find things in a sorted list much faster using what's called a *divide and conquer* approach. The main idea is to divide the list of records we're searching through in half at each point in our search. We start by looking in the middle of the list. If the record we're looking for is the same as the middle element of the list, we are done. If it's smaller than the middle record, we only need to look in the first half of the list, and if it's bigger, we only need to look in the second half. This way of searching for something is often called *binary search*. Because each pass of binary search at worst splits the search space in half, we would expect the time taken to be at worst a multiple of $\log(n)$, where n is the size of the list. (In symbols we say that the time is $O(\log(n))$, pronounced "big oh of log en," which means that for all but perhaps finitely many exceptions, it is known to lie below a constant multiple of $\log(n)$.) For large values of n, this is an enormous improvement because, for example, $\log_2(1,000,000) \approx 20$, a speed-up factor of $1,000,000/20 = 50,000$.

But we run into trouble when we try to code this up because we can't get to the middle of a list quickly. In fact, the time it takes to get that middle element is long enough to make the binary search algorithm as slow as doing the straightforward linear search that constituted our first and second approaches. Can we do something to our list that is more drastic than just sorting it? In other words, can we somehow arrange the video records so that we could efficiently implement the binary search algorithm? We would need to be able to easily access the middle element (i.e., the one where half the remaining records are larger than it and half are smaller). We would also need to be able to access the records that are smaller than the middle record, as well as those which are larger. Furthermore, both halves should be structured in exactly the same way as the whole set of video records, so we can search the relevant half in the same way.

How do we create such a structure? The answer is to use a data structure based on the above description. Our new data type will have three elements: one movie record (the "middle" one) and two collections of movie records (those that are smaller and those that are larger). This way, we can get at any of the three parts we need by just using the appropriate selector.

This type of structure is called a *binary search tree*. There is the hint of a recursive definition in the preceding discussion: Most binary search trees have a middle element and two subtrees, which are also binary search trees. We need to make this more precise. First, we skipped over the base case: an empty tree. Secondly, we need to define what we mean by a middle element. This is simply one that is greater than every element in one subtree and less than every element in the other subtree. Thus we can make the following definition:

Binary search tree: A binary search tree is either empty or it consists of three parts: the root, the left subtree, and the right subtree. The left and right subtrees are themselves binary search trees. The root is an element that is greater than or equal to each of the elements in the left subtree and less than or equal to each of the elements in the right subtree.

Notice that there is no guarantee in this definition that the root is the median element (i.e., that half of the elements in the tree are less than it and half are greater than it). When the root of a tree is the median, and similarly for the roots of the subtrees, sub-subtrees, etc., the tree will be as short as possible. We will see in the next section that such trees are the binary search trees that are most efficient for searching.

For the remainder of this section, we will work with two kinds of binary search trees, ones that have numbers as their elements and ones that have video records. Because trees with numbers are easier to conceptualize, we will write procedures that work with them first. Then we can easily modify these procedures to work with trees of video records.

In the numerical trees, we will assume that there are no duplicate items. In this case, we say that the tree is strictly ordered. In the video record trees, there are probably lots of "duplicates." Recall that we compare two records by comparing their directors. Because some people direct many videos, we would expect to see one entry for each of these videos in the tree.

Binary search trees can be represented visually by diagrams in which each tree is a box. Empty trees are represented by empty boxes, and nonempty trees are represented by boxes containing the root value and the boxes for the two subtrees. For example, a small binary search tree with seven elements looks like the following:

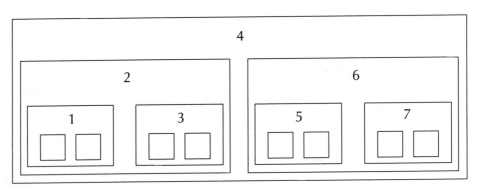

Note that the root of the tree, which is 4, is at the top, and the subtrees branch downward. For some obscure reason, mathematicians and computer scientists almost always draw their trees so that they grow upside down. The left subtree of this example tree has 2 for its root. Notice that this subtree is a box much like the outer one, and so we can talk about its subtrees in turn (with roots 1 and 3), just as we talked about the subtrees of the original tree.

This sort of boxes-within-boxes diagram is probably the best way to think of a tree because it emphasizes the recursive three-part structure. However, another style of diagram is so traditional that it is worth getting used to as well. In this traditional style of tree diagram, the same binary search tree would look like the following:

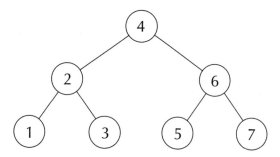

Here you have to mentally recognize the whole collection of seven "nodes" as a single tree, with the top node as the root, the three nodes on the left grouped together in your mind as one subtree, and the three nodes on the right similarly grouped together as the other subtree. You also have to remember that the "leaves" at the bottom of the tree (1, 3, 5, and 7) are really roots of trees with empty subtrees that are invisible in this style of diagram.

We can implement binary search trees by using lists with three elements. Using the convention that the first element is the root, and the second and third elements are the left and right subtrees, respectively, the list representation of the preceding tree would be

(4 (2 (1 () ()) (3 () ())) (6 (5 () ()) (7 () ())))

Its tree structure is much easier to see if we write it on several different lines:

(4
 (2
  (1 () ())
  (3 () ()))
 (6
  (5 () ())
  (7 () ())))

What sort of operations do we need to implement binary search trees? We use two constructors:

```
(define make-empty-tree
  (lambda () '()))

(define make-nonempty-tree
  (lambda (root left-subtree right-subtree)
    (list root left-subtree right-subtree)))
```

and four selectors:

```
(define empty-tree? null?)

(define root car)

(define left-subtree cadr)

(define right-subtree caddr)
```

These procedures are all we need to implement the binary search algorithm given above. Initially, we assume that we're dealing with a binary search tree that has numerical elements and does not have duplicate entries:

```
(define in?
  (lambda (value tree)
    (cond
      ((empty-tree? tree) #f)
      ((= value (root tree)) #t)
      ((< value (root tree)) (in? value (left-subtree tree)))
      (else ; the value must be greater than the root
       (in? value (right-subtree tree))))))
```

Notice how closely this procedure follows the definition of binary search trees. If the tree is empty, the value can't be in the tree. On the other hand, if the tree is not empty, the value is either equal to the root or it's in one of the subtrees. Furthermore, we can tell which subtree it's in by how it compares to the root.

There are two related points worth noting here because they will crop up time and time again. One is the parallelism between the recursive structure of the data and that of the procedure that operates on it. The other is that our one-layer thinking about the design of the procedure goes along with a one-layer perspective on the structure of the data. We don't think about searching through a succession of values in the tree, but rather about looking at the root and then one or the other subtree. Similarly, we don't view the tree as composed of a bunch of values, but rather of a root and two subtrees. We can summarize these points as a general principle for future reference:

The one-layer data structure principle: Hierarchical data structures should not be thought of in their entirety but rather in a one-layer fashion, as a recursive composition of substructures. This one-layer thinking guides one to write recursive procedures that naturally parallel the recursive structure of the data.

▸ **Exercise 8.1**

Write a procedure called `minimum` that will find the smallest element in a nonempty binary search tree of numbers.

▸ **Exercise 8.2**

Write a procedure called `number-of-nodes` that will count the number of elements in a binary search tree.

In the video catalog example, we will want a version of `in?` that returns a list of all the videos directed by a given person. Therefore, we will need a procedure that takes a video record and a director's name and determines how the name of the director of the video compares alphabetically to the given name. The director field of the video record is often called the *key* field; the particular name that we're searching for is called the *key value*. Now, any two names could be identical, the first one could come before the second in alphabetical order, or the first one could come after the second. Therefore we'll assume our comparison procedure returns one of three symbols, =, <, or >.

```
(define compare-by-director
  (lambda (video-record name)
    ; Returns one of the symbols <, =, or > according to how the
    ; director in video-record compares alphabetically to name.
    ; For example, if video-record's director alphabetically
    ; precedes name, < would be returned.
    the code implementing this would go here))
```

We're now in a position to modify `in?` so that it can list all of the videos in a binary search tree that are directed by a given person. The basic idea is to traverse the tree looking for a node whose director is the same as the given key value. Once we find such a subtree, we must still search both halves of it, looking for all of the other records that match the key value. This may seem to defeat the efficiency of the procedure. However, it can be shown that so long as the tree isn't unnecessarily tall and skinny, this search method is in fact very efficient.

To make our procedure work generally, and not just for the director, let's suppose that we have a general comparison operator (such as `compare-by-director`). Such a procedure takes a video record and a key value, compares the appropriate field of the record to the key value, and returns exactly one of the symbols =, <, or >. We can then write a procedure that returns the list of records matching a given key value as follows:

```
(define list-by-key
  (lambda (key-value comparator tree)
    (if (empty-tree? tree)
        '()
        (let ((comparison-result (comparator (root tree)
                                             key-value)))
          (cond
           ((equal? comparison-result '=)
            (cons (root tree)
                  (append (list-by-key key-value comparator
                                       (left-subtree tree))
                          (list-by-key key-value comparator
                                       (right-subtree tree)))))
           ((equal? comparison-result '<)
            (list-by-key key-value comparator
                         (right-subtree tree)))
           (else ;it must be the symbol >
            (list-by-key key-value comparator
                         (left-subtree tree)))))))))
```

Of course, because we haven't explained how to do alphabetical comparison, you're not in a very good position to complete the **compare-by-director** procedure above. You could, of course, try **list-by-key** out with an analogous **compare-by-year** instead, or alternatively consult a Scheme reference manual to learn how to do alphabetical comparisons. However, our main point was to illustrate the nature of accessing a binary search tree, not to get into the details of the specific kind of comparison used.

The procedure **list-by-key** typifies a process called *tree traversal*. We call it a *preorder* traversal because we consider the root of the tree first and then the left and right subtrees, in that order. When the root of the tree should be included in the result, it is consed on in front of the elements from the left and right subtrees. The lists from the left and right subtrees are appended together using a built-in procedure we haven't seen before, **append**. Here is a simpler example of **append**:

```
(append '(a b c) '(1 2 3 4))
(a b c 1 2 3 4)
```

We can use this idea of preorder traversal with **cons** and **append** to produce a list of all the nodes in the tree:

```
(define preorder
  (lambda (tree)
    (if (empty-tree? tree)
        '()
        (cons (root tree)
              (append (preorder (left-subtree tree))
                      (preorder (right-subtree tree)))))))
```

The `append` in this procedure can be avoided if we generalize to a `preorder-onto` procedure that conses the tree's nodes onto the front of a specified list. This is analogous to our definition of `reverse` in terms of `reverse-onto` and is motivated by the same concern: efficiency.

```
(define preorder
  (lambda (tree)
    (preorder-onto tree '())))

(define preorder-onto
  (lambda (tree list)
    (if (empty-tree? tree)
        list
        (cons (root tree)
              (preorder-onto (left-subtree tree)
                             (preorder-onto (right-subtree tree)
                                            list))))))
```

> ### Exercise 8.3

Use this technique to eliminate the `append` from `list-by-key`.

One of the problems with `preorder` is that the list it produces is not sorted. We can get a list of the nodes that's sorted by doing what's called an *in order* traversal of the tree. The "in" refers to the fact that you include the root of the tree in between the left and right subtrees:

```
(define inorder
  (lambda (tree)
    (if (empty-tree? tree)
        '()
        (append (inorder (left-subtree tree))
                (cons (root tree)
                      (inorder (right-subtree tree)))))))
```

Now when we call `inorder` on a binary search tree, the resulting list has the elements in it listed in increasing order.

Exercise 8.4

Again, eliminate `append` by using an "onto" parameter.

Exercise 8.5

The third standard way of traversing a tree is called a *postorder* traversal. Here, you enumerate the left subtree, then the right subtree, and finally the root. Write a procedure that takes a binary search tree and produces the list of nodes that describe a postorder traversal of the tree.

Exercise 8.6

Suppose we want to create a new binary search tree by adding another element to an already existing binary search tree. Where is the easiest place to add such an element? Write a procedure called `insert` that takes a number and a binary search tree of numbers and returns a new binary search tree whose elements consist of the given number together with all of the elements of the binary search tree. You may assume that the given number isn't already in the tree.

Exercise 8.7

Using the procedure `insert`, write a procedure called `list->bstree` that takes a list of numbers and returns a binary tree whose elements are those numbers. Try this on several different lists and draw the corresponding tree diagrams. What kind of list gives you a short bushy tree? What kind of list gives a tall skinny tree?

8.2   Efficiency Issues with Binary Search Trees

Now that we have some experience with binary search trees, we need to ask if they really are a better structure for storing our catalog of videos than sorted lists. In order to do that, we first look at a general binary tree and get some estimates on the number of nodes in a tree. We start with some definitions.

If we ignore the ordering properties that are part of a binary search tree's definition, we get something called a *binary tree*. More precisely,

Binary tree: A binary tree is either empty or it consists of three parts: the root, the left subtree, and the right subtree. The left and right subtrees are themselves binary trees.

Needless to say, binary search trees are special cases of binary trees. Furthermore, we set up the basic constructors and selectors for binary search trees so that they work equally well for implementing binary trees.

There is an enormous amount of terminology commonly used with binary trees. The elements that make up roots of binary trees (or roots of subtrees of binary trees) are called the *nodes* of the tree. In the graphical representation of a tree, the nodes are often represented by circles with values inside them. If a particular node in a binary tree is the root of a subtree that has two empty subtrees, that node is called a *leaf*. On the other hand, if a node is the root of a subtree that has at least one nonempty subtree, that node is called an *internal node*. If you look at the graphical representation, the leaves of a tree are the nodes at the very bottom of the tree and all of the rest of the nodes are internal ones. Of course, if we drew out trees with the root at the bottom of the diagram, the leaves would correspond more closely to real leaves on real trees. The two subtrees of a binary tree are often labeled as the left subtree and the right subtree. Sometimes these subtrees are called the left child or the right child. More commonly, we define a parent-child relationship between nodes. If an internal node has a nonempty left subtree, the root of that left subtree is called the *left child* of the node. The right child is similarly defined. The internal node is the parent node of its children. The parent-child relationship is indicated graphically by drawing an edge between the two nodes. The root of the whole tree has no parent, all internal nodes have at least one and at most two children, and the leaves in a tree have no children at all.

Imagine traveling through a binary tree starting at the root. At each point, we make a choice to go either left or right. If we only travel downward (i.e., without backing up), there is a unique path from the root to any given node. The *depth* of a node is the length of the path from the root to that node, where we define the *length of a path* to be the number of edges that we passed along. For example, if we travel from 7 to 2 to 3 in the tree

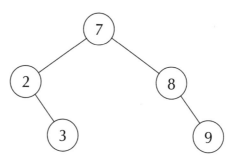

we take a path of length 2. The *height* of a tree is the length of the longest path from the root down to a leaf without any doubling back. In other words, it is the maximum depth of the nodes in the tree. Thus, the height of the above tree is 2 because every path from the root to a leaf has length 2. According to our definition, a tree having a single node will have height 0. The height of an empty tree is undefined; in the remainder of this section, we'll assume all the trees we're talking about are nonempty.

Exercise 8.8

Write a predicate that will return true if the root node of a tree is a leaf (i.e., the tree has only one node).

Exercise 8.9

Write a procedure that will compute the height of a tree.

Suppose we have a binary tree of height h. What is the maximum number of nodes that it can have? What is the maximum number of leaves that it can have? These maximum values occur for *complete trees*, where a complete tree of height h is one where all of the leaves occur at depth h and all of the internal nodes have exactly two children. (Why is the number of leaves maximum then?) Let's let *leaves*(h) and *nodes*(h), respectively, denote the maximum number of leaves and nodes of a tree of height h and look at a few small examples to see if we can determine a general formula. A tree of height 0 has one node and one leaf. A tree of height 1 can have at most two leaves, and those plus the root make a total of three nodes. A tree of height 2 can have at most four leaves, and those plus the three above make a maximum of seven nodes.

In general, the maximum number of leaves doubles each time h is increased by 1. This combined with the fact that *leaves*(0) = 1 implies that *leaves*(h) = 2^h. On the other hand, because every node in a complete tree is either a leaf or a node that would remain were the tree shortened by 1, the maximum number of nodes of a tree of height $h > 0$ is equal to the maximum number of leaves of a tree of height h plus the maximum number of nodes of a tree of height $h - 1$. Thus, we have derived the following recursive formula, or *recurrence relation*:

$$nodes(h) = \begin{cases} 1 & \text{if } h = 0 \\ leaves(h) + nodes(h-1) & \text{if } h > 0 \end{cases}$$

If we take the second part of this recurrence relation, *nodes*(h) = *leaves*(h) + *nodes*($h - 1$), and substitute in our earlier knowledge that *leaves*(h) = 2^h, it follows that when h is positive, *nodes*(h) = 2^h + *nodes*($h - 1$). Similarly, for $h > 1$, we could show that $nodes(h-1) = 2^{h-1} + nodes(h-2)$, so $nodes(h) = 2^h + 2^{h-1} + nodes(h-2)$. Continuing this substitution process until we reach the base case of $nodes(0) = 1$, we find that $nodes(h) = 2^h + 2^{h-1} + 2^{h-2} + \cdots + 4 + 2 + 1$. This sum can be simplified by taking advantage of the fact that multiplying it by 2 effectively shifts it all over by one position, that is, $2 \times nodes(h) = 2^{h+1} + 2^h + 2^{h-1} + \cdots + 8 + 4 + 2$. The payoff comes if we now subtract $nodes(h)$ from this:

$$
\begin{array}{rl}
2 \times nodes(h) = & 2^{h+1} + 2^h + 2^{h-1} + \cdots + 4 + 2 \\
-\quad nodes(h) = & \qquad\quad\; 2^h + 2^{h-1} + \cdots + 4 + 2 + 1 \\
\hline
nodes(h) = & 2^{h+1} \qquad\qquad\qquad\qquad\quad\; - 1
\end{array}
$$

▶ **Exercise 8.10**

You can also use the recurrence relation together with induction to prove that $nodes(h) = 2^{h+1} - 1$. Do so.

▶ **Exercise 8.11**

In many applications, binary trees aren't sufficient because we need more than two subtrees. An m-ary tree is a tree that is either empty or has a root and m subtrees, each of which is an m-ary tree. Generalize the previous results to m-ary trees.

Now suppose we have a binary tree that has n nodes total. What could the height of the tree be? In the worst-case scenario, each internal node has one nonempty child and one empty child. For example, imagine a tree where the left subtree of every node is empty (i.e., it branches only to the right). (This will happen with a binary search tree if the root at each level is always the smallest element.) In this case, the resulting tree is essentially just a list. Thus the maximum height of a tree with n nodes is $n - 1$.

What about the minimum height? We saw that a tree of height h can accommodate up to $2^{h+1} - 1$ nodes. On the other hand, if there are fewer than 2^h nodes, even a tree of height $h - 1$ would suffice to hold them all. Therefore, for h to be the minimum height of any tree with n nodes, we must have $2^h \le n < 2^{h+1}$. If we take the logarithm base 2 of this inequality, we find that

$$ h \le \log_2(n) < h + 1 $$

In other words, the minimum height of a tree with n nodes is $\lfloor \log_2(n) \rfloor$. (The expression $\lfloor \log_2(n) \rfloor$ is pronounced "the floor of log en." In general, the floor of a real number is the greatest integer that is less than or equal to that real number.)

Because searching for an element in a binary search tree amounts to finding a path from the root node to a node containing that element, we will clearly prefer trees of *minimum height* for the given number of nodes. In some sense, such trees will be as short and bushy as possible. There are several ways to guarantee that a tree with *n* nodes has minimum height. One is given in Exercise 8.12. In Chapter 13 we'll consider the alternative of settling for trees that are no more than 4 times the minimum height.

We now have all of the mathematical tools we need to discuss why and when binary search trees are an improvement over straightforward lists. We will consider the procedure `in?` because it is somewhat simpler than `list-by-key`. However, similar considerations apply to the efficiency of `list-by-key`, just with more technical difficulties. Remember that with the `in?` procedure, we are only concerned with whether or not a given element is in a binary search tree, whereas with `list-by-key` we want to return the list of all records matching a given key.

Let's consider the time taken by the procedure `in?` on a tree of height *h* having *n* nodes. Searching for an element that isn't in the tree is equivalent to traveling from the root of the tree to one of its leaves. In this case, we will pass through at most $h + 1$ nodes. If we're searching for an element that is in the tree, we will encounter it somewhere along a path from the root to a leaf. Because the number of operations performed by `in?` is proportional to the number of nodes encountered, we conclude that in either case, searching for an element in the tree takes $O(h)$ time. If the tree has minimum height, this translates to $O(\log(n))$. In the worst case, where the height of the tree is $n - 1$, this becomes $O(n)$.

> ### Exercise 8.12

In Exercise 8.7, you wrote a procedure `list->bstree` that created a binary search tree from a list by successively inserting the elements into the tree. This procedure can lead to trees that are far from minimum height—surprisingly, the worst case occurs if the list is in sorted order. However, if you know the list is already in sorted order, you can do much better: Write a procedure `sorted-list->min-height-bstree` that creates a minimum height binary search tree from a sorted list of numbers. *Hint:* If the list has more than one element, split it into three parts: the middle element, the elements before the middle element, and the elements after. Construct the whole tree by making the appropriate recursive calls on these sublists and combining the results.

> ### Exercise 8.13

Using `sorted-list->min-height-bstree` and `inorder` (which constructs a sorted list from a binary search tree), write a procedure `optimize-bstree` that optimizes a binary search tree. That is, when given an arbitrary binary search tree, it should produce a minimum-height binary search tree containing the same nodes.

Exercise 8.14

Using `list->bstree` and `inorder`, write a procedure **sort** that sorts a given list.

▶ Privacy Issues

How would you feel if you registered as a child at a chain ice-cream parlor for their "birthday club" by providing name, address, and birth date, only to find years later the Selective Service using that information to remind you of your legal obligation to register for the draft?

This case isn't a hypothetical one: It is one of many real examples of personal data voluntarily given to one organization for one purpose being used by a different organization for a different purpose.

Some very difficult social, ethical, and legal questions occur here. For example, did the ice-cream chain "own" the data it collected and hence have a right to sell it as it pleased? Did the the government step outside of the Bill of Rights restrictions on indiscriminate "dragnet" searches? Did the social good of catching draft evaders justify the means? How about if it had been tax or welfare cheats or fathers delinquent in paying child support? (All of the above have been tracked by computerized matching of records.) Should the computing professionals who wrote the "matching" program have refused to do so?

The material we have covered on binary search trees may help you to define efficient structures to store and retrieve data. However, because many information storage and retrieval systems are used to store personal information, we urge you to also take the following to heart when and if you undertake such a design. The Code of Ethics and Professional Conduct of the Association for Computing Machinery, or ACM (which is the major computing professional society) contains as General Moral Imperative 1.7:

Respect the privacy of others
Computing and communication technology enables the collection and exchange of personal information on a scale unprecedented in the history of civilization. Thus there is increased potential for violating the privacy of individuals and groups. It is the responsibility of professionals to maintain the privacy and integrity of data describing individuals. This includes taking precautions to ensure the accuracy of data, as well as protecting it from unauthorized access or accidental disclosure to inappropriate individuals. Furthermore, procedures must be established to allow individuals to review their records and correct inaccuracies.

(Continued)

▶ **Privacy Issues (Continued)**

This imperative implies that only the necessary amount of personal information be collected in a system, that retention and disposal periods for that information be clearly defined and enforced, and that personal information gathered for a specific purpose not be used for other purposes without consent of the individual(s). These principles apply to electronic communications, including electronic mail, and pro-hibit procedures that capture or monitor electronic user data, including messages, without the permission of users or bona fide authorization related to system operation and maintenance. User data observed during the normal duties of system operation and maintenance must be treated with strictest confidentiality, except in cases where it is evidence for the violation of law, organizational regulations, or this Code. In these cases, the nature or contents of that information must be disclosed only to proper authorities.

8.3   Expression Trees

So far, we've used binary trees and binary search trees as a way of storing a collection of numbers or records. What makes these trees different from lists is the way we can access the elements. A list has one special element, the first element, and all the rest of the elements are clumped together into another list. Binary trees also have a special element, the root, but they divide the rest of the elements into *two* subtrees, instead of just one, which gives a hierarchical structure that is useful in many different settings. In this section we'll look at another kind of tree that uses this hierarchical structure to represent arithmetical expressions. In these trees, the way a tree is structured indicates the operands for each operation in the expression.

Consider an arithmetic expression, such as the one we'd write in Scheme notation as (+ 1 (* 2 (- 3 5))). We can think of this as being a tree-like structure with numbers at the leaves and operators at the other nodes:

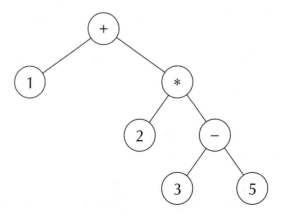

Such a structure is often called an *expression tree*. As we did with binary trees, we can define an expression tree more precisely:

Expression tree: An expression tree is either a number or it has three parts, the name of an operator, a left operand and a right operand. Both the left and right operands are themselves expression trees.

There are several things to notice about this definition:

- We are restricting ourselves to expressions that have *binary operators* (i.e., operators that take exactly two operands).
- We are also restricting ourselves to having numbers as our *atomic expressions*. In general, expression trees also include other kinds of constants and variable names as well.
- There is nothing in the definition that says an expression tree must be written in *prefix* order, that is, with the name of the operator preceding the two operands. Indeed, most people would find *infix* order more natural. An infix expression has the name of the operator in between the two operands.

How do we implement expression trees? We will do it in much the same way that we implemented binary trees, except that we will follow the idea of the last note in the preceeding list and list the parts of an expression in infix order:

```
(define make-constant
  (lambda (x) x))

(define constant? number?)

(define make-expr
  (lambda (left-operand operator right-operand)
    (list left-operand operator right-operand)))

(define operator cadr)

(define left-operand car)

(define right-operand caddr)
```

Now that we have a way of creating expressions, we can write the procedures necessary to evaluate them using the definition to help us decide how to structure our code. To buy ourselves some flexibility, we'll use a procedure called `look-up-value` to map an operator name into the corresponding operator procedure. Then the main `evaluate` procedure just needs to apply that operator procedure to the values of the operands:

```
(define evaluate
  (lambda (expr)
    (cond ((constant? expr) expr)
          (else ((look-up-value (operator expr))
                 (evaluate (left-operand expr))
                 (evaluate (right-operand expr)))))))

(define look-up-value
  (lambda (name)
    (cond ((equal? name '+) +)
          ((equal? name '*) *)
          ((equal? name '-) -)
          ((equal? name '/) /)
          (else (error "Unrecognized name" name)))))
```

With these definitions, we would have the following interaction:

```
(evaluate '(1 + (2 * (3 - 5))))
-3
```

▶ **Exercise 8.15**

In the preceding example, we've "cheated" by using a quoted list as the expression to evaluate. This method relied on our knowledge of the representation of expression trees. How could the example be rewritten to use the constructors to form the expression?

We can do more with expression trees than just finding their values. For example, we could modify the procedure for doing a postorder traversal of a binary search tree so that it works on *expression trees* instead. In this case, our base case will be when we have a constant, or a leaf, instead of an empty tree:

```
(define post-order
  (lambda (tree)
    (define post-order-onto
      (lambda (tree list)
        (if (constant? tree)
            (cons tree list)
            (post-order-onto (left-operand tree)
                             (post-order-onto
                              (right-operand tree)
                              (cons (operator tree) list))))))
    (post-order-onto tree '())))
```

If we do a postorder traversal of the last tree shown, we get:

```
(post-order '(1 + (2 * (3 - 5)))))
(1 2 3 5 - * +)
```

This result is exactly the sequence of keys that you would need to punch into a Hewlett-Packard calculator in order to evaluate the expression. Such an expression is said to be a *postfix* expression.

> **Exercise 8.16**

Define a procedure for determining which operators are used in an expression.

> **Exercise 8.17**

Define a procedure for counting how many operations an expression contains.

Note that all of the operators in our expressions were binary operators, and thus we needed nodes with two children to represent them; we say the operator nodes all have *degree* 2. If we had operators that took m expressions instead of just two, we would need nodes with degree m (i.e., trees that have m subtrees).

The kind of tree we've been using in this section differs subtly from the binary and m-ary trees we saw earlier in the chapter. In those *positional trees*, it was possible to have a node with a right child but no left child, for example. In the *ordered trees* we're using for expressions, on the other hand, there can't be a second operand unless there is a first operand. Other kinds of trees exist as well, for example, trees in which no distinction is made among the children—none is first or second, left or right; they are all just children. Most of the techniques and terminology carry over for all kinds of trees.

8.4 An Application: Automated Phone Books

Have you ever called a university's information service to get the phone number of a friend and, instead of talking to a human operator, found yourself following instructions given by a computer? Perhaps you were even able to look up the friend's phone number using the numbers on the telephone keypad. Such automated telephone directory systems are becoming more common. In this section we will explore one version of how such a directory might be implemented.

In this version, a user looks up the telephone number of a person by spelling the person's name using the numbers on the telephone keypad. When the user has entered enough numbers to identify the person, the system returns the telephone number. Can we rephrase this problem in a form that we can treat using Scheme? Suppose that we have a collection of pairs, where each pair consists of a person's name and phone number. How could we store the pairs so that we can easily retrieve a person's phone number by giving the sequence of digits (from 2 to 9) corresponding to the name? Perhaps our system might do even more: For example, we could have our program repeatedly take input from the user until the identity of the desired person is determined, at which point the person's name and phone number is given.

Notice the similarity between this problem and the video catalog problem considered in Section 8.1. There we wanted to store the videos in a way that allowed us to efficiently find all videos with a given director. Our desire to implement binary search led us to develop the binary search tree ADT. Searching was accomplished by choosing the correct child of each subtree and therefore amounted to finding the path from the root node to the node storing the desired value.

We are also searching for things with the automated phone book, but the difference is the method of retrieval: we want to retrieve a phone number by successively giving the digits corresponding to the letters in the person's name. How should we structure our data in a way that facilitates this type of retrieval? Suppose we use a tree to store the phone numbers. What type of tree would lend itself to such a search?

If we are going to search by the sequence of digits corresponding to the person's name, then these digits could describe the path from the root node to the node storing the desired value. Each new digit would get us closer to our goal. The easiest way to accomplish this is to have the subtrees of a given node labeled (indexed) by the digits themselves. Then the sequence of digits would exactly describe the path to the desired node because we would always choose the subtree labeled by the next digit in our sequence. Such a tree is called a *trie*. This name is derived from the word re*trie*val, though the conventional pronunciation has become "try" rather than the logical but confusing "tree." More precisely,

> **Trie:** A trie is either empty or it consists of two parts: a list of root values and a list of subtries, which are indexed by labels. Each subtrie is itself a trie.

Because we have the eight digits from 2 to 9 as labels in our example, our tries will be 8-ary trees. The first child of a node will be implicitly labeled as the "2" child, the second as the "3" child, etc. In other words, the digits the user enters describe a path starting from the root node. If the user types a 2, we move to the first child of the root node. If the user types a 3 next, we then move to the second child of that node.

The values stored at a particular node are those corresponding to the path from the root of the trie to that node. If anyone had an empty name (i.e., zero letters long), that name and number would be stored on the root node of the trie. Anyone with the one-letter name A, B, or C would be on the first child of the root (the one for the digit 2 on the phone keypad, which is also labeled ABC). Anyone with the

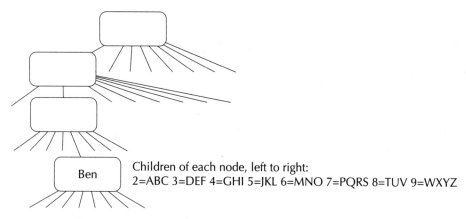

Children of each node, left to right:
2=ABC 3=DEF 4=GHI 5=JKL 6=MNO 7=PQRS 8=TUV 9=WXYZ

Figure 8.1 An example phone trie, with Ben's position indicated

one-letter name D, E, or F would be on the second child of the root. Anyone with any of the two-letter names Ad, Ae, Af, Bd, Be, Bf, Cd, Ce, or Cf would be on the second child of the first child of the root. For example, the trie in Figure 8.1 shows where the name and number of someone named Ben would be stored.

Note that a given node may or may not store a value: In our example, the nodes encountered on the way to Ben's node don't have any values because no one has an empty name, the one-letter name A, B, or C, or any of the 9 two-letter names listed above. Not all the values need be at leaf nodes, however. For example, Ben's name corresponds on a phone to the digits 2-3-5. However, these are also the first three digits in the name Benjamin, and in fact even the first three digits in the name Adonis, because B and A share a phone digit, as do E and D and also N and O. Therefore, the node in our trie that stores the value Ben may also be encountered along a path to a deeper node that stores Benjamin or Adonis.

We must also allow more than one value to be stored at a given node, because, for example, Jim and Kim would be specified by the same sequence of digits (5-4-6) on the telephone. Therefore, we have a *list* of root values in our definition.

How can we implement tries? As described above, we will implement them as 8-ary trees, where every tree has *exactly* eight subtrees, even if some (or all) of them are empty. These subtrees correspond to the digits 2 through 9, which have letters on a phone keypad. We call these digits 2 through 9 the "labels" of the subtrees and define a selector called `subtrie-with-label` that returns the subtrie of a nonempty trie that corresponds to a given label:

```
(define make-empty-trie
  (lambda () '()))
```

```
(define make-nonempty-trie
  (lambda (root-values ordered-subtries)
    (list root-values ordered-subtries)))


(define empty-trie? null?)


(define root-values car)


(define subtries cadr)


(define subtrie-with-label
  (lambda (trie label)
    (list-ref (subtries trie) (- label 2))))
```

Note that the constructor `make-nonempty-trie` assumes that the subtries are given to it in order (including possibly some empty subtries). Constructing a specific phone trie is a somewhat difficult task that we will consider later in this section. In fact, we will write a procedure `values->trie` that takes a list of values (people's names and phone numbers) and returns the trie containing those values. Note also that the procedure `subtrie-with-label` must subtract 2 from the label because list convention refers to the first element (corresponding to the digit 2) as element number zero.

The values in our automated phone book are the phone numbers of various people. In order to store the person's name and phone number together, we create a simple record-structured ADT called *person*:

```
(define make-person
  (lambda (name phone-number)
    (list name phone-number)))


(define name car)


(define phone-number cadr)
```

How do we construct the trie itself? As we said in the preceeding, we will do this later in the section by writing a procedure `values->trie` that creates a trie from a list of values. For example, a definition of the form:

```
(define phone-trie
  (values->trie (list (make-person 'lindt      7483)
                      (make-person 'cadbury    7464)
                      (make-person 'wilbur     7466)
                      (make-person 'hershey    7482)
```

```
(make-person 'spruengli        7009)
(make-person 'merkens          7469)
(make-person 'baker            7465)
(make-person 'ghiradelli       7476)
(make-person 'tobler           7481)
(make-person 'suchard          7654)
(make-person 'callebaut        7480)
(make-person 'ritter           7479)
(make-person 'maillard         7477)
(make-person 'see              7463)
(make-person 'perugina         7007)))))
```

will define `phone-trie` to be the trie containing the given people, which can then
be used to look up phone numbers. You can work on other exercises involving tries
before we write `values->trie` because we've included an alternate definition on
the web site for this book, which simply defines `phone-trie` as a quoted list.

Using what we have already developed, we can implement a simple automated
phone book as follows:

```
(define look-up-with-menu
  (lambda (phone-trie)
    (menu)
    (look-up-phone-number phone-trie)))

(define menu
  (lambda ()
    (newline)
    (display "Enter the name, one digit at a time.")
    (newline)
    (display "Indicate you are done by 0.")
    (newline)))

(define look-up-phone-number
  (lambda (phone-trie)
    (newline)
    (if (empty-trie? phone-trie)
        (display "Sorry we can't find that name.")
        (let ((user-input (read)))
          (if (= user-input 0)
              (display-phone-numbers (root-values phone-trie))
              (look-up-phone-number (subtrie-with-label
                                      phone-trie
                                      user-input)))))))
```

```
(define display-phone-numbers
  (lambda (people)
    (define display-loop
      (lambda (people)
        (cond ((null? people) 'done)
              (else (newline)
                    (display (name (car people)))
                    (display "'s phone number is ")
                    (display (phone-number (car people)))
                    (display-loop (cdr people)))))))
    (if (null? people)
        (display "Sorry we can't find that name.")
        (display-loop people)))))
```

Here is how you could use `look-up-with-menu` to look up the telephone number of Spruengli, for example:

```
(look-up-with-menu phone-trie)
```
Enter the name, one digit at a time.
Indicate you are done with 0.

```
7
7
7
8
3
6
4
5
4
0
```
spruengli's phone number is 7009

This method is certainly progress, but it is also somewhat clunky. After all, in our example Spruengli is already determined by the first two digits (7 and 7). It seems silly to require the user to enter more digits than are necessary to specify the desired person. We could make our program better if we had a procedure that tells us when we have exactly one remaining value in a trie, and another procedure that returns that value.

We can write more general versions of both of these procedures; one would return the number of values in a trie and the other the list of values. Notice that these two procedures are quite similar. In either case you can compute the answer by taking the number of values (respectively, the list of values) at the root node and adding that to the number of values (respectively, the list of values) in each of the subtries. The difference is that in the former case you add the numbers by regular addition, whereas in the latter case you add by appending the various lists.

Exercise 8.18

Write the procedure **number-in-trie** that calculates the total number of values in a trie. *Hint:* In the general case, you can compute the list of numbers in the various subtries by using **number-in-trie** in conjunction with the built-in Scheme procedure **map**. The total number of values in all the subtries can then be gotten by applying the **sum** procedure from Section 7.3. Of course, you have to take into account the values that are at the root node of the trie.

Exercise 8.19

Write the procedure **values-in-trie** that returns the list of all values stored in a given trie. It should be very similar in form to **number-in-trie**. You may find your solution to Exercise 7.5 on page 173 useful. In fact, if you rewrote **number-in-trie** to use Exercise 7.5's solution in place of **sum**, **values-in-trie** would be nearly identical in form to **number-in-trie**.

Exercise 8.20

Let's use these procedures to improve what is done in the procedure **look-up-phone-number**.

a. Use **number-in-trie** to determine if there are fewer than two values in *phone-trie* and immediately report the appropriate answer if so, using **values-in-trie** and **display-phone-numbers**.

b. Further modify **look-up-phone-number** so that if the user enters 1, the names of all the people in the current trie will be reported, but the procedure **look-up-phone-number** will continue to read input from the user. You will also want to make appropriate changes to **menu**.

We now confront the question of how these tries we have been working with can be created in the first place. As we indicated earlier, we will write a procedure **values->trie** that will take a list of values (i.e., people) and will return the trie containing them. First some remarks on vocabulary: Because we have so many different data types floating around (and we will soon define one more), we need to be careful about the words we use to describe them. A *value* is a single data item (in our case a person, that is, name and phone number) being stored in a trie. A *label* is in our case a digit from 2 to 9; it is what is used to select a subtrie. Plurals will always indicate lists; for example, *values* will mean a list of values and *labels* will mean a list of labels. This may seem trivial, but it will prove very useful for understanding the meanings of the following procedures and their parameters.

Exercise 8.21

Write a procedure `letter->number` that takes a letter (i.e., a one-letter symbol) and returns the number corresponding to it on the telephone keypad. For *q* and *z* use 7 and 9, respectively. *Hint:* The easiest way to do this exercise is to use a **cond** together with the list membership predicate **member** we introduced in the previous chapter.

Exercise 8.22

To break a symbol up into a list of one-character symbols, we need to use some features of Scheme that we'd rather not talk about just now. The following `explode-symbol` procedure uses these magic features of Scheme so that `(explode-symbol 'ritter)` would evaluate to the list of one-letter symbols `(r i t t e r)`, for example:

```
(define explode-symbol
  (lambda (sym)
    (map string->symbol
         (map string
              (string->list (symbol->string sym))))))
```

Use this together with `letter->number` to write a procedure `name->labels` that takes a name (symbol) and returns the list of numbers corresponding to the name. You should see the following interaction:

```
(name->labels 'ritter)
(7 4 8 8 3 7)
```

To make a trie from a list of values, we will need to work with the labels associated with each of the values. One way is to define a simple ADT called *labeled-value* that packages these together. This could be done as follows:

```
(define make-labeled-value
  (lambda (labels value)
    (list labels value)))
```

```
(define labels car)

(define value cadr)
```

Because we will use this abstraction to construct tries, we will need some procedures that allow us to manipulate labeled values.

> ### Exercise 8.23

Write a procedure `empty-labels?` that takes a labeled value and returns true if and only if its list of labels is empty.

> ### Exercise 8.24

Write a procedure `first-label` that takes a labeled value and returns the first label in its list of labels.

> ### Exercise 8.25

Write a procedure `strip-one-label` that takes a labeled value and returns the labeled value with one label removed. For example, you would have the following interaction:

```
(define labeled-ritter
  (make-labeled-value '(7 4 8 8 3 7)
                      (make-person 'ritter 7479)))

(labels (strip-one-label labeled-ritter))
(4 8 8 3 7)

(name (value (strip-one-label labeled-ritter)))
ritter

(phone-number (value (strip-one-label labeled-ritter)))
7479
```

> ### Exercise 8.26

Write a procedure `value->labeled-value` that takes a value (person) and returns the labeled value corresponding to it. You must of course use the procedure `name->labels`.

We can now write `values->trie` in terms of a yet to be written procedure that operates on labeled values:

```
(define values->trie
  (lambda (values)
    (labeled-values->trie (map value->labeled-value
                               values))))
```

How do we write `labeled-values->trie`? The argument to this procedure is a list of labeled values, and we must clearly use the labels in the trie construction. If a given labeled value has the empty list of labels (in other words, we have gotten to the point in the recursion where all of the labels have been used), the associated value should be one of the values at the trie's root node. We can easily isolate these labeled values using the `filter` procedure from Section 7.3, as in:

```
(filter empty-labels? labeled-values)
```

We can similarly isolate those with nonempty labels, which belong in the subtries; the first label of each labeled value determines which subtrie it goes in.

> ### Exercise 8.27

Write a procedure `values-with-first-label` that takes a list of labeled values and a label and returns a list of those labeled values that have the given first label, but with that first label removed. You may assume that none of the labeled values has an empty list of labels. Thus, the call `(values-with-first-label labeled-values 4)` should return the list of those labeled values in `labeled-values` with a first label of 4, but with the 4 removed from the front of their lists of labels. (This would only be legal assuming each labeled value in `labeled-values` has a nonempty list of labels.) Stripping off the first label makes sense because it was used to select out the relevant labeled values, which will form one subtrie of the overall trie. Within the subtrie, that first label no longer plays a role.

> ### Exercise 8.28

Using the procedure `values-with-first-label`, write a procedure `categorize-by-first-label` that takes a list of labeled values, each with a nonempty list of labels, and returns a *list of lists* of labeled values. The first list in the list of lists should contain all those labeled values with first label 2, the next list, those that start with 3, etc. (If there are no labeled values with a particular first label, the corresponding list will be empty. There will always be eight lists, one for each possible first label,

Case 1, labeled-values is empty

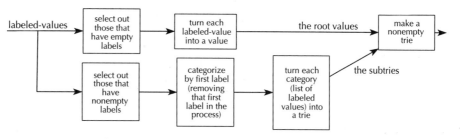

Case 2, labeled-values is nonempty

Figure 8.2   The design of the `labeled-values->trie` procedure

ranging from 2 to 9.) Each labeled value should have its first label stripped off, which `values-with-first-label` takes care of. (Thus the labeled values in the first list, for example, no longer have the label of 2 on the front.)

Exercise 8.29

Finally, write the procedure `labeled-values->trie`. If the list of labeled values is empty, you can just use `make-empty-trie`. On the other hand, if the list is not empty, you can isolate those labeled values with empty labels and those with nonempty labels, as indicated above. You can turn the ones with empty labels into the root values by applying `value` to each of them. You can turn the ones with nonempty labels into the subtries by using `categorize-by-first-label`, `map`, and `labeled-values->trie`. Once you have the root values and the subtries, you can use `make-nonempty-trie` to create the trie. Figure 8.2 illustrates this design.

Review Problems

Exercise 8.30

Fill in the following definition of the procedure `successor-of-in-or`. This procedure should take three arguments: a value (*value*), a binary search tree (*bst*), and a value to return if no element of the tree is larger than *value* (*if-none*). If there is any element, *x*, of *bst* such that *x* > *value*, the smallest such element should be returned. Otherwise, *if-none* should be returned.

```
(define successor-of-in-or
  (lambda (value bst if-none)
    (cond ((empty-tree? bst)
           _____)
          ((<= (root bst) value)
           (successor-of-in-or _____

                               _____

                               _____))
          (else
           (successor-of-in-or _____

                               _____

                               _____)))))
```

▷ **Exercise 8.31**

Write a procedure that takes as arguments a binary search tree of numbers, a lower bound, and an upper bound and counts how many elements of the tree are greater than or equal to the lower bound and less than or equal to the upper bound. Assume that the tree may contain duplicate elements. Make sure your procedure doesn't examine more of the tree than is necessary.

▷ **Exercise 8.32**

Write a procedure that takes as arguments a binary search tree of numbers, a lower bound, and an upper bound and returns an ordered list of those elements of the tree that are greater than or equal to the lower bound and less than or equal to the upper bound. Assume that the tree may contain duplicate elements. Use the technique of an "onto" parameter to avoid unnecessary appending of lists, and make sure your procedure doesn't examine more of the tree than is necessary.

Chapter Inventory

Vocabulary

divide and conquer	leaf
binary search	internal node
root	child
subtree	parent
strictly ordered	tree traversal
node	preorder

in-order
postorder
depth
length of a path
height
complete tree
recurrence relation
⌊⌋ (floor)
minimum height binary tree
The Code of Ethics and
Professional Conduct

Association for Computing
Machinery (ACM)
binary operator
atomic expression
prefix
infix
postfix
degree
positional tree
ordered tree

Slogans

The one-layer data structure principle

Abstract Data Types

binary search tree
binary tree
expression tree

trie
person
labeled value

New Predefined Scheme Names

append

Scheme Names Defined in This Chapter

```
make-empty-tree
make-nonempty-tree
empty-tree?
root
left-subtree
right-subtree
in?
minimum
number-of-nodes
list-by-key
preorder
preorder-onto
inorder
insert
list->bstree
sorted-list->min-height-bstree
optimize-bstree
```

```
sort
make-constant
constant?
make-expr
operator
left-operand
right-operand
look-up-value
evaluate
post-order
make-empty-trie
make-nonempty-trie
empty-trie?
root-values
subtries
subtrie-with-label
values->trie
```

```
make-person               name->labels
name                      make-labeled-value
phone-number              labels
phone-trie                value
look-up-with-menu         empty-labels?
menu                      first-label
look-up-phone-number      strip-one-label
display-phone-numbers     value->labeled-value
number-in-trie            labeled-values->trie
values-in-trie            values-with-first-label
letter->number            categorize-by-first-label
explode-symbol            successor-of-in-or
```

Sidebars

Privacy Issues

Notes

As with Θ in Chapter 4, the conventional definition of O allows any number of exceptions up to some cutoff point, rather than finitely many exceptions as we do. Again, so long as n is restricted to the nonnegative integers, our definition is equivalent.

The example of personal information divulged to an ice-cream parlor "birthday club" winding up in the hands of the Selective Service is reported in [24].

The ACM Code of Ethics and Professional Conduct can be found in [17]; a set of illustrative case studies accompanies it in [4].

Regarding the pronunciation of "trie," we've had to take Aho and Ullman's word for it—none of us can recall ever having heard "trie" said aloud. Aho and Ullman should know, though and they write on page 217 of their *Foundations of Computer Science* [3] that "it was originally intended to be pronounced 'tree.' Fortunately, common parlance has switched to the distinguishing pronunciation 'try.'"

CHAPTER NINE

Generic Operations

9.1 Introduction

We described data abstraction in Chapter 6 as a barrier between the way a data type is used and the way it is represented. There are a number of reasons to use data abstraction, but perhaps its greatest advantage is that the programmer can rely on an *abstract mental model* of the data rather than worrying about such mundane details as how the data is represented. For example, we can view the game-state ADT from Chapter 6 as a snapshot picture of an evolving Nim game and can view lists as finite sequences of objects. The simplification resulting from using abstract models is essential for many of the complicated problems programmers confront. In this chapter we will exploit and extend data abstraction by introducing *generic operations*, which are procedures that can operate on several different data types.

We rely on our mental model of an ADT when pondering how it might be used in a program. To actually work with the data, however, we need procedures that can manipulate it; these procedures are sometimes called the ADT's *interface*. For example, all of the procedures Scheme provides for manipulating lists comprise the list type's interface. The barrier between an ADT's use and its implementation results directly from the programming discipline of using the interface procedures instead of explicitly referring to the underlying representation. The interface must give us adequate power to manipulate the data as we would expect, given our mental model of the data, but we still have some flexibility in how the interface is specified. On the other hand, once we have specified the interface, we can easily imagine that some of the interface procedures would be appropriate for other data types. For example, most ADTs could benefit from a type-specific display procedure, if only for debugging purposes; such a procedure should "do the right thing" for its data, regardless of how the data is represented. Generic operators allow us to share common operators among several different data types.

Another advantage of generic operators is that they can be used to maintain a uniform interface over similar data types that have entirely different representations. One example of this occurs when a data type can be represented in significantly different ways. For instance, suppose we wish to implement an ADT *date* to represent the date (i.e., the day, month, and year) when something occurs. One way to do this would be by using a three-part data structure containing integers representing the day, month, and year in the obvious manner (e.g., May 17, 1905, would be represented by the triple $(17, 5, 1905)$). An altogether different way would be to represent a date by the integer that equals the number of days that date fell after January 1, 1900 (January 1, 1901, would be represented by 365 and May 17, 1905, by 1962). Which representation we use can have a significant impact on performance. For example, if we want to determine whether a given date occurs in the month of May, that would be easier to do using the first representation than the second. On the other hand, if we want to find the number of days between two dates, the relative difficulty would be reversed. Of course we can convert between the two representations, but the formula would be quite messy in this case and in general might entail significant computational complexity.

When forced to decide between significantly different representations, the programmer must make a judgment based on how the ADT is likely to be used. However, in this chapter we'll discover another option open to the programmer: allow multiple representations for the same abstract data type to coexist simultaneously. There are cases where this proves advantageous. We work through the details of such an example in Section 9.2.

More generally, it is not hard to imagine distinct data types that nonetheless share some commonality of form or purpose. For example, a library catalog will contain records of various kinds of items, say, books, movies, journals, and CDs. To a greater or lesser extent, all of these types of catalog items share some common attributes such as title, year of publication, and author (respectively, director, editor, and artist). Each kind of catalog item might have a separate interface (such as the interface we described for the movie ADT in Chapter 7). When combining the various types of catalog items into a common database, however, it would be greatly advantageous if they shared a common interface. We work through the details of this example in Section 9.3.

9.2　Multiple Representations

Scheme represents lists of values by explicitly consing together the elements in the list. Therefore there will be one **cons** pair per element in the list, which potentially requires a considerable amount of computer memory. Other lists can be represented more efficiently, however, especially if the lists have some regularity in them. For example, if we know that a list consists of increasing consecutive integers in a given range (for example, 3 through 100), rather than storing the list (3 4 5 ... 100), we could instead store the first and last elements of the range (3 and 100). Note that the standard list procedures can be easily computed in terms of the first and last elements. For example, the length of the example list is $100-3+1 = 98$ and its "`cdr`" is the increasing consecutive list with first element 4 and last element 100. In this section, we'll show how we can allow this new representation to coexist seamlessly with regular Scheme lists. To avoid confusion, we'll think of both representations as implementations of *sequences* and use the term *list* to mean Scheme lists. Similarly, we'll reserve the normal list notation, such as (1 2 3), for genuine Scheme lists, and when we want to write down the elements of a sequence, we will do so as $\langle 1, 2, 3 \rangle$, for example.

Let's step back a moment to consider how Scheme deals with lists. We remarked in Chapter 7 that the choice of `cons`, `car`, `cdr`, and `null?` as the basic constructor and selectors for lists ran counter to good data-abstraction practice because they don't sufficiently separate the use of lists from their representation. Even if we used more descriptive names like `make-list`, `head`, `tail`, and `empty-list?`, the underlying representation would be obscured but not fully hidden—`head` and `tail` are after all the two components of the underlying representation (the "two-part list viewpoint"). We will use more descriptive names like `head` and `tail` in our implementation of sequences, but these two procedures will not have the same "core" status as they do with Scheme lists.

In general, at least some of an ADT's interface procedures must have direct access to the underlying representation, whereas others might well be implemented in terms of this basic set without direct reference to the underlying representation. For example, we indicated in Chapter 7 how `cons`, `car`, `cdr`, and `null?` formed such an essential set by showing how other list procedures such as `length`, `list-ref`, and `map` could be written in terms of them. However, Scheme itself may have a more complex representation that allows the other interface procedures to be more efficiently implemented. For example, the representation might keep track of the list's length so that the length doesn't have to be recalculated each time by cdring down the list. To allow our implementation of sequences to provide all operations as efficiently as possible, there will be no designated minimal set of core procedures. Instead, we will view the ADT *sequence* as being specified by its entire interface. That interface is implemented separately in terms of each underlying representation.

So how do we implement sequences in a manner that allows these two (and perhaps other) representations to coexist in a transparent manner? To start out, let's suppose that we will have a variety of constructors (at least one for each representation) but will limit ourselves to the following selectors, which are modeled after the corresponding list procedures:

```
(head sequence)
  ; returns the first element of sequence, provided sequence is
  ; nonempty

(tail sequence)
  ; returns all but the first element of sequence as a
  ; sequence, provided sequence is nonempty

(empty-sequence? sequence)
  ; returns true if and only if sequence is empty

(sequence-length sequence)
  ; returns the length of sequence
```

We will implement sequences using a style of programming called *message-passing*, which exploits the fact that procedures are first-class data objects in Scheme. The data objects representing our sequences will not be passive: They will instead be procedures that respond appropriately to "messages," which are symbols representing the various interface operations.

For example, we could write a procedure `sequence-from-to` that returns an increasing sequence of consecutive integers in a given range as follows:

```
(define sequence-from-to
  (lambda (low high)
    (lambda (op)
      (cond ((equal? op 'empty-sequence?)
             (> low high))
            ((equal? op 'head)
             low)
            ((equal? op 'tail)
             (sequence-from-to (+ low 1)  high))
            ((equal? op 'sequence-length)
             (if (> low high) 0 (+ (- high low) 1)))
            (else (error "illegal sequence operation" op))))))
```

In this code, `op` is a symbol (the "message") that represents the desired operator. After evaluating the procedure above, we might then have the following interaction:

```
(define seq-1 (sequence-from-to 3 100))

(seq-1 'head)
3
```

```
(seq-1 'sequence-length)
```
98

```
(seq-1 'tail)
```
#<procedure>

```
((seq-1 'tail) 'head)
```
4

Although this style of programming will probably appear quite odd the first few times you see it, a number of programming languages (notably *Smalltalk* and other *object-oriented* languages) successfully exploit the message-passing approach. Nevertheless, we can layer the more traditional interface on top of message-passing by defining the interface procedures as follows:

```
(define head
  (lambda (sequence)
    (sequence 'head)))

(define tail
  (lambda (sequence)
    (sequence 'tail)))

(define empty-sequence?
  (lambda (sequence)
    (sequence 'empty-sequence?)))

(define sequence-length
  (lambda (sequence)
    (sequence 'sequence-length)))
```

Our earlier interaction would then contain the following more familiar code:

```
(head seq-1)
```
3

```
(sequence-length seq-1)
```
98

```
(head (tail seq-1))
```
4

▷ **Exercise 9.1**

As is evident from the the output given above, we would be better able to check our procedures if we could easily display the sequences we construct. Instead of writing an ADT display procedure for sequences, an easier approach is to write a procedure `sequence->list` that converts a sequence to the corresponding Scheme list, which can then be directly displayed. Write this procedure, accessing the sequence only through the interface procedures `head`, `tail`, and `empty-sequence?`.

▷ **Exercise 9.2**

The sequences we just described are restricted to consecutive increasing sequences of integers (more precisely, to increasing arithmetic sequences where consecutive elements differ by 1). We can easily imagine similar but more general sequences such as $\langle 6, 5, 4, 3, 2 \rangle$ or $\langle 5, 5.1, 5.2, 5.3, 5.4, 5.5 \rangle$—in other words, general *arithmetic sequences* of a given length, starting value, and increment (with decreasing sequences having a negative increment value).

a. Write a procedure `sequence-with-from-by` that takes as arguments a length, a starting value, and an increment and returns the corresponding arithmetic sequence. Thus, (`sequence-with-from-by 5 6 -1`) would return the first and (`sequence-with-from-by 6 5 .1`) would return the second of the two preceding sequences. Remember that sequences are represented as procedures, so your new sequence constructor will need to produce a procedural result.

b. The procedure `sequence-from-to` can now be rewritten as a simple call to `sequence-with-from-by`. The original `sequence-from-to` procedure made an empty sequence if its first argument was greater than its second, but you should make the new version so that you can get both increasing and decreasing sequences of consecutive integers. Thus, (`sequence-from-to 3 8`) should return $\langle 3, 4, 5, 6, 7, 8 \rangle$, whereas (`sequence-from-to 5 1`) should return $\langle 5, 4, 3, 2, 1 \rangle$.

c. Write a procedure `sequence-from-to-with` that takes a starting value, an ending value, and a length and returns the corresponding arithmetic sequence. For example, (`sequence-from-to-with 5 11 4`) should return $\langle 5, 7, 9, 11 \rangle$.

Having given constructors for arithmetic sequences, we can add sequences represented by traditional Scheme lists by writing a procedure `list->sequence` that returns the sequence corresponding to a given list:

```
(define list->sequence
  (lambda (lst)
    (lambda (op)
      (cond ((equal? op 'empty-sequence?)
             (null? lst))
            ((equal? op 'head)
             (car lst))
            ((equal? op 'tail)
             (list->sequence (cdr lst)))
            ((equal? op 'sequence-length)
             (length lst))
            (else (error "illegal sequence operation" op))))))))
```

In essence, we are off-loading each of the sequence procedures to the corresponding list procedure. Note that to the user, the various representations of sequences work together seamlessly and transparently:

```
(define seq-2 (sequence-with-from-by 6 5 -1))

(define seq-3 (list->sequence '(4 3 7 9)))

(head seq-2)
5

(head seq-3)
4
```

In a sense, each of the interface procedures triggers a representation-specific behavior that knows how to "do the right thing" for its representation.

> **Exercise 9.3**

Use `list->sequence` to write a procedure `empty-sequence` that takes no arguments and returns an empty sequence.

> **Exercise 9.4**

One disadvantage with the preceding version of `list->sequence` is that the Scheme procedure `length` normally has linear complexity in the list's length (unless the version of Scheme you use does something like the trick we will now describe that reduces `sequence-length` to constant complexity).

a. Modify `list->sequence` so that it has a `let` expression that computes the list's length once at sequence construction time and then uses that value when asked for the sequence's length.

b. The problem with the solution in part **a** is that the tail's length is computed each time you return the tail. Because the complexity of calculating a list's length is proportional to the length, if you do the equivalent of cdring down the sequence, the resulting complexity is quadratic in the list-sequence's length, certainly an undesirable consequence.

One solution to this problem is to write an auxiliary procedure `list-of-length->sequence` that is passed both a list and its length and returns the corresponding sequence. This procedure can efficiently compute its tail, and `list->sequence` can be reimplemented as a call to `list-of-length->sequence`. Carry out this strategy.

This solution seems to nicely accomplish our goal of seamlessly incorporating different underlying representations, but because we have only implemented the four selectors `head`, `tail`, `empty-sequence?`, and `sequence-length`, we have not really tested the limits of this approach. To do so, let's attempt to add the selector and constructors corresponding to `list-ref`, `cons`, `map`, and `append`.

The selector that corresponds to `list-ref` differs significantly from the other selectors we've seen so far. Each of those takes only one parameter (the sequence) and, as a result, always returns the same value for a given sequence. In contrast, `sequence-ref` will take two parameters, a sequence and an integer index, and the value returned will depend on both the sequence and the index. Consequently, the `cond` branch corresponding to sequence reference in `sequence-from-to` or `list->sequence` should be a *procedure* that takes an integer index n and returns the nth number in the sequence. To see how this works, here is the expanded version of `sequence-from-to` that includes a branch for sequence reference:

```
(define sequence-from-to
  (lambda (low high)
    (lambda (op)
      (cond ((equal? op 'empty-sequence?)
             (> low high))
            ((equal? op 'head)
             low)
            ((equal? op 'tail)
             (sequence-from-to (+ low 1)  high))
            ((equal? op 'sequence-length)
             (if (> low high) 0 (+ (- high low) 1)))
            ;;(continued)
```

```
((equal? op 'sequence-ref)
 (lambda (n)
   (if (and (<= 0 n) (<= n (- high low)))
       (+ low n)
       (error "sequence-from-to: index out of range"
              n)))))))))
```

We can then implement `sequence-ref` as follows:

```
(define sequence-ref
  (lambda (sequence n)
    ((sequence 'sequence-ref) n)))
```

▶ Exercise 9.5

Rewrite `list->sequence` so that it has a branch for sequence reference.

The remaining three operators we will add to sequences correspond to the list operators `cons`, `map`, and `append`; for simplicity, we will call these operators `sequence-cons`, `sequence-map`, and `sequence-append`. Note that all three of these operators are in fact constructors, because their agenda is to create a *new* sequence from the given data. Therefore, rather than being implemented as branches of the `cond`s of the other sequence constructors, we should simply write a new sequence constructor for each of these operators.

Consider `sequence-cons`, which is passed an element (to become the `head`) and an already-constructed sequence (to become the `tail`). Following is an implementation of `sequence-cons` that uses a `let` in order to calculate its length once and for all:

```
(define sequence-cons
  (lambda (head tail)
    (let ((new-length (+ 1 (sequence-length tail))))
      (lambda (op)
        (cond ((equal? op 'empty-sequence?)
               #f)
              ((equal? op 'head)
               head)
              ((equal? op 'tail)
               tail)
              ((equal? op 'sequence-length)
               new-length)
              ;;(continued)
```

```
          ((equal? op 'sequence-ref)
           (lambda (n)
             (if (= n 0)
                 head
                 (sequence-ref tail (- n 1)))))))
           (else (error "illegal sequence operation" op)))))))
```

Note that we need not worry what "kind" of sequence `tail` is, because we are assured that whichever representation `tail` uses, it knows how to appropriately calculate `sequence-length` and `sequence-ref`. In particular, we can be sure that computational efficiencies constructed into `tail` (for example, in `sequence-length`) are maintained in `sequence-cons`.

▶ **Exercise 9.6**

Write the sequence constructor `sequence-map`, that outwardly acts like the list procedure `map`. However unlike `map`, which applies the procedural argument to all the list elements, `sequence-map` should not apply the procedural argument at all yet. Instead, when an element of the resulting sequence (such as its head) is accessed, that is when the procedural argument should be applied.

We finally arrive at the sequence constructor `sequence-append`. Just as we've shown how `append` can be used to append together two lists, we'll write `sequence-append` such that it can append together any two sequences:

```
(define sequence-append
  (lambda (seq-1 seq-2)
    (cond ((empty-sequence? seq-1) seq-2)
          ((empty-sequence? seq-2) seq-1)
          (else
           (let ((seq-1-length (sequence-length seq-1))
                 (seq-2-length (sequence-length seq-2)))
             (lambda (op)
               (cond ((equal? op 'empty-sequence?)
                      #f)
                     ((equal? op 'head)
                      (head seq-1))
                     ((equal? op 'tail)
                      (sequence-append (tail seq-1) seq-2))
                     ((equal? op 'sequence-length)
                      (+ seq-1-length seq-2-length))
                     ;;(continued)
```

```
((equal? op 'sequence-ref)
 (lambda (n)
   (cond ((< n seq-1-length)
          (sequence-ref seq-1 n))
         (else
          (sequence-ref seq-2
                        (- n seq-1-length)))))))
(else (error "illegal sequence operation"
             op)))))))))
```

As with `sequence-cons`, the `let` expression is used primarily for efficiency. Note, however, that the length of the first subsequence is also used in `sequence-ref` to determine which subsequence to reference at what index.

9.3 Exploiting Commonality

Imagine that you have parlayed the movie query system from Chapter 7 into such an enormous success that it is currently being used by three major video store chains (not to mention the pirated versions being used by less honorable dealers). You have extended the natural language interface of your program (which you nicknamed Roger) to such an extent that many people think of Roger as a friend, and a few even consult him about their love life and other such befuddling aspects of their existence.

You were recently contacted by the owner of the Twilight Coffeehouse/Bookstore, who, in addition to selling books, also sells compact discs and rents obscure but interesting videos. She is very interested in extending Roger so that he could be consulted about books and CDs as well as videos. She already has two database programs, one for her books and and one for her CDs (surprisingly, done in Scheme as well), but she prefers the Roger interface. What she would like to do is to combine these two databases and your video database into one large database. A tantalizing idea indeed, but how could it be done?

Combining the three databases involves more than just gluing the lists of records together; you also need to provide procedures that operate on the individual records in this new database. But there's a catch here: Each of those individual records could represent a book, a video, or a CD. Books, videos, and CDs have many properties in common; for example, each has a title and a year released. Also, the book's author more or less corresponds to the movie's director and the CD's recording artist. On the other hand, some attributes do not have obvious correlates from one data type to another (e.g., the actors in a movie have no obvious analogue in books or CDs). Ideally, we would like to have an interface that is as uniform as possible across the three underlying data types.

But speaking of an interface seems premature. After all, we defined an interface as the set of procedures that operate on an ADT, and we do not yet have a single ADT. From the point of view of generic operations, we can get around this problem by hypothesizing an ADT *catalog-item* that captures the *commonality* among the three underlying ADTs. Any given catalog-item will in fact be a movie, book, or CD (or any other catalog-item-like type we might later add), so movies, for example, might be called a "class" of catalog items. (We are essentially introducing here a form of *class hierarchy* that is a core concept in *object-oriented programming*, which we will describe in detail in Chapter 14.)

In order to fully specify the interface for catalog items, let's write down the operations for each of the databases, grouping together those that are similar. Thus, we have three different operations for finding a title, three different operations for finding the year in which an object was made, and so on. The result is the table in Figure 9.1. The individual entries of the table are the procedures that operate on data of the given type. The columns of the table organize the operations by type, and the rows of the table group the analogous operations among the three types under a generic name indicating what is being done. In some cases (`title`, `year-made`, and `display-item`) there are obvious correlates for each of the three types. In other cases, such as `actors`, there are no obvious correlates, which leads to blanks in the table. In some cases, however, there are close analogues that we wrote in the table under more generic names (`creator` and `company`). Note that `company` applies to only two of the three data types because our movie database didn't contain information about movies' distributors. The names of the rows are precisely the generic operators we want to implement as the interface for catalog items.

We are left with the question of how we actually implement these generic operators. (Note that we are assuming that the three underlying types are already fully implemented, and our goal is to combine them in as transparent a manner as possible.) One method of accomplishing this would be to use the message-passing style of Section 9.2; we choose not to do it that way, mainly because we will take this opportunity to introduce another approach to genericity that involves tagging the

	movie	book	cd
title	movie-title	book-title	cd-title
year-made	movie-year-made	book-year-made	cd-year-made
display-item	display-movie	display-book	display-cd
creator	movie-director	book-author	cd-artist
company		book-publisher	cd-record-company
actors	movie-actors		

Figure 9.1　Operation table for Movies, Books, and CDs

data with its type. In addition to allowing us to explore a new technique, this latter approach is slightly more suited to the integration of already-existing types than message-passing. We will work through two variants of this type-tagging approach.

Generic Operations through Symbolic Type Tags

Our first variant of the type-tagging approach involves attaching a symbolic tag, or label, to each piece of data that indicates whether the datum is a book, video, or CD. Then, when we write a generic procedure, we take a tagged datum, look at its tag, and use that to determine which operation to apply.

Tagging data is fairly simple. We need to create an ADT that binds together each datum with its tag. For example, we can do the following:

```
(define tagged-datum
  (lambda (type value)
    (cons type value)))

(define type car)

(define contents cdr)
```

The type argument could in general be various things; for now it will be a symbol that "names" the given type.

▶ Exercise 9.7

Write a procedure `list->tagged-list` that takes a list of untagged elements and a type and returns the corresponding list where each element has been tagged by the given type tag. Thus, if `movies` is a list of movie records, you can define a (symbolically) tagged list of movie records by evaluating:

```
(define tagged-movies
  (list->tagged-list movies 'movie))
```

If our three databases are lists called `movies`, `books`, and `cds`, then we could create the combined database as follows:

```
(define database
  (append (list->tagged-list movies 'movie)
          (list->tagged-list books  'book)
          (list->tagged-list cds    'cd)))
```

How can we implement the generic operations? Probably the most obvious way is to do so one operation at a time. Viewed in terms of the table in Figure 9.1, we are filling out the table row by row. Assume that the data has been tagged as in Exercise 9.7, with each element tagged with one of the symbols movie, book, or cd. We can then easily test the type of a given item by using the following predicates:

```
(define movie?
  (lambda (x)
    (equal? (type x) 'movie)))
```

```
(define book?
  (lambda (x)
    (equal? (type x) 'book)))
```

```
(define cd?
  (lambda (x)
    (equal? (type x) 'cd)))
```

Using these predicates, the generic operations become easy to write. For example, here is title:

```
(define title
  (lambda (x)
    (cond ((movie? x) (movie-title (contents x)))
          ((book? x)  (book-title (contents x)))
          ((cd? x)    (cd-title (contents x)))
          (else (error "unknown object in title"  x)))))
```

Exercise 9.8

In the course of integrating databases, some of the operations that seem analogous between types might have some annoying differences. For example, suppose that the movie directors and actors have their names stored as lists with the family names last, whereas for books and CDs the authors' and artists' names are stored with family names first. Suppose that you decide for consistency's sake and ease of display to have all of the generic procedures return the names with the family name last.

a. Write a procedure family-name-last that takes a name (as a list of symbols) with family name first and returns the corresponding list with family name last.

b. Use family-name-last to write a generic operation creator that returns the name with the family name last in all cases.

Implementing generic operations becomes somewhat more delicate when an operation doesn't apply across the three types, say, for example, `actors`. One possibility would be to signal an error when this occurs. For example, we could handle the operation `actors` by using `error`:

```
(define actors
  (lambda (x)
    (cond ((movie? x) (movie-actors (contents x)))
          (else (error "Cannot find the actors of the given type"
                    (type x))))))
```

If we choose this approach, we must modify the query system appropriately. For example, suppose Roger were asked the following question:

```
(what films was randy quaid in)
```

Then the action matching this pattern must not apply the operation `actors` to all items in the database because otherwise it will signal an error. This means that in this case the database must first be filtered by the predicate `movie?`. In general, patterns that clearly indicate the type of the desired records should first filter the database by the type's predicate.

Exercise 9.9

An alternative approach to this problem is to return a testable value, for example, the empty list, if there is no procedure for the given operation and type. Discuss this approach, especially as it pertains to Roger.

Exercise 9.10

Because we have posed our problem in terms of integrating databases, we should not assume that the result will be the last word in entertainment databases. After all, we might add a new type (say magazines), a new piece of information (perhaps the cost for rental or purchase), or some other increased functionality. Let's consider how difficult these tasks would be using the current approach to generic operations.

a. Discuss what you would need to do to integrate a magazine database into the current one consisting of movies, books, and CDs. What changes would you have to make to the generic operations you have already written?

b. Discuss what you would need to do to add a new generic operation, for example, the cost for rental or purchase of the given item.

c. Discuss what you would need to do to add a single entry to the operation table, for example, adding a way of finding a movie's distributor to the "company" row of the table.

Operation Tables as Type Tags

In the variant of the type-tagging approach described above, we symbolically tagged the data as being of a given type and wrote the generic operations using a `cond` that branched on the allowable types for the operation. Viewed in terms of the operation table of Figure 9.1, this approach fills the table out row by row, which is to say operation by operation. One could argue that there would be advantages to an approach that more directly mirrors how the individual databases were originally constructed, namely, type by type. If we had used message-passing as suggested at the beginning of this section, we would have had a separate constructor for each underlying type, precisely this desired approach. But there would also be a great deal of redundancy in the message-passing implementation: After all, each of the movies contains a variant of the same general method for responding to the operations; individual movies only differ in their "content" data. You might well argue that this is precisely the point, and you would be correct. But somehow or other, these general methods of responding seem more appropriately associated with the type than with each of the separate data objects.

Is there some way to combine the two approaches? One way to do this would be to tag the data as in the preceding subsection but let the type tags provide the general procedures for performing the operations instead of merely being symbolic type names. In other words, the tags would correspond to the columns of the operation table. In effect, each type would be a one-dimensional table that stores the particular procedure to be used for each of the various generic operations.

Let's implement a *type* ADT, which contains the name of the type as well as the operation table, because it will prove useful to know the name of the type when reporting errors:

```
(define make-type
  (lambda (name operation-table)
    (cons name operation-table)))

(define type-name car)

(define type-operation-table cdr)
```

We implement one-dimensional tables (the columns of the full operation table) as an abstract data type with a constructor `make-table` that will make a table from a list of the symbols denoting the operations and a list of the corresponding procedures to be used for those operations on the given type. For example, we would define the type `movie` as

```
(define movie
  (make-type 'movie
             (make-table
              '(title year-made director actors creator display-item)
              (list movie-title movie-year-made movie-director
                    movie-actors movie-director display-movie))))
```

Having defined the types `book` and `cd` as well, we could then define our tagged database as follows:

```
(define database
  (append (list->tagged-list movies movie)
          (list->tagged-list books  book)
          (list->tagged-list cds    cd)))
```

Notice that the tags are no longer simply symbols but are instead type objects that also contain the column of the operation table corresponding to the type of the tagged data item.

At this point each data object includes not only its particular component values but also has access to the column of the operation table that tells how to do the various operations. What we need now is a procedure, which we will call `operate`, that when given the name of an operation and a tagged data value, looks up the appropriate procedure in the data value's operation table and applies that procedure to the contents of the (tagged) data value. Thus we could use `operate` to define the generic operation `title` as follows:

```
(define title
  (lambda (tagged-datum)
    (operate 'title tagged-datum)))
```

How do we define `operate`? Clearly we must look up the operation name in the operation table and apply the corresponding procedure (if it exists) to the contents of the given data object. If no such procedure is found for the given operation, an error should be reported. This process is complicated. It would probably be best to have `operate` spin the table-searching tasks off onto another more general table-lookup procedure, to which it passes the necessary arguments. We will define a procedure `table-find`, which is passed the operation table, the name of the operation, a procedure that describes what to do if the operation is found in the given table,

and a procedure that describes what to do if it is not found. Thus, we would call
`table-find` as follows:

```
(define operate
  (lambda (operation-name value)
    (table-find (type-operation-table (type value))
                operation-name
                (lambda (procedure) ; use this if found
                  (procedure (contents value)))
                (lambda ()            ; use this if not found
                  (error "No way of doing operation on type"
                         operation-name
                         (type-name (type value)))))))
```

Note that the procedure that `operate` supplies to `table-find` for use if the table
lookup is successful takes one argument, namely, the procedure that was found in
the table. In contrast, the procedure that `operate` supplies to `table-find` for the
not-found case takes no arguments; it simply reports the error that occurred.

At this point, we need to define the table ADT, with its `make-table` and
`table-find` operations. There are many plausible representations for tables; here,
we'll opt for simplicity and just cons together into a pair the list of keys and the list
of values:

```
(define make-table
  (lambda (keys values)
    (cons keys values)))
```

The procedure `table-find` simply cdrs down the two lists, looking in the list of
keys for the desired key, (i.e., the operation name):

```
(define table-find
  (lambda (table key what-if-found what-if-not)
    (define loop
      (lambda (keys values)
        (cond ((null? keys) (what-if-not))
              ((equal? key (car keys))
               (what-if-found (car values)))
              (else
               (loop (cdr keys) (cdr values))))))
    (loop (car table) (cdr table))))
```

> **Exercise 9.11**

How would you implement the type predicates such as `movie?` using this representation with type tags containing operation tables?

> **Exercise 9.12**

Discuss the questions from Exercise 9.10 in terms of the operation-table type-tag representation.

> **Exercise 9.13**

Through this entire section, we've been glossing over a minor difficulty, namely, that many books are coauthored. Thus, it would be more likely that the book database actually supported a `book-authors` operation, which returns a list of authors, rather than the `book-author` operation we've been presuming. The primary difficulty this would cause is that we'd wind up with a `creator` generic operation that returns a single director for a movie, but a list of authors for a book. If we were processing a query like (`what do you have by John Doe`), we would have to in some cases test for equality between (`John Doe`) and the creator and in other cases test for membership of (`John Doe`) in the creator list.

a. How would you arrange, at database integration time, for there to be a `creators` generic operation that returned a list of creators for any type of object, even a movie? Assume that the movie database is unchanged, so there is still just a singular director, whereas the book database is now presumed to have the `book-authors` operation. (Which assumption seems more plausible for CDs?)

b. An alternative would be to change the movie database to directly support a list of directors, rather than a single director, for each movie. What are the relative advantages and disadvantages of the two approaches?

In the next section you'll have an opportunity to apply the technology of generic operations; we also use it as a tool while covering other topics in the next two chapters. We'll return to our consideration of generic operations as a topic of study in its own right in Chapter 14, which discusses object-oriented programming. The implementation technique we use there is a variant of the "operation tables as type tags" theme, with techniques we'll encounter in the meantime used to improve the efficiency of the table lookup.

9.4　An Application: Computer Graphics

In this section, we'll look inside graphics operations like those used in Chapters 1 through 4. We'll show how to use the message-passing technique to implement those graphics operations in terms of lower-level ones. In fact, we'll serve up a double helping of generic operations because there are two different abstract data types we'll use:

- Drawing media, on which we can perform the basic graphics operations of drawing lines and filled triangles

- Images, which can be arbitrarily complex assemblies so long as they know how to draw themselves onto a medium

First, let's consider why we want to treat images as an abstract data type with generic operations that can be used across multiple implementations. We have lots of different kinds of images from simple ones such as lines and filled triangles to more complex images such as pinwheeled quilts and c-curve fractals. Nonetheless, there are certain operations we want to perform on any image, without needing to know what kind of image it is. For example, we should be able to find the width and height of any image. If nothing else, this information is needed for error checking when we perform stacking and overlaying operations. (Only images of the same width can be stacked, and only images of the same width and height can be overlaid.) We also want to be able to draw an image onto a drawing medium in a single simple operation, without concerning ourselves with what conglomeration of lines and triangles may need to be drawn.

The situation with drawing media is a bit more interesting. First, there can be multiple forms of graphics output. For example, we can draw onto an on-screen window, or we can "draw" by writing to a file stored in some graphics file format, for later use. Thus we can foresee having at least two kinds of drawing media: windows and files. We can perform the same basic operations of drawing lines and filled triangles in either case but with different results depending on the kind of medium we are drawing on. Because we'll use generic operations to uniformly access any medium, we'll be able to construct complex images that know how to "draw themselves" on any medium, without the images needing to be aware of the different kinds of media. Additionally, we will show how we can layer a new "virtual medium" on top of an existing medium. We do this layering to make it easy to perform a transformation, such as turning an image.

Before we begin looking closely at images and drawing media, we need to take care of two details. First, both images and drawing media use a two-dimensional coordinate system. For example, if we wanted to create an image with a line, we would specify the two coordinates for each of the line's two endpoints. Now that we've learned how to make compound data, we can make a point ADT. We define the constructor and selectors for points as follows:

```
(define make-point cons)
```

```
(define x-coord car)
```

```
(define y-coord cdr)
```

We'll use the convention that *x* coordinates increase from left to right and *y* coordinates increase from bottom to top. This is mathematically conventional but not in agreement with all computer systems' conventions. On some computer systems, the *y* coordinates in a window start with 0 at the top and increase as you go down the screen. On such a system, the low-level type of drawing medium for drawing on windows will need to take care of reversing the *y* coordinates.

We will, however, use two different ranges of coordinate values. One range is for images and so will be used for the arguments the user provides to the constructors of fundamental images, `make-line` and `make-filled-triangle`. For convenience and consistency with earlier chapters, these two constructors expect points with coordinates in the range from −1 to 1.

Our other range of coordinates will be used for doing the actual drawing on drawing media. For this drawing, we'll use coordinates that range from 0 up to the width or height of the medium. What units do we use to measure the width and height? We do not specify the unit of measure, but one reasonable unit for images displayed on a computer screen would be the size of a *pixel*, that is, one of the little dots that the computer can individually light up. For example, a 100×200 medium might be drawing to a window of those dimensions so that valid *x* coordinates for drawing on the medium range from 0 at the far left to 100 at the far right, whereas the valid *y* coordinates range from 0 at the bottom to 200 at the top. We chose this coordinate system, with the origin in the lower left-hand corner rather than in the center, because it will simplify the calculations needed to stack images.

The second detail we need to take care of is providing an interface that hides our decision to use the message-passing style. That is, each image or drawing medium will be represented as a procedure that can perform the various operations when passed an appropriate symbolic message indicating the desired operation. However, our users will be thinking that various operations are performed on the images. Thus, we'll define the following interface procedures:

```
;; Interface to image operations
```

```
(define width
  (lambda (image)
    (image 'width)))
```

```
(define height
  (lambda (image)
    (image 'height)))

(define draw-on
  (lambda (image medium)
    ((image 'draw-on) medium)))

;; Interface to drawing medium operations

(define draw-line-on
  (lambda (point0 point1 medium)
    ((medium 'draw-line) point0 point1)))

(define draw-filled-triangle-on
  (lambda (point0 point1 point2 medium)
    ((medium 'draw-filled-triangle) point0 point1 point2)))
```

At this point, we know what operations we can invoke on an image or a medium, even though we don't have any images or media on which to invoke those operations. Conversely, we know what operations any image or medium we construct will need to support. By putting these two kinds of information together, we can begin to write some constructors. We'll start with the constructors for two fundamental images, `make-line` and `make-filled-triangle`. (We've chosen to call these procedures `make-line` and `make-filled-triangle`, rather than `line` and `filled-triangle`, to help you distinguish the procedures we're writing in this section from the predefined ones we used in the earlier chapters. We'll similarly avoid reusing other names.) These images support the `draw-on` operation for drawing themselves on a medium by using the `draw-line-on` and `draw-filled-triangle-on` interface operations specified above for media.

We'll need to make a rather arbitrary choice of size for these two fundamental images. (Other images, formed by stacking, turning, etc., will have sizes that derive from this basic image size.) The best choice depends on where the medium is doing its drawing; for example, if the medium is drawing on your computer screen, the best choice depends on such issues as the size of your computer's screen. However, the following value is probably in a plausible range:

```
(define basic-image-size 100)
```

Recall that `make-line` and `make-filled-triangle` need to convert from the user's coordinate range of -1 to 1 into the drawing medium's coordinate range, which will

be from 0 to `basic-image-size`. We can convert a point from one range to the
other using the following procedure:

```
(define transform-point ; from -1 to 1 into 0 to basic-image-size
  (lambda (point)
    (define transform-coord
      (lambda (coord)
        (* (/ (+ coord 1) 2)  ; fraction of the way to top or right
           basic-image-size)))
    (make-point (transform-coord (x-coord point))
                (transform-coord (y-coord point)))))
```

With these preliminaries in place, we can write our first image constructor:

```
(define make-line
  (lambda (point0 point1)
    (lambda (op)
      (cond
        ((equal? op 'width) basic-image-size)
        ((equal? op 'height) basic-image-size)
        ((equal? op 'draw-on)
         (lambda (medium)
           (draw-line-on (transform-point point0)
                         (transform-point point1)
                         medium)))
        (else (error "unknown operation on line" op))))))
```

As you can see, a line responds to queries about its width and height by reporting
our `basic-image-size`, and it draws itself on a medium in the obvious way, by
drawing a single line on that medium. So far, the image hasn't added any interesting
functionality to that provided by the drawing medium itself. But remember, images
can be more complex. For example, we could have an image that was a c-curve
fractal of level 10. When we invoke its **draw-on** operation to draw it on a medium,
1024 **draw-line-on** operations will be performed on the medium for us.

So that you can test the preceding line constructor, we need to give you some
way of making a drawing medium that actually displays an image on your screen.
Later in this section we'll show how drawing media can be constructed, by working
through the example of a type of drawing medium that writes a particular graphics
file format. Meanwhile, you can use a procedure called **show** that's provided on
the web site for this book. We provide specific versions of **show** for various different
computer systems. You apply **show** to an image that needs to be shown, as in the call

```
(show (make-line (make-point 0 0) (make-point 1 1)))
```

The show procedure is more than just a drawing medium, however. First, show takes care of some system-dependent matters, such as opening a window that is the same size as the image. Then show constructs a drawing medium for drawing on that window (in some system-dependent way) and passes it to the image's draw-on procedure. When the drawing is all done, show takes care of any system-dependent wrap-up that needs to be done, such as notifying the system that the window is complete.

In the earlier chapters, we assumed that images constructed using the predefined image procedures were automatically shown, without needing to explicitly use a procedure such as show. The way this is implemented is that the Scheme system itself applies show when the value of a computation is an image, just as when the value is a number, it displays the digits representing the number. Thus show (or an analogue) was really at work behind the scenes. In this chapter we make it explicit.

We mentioned above that the images can be much more complex, like that 1024-line level-10 c-curve. However, before we move on to how these complex images are constructed, one other image type directly reflects the abilities of drawing media.

> ### Exercise 9.14

Write the make-filled-triangle image constructor. It should take three points as arguments, each with coordinates in the −1 to 1 range. It should produce an image with the basic-image-size as its width and height, drawn on a medium as a filled triangle.

Now we are ready to consider how to build more complex images. We'll start with overlaying two images, because that is all we need to construct our c-curve example. Such an image should be able to report its height or width and should be able to draw itself. The size issue is fairly simple to deal with, but how do we get an overlaid image to draw itself? The answer is to use the fact that an overlaid image is a composite of two other images. When the overlaid image is asked to draw itself on a medium, it simply passes the buck to its two constituent images by asking them to draw themselves on that medium. This leads to the following constructor:

```
(define make-overlaid-image
  (lambda (image1 image2)
    (if (not (and (= (width image1) (width image2))
                  (= (height image1) (height image2))))
        (error "can't overlay images of different sizes")
        (lambda (op)
          (cond ((equal? op 'width) (width image1))
                ((equal? op 'height) (height image1))
                ;;(continued)
```

```
((equal? op 'draw-on)
 (lambda (medium)
   (draw-on image1 medium)
   (draw-on image2 medium)))
(else
 (error "unknown operation on overlaid image"
        op)))))))
```

Notice that this is both a producer and a consumer of the interface we specified for images. Because what it produces is an image, the result needs to provide the width, height, and draw-on operations. Because that composite image is built from two preexisting images, it can count on image1 and image2 to be able to report their own width and height and to draw themselves appropriately. That way we don't need to care what sort of images are being overlaid.

You can try out the code thus far by using the c-curve procedure, rewritten in terms of our new constructors:

```
(define c-curve
  (lambda (x0 y0 x1 y1 level)
    (if (= level 0)
        (make-line (make-point x0 y0) (make-point x1 y1))
        (let ((xmid (/ (+ x0 x1) 2))
              (ymid (/ (+ y0 y1) 2))
              (dx (- x1 x0))
              (dy (- y1 y0)))
          (let ((xa (- xmid (/ dy 2)))
                (ya (+ ymid (/ dx 2))))
            (make-overlaid-image
             (c-curve x0 y0 xa ya (- level 1))
             (c-curve xa ya x1 y1 (- level 1)))))))))
```

With this definition in place, and using the show procedure we mentioned earlier to provide an appropriate on-screen drawing medium, you could do (show (c-curve 0 -1/2 0 1/2 8)) to see a level-8 c-curve.

Let's now consider the example of turning an image a quarter turn to the right, as we did in designing quilt covers. We can use the ability to have different kinds of drawing media to great advantage here. When we want a turned image to draw itself on a particular medium, the turned image will create a new "virtual" medium layered on top of the given medium. This new medium takes care of doing the turning. In other words, when a turned image is asked to draw itself onto a base medium, it will pass the buck to the original image by asking it to draw itself on the virtual medium. The original image then asks the virtual medium to draw some lines and/or triangles. The virtual medium responds to each of these requests by asking the base medium to draw a rotated version of the requested line or triangle.

How does the virtual medium turn the lines and triangles? The key to this turning is that we really only need to move the endpoints of the lines or the vertices of the triangle. A point that is near the left end of the medium's top edge will need to transformed to a point near the top of the right-hand edge of the base medium, and a point at the center of the left edge will be transformed to a point at the center top. To turn a line connecting these two points, the virtual medium simply transforms each of the points and then asks the base medium to draw a line connecting the two transformed points.

When we write the constructor for this virtual medium, we'll assume that we have a **transform** procedure that can take care of transforming one point. That is, if we apply **transform** to the top center point, we get the center point of the right edge back. Given this point transformer, we can build the transformed medium using the following constructor:

```
(define make-transformed-medium
  (lambda (transform base-medium)
    (lambda (op)
      (cond
        ((equal? op 'draw-line)
         (lambda (point0 point1)
           (draw-line-on (transform point0) (transform point1)
                         base-medium)))
        ((equal? op 'draw-filled-triangle)
         (lambda (point0 point1 point2)
           (draw-filled-triangle-on (transform point0)
                                    (transform point1)
                                    (transform point2)
                                    base-medium)))
        (else
         (error "unknown operation on transformed medium"
                op))))))
```

Just as **make-overlaid-image** was both a producer and a consumer of the image interface, so too is **make-transformed-medium** both a producer and a consumer of the drawing medium interface. It constructs the new medium as a "wrapper" around the old medium—all operations on the new medium are translated into operations on the old medium.

For the specific problem of turning an image a quarter turn to the right, consider the quarter turn illustrated in Figure 9.2. Clearly the width and height are interchanged in the turned image, and the *x* coordinate of a transformed point is the

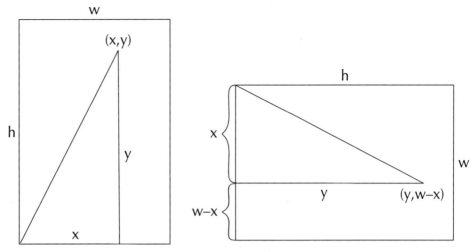

Figure 9.2 Illustration of what happens to the width, height, and a point (x, y) when an image is turned. The turned point has coordinates $(y, w - x)$ where w is the width of the base image.

original point's y coordinate. (In our earlier example, this explains why a point on the top edge maps into a point on the right-hand edge.) Furthermore, we can obtain the transformed point's y coordinate by subtracting the original point's x coordinate from the new height, which is the old width. This leads to the following code:

```
(define make-turned-image   ; quarter turn to the right
  (lambda (base-image)
    (define turn-point
      (lambda (point)
        ;; y becomes x, and the old width minus x becomes y
        (make-point (y-coord point)
                    (- (width base-image) (x-coord point)))))
    (lambda (op)
      (cond
        ((equal? op 'width) (height base-image))
        ((equal? op 'height) (width base-image))
        ((equal? op 'draw-on)
         (lambda (medium)
           (draw-on base-image
                    (make-transformed-medium turn-point medium))))
        (else (error "unknown operation on turned image" op))))))
```

You could test this out using lines, but if you've written `make-filled-triangle`, you can also try quarter turns out in their familiar context of quilting basic blocks, such as the two below:

```
(define test-bb
  (make-filled-triangle (make-point 0 1)
                        (make-point 0 -1)
                        (make-point 1 -1)))

(define nova-bb
  (make-overlaid-image
   (make-filled-triangle (make-point 0 1)
                         (make-point 0 0)
                         (make-point -1/2 0))
   (make-filled-triangle (make-point 0 0)
                         (make-point 0 1/2)
                         (make-point 1 0))))
```

Of course, we don't have to limit ourselves to just explicating the kind of image operations we used in earlier chapters. We can also add some new operations to our repertory.

Exercise 9.15

Write a `make-mirrored-image` constructor. It should take a single image as an argument, like `make-turned-image` does. The image it produces should be the same size as the original but should be flipped around the vertical axis so that what was on the left of the original image is on the right of the mirrored image, and vice versa, as though the original image had been viewed in a mirror.

Exercise 9.16

Write a `make-scaled-image` constructor. It should take a real number and an image as its arguments. The image it makes should be a magnified or shrunken version of the original image, under the control of the numeric scale argument. For example, (`make-scaled-image 2 test-bb`) should make an image twice a big as `test-bb`, whereas (`make-scaled-image 1/4 test-bb`) should make one one-quarter as big as `test-bb`. (Of course, you can scale other images, like c-curves, as well.) Don't just scale the image's width and height; you also need to arrange for the scaling when the image is drawn.

To get full quilt covers, we also still need a way of stacking one image on top of another, making a new image with the combined heights. This is rather similar to `make-overlaid-image`, except that the top image will need to be fooled into drawing higher up on the drawing medium than it normally would so that its drawing goes above that of the bottom image. This can be achieved by giving it a transformed medium to draw on. It will draw on that transformed medium using *y* coordinates that start at 0, but the transformed medium will translate that into drawing commands on the base medium that have larger *y* coordinate values.

Exercise 9.17

Using this approach, write a `make-stacked-image` constructor that takes the top and bottom images as its arguments. You should initially test out your constructor by doing such simple evaluations as (`make-stacked-image test-bb nova-bb`). Once it seems to work, you can make fancier quilt patterns as described below.

Using your `make-stacked-image` procedure along with our earlier `make-turned-image` procedure, the `pinwheel` procedure can be rewritten as follows:

```
(define pinwheel
  (lambda (image)
    (let ((turned (make-turned-image image)))
      (let ((half (make-turned-image (make-stacked-image turned
                                                         image))))
        (make-stacked-image half
                            (make-turned-image
                             (make-turned-image half)))))))
```

With this in hand, you can make quilt covers by doing evaluations such as (`show (pinwheel (pinwheel nova-bb))`). For large covers, you probably will want to show scaled-down versions made using `make-scaled-image`.

You may be feeling a bit ripped off because so far we haven't shown how a "real" drawing medium can be constructed, that is, one that doesn't just pass the buck in some transformed way to an underlying base medium. If you look on the web site for this book, you can find several system-dependent versions of the `show` procedure, each of which constructs some particular kind of on-screen drawing medium. At this point, we'll take a look at constructing a drawing medium that "draws" by writing to a file. This further highlights the benefits of generic operations. All of the image constructors we defined above are just as good for producing a graphical file as they are for drawing on the screen. That's because each of them draws on an arbitrary drawing medium, using the specified interface that all drawing media share.

The file format we'll write is one known as *Encapsulated PostScript*, or *EPS*. It is a popular format, which on many systems you'll be able to preview on-screen or include as illustrations in documents. (For example, you could write a c-curve or quilt pattern to an EPS file and then include that EPS file in a word-processed report. We used this technique to make illustrations for this book.) In addition to the EPS format's popularity and versatility, it has the advantage of being a relatively straightforward textual format. For example, to draw a line from $(0, 0)$ to $(100, 100)$, we would put the following into the EPS file:

```
0 0 moveto 100 100 lineto stroke
```

Similarly, to draw a filled triangle with vertices $(0, 0)$, $(100, 0)$, and $(50, 100)$, we would put the following line into the file:

```
0 0 moveto 100 0 lineto 50 100 lineto closepath fill
```

Although this notation is likely to be unfamiliar to you, at least it is readable, unlike some other graphics file formats.

By using the `display` and `newline` procedures, we could write the EPS output to your computer's screen for you to see. That is, you'd wind up seeing a bunch of textual descriptions of graphical objects, like the examples given above. However, doing so would not be very useful. Instead, we'll write the EPS output into a file stored on your computer, ready for you to view using a previewer program or to incorporate into a word-processed document. To write this output to a file, we'll use a predefined Scheme procedure called `with-output-to-file`. It reroutes the output produced by procedures like `display` and `newline` so that they go into the file instead of to your screen. For example,

```
(with-output-to-file "foo"
  (lambda ()
    (display "hello, world")
    (newline)))
```

would create a one-line file called **foo** containing the message *hello, world*.

We'll write a procedure called **image->eps** that writes an EPS version of a given image into a file with a given filename. Just like **show**, this procedure will take care of some start-up details before asking the image to draw itself. The procedure first writes a bit of header information to the file, including the information about how big the image is. Then, **image->eps** asks the image to draw itself on a specially constructed drawing medium called **eps-medium** that outputs the EPS commands for drawing the lines or filled triangles.

```
(define image->eps
  (lambda (image filename)
    (with-output-to-file filename
      (lambda ()
        (display "%!PS-Adobe-3.0 EPSF-3.0")
```

```
(newline)
(display "%%BoundingBox: 0 0 ")
;; We need to make sure the bounding box is expressed
;; using only exact integers, as required by PostScript.
;; Therefore we process the width and height of the
;; image using round and then inexact->exact. The
;; round procedure would convert 10.8 into the inexact
;; integer 11., which the inexact->exact then converts
;; to the exact integer 11
(display (inexact->exact (round (width image))))
(display " ")
(display (inexact->exact (round (height image))))
(newline)
;; Now do the drawing
(draw-on image eps-medium)))))
```

How does `eps-medium` work? It simply needs to draw lines and filled triangles in the EPS manner illustrated earlier, which leads to the following definition:

```
(define eps-medium
  (lambda (op)
    (cond ((equal? op 'draw-line)
           (lambda (point0 point1)
             (display-eps-point point0)
             (display "moveto")
             (display-eps-point point1)
             (display "lineto stroke")
             (newline)))
          ((equal? op 'draw-filled-triangle)
           (lambda (point0 point1 point2)
             (display-eps-point point0)
             (display "moveto")
             (display-eps-point point1)
             (display "lineto")
             (display-eps-point point2)
             (display "lineto closepath fill")
             (newline)))
          (else
           (error "unknown operation on EPS medium"
                  op)))))
```

The `display-eps-point` procedure this uses simply writes out the *x* and *y* coordinates in a format suitable for PostScript. In particular, PostScript can't handle a fraction written with a slash, such as 1/2. Therefore, we use the predefined procedure `exact->inexact` to convert numbers that aren't integers into their "inexact" form, which gets displayed as .5 (for example) rather than 1/2. (The procedure `exact->inexact` returns unchanged any number that is already inexact.)

```
(define display-eps-point
  (lambda (point)
    (define display-coord
      (lambda (coord)
        (if (integer? coord)
            (display coord)
            (display (exact->inexact coord)))))
    (display " ")
    (display-coord (x-coord point))
    (display " ")
    (display-coord (y-coord point))
    (display " ")))
```

Exercise 9.18

Write a procedure `summarize-image` that takes an image as its argument and uses `display` to give you a summary of that image as follows. For each line segment the image contains, a letter l should be displayed, and for each filled triangle, a letter t. For example, if you evaluate (`summarize-image (c-curve 0 -1/2 0 1/2 3)`), you should see eight l's because the level-3 c-curve is constituted out of eight line segments.

Review Problems

Exercise 9.19

You are hired to supervise a team of programmers working on a computerized geometry system. It is necessary to manipulate various geometric figures in standard ways. As project manager, you have to select an organizational strategy that will allow all different shapes of geometric figures to be be accessed using generic selectors for such information as the *x* and *y* coordinates of the figure and the area.

State which strategy you have chosen and briefly justify your choice (e.g., use one to three sentences). For your programmers' benefit, illustrate how your choice would be used to implement constructors `make-square` and `make-circle` and generic selectors `center-x`, `center-y`, and `area`. The two constructors each take three arguments; in both cases, the first two are the x and y coordinates of the center of the figure. The third argument specifies the length of the side for a square and the radius for a circle. The selectors should be able to take either a square or a circle as their argument and return the appropriate numerical value.

Exercise 9.20

Global Amalgamations Corp. has just acquired yet another smaller company and is busily integrating the data processing operations of the acquired company with that of the parent corporation. Luckily, both companies are using Scheme, and both have set up their operations to tolerate multiple representations. Unfortunately, one company uses operation tables as type tags, and the other uses procedural representations (i.e., message passing). Thus, not only are multiple representations now co-existing, but some of them are type-tagged data and others are message-passing procedures. You have been called in as a consultant to untangle this situation.

What is the minimum that needs to be done to make the two kinds of representation happily coexist? Illustrate your suggestion concretely using Scheme as appropriate. You may want to know that there is a built-in predicate `pair?` that tests whether its argument is a pair, and a similar one, `procedure?`, that tests whether its argument is a procedure.

Exercise 9.21

One way we can represent a set is as a predicate (i.e., a procedure that returns true or false). The idea is that to test whether a particular item is in the set, we pass it to the procedure, which provides the answer. For example, using this representation, the built-in procedure `number?` could be used to represent the (infinite) set of all numbers.

a. Implement `element-of-set?` for this representation. It takes two arguments, an element and a set, and returns true or false depending on whether the element is in the set or not.

b. Implement `add-to-set` for this representation. It takes two arguments, an element and a set, and returns a new set that contains the specified element as well as everything the specified set contained. *Hint: Remember that a set is represented as a procedure.*

c. Implement `union-set` for this representation. It takes two arguments—two sets— and returns a new set that contains anything that either of the provided sets contains.

d. Write a paragraph explaining why you think the authors included this exercise in this chapter rather than elsewhere in the book.

▷ **Exercise 9.22**

Assume that `infinity` has been defined as a special number that is greater than all normal (finite) numbers and that when added to any finite number or to itself, it yields itself. (In some Scheme systems you can define it as follows: `(define infinity (/ 1.0 0.0))`.) Now there is no reason why sequences need to be of finite length. Write a constructor for some interesting kind of infinite sequence.

▷ **Exercise 9.23**

Show how the movie, book, and CD databases could be combined using message-passing instead of type-tagging.

Chapter Inventory

Vocabulary

abstract mental model	commonality
generic operation	class hierarchy
interface	object-oriented programming
multiple representations	type tag
message-passing	operation table
Smalltalk	pixel
object-oriented language	Encapsulated PostScript (EPS)
arithmetic sequence	

Abstract Data Types

date	table
sequence	drawing medium
catalog-item	image
tagged datum	point
type	

New Predefined Scheme Names

```
with-output-to-file
pair?
procedure?
```

Scheme Names Defined in This Chapter

`head`	`sequence-length`
`tail`	`sequence-from-to`
`empty-sequence?`	`sequence->list`

sequence-with-from-by
sequence-from-to-with
list->sequence
empty-sequence
list-of-length->sequence
sequence-ref
sequence-cons
sequence-map
sequence-append
title
year-made
display-item
creator
company
actors
tagged-datum
type
contents
list->tagged-list
tagged-movies
database
movie?
book?
cd?
family-name-last
make-type
type-name
type-operation-table
make-table
movie
operate

table-find
make-point
x-coord
y-coord
make-line
make-filled-triangle
width
height
draw-on
draw-line-on
draw-filled-triangle-on
basic-image-size
transform-point
show
make-overlaid-image
make-transformed-medium
make-turned-image
make-mirrored-image
make-scaled-image
make-stacked-image
image->eps
summarize-image
make-square
make-circle
center-x
center-y
area
element-of-set?
add-to-set
union-set

CHAPTER TEN

Implementing Programming Languages

10.1 Introduction

The Scheme system you've been using as you work through this book is itself a program, one that repeatedly reads in an expression, evaluates it, and prints out the value. The main procedure in this system is a *read-eval-print loop*. In this chapter, we'll see how such a system could have been written by building a read-eval-print loop for a somewhat stripped down version of Scheme we call Micro-Scheme.

The previous paragraph announced without any fanfare one of the deepest truths of computer science: The fully general ability to perform any computation whatsoever is itself one specific computation. The read-eval-print loop, like any other procedure, performs the one specialized task it has been programmed to do. However, its specific task is to do whatever it is told, including carrying out any other procedure. It exemplifies the *universality principle*:

> **The universality principle:** There exist universal procedures (such as the read-eval-print loop) that can perform the work of any other procedure. Like any other procedure, they are specialized, but what they specialize in is being fully general.

In the next section, we'll first describe exactly what Micro-Scheme expressions look like by using a special notation called *Extended Backus-Naur Form*. In the third section, we'll build the read-eval-print loop for Micro-Scheme. Because definitions are among the features of Scheme missing from Micro-Scheme, there is no convenient way to create recursive procedures. To overcome this, in the fourth section we'll add global definitions to Micro-Scheme, resulting in Mini-Scheme. Finally, in the application section at the end of the chapter you'll have the opportunity to modify the Mini-Scheme system so that it prints out each of the steps involved in evaluating the main problem, each subproblem, sub-subproblem, etc., much like the diagrams from the early chapters. That way, you'll have a useful tool for helping to understand Scheme evaluation.

Before launching into the development of Micro-Scheme, let's consider why we would want to build a Scheme system when we already have one available:

- As mentioned in the preceding paragraph, in the application section you'll add explanatory output that is helpful in understanding Scheme evaluation. Adding this output to the Scheme system you've been using would probably not be as easy.

- In fact, even without adding any explanatory output, you'll probably come to understand Scheme evaluation better, simply by getting an insider's perspective on it.

- You'll also be able to experiment with changes in the design of the programming language. For example, if you have been wishing that Scheme had some feature, now you'll have the opportunity to add it.

- You'll even be in a good position to implement a whole new programming language that isn't a variant of Scheme at all. Many of the general ideas of programming language implementation are independent of the specific language being implemented. The main reason why this chapter is focused on the nearly circular implementation of Mini-Scheme in Scheme is simply to avoid introducing another language for you to understand.

10.2 Syntax

The read-eval-print loop for Micro-Scheme uses many of the ideas from the movie query application in Section 7.6. There, we had a procedure, `query-loop`, that read in a query, matched it to one of a variety of patterns, took the appropriate action, and printed the result. Here, we have a loop that reads in an expression and uses a similar matching algorithm to determine what kind of expression it has. This information is then used to compute and print the value of the expression.

Recall that in the query loop, we knew that there would be some queries that didn't match any of the patterns in our database. Similarly, in the Micro-Scheme loop, there will be expressions that don't match any of the valid forms for Micro-Scheme expressions. For example, the expression (if (not (= x 0)) (/ 2 x) (display "tried to divide by 0") 17) is not a valid Micro-Scheme expression because there are four expressions following the symbol `if` and only three are allowed. Expressions that don't have a valid form are said to be *syntactically incorrect*;

those that are well formed are, of course, syntactically correct. Note that the emphasis is on *form*; for example, the expression (3 2) is syntactically correct because 2 and 3 are both valid expressions, and any collection of one or more valid expressions surrounded by parentheses is also a valid expression. However, that expression doesn't have any meaning or value. Such an error is called a *semantic error*.

The input to the movie query system was fairly easy to specify—it was a list of symbols—but the input to the Micro-Scheme read-eval-print loop has considerably more structure. Micro-Scheme is just a stripped down version of Scheme; essentially it has all the features of Scheme that we've seen up until now except define, cond, let, and, or, and most of the built-in Scheme procedures. This means that a Micro-Scheme expression could be a symbol, a constant (i.e., a number, boolean, or string), or a list of Micro-Scheme expressions and keywords. The *keywords* are the special symbols if, lambda, and quote; we'll say more about quote, which you haven't previously seen, in a bit. Not everything a Micro-Scheme user types in is going to be a valid Micro-Scheme expression, so we'll call each input to the read-eval-print loop a *potential Micro-Scheme expression*, or *PMSE* for short. We can give a recursive definition of a PMSE:

PMSE: A PMSE is a symbol, a number, a string, a boolean, or a list of PMSEs.

The main task of this section is to describe which PMSEs are actually Micro-Scheme expressions. To do this, we'll use a concise notation called EBNF that is commonly used for defining the syntax of formal languages, such as programming languages. The name EBNF stands for Extended Backus-Naur Form, because this notation is an extension to a form of syntax definition that John Backus developed and Peter Naur popularized by using it in the published definition of the programming language Algol, which he edited.

EBNF is one example of a notation for language *grammars*, which specify how *syntactic categories* are recursively structured. The basic idea is to be able to say things like "any collection of one or more expressions surrounded by parentheses is also an expression," which is an inherently recursive statement. The only difference is that rather than saying it in English, we have a notation for saying it that is both more precise and more concise. Regarding precision, notice that the English version could be misread as saying that each of the individual expressions is surrounded by parentheses, rather than the whole collection. Regarding concision, here is the EBNF version:

⟨expression⟩ ⟶ (⟨expression⟩⁺)

This collection of symbols with an arrow in it is called a *production* of the grammar. The arrow separates the production into two sides, the left-hand and the right-hand sides. The word ⟨expression⟩ with the angle brackets around it is a *syntactic category name* or *nonterminal*. A grammar is a collection of productions that is used to define one specific *syntactic category*; for Micro-Scheme it would be ⟨expression⟩. However, along the way we may want to define other syntactic categories, such as ⟨conditional⟩. The meaning of a production is that the right-hand side specifies one form that is permissible for the syntactic category listed on the left-hand side. For example, the above production gives one form that an ⟨expression⟩ can have.

The parentheses in the example production's right-hand side are necessary symbols that must appear in any ⟨expression⟩ of that form; these are called *terminal* symbols. For another example, the production

⟨expression⟩ ⟶ (if ⟨expression⟩ ⟨expression⟩ ⟨expression⟩)

contains the keyword if as a terminal symbol as well as the parentheses.

At this point we have two productions for ⟨expression⟩, because we have given two different forms that ⟨expression⟩s can have. This is normal; many syntactic categories will be specified by a collection of productions specifying alternative forms the category can have. The grammar is easier to read if all the productions for a particular category are grouped together; a notational shorthand is generally used for this. In the case of our two productions for ⟨expression⟩, this shorthand notation would be as follows:

⟨expression⟩ ⟶ (⟨expression⟩$^+$)
    | (if ⟨expression⟩ ⟨expression⟩ ⟨expression⟩)

The vertical bar is used to indicate that another production for the same left-hand side follows. Any number of productions can be grouped together in this way. If the right-hand sides are short, they can be listed on the same line, as follows:

⟨digit⟩ ⟶ 0 | 1 | 2 | 3 | 4 | 5 | 6 | 7 | 8 | 9

Note, incidentally, that none of these productions for ⟨digit⟩ contains any nonterminal symbols on the right-hand side. Every grammar must have some productions like that to provide the base case for the recursion inherent in grammars.

The first production given for ⟨expression⟩ had a superscript plus sign in its right-hand side; this is a special notation that means "one or more." In particular, ⟨expression⟩$^+$ is the EBNF way to say "one or more ⟨expression⟩s," which was used to say that one form an ⟨expression⟩ can have is a pair of parentheses surrounding one or more ⟨expressions⟩s.

There is another very similar notation that can be used to say "zero or more." For example, suppose we want to specify the syntax of lambda expressions. We'll limit the body to a single ⟨expression⟩ but will allow the parameter list to have zero or more ⟨name⟩s in it so that we can have procedures with any number of parameters, including parameterless procedures. This would be expressed as follows:

⟨expression⟩ ⟶ (**lambda** (⟨name⟩*) ⟨expression⟩)

The general rule is that a syntactic category name with a superscript asterisk indicates zero or more instances of the category, whereas a syntactic category name with a superscript plus sign indicates one or more instances of the category.

Now that we have the basics of EBNF, we can use it to describe all of Micro-Scheme. Recall that Micro-Scheme is a stripped-down version of Scheme; specifically, it includes many of the features of Scheme that we've seen up until now. The basic syntactic category in Micro-Scheme is the expression.

⟨expression⟩ ⟶ ⟨name⟩ | ⟨constant⟩ | ⟨conditional⟩ | ⟨abstraction⟩
   | ⟨application⟩

⟨constant⟩ ⟶ ⟨literal⟩ | ⟨quotation⟩

⟨literal⟩ ⟶ ⟨number⟩ | ⟨boolean⟩ | ⟨string⟩

⟨conditional⟩ ⟶ (**if** ⟨expression⟩ ⟨expression⟩ ⟨expression⟩)

⟨abstraction⟩ ⟶ (**lambda** (⟨name⟩*) ⟨expression⟩)

⟨quotation⟩ ⟶ (**quote** ⟨datum⟩)

⟨application⟩ ⟶ (⟨expression⟩⁺)

⟨name⟩ ⟶ *any symbol allowed by the underlying Scheme except* **lambda**, **quote**,
        and **if**
⟨number⟩ ⟶ *any number allowed by the underlying Scheme*
⟨string⟩ ⟶ *any string allowed by the underlying Scheme*
⟨boolean⟩ ⟶ *any boolean allowed by the underlying Scheme*
⟨datum⟩ ⟶ *any datum allowed by the underlying Scheme*

You will notice that there are five syntactic categories at the end of the grammar that are defined in terms of the underlying Scheme. The last one, ⟨datum⟩, includes the other four as well as lists and a couple other Scheme types we have not yet discussed; specifically, ⟨datum⟩ consists of everything that Scheme will successfully read using the built-in **read** procedure. In fact, the main reason that we describe ⟨name⟩s, ⟨number⟩s, ⟨string⟩s, ⟨boolean⟩s, and ⟨datum⟩s in terms of the underlying Scheme is that we're using the built-in **read** procedure for reading in the PMSEs. Once we've read in a PMSE, the underlying Scheme has it all nicely packaged for us so we can tell if it's a symbol, a number, a boolean, a string, a list, or none of the above simply by using predicates such as **symbol?**, **number?**, and so on.

Our grammar provides two ways to specify a ⟨constant⟩. One is as a ⟨literal⟩, such as 31, #t, or "hello". The other way is as a ⟨quotation⟩, such as (quote x) or (quote (1 2)). In normal Scheme, you are used to seeing quotations written a different way, as 'x or '(1 2), which is really just a shorthand notation; when the read procedure sees 'x in the input, it returns the list (quote x).

Finally, you'll notice that we used an unfamiliar name for the syntactic category of lambda expressions: We called them ⟨abstraction⟩s. We didn't want to name the syntactic category ⟨lambda-expression⟩ because that would be naming it after the keyword occurring in it—naming it after what the expressions look like rather than after their meaning. (An analogy would be if we had named ⟨application⟩s "parenthesized expressions" because they have parentheses around them, rather than focusing on the fact that they represent the application of a procedure to its arguments.) We didn't want to call these expressions ⟨procedure⟩s either because a procedure is the value that results from evaluating such an expression, and we want to distinguish the expression from the value. There is a long tradition of calling this kind of expression an *abstraction*, so we adopted this name.

▶ Exercise 10.1

The categories ⟨number⟩, ⟨string⟩, and ⟨boolean⟩ are directly testable by the corresponding Scheme procedures number?, string?, and boolean?, but ⟨name⟩ does not have an exact Scheme correlate. You will write one in this exercise.

a. Recall that the symbols lambda, quote, and if that are disallowed as names because of their special usage in Micro-Scheme are called *keywords*. Write a predicate keyword? that tests whether its argument is a keyword.
b. Write the predicate name?. You will need to use the built-in Scheme procedure symbol?.

▶ Exercise 10.2

Even when a category is directly testable by Scheme, using EBNF to express it at a more primitive level can help you appreciate the expressive power of EBNF. In this exercise you will use EBNF to describe certain kinds of numbers—a small subset of those allowed by Scheme.

a. Write a production for ⟨unsigned-integer⟩. You can use the productions for ⟨digit⟩ given above.
b. Next write productions for ⟨integer⟩; an ⟨integer⟩ may start with a − sign, a + sign, or neither.
c. Finally, write productions for ⟨real-number⟩, which are (possibly) signed numbers that may have a decimal point. Note that if the real number has a decimal point,

there must be at least one digit to the left or to the right (or both) of the decimal point. Thus, −43., .43, 43, +43.21, and 43.0 are all valid real numbers.

▶ Exercise 10.3

In Section 8.3 we considered expression trees for simple arithmetic expressions. All such expressions are either numbers or lists having an operator (one of +, -, *, or /) and two operands. Actually, there are three important variants, depending on where the operator occurs: in the first position (prefix or Scheme notation), the second position (infix or standard notation), or the third position (postfix, also known as Reverse Polish notation, or RPN). Let's consider how such expressions can be specified using EBNF.

a. Write productions for ⟨arithmetic-prefix-expression⟩.
b. Write productions for ⟨arithmetic-infix-expression⟩.
c. Write productions for ⟨arithmetic-postfix-expression⟩.
d. As noted in Section 8.3, a postorder traversal of an expression tree results in a list of the nodes that is identical to the language specified by ⟨arithmetic-postfix-expression⟩, except that subexpressions are not parenthesized. Revise the productions for ⟨arithmetic-postfix-expression⟩ so that subexpressions are not parenthesized. (The overall top-level expression needn't be parenthesized either.)

▶ Exercise 10.4

Let's consider two possible additions to our Micro-Scheme grammar involving regular Scheme expressions.

a. Write a production for **let** expressions. Remember that **let** expressions allow zero or more bindings (i.e., parenthesized name/expression pairs), and the body of the **let** contains one or more expressions. You should define a separate syntactic category for ⟨binding⟩.
b. Write productions for **cond** expressions. Remember that **cond** expressions allow one or more branches, the last of which may be an **else**, and each branch has one or more expressions following the test condition.

▶ Exercise 10.5

Our grammar for Micro-Scheme says that an ⟨application⟩ is of the form (⟨expression⟩⁺). Some authors prefer to instead say that it is of the form (⟨expression⟩

⟨expression⟩*), even though this is longer and is equivalent. Speculate why it might be preferred.

We can use the productions for ⟨expression⟩ to determine whether or not (+ 2 3) is a syntactically valid Micro-Scheme expression. Because it matches the production for an ⟨application⟩, it will be a valid Micro-Scheme expression if and only if +, 2, and 3 are valid. Now, + is a symbol in Scheme and not a keyword, so it is a

---

◢ The Expressiveness of EBNF

If we weren't allowed to use the superscript asterisk and plus sign in EBNF, we wouldn't lose anything in terms of the power of the notation: We could still represent all the same language constructs, just using recursion. For example, rather than

⟨application⟩ ⟶ (⟨expression⟩$^+$)

we could write

⟨application⟩ ⟶ (⟨expressions⟩)

⟨expressions⟩ ⟶ ⟨expression⟩
    | ⟨expressions⟩ ⟨expression⟩

As the above example shows, although the superscripted asterisk and plus sign don't add anything to the range of languages the EBNF notation can describe, they do contribute to keeping our grammars short and easy to understand.

Having seen what happens if we eliminate the "repetition" constructs and rely only on recursion, now let's consider the reverse. Suppose we forbid all use of recursion in EBNF but allow the superscript asterisk and plus sign. We have to be clear what it means to rule out recursion: Not only are we forbidding syntactic categories from being directly defined in terms of themselves (as ⟨expressions⟩ is in the preceding), but we are also forbidding indirect recursions, such as the definition of ⟨expression⟩ in terms of ⟨application⟩, which is itself defined in terms of ⟨expression⟩. This restriction cuts into the range of languages that is specifiable. For example, consider the language specified by the following recursive EBNF grammar:

⟨parens⟩ ⟶ ()
    | (⟨parens⟩)

(Continued)

> **The Expressiveness of EBNF (Continued)**

Any string of one or more left parentheses followed by the same number of right parentheses is a ⟨parens⟩. Suppose we have a nonrecursive grammar that also matches all these strings (but possibly others as well). Consider a very long string of left parentheses followed by the same number of right parentheses. If the string is long relative to the size of the nonrecursive grammar, the only way this can happen is if the asterisk or plus sign is being used at some point to match a repeated substring. The part being repeated has to contain either only left parentheses or only right parentheses because otherwise its repetition would cause a right parenthesis to come before a left parenthesis. However, if the repeated part contains only one kind of parenthesis, and if we simply repeat that part more times (which the asterisk or plus sign allows), we'll wind up with an imbalance between the number of left and right parentheses. Thus the nonrecursive grammar, if it matches all the strings that ⟨parens⟩ does, must match some other strings as well that ⟨parens⟩ doesn't; in other words, we've got a language that can be specified using a recursive grammar but not a nonrecursive one.

Even with recursion allowed, EBNF isn't the ultimate in language specification; it can't specify some very simple languages. For example, suppose we want the language to allow any number of left parentheses followed by the same number of letter a's followed by the same number of right parentheses. For example, (a) and ((aa)) would be legal but ((a)) and ((aa) wouldn't be. There is no way to specify this language using EBNF. Even sketching the proof of this would go beyond the scope of this book, but you'll see it in a course on formal languages and automata theory. Such courses, also sometimes called "mathematical theory of computation" or "foundations of computation," go into more details on the other issues we covered in this sidebar and cover related topics as well.

⟨name⟩ in Micro-Scheme, and thus + is a valid Micro-Scheme expression. Similarly, 2 and 3 are numbers, so they are Micro-Scheme ⟨constant⟩s. Thus, they too are valid Micro-Scheme expressions. Hence, the whole expression (+ 2 3) is also valid.

> **Exercise 10.6**

Determine which of the following PMSEs are syntactically valid Micro-Scheme expressions and explain why.

a. (if 3 1 5)
b. (lambda x (+ x 2))
c. (((a ((b))) c))

d. (lambda (lambda) 3)

e. (lambda () lambda)

f. (lambda (x) (if (> x 0) x (- x) 0))

g. (lambda () x)

h. (lambda ())

i. (/)

j. (#t #f)

As you did the exercise above, you probably matched a PMSE against the productions for a Micro-Scheme ⟨expression⟩. Whenever you found a match, you took the various parts of the PMSE and checked to see whether they were valid as well. Note that this is a form of pattern-matching similar to what you did in Section 7.6 to determine the form of a query in the movie query system.

We can use the pattern-matching mechanism from Section 7.6 to determine whether or not a PMSE is a syntactically correct Micro-Scheme expression. In particular, we'll use the procedures **matches?** and **substitutions-in-to-match**, together with a pattern/action list appropriate for Micro-Scheme. This list will have one pattern/action pair for each kind of compound expression—⟨conditional⟩, ⟨abstraction⟩, and ⟨application⟩. The matching will determine whether or not a PMSE has the correct number of "sub-PMSEs" in the correct places, and the actions will check to see if these sub-PMSEs are valid expressions. The pattern/action list will also take care of ⟨quotation⟩s, whereas we'll have to use separate checks to determine whether or not we have one of the simplest kinds of Micro-Scheme expressions, ⟨name⟩ and ⟨literal⟩, neither of which has any sub-PMSE.

Here, then, is the code for a syntax checking predicate **syntax-ok?**, together with the pattern/action list. The procedure **all-are** is a higher-order procedure from Exercise 7.49 on page 208. It takes a predicate, such as **name?** or **syntax-ok?**, and returns a procedure that determines whether or not everything in a list satisfies the original predicate. Thus, for example, the action for the pattern starting with **lambda** includes a check that all of the parameters are really names.

```
(define syntax-ok?
  (lambda (pmse)
    (define loop   ;main procedure is on next page
      (lambda (p/a-list)
        (cond ((null? p/a-list) #f)
              ((matches? (pattern (car p/a-list)) pmse)
               (apply (action (car p/a-list))
                      (substitutions-in-to-match
                       (pattern (car p/a-list))
                       pmse)))
              (else (loop (cdr p/a-list)))))))) ;end of loop
```

```
    (cond ((or (number? pmse) ;main syntax-ok? procedure
               (string? pmse)
               (boolean? pmse)) ;pmse is a literal
           #t)
          ((name? pmse) #t)
          ((list? pmse) ;try matching it against the patterns
           (loop micro-scheme-syntax-ok?-p/a-list))
          (else #f))))

(define micro-scheme-syntax-ok?-p/a-list
  (list
   (make-pattern/action '(if _ _ _)
                        (lambda (test if-true if-false)
                          (and (syntax-ok? test)
                               (syntax-ok? if-true)
                               (syntax-ok? if-false))))
   (make-pattern/action '(lambda _ _)
                        (lambda (parameters body)
                          (and (list? parameters)
                               ((all-are name?) parameters)
                               (syntax-ok? body))))
   (make-pattern/action '(quote _)
                        (lambda (datum) #t))
   (make-pattern/action '(...)    ; note that this *must* come last
                        (lambda (pmses)
                          ((all-are  syntax-ok?) pmses)))))
```

Let's look at what happens if we call **syntax-ok?** on a list-structured PMSE, say, (if 3 1 5). This PMSE will match the first pattern in the pattern/action list because (if 3 1 5) is a list with four elements and the first element is the symbol **if**. The last three elements in the PMSE are the test expression, the expression to evaluate if the test expression is true, and the expression to evaluate if the test is false. The action that corresponds to this pattern is to recursively check to see if all three of these expressions are really well-formed Micro-Scheme expressions by using the procedure **syntax-ok?** and the special form **and**.

In the example above a *mutual recursion* occurs between **syntax-ok?** and the action procedures, much like with **even-part** and **odd-part** in Section 7.5. That is, **syntax-ok?** doesn't directly invoke itself to check the validity of sub-PMSEs but rather invokes an action procedure that in turn invokes **syntax-ok?** on the sub-PMSEs. Because this will in general result in more than one recursive call to **syntax-ok?** (for example, conditionals result in three recursive calls), the net result is tree recursion. Micro-Scheme expressions have a tree-like structure similar to the expression trees in Section 8.3. The tree recursion resulting from a call to `syntax-ok?` exactly parallels the tree-like structure of the given PMSE.

▶ Exercise 10.7

Why does the mutual recursion between `syntax-ok?` and the action procedures eventually stop when we check the syntax of (`if 3 1 5`)? Why will it eventually stop on any list-structured PMSE?

▶ Exercise 10.8

What happens if the PMSE being checked is the empty list?

Note that there are plenty of syntactically valid Micro-Scheme expressions that are nevertheless completely nonsensical: consider, for example, (`1 5`). This expression is a syntactically valid Micro-Scheme expression (and a syntactically valid Scheme one, too), but it doesn't have a value, because the value of `1` is the number 1, not a procedure. The point is that this expression has the correct form for Micro-Scheme expressions, and form is the only thing that EBNF specifies. The big gain with EBNF is that the productions for a language translate fairly simply into a syntax checker such as `syntax-ok?`. In the next section, we'll see that the same productions can also serve as the basis for categorizing expressions and identifying their parts in preparation for evaluating them.

Finally, we make one important remark concerning the structure of the pattern/action list. Note that the first three patterns in the pattern/action list describe list-structured PMSEs that can be identified by their size and their first element. Because of the way the pattern/action list is structured, any other nonempty list is considered to be an application. When we extend Micro-Scheme by adding new productions, we will want to maintain this property by keeping the pattern for applications at the end of the pattern/action list.

10.3   Micro-Scheme

Now that we know the syntax for Micro-Scheme, we can build a read-eval-print loop for it. The Micro-Scheme read-eval-print loop itself is quite straightforward:

```
(define read-eval-print-loop
  (lambda ()
    (display ";Enter Micro-Scheme expression:")
    (newline)
    ;;(continued)
```

```
(let ((expression (read)))
  (let ((value (evaluate (parse expression))))
    (display ";Micro-Scheme value: ")
    (write value)
    (newline)))
(read-eval-print-loop)))
```

Each expression is read in with **read**, then *parsed* and *evaluated*, and finally the value is written back out using **write**, with some frills provided by **newline** and **display**. (The built-in procedure **write** is just like **display** except for some details such as providing double quote marks around strings. That way you can see the difference between the string **"foo"** and the symbol **foo**, unlike when they are **displayed**.)

The core of this read-eval-print loop is a two-step process that uses the two procedures **parse** and **evaluate**. In order to understand the separate tasks of these two procedures, let's first consider the arithmetic expressions described in Exercise 10.3. No matter which way we denote arithmetic expressions (infix, prefix, and postfix), each expression gives rise to a unique expression tree, as described in Section 8.3. Parsing is the process of converting an actual expression to the corresponding expression tree. But why should we go through this intermediate stage (the expression tree) rather than simply evaluating the expression directly? Separating the parsing from the evaluation allows us to make changes in the superficial form or syntax of expressions (such as whether we write our arithmetic expressions in prefix, infix, or postfix) without needing to change the evaluation procedure. Furthermore, evaluation itself is made easier, because the expression tree data type can be designed for ease of evaluation rather than for ease of human writing.

Arithmetic expressions are considerably simpler than Micro-Scheme expressions in one sense, however. Namely, there were only two kinds of nodes in our expression trees: constants, which were leaves, and operators, which were internal nodes. We needed to distinguish between constants and operators in Section 8.3's **evaluate** procedure, but all internal nodes were treated the same way: by looking up and applying the specified Scheme procedure.

If you think instead about how Micro-Scheme works, it would be natural for expression trees to have two kinds of leaves, corresponding to the syntactic categories ⟨name⟩ and ⟨constant⟩. Each of these will need to be evaluated differently. Similarly, there are three natural candidates for kinds of internal nodes, corresponding to ⟨conditional⟩, ⟨abstraction⟩, and ⟨application⟩, because these syntactic categories have subexpressions that would correspond to subtrees. Again, the way each of these expressions is evaluated depends on what kind of expression it is. For example, think about the difference between the way (+ (square 2) (square 3)) is evaluated and the way (if (= x 0) 1 (/ 5 x)) is. Because we need to know what kind of expression we have in order to evaluate it, parsing must identify and mark what sort of expression it is considering and break it down into its component parts. In our example above, the expression (+ (square 2) (square 3)) is an application, whose operator is + and whose operands are (square 2) and (square 3). Each of these operands is itself an application with an operator, which is square, and an operand, which is either 2 or 3.

So, the value of parse will be a tree-structured data type, which is typically called an *Abstract Syntax Tree*, or *AST*. The AST for an expression indicates what kind of expression it is and what its components are. Furthermore, the components are themselves typically ASTs. The evaluation process itself can be carried out on the AST rather than the original expression; as described above, this approach has the advantage that if the language is redesigned in ways that change only the superficial syntax of expressions, only parse (not evaluate) needs to be changed.

ASTs are an abstract data type, which means we shouldn't worry too much for now about how they are represented (what they "look like") so long as they provide the appropriate operations, notably the evaluate operation. However, it is easier to think about ASTs if you have something concrete you can think about, so we will present here a pictorial version of ASTs that you can use when working through examples with paper and pencil. Each AST is visually represented as a tree whose root node has a label indicating what kind of AST it is. The leaf nodes, which correspond to the syntactic categories ⟨name⟩ and ⟨constant⟩, are fairly simple. For example,

┌─ **Name** ─┐
│ name: + │ is the name AST corresponding to the name +, and

┌─ **Constant** ─┐
│ value: 2 │
is the constant AST corresponding to 2. Note that in addition to the labels (that designate their syntactic categories Name and Constant), both of these ASTs contain information specifying which particular name or constant they represent (name: + and value: 2).

The other three syntactic categories (⟨conditional⟩, ⟨abstraction⟩, and ⟨application⟩) correspond to internal nodes because they each contain subexpressions that themselves result in ASTs. In contrast to the expression trees in Section 8.3, which always had exactly two children, the number of children of an internal node in these ASTs will vary. This number depends partially on the syntactic category; for example, the root node corresponding to the category ⟨conditional⟩ will always have three children: one each for the test, if-true, and if-false subexpressions. On the other hand, the number of children of the root node corresponding to the category ⟨application⟩ varies: The operator is one child, and the operands are the others.

First consider the ⟨application⟩ category. If we parse the Micro-Scheme expression (+ 2 3), we get the following application AST:

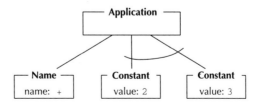

The three children are the ASTs corresponding to the three subexpressions of the expression. The leftmost child corresponds to the operator +, which is a name AST, and the other children correspond to the two operands; we put a curved line in the diagram to indicate that these latter subtrees are grouped together as a *list* of operands. As noted above, the number of subtrees varies with the application; for example, parsing the expression (+ 2 3 4) would result in the following application AST:

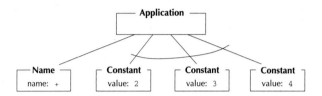

We have two other kinds of ASTs: conditional ASTs, which result from parsing `if` expressions, and abstraction ASTs, which result from parsing `lambda` expressions. The conditional AST resulting from the expression (if (= x 0) 1 (/ 5 x)) is diagrammed in Figure 10.1, and the abstraction AST resulting from the expression (lambda (x) (* x x)) is diagrammed in Figure 10.2. Notice that the abstraction AST contains the list of parameter names and has a single sub-AST, corresponding to the body of the abstraction.

Recall that we are doing evaluation in a two-step process: first parse the expression, then evaluate the resulting AST. Thus, if we use A as a name for the first application AST shown above, the Scheme (not Micro-Scheme) expression (**parse** '(+ 2 3)) has A as its value, and the Scheme expression (**evaluate** A) has 5 as its value. Those are the two steps that the Micro-Scheme read-eval-print loop goes through after reading in (+ 2 3): It first parses it into the AST A, and then evaluates the AST A to get 5, which it writes back out.

What do we gain by using this two-step evaluation process? As we said at the outset, part of the gain is the decoupling of the superficial syntax (**parse**'s concern)

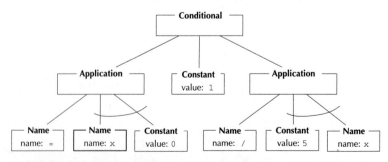

Figure 10.1   Conditional AST parsed from (if (= x 0) 1 (/ 5 x))

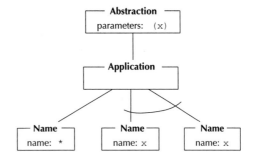

Figure 10.2   Abstraction AST parsed from (`lambda (x) (* x x)`)

from the deeper structure (**evaluate**'s concern). Perhaps more important, however, is the other advantage we mentioned: The tree structure of ASTs greatly facilitates the evaluation process. ASTs are made to be evaluated. Now that we have seen AST diagrams, we can understand why this is. First, each AST has an explicit type, which controls how it is evaluated. For example, consider the two kinds of leaf nodes, name ASTs and constant ASTs. Evaluating a constant AST is trivial, because we simply return the value that it stores. Evaluating a name AST is slightly more complicated but only requires looking up its name somewhere.

As for the more complicated ASTs, their recursive structure guides the evaluation. Let's just consider how we might evaluate a conditional AST, for example, the one in Figure 10.1. In evaluating such an AST, the left child gets evaluated first, and depending on whether its value is true or false, either the second or third child is evaluated and its value is returned. The evaluation of the sub-ASTs is done recursively; how precisely a given sub-AST is evaluated depends on which kind of AST it is.

Before we start worrying about how to implement the data type of ASTs, we'll first write the procedure **parse**, assuming that we have all the constructors (**make-abstraction-ast**, **make-application-ast**, etc.) we need.

The procedure **parse** will look almost the same as the procedure **syntax-ok?** in that we need to look at the expression and see if it matches one of the forms of the expressions in our language. The only difference is that instead of returning a boolean indicating whether the syntax is okay, **parse** will return an AST. Here is the code for **parse**, together with a new pattern/action list:

```
(define parse
  (lambda (expression)
    (define loop
      (lambda (p/a-list)
        (cond ((null? p/a-list)
               (error "invalid expression" expression))
```

```
                    ((matches? (pattern (car p/a-list)) expression)
                     (apply (action (car p/a-list))
                            (substitutions-in-to-match
                             (pattern (car p/a-list))
                             expression)))
                    (else (loop (cdr p/a-list))))))) ;end of loop
           (cond ((name? expression) ;start of main parse procedure
                  (make-name-ast expression))
                 ((or (number? expression)
                      (string? expression)
                      (boolean? expression))
                  (make-constant-ast expression))
                 ((list? expression)
                  (loop micro-scheme-parsing-p/a-list))
                 (else (error "invalid expression" expression)))))) 


  (define micro-scheme-parsing-p/a-list
    (list
     (make-pattern/action '(if _ _ _)
                          (lambda (test if-true if-false)
                            (make-conditional-ast (parse test)
                                                  (parse if-true)
                                                  (parse if-false))))
     (make-pattern/action '(lambda _ _)
                          (lambda (parameters body)
                            (if (and (list? parameters)
                                     ((all-are name?) parameters))
                                (make-abstraction-ast parameters
                                                      (parse body))
                                (error "invalid expression"
                                       (list 'lambda
                                             parameters body)))))
     (make-pattern/action '(quote _)
                          (lambda (value)
                            (make-constant-ast value)))
     (make-pattern/action '(...)    ; note that this *must* come last
                          (lambda (operator&operands)
                            (let ((asts (map parse
                                             operator&operands)))
                              (make-application-ast (car asts)
                                                    (cdr asts)))))))
```

Exercise 10.9

The action for `ifs` parses all three subexpressions into ASTs and passes the three resulting ASTs to `make-conditional-ast`. Similarly, the action for `lambda` expressions parses the body. However, it doesn't parse the parameters. Why not?

Our next task, then, is to implement the AST data structure. How are we going to do this? Although the various `make-...-ast` procedures make lots of different kinds of ASTs (one for each kind of expression), we want to be able to apply one operation to any one of them: `evaluate`. Thus, to implement ASTs we need to do so in a way that accommodates generic operations. We choose to use procedural representations, leading to the following definition of `evaluate`:

```
(define evaluate
  (lambda (ast)
    (ast 'evaluate)))
```

We'll evaluate expressions much the way we showed in Chapter 1, using the substitution model, which means that when a procedure is applied to arguments, the argument values are substituted into the procedure's body where the parameters appear, and then the result is evaluated. This process leads us to need an additional generic operator for ASTs, one that substitutes a value for a name in an AST:

```
(define substitute-for-in
  (lambda (value name ast)
    ((ast 'substitute-for) value name)))
```

Note that we've set this up so that when the AST is given the message `substitute-for`, it replies with a procedure to apply to the value and the name. That way ASTs can always expect to be given a single argument, the message (`evaluate` or `substitute-for`), even though in one case there are two more arguments to follow.

Let's look at the evaluation process and see how substitution fits into it, using our pictorial version of ASTs. We'll introduce one minor new element into our pictures, additional labels on the ASTs so that we can more easily refer to them. For example, when we talk about the AST A_2 in Figure 10.3, we mean the AST whose root node has the naming label A_2, in other words, the abstraction AST that is the full AST's first child. Suppose we parse the Micro-Scheme expression `((lambda (x) (* x x)) (+ 2 3))`, which results in the AST A_1 shown in Figure 10.3. Now let's look in detail at what happens when we evaluate A_1.

Because A_1 is an application AST, evaluating it involves first evaluating the operator AST, A_2, and the operand ASTs, of which there is only one, A_7. Because A_2 is an abstraction AST, evaluating it creates an actual procedure; let's call that procedure

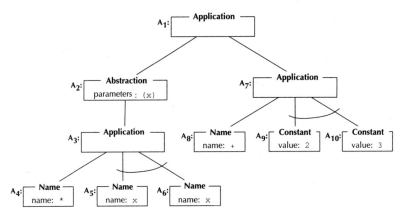

Figure 10.3 The AST corresponding to ((lambda (x) (* x x)) (+ 2 3)).

P_1 for reference. The procedure P_1 has a parameter list that contains only x and has the AST A_3 as its body. Next we need to evaluate the operand, A_7, to find out what value P_1 should be applied to. Because A_7 is again an application AST, its evaluation proceeds similarly to that of A_1; we need to evaluate its operator AST, A_8, and its operand ASTs, A_9 and A_{10}. Because A_8 is a name AST, evaluating it simply involves looking up what the name + is a name for. The answer is that it is a name for the built-in addition procedure, which we can call P_2. Evaluating A_9 and A_{10} is even simpler, because they are constant ASTs. Each evaluates to the value shown in the AST itself: 2 for A_9 and 3 for A_{10}. Now that A_7's operator and operands have been evaluated, we can finish off evaluating A_7 by applying P_2 to 2 and 3. Doing so produces 5, because P_2 is the built-in addition procedure. Now we know that A_2's value is the procedure P_1 and that A_7's value is 5. Thus we can finish off the evaluation of A_1 by applying P_1 to 5.

Because P_1 is not a built-in procedure (unlike P_2), but rather is one that the user wrote in Micro-Scheme, we need to use the substitution model. We take P_1's body, which is the AST A_3, and replace each name AST that is an occurrence of the parameter name, x, by a constant AST containing the argument value, 5. We can do this task as (substitute-for-in 5 'x A_3). The result of this substitution is the AST A_{11} shown in Figure 10.4. Notice that the AST A_4, which was the operator AST

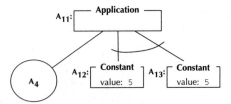

Figure 10.4 The AST resulting from (substitute-for-in 5 'x A_3). Note that the circled A_4 indicates that an already existing AST, A_4, is being reused here.

of A_3, is also serving as the operator AST of our new A_{11}, which is what the circled A_4 indicates. Also, notice that each place where the value 5 was substituted for the name x, it was packaged into a constant AST; this resulted in ASTs A_{12} and A_{13}. This packaging is necessary because we can't use a naked value where a sub-AST is expected. Next we evaluate A_{11}, which involves evaluating its operator AST, A_4, and its operand ASTs, A_{12} and A_{13}. A_4 evaluates to the built-in multiplication procedure, and A_{12} and A_{13} each evaluate to 5. Finally, the built-in multiplication procedure can be applied to 5 and 5, producing the final answer of 25. This process can be shown in a diagram, as in Figure 10.5. Of course, this can also be abbreviated, for example, by leaving out the details of how substituting 5 for x in A_3 results in A_{11}.

We can evaluate conditional ASTs similarly to what is shown in the foregoing, but there is a bit of a twist because we first evaluate the test AST and then depending on whether its value is true or false, evaluate one of the other two sub-ASTs to provide the conditional AST's value. This process is illustrated in Figure 10.6, which shows the evaluation of an AST (A_{14}) that results from parsing (if #f 1 2).

Exercise 10.10

Draw a diagram showing the AST resulting from parsing ((lambda (x) (if (> x 0) x 0)) (- 0 3)). Now step through the process of evaluating that AST, analogously to the above evaluations of A_1 and A_{14}.

Now we're in a position to start writing the various AST constructors, each with its own method of evaluating and substituting. We start with the simplest ASTs, names and constants.

Names can be evaluated using the **look-up-value** procedure from Chapter 8; substituting a value for a name in a name AST is either a nonevent or a real substitution, depending on whether the two names are equal or not:

```
(define make-name-ast
  (lambda (name)
    (define the-ast
      (lambda (message)
        (cond ((equal? message 'evaluate) (look-up-value name))
              ((equal? message 'substitute-for)
               (lambda (value name-to-substitute-for)
                 (if (equal? name name-to-substitute-for)
                     (make-constant-ast value)
                     the-ast)))
              (else (error "unknown operation on a name AST"
                      message)))))
    the-ast))
```

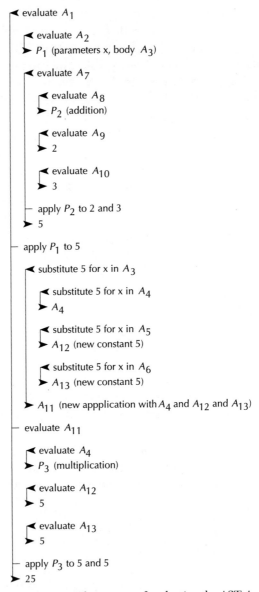

Figure 10.5　The process of evaluating the AST A_1

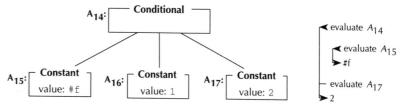

Figure 10.6   The process of evaluating a conditional AST

> ### Exercise 10.11
>
> Extend `look-up-value` to include all your other favorite Scheme predefined names so that they are available in Micro-Scheme as well.

> ### Exercise 10.12
>
> Further extend `look-up-value` so that some useful names are predefined in Micro-Scheme that *aren't* predefined in Scheme.

Constants are the ASTs that have the most straightforward implementation:

```
(define make-constant-ast
  (lambda (value)
    (define the-ast
      (lambda (message)
        (cond ((equal? message 'evaluate) value)
              ((equal? message 'substitute-for)
               (lambda (value name)
                 the-ast))
              (else (error "unknown operation on a constant AST"
                           message)))))
    the-ast))
```

The compound ASTs are much more interesting to implement, mostly because evaluating them usually involves evaluating one or more of their components. Here is the AST for conditional expressions (`if`s):

```
(define make-conditional-ast
  (lambda (test-ast if-true-ast if-false-ast)
    (lambda (message)
      (cond ((equal? message 'evaluate)
             ;;(continued)
```

```
        (if (evaluate test-ast)
            (evaluate if-true-ast)
            (evaluate if-false-ast)))
     ((equal? message 'substitute-for)
      (lambda (value name)
        (make-conditional-ast
          (substitute-for-in value name test-ast)
          (substitute-for-in value name if-true-ast)
          (substitute-for-in value name if-false-ast))))
     (else (error "unknown operation on a conditional AST"
              message))))))
```

This code follows a very simple pattern: Evaluating the conditional AST involves evaluating component ASTs (first the test and then one of the others based on the result of that first evaluation), and similarly, substituting into the AST involves substituting into the constituent AST components.

Evaluating an application is similar to evaluating a conditional. First, we need to evaluate the operator and each of the operands. Then we should apply the operator's value to the values of the operands, using the built-in procedure **apply**, which assumes that an operator's value is actually a Scheme procedure. Doing a substitution on an application involves substituting into the operator and each of the operands. Therefore, in Scheme, we have

```
(define make-application-ast
  (lambda (operator-ast operand-asts)
    (lambda (message)
      (cond ((equal? message 'evaluate)
             (let ((procedure (evaluate operator-ast))
                   (arguments (map evaluate operand-asts)))
               (apply procedure arguments)))
            ((equal? message 'substitute-for)
             (lambda (value name)
               (make-application-ast
                (substitute-for-in value name operator-ast)
                (map (lambda (operand-ast)
                       (substitute-for-in value name operand-ast))
                     operand-asts))))
            (else (error "unknown operation on an application AST"
                     message))))))
```

The most complicated ASTs are probably those for abstractions (**lambda** expressions). As we mentioned previously, the result of evaluating an abstraction AST should be an actual Scheme procedure; we'll ignore that for now by assuming that we can write a procedure called `make-procedure` that will make this Scheme procedure for us. The method for handling substitutions is worth looking at closely:

```
(define make-abstraction-ast
  (lambda (parameters body-ast)
    (define the-ast
      (lambda (message)
        (cond ((equal? message 'evaluate)
               (make-procedure parameters body-ast))
              ((equal? message 'substitute-for)
               (lambda (value name)
                 (if (member name parameters)
                     the-ast
                     (make-abstraction-ast
                      parameters
                      (substitute-for-in value name body-ast)))))
              (else (error "unknown operation on an abstraction AST"
                           message)))))
    the-ast))
```

You should have noticed that if a substitution is performed where the name being substituted for is one of the parameters, the AST is returned unchanged. Only if the name isn't one of the parameters is the substitution done in the body. In other words, if we substitute 3 for x in (lambda (x) (+ x y)), we get (lambda (x) (+ x y)) back unchanged, but if we substitute 3 for y in (lambda (x) (+ x y)), we get (lambda (x) (+ x 3)). This rule is what is called only substituting for *free* occurrences of the name rather than also *bound* occurrences. This limited form of substitution is the right thing to do because when we are evaluating an expression like

```
((lambda (x)
   (+ x
      ((lambda (x) (* x x))
       5)))
 3)
```

we want to substitute the 3 only for the outer x, not the inner one, which will later have 5 substituted for it. That way we get 28 rather than 12.

Exercise 10.13

Draw the pictorial form of the AST that would result from parsing the above expression, and carefully step through its evaluation, showing how the value of 28 is arrived at. As additional checks on your work, the parsing step should result in 13 ASTs (the main AST with 12 descendant ASTs below it), and six more ASTs should be created in the course of the evaluation so that if you sequentially number the ASTs, the last one will be numbered 19. Be sure you have enough space to work in; it is also helpful to do this exercise with a partner so that you can catch each other's slips because it requires so much attention to detail.

All that is left at this point to have a working Micro-Scheme system is the `make-procedure` procedure:

```
(define make-procedure
  (lambda (parameters body-ast)
    (lambda arguments
      (define loop
        (lambda (parameters arguments body-ast)
          (cond ((null? parameters)
                 (if (null? arguments)
                     (evaluate body-ast)
                     (error "too many arguments")))
                ((null? arguments)
                 (error "too few arguments"))
                (else
                 (loop (cdr parameters) (cdr arguments)
                       (substitute-for-in (car arguments)
                                          (car parameters)
                                          body-ast))))))
      (loop parameters arguments body-ast))))
```

One minor new feature of Scheme is shown off in the above procedure, where it has `(lambda arguments ...)` instead of the usual `(lambda (...) ...)`. This expression makes a procedure that will accept any number of arguments; they get packaged together into a list, and that list is called `arguments`.

> ### Exercise 10.14

Suppose we define (in Scheme, not Micro-Scheme) the procedure `foo` as follows:

```
(define foo (lambda x x))
```

What predefined Scheme procedure behaves exactly like `foo`?

Now that we have a working Micro-Scheme system, we can extend it either in ways that make it more similar to Scheme or in ways that make it less similar.

> **Exercise 10.15**

Add `let` expressions to Micro-Scheme, like those in Scheme.

> **Exercise 10.16**

Add a `with` expression to Micro-Scheme that can be used like this:

```
;Enter Micro-Scheme expression:
(with x = (+ 2 1) compute (* x x))
;Micro-Scheme value: 9
```

The meaning is the same as `(let ((x (+ 2 1))) (* x x))` in Scheme; unlike `let`, only a single name and a single body expression are allowed.

> **Exercise 10.17**

Add some other Scheme feature of your choice to Micro-Scheme.

> **Exercise 10.18**

Add some other non-Scheme feature of your choice to Micro-Scheme.

10.4   Global Definitions: Turning Micro-Scheme into Mini-Scheme

Using the Micro-Scheme language you can make procedures and apply them to arguments. For example, we can make a squaring procedure and apply it to 3 as follows:

```
((lambda (x) (* x x))
 3)
```

You can also give names to procedures, which will be easiest if you've added `let` expressions to Micro-Scheme, as in Exercise 10.15. In that case, you can write

```
(let ((square (lambda (x) (* x x))))
  (square 3))
```

You can even build up a succession of procedures, where later procedures make use of earlier ones. For example,

```
(let ((square (lambda (x) (* x x))))
  (let ((cylinder-volume (lambda (radius height)
                           (* (* 3.1415927 (square radius))
                              height)))))
    (cylinder-volume 5 4)))
```

However, all is not well. With the language as it stands, there is no easy way to write recursive procedures (i.e., procedures that use themselves), which is a major problem, considering all the use we've been making of recursive procedures.

To resolve this problem, we'll add definitions to our language so that we can say things like

```
(define factorial
  (lambda (n)
    (if (= n 1)
        1
        (* (factorial (- n 1))
           n))))
```

To keep matters simple, we'll stick with *global* or *top-level* definitions that are given directly to the read-eval-print loop. We won't add internal definitions nested inside other procedures. Even with only global definitions, our language suddenly becomes much more practical, so we'll rename it Mini-Scheme to distinguish it from the nearly useless Micro-Scheme.

To support global definitions and recursive procedures, we need to introduce the notion of a *global environment*. A global environment is a collection of name/value associations that reflects the global definitions that have been entered up to some point. The read-eval-print loop starts out with an initial global environment that contains the predefined names, such as +. Every time the read-eval-print loop is given a new global definition, a new global environment is formed that reflects that new definition as well as all prior ones. When the read-eval-print loop is given an expression, it is evaluated *in the current global environment* rather than simply being evaluated. We need to talk about evaluating in a global environment, rather than just evaluating, because evaluating (factorial 5) is quite different after factorial has been defined than it is before. Here is the Mini-Scheme read-eval-print loop that reflects these considerations:

```
(define read-eval-print-loop
  (lambda ()
    (define loop
      (lambda (global-environment)
        (display ";Enter Mini-Scheme expr. or definition:")
        (newline)
        (let ((expression-or-definition (read)))
          (if (definition? expression-or-definition)
              (let ((name (definition-name
                            expression-or-definition))
                    (value (evaluate-in
                             (parse (definition-expression
                                      expression-or-definition))
                             global-environment)))
                (display ";Mini-scheme defined: ")
                (write name)
                (newline)
                (loop (extend-global-environment-with-naming
                        global-environment
                        name value)))
              (let ((value (evaluate-in
                             (parse expression-or-definition)
                             global-environment)))
                (display ";Mini-scheme value: ")
                (write value)
                (newline)
                (loop global-environment))))))
    (loop (make-initial-global-environment))))
```

This new read-eval-print loop distinguishes between definitions and expressions using the predicate `definition?` and selects out the two components of a definition using `definition-name` and `definition-expression`. Before we move onto the more meaty issues surrounding global environments, here are simple definitions of these more superficial procedures:

```
(define definition?
  (lambda (x)
    (and (list? x)
         (matches? '(define _ _) x))))

(define definition-name cadr)

(define definition-expression caddr)
```

Returning to global environments, we now have a good start on considering them operationally, as an abstract data type. We have seen that we need two constructors, `make-initial-global-environment` and `extend-global-environment-with-naming`. The former produces a global environment that contains the predefined names, and the latter makes a new global environment that is the same as a preexisting global environment except for one new name/value association. What about selectors? We'll need a `look-up-value-in` selector, which when given a name and a global environment finds the value associated with that name in that global environment.

To see how this selector winds up getting used, we need to consider `evaluate-in`, which is the Mini-Scheme analog of Micro-Scheme's `evaluate`:

```
(define evaluate-in
  (lambda (ast global-environment)
    ((ast 'evaluate-in) global-environment)))
```

As before, the actual knowledge regarding how to evaluate is localized within each kind of AST. The only difference is that now an `evaluate-in` operation, rather than `evaluate`, is provided by each kind of AST. This new operation is applied to the global environment in which the evaluation is to occur.

When we look at name ASTs, we see the key difference between the Mini-Scheme `evaluate-in` operation, which looks up the name in the specified global environment, and the old Micro-Scheme `evaluate`:

```
(define make-name-ast
  (lambda (name)
    (define the-ast
      (lambda (message)
        (cond ((equal? message 'evaluate-in)
               (lambda (global-environment)
                 (look-up-value-in name global-environment)))
              ((equal? message 'substitute-for)
               (lambda (value name-to-substitute-for)
                 (if (equal? name name-to-substitute-for)
                     (make-constant-ast value)
                     the-ast)))
              (else (error "unknown operation on a name AST"
                           message)))))
    the-ast))
```

Constant ASTs can be implemented in a way that is very similar to Micro-Scheme, because the global environment is completely irrelevant to their evaluation:

```
(define make-constant-ast
  (lambda (value)
    (define the-ast
      (lambda (message)
        (cond ((equal? message 'evaluate-in)
               (lambda (global-environment)
                 value))
              ((equal? message 'substitute-for)
               (lambda (value name)
                 the-ast))
              (else (error "unknown operation on a constant AST"
                           message)))))
    the-ast))
```

For conditional ASTs (i.e., if expressions), the global environment information is simply passed down to the evaluations of subexpression ASTs:

```
(define make-conditional-ast
  (lambda (test-ast if-true-ast if-false-ast)
    (lambda (message)
      (cond ((equal? message 'evaluate-in)
             (lambda (global-environment)
               (if (evaluate-in test-ast global-environment)
                   (evaluate-in if-true-ast global-environment)
                   (evaluate-in if-false-ast global-environment))))
            ((equal? message 'substitute-for)
             (lambda (value name)
               (make-conditional-ast
                (substitute-for-in value name test-ast)
                (substitute-for-in value name if-true-ast)
                (substitute-for-in value name if-false-ast))))
            (else (error "unknown operation on a conditional AST"
                         message))))))
```

As with the constant ASTs, the global environment is irrelevant to the evaluation of abstraction ASTs (i.e., lambda expressions):

```
(define make-abstraction-ast
  (lambda (parameters body-ast)
    (define the-ast
      (lambda (message)
        ;;(continued)
```

```
            (cond ((equal? message 'evaluate-in)
                   (lambda (global-environment)
                     (make-procedure parameters body-ast)))
                  ((equal? message 'substitute-for)
                   (lambda (value name)
                     (if (member name parameters)
                         the-ast
                         (make-abstraction-ast
                          parameters
                          (substitute-for-in value name body-ast)))))
                  (else (error "unknown operation on an abstraction AST"
                               message)))))
      the-ast))
```

The last AST to consider is the application AST. When a procedure is applied, its body is evaluated (with appropriate parameter substitutions done) in the current global environment. Thus, we need to keep track of that global environment. In order to do this, we'll pass in the global environment as an extra argument to the Mini-Scheme procedure, before the real ones:

```
(define make-application-ast
  (lambda (operator-ast operand-asts)
    (lambda (message)
      (cond ((equal? message 'evaluate-in)
             (lambda (global-environment)
               (let ((procedure (evaluate-in operator-ast
                                             global-environment))
                     (arguments (map (lambda (ast)
                                       (evaluate-in
                                        ast
                                        global-environment))
                                     operand-asts)))
                 (apply procedure
                        (cons global-environment arguments)))))
            ((equal? message 'substitute-for)
             (lambda (value name)
               (make-application-ast
                (substitute-for-in value name operator-ast)
                ;;(continued)
```

```
                    (map (lambda (operand-ast)
                           (substitute-for-in value
                                              name
                                              operand-ast))
                        operand-asts))))
                  (else (error "unknown operation on an application AST"
                             message))))))
```

Of course, we'll have to change `make-procedure` so that it expects this extra first
argument and uses it appropriately:

```
(define make-procedure
  (lambda (parameters body-ast)
    (lambda global-environment&arguments
      (let ((global-environment (car global-environment&arguments))
            (arguments (cdr global-environment&arguments)))
        (define loop
          (lambda (parameters arguments body-ast)
            (cond ((null? parameters)
                   (if (null? arguments)
                       (evaluate-in body-ast global-environment)
                       (error "too many arguments")))
                  ((null? arguments)
                   (error "too few arguments"))
                  (else
                   (loop (cdr parameters) (cdr arguments)
                         (substitute-for-in (car arguments)
                                            (car parameters)
                                            body-ast))))))
        (loop parameters arguments body-ast)))))
```

> ### Exercise 10.19

Look up `lambda` expressions in the R^{4}RS (available from the web site for
this book) and figure out how to rewrite `make-procedure` so that it has
`(lambda (global-environment . arguments) ...)` where the above version
has `(lambda global-environment&arguments ...)`.

Finally, we need to implement global environments. Because global environments
are used to find a value when given a name, one simple implementation is to use
procedures. Thus a global environment is a procedure that takes a name as its
parameter and returns the corresponding value:

```
(define look-up-value-in
  (lambda (name global-environment)
    (global-environment name)))

(define make-initial-global-environment
  (lambda ()
    (lambda (name)
      return the built-in procedure called name)))

(define extend-global-environment-with-naming
  (lambda (old-environment name value)
    (lambda (n)
      (if (equal? n name)
          value
          (old-environment n)))))
```

As you can see, we still need to finish writing `make-initial-global-environment`. The procedure it produces, for converting a name (such as `+`) to a built-in procedure (such as the addition procedure), is very similar to `look-up-value`. However, there is one important difference. In Micro-Scheme, we could directly use the built-in procedures (such as addition) from normal Scheme; thus, `look-up-value` could return these procedures, such as the Scheme procedure called `+`. However, in Mini-Scheme this is no longer the case. In Mini-Scheme, the evaluation of an application AST no longer applies the procedure to just its arguments. Instead, it slips in the global environment as an extra argument before the real ones. Thus, if we were to use normal Scheme's `+` as Mini-Scheme's `+`, when we tried doing even something as simple as `(+ 2 2)`, we'd get an error message because the Scheme addition procedure would be applied to three arguments: a global environment, the number 2, and the number 2 again.

To work around this problem, we'll make a Mini-Scheme version of `+` and of all the other built-in procedures. The Mini-Scheme version will simply ignore its first argument, the global environment. We can make a Mini-Scheme version of any Scheme procedure using the following converter:

```
(define make-mini-scheme-version-of
  (lambda (procedure)
    (lambda global-environment&arguments
      (let ((global-environment (car global-environment&arguments))
            (arguments (cdr global-environment&arguments)))
        (apply procedure arguments)))))
```

For example, this procedure could be used as follows:

```
(define ms+ (make-mini-scheme-version-of +))

(ms+ (make-initial-global-environment) 2 2)
4
```

Now, we can finish writing `make-initial-global-environment`:

```
(define make-initial-global-environment
  (lambda ()
    (let ((ms+ (make-mini-scheme-version-of +))
          (ms- (make-mini-scheme-version-of -))
          ;; the rest get similarly converted in here
          )
      (lambda (name)
        (cond ((equal? name '+) ms+)
              ((equal? name '-) ms-)
              ;; the rest get similarly selected in here
              (else (error "Unrecognized name" name)))))))
```

> ### Exercise 10.20

Flesh out `make-initial-global-environment`.

> ### Exercise 10.21

Extend your solution of Exercise 10.19 to `make-mini-scheme-version-of`.

10.5   An Application: Adding Explanatory Output to Mini-Scheme

In this section, you'll modify the Mini-Scheme implementation so that each expression being evaluated is displayed. You'll then further modify the system so that varying indentation is used to show whether an expression is being evaluated as the main problem, a subproblem, a sub-subproblem, etc. You'll also modify the system to display the value resulting from each evaluation.

To display each expression as it is evaluated, we can modify the `evaluate-in` procedure. At first you might think something like the following would work:

```
(define evaluate-in     ; Warning: this version doesn't work
  (lambda (ast global-environment)
    (display ";Mini-Scheme evaluating: ")
    (write ast)
    (newline)
    ((ast 'evaluate-in) global-environment)))
```

Unfortunately, this code displays the AST being evaluated, and what the user would really like to see is the corresponding expression. Therefore, we'll instead define `evaluate-in` as follows:

```
(define evaluate-in
  (lambda (ast global-environment)
    (display ";Mini-Scheme evaluating: ")
    (write (unparse ast))
    (newline)
    ((ast 'evaluate-in) global-environment)))
```

This code uses a new generic operation on ASTs, `unparse`. This operation should recreate the expression corresponding to an AST. The `unparse` procedure itself looks much like any generic operation:

```
(define unparse
  (lambda (ast)
    (ast 'unparse)))
```

Now we have to modify each AST constructor to provide the `unparse` operation. Here, for example is `make-application-ast`:

```
(define make-application-ast
  (lambda (operator-ast operand-asts)
    (lambda (message)
      (cond ((equal? message 'unparse)
             (cons (unparse operator-ast)
                   (map unparse operand-asts)))
            ((equal? message 'evaluate-in)
             unchanged)
            ((equal? message 'substitute-for)
             unchanged)
            (else (error "unknown operation on an application AST"
                         message))))))
```

► **Exercise 10.22**

Add the `unparse` operation to each of the other AST constructors. When you add `unparse` to `make-constant-ast`, keep in mind that some constants will need to be expressed as quotations. For example, a constant with the value 3 can be unparsed into 3, but a constant that has the symbol x as its value will need to be unparsed into (quote x). You can look at the **parse** procedure to see what kinds of values can serve as constant expressions without being wrapped in a quotation.

> **Exercise 10.23**
>
> Adding the **unparse** operation has rather unfortunately destroyed the separation of concerns between **parse** and the AST types. It used to be that only **parse** needed to know what each kind of expression looked like. In fact, most of the knowledge regarding the superficial appearance of expressions was concentrated in the parsing pattern/action list. Now that same knowledge is being duplicated in the implementation of the **unparse** operation. Suggest some possible approaches to recentralizing the knowledge of expression appearance. You need only outline some options; actually implementing any good approach is likely to be somewhat challenging.

At this point, you should be able to do evaluations (even fairly complex ones, like (factorial 5)) and get a running stream of output from Mini-Scheme explaining what it is evaluating. However, no distinction is made between evaluations that are stages in the evolution of the main problem and those that are subproblems (or subsubproblems or . . .), which makes the output relatively hard to understand. We can rectify this problem by replacing evaluate-in with evaluate-in-at, which takes not only an expression to evaluate and a global environment to evaluate it in, but also a *subproblem nesting level* at which to do the evaluation. The actual evaluation is no different at one level than at another, but the explanatory output is indented differently:

```
(define evaluate-in-at
  (lambda (ast global-environment level)
    (display ";Mini-Scheme evaluating:")
    (display-times " " level)
    (write (unparse ast))
    (newline)
    ((ast 'evaluate-in-at) global-environment level)))

(define display-times
  (lambda (output count)
    (if (= count 0)
        'done
        (begin (display output)
               (display-times output (- count 1))))))
```

The AST constructors also need to be modified to accommodate this new evaluate-in-at operation. Here's the new **make-application-ast**, which evaluates the operator and each operand at one subproblem nesting level deeper:

```
(define make-application-ast
  (lambda (operator-ast operand-asts)
    (lambda (message)
      (cond ((equal? message 'unparse)
             unchanged)
            ((equal? message 'evaluate-in-at)
             (lambda (global-environment level)
               (let ((procedure (evaluate-in-at operator-ast
                                                 global-environment
                                                 (+ level 1)))
                     (arguments (map (lambda (ast)
                                       (evaluate-in-at
                                        ast
                                        global-environment
                                        (+ level 1)))
                                     operand-asts)))
                 (apply procedure
                        (cons global-environment
                              arguments)))))
            ((equal? message 'substitute-for)
             unchanged)
            (else (error "unknown operation on an application AST"
                         message))))))
```

▷ **Exercise 10.24**

Modify the other AST constructors to support the **evaluate-in-at** operation. For conditionals, the test should be evaluated one nesting level deeper than the overall conditional, but the if-true or if-false part should be evaluated at the same level as the overall conditional. (This distinction is because the value of the test is not the value of the overall conditional, so it is a subproblem, but the value of the if-true or if-false part *is* the value of the conditional, so whichever part is selected is simply a later stage in the evolution of the same problem rather than being a subproblem. This reasoning is illustrated in Figure 1.2 on page 14 and Figure 10.6.)

> **Exercise 10.25**

Modify the `read-eval-print-loop` so that it does its evaluations at subproblem nesting level 1.

> **Exercise 10.26**

Modify `make-procedure` so that the procedures it makes expect to receive an extra level argument after the global environment argument, before the real arguments. The procedure body (after substitutions) should then be evaluated at this level. You'll also need to change `make-application-ast` to supply this extra argument and change `make-mini-scheme-version-of` to produce procedures that expect (and ignore) this extra argument.

At this point, if you try doing some evaluations in Mini-Scheme, you'll get output like the following:

```
;Enter Mini-Scheme expr. or definition:
(+ (* 3 5) (* 6 7))
;Mini-Scheme evaluating: (+ (* 3 5) (* 6 7))
;Mini-Scheme evaluating:  +
;Mini-Scheme evaluating:  (* 3 5)
;Mini-Scheme evaluating:   *
;Mini-Scheme evaluating:   3
;Mini-Scheme evaluating:   5
;Mini-Scheme evaluating:  (* 6 7)
;Mini-Scheme evaluating:   *
;Mini-Scheme evaluating:   6
;Mini-Scheme evaluating:   7
;Mini-scheme value: 57
```

On the positive side, it is now possible to see the various subproblem nesting levels. For example, +, (* 3 5), and (* 6 7) are subproblems of the main problem, and *, 3, 5, * (again), 6, and 7 are sub-subproblems. On the negative side, this output is still lacking any indication of the values resulting from the various nested problems (other than the final value shown for the main problem). For example, we can't see that the two multiplications produced 15 and 42 as their values. We can arrange for the value produced by each evaluation to be displayed, indented to match the "Mini-Scheme evaluating" line:

```
(define evaluate-in-at
  (lambda (ast global-environment level)
    (display ";Mini-Scheme evaluating:")
    (display-times " " level)
    (write (unparse ast))
    (newline)
    (let ((value ((ast 'evaluate-in-at) global-environment level)))
      (display ";Mini-Scheme value     :")
      (display-times " " level)
      (write value)
      (newline)
      value)))
```

With this change, we can see the values of the two multiplication subproblems as well as the addition problem. However, as you can see below, the result is such a muddled mess as to make it questionable whether we've made progress:

```
;Enter Mini-Scheme expr. or definition:
(+ (* 3 5) (* 6 7))
;Mini-Scheme evaluating: (+ (* 3 5) (* 6 7))
;Mini-Scheme evaluating:  +
;Mini-Scheme value     :  #<procedure>
;Mini-Scheme evaluating:  (* 3 5)
;Mini-Scheme evaluating:   *
;Mini-Scheme value     :   #<procedure>
;Mini-Scheme evaluating:  3
;Mini-Scheme value     :  3
;Mini-Scheme evaluating:  5
;Mini-Scheme value     :  5
;Mini-Scheme value     :  15
;Mini-Scheme evaluating:  (* 6 7)
;Mini-Scheme evaluating:   *
;Mini-Scheme value     :   #<procedure>
;Mini-Scheme evaluating:  6
;Mini-Scheme value     :  6
;Mini-Scheme evaluating:  7
;Mini-Scheme value     :  7
;Mini-Scheme value     :  42
;Mini-Scheme value     : 57
;Mini-scheme value: 57
```

This explanatory output is so impenetrable that we clearly are going to have to find a more visually comprehensible format. We'll design an idealized version of our format first, without regard to how we are going to actually produce that output. While we are at it, we can also solve another problem with our existing output: We don't currently have any way of explicitly showing that an evaluation problem is converted into another problem of the same level with the same value. Instead, the new and old problems are treated independently, and the value is shown for each (identically). For an iterative process, we'll see the same value over and over again. For example, if we computed the factorial of 5 iteratively, we'd get shown the value 120 not only as our final value but also as the value of each of the equivalent problems, such as $1 \times 5!$, $5 \times 4!$, $20 \times 3!$, etc. Yet we'd really like to see each problem converted into the next with a single answer at the bottom.

An example of our idealized format is shown in Figure 10.7; as you can see, it is closely based on the diagrams we used to explain AST evaluation. Notice that we

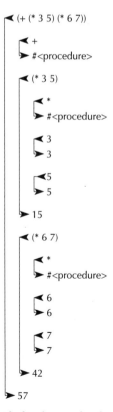

Figure 10.7   An idealized example of explanatory output

are still using indentation to show the subproblem nesting levels, but now we are also using lines with arrowheads to show the connection between each expression and its value. We can also use a similar format to show several expressions sharing the same value, as in Figure 10.8. Here three expressions all share the value 9. The first is an application expression, and the second results from it by substituting the

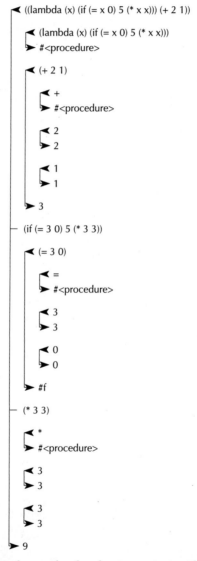

Figure 10.8 Another idealized example of explanatory output, with three equivalent problems sharing the value 9

argument value, 3, into the procedure body in place of the parameter name, x. The resulting conditional expression, (if (= 3 0) 5 (* 3 3)), is in turn converted into the third equivalent expression, (* 3 3), because the condition evaluates to a false value.

If we want to approximate these diagrams, but do so using the normal Scheme display procedure, which produces textual output, we'll have to settle for using characters to approximate the lines and arrowheads. Our two examples are shown in this form in Figures 10.9 and 10.10.

```
+-< (+ (* 3 5) (* 6 7))
|
| +-< +
| +-> #<procedure>
|
| +-< (* 3 5)
| |
| | +-< *
| | +-> #<procedure>
| |
| | +-< 3
| | +-> 3
| |
| | +-< 5
| | +-> 5
| |
| +-> 15
|
| +-< (* 6 7)
| |
| | +-< *
| | +-> #<procedure>
| |
| | +-< 6
| | +-> 6
| |
| | +-< 7
| | +-> 7
| |
| +-> 42
|
+-> 57
```

Figure 10.9   Explanatory output with lines and arrowheads approximated using characters

```
+-< ((lambda (x) (if (= x 0) 5 (* x x))) (+ 2 1))
|
| +-< (lambda (x) (if (= x 0) 5 (* x x)))
| +-> #<procedure>
|
| +-< (+ 2 1)
| |
| | +-< +
| | +-> #<procedure>
| |
| | +-< 2
| | +-> 2
| |
| | +-< 1
| | +-> 1
| |
| +-> 3
|
+-- (if (= 3 0) 5 (* 3 3))
|
| +-< (= 3 0)
| |
| | +-< =
| | +-> #<procedure>
| |
| | +-< 3
| | +-> 3
| |
| | +-< 0
| | +-> 0
| |
| +-> #f
|
+-- (* 3 3)
|
| +-< *
| +-> #<procedure>
|
| +-< 3
| +-> 3
|
| +-< 3
| +-> 3
|
+-> 9
```

Figure 10.10   Second example of explanatory output using characters

In the character-based version of the explanatory output, there are two kinds of lines: lines that have something on them, like

```
| +-< (+ 2 1)
```

or

```
| +-> 3
```

or

```
+-- (* 3 3)
```

and those that are blank aside from the vertical connecting lines, such as

```
| |
```

We can use two procedures for producing these two kinds of line. For the ones that have content, we need to specify the thing to write (which might be an expression or a value), the "indicator" that shows what kind of line this is (< or > or -), and the nesting level. For blank lines, only the nesting level is needed:

```
(define write-with-at
  (lambda (thing indicator level)
    (display-times "| " (- level 1))
    (display "+-")
    (display indicator)
    (display " ")
    (write thing)
    (newline)))

(define blank-line-at
  (lambda (level)
    (display-times "| " level)
    (newline)))
```

Now we have to insert the appropriate calls to these procedures into our evaluator. We'll need to differentiate between two kinds of evaluations: those that should have lines with leftward pointing arrowheads (initial evaluations) and those that should have arrowheadless connecting lines (additional evaluations sharing the same ultimate value). The additional evaluations, with the arrowheadless line, originate from two sources: evaluating the body of a procedure with the argument values substituted in and evaluating one or the other alternative of a conditional. Both are shown in our example of evaluating `((lambda (x) (if (= x 0) 5 (* x x))) (+ 2 1))`. We can handle initial and additional evaluations differently by using two separate procedures. For initial evaluations we'll use our existing `evaluate-in-at`, which provides the left-arrow line and also is responsible for the right-arrow line at the end with the value. We'll use a new procedure, `evaluate-additional-in-at`, for the additional evaluations, which just "hook into" the existing evaluation's line:

```
(define evaluate-in-at
  (lambda (ast global-environment level)
    (blank-line-at (- level 1))
    (write-with-at (unparse ast) "<" level)
    (let ((value ((ast 'evaluate-in-at) global-environment level)))
      (write-with-at value ">" level)
      value)))
```

```
(define evaluate-additional-in-at
  (lambda (ast global-environment level)
    (blank-line-at level)
    (write-with-at (unparse ast) "-" level)
    ((ast 'evaluate-in-at) global-environment level)))
```

> **Exercise 10.27**

Three calls to `evaluate-in-at` need to be changed to `evaluate-additional-in-at`. Change them.

> **Exercise 10.28**

To make the output look as shown, it is also necessary to provide a blank line before the value of a built-in procedure. Put the appropriate call to `blank-line-at` into the procedures generated by `make-mini-scheme-version-of`.

> **Exercise 10.29**

When an application expression is evaluated, it might be desirable to explicitly show that a procedure is being applied and what argument values it is being applied to, after the operator and operands have been evaluated. Figure 10.11 shows an example of this. Add this feature.

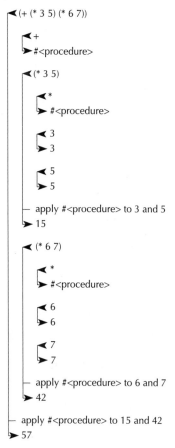

Figure 10.11 Explanatory output with applications shown

► Exercise 10.30

Decide what further improvements you'd like to have in the explanatory output and make the necessary changes.

Review Problems

▷ Exercise 10.31

Use EBNF to write a grammar for the language of all strings of one or more digits that simultaneously meet both of the following requirements:

a. The digits alternate between even and odd, starting with either.
b. The string of digits is the same backward as forward (i.e., is palindromic).

Your grammar may define more than one syntactic category name (nonterminal), but be sure to specify which one generates the language described above.

▷ **Exercise 10.32**

Suppose the following Micro-Scheme expression is parsed:

```
((lambda (x) x) (if (+ 2 3) + 3))
```

a. Draw the AST that would result.

b. If this AST were evaluated, two of the ASTs it contains (as sub-ASTs or sub-sub-ASTs, etc.) would not wind up getting evaluated. Indicate these two by circling them, and explain for each of them why it doesn't get evaluated.

▷ **Exercise 10.33**

In Scheme, Micro-Scheme, and Mini-Scheme, it is an error to evaluate ((+ 2 3) (* 5 7) 16) because this will try to apply 5 to 35 and 16, and 5 isn't a procedure. It would be possible to change the language so that instead of this construction being an error, it would evaluate to the three-element list (5 35 16). That is, when the "operator" subexpression of an "application" expression turns out not to evaluate to a procedure, a list of that value and the "operand" values is produced.

a. Change Micro-Scheme or Mini-Scheme to have this new feature.

b. Argue that this is an improvement to the language.

c. Argue that it makes the language worse.

▷ **Exercise 10.34**

Suppose that the Micro-Scheme `make-conditional-ast` were changed to the following:

```
(define make-conditional-ast
  (lambda (test-ast if-true-ast if-false-ast)
    (lambda (message)
      (cond ((equal? message 'evaluate)
             (let ((test-value (evaluate test-ast))
                   (if-true-value (evaluate if-true-ast))
                   (if-false-value (evaluate if-false-ast)))
               ;;(continued)
```

```
    (if test-value
        if-true-value
        if-false-value)))
 ((equal? message 'substitute-for)
  (lambda (value name)
    (make-conditional-ast
     (substitute-for-in value name test-ast)
     (substitute-for-in value name if-true-ast)
     (substitute-for-in value name if-false-ast))))
 (else (error "unknown operation on a conditional AST"
              message))))))
```

a. Give an example of a conditional expression where this new version of `make-conditional-ast` would produce an AST that evaluates to the same value as the old version would.

b. Give an example of a conditional expression where evaluating the AST constructed by the new version would produce different results from evaluating the AST produced by the old version.

c. Is this change a good idea or a bad one? Explain.

▷ Exercise 10.35

Rewrite `look-up-value` to use a table of names and their corresponding values, rather than a large `cond`.

▷ Exercise 10.36

Replace the global-environment ADT implementation with an alternative representation based on a list of name/value pairs.

▷ Exercise 10.37

Some programming languages have a so-called `arithmetic-if` expression that is similar to Scheme's `if` expression, except that instead of having a boolean test condition and two other subexpressions (the if-true and if-false subexpressions), it has a numerical test expression and *three* other subexpressions (the if-negative, the if-zero, and the if-positive subexpressions). To evaluate an `arithmetic-if` expression, you first evaluate the test expression, and then, depending upon whether that value is negative, zero, or positive, the corresponding subexpression is evaluated. For example, if you wanted to define an `expt` procedure that appropriately dealt with both positive and negative integers, you could write

```
(define expt
  (lambda (b n)
    (arithmetic-if n
                   (/ 1 (expt b (- n)))
                   1
                   (* b (expt b (- n 1)))))))
```

You will work through the details of adding `arithmetic-if`'s to Mini-Scheme in this problem. To get you started, let's choose to implement `arithmetic-if`s using a new AST constructor `make-arithmetic-if-ast`. The skeleton for `make-arithmetic-if-ast`, with the important code left out, is as follows (note that all subexpressions are passed in parsed):

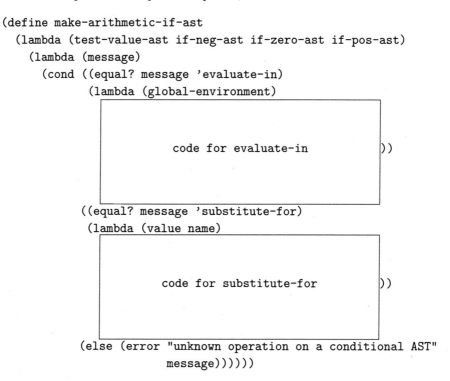

```
(define make-arithmetic-if-ast
  (lambda (test-value-ast if-neg-ast if-zero-ast if-pos-ast)
    (lambda (message)
      (cond ((equal? message 'evaluate-in)
             (lambda (global-environment)


                        code for evaluate-in              ))


            ((equal? message 'substitute-for)
             (lambda (value name)


                        code for substitute-for           ))


            (else (error "unknown operation on a conditional AST"
                         message)))))))
```

a. Add the code for `evaluate-in`.
b. Add the code for `substitute-for`.
c. Add the appropriate pattern/action to the `micro-scheme-parsing-p/a-list`.

▷ **Exercise 10.38**

Suppose we add a new kind of expression to the Micro-Scheme language, the `uncons` expression. The EBNF for it is as follows:

```
(uncons ⟨expression⟩ into ⟨name⟩ and ⟨name⟩ in ⟨expression⟩)
```

This kind of expression is evaluated as follows:

- The first ⟨expression⟩ is evaluated. Its value must be a pair (such as cons produces); otherwise, an error is signaled.
- The car of that pair is substituted for the first ⟨name⟩, and the cdr for the second ⟨name⟩, in the second ⟨expression⟩.
- After these substitutions have been made, the second ⟨expression⟩ (as modified by the substitutions) is then evaluated. Its value is the value of the overall uncons expression.

For a simple (and stupid) example, the expression

```
(uncons (cons 3 5) into x and y in (+ x y))
```

would evaluate to 8.

Parsing an uncons expression involves parsing the constituent expressions, which we can call the pair-expression and the body-expression. The resulting two ASTs, which we can call the pair-ast and body-ast, get passed into the make-uncons-ast constructor, along with the two names, which we can call the car-name and cdr-name. Here is the outline of make-uncons-ast; write the two missing pieces of code.

```
(define make-uncons-ast
  (lambda (pair-ast body-ast car-name cdr-name)
    (lambda (message)
      (cond ((equal? message 'evaluate)


                         code for evaluate                    )


            ((equal? message 'substitute-for)
             (lambda (value name)


                    code for substitute-for           ))


            (else (error "unknown operation on a for AST"
                         message))))))
```

Chapter Inventory

Vocabulary

read-eval-print loop
Extended Backus-Naur Form (EBNF)
syntactic correctness
semantic error
keyword
grammar
syntactic category
production
nonterminal

terminal
abstraction
parsing
free
bound
global or top-level definition
global environment
subproblem nesting level
arithmetic if

Slogans

The universality principle

Abstract Data Types

abstract syntax tree (AST)

New Predefined Scheme Names

```
symbol?
string?
```

```
boolean?
write
```

New Scheme Syntax

```
quote
```
lambda expressions accepting variable
numbers of arguments

Scheme Names Defined in This Chapter

```
keyword?
name?
syntax-ok?
micro-scheme-syntax-ok?-p/a-list
read-eval-print-loop
parse
micro-scheme-parsing-p/a-list
evaluate
substitute-for-in
make-name-ast
make-constant-ast
```

```
make-conditional-ast
make-application-ast
make-abstraction-ast
make-procedure
definition?
definition-name
definition-expression
evaluate-in
look-up-value-in
make-initial-global-environment
```

```
extend-global-environment-        write-with-at
    with-naming                   blank-line-at
make-mini-scheme-version-of       evaluate-additional-in-at
unparse                           make-arithmetic-if-ast
evaluate-in-at                    make-uncons-ast
display-times
```

Sidebars

The Expressiveness of EBNF

Notes

We motivated Mini-Scheme with the remark that Micro-Scheme provides no easy way to express recursive procedures. As an example of the not-so-easy ways of expressing recursion that *are* possible even in Micro-Scheme, we offer the following:

```
;; factorial-maker makes factorial when given factorial-maker
(let ((factorial-maker
        (lambda (factorial-maker)
          (lambda (n)
            (if (= n 0)
                1
                (let ((factorial
                        (factorial-maker factorial-maker)))
                  (* (factorial (- n 1))
                     n)))))))
  (let ((factorial (factorial-maker factorial-maker)))
    (factorial 52)))
```

PART III

Abstractions of State

In the previous part, we characterized each type of data by the collection of operations that could be performed on data of that type. However, there were only two fundamental kinds of operations: those that constructed new things and those that asked questions about existing things. In this part, we'll add a third, fundamentally different, kind of operation, one that modifies an existing object. This kind of operation also raises the possibility that two concurrently active computations will interact because one can modify an object the other is using. Therefore, at the conclusion of this part we'll examine concurrent, interacting computations.

We will lead into our discussion of changeable objects by looking at how computers are organized and how they carry out computations. The relevance of this discussion is that the storage locations in a computer's memory constitute the fundamental changeable object. We'll look next at how numerically indexed storage locations, like a computer's memory, can be used to make some computational processes dramatically more efficient by eliminating redundant recomputations of subproblem results. Then we'll look at other forms of modifiable objects, where the operations don't reflect the computer's numbered storage locations but rather reflect application-specific concerns. We'll then build this technique into object-oriented programming by blending in the idea that multiple concrete kinds of objects can share a common interface of generic operations. Finally, we will show how to transplant these same ideas into another programming language, Java, that we will use to introduce programs that have concurrent, interacting components.

CHAPTER ELEVEN

Computers with Memory

11.1 Introduction

In the first two parts of the book we looked at computational processes from the perspective of the procedures and the data on which those procedures describe operations, but we've not yet discussed the computer that does the processing. In this chapter, we'll look at the overall structure of a typical present-day computer and see how such a computer is actually able to carry out a procedurally specified computational process.

One of the most noteworthy components we'll see that computers have is *memory* (specifically, *Random Access Memory* or *RAM*). What makes memory so interesting is that it is unlike anything we've seen thus far—it is not a process or a procedure for carrying out a process, and it is also not simply a value or a collection of values. Rather, it is a collection of *locations* in which values can be stored; each location has a particular value at any one time, but the value can be changed so that the location contains a different value than it used to.

After seeing collections of memory locations as a component of computers, we'll see how they are also available for our use when programming in Scheme, as so-called *vectors*. In this chapter, we introduce vectors and use them to build a computer simulator in Scheme. In the following chapters we look at ways in which these locations can be used to improve the efficiency of computational processes and to construct software systems that are modular and naturally reflect the structure of noncomputational systems that the software models.

11.2 An Example Computer Architecture

In this section, we will attempt to "open the hood" of a computer like the one you have been using while working through this book. However, because so many different types of computers exist, and because actual computers are highly complex machines involving many engineering design decisions, we will make two simplifications. First, rather than choosing any one real computer to explain, we've made up our own simple, yet representative, computer, the Super-Lean Instruction Machine, also known as SLIM. Second, rather than presenting the design of SLIM in detail, we describe it at the *architectural* level. By *architecture* we mean the overall structure of the computer system to the extent it is relevant to the computer's ability to execute a program.

You might well wonder whether an actual SLIM computer exists that meets the specifications of our architectural design. To our knowledge, no such computer does exist, although in principle one could be fabricated. (Before construction could begin, the specifications would need to be made more complete than the version we present here.) Because you are unlikely to find a real SLIM, we provide a simulated SLIM computer on the web site for this book; we will say more about this simulated computer in the next section. In fact, this chapter's application section involves writing another simulator for SLIM.

Even at the architectural level, we have many options open to us as computer designers. We use the SLIM architecture to focus on a single representative set of choices rather than illustrating the entire range of options. These choices were made to be as simple as possible while still remaining broadly similar to what is typical of today's architectures. We point out a few specific areas where alternative choices are common, but you should keep in mind that the entire architecture consists of nothing but decisions, none of which is universal. A good successor course on computer organization and architecture will not only show you the options we're omitting but will also explain how a designer can choose among those options to rationally balance price and performance.

SLIM is a *stored program computer*. By this we mean that its behavior consists of performing a sequence of operations determined by a *program*, which is a list of *instructions*. The set of possible instructions, called the computer's *instruction set*, enumerates the computer's basic capabilities. Each instruction manipulates certain objects in the computer—for example, reading input from the keyboard, storing some value in a memory location, or adding the values in two memory locations and putting the result into a third. The way that an actual computer accomplishes these tasks is a very interesting story but not one we will pursue here. Viewing SLIM as a stored program computer allows us to focus on the computational core of computers.

You might well ask, "How does this information relate to my computer? I don't recall ever specifically telling my computer to run through a list of instructions." In fact, you probably have done so, regardless of how primitive or advanced your computer is. Turning on (or "booting up") the computer implicitly loads in and starts running an initial program known as an *operating system*, part of whose task is to make it easy to run other programs. The applications you use on your computer (such as your Scheme system) are programs stored in the computer's memory. When you

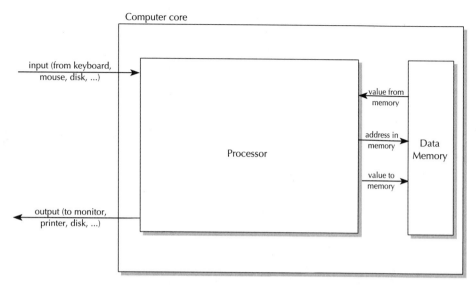

Figure 11.1   High-level view of SLIM

invoke one of these applications, perhaps by using a mouse to click on an icon, you are causing the operating system to load the application program into the computer's instruction memory and start execution at the program's first instruction.

We start with a *structural* description of SLIM: Figure 11.1 shows a high-level, coarse-grained view of its architecture. The boxes in this diagram represent SLIM's functional units, and the arrows show paths for the flow of data between these units. Our structural description will involve describing the tasks of the functional units, successively "opening them up" to reveal their functional subunits and internal data paths. We will stop at a level detailed enough to give an understanding of how a stored program works rather than continuing to open each unit until we get to the level of the electrical circuits that implement it. In the next section we will turn our attention to an *operational* understanding of the architecture, and will enumerate the instructions it can execute.

The *computer core* is an organizing concept referring to those parts of SLIM except its input and output devices—imagine it as your computer minus its keyboard, mouse, monitor, and disk drive. Because SLIM is a stored program computer, the task of the computer is to *run* (or *execute*) a program, which takes in input and produces output. Instead of considering all of the possible *input* and *output devices* enumerated in the diagram, we will make the simplifying assumption that input comes from the keyboard and output goes to the monitor screen.

The *processor* performs the operations that constitute the execution of a program, using the *data memory* to store values as needed for the program. When a processor operation requires that values be stored into or retrieved from memory, it sends to the memory unit the *address* (described below) of the memory location. The memory unit remembers what value was most recently stored by the processor into each location. When the processor then asks the memory to retrieve a value from a particular location, the memory returns to the processor that most recently stored value, leaving it in the location so that the same value can be retrieved again. The processor can also consume input and produce output.

Even at this very crude level, our architecture for SLIM already embodies important decisions. For example, we've decided not to have multiple independently operating processors, all storing to and retrieving from a single shared memory. Yet in practice, such *shared-memory multiprocessor* systems are becoming relatively common at the time of this writing. Similarly, for simplicity we've connected the input and output devices only to the processor in SLIM, yet real architectures today commonly include *Direct Memory Access* (DMA), in which input can flow into memory and output can be retrieved directly from memory without passing through the processor.

Now we need to examine each of the boxes in the computer core more closely. The memory component is the simpler one. Conceptually, it is a long sequence of "slots" (or "boxes") that are the individual memory locations. In order to allow the processor to uniquely specify each location, the slots are sequentially numbered starting at 0. The number corresponding to a given slot is called its *address*. When the processor asks the memory to store 7 at address 13, the memory unit throws away the value that is in the slot numbered 13 and puts a 7 into that slot, as shown in Figure 11.2. At any later time, as long as no other store into location 13 has been done in the meantime, the processor can ask the memory to retrieve the value from

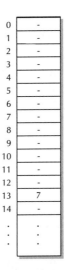

Figure 11.2   Memory, with 7 stored at address 13

address 13 and get the 7 back. (Note that the location numbered 13 is actually the fourteenth location because the first address is 0.)

The processor has considerably more internal structure than the memory because it needs to

- Keep track of what it is supposed to do next as it steps through the instructions that constitute the program
- Locally store a limited number of values that are actively being used so that it doesn't need to send store and retrieve requests to the memory so frequently
- Do the actual arithmetic operations, such as addition

The three subcomponents of the processor responsible for these three activities are called the *control unit,* the *registers,* and the *arithmetic logical unit* (or ALU), respectively. Figure 11.3 illustrates these three units and the main data paths between them. As you can see, in SLIM everything goes to or from the registers. (Registers are locations, like those in the memory: They can be stored into and retrieved from.) The ALU receives the operands for its arithmetic operations from registers and stores the result back in a register. If values stored in memory are to be operated on, they first have to be loaded into registers. Then the arithmetic operation can be performed, and the result will be stored in a register. Finally, the result can be stored in memory, if desired, by copying it from the register.

In addition to the data paths shown in the diagram, additional paths lead out of the control unit to the other units that allow the control unit to tell the ALU which arithmetic operation to do (addition, subtraction, multiplication, ...), to tell the register set which specific registers' values are to be retrieved or stored, and to

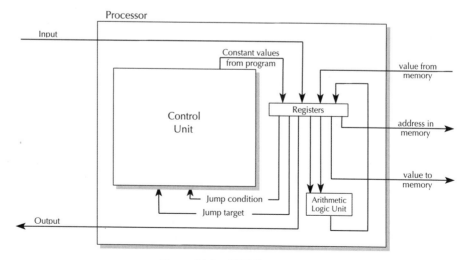

Figure 11.3   SLIM's processor

tell the memory whether a value is to be stored into the specified address or retrieved from it. We don't show these control paths because they complicate the diagram. Keep in mind, however, that whenever we describe some capability of one of the units, we are implicitly telling you that there is a connection from the control unit to the unit in question that allows the control unit to cause that capability to be used. For example, when we tell you that the ALU can add, we are telling you that there is a path leading from the control unit to the ALU that carries the information about whether the control unit wishes the ALU to add. From the operational viewpoint of the next section, therefore, an *add* instruction is in SLIM's instruction set.

Zooming in another level of detail, we examine each of the boxes shown in the processor diagram more closely, starting with the registers. The registers unit is just like the memory, a numbered collection of locations, except that it is much smaller and more intimately connected with the rest of the processor. SLIM has 32 registers, a typical number currently. (In contrast, the data memory has at least tens of thousands of locations and often even millions.) The registers are numbered from 0 to 31, and these register numbers play an important role in nearly all of the computer's instructions. For example, an instruction to perform an addition might specify that the numbers contained in registers 2 and 5 should be added together, with the sum to be placed into register 17. Thus, the addition instruction contains three register numbers: two *source registers* and one *destination register*. An instruction to store a value into memory contains two register numbers: the source register, which holds the value to store, and an *address register*, which holds the memory address for storing that value.

The ALU can perform any of the arithmetic operations that SLIM has instructions for: addition, subtraction, multiplication, division, quotient, remainder, and numeric comparison operations. The numeric comparison operations compare two numbers and produce a numeric result, which is either 1 for true or 0 for false. The ALU can do six kinds of comparison: $=$, $\neq$, $<$, $>$, $\leq$, and $\geq$. This is a quite complete set of arithmetic and comparison operations by contemporary standards; some real architectures don't provide the full set of comparison operations, for example, or they require multiplication and division to be done with a sequence of instructions rather than a single instruction.

The control unit, shown in Figure 11.4, contains the program to execute in an *instruction memory*. Like the main (data) memory, the instruction memory has numbered locations, and we call the location numbers addresses. The difference is that instead of containing values to operate on, these locations contain the instructions for doing the operating. For example, the instruction at address 0 might say to load a 7 into register number 3. (Many architectures share a single memory for both instructions and data; the kind of architecture we've chosen, with separate memories, is known as a *Harvard architecture*.)

At any time, the computer is executing one particular instruction from the instruction memory, which we call the *current instruction*. The address in the instruction

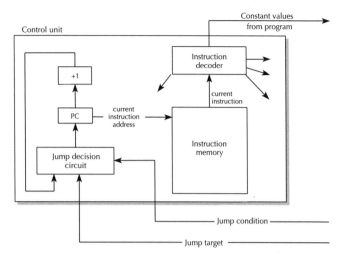

Figure 11.4   SLIM's control unit

memory at which this current instruction appears is the *current instruction address*. A special storage location, called the *program counter*, or *PC*, is used to hold the current instruction address. When the computer is first started, a 0 is placed into the PC, so the first instruction executed will be the one at address 0 (i.e., the first one in the instruction memory). Thereafter, the computer normally executes consecutive instructions (i.e., after executing the instruction at address 0, the computer would normally execute the instruction at address 1, then 2, etc.). This is achieved by having a unit that can add 1 to the value in the PC and having the output from this adder feed back into the PC. However, there are special *jump* instructions that say to *not* load the PC with the output of the adder but instead to load it with a new instruction address (the *jump target address*) taken from a register. Thus, there is a jump decision circuit that controls whether the PC is loaded from the adder (which always adds 1), for continuing on to the next instruction, or from the jump target address (which comes from the registers unit), for shifting to a different place in the instruction sequence when a jump instruction is executed. This jump decision circuit can decide whether to jump based on the jump condition value, which also comes from the registers unit.

   The PC provides the current instruction address to the instruction memory, which in turn provides the current instruction to the *instruction decoder*. The instruction decoder sends the appropriate control signals to the various units to make the instruction actually happen. For example, if the instruction says to add the contents of registers 2 and 5 and put the sum in register 17, the control unit would send *control signals* to the registers to retrieve the values from registers 2 and 5 and pass those values to the ALU. Further control signals would tell the ALU to add the values it received. And finally, control signals would tell the registers to load the value

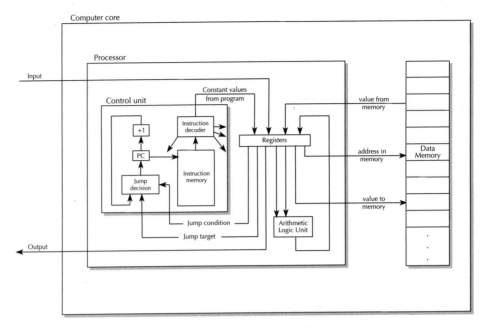

Figure 11.5 The entire SLIM architecture

received from the ALU into register 17. The other connection from the control unit to the rest of the processor allows instructions to include constant values to load into a register; for example, if an instruction said to load a 7 into register 3, the control unit would send the 7 out along with control signals saying to load this constant value into register 3.

We could in principle continue "opening up" the various boxes in our diagrams and elucidating their internal structure in terms of more specialized boxes until ultimately we arrived at the level of individual transistors making up the computer's circuitry. However, at this point we'll declare ourselves satisfied with our *structural* knowledge of the computer architecture. In the next section we will turn our attention to an *operational* understanding of the architecture and will enumerate the instructions it can execute. Our structural knowledge of the SLIM architecture is summarized in Figure 11.5, which combines into a single figure the different levels of detail that were previously shown in separate figures.

11.3 Programming the SLIM

In this section, we will examine the instructions that SLIM can execute. Each instruction can be written in two notations. Within the computer's instruction memory, each location contains an instruction that is encoded in *machine language*, which is a notation for instructions that is designed to be easy for the computer to decode and execute rather than to be easy for humans to read and write. Therefore, for human convenience we also have an *assembly language* form for each instruction, which is the form that we use in this book. A program known as an *assembler* can mechanically translate the instructions constituting a program from assembly language to machine language; the result can then be loaded into the instruction memory for running. (The machine language form of an instruction in instruction memory is a pattern of *bits*, that is, of 0s and 1s. The sidebar What Can Be Stored in a Location? explains that memory locations fundamentally hold bit patterns; in instruction memory, those bit patterns represent instructions.)

Each instruction contains an *operation code*, or *opcode*, that specifies what operation should be done, for example, an addition or store. In the assembly language we will use, the opcode always will be a symbol at the beginning of the instruction; for example, in the instruction add 17, 2, 5, the opcode is add and indicates that an addition should be done. After the opcode, the remainder of the instruction consists of the *operand specifiers*. In the preceding example, the operand specifiers are 17, 2, and 5. In the SLIM instruction set, most operand specifiers need to be register numbers. For example, this instruction tells the computer to add the contents of registers 2 and 5 and store the sum into register 17. (Note that the first operand specifies where the result should go.) To summarize, we say that the form of an addition instruction is add *destreg*, *sourcereg*$_1$, *sourcereg*$_2$. We'll use this same notation for describing the other kinds of operations as well, with *destreg* for operand specifiers that are destination register numbers, *sourcereg* for operand specifiers that are source register numbers, *addressreg* for operand specifiers that are address register numbers (i.e., register numbers for registers holding memory addresses), and *const* for operand specifiers that are constant values.

Each of the 12 arithmetic operations the ALU can perform has a corresponding instruction opcode. We've already seen add for addition; the others are sub for subtraction, mul for multiplication, div for division, quo for quotient, rem for remainder, seq for =, sne for ≠, slt for <, sgt for >, sle for ≤, and sge for ≥. The overall form of all these instructions is the same; for example, for multiplication it would be mul *destreg*, *sourcereg*$_1$, *sourcereg*$_2$. Recall that the comparison operations all yield a 0 for false or a 1 for true. So, if register 7 contains a smaller number than register 3 does, after executing the instruction slt 5, 7, 3, register number 5 will contain a 1. The s on the front of the comparison instructions is for "set," because they set the destination register to an indication of whether the specified relationship holds between the source registers' values.

There are two instructions for moving values between registers and memory. To *load* a value into a register from a memory location, the ld opcode is used: ld *destreg*, *addressreg*. To *store* a value from a register into a memory location, the st opcode is used: st *sourcereg*, *addressreg*. As an example, if register 7 contains 15, and memory location 15 contains 23, after executing the instruction ld 3, 7,

> ## What Can Be Stored in a Location?
>
> One of the many issues we gloss over in our brief presentation of computer architecture is the question of what values can be stored in a memory location or register. Until now we have acted as though any number could be stored into a location. The purpose of this sidebar is to confess that locations in fact have a limited size and as such can only hold a limited range of numbers.
>
> Each storage location has room for some fixed number of units of information called *bits*. Each bit-sized piece of storage is so small that it can only accommodate two values, conventionally written as 0 and 1. Because each bit can have two values, 2 bits can have any of four bit patterns: $(0,0)$, $(0,1)$, $(1,0)$, and $(1,1)$; similarly 3 bits worth of storage can hold eight different bit patterns: $(0,0,0)$, $(0,0,1)$, $(0,1,0)$, $(0,1,1)$, $(1,0,0)$, $(1,0,1)$, $(1,1,0)$, and $(1,1,1)$. In general, with n bits it is possible to store 2^n different patterns. The number of bits in a storage location is called the *word size* of the computer. Typical present-day computers have word sizes of 32 or 64 bits. With a 64-bit word size, for example, each storage location can hold 2^{64}, or 18,446,744,073,709,551,616 distinct patterns.
>
> It is up to the computer's designer to decide what values the 2^n bit patterns that can be stored in an n-bit *word* represent. For example, the 2^{64} bit patterns that can be stored in a 64-bit word could be used to represent either the integers in the range from 0 to $2^{64} - 1$ or the integers in the range from -2^{63} to $2^{63} - 1$ because both ranges contain 2^{64} values. It would also be possible to take the bit patterns as representing fractions with numerator and denominator both in the range -2^{31} to $2^{31} - 1$ because there are 2^{64} of these as well. Another option, more popular than fractions for representing nonintegral values, is so-called *floating point* numerals of the form $m \times 2^e$, where the *mantissa, m,* and the *exponent, e,* are integers chosen from sufficiently restricted ranges that both integers' representations can be packed into the word size. In our example of a 64-bit word, it would be typical to devote 53 bits to the the mantissa and 11 bits to the exponent. If each of these subwords were used to encode a signed integer in the conventional way, this would allow m to range from -2^{52} to $2^{52} - 1$ and e to range from -2^{10} to $2^{10} - 1$. Again, this results in a total of 2^{64} numerals.
>
> Of course, the circuitry of the ALU will have to reflect the computer designer's decision regarding which number representation is in use. This is because the ALU is in the business of producing the bit pattern that represents the result of an arithmetic operation on the numbers represented by two given bit patterns. Many computers actually have ALUs that can perform arithmetic operations on several different representations; on such a machine, instructions to carry out arithmetic operations specify not only the operation but also the representation. For example,
>
> (Continued)

> **What Can Be Stored in a Location? (Continued)**

one instruction might say to add two registers' bit patterns interpreted as integers, whereas a different instruction might say to add the bit patterns interpreted as floating point numerals.

Whatever word size and number representation the computer's designer chooses will impose some limitation on the values that can be stored in a location. However, the computer's programmer can represent other kinds of values in terms of these. For example, numbers too large to fit in a single location can be stored in multiple locations, and nonnumeric values can be encoded as numbers.

register 3 will also contain 23. If register 4 contains 17 and register 6 contains 2, executing `st 4, 6` will result in memory location 2 containing a 17.

To read a value into a register from the keyboard, the instruction `read` *destreg* can be used, whereas to write a value from a register onto the display, the instruction would be `write` *sourcereg*. We've included these instructions in the SLIM architecture in order to make it easier to write simple numeric programs in assembly language, but a real machine would only have instructions for reading in or writing out individual characters. For example, to write out 314, it would have to write out a 3 character, then a 1, and finally a 4. The programming techniques shown later in this chapter would allow you to write assembly language subprograms to perform numeric input and output on a variant of the SLIM architecture that only had the read-a-character and write-a-character operations. Thus, by assuming that we can input or output an entire number with one instruction, all we are doing is avoiding some rather tedious programming.

The one other source for a value to place into a register is a constant value appearing in the program. For this the so-called *load immediate* opcode, `li`, is used: `li` *destreg, const*. For example, a program that consisted of the two instructions:

```
li 1, 314
write 1
```

would display a 314 because it loads that value into register 1 and then writes out the contents of register 1 to the display.

Actually, the preceding two-instruction program above isn't quite complete because nothing stops the computer from going on to the third location in its instruction memory and executing the instruction stored there as well; we want to have some way to make the computer stop after the program is done. This action can be arranged by having a special `halt` instruction, which stops the computer. So, our first real program is as follows:

```
li 1, 314
write 1
halt
```

> ▶ **Exercise 11.1**

Suppose you want to store the constant value 7 into location 13 in memory. Let's see what is involved in making this store happen. You'll need a copy of Figure 11.5 for this exercise (that figure is the diagram of the entire SLIM architecture).

a. Use color or shading to highlight the lines in the diagram that the value 7 will travel along on its way from the instruction memory to the main memory.
b. Similarly, use another color or shading style to highlight the lines in the diagram that the address 13 will travel along on its way from the instruction memory to the main memory.
c. Finally, write a sequence of SLIM instructions that would make this data movement take place.

As mentioned above, a simulated SLIM computer is on the web site for this book. It is called SLIME, which stands for SLIM Emulator. SLIME has the functionality of an assembler built into it, so you can directly load in an assembly language program such as the preceding one, without needing to explicitly convert it from assembly language to machine language first. Once you have loaded in your program, you can run it in SLIME either by using the Start button to start it running full speed ahead or by using the Step button to step through the execution one instruction at a time. Either way, SLIME shows you what is going on inside the simulated computer by showing you the contents of the registers, memories, and program counter.

In designing SLIME, we needed to pin down what range of numbers the storage locations can hold, as described in the preceding sidebar. Our decision was to allow only integers in the range from -2^{31} through $2^{31} - 1$. Because we are only allowing integers, we made the `div` instruction (division) completely equivalent to `quo` (quotient). The two opcodes are different because other versions of SLIM might allow fractions or floating point numerals. Also, any arithmetic operation that would normally produce a result bigger than $2^{31} - 1$ or smaller than -2^{31} gets mapped into that range by adding or subtracting the necessary multiple of 2^{32}. This produces a result that is congruent to the real answer, modulo 2^{32}. For example, if you use SLIME to compute factorials, it will correctly report that $5! = 120$ but will falsely claim that 14! is 1,278,945,280; the real answer is larger than that by 20×2^{32}.

For another example of assembly language programming, suppose you want to write a program that reads in two numbers and then displays their product. This is accomplished by reading the input into two registers, putting their product into a third, and then writing it out:

```
read 1
read 2
mul 3, 1, 2
write 3
halt
```

Note that we didn't actually need to use the third register: we could have instead written `mul 2, 1, 2`, storing the result instead in register 2; we would then have to also change `write 3` to `write 2`. In a larger program, this might help us stay within 32 registers; it would only be possible, however, if the program didn't need to make any further use of the input value after the product has been calculated.

▶ **Exercise 11.2**

Write a program that reads in two numbers and then displays the sum of their squares.

Now we only have one more kind of instruction, the instructions for jumping, or causing some instruction other than the one in the immediately following location in instruction memory to be executed next. SLIM follows tradition by having two kinds of jump instructions, *conditional jumps*, which under some conditions jump and other conditions *fall through* to the next instruction, and *unconditional jumps*, which jump under all circumstances. For simplicity, we've designed SLIM to only have a single conditional jump opcode: jump if equal to zero, or `jeqz`. The way this code is used is that `jeqz` *sourcereg, addressreg* will cause the computer to check to see if the *sourcereg* register contains zero or not. If it doesn't contain zero, execution falls through to the next instruction, but if it does contain zero, the contents of the *addressreg* register is used as the address in instruction memory at which the execution should continue. Because the comparison instructions, such as `slt`, use 0 for false and 1 for true, you can also think of `jeqz` as being a "jump when false" instruction. The unconditional jump, `j` *addressreg*, will always use the number stored in the *addressreg* register as the next instruction address.

The following simple program reads in two numbers and then uses conditional jumping to display the larger of the two. We include comments, written with a semicolon just like in Scheme:

```
read 1       ; read input into registers 1 and 2
read 2
sge 3, 1, 2 ; set reg 3 to 1 if reg 1 >= reg 2, otherwise 0
li 4, 7      ; 7 is address of the "write 2" instruction, for jump
jeqz 3, 4    ; if reg 1 < reg 2, jump to instruction 7 (write 2)
write 1      ; reg 1 >= reg 2, so write reg 1 and halt
halt
write 2      ; reg 1 < reg 2, so write reg 2 and halt
halt
```

Notice that we must figure out the instruction number (i.e., the address in instruction memory) of the jump target for the `jeqz` instruction, which is 7 (not 8) because we start at instruction number 0. We also need to load the 7 into a register (in this case register 4) because jump instructions take their jump target from a register (the *address register*) rather than as an immediate, constant value. The need to determine the address of some instructions is one factor that contributes to the difficulty of writing, and even more of understanding, assembly language programs. It is even worse if you need to modify a program because if your change involves adding or deleting instructions, you might well have to recalculate the addresses of all potential jump targets and change all references to those addresses. As you can imagine, this problem would make program modification very difficult indeed.

Another factor contributes to the difficulty of programming in assembly language, which also relates to numbers within a program. We reference the value in a register by its register number; thus, we write the instruction `sge 3, 1, 2` knowing that registers 1 and 2 contain the input values and register 3 will contain the value indicating which is larger. In a simple program, this is not much of a problem (especially if the comments are adequate), but you can probably imagine that this can make larger programs very hard to understand and nearly impossible to modify.

Both of these difficulties would be reduced if we had a way to use names to make our programs more understandable. Assemblers typically have such a capability; the one we have built into SLIME is no exception. Our assembler allows names to be assigned to registers and allows us to embed symbolic *labels* at points within our program; both types of names can be used within assembly language instructions. Thus, we could rewrite the program as follows:

```
allocate-registers input-1, input-2
allocate-registers comparison, jump-target

read input-1
read input-2
sge comparison, input-1, input-2
li jump-target, input-2-larger
jeqz comparison, jump-target

write input-1
halt

input-2-larger:    ; an instruction label, referring to the
   write input-2   ; write input-2 instruction
   halt
```

We use blank lines to indicate the basic logical blocks within the program and indent all the lines except labels to make the labels more apparent.

The designation of register names is done using the `allocate-registers` lines, which instruct the assembler to choose a register number (between 0 and 31) for each of the names. The division into two separate `allocate-registers` lines is simply to avoid having one very long line. Either way, each name is assigned a different register number. The register names can be used exactly as register numbers would be, to specify the operands in assembly language instructions. Note that there is no guarantee as to which register number is assigned to a given name, and there is a limit of 32 names. In fact, if you use register names, *do not* refer to registers by number because you may be using the same register as a symbolically named one.

In addition to these names for register numbers, our assembler (like most) allows names to be given to instruction numbers by using labels within the program, such as `input-2-larger:`. The labels end with a colon to distinguish them from instructions. A label can be used as a constant would be, in an `li` instruction, as illustrated previously. Notice that the colon doesn't appear in the `li` instruction, just where the label is actually labeling the next instruction.

The key point to keep in mind about register names and instruction labels is that they are simply a convenient shorthand notation, designed to let the assembler do the counting for you. The two versions of the preceding program will be completely identical by the time they have been translated into machine language and are being executed by the machine. For example, the instruction label `input-2-larger` in the `li` instruction will have been replaced by the constant 7 in the course of the assembly process.

▶ Exercise 11.3

The quadratic formula states that the roots of the quadratic equation $ax^2 + bx + c = 0$ (where $a \neq 0$) are given by the formula

$$\frac{-b \pm \sqrt{b^2 - 4ac}}{2a}$$

Therefore, the equation will have 0, 1, or 2 real roots depending on whether $b^2 - 4ac$ is < 0, $= 0$, or > 0.

Write an assembly language program that reads in three values (corresponding to a, b, and c) and writes out whether the equation $ax^2 + bx + c = 0$ has 0, 1, or 2 real roots.

Even with our ability to use names, assembly language programming is still excruciatingly detail-oriented, which is why we normally program in a language like Scheme instead. Even though SLIM (like real computers) can only execute instructions in its own machine language, we can still use Scheme to program it in either of two ways:

1. We can write a single assembly language program, namely, for a Scheme read-eval-print-loop, like the one we programmed in Scheme in the previous chapter. From then on, the computer can just run the result of assembling that one program, but we can type in whatever Scheme definitions and expressions we want. This is called using an *interpreter*.

2. We can write a program (in Scheme) that translates a Scheme program into a corresponding assembly language or machine language program. This is known as a *compiler*. Then we can use the compiler (and the assembler, if the compiler's

---

▶ SLIM's Instruction Set

```
add destreg, sourcereg₁, sourcereg₂
sub destreg, sourcereg₁, sourcereg₂
mul destreg, sourcereg₁, sourcereg₂
div destreg, sourcereg₁, sourcereg₂
quo destreg, sourcereg₁, sourcereg₂
rem destreg, sourcereg₁, sourcereg₂

seq destreg, sourcereg₁, sourcereg₂
sne destreg, sourcereg₁, sourcereg₂
slt destreg, sourcereg₁, sourcereg₂
sgt destreg, sourcereg₁, sourcereg₂
sle destreg, sourcereg₁, sourcereg₂
sge destreg, sourcereg₁, sourcereg₂

ld destreg, addressreg
st sourcereg, addressreg

li destreg, const

read destreg
write sourcereg

jeqz sourcereg, addressreg
j addressreg

halt
```

output is assembly language) to translate our Scheme programs for execution by the computer.

For your convenience, a complete list of SLIM's instructions is given in a sidebar.

11.4   Iteration in Assembly Language

The previous sections described the capabilities of a computer by showing the structure of SLIM and enumerating the instructions it can carry out. We also wrote some simple programs in assembly language that used the naming and labeling capabilities of the assembler. In this section, we turn our attention to extending our programming skills by writing programs in SLIM's assembly language for carrying out iterative processes. We extend this skill to recursive processes in the next section.

You may recall that in Part I of this book we introduced recursion before iteration. This order was because in our experience students find many problems easier to solve using the recursion strategy rather than the iteration strategy. However, by now you should be experienced at solving problems both ways, and iterative solutions can be more naturally expressed in assembly language than can recursive solutions. Therefore, we've reversed the order of presentation here, starting with iteration and then moving on to recursion in the next section. The reason why it is straightforward to write assembly language programs that generate iterative processes is that iterative behavior is fairly easy to achieve through programming *loops* caused by jumps in the code.

Consider the simple problem of printing out the numbers from 1 to 10. One solution is described in the *flow chart* in Figure 11.6. The loop is visually apparent in the flow chart and is accomplished in assembly language as follows:

```
allocate-registers count, one, ten, loop-start, done

    li count, 1
    li one, 1
    li ten, 10
    li loop-start, the-loop-start

the-loop-start:
    write count
    add count, count, one
    sgt done, count, ten
    jeqz done, loop-start

    halt
```

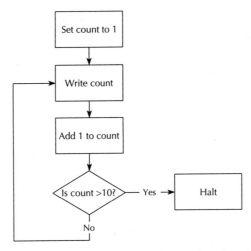

Figure 11.6   Flow chart for printing the numbers from 1 to 10

Before going on, be sure to compare the flow chart with the program and see how completely they parallel each other.

Having now written a simple iterative program, we can write more interesting programs, perhaps drawing from iterative procedures we have written in Scheme. For example, we can write a program to read in a number, iteratively calculate its factorial, and print out the result, similar to the following Scheme program:

```
(define factorial-product
  (lambda (a b) ; computes a * b!, provided b is a nonnegative integer
    (if (= b 0)
        a
        (factorial-product (* a b) (- b 1)))))

(define factorial
  (lambda (n)
    (factorial-product 1 n)))
```

Just as this Scheme program has a comment explaining what the `factorial-product` procedure does, so too our assembly language version has a comment saying what we can expect to happen when execution reaches the instruction labeled `factorial-product-label`:

```
allocate-registers a, b, one, factorial-product, end

li a, 1
read b
li one, 1
li factorial-product, factorial-product-label
li end, end-label

factorial-product-label:
    ;; computes a * b! into a and then jumps to end
    ;; provided that b is a nonnegative integer;
    ;; assumes that the register named one contains 1 and
    ;; the factorial-product register contains this address;
    ;; may also change the b register's contents
    jeqz b, end   ; if b = 0, a * b! is already in a

    mul a, a, b   ; otherwise, we can put a * b into a
    sub b, b, one ; and b - 1 into b, and start the
    j factorial-product           ; iteration over

end-label:
    write a
    halt
```

> ### Exercise 11.4

Translate into SLIM assembly language the procedure for raising a base to a power given in Section 3.2.

> ### Exercise 11.5

SLIME has a counter that shows how many instructions have been executed. This counter can be used to carefully compare the efficiency of different algorithms. Translate into SLIM assembly language the following alternative **power-product** procedure and compare its efficiency with that of your program from the preceding exercise, with increasingly large exponents. (*Hint:* You'll need an extra register in which to store the remainder of e divided by 2. You'll also need one more label because the **cond** has three cases; another register to hold the numeric value of that label will also come in handy.) You should be able to predict the instruction counts by carefully analyzing your programs; that way the simulator's instruction counts can serve as empirical verification of your prediction, showing that you have correctly understood the programs.

```
(define power-product
   (lambda (a b e)    ; returns a times b to the e power
      (cond ((= e 0) a)
            ((= (remainder e 2) 0)
             (power-product a (* b b) (/ e 2)))
            (else (power-product (* a b) b (- e 1)))))))
```

■▶ **Exercise 11.6**

Translate into SLIM assembly language your procedure for finding the exponent of 2 in a positive integer, from Exercise 3.2.

■▶ **Exercise 11.7**

Translate into SLIM assembly language the procedure for finding a Fermat number by repeated squaring given in Section 3.2.

One aspect of the iterative factorial program to note carefully is the order of the multiplication and subtraction instructions. Because the multiplication is done first, the old value of b is multiplied into a; only afterward is b reduced by 1. If the order of these two instructions were reversed, the program would no longer compute the correct answer. In Scheme terms, the correct version of the SLIM program is like the following Scheme procedure:

```
(define factorial-product
   (lambda (a b) ; computes a * b!, given b is a nonnegative integer
      (if (= b 0)
          a
          (let ((a (* a b)))
             (let ((b (- b 1)))
                (factorial-product a b))))))
```

If the multiplication and subtraction were reversed, it would be like this (incorrect) Scheme procedure:

```
(define factorial-product ; this version doesn't work
   (lambda (a b) ; computes a * b!, given b is a nonnegative integer
      ;;(continued)
```

```
(if (= b 0)
    a
    (let ((b (- b 1)))
      (let ((a (* a b))) ; note that this uses the new b
        (factorial-product a b))))))
```

In the `factorial-product` procedure, the new value for b is calculated without making use of the (old) value of a, so we can safely "clobber" a and then compute b. Other procedures may not be so lucky in this regard; there may be two arguments where each needs to have its new value computed from the old value of the other one. In these cases, it is necessary to use an extra register to temporarily hold one of the values. For example, consider translating into the SLIM assembly language the following Scheme procedure for computing a greatest common divisor:

```
(define gcd
  (lambda (x y)
    (if (= y 0)
        x
        (gcd y (remainder x y)))))
```

Here the new value of x is computed using the old value of y (in fact, it is simply the same as the old value of y), and the new value of y is computed using the old value of x; thus, it appears neither register can receive its new value first because the old value of that register is still needed for computing the new value of the other register. The solution is to use an extra register; we can model this solution in Scheme using `let`s as follows:

```
(define gcd
  (lambda (x y)
    (if (= y 0)
        x
        (let ((old-x x))
          (let ((x y))                           ; x changes here
            (let ((y (remainder old-x y))) ; but isn't used here
              (gcd x y)))))))
```

▶ Exercise 11.8

Translate `gcd` into a SLIM assembly language program for reading in two numbers and then computing and writing out their greatest common divisor. (*Hint:* To copy a value from one register to another, you can add it to zero.)

Returning to the iterative factorial program, another more subtle point to note is that the comment at the `factorial-product-label` specifies the behavior that will result in terms of the values in three kinds of registers:

1. The `a` and `b` registers correspond to the arguments in the Scheme procedure. These control which specific computation the loop will carry out, within the range of computations it is capable of.

2. The `one` register, which is assumed to have a 1 in it whenever execution reaches the label, has no direct analog in the Scheme procedure. This register isn't intended to convey information into the loop that can be varied to produce varying effects, the way the `a` and `b` registers can. Instead, it is part of the specification for efficiency reasons only. Instead of requiring that a 1 be in the `one` register whenever execution reaches the label, it would be possible to load the 1 in after the label. However, that would slow the program down because the loading would be needlessly done each time around the loop. The same considerations apply to the `factorial-product` register, which also holds a constant value, the starting address of the loop.

3. The `end` register is perhaps the most interesting of all. It is what we call a *continuation register* because it holds the *continuation address* for the `factorial-product` procedure. That is, this register holds the address that execution should continue at after the `factorial-product` computation is completed. Once the computer has finished computing $a \times b!$, it jumps to this continuation address, providing another opportunity to control the behavior of this looping procedure, as we'll see shortly. Namely, in addition to varying what numbers are multiplied, we can also vary where execution continues afterward.

To see how we would make more interesting use of a continuation register, consider writing a procedure for computing $n! + (2n)!$ as follows:

```
(define factorial-product ; unchanged from the above
  (lambda (a b) ; computes a * b!, given b is a nonnegative integer
    (if (= b 0)
        a
        (factorial-product (* a b) (- b 1)))))

(define two-factorials
  (lambda (n)
    (+ (factorial-product 1 n)
       (factorial-product 1 (* 2 n)))))
```

Clearly something different should happen after `factorial-product` is done with its first computation than after it is done with its second computation. After the first computation, it is still necessary to do the second computation, whereas after the second computation, it is only necessary to do the addition and write the result out. So, not only will different values be passed in the b register, but different values will be passed in the end continuation register as well:

```
allocate-registers a, b, one, factorial-product
allocate-registers end, n, result, zero

li one, 1
li zero, 0
li factorial-product, factorial-product-label
read n
li a, 1
add b, zero, n ; copy n into b by adding zero
li end, after-first ; note continuation is after-first

factorial-product-label:
    ;; computes a * b! into a and then jumps to end
    ;; provided that b is a nonnegative integer;
    ;; assumes that the register named one contains 1 and
    ;; the factorial-product register contains this address;
    ;; may also change the b register's contents
    jeqz b, end   ; if b = 0, a * b! is already in a

    mul a, a, b  ; otherwise, we can put a * b into a
    sub b, b, one ; and b - 1 into b, and start the
    j factorial-product      ; iteration over

after-first:
    add result, zero, a   ; save n! away in result
    li a, 1
    add b, n, n              ; and set up to do (2n)!,
    li end, after-second  ; continuing differently after
    j factorial-product   ; this 2nd factorial-product,

after-second:               ; namely, by
    add result, result, a ; adding (2n!) in with n!
    write result          ; and displaying the sum
    halt
```

To understand the role that the n and **result** registers play in the two-factorials program, it is helpful to contrast it with the following double-factorial program. If we refer to the value the double-factorial program reads in as *n*, what it is computing and displaying is (*n*!)!:

```
allocate-registers a, b, one, factorial-product, end, zero

li one, 1
li zero, 0
li factorial-product, factorial-product-label
li a, 1
read b ; the first time, the read-in value is b
li end, after-first ; and the continuation is after-first

factorial-product-label:
    ;; computes a * b! into a and then jumps to end
    ;; provided that b is a nonnegative integer;
    ;; assumes that the register named one contains 1 and
    ;; the factorial-product register contains this address;
    ;; may also change the b register's contents
    jeqz b, end  ; if b = 0, a * b! is already in a

    mul a, a, b  ; otherwise, we can put a * b into a
    sub b, b, one ; and b - 1 into b, and start the
    j factorial-product    ; iteration over

after-first:
    add b, zero, a ; move the factorial into b by adding zero
    li a, 1         ; so that we can get the factorial's factorial
    li end, after-second ; continuing differently after
    j factorial-product  ; this second factorial-product,

after-second:            ; namely, by
    write a              ; displaying the result
    halt
```

This latter program reads the *n* value directly into the b register, ready for computing the first factorial. The earlier two-factorials program, in contrast, read *n* into a separate n register and then copied that register into b before doing the first factorial. The reason why the two-factorials program can't read the input value directly into b the way double-factorial does is that it will need the *n* value again, after *n*! has been computed, to compute (2*n*)!. Therefore, this *n* value needs to be stored somewhere "safe" while the first factorial is being computed. The b register isn't a safe place because the factorial-product loop changes that register (as its comment warns). Thus, a separate **n** register is needed.

The **result** register is needed for a similar reason, to be a safe holding place for $n!$ while $(2n)!$ is being computed; clearly the result of $n!$ can't be left in the **a** register while the second factorial is being computed. In double-factorial, on the other hand, the result of $n!$ isn't needed after $(n!)!$ is computed, so it doesn't need to be saved anywhere.

> ### Exercise 11.9

Write a SLIM program for reading in four numbers, x, y, n, and m, and computing $x^n + y^m$ and displaying the result. Your program should reuse a common set of instructions for both exponentiations.

To review, we've learned two lessons from the two-factorials program:

1. If a procedure within the program is invoked more than once, a continuation register can be used to make the procedure continue differently when it is done with one invocation than when it is done with another.
2. If a value needs to be preserved across a procedure invocation, it shouldn't be stored in a register that will be clobbered (i.e., stored into) by the procedure. Instead, the value should be moved somewhere "safe," a location *not* stored into by the procedure.

11.5 Recursion in Assembly Language

In the previous section, we wrote assembly language procedures that generated iterative processes. Along the way, we learned two important lessons: the use of a continuation register and the importance of choosing a safe location for values that must be preserved across a procedure invocation. With these two lessons in mind, it is time to consider recursive processes. Sticking with factorials, we'll use the following Scheme procedure as our starting point:

```
(define factorial
  (lambda (n)
    (if (= n 0)
        1
        (* (factorial (- n 1))
           n))))
```

Consider using a SLIM program based on this procedure to compute 5! by computing 4! and then multiplying the result by 5. What needs to be done after the factorial procedure has finished computing 4!? What needs to be done after the factorial procedure has finished computing 5!? Are these the same? This should bring to mind the first of the two lessons from two-factorials: A continuation register can be used to make the factorial procedure continue differently after computing 4! than after computing 5!. After computing 4!, the computer needs to multiply the result by 5, whereas after computing 5!, the computer needs to display the final result. Tentatively, then, we'll assume we are going to use three registers: an n register for the argument to the factorial procedure, a `cont` register for the procedure's continuation address, and a `val` register to hold the resulting value of $n!$.

Next question: Do any values need preserving while the computation of 4! is underway? Yes, the fact that n is 5 needs to be remembered so that when 4! has been computed as 24, the computer knows to use 5 as the number to multiply 24 by. The computer also needs to save the 5! computation's continuation address across the 4! computation so that once it has multiplied 24 by 5 and gotten 120, it knows what to do next. It isn't obvious that the continuation will be to display the result—the computation of 5! *might* have been as a step in computing 6!. So, the continuation address needs to be preserved as the source of this information on how to continue. Thus, two values must be preserved across the recursive factorial subproblem: the main factorial problem's value of n and the main factorial problem's continuation address.

The second of the two lessons we learned from two-factorials leads us to ask: What are safe locations to hold these values so they aren't overwritten? Clearly the n register is not a safe place to leave the value 5 while computing 4!, because in order to compute 4!, we'll store 4 into n. Similarly, the `cont` register is not a safe place to leave the continuation address for the computation of 5! while the computation of 4! is underway, because the continuation address for the 4! computation will be stored there. Should we introduce two more registers to hold the main problem's n value and continuation address while the subproblem uses the n and cont registers?

If there were only two levels of procedure invocation—the main problem and the subproblem—the proposed solution of using two more registers would be reasonable. Unfortunately, the subproblem of computing 4! itself involves the sub-subproblem of computing 3!, which involves the sub-sub-subproblem of computing 2!, and so forth down to the base case. Each level will have two values to preserve, but we can't use two registers per level; among other things we only have 32 registers total, so we'd never be able to compute 52! if we used two registers per level.

The need for two safe storage locations per level (i.e., two locations that won't be stored into by the other levels) is real. So, having seen that registers won't suffice, we turn to our other, more plentiful, source of storage locations, the data memory. The top-level problem can store its n value and continuation address into the first two memory locations for safekeeping (i.e., it can store them at addresses 0 and 1). The subproblem would then similarly use the next two memory locations, at addresses 2 and 3, the sub-subproblem would use addresses 4 and 5, etc. Because each level uses different locations, we cannot clobber values, and because the memory is large, the maximum recursion depth attainable, although limited, will be sufficient for most purposes. (You may have noticed that this example is our first use of memory. In the following section and subsequent chapters we'll see other uses, so recursion isn't the only reason for having memory. It is one important reason, however.)

To keep track of how much of the memory is already occupied by saved values, we'll use a register to hold the number of locations that are in use. When a procedure starts executing, this register's value tells how much of memory should be left untouched and also tells which memory locations are still available for use. If the register holds 4, that means that the first four locations should be left alone, but it also means that 4 is the first address that is up for grabs, because the four locations in use are at addresses 0 through 3.

The procedure can therefore store its own values that need safekeeping into locations 4 and 5; it should increase the memory-in-use register's value by 2 to reflect this fact. When the procedure later retrieves the values from locations 4 and 5, it can decrease the count of how many memory locations are in use by 2. Thus, when the procedure exits, the memory-in-use register is back to 4, the value it had on entry.

This very simple idea of having procedures "clean up after themselves," by deallocating the memory locations they've allocated for their own use, is known as *stack discipline*. (When we speak of allocating and deallocating memory locations, we're referring to increasing and decreasing the count of how many locations are in use.) The reason for the name *stack discipline* is that the pattern of growth and shrinkage in the memory's use is like piling things up on a stack and then taking them off. The most recently piled item is on top of the stack, and that is the one that needs to be taken off first. So too with the *stack* in the computer's memory; locations 0 and 1 were allocated first, then 2 and 3 "on top" of those, and then 4 and 5 "on top" of those. Now, the first locations to be deallocated are 5 and 4—the stack shrinks from the top. Computer scientists traditionally refer to putting items on a stack as *pushing* onto the stack and removing items from the stack as *popping*. The register that records how much of the memory is currently occupied by the stack is known as the *stack pointer*, or *SP*. We'll use the register name `sp` in the program below. The stack pointer is a procedure's indication of what locations in memory to use for its saved values, as in the following recursive factorial program:

```
allocate-registers n, cont ; the argument, continuation,
allocate-registers val     ; and result of factorial procedure
allocate-registers factorial, base-case ; hold labels' values
allocate-registers sp ; the "stack pointer", it records how many
                      ; memory locations are occupied by saved
                      ; values (starting at location 0)
allocate-registers one ; the constant 1, used in several places
```

```
;; set up the constants
li one, 1
li factorial, factorial-label
li base-case, base-case-label
;; initialize the stack pointer (nothing saved yet)
li sp, 0
;; set up for the top level call to factorial
read n   ; the argument, n, is read in
li cont, after-top-level ; the continuation is set
;; and then we can fall right into the procedure

factorial-label:
    ;; computes the factorial of n into val and jumps to cont;
    ;;   doesn't touch the first sp locations of memory and
    ;;   restores sp back to its entry value when cont is jumped to;
    ;;   assumes the factorial, base-case, and one registers hold the
    ;;   constant values established at the beginning of the program
    jeqz n, base-case

    ;; if n isn't zero, we save n and cont into memory for
    ;; safe keeping while computing (n-1)!; sp tells us where in
    ;; memory to save them (so as not to clobber other, previously
    ;; saved values), and we adjust sp to reflect the new saves
    st n, sp
    add sp, sp, one
    st cont, sp
    add sp, sp, one
    ;; now that we're done saving, we can set up for (n-1)!
    sub n, n, one   ; using n-1 as the new n argument
    li cont, after-recursive-invocation ; the continuation
    j factorial                         ;   after this call

after-recursive-invocation:            ;   is down here
    ;; having made it through the recursive call, the saved
    ;; values of cont and n can be restored to their registers
    ;; from memory; note that they are "popped" from the stack
    ;; in the opposite order they were "pushed" onto the stack,
    ;; since the second one pushed wound up "on top" (i.e., later
    ;; in memory), so should be retrieved first
    sub sp, sp, one
    ld cont, sp
    sub sp, sp, one
```

```
ld n, sp
;; having retrieved n and cont and set sp back to the way it
;; was on entry (since it went up by two and back down by two)
;; we are ready to compute n! as (n-1)! * n, i.e. val * n,
;; putting the result into val, and jump to the continuation
mul val, val, n
j cont

base-case-label:
    ;; this is the n = 0 case, which is trivial
    li val, 1
    j cont

after-top-level:
    ;; when the top level factorial has put n! in val, it jumps here
    write val ; to display that result
    halt
```

Exercise 11.10

Write a SLIM program based on the recursive **power** procedure you wrote in Exercise 2.1 on page 28. Try not to save any more registers to the stack than are needed. You should use SLIME to compare the efficiency of this version with the two iterative versions you wrote in Exercises 11.4 and 11.5. (As before, it should be possible for you to predict the instruction counts in advance by analyzing the programs; the simulator can then serve to verify your prediction.)

Exercise 11.11

Write a SLIM program based on your procedure for recursively computing the sum of the digits in a number; you wrote this procedure in Exercise 2.11 on page 39.

Exercise 11.12

Write a SLIM program based on your procedure for recursively computing the exponent of 2 in a number; you wrote this procedure in Exercise 2.12 on page 40.

11.6   Memory in Scheme: Vectors

In the previous sections of this chapter we've looked "under the hood" at computer architecture and assembly language programming. This introduction is valuable in its own right because it provided you with a clearer understanding of how computation actually happens. However, it had an important side benefit as well: We encountered a new kind of programming, based on sequentially retrieving values from locations, computing new values from them, and storing the new values back into the locations. This style is known as the *imperative style* or *imperative paradigm* of programming because each instruction is issuing a command to the computer to carry out a particular action. The imperative style is closely tied to the concept of *state* (i.e., that actions can change something about the computer that affects future actions). It is what ties together the disjointed sequence of commands into a purposeful program — the fact that each changes something that future instructions examine. In SLIM, as in most computers today, the primary form of state is the storage locations.

In the following chapters we'll see some interesting applications of state and imperative programming. However, before we do so, it is worth recapturing what we lost in moving from Scheme to assembly language. As an example of what we've lost, consider storing $(x + y) \times (z + w)$ into some memory location. In Scheme, we could express the product of sums as exactly that, a product of sums: (* (+ x y) (+ z w)). However, we haven't yet seen any way to store the resulting value into a location. (That's about to change.) In assembly language, on the other hand, we'd have no problem storing the result into a location, but we'd also be forced to store the component sums into locations, whether we wanted to or not. We'd need to compute the first sum and store it somewhere — and we'd have to pick the location to store it into. Then we could do the second sum and again store it somewhere we'd have to choose. Finally, we could compute the product we wanted and store it as desired. The result is that what was a natural nesting of computations got painstakingly *linearized* into a sequence of steps, and the new ability to store values into locations spread like a cancer into even those parts of the computation where it didn't naturally belong.

The ability to nest computations (like the product of sums) and avoid storing intermediate results is a large part of what makes a higher-level programming language like Scheme so much more convenient than assembly language. Nesting of computations works naturally when the computations correspond to mathematical functions, which compute result values from argument values. The programming we've done in Scheme up until now has all had this *functional* character — we say that we were programming in the *functional style* or *functional paradigm*. In functional programming the natural way to combine computations is through structured nesting, whereas in imperative programming, the natural means of combination is through linear sequencing. An important open research topic in computer programming language design is to find natural ways to use richer structures of combination with state. For now, we'll tackle a simpler goal: integrating the two styles of programming so that the *value-oriented* portions of a program can use the full power of functional programming, whereas the *state-oriented* portions will have an imperative flavor. To do this, we introduce memory into Scheme.

Chunks of memory in Scheme are called *vectors*. Each vector has a size and contains that many memory locations. Vectors are made by the `make-vector` procedure, which must be told how big a vector to make. For example `(make-vector 17)` will make a vector with 17 locations in it. The locations are numbered starting from 0 in each vector, so the locations in the example vector would be numbered from 0 to 16. A simple example follows of creating and using a vector; it shows how values can be stored into and retrieved from the vector's locations and how the size of a vector can be determined:

```
(define v (make-vector 17))

(vector-length v)     ; find out how many locations
17

(vector-set! v 13 7) ; store a 7 into location 13

(vector-ref v 13)     ; retrieve what's in location 13
7

(vector-set! v 0 3)  ; put a 3 into the first location (location 0)

(vector-ref v 13)     ; see if location 13 still intact
7

(vector-set! v 13 0) ; now clobber it

(vector-ref v 13)     ; see that location 13 did change
0
```

Notice that the procedure for changing the contents of one of a vector's locations is called `vector-set!`, with an exclamation point at the end of its name. This is an example of a convention that we generally follow, namely, that procedures for changing an object have names that end with an exclamation point. Just as with the question mark at the end of a predicate's name, this naming convention is purely for better communication among humans; the Scheme language regards the exclamation point or question mark as no different than a letter. Another point to notice is that we didn't show any value for the evaluations that applied `vector-set!`. This is because the definition of the Scheme programming language leaves this value unspecified, so it can vary depending on the particular Scheme system you are using. Your particular system might well return something useful (like the old value that was previously stored in the location), but you shouldn't make use of that because doing so would render your programs nonportable.

As an example of how a vector could be used, consider making a *histogram* of the grades the students in a class received on an exam. That is, we'd like to make a bar chart with one bar for each grade range, where the length of the bar corresponds to how many students received a grade within that range. A simple histogram might look as follows:

```
90-99: XXXXXXX
80-89: XXXXXXXXX
70-79: XXXXXX
60-69: XXX
50-59: XXXX
40-49: XXX
30-39: XX
20-29:
10-19: X
00-09:
```

This histogram shows, for example, that two students received grades in the 30s; one X appears for each student in the grade range.

The obvious way to make a histogram like this one is to go through the students' grades one by one, keeping 10 counts, one for each grade range, showing how many students have been discovered to be in that range. Initially each count is 0, but as a grade of 37 is encountered, for example, the counter for the 30s range would be increased by 1. At the end, the final counts are used in printing out the histogram to determine how many Xs to print in each row. The fact that the counts need to change as the grades are being processed sounds like storage locations; the fact that we need 10 of them sounds like we need a vector of length 10. So, we have a plan for our program:

1. Make a vector of length 10.
2. Put a 0 into each location in the vector.
3. Read in the grades one by one. For each, increment the appropriate location or "bin" within the vector.
4. Display the vector as a histogram.

Writing this in Scheme, we get the following:

```
(define do-grade-histogram
  (lambda ()
    (let ((histogram (make-vector 10)))
      (define read-in-grades-loop
        (lambda ()
          (let ((input (read)))
            ;;(continued)
```

```
              (if (equal? input 'done)
                  'done-reading
                  (let ((bin (quotient input 10)))
                    (vector-set! histogram bin
                                 (+ 1 (vector-ref histogram bin)))
                    (read-in-grades-loop)))))))) ;end of loop
        (zero-out-vector! histogram) ;start of main procedure
        (newline)
        (display
         "Enter grades in the range 0 - 99; enter done when done.")
        (newline)
        (read-in-grades-loop)
        (display-histogram histogram)))))
```

This relies on two other procedures: zero-out-vector! puts the initial 0 into each location, and display-histogram displays the vector as a histogram. They can be written as follows:

```
(define zero-out-vector!
  (lambda (v)
    (define do-locations-less-than
      (lambda (limit)
        (if (= limit 0)
            'done
            (let ((location (- limit 1)))
              (vector-set! v location 0)
              (do-locations-less-than location)))))
    (do-locations-less-than (vector-length v))))

(define display-histogram
  (lambda (histogram)
    (define display-row
      (lambda (number)
        (display number)
        (display "0-")
        (display number)
        (display "9: ")
        ;; display-times from page 313 useful here
        (display-times "X" (vector-ref histogram number))
        (newline)))
    ;;(continued)
```

```
(define loop
  (lambda (counter)
    (if (< counter 0)
        'done
        (begin (display-row counter)
               (loop (- counter 1))))))
(newline)
(loop 9)
(newline)))
```

> **Exercise 11.13**

Some students earn grades of 100 for their exams, rather than just 0 to 99. There is no one clearly right way to modify the histograms to accommodate this. Consider some of the options, choose one, justify your choice, and implement it.

The previous program used one X per student. This works for those of us fortunate enough to have small classes, but in a large course at a large university, some of the bars of Xs would no doubt run off the edge of the computer's screen. This problem can be resolved by scaling the bars down so that each X represents 10 students instead of 1, for example. The scaling factor can be chosen automatically to make the longest bar fit on the screen. For example, we could choose as the number of students per X the smallest positive integer that makes the longest bar no longer than 70 Xs. Here is a version of `display-histogram` that does this:

```
(define maximum-bar-size 70)

(define display-histogram
  (lambda (hist)
    (let ((scale (ceiling  ; i.e., round up to an integer
                   (/ (largest-element-of-vector hist)
                      maximum-bar-size))))
      (define display-row
        (lambda (number)
          (display number)
          (display "0-")
          (display number)
          (display "9: ")
          (display-times "X" (quotient
                               (vector-ref hist number)
                               scale))
          (newline)))
      ;;(continued)
```

```
(define loop
  (lambda (counter)
    (if (< counter 0)
        'done
        (begin (display-row counter)
               (loop (- counter 1)))))))
(newline)
(display "Each X represents ")
(display scale)
(newline)
(loop 9)
(newline))))
```

▷ **Exercise 11.14**

Write the `largest-element-of-vector` procedure that it takes to make this work.

11.7   An Application: A Simulator for SLIM

Because vectors in Scheme are so similar to SLIM's memory and registers, we can use vectors to build a *model* of SLIM as the core of a Scheme program that simulates the execution of SLIM programs. In this section, we'll build such a simulator. It won't be as fancy as SLIME, but it will suffice to execute any SLIM program. Our ultimate goal is to write a procedure called `load-and-run` that executes a given machine language program, but of course we'll write a lot of other procedures along the way. The `load-and-run` procedure will receive the program to run as a vector of machine language instructions; later we'll see how those instructions can be constructed.

In attacking a project as large as the SLIM simulator, it is helpful to divide it up into separate *modules* and understand the interfaces between the modules first, before actually doing any of the programming. For our simulator, we'll use three modules (one of which, the instructions module, is shared with the assembler):

1. The first module provides an abstract data type called the *machine model*. A machine model keeps track of the state of the simulated machine, which is where the contents of the simulated machine's registers, memory, and program counter are stored. Whether the machine is in the special halted state is also stored here.

   More specifically, this module provides the rest of the program with a `make-machine-model` procedure, which can be used to make a new machine model, with all the locations holding 0 and with the machine not halted. This module then allows the rest of the program to inspect and modify the state of that machine model by using procedures such as `get-pc` for getting the current contents of the program counter and `set-pc!` for changing the program counter's contents. Other interface procedures are `get-reg` and `set-reg!` for registers, `get-mem` and `set-mem!` for memory, and `halted?` and `halt!` for haltedness. All the procedures except `make-machine-model` take a machine model as their first argument. The procedures that concern registers and memory take a register number or memory address as the second argument. All the `set-...!` procedures take the new value as the final argument. For example, `set-reg!` takes a machine model, a register number, and a new value for the register as its arguments.

2. The instructions module provides the assembler with constructors for each kind of machine language instruction. It also provides the simulator with a `do-instruction-in-model` procedure, which takes one of the machine language instructions and a machine model and carries out the effects of that instruction in the model. Notice that nothing outside of this module needs to care what the encoding of a machine language instruction is. Also, this module's `do-instruction-in-model` procedure doesn't need to care about the representation for machine models because it can use the access and updating procedures previously described. Part of the effect of every instruction on a model is to update that model's program counter, using `set-pc!`. This effect exists even for nonjumping instructions, which set the PC to 1 more than its previous value.

   The instruction constructors are `make-load-inst`, `make-store-inst`, `make-load-immediate-inst`, `make-add-inst`, `make-sub-inst`, `make-mul-inst`, `make-div-inst`, `make-quo-inst`, `make-rem-inst`, `make-seq-inst`, `make-sne-inst`, `make-slt-inst`, `make-sgt-inst`, `make-sle-inst`, `make-sge-inst`, `make-jeqz-inst`, `make-jump-inst`, `make-read-inst`, `make-write-inst`, and `make-halt-inst`. Each of these takes one argument per operand specifier in the same order as the operand specifiers appear in the assembly language instruction. For example, `make-load-inst` takes two arguments because load instructions have two operand specifiers. The two arguments in this case are the register numbers. (They must be numbers, not names.) For `make-load-immediate-inst`, the second argument must be the actual numeric constant value.

3. Finally, there is the main module that provides the `load-and-run` procedure. It makes heavy use of the services provided by the other two modules, concerning itself primarily with the overall orchestration of the execution of the simulated program. Its argument is a vector of instructions; at each step (so long as the machine isn't halted), it retrieves from this vector the instruction addressed by the model's program counter and does that instruction in the model. Once the model indicates that the machine has halted, the `load-and-run` procedure returns a count of how many instructions were executed.

The main module is the simplest, so let's start there. It needs only to provide the `load-and-run` procedure. Having identified that the machine model module makes the `make-machine-model`, `halted?` and `get-pc` procedures available, and that the instructions module makes the `do-instruction-in-model` procedure available, we can write `load-and-run` as follows:

```
(define load-and-run
  (lambda (instructions)
    (let ((model (make-machine-model))
          (num-instructions (vector-length instructions)))
      (define loop
        (lambda (instructions-executed-count)
          (if (halted? model)
              instructions-executed-count
              (let ((current-instruction-address (get-pc model)))
                (cond
                  ((= current-instruction-address num-instructions)
                   (error "Program counter ran (or jumped) off end"))
                  ((> current-instruction-address num-instructions)
                   (error
                     "Jump landed off the end of program at address"
                     current-instruction-address))
                  (else
                   (do-instruction-in-model
                    (vector-ref instructions
                                current-instruction-address)
                    model)
                   (loop (+ instructions-executed-count 1)))))))))
      (loop 0))))
```

Either of the other two modules could be done next or they could even be done simultaneously by two different programmers. In this textbook, we choose to focus on the machine model module first. Recall that it provides a constructor, `make-machine-model`, and various procedures for examining and updating machine models (we call these latter procedures *selector* and *mutator* procedures, respectively). A machine model needs to contain models of the machine's memory, registers, and the two miscellaneous items of state, the program counter and the haltedness indicator. The obvious representation for the memory is as a vector that is as large as the simulated memory. Similarly, it seems natural to use a vector of length 32 to model the machine's bank of 32 registers. We'll lump the other two pieces of state into a third vector, of length 2; this leads to the following constructor:

```
(define mem-size 10000)
(define reg-bank-size 32)
```

```
(define make-machine-model
  (lambda ()
    (let ((memory (make-vector mem-size))
          (registers (make-vector reg-bank-size))
          (misc-state (make-vector 2)))
      (zero-out-vector! memory)
      (zero-out-vector! registers)
      (vector-set! misc-state 0 0) ; PC = 0
      (vector-set! misc-state 1 #f) ; not halted
      (list memory registers misc-state))))
```

This constructor produces machine models that are three element lists, consisting of the memory vector, the registers vector, and the miscellaneous state vector. This latter vector has the PC in location 0 and the haltedness is location 1. Using this information, we can now write the four selectors and four mutators. Here, for example, are the selector and mutator for the registers:

```
(define get-reg
  (lambda (model reg-num)
    (vector-ref (cadr model) reg-num)))

(define set-reg!
  (lambda (model reg-num new-value)
    (vector-set! (cadr model) reg-num new-value)))
```

> **Exercise 11.15**

Write the remaining selectors and mutators: get-pc, set-pc!, halted?, halt!, get-mem, and set-mem!.

Moving to the instructions module, we could choose from many possible representations for machine language instructions. Some would be more realistic if the machine language were actually to be loaded into a hardware SLIM, built from silicon and copper. Here we'll cop out and use a representation that makes the simulator easy to develop. If the representation used by this module were changed, both the assembler (which uses this module's instruction constructors) and the main part of the simulator would remain unchanged; therefore, we can afford to cop out now, knowing that the decision is reversible if we ever get serious about building hardware.

Specifically, we'll represent each machine language instruction as a procedure for suitably updating the machine model, when passed that model as its argument. In other words, we'll have a trivial do-instruction-in-model :

```
(define do-instruction-in-model
  (lambda (instruction model)
    (instruction model)))
```

Even though this pushes off all the real work to the instruction constructors, they aren't especially hard to write either, thanks to the support provided by the machine model module. Here is an example:

```
(define make-load-inst
  (lambda (destreg addressreg)
    (lambda (model)
      (set-reg! model
                destreg
                (get-mem model
                         (get-reg model addressreg)))
      (set-pc! model (+ (get-pc model) 1)))))
```

> ### Exercise 11.16

Write the other instruction constructors: `make-store-inst`, `make-load-immediate-inst`, `make-add-inst`, `make-sub-inst`, `make-mul-inst`, `make-div-inst`, `make-quo-inst`, `make-rem-inst`, `make-seq-inst`, `make-sne-inst`, `make-slt-inst`, `make-sgt-inst`, `make-sle-inst`, `make-sge-inst`, `make-jeqz-inst`, `make-jump-inst`, `make-read-inst`, `make-write-inst`, and `make-halt-inst`.

At this point, you should be able to try out the simulator. Here is an example that avoids using the assembler; it is the program that we presented in Section 11.3 as our first complete program, the one for displaying 314 and then halting:

```
(let ((instructions (make-vector 3)))
  (vector-set! instructions 0
               (make-load-immediate-inst 1 314))
  (vector-set! instructions 1
               (make-write-inst 1))
  (vector-set! instructions 2
               (make-halt-inst))
  (load-and-run instructions))
```

Of course, there is no need to make all your instructions by hand this way, when an assembler can do the work for you. Writing an assembler in Scheme that could read in the exact assembly notation we showed earlier would distract us with various

```
(define write-larger
  (assemble
    '((allocate-registers input-1 input-2 comparison jump-target)

      (read input-1)
      (read input-2)
      (sge comparison input-1 input-2)
      (li jump-target input-2-larger)
      (jeqz comparison jump-target)

      (write input-1)
      (halt)

      input-2-larger
      (write input-2)
      (halt))))
```

Figure 11.7 Assembling a program using our variant notation. This definition would result in `write-larger` being a vector of machine language instructions; you could then do (`load-and-run write-larger`). Note in particular that labels don't end with colons.

messy details, like how to strip the colon off the end of a label. On the other hand, if we are willing to accept the variant notation illustrated in Figure 11.7, the assembler becomes a straightforward application of techniques from earlier chapters, such as the pattern/action list. An assembler written in this way is included in the software on the web site for this book. We won't include a printed version of it here, but you might be interested in looking at it on your computer.

Review Problems

▷ **Exercise 11.17**

Suppose you wanted to make SLIM cheaper to build by eliminating some of the six comparison instructions.

a. If you were only willing to modify your programs in ways that didn't make them any longer, how many of the comparison operations could you do without? Explain.

b. Suppose you were willing to lengthen your programs. Now how many of the comparison operations do you really need? Explain.

▷ **Exercise 11.18**

Write a SLIM program to read in one or more single-digit numbers, followed by a negative number to indicate that the digits are over. The program should then write out the number those digits represent, treated as a decimal integer. The first digit read in should be the most significant digit. So, for example, if the program reads in 3, 1, 4, and then -1, it should output the number 314. If you had a machine similar to SLIM but (more realistically) only able to input a single character at a time, this is how you would have to input numbers.

▷ **Exercise 11.19**

Write a SLIM program to read a nonnegative integer in and then display its digits one by one, starting with the leftmost digit. If you had a machine similar to SLIM but it was (more realistically) only able to output a single character at a time, this method is how you would have to output numbers. (*Hint:* Your solution will probably be similar to the one for Exercise 11.11.)

▷ **Exercise 11.20**

Suppose you bought a second-hand SLIM dirt cheap, only to find that the j instruction on it didn't work. Explain how you could rewrite all your programs to not use this instruction.

▷ **Exercise 11.21**

Write a procedure in Scheme that when given a vector and two integers specifying locations within the vector, it swaps the contents of the specified locations.

▷ **Exercise 11.22**

Write a procedure in Scheme that when given a vector, it stores 0 into location 0 of that vector, 1 into location 1, 2 into location 2, etc.

▷ **Exercise 11.23**

We can represent a deck of cards as a 52-element vector, initialized to hold the values 0 through 51 using the procedure from Exercise 11.22. If we wish to randomize the order of the "cards" (i.e., values) prior to using the deck in a game, we can use the following plan:

1. Randomly pick an integer in the range from 0 to 51; we'll call this integer *i*.
2. Swap the contents of locations *i* and 51 of the vector, using the swapping procedure from Exercise 11.21.
3. Now similarly pick a random number in the range from 0 to 50, and swap that location with location 50.
4. Continue in this way with progressively smaller prefixes of the vector, swapping a randomly chosen location within the range with the last element of the range.
5. Once a random choice of either location 0 or 1 has been swapped with location 1, the vector has been totally randomized.

Implement this randomization procedure in Scheme; the procedure should take the vector to randomize as its argument and should work for vectors of sizes other than 52.

▷ **Exercise 11.24**

Write a procedure, `shift!`, which takes a vector as its one argument and modifies that vector by shifting its contents down one position as follows. If the length of the vector is *n*, for *k* in the range $0 \leq k < n - 1$, position *k* of the vector should be modified to hold the value that was originally in position $k + 1$. The last element of the vector should be left unchanged. Warning: It matters whether you loop upward from the beginning of the vector to the end or downward from the end of the vector to the beginning.

▷ **Exercise 11.25**

The following SLIM assembly language program reads in two integers, *x* and *y*, computes some function of them, and writes out the answer. You may assume that neither *x* nor *y* is negative and that the arithmetic operations done by the program never overflow (i.e., never produce a result too large or small to represent). Express in a simple mathematical formula what function of *x* and *y* the program computes. Explain the reasoning behind your answer.

```
allocate-registers x, y, z, one, loop-reg, end-reg

read x
read y
li one, 1
li loop-reg, loop
li end-reg, end
```

```
loop:
    jeqz y, end-reg
    add z, x, x
    add z, z, z
    sub x, x, z
    sub y, y, one
    j loop-reg

end:
    write x
    halt
```

▷ **Exercise 11.26**

Consider the following iterative procedure that computes the sum of digits of a nonnegative number:

```
(define sum-of-digits
  (lambda (n) ; assume n >= 0
    (define iter
      (lambda (n acc)
        (if (= n 0)
            acc
            (let ((last-digit (remainder n 10)))
              (iter (quotient n 10)
                    (+ acc last-digit))))))
    (iter n 0)))
```

Write a SLIM assembly language program that reads in an integer *n* (which you may assume is nonnegative) and writes out the sum of its digits, using the algorithm described in the previous Scheme procedure.

▷ **Exercise 11.27**

Write a procedure `multiply-by!` that takes a vector and a number and changes the vector by multiplying each value in the vector by that number. You may assume that the vector itself is filled with numbers. As an example, you should have the following interaction:

```
(define v (vector 2 1 4 5))

v
#(2 1 4 5) ; <-- this is the way Scheme displays vectors

(multiply-by! v 3)
done

v
#(6 3 12 15)

(multiply-by! v 2)
done

v
#(12 6 24 30)
```

▷ **Exercise 11.28**

Write a SLIM assembly language program that reads in an integer *n* (which you may assume is positive) and writes out its largest odd divisor, using the algorithm described in the Scheme procedure of Exercise 3.13 on page 69.

Hint: You can test whether the contents of a given register is odd by using the SLIM instruction **rem** to check whether its remainder upon division by 2 is 1.

Chapter Inventory

Vocabulary

memory
Random Access Memory (RAM)
locations
vectors
Super-Lean Instruction
    Machine (SLIM)
architecture
stored program computer
program
instructions
instruction set
operating system
computer core
run a program

execute a program
input device
output device
processor
data memory
address
shared-memory multiprocessor
Direct Memory Access (DMA)
control unit
registers
arithmetic logical unit (ALU)
source registers
destination register
address register

instruction memory
Harvard architecture
current instruction
current instruction address
program counter (PC)
jump
jump target address
instruction decoder
control signals
bits
word size
word
floating point
mantissa
exponent
machine language
assembly language
assembler
operation code
opcode
operand specifiers
load
store
conditional jumps

fall through
unconditional jumps
labels
interpreter
compiler
loops
flow chart
continuation register
continuation address
stack discipline
stack
push
pop
stack pointer (SP)
imperative style or paradigm
state
linearization
functional style or paradigm
value oriented
state oriented
vectors
module
selector
mutator

Abstract Data Types

machine models
machine language instructions

New Predefined Scheme Names

make-vector
vector-length

vector-set!
vector-ref

Scheme Names Defined in This Chapter

power-product
gcd
two-factorials
do-grade-histogram
zero-out-vector!
display-histogram
maximum-bar-size

largest-element-of-vector
load-and-run
make-machine-model
get-pc
set-pc!
get-reg
set-reg!

get-mem	make-slt-inst
set-mem!	make-sgt-inst
halted?	make-sle-inst
halt!	make-sge-inst
do-instruction-in-model	make-jeqz-inst
make-load-inst	make-jump-inst
make-store-inst	make-read-inst
make-load-immediate-inst	make-write-inst
make-add-inst	make-halt-inst
make-sub-inst	mem-size
make-mul-inst	reg-bank-size
make-div-inst	write-larger
make-quo-inst	assemble
make-rem-inst	shift!
make-seq-inst	sum-of-digits
make-sne-inst	multiply-by!

Sidebars

What Can Be Stored in a Location?
SLIM Instruction Set

Notes

Our SLIM architecture is similar to that of many modern RISC instruction set architectures, such as the MIPS architecture described by Kane and Heinrich [30]. A good next step if you are interested in computer organization and assembly language programming is Patterson and Hennessy's book [39]. (That book uses the MIPS architecture for its examples, so the transition from SLIM should be relatively smooth.)

One key difference to be aware of if you compare our treatment of assembly language programming with that of other authors is that what we refer to as a *continuation address* is called a *return address* by most other authors; similarly, they refer to a *return address register* rather than a *continuation register*. This alternate name reflects the fact that the continuation of a procedure often is directly after the corresponding call, so the procedure continues by returning whence it came. Our choice of name reflects the fact that although this returning behavior is common, it isn't universal, so we'd rather use the more neutral name *continuation address*.

CHAPTER TWELVE

Dynamic Programming

12.1 Introduction

In the previous chapter, we introduced the notion of storage, embodied in Scheme by vectors. The point of storage is to allow one part of a computation to store a value that a later part of the computation will retrieve. However, this leaves open the question of what ultimate objectives can be served by this "squirreling away" of information.

In this chapter, we'll introduce one important use for storage, a technique that can be used to make some computations dramatically more efficient. In particular, we'll look at tree-recursive processes that naturally wind up repeatedly recomputing the solution to identical subproblems. By using storage, we can keep track of which computations have already been done and what the results were so that we can reuse the results rather than recompute them. We'll look at two variants on this theme, one in which results are stashed away on an "opportunistic" basis as they need to be computed and another in which we systematically precompute results before we have any need for them. Although we'll look at the differences between these two variants, we'll also emphasize their commonality. Both have the power to turn a computation that takes too long to be feasible into one that completes in an instant.

We'll start with an overview section, in which we take a single simple example problem through all three different versions: the original tree-recursive form, the version that opportunistically stores results (memoization), and the version that precomputes results (dynamic programming). We'll then have a section apiece devoted to memoization and dynamic programming, in which we work through more examples, addressing some side issues that don't arise in our simple introductory example. A short section brings the two variants back together in order to compare their relative advantages. Finally, you will apply these techniques to the problem of breaking paragraphs into lines in a visually pleasing way.

12.2 Revisiting Tree Recursion

During summer vacation this year, two of us decided to add a path from our back door to the garden. We had two different lengths of paving stones available to us; one was 1 foot long and the other was 2 feet. (Both were wide enough for the kind of path we had in mind.) We were willing to use any combination of the two sizes, provided that the total length worked out correctly. When we tried to decide the exact pattern of stones, however, we found that we could not agree on which pattern to follow. At that point, the third author suggested that we use Scheme to generate all the possible patterns, present them to him, and he would pick the most pleasing one. For example, if the path was only 4 feet long, there would be five patterns that look like these:

As we headed indoors to try this idea out, one of us had second thoughts and became concerned about the number of pictures we might wind up generating. We decided to first write a procedure that would count the number of different ways to make a path using these pavers.

To write this procedure, we can concentrate on the length of the path. If the length is 1 foot, there is only one way to form it, because we must use one of the pavers that are 1 foot long. If the length is 0 feet, there is only one way to form it, by using no pavers at all. On the other hand, if the length is 2 or more feet, we have two choices for the first paver. If we use a 1-foot paver as the first paver, the number of ways to pave the remainder of the walk is the same as the number of ways to construct a walk that is 1 foot shorter. Similarly, if the first stone is a 2-foot paver, the number of ways to complete the path is the number of ways to construct a path that is 2 feet shorter. Thus, the total number of ways (starting with either size paver) to construct a path that is a given length will be the sum of the number of ways to construct a path that is 1 foot shorter and the number of ways to construct a walk 2 feet shorter:

```
(define walk-count
  (lambda (feet)
    (cond ((= feet 0) 1)
          ((= feet 1) 1)
          (else (+ (walk-count (- feet 1))
                   (walk-count (- feet 2))))))))
```

We tested this out on some relatively small numbers, and it seemed to work. For example, it correctly told us that there are five ways to pave a 4-foot walk, as shown by the preceding pictures. So, we moved to our real question, which was how many ways there were to pave the 30-foot path in the back yard. After waiting over a minute without getting an answer, we got impatient and gave up. Interestingly, the answer was nowhere near as slow in arriving for only slightly shorter paths; for example, we were able to find in under a second that there are 10,946 different ways to pave a 20-foot path. Later, when we were feeling more patient, we timed the procedure for all lengths from 20 to 30 feet and constructed the following table:

Path length	Ways to pave	Seconds to find
20	10,946	0.83
21	17,711	1.32
22	28,657	2:14
23	46,368	3.49
24	75,025	5.61
25	121,393	9.08
26	196,418	14.51
27	317,811	23.56
28	514,229	37.87
29	832,040	61.28
30	1,346,269	99.67

As you can see from the table, although our tree-recursive procedure is very elegant, it also takes an enormous amount of time except for very small path lengths. Remembering the asymptotic outlook from Chapter 4, what is happening is that the time is growing quickly as the path length increases. You may notice that the number of ways to pave the path is also growing similarly quickly. If you compare adjacent rows of the table, you'll see that neither the number of ways to pave nor the number of seconds taken is growing so fast as to double with each additional foot of path. On the other hand, if you compare a row with the one two rows down from it, you'll see that both the number of pavings and the number of seconds are growing quickly enough that they more than double with each additional 2 feet of path. So, if we use n to denote the path length in feet, the empirical evidence seems to suggest that both the number of pavings and the time taken have order of growth $\Theta(b^n)$ where the base of the exponent, b is somewhat more than $\sqrt{2}$ but less than 2. (*Exponential growth* with a base of 2 would double each foot, whereas with a base of $\sqrt{2}$, it would double every 2 feet.) It turns out that it isn't hard to show that the number of pavings and the time grow faster than $(\sqrt{2})^n$ and slower than 2^n. We'll take a minute to do the necessary math and then move on to our real goal, which is to show how to use memory in the form of vectors to dramatically reduce the order of growth of tree-recursive processes like this one.

Before doing the mathematical analysis, we'll give a more compact name to the number of ways to pave an n-foot path using any mixture of 1- and 2-foot pavers.

Traditionally mathematicians use the symbol F_{n+1} for this number. That is, F_1 is the number of ways to pave a 0-foot walk, F_2 is the number of ways to pave a 1-foot walk, etc. The letter F stands for Fibonacci, because these numbers are known as the *Fibonacci numbers*. These numbers were originally popularized by a problem concerning rabbit reproduction in an early thirteenth-century arithmetic book whose author, Leonardo Pisano, was sometimes known by the patronymic Fibonacci.

At any rate, our definition is that $F_1 = 1$, $F_2 = 1$, and for any $n > 2$, $F_n = F_{n-1} + F_{n-2}$. You can convince yourself that after the first two Fibonacci numbers, they get steadily larger, that is, $F_n > F_{n-1}$ for all $n > 2$. (All the Fibonacci numbers are positive because adding positives yields a positive; thus, because F_n is the sum of F_{n-1} and the positive number F_{n-2}, it must be larger than F_{n-1}.) We can get some handle on how fast the Fibonacci numbers grow by observing that $F_n = F_{n-1} + F_{n-2}$, and because the numbers are increasing in size, we have $F_{n-1} > F_{n-2}$ (for $n > 3$). Therefore, F_n must be larger than twice F_{n-2} but not as large as twice F_{n-1} (again, for $n > 2$). Thus we have shown that the number of ways to pave a path more than doubles with every 2 feet in length but doesn't grow quickly enough to double every foot, in keeping with the empirical evidence.

All that remains is to show that the time our tree-recursive procedure takes to compute F_{n+1} grows at the same order of growth as F_{n+1} itself. If you look at the procedure, you can see that all it does is add up lots of 1s to get its answer. The base case invocations supply the 1s, and the remaining procedure invocations add them up. To get a total answer of F_{n+1}, there must be F_{n+1} 1s being added together, so the recursion tree must have F_{n+1} base-case leaves. Imagine starting with those F_{n+1} 1s in a pile and repeatedly taking two numbers out of the pile, adding them together, and putting the sum back into the pile. Continue until there is only one number left in the pile. How many additions did you do? Well, each addition reduced the number of numbers by one because you took two numbers out of the pile and put one back in. You started with F_{n+1} numbers (the 1s) and ended with one number (F_{n+1} itself). Thus, the number of numbers went down by $F_{n+1} - 1$, and that must be the number of additions. This tells us how many invocations of the **walk-count** procedure there are when you start by doing (**walk-count** n). The answer is F_{n+1} base-case invocations plus $F_{n+1} - 1$ adding-up invocations, for a grand total of $2F_{n+1} - 1$. Thus, the amount of work done has the same order of growth as F_{n+1} does, namely, a quickly growing exponential growth.

From the foregoing analysis, and our earlier table of ways to pave paths of length 20 through 30 feet, we can see that evaluating (**walk-count** 30) winds up involving over 2.6 million invocations of **walk-count**. On the other hand, there isn't much variety in these invocations. Because the **walk-count** for a particular path length is computed only from the counts for smaller path lengths, there are at most 31 differ-ent **walk-counts** that can be involved in the computation of (**walk-count** 30): (**walk-count** 0) up through (**walk-count** 30). Since we have over 2.6 million invocations of **walk-count**, but at most 31 different ones, there clearly must be a great deal of repetition. This is our sign that there is a substantial opportunity for improvement. This is a general sign, worth being on the lookout for in the future. Therefore, we'll give it a name:

> **The much computation, little variety sign:** If a procedure does a great number of subcomputations, but there isn't much room for variety in the subcomputations that can arise, a lot of repeated computations must occur. That is a sign that a large performance improvement may be possible.

With this sign to motivate us, we'll turn to how we can use memory to get a more reasonable order of growth. We will look at two techniques, memoization and dynamic programming. We don't actually need either of these techniques to write an efficient version of the `walk-count` procedure—we could instead just write an iterative version. However, we're going to need memoization and dynamic programming in our tool kit when we encounter harder problems. Rather than waiting for those problems, we'll learn the essential ideas of memoization and dynamic programming in the comparatively simple context of the `walk-count` procedure. Moreover, the iterative version we're choosing not to write isn't fundamentally very different from the dynamic programming version.

The first technique we look at is called *memoization*. The basic idea behind memoization is to use memory to store a table of the values that we've already calculated. Then we can take advantage of the fact that once we've calculated a particular Fibonacci number, we will never need to recalculate it.

With memoization, we need to make a slight change in how we calculate Fibonacci numbers. Whenever we need to know a smaller Fibonacci number, as a subproblem, we don't want to just blindly go ahead and calculate it. Instead, we want to first check to see if it is already in our table of values; if not, we compute it and put it in the table. To accommodate this change, we'll slightly modify `walk-count` so that rather than directly invoking itself for the recursive calls, it invokes a separate `walk-count-subproblem` procedure:

```
(define walk-count
  (lambda (n)
    (cond ((= n 0) 1)
          ((= n 1) 1)
          (else (+ (walk-count-subproblem (- n 1))
                   (walk-count-subproblem (- n 2))))))))
```

Before we define `walk-count-subproblem`, and see how it stores the subproblem values in a table for reuse, let's address the question of where the table comes from. What we can do is define a `memoized-walk-count` procedure that creates the table (as an *n*-element vector), then has internal definitions of our modified `walk-count`, `walk-count-subproblem`, and other helping procedures, and finally calls the modified `walk-count` to do the actual computation. That is, the overall template looks like this:

```
(define memoized-walk-count
  (lambda (n)
    (let ((table (make-vector n)))
      (define walk-count
        (lambda (n)
          (cond ((= n 0) 1)
                ((= n 1) 1)
                (else (+ (walk-count-subproblem (- n 1))
                         (walk-count-subproblem (- n 2)))))))
      (define walk-count-subproblem
        (lambda (n)
          we still need to define this))
      there will be some other helping stuff here
      (walk-count n))))
```

Of course, we could have named the outer `memoized-walk-count` procedure `walk-count` as well, which would have the advantage that any callers of the old, slow, tree-recursive `walk-count` procedure would automatically now be calling the sleek, new, memoized version. We've chosen to give it a distinctive name so that we can more easily compare the two versions.

We can write `walk-count-subproblem` as a two-step process: first ensure that the value is in the table (i.e., put it there if it isn't already), and then in any case return the value found in the table:

```
(define walk-count-subproblem
  (lambda (n)
    (ensure-in-table! n)
    (vector-ref table n)))
```

To ensure that a value is in the table, we will first check to see if the table has a value already stored in the position *n*; if not, we store one there. This leaves the question: How do we check? We'll take the approach of initially storing the false value, `#f`, into all the table entries. That way when an actual value is stored into one of the entries, it will change from being false to being something nonfalse. Because Scheme interprets anything other than false as being true, we can write the procedure as follows:

```
(define ensure-in-table!
  (lambda (n)
    (if (vector-ref table n) ; anything but #f ?
        'done
        (store-into-table! n)))))
```

The `store-into-table!` procedure itself is trivial:

```
(define store-into-table!
  (lambda (n)
    (vector-set! table n (walk-count n)))))
```

The only missing step is initially filling the whole table with #f values. That can be done using a procedure called `vector-fill!`, which we we would use as follows:

```
(vector-fill! table #f)
```

The procedure `vector-fill!` is very similar to the procedure `zero-out-vector!` in Section 11.6 in that it puts a particular value in each location of a vector. This procedure is specified by the R^{4}RS Scheme standard as being "inessential" (i.e., not every Scheme implementation is required to provide it).

▷ **Exercise 12.1**

Write the procedure `vector-fill!`

At this point, we've seen all the pieces of `memoized-walk-count` and merely need to put them together in one place:

```
(define memoized-walk-count
  (lambda (n)
    (let ((table (make-vector n)))
      (define walk-count
        (lambda (n)
          (cond ((= n 0) 1)
                ((= n 1) 1)
                (else (+ (walk-count-subproblem (- n 1))
                         (walk-count-subproblem (- n 2)))))))
      (define walk-count-subproblem
        (lambda (n)
          (ensure-in-table! n)
          (vector-ref table n)))
```

```
      (define ensure-in-table!
        (lambda (n)
          (if (vector-ref table n)
              'done
              (store-into-table! n))))
      (define store-into-table!
        (lambda (n)
          (vector-set! table n (walk-count n))))
      (vector-fill! table #f)
      (walk-count n))))
```

Now let's take a careful look at how the table gets filled in. As soon as a value is calculated for the first time, it is placed in the table. On the other hand, we can't compute a value until we have computed the previous two values. Thus, the very first values that go in the table are F_1 and F_2, then F_3, F_4, and so on. This suggests an iterative way of computing Fibonacci numbers, using a vector. The basic idea is to construct a vector of values as we did in the memoized approach, but instead of filling this vector in as needed, we start at the beginning (at index 0) and fill in the whole vector systematically, start to finish. This second approach to using memory to improve the time complexity of a procedure is called *dynamic programming*; we'll abbreviate dynamic programming to dp and call this version of the procedure dp-walk-count:

```
(define dp-walk-count
  (lambda (n)
    (let ((table (make-vector n)))
      (define walk-count
        (lambda (n)
          (cond ((= n 0) 1)
                ((= n 1) 1)
                (else (+ (walk-count-subproblem (- n 1))
                         (walk-count-subproblem (- n 2)))))))
      (define walk-count-subproblem
        (lambda (n)
          ;; no need to ensure in table, given systematic filling in
          (vector-ref table n)))
      (define store-into-table!
        (lambda (n)
          (vector-set! table n (walk-count n))))
      (define store-into-table-from!
        ;; does store-into-table! for values from start through n-1
```

```
      (lambda (start)
        (if (= start n)
            'done
            (begin
              (store-into-table! start)
              (store-into-table-from! (+ start 1))))))
      (store-into-table-from! 0)
      (walk-count n))))
```

> ### Exercise 12.2

Make a list of the parts of `memoized-walk-count` and `dp-walk-count` that are identical and a list of those that are different.

> ### Exercise 12.3

Compute by hand the value of (`walk-count` 10) (i.e., F_{11}).

If you compare the procedure `store-into-table-from!` to your code for `vector-fill!`, you will probably notice that the two procedures are very similar. Both of these have the same basic structure of evaluating an expression for the integers ranging from some initial value up to some final value. We can abstract these procedures by writing a higher-order procedure called `from-to-do`:

```
(define from-to-do
  (lambda (start stop body)
    (if (> start stop)
        'done
        (begin (body start)
               (from-to-do (+ 1 start) stop body)))))
```

We can then rewrite `dp-walk-count` using `from-to-do`:

```
(define dp-walk-count-2
  (lambda (n)
    (let ((table (make-vector n)))
      (define walk-count
        (lambda (n)
          (cond ((= n 0) 1)
                ((= n 1) 1)
                (else (+ (walk-count-subproblem (- n 1))
                         (walk-count-subproblem (- n 2))))))))))
```

```
(define walk-count-subproblem
  (lambda (n)
    ;; no need to ensure in table
    (vector-ref table n)))
(define store-into-table!
  (lambda (n)
    (vector-set! table n (walk-count n))))
(from-to-do 0 (- n 1) store-into-table!)
(walk-count n))))
```

The most important point to make is that both the memoized and the dynamic programming versions are *huge* improvements over the original tree recursive version. You may recall that the original version took times ranging from 0.83 seconds to compute F_{21} up to 99.67 seconds to compute F_{31} on our computer. By contrast, the memoized and dynamic programming versions ranged from 0.002 or 0.003 seconds for F_{21} only up to 0.003 or 0.004 seconds for F_{31}.

Because the two techniques are so similar and lead to such similarly dramatic performance improvements, you may wonder why we've bothered to present both. Each technique turns out to have its own advantages; however, they don't show up very clearly in this simple example. Therefore, we'll wait until we've seen more examples of memoization and dynamic programming (in the next two sections) before presenting a comparison of the relative strengths of these two techniques. The key point to remember, though, is that the differences between memoization and dynamic programming are nowhere near as dramatic as those between either one of them and tree recursion.

Although we probably could have figured out the dynamic programming version of `walk-count` without writing the memoized version first, we will find that with more complicated problems, doing a memoized version helps us visualize the table without having to worry about how it gets filled in. In the rest of this chapter, we will look at several problems, first concentrating on how to make a memoized version and then looking at how to write dynamic programming solutions.

12.3　Memoization

In this section, we consider the *binomial coefficients* that are calculated by the solution to Exercise 4.17 on page 103. These numbers describe the number of ways to select a subset of k objects from a set of n distinct objects, for values of k and n such that $0 \leq k \leq n$. To choose k of n items, we can either choose the first item and $k - 1$ of the remaining $n - 1$ or not choose the first item and choose k of the remaining $n - 1$. This provides the recursive case of our procedure:

```
(define choose
  (lambda (n k)
    (cond ((= n k) 1)
          ((= k 0) 1)
          (else (+ (choose (- n 1) (- k 1))
                   (choose (- n 1) k)))))))
```

We can measure the time complexity of choose by counting the number of additions that are needed to compute (choose n k). Because the base cases only contribute a value of 1, we can use the same argument as we did with walk-count to show that the number of additions needed to compute (choose n k) must be one less than its actual value. However, finding bounds on the size of $C(n, k)$ is very complicated (and beyond the scope of this text). Even if n grows large, $C(n, k)$ won't grow rapidly larger if k stays small. In particular, $C(n, 0) = 1$ and $C(n, 1) = n$, neither of which is rapidly growing. Similarly, if k stays close to n as n grows, $C(n, k)$ again won't grow rapidly; as examples, consider that $C(n, n) = 1$ and $C(n, n - 1) = n$. The most rapidly growing case is when k is midway in between these extremes, that is, when we're looking at $C(2k, k)$ as k grows large. This case grows very large very fast, as shown in the following table:

k	$C(2k, k)$
1	2
2	6
3	20
4	70
5	252
6	924
7	3,432
8	12,870
9	48,620
10	184,756
11	705,432
12	2,704,156
13	10,400,600
14	40,116,600
15	155,117,520
16	601,080,390
17	2,333,606,220
18	9,075,135,300
19	35,345,263,800
20	137,846,528,820

Thus, it is clear that our tree-recursive **choose** procedure, which adds up 1s one at a time, is going to take an unreasonable amount of time even to solve such a small problem as $C(40, 20)$.

> **Exercise 12.4**

Draw a tree, analogous to Figure 4.4 on page 92, showing how the value of $C(4, 2)$ is computed by **choose**. Your tree should have $C(4, 2)$ at the root and six 1s as its leaves.

> **Exercise 12.5**

Explain how the "much computation, little variety sign" applies to this problem. In particular, we showed that $C(40, 20) = 137{,}846{,}528{,}820$, which the tree-recursive **choose** procedure computes by adding up 137,846,528,820 1s, clearly a great deal of computation. What about the variety side of the picture? In the course of computing $C(40, 20)$, the tree-recursive **choose** procedure winds up computing $C(n, k)$ for other values of n and k. Can you say anything about how many different combinations of n and k might arise?

We will first improve the time complexity of **choose** by using memoization, just as we did with the Fibonacci numbers. In the next section, we will look at a dynamic programming solution to computing **choose**.

There is one major difference between **choose** and **walk-count**. Whereas **walk-count** has only one parameter and thus can easily use a vector to store the calculated values, **choose** has two parameters. If we think of the **walk-count** value vector as being a table, we see that we were using a one-dimensional table there. For **choose** we'll need a two-dimensional table, or a grid. Such a table would have two sets of indices, one for the rows and one for the columns. Each element in the table can be located by two numbers—one that identifies which row the element is in and one that identifies which column it's in. A typical picture would then be something like the following

In this example, the element in row 2 and column 4 is 6, and the height of the table (number of rows) is 4, whereas the width (number of columns) is 6. Note that the rows and columns are numbered starting from 0.

Unfortunately, Scheme does not provide two-dimensional tables for us. We can define an abstract data type for them; we'll need to have a procedure that constructs tables, a procedure that looks up a value in a table, and a procedure that changes the value of a given location in a table. We could also have selectors that tell us how many rows or columns a particular table has. Assume that these procedures are specified by the following definitions:

```
(define make-table
  (lambda (number-of-rows number-of-columns)
    ...))

(define table-ref
  (lambda (table row column)
    ...))

(define table-set!
  (lambda (table row column value)
    ...))

(define table-height
  (lambda (table)
    ...))

(define table-width
  (lambda (table)
    ...))
```

> ### Exercise 12.6

Using these procedures, write

a. A procedure called `table-fill!` that takes a table and an element and sets every entry in the table to the given element. For example, `(table-fill! table 0)` would have a similar effect to that of `zero-out-vector!` in Section 11.6.

b. A procedure called `display-table` that nicely displays its table parameter.

How do we implement tables? We want to use vectors because they allow us to store results. But somehow we need to create a two-dimensional table out of a one-dimensional vector. One way to do this is to think of a table as a sequence of rows (i.e., a vector of rows). Each row is then divided up into a sequence of elements, one per column; in other words, each row is itself a vector. When we want the element in row *r* and column *c*, we look at the vector in position *r* of our table and find the element in position *c* of that vector. Thus, the procedure `table-ref` is defined by

```
(define table-ref
  (lambda (table row col)
    (vector-ref (vector-ref table row) col)))
```

> ### Exercise 12.7

Write the procedure `table-set!`

> ### Exercise 12.8

Write the procedures `table-height` and `table-width`. Each of these should take a table as a parameter and return the number of rows or columns in that table.

Creating the table is fairly straightforward. We want to first create a vector for the rows. Then we want to fill this vector with vectors:

```
(define make-table
  (lambda (r c)
    (let ((table (make-vector r)))
      (from-to-do  0 (- r 1)
                   (lambda (i)
                     (vector-set! table i (make-vector c))))
      table)))
```

Now that we have tables, we can make a memoized version of **choose**, which is very similar to making a memoized version of **walk-count**. As before, we will construct a table, although this one is a two-dimensional table instead of a one-dimensional one. We will initially set all of the entries of this table to false. Before using any element of the table, we ensure that it has been filled in:

```
(define memoized-choose
  (lambda (n k)
    (let ((table (make-table n (+ k 1))))
      (define choose
        (lambda (n k)
          (cond ((= n k) 1)
                ((= k 0) 1)
```

```
        (else (+ (choose-subproblem (- n 1) (- k 1))
                 (choose-subproblem (- n 1) k)))))))
  (define choose-subproblem
    (lambda (n k)
      (ensure-in-table! n k)
      (table-ref table n k)))
  (define ensure-in-table!
    (lambda (n k)
      (if (table-ref table n k)
          'done
          (store-into-table! n k))))
  (define store-into-table!
    (lambda (n k)
      (table-set! table n k (choose n k))))
  (table-fill! table #f)
  (choose n k))))
```

As you can see, the relationship between `memoized-choose` and `choose` is essentially identical to the relationship between `memoized-walk-count` and `walk-count`, except `make-table`, `table-ref`, `table-set!`, and `table-fill!` are used in place of `make-vector`, `vector-ref`, `vector-set!`, and `vector-fill!`.

One subtle point is the size chosen for the table: n rows and $k + 1$ columns. The n rows are enough because the first argument to `choose-subproblem` will never be any larger than $n - 1$. (Remember, with n rows, the indices can run from 0 to $n - 1$.) By contrast, the second argument to `choose-subproblem` can be as large as k. Therefore, $k + 1$ columns are needed. That way the legal range for column indices includes k.

One of the nice features about the memoized version of `choose` is the relationship between the indices of the table entries and the values of those entries. More precisely, `(choose i j)` has the same value as `(table-ref table i j)`, assuming that the table has been filled in at that position. In the next example, we consider a situation where this relationship is not as direct.

This second example is a chocolate version of a famous problem in computer science. Suppose we are at a chocolate candy store and want to assemble a kilogram box of chocolates. Some of the chocolates (such as the caramels) at this store are absolutely the best in the world, and others are only so-so. In fact, we've rated each one on a scale of 1 to 10, with 10 being the highest. Furthermore, we know the weight of a piece of each kind; for example, a caramel weighs 13 grams. How do we put together the best box weighing at most 1 kilogram? (The more well-known version of this problem is known as the *knapsack problem*, but we have trouble imagining packing chocolates into a knapsack rather than a box and trouble imagining anything other than chocolate being of sufficient value to warrant optimization.)

Before we start writing a Scheme procedure to solve this problem, we need to construct abstract data types for chocolates and boxes of chocolates and to define what we mean by "the best" box.

Defining chocolates is quite easy. At the candy store, each chocolate has a filling (e.g., caramel, marshmallow, maple cream) and a coating of dark, milk, or white chocolate. We also know the weight of an individual piece of chocolate as well as a number that describes its desirability. We will glue these four attributes together in a list and use `car` and `cdrs` for selectors:

```
(define make-chocolate
  (lambda (filling covering weight desirability)
    (list filling covering weight desirability)))
```

```
(define chocolate-filling car)
(define chocolate-covering cadr)
(define chocolate-weight caddr)
(define chocolate-desirability cadddr)
```

Boxes of chocolates are just collections of pieces of chocolate. Some boxes are empty (indeed, in one author's office, all the boxes are empty); some contain several pieces. The weight of a box of chocolates is the sum of the weights of the pieces. Similarly, the desirability of a box is the sum of the desirabilities of the pieces. The best box, then, is the one with a maximum desirability.

As an abstract data type, we will want to know what chocolates are in the box, what the weight of a box is, and what the desirability of a box is. We will also need to compare two boxes to see which one is better. For constructors, we will need to be able to make an empty box, and we will also need to be able to add a chocolate to a box. Because we're concentrating on buying the box, we won't worry about taking chocolates out of the box.

Initially, we might be tempted to use lists of chocolates to implement our box ADT. To find the weight of a box, we would just cdr down the list that represents it and add up the weights of the individual pieces, and we would find the desirability in a similar fashion. However, this approach can be time-consuming if we do a lot of `box-weight` or `box-desirability` operations. Because we want to use this ADT in a procedure that finds the most desirable box subject to a given weight limit, we are likely to be doing exactly that.

We can improve on using just lists to represent boxes by using a combination of a list of chocolates, a weight, and a desirability. We will need to be sure that the weight of a box is actually equal to the sum of the weights of the chocolates in the list and, similarly, that the desirability is the sum of the desirabilities of the chocolates. Therefore, whenever we add a piece of chocolate to a box, we will want to cons it onto the list, add its weight to the weight and add its desirability to the desirability. Furthermore an empty box will have a weight of 0 and a desirability of 0:

```
(define make-empty-box
  (lambda ()
    (list '() 0 0)))

(define box-chocolates car)
(define box-weight cadr)
(define box-desirability caddr)

(define add-chocolate-to-box
  (lambda (choc box)
    (list (cons choc
                (box-chocolates box))
          (+ (chocolate-weight choc)
             (box-weight box))
          (+ (chocolate-desirability choc)
             (box-desirability box)))))
```

> **Exercise 12.9**

Using these procedures, write a procedure called `better-box` that takes two boxes of chocolates and returns the one that is more desirable. If they are equally desirable, you should return whichever one you choose.

How do we find the most desirable box weighing 1 kilogram or less? As with `choose`, we will first concentrate on finding a tree-recursive procedure to pick a box and then will write a memoized version of that. The input to the procedure will be the weight of the box we would like to buy and a list of all the chocolates that are available in the store. Here is an example of one such list, constructed from the chocolates available at a small store in Ohio:

```
(define shirks-chocolates-rated-by-max
  (list (make-chocolate 'caramel 'dark 13 10)
        (make-chocolate 'caramel 'milk 13 3)
        (make-chocolate 'cherry 'dark 21 3)
        (make-chocolate 'cherry 'milk 21 1)
        (make-chocolate 'mint 'dark 7 3)
        (make-chocolate 'mint 'milk 7 2)
        (make-chocolate 'cashew-cluster 'dark 8 6)
        (make-chocolate 'cashew-cluster 'milk 8 4)
        (make-chocolate 'maple-cream 'dark 14 1)
        (make-chocolate 'maple-cream 'milk 14 1)))
```

▷ **Exercise 12.10**

Although our program won't be designed to take advantage of the peculiarities of the above list, we should notice them so that we can check the program's output more easily.

a. Only three of the above ten kinds of chocolate can ever show up in an optimal box of chocolates, no matter what the box's weight limit is. Which three are they?

b. Figure out by hand the optimal box weighing no more than 20 grams and the optimal box weighing no more than 25 grams.

To write a tree-recursive procedure to find the best box for Max, we will concentrate on the first chocolate in the list. We will find the best box of chocolates that doesn't have any dark chocolate-covered caramels in it, we'll find the best box of chocolates that has at least one dark caramel in it, and we'll take the better of these two. To make the best 1000-gram (or less) box that has at least one dark caramel in it, we can make the best 987-gram (or less) box of any kind and then add one (13-gram) dark chocolate caramel to it. Note that in the case where we exclude the dark chocolate caramels, we have to find the best box of chocolates using a smaller list of available chocolates, whereas in the case where we commit 13 grams of our weight limit for the dark chocolate caramel, we have to assemble the rest of the box with a smaller remaining weight limit. Thus, our base cases would occur when the list of available chocolates is empty or when the weight limit is zero. We also need to remember that if the weight limit is less than 13 grams, we *can't* choose to include a caramel!

```
(define pick-chocolates
  (lambda (chocolates weight-limit)
    (cond ((null? chocolates) (make-empty-box))
          ((= weight-limit 0) (make-empty-box))
          ((> (chocolate-weight (car chocolates)) ; first too heavy
              weight-limit)
           (pick-chocolates (cdr chocolates) weight-limit))
          (else
           (better-box
            (pick-chocolates (cdr chocolates) ; none of first kind
                             weight-limit)
            (add-chocolate-to-box
             (car chocolates)        ; at least one of the first kind
             (pick-chocolates chocolates
                              (- weight-limit
                                 (chocolate-weight
                                  (car chocolates)))))))))))
```

This procedure is similar to `choose` in that the `else` clause has two recursive calls; thus we would expect a worse-case scenario where the time complexity is roughly exponential. To improve the time complexity, we will try to memoize `pick-chocolates`. As with `choose`, we will need a two-dimensional table. One dimension will correspond to the weight. In other words, we can use the numbers from zero up to and including the weight limit to index the columns, say. The other dimension will correspond to the list of available chocolates in some way. But we must use integers for indexing the rows; we can't use lists. One way to get around this problem is to use the length of each list. Thus, if we're using the list of Shirk's chocolates given above, the row with index 10 would correspond to the whole list of chocolates, the row with index 9 would correspond to the cdr of that list, and so on. The entries of the table will be boxes of chocolates. To be precise, the entry in the ith row and jth column will be the best box of chocolates weighing at most j grams and restricted to the last i elements of the list of available chocolates.

> ### Exercise 12.11

We assume that the weight limit and the weight of each kind of chocolate is an integer number of grams. Why is this assumption necessary?

Now that we know how our table works, writing the memoized version of `pick-chocolates` is very straightforward. As with `choose` and `walk-count`, we will want to construct a table and fill it with the value `#f`. The rest of the construction is also essentially the same as before. The one substantial novelty is that we will need to use the *length* of the chocolates list for indexing the rows of the table:

```
(define memoized-pick-chocolates
  (lambda (chocolates weight-limit)
    (let ((table (make-table (+ (length chocolates) 1)
                             (+ weight-limit 1))))
      (define pick-chocolates
        (lambda (chocolates weight-limit)
          (cond ((null? chocolates) (make-empty-box))
                ((= weight-limit 0) (make-empty-box))
                ((> (chocolate-weight (car chocolates))
                    weight-limit)                        ; first too heavy
                 (pick-chocolates-subproblem (cdr chocolates)
                                             weight-limit))
                (else
                 ;;(continued)
```

```
                          (better-box
                           (pick-chocolates-subproblem
                            (cdr chocolates) ; none of first kind
                            weight-limit)
                           (add-chocolate-to-box
                            (car chocolates) ; at least one of the first kind
                            (pick-chocolates-subproblem
                             chocolates
                             (- weight-limit
                                (chocolate-weight (car chocolates)))))))))))
              (define pick-chocolates-subproblem
                (lambda (chocolates weight-limit)
                  (ensure-in-table! chocolates weight-limit)
                  (table-ref table (length chocolates) weight-limit)))
              (define ensure-in-table!
                (lambda (chocolates weight-limit)
                  (if (table-ref table (length chocolates) weight-limit)
                      'done
                      (store-into-table! chocolates weight-limit))))
              (define store-into-table!
                (lambda (chocolates weight-limit)
                  (table-set! table (length chocolates) weight-limit
                              (pick-chocolates chocolates weight-limit))))
              (table-fill! table #f)
              (pick-chocolates chocolates weight-limit))))
```

> ### Exercise 12.12

We used a tree-recursive procedure, `count-combos`, in Section 7.5 to determine how many ways there were to redeem for prizes the 10 tickets one of our sons won playing Whacky Gator at the local arcade.

a. Since we wrote Chapter 7, our children have grown older and are better Gator Whackers. Empirically see how well (or poorly) the tree-recursive `count-combos` procedure you wrote in Chapter 7 can accommodate this by seeing how the time grows as the number of tickets to redeem grows.

b. Write a memoized version, and empirically compare it with your prior version.

12.4 Dynamic Programming

Although memoization can dramatically improve the performance of a tree-recursive procedure, the memoized procedure still generates a recursive process. We saw that we could fill out the table in an iterative fashion with the Fibonacci example, using dynamic programming. In this section, we will show how to use dynamic programming to rewrite `choose`. Then we will consider another example, with applications ranging from document management to molecular biology.

First, let's look at the binomial coefficients, that is, the numbers calculated by the procedure `choose`. If we look at the table of values at the end of computing (`memoized-choose 9 4`), the table is as follows:

```
#f #f #f #f #f
1  1  #f #f #f
1  2  1  #f #f
1  3  3  1  #f
1  4  6  4  1
1  5  10 10 5
#f 6  15 20 15
#f #f 21 35 35
#f #f #f 56 70
```

As you can see, not all of the entries in the table wound up getting filled in because not all of them had any bearing on computing $C(9, 4)$. For example, the `#f` in the lower left corner corresponds to $C(8, 0)$; although this entry could legally be filled in with the value 1, there was no reason to do so, because it did not arise as a subproblem in computing $C(9, 4)$. The `#f` values in the upper right portion of the table are more interesting. These correspond to values of $C(i, j)$ where $i < j$. In particular, the far upper right entry is for $C(0, 4)$, the number of ways of choosing four items when you don't have any to choose from. As before, these entries play no role in computing $C(9, 4)$. However, they are a little different from the values in the lower left: Up until now we haven't specified what the correct value is for $C(i, j)$ when $i < j$; our `choose` procedure doesn't handle this case. To keep our dynamic programming version of `choose` simple, we'll have it fill in the whole table. To make this possible, we'll have to add one more case to the definition of `choose`. If you ask how many ways there are to choose k items out of n, and $k > n$, there are 0 ways to do it. Thus, the table as filled in by the dynamic programming version will be

```
1  0  0  0  0
1  1  0  0  0
1  2  1  0  0
1  3  3  1  0
1  4  6  4  1
1  5  10 10 5
1  6  15 20 15
1  7  21 35 35
1  8  28 56 70
```

Now that we've straightened out what needs doing—and in particular, that the upper right triangular portion of the table gets filled in with zeros—we can write the dynamic programming version much as before:

```
(define dp-choose
  (lambda (n k)
    (let ((table (make-table n (+ k 1))))
      (define choose
        (lambda (n k)
          (cond ((< n k) 0)   ; this is the new case
                ((= n k) 1)
                ((= k 0) 1)
                (else (+ (choose-subproblem (- n 1) (- k 1))
                         (choose-subproblem (- n 1) k))))))
      (define choose-subproblem
        (lambda (n k)
          (table-ref table n k)))
      (define store-into-table!
        (lambda (n k)
          (table-set! table n k (choose n k))))
      (from-to-do 1 (- n 1)
                  (lambda (row)
                    (from-to-do 0 k
                                (lambda (col)
                                  (store-into-table! row col)))))
      (choose n k))))
```

> ### Exercise 12.13

Now that we have added a case for $n < k$, we could eliminate the case for $n = k$. Explain why.

> ### Exercise 12.14

Write a dynamic programming version of the chocolate box problem in the previous section. You'll find it helpful to first write a procedure that when given a number, n, returns the last n elements of the list of chocolates.

For our second example, consider a problem that occurs in systems that keep multiple old versions of large files. For example, in writing this book, we used a program that kept each draft of a chapter. After the first few versions of a given chapter, the number of changes from one draft to the next was relatively small, whereas the size of each draft was relatively large. Rather than storing all of the different versions, our system stores only the current one. For each prior draft, it stores a list of the changes between that draft and the next. Now, the smaller this list of changes is, the less space we'll need to store it. Thus we'd like to find the smallest possible list of changes to convert one version into the next.

We will look at a somewhat simplified version of this problem. To be more precise, suppose we have two vectors of symbols, and we want to convert the first vector to the second by doing one of three things. We can insert a symbol into the first vector (in any one position), we can delete one occurrence of a symbol from the first vector, or we can replace one occurrence of a symbol with another symbol. What is the minimal number of changes we need to make to convert the first vector to the second? What are the changes that need to be made? We will answer the first question using dynamic programming and then outline a way of modifying that solution to find an answer to the second. Even without the modifications our procedure could be useful—it could be used to determine how similar two documents are, or, equally well, how similar two DNA sequences are.

We'll start by concentrating on the sizes of the two vectors, which we'll call *vector1* and *vector2*. Suppose *vector1* has n elements and *vector2* has m elements. If $n = 0$, the minimal number of changes we need to make is m because we will have to insert each element of that second vector into the first one. Similarly, if $m = 0$, the minimal number of changes we need to make is n because we'll need to do n deletions.

Now suppose both sizes are nonzero. We can look at the last element in each vector and determine what to do by seeing if these elements are the same or not. If they are the same, we simply need to find out how many changes are needed to convert the first $n - 1$ elements of *vector1* into the first $m - 1$ elements of *vector2*.

If, on the other hand, the last elements differ, we have three options:

1. We could delete the last element of *vector1* and then find the minimum number of changes needed to convert the first $n - 1$ elements of *vector1* into all of *vector2*.
2. We could find the minimum number of changes needed to convert all of *vector1* into the first $m - 1$ elements of *vector2* and then insert the last element of *vector2* at the end.
3. We could replace the last element of *vector1* with the last element of *vector2* and then find the minimum number of changes needed to convert the first $n - 1$ elements of *vector1* into the first $m - 1$ elements of *vector2*.

Note that in each of these cases, we decrease the size of at least one of the vectors, in the sense that we are looking at one fewer element. The vectors themselves don't shrink; we just focus attention on the first $n - 1$ or $m - 1$ elements rather than all n or m. For this reason, the `changes` procedure that follows is written in terms of an internal procedure named `changes-in-first-and-elements`, where (`changes-in-first-and-elements` i j) computes the minimum number of changes needed to turn the first i elements of *vector1* into the first j elements of *vector2*. That is, it determines the number of changes needed in the first i and j elements (of vectors 1 and 2, respectively), hence the name. This will involve comparing the ith element of *vector1* with the jth element of *vector2* rather than comparing the last elements of the vectors. (Note that the ith and jth elements are in locations $i - 1$ and $j - 1$ because the locations are numbered from 0.)

Returning to the three possibilities listed above, let's quantify how many changes are needed in each case. We'll use $D(i, j)$ as a notation for the number of changes needed to transform the first i elements of *vector1* into the first j elements of *vector2*. Then in the first case we have the one deletion of the ith element of *vector1* plus the $D(i - 1, j)$ changes needed to finish the job, for a total of $1 + D(i - 1, j)$. Similarly, in the other two cases we get $1 + D(i, j - 1)$ and $1 + D(i - 1, j - 1)$ as the number of changes. Because we are interested in finding the *minimum* number of changes, we simply need to select whichever of these three possibilities is smallest; the built-in Scheme procedure `min` can do this for us.

In summary, here is the Scheme version of this algorithm:

```
(define changes
  (lambda (vector1 vector2)
    (let ((n (vector-length vector1))
          (m (vector-length vector2)))
      (define changes-in-first-and-elements
        (lambda (i j)
          (cond
            ((= i 0) j)
            ((= j 0) i)
            (else
             (if (equal? (vector-ref vector1 (- i 1))
                         (vector-ref vector2 (- j 1)))
                 (changes-in-first-and-elements (- i 1) (- j 1))
                 (min (+ 1 (changes-in-first-and-elements
                            (- i 1) j))
                      (+ 1 (changes-in-first-and-elements
                            i (- j 1)))
                      (+ 1 (changes-in-first-and-elements
                            (- i 1) (- j 1)))))))))
      (changes-in-first-and-elements n m))))
```

Because of those three recursive calls in the `else` clause, this algorithm is a very good candidate for either memoization or dynamic programming. In both cases,

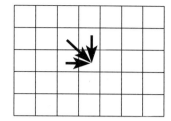

Figure 12.1 The three locations that influence a table entry are those above, to the left, and diagonally up and to the left.

we'll need to construct a table. We can use i and j to index the table, so we'll use a table with $n + 1$ rows and $m + 1$ columns, and we'll assume that the table entry in position (i, j) is $D(i, j)$, the minimal number of changes needed to convert the first i elements of the first vector to the first j elements of the second.

▶ Exercise 12.15

Write a memoized version of **changes**.

To write the dynamic programming version of this procedure, note that to compute one element of the table, we need to have already computed the element immediately above it, the one immediately to its left, and the one that is one row above and one column to the left of it. In other words, the table entry at position (i, j) is computed from the entries in positions $(i, j - 1), (i - 1, j)$, and $(i - 1, j - 1)$, as shown in Figure 12.1. This means that we should fill out the table in an order such that the three entries at the tails of the three arrows are filled in *before* the entry at the heads of the arrows. There are several such orders; the most obvious two are either to go left to right across the top row, then left to right across the next row, etc., or alternatively to go top to bottom down the leftmost column, then top to bottom down the second column, etc. If we arbitrarily choose the former of these options (the row by row approach), we get this program:

```
(define dp-changes
  (lambda (vector1 vector2)
    (let ((n (vector-length vector1))
          (m (vector-length vector2)))
      (let ((table (make-table (+ n 1) (+ m 1))))
        (define changes-in-first-and-elements
          (lambda (i j)
            (cond
              ((= i 0) j)
```

```
                            ((= j 0) i)
                            (else
                             (if (equal? (vector-ref vector1 (- i 1))
                                         (vector-ref vector2 (- j 1)))
                                 (changes-in-first-and-elements-subproblem (- i 1)
                                                                           (- j 1))
                                 (min
                                  (+ 1 (changes-in-first-and-elements-subproblem
                                        (- i 1) j))
                                  (+ 1 (changes-in-first-and-elements-subproblem
                                        i (- j 1)))
                                  (+ 1 (changes-in-first-and-elements-subproblem
                                        (- i 1) (- j 1)))))))))
        (define changes-in-first-and-elements-subproblem
          (lambda (i j)
            (table-ref table i j)))
        (define store-in-table!
          (lambda (i j)
            (table-set! table i j
                        (changes-in-first-and-elements i j))))
        (from-to-do 0 n
                    (lambda (row)
                      (from-to-do 0 m
                                  (lambda (col)
                                    (store-in-table! row col)))))
        (changes-in-first-and-elements n m)))))
```

> ### Exercise 12.16

We mentioned that this procedure uses just one possible valid ordering.

a. Change the procedure to the other (column by column) valid ordering we mentioned, and verify that it still works.
b. Give an example of an invalid order in which to fill in the table.
c. Give a third example of a valid order.

> ### Exercise 12.17

The last line of the **dp-changes** procedure calculates $D(n, m)$ using the expression

```
(changes-in-first-and-elements n m)
```

It would be possible to instead just look this value up from the already filled-in table by changing the above expression to

```
(changes-in-first-and-elements-subproblem n m)
```

The analogous modification would not have been legal in `dp-choose`, however. Explain what the relevant difference is between the two procedures.

> ### Exercise 12.18

The previous versions of `changes` all used as their base cases $D(0,j) = j$ and $D(i,0) = i$. As preparation for the next exercise, modify `dp-changes` so that the only base case is $D(0,0) = 0$. You'll need to recursively define $D(0,j)$ as $1 + D(0,j-1)$ for $j > 0$ and similarly define $D(i,0)$ as $1 + D(i-1,0)$ for $i > 0$.

> ### Exercise 12.19

In this problem, we outline a way to modify the `dp-changes` from the previous exercise so that it produces a list of the changes to make to *vector1* in order to get *vector2*.

a. First we need an ADT for the changes. Each change will have a certain type (replace, insert, or delete) and a position at which to do the change. Insertions and replacements will also need to know what symbol to use for the insertion or replacement. Construct a suitable ADT, with three constructors and three selectors.

b. Next, we'll need an ADT for *collections of changes*, which is like a box of chocolates in the previous section—the point of using a "collection" ADT rather than a list is so that the number of changes in the collection can be kept track of, rather than repeatedly counted with `length`. You'll need `make-empty-collection` and `add-change-to-collection` constructors and `collection-size` and `collection-list` selectors.

c. We will change the values in the table so that they are collections of changes rather than integers that indicate the minimum number of changes. In that case, instead of using the procedure `min` to select the smallest of three numbers, we'll need to select the smallest of three collections of changes. Write a procedure that gets three collections of changes, determines which has the smallest size, and returns that collection.

d. Finally, write a version of `dp-changes` that produces the list of changes to make rather than the number of them.

12.5 Comparing Memoization and Dynamic Programming

Having seen a number of examples of both memoization and dynamic programming, let's consider what their relative strong points are. Keep in mind, though, that we're talking here about relatively fine differences between two very similar and similarly powerful techniques.

One benefit of memoization is that only those table entries that are needed are computed, whereas in dynamic programming all table entries get systematically computed in case they turn out to be needed. For some procedures this systematicness makes no difference; for example, the `memoized-walk-count` procedure fills in the whole table anyhow because it is all needed. However, consider the memoized and dynamic programming versions of `choose`. As the example tables in Section 12.4 show, the dynamic programming version can compute significantly more table entries. For some other problems, the difference is even more substantial.

The other principal advantage of memoization, relative to dynamic programming, is that the programmer doesn't have to figure out in what order the table needs to be filled. For the procedures we've seen (and most encountered in practice), this wasn't difficult. Occasionally, however, one encounters a problem where the correct ordering of the subproblems is a stumper, and then it is wise not to bother figuring it out but rather to simply use memoization.

One of the biggest advantages of dynamic programming is that for some problems—such as computing Fibonacci numbers—the dynamic programming solution can be modified to use asymptotically less memory (in the case of `dp-walk-count`, $\Theta(1)$ instead of $\Theta(n)$). This is possible because the Fibonacci recurrence, $F_n = F_{n-1} + F_{n-2}$, is an example of a *limited history recurrence*, in which only a limited number of preceding values (here 2) need to be remembered in order to compute a new value. Thus, rather than using an n-element vector for the table of values, it is possible to just keep cycling through the positions in a two-element vector, reusing the same two storage locations over and over for the most recent two Fibonacci numbers. A similar savings is possible in other limited-history recurrences.

As you can see, the most substantial differences between memoization and dynamic programming only arise in some problems, not in all. For those problems where none of these special considerations apply, professional programmers generally choose dynamic programming because if one is careful about the programming details, it can be slightly more efficient (by a constant factor—not a better asymptotic order of growth). On the other hand, memoization is a tool you can quickly and easily reach for, with less careful analysis.

12.6 An Application: Formatting Paragraphs

In this section we consider a problem that is encountered by many text formatting or word processing programs. How do we find the best way to break a paragraph into separate lines? To be more precise, suppose we have all the words and punctuation marks in a paragraph typed in somehow, and we need to decide how to break that paragraph into lines. We are only allowed to break lines in between words; that is, we can't hyphenate words. We are also concerned about the amount of white space that is left over on the lines. Ideally, the words on each line and the spaces between those words would fill the entire width of the line, with no leftover space. Moreover, if there is leftover space, we'd prefer that it was reasonably evenly spread among the lines, with just a little per line, rather than some lines having large amounts of excess space. Of course, we realize that the last line of the paragraph may need to have a large chunk of white space, so we won't count the amount of leftover white space that appears on that line.

Let's assume that the input to this problem will be a list of words, where each word is a string that can contain letters, digits, punctuation marks, etc., but not any spaces. We can find the width a word will occupy on the printed page by using a `string-width` procedure. A simple version of this procedure would simply say that each character occupies one unit of space; that works for fixed-width type fonts `like this one`. If we make that simplifying assumption, the width of a string would be the same as its length in characters, and we could simply do the following definition:

```
(define string-width string-length)
```

If you want to make our program work with type fonts in which the characters vary in width, you'll simply need to redefine `string-width` to take this fact into account. We will also assume that we know the maximum width of a line, measured in the same units as `string-width` uses. So, because our simple `string-width` returns the width measured in characters, the maximum line width would be expressed in characters too.

We would like the output from our formatting procedure to be a list of lists of words. Each list of words represents a line in the paragraph. The amount of space that a given line takes up will be the sum of the widths of the words in that line plus the width of the spaces that go in between the words. The width of each space can be given the name `space-width`; with widths measured in characters this would simply be

```
(define space-width 1)
```

If `string-width` were changed to report widths in some other unit to accommodate a variable-width font, `space-width` would need to be changed to reflect the width of the space character in that font. The leftover space on a line is simply the difference between the maximum line width and the amount of space that the line uses. The amount of space the line uses can be computed as follows, using the `sum` procedure from Chapter 7:

```
(define line-width
  (lambda (word-widths)
    (+ (sum word-widths) ; total width of words
       (* (- (length word-widths) 1) ; number of spaces
          space-width)))) ; each this wide
```

If we didn't care about having a large chunk of white space on any one line, we could measure how good a particular solution to our problem is by simply adding up the amount of leftover space on all of the lines but the last one. The smaller this number is, the better the solution is. However, we really do care about huge chunks of white space. In other words, having nine excess spaces on one line and one on another is not as good as having five on each. One way to adjust for this problem would be to add up the cubes of the amounts of leftover space, because cubing would make that huge chunk count for a lot more. (We could take some other power, as well. In general, the higher the power, the greater the penalty is for having one or two big amounts of leftover space.) We call this cubed leftover space the *cost*; the following procedure computes the cost of a line:

```
(define line-cost
  (lambda (word-widths max-line-width)
    (expt (- max-line-width (line-width word-widths))
          3)))
```

In summary, we want to find the best way to break our paragraph into lines, where *best* means that we want to minimize the sum of the line costs on all of the lines except for the very last line. We will assume that we're given as input the maximum line width and a list of strings. Our output is a list of lists of strings.

One approach to this problem is to first simplify it somewhat by taking the list of strings and converting it into a list of numbers, namely, the widths of the strings. Working from this list of widths, we will initially produce as output simply a list of integers, where each of these integers specifies how many words are in the corresponding line. Using this list, we can then chop up the original list of strings into the final list of lists of strings. In other words, our overall formatting process has three phases: preprocessing the list of strings into a list of widths, doing the main decision-making about how many words to put on each line, and then postprocessing to get a list of lists of strings. The following two exercises take care of the preprocessing and postprocessing stages.

Exercise 12.20

Write a procedure that will take a list of strings and convert it into a list of numbers that correspond to the string widths.

> **Exercise 12.21**

Write a procedure called `make-lines` that takes a list of elements and a list of integers and breaks the list of elements into sublists. For example, (`make-lines` `'(a b c d e f g h i j) '(2 3 5))` has a value of ((a b) (c d e) (f g h i j)). You should assume that the integers in the second list add up to the number of elements in the first list.

Now we can assume that our problem is to take a list of word widths and find the best number of words to put on each line. We will work recursively by concentrating on the first line. Suppose that we have n words total and we decide to put some number of them, k, on the first line. If we break the remaining $n - k$ words into lines in the best possible way, the overall line breaking will be the best that is possible given the decision to put k words on the first line. Therefore, all we have to do is experiment with different values of k and see which gives the best result, in each case recursively invoking the procedure to optimally divide up the remaining $n - k$ words.

As we experiment with different values of k, we are looking to see which results in the best solution to the line-breaking problem. How do we tell which solution is best? One way to do this is to associate a cost with each solution. The cost of a solution is the sum of the costs of all of the lines except for the last one. The best solution is one with a minimal cost.

Now, our solutions will consist of a list of numbers that tell us how many words to put onto each line. We can improve the efficiency of our program by connecting this list with its associated cost.

> **Exercise 12.22**

Construct an abstract data type for solutions that will glue together a list of integers, called `breaks`, and a number, called `cost`. You should have one constructor and two selectors:

(`make-solution` *breaks cost*)
(`breaks` *solution*)
(`cost` *solution*)

> **Exercise 12.23**

Write a procedure `better-solution` that when given two solutions returns the one with the lower cost. If the two have equal costs, either can be returned.

As the paragraph formatting procedure systematically experiments with varying numbers of words on the first line, it needs to determine the best solution that results. One way we can arrange for this is with a higher-order procedure, `best-solution-from-to-of`, much like `from-to-do`. Like `from-to-do`, it will apply a procedure to each integer in a range. Each time the procedure is applied, it is expected to produce a solution as its result, and the best of these (as determined by your `better-solution` procedure) gets returned:

```
(define best-solution-from-to-of
  (lambda (low high procedure)
    (if (= low high)
        (procedure low)
        (better-solution (procedure low)
                         (best-solution-from-to-of (+ low 1) high
                                                   procedure)))))
```

When this `best-solution-from-to-of` procedure is used to try out the different possibilities for how many words go on the first line, the first argument (low) will be 1, because that is the minimum number of words that can be put on a line. How about the second argument? What is the maximum number of words that can be put on the first line? This depends on how wide the words are and what the maximum line width is.

Exercise 12.24

Write a procedure `num-that-fit` that takes two arguments. The first is a list of word widths and the second is the maximum line width. Your procedure should determine how many of the words (from the beginning of the list) can be fit onto a line. Remember to account for the spaces between the words, each of which has the width named `space-width`.

At this point, we are ready to write the `format-paragraph` procedure itself. It takes as arguments the list of word widths for the paragraph and the maximum line width. It returns a solution object, which contains the best possible set of breaks together with the cost of that set of breaks. (Remember that the breaks are the number of words on each line.) This procedure first checks for two special cases:

1. If all the words can be fit on a single line, that is the best solution and has cost 0 because excess space on the last line isn't counted.
2. If no words can be put on the first line without overfilling it (i.e., even the first word alone is too wide for the maximum line width), an error message is given because the given formatting problem is insoluble.

Other than these two special cases, the procedure follows the strategy we outlined earlier of systematically trying all the possibilities for how many words to put on the first line:

```
(define format-paragraph  ;returns solution
  (lambda (word-widths max-line-width)
    (let ((most-on-first (num-that-fit word-widths max-line-width)))
      (cond ((= most-on-first (length word-widths))
             (make-solution (list most-on-first) 0))  ; all on first
            ((= most-on-first 0)
             (error "impossible to format; use shorter words"))
            (else
             (best-solution-from-to-of
              1 most-on-first
              (lambda (num-on-first)
                (let ((solution-except-first-line
                       (format-paragraph (list-tail word-widths
                                                    num-on-first)
                                         max-line-width)))
                  (make-solution
                   (cons num-on-first
                         (breaks solution-except-first-line))
                   (+ (cost solution-except-first-line)
                      (line-cost (first-elements-of
                                  num-on-first
                                  word-widths)
                                 max-line-width)))))))))))
```

Exercise 12.25

Put this procedure together with the ones you wrote for computing the list of widths from a list of strings, the **breaks** selector you wrote, and the **make-lines** procedure you wrote. This should let you format a list of words into a list of lists of words, one per line. Try this out with some short lists of words and narrow maximum line widths. Try scaling up the number of words and/or the maximum line width; how tolerable is the growth in time?

Of all of the procedures we've considered so far, this one probably makes the most tree-recursive calls because it tries out all possible numbers of words to place on each line. This fact makes it a very good candidate for memoizing or for using dynamic programming.

The various subproblems solved in the course of formatting a paragraph consist of formatting tails of that paragraph, but with the same maximum line width. Thus only a one-dimensional table (vector) is needed, indexed by the number of words. That is, the entry at position n in the vector will contain the solution object showing the best way to break the last n words of the paragraph into lines, which means that the length of the word-widths list is used to index the table, much as the length of the chocolates list was used as an index in the chocolate box problem.

▶ **Exercise 12.26**

Write a memoized version of format-paragraph. Test your memoized version to be sure it produces the same answers as the nonmemoized version. Also, empirically compare their speed as the number of words and/or the maximum line width grows.

In writing a dynamic programming version, it will be helpful to have a procedure that given a number n computes the tail of length n of the word-widths list. Again, this problem is analogous to the situation in the chocolate-box problem.

▶ **Exercise 12.27**

Following the hint just given, write a dynamic programming version of format-paragraph. Again, test that it produces the same results as the other versions and empirically compare its performance.

Review Problems

▷ **Exercise 12.28**

We implemented two-dimensional tables in terms of one-dimensional vectors by representing each table as a vector of vectors, one per row. The most obvious alternative would be to continue to have a vector of vectors but make it be one per column. However, we have another, less obvious alternative: We can store all the elements of an $n \times m$ table in a single vector of length nm. For example, the 15 elements of a 3×5 table can be stored in the 15 elements of a vector of length 15. The two most straightforward ways to do this alternative are either to store first the elements from the first row, then those from the second row, etc., or to start with the elements from the first column, then those from the second column, etc. Note that in either case you will need to store the width and height of the table, not only because table-width and table-height are selectors for the table ADT, but more crucially in order to calculate the appropriate index into the vector of table values. One easy thing we can do is to let a table be represented by a three-element vector, where the first two elements represent the width and height and the third element is the vector that stores the table values. Reimplement the table ADT using either of these variations (i.e., storing the elements row by row or column by column in a single vector).

▷ **Exercise 12.29**

Suppose you are the instructor of a course with n students, and you want to divide the students into k teams for a project. You don't care how many students are on each team (for example, that they be equal), except that each team must have at least one student on it, because otherwise there wouldn't really be k teams. How many ways can you divide the students up?

This problem can be analyzed much as we analyzed `choose`. The first student can either be in a team alone or in a team with one or more others. In the first case, the remaining $n - 1$ students need to be divided into $k - 1$ teams. In the second case, the remaining $n - 1$ students need to be divided into k teams, and then one of those k teams needs to be chosen to add the first student to. So, if we use $S(n, k)$ to denote our answer, we have $S(n, k) = S(n - 1, k - 1) + kS(n - 1, k)$. (We're using the letter S because numbers computed in this way are conventionally called *Stirling numbers of the second kind*.) Of course, this equation is only the recursive case; you'll need one or more base cases as well.

Write a tree-recursive procedure for computing $S(n, k)$ and then make it more efficient using memoization or dynamic programming. (Or you could first rewrite it using memoization and then using dynamic programming.)

▷ **Exercise 12.30**

We defined the procedure `from-to-do` earlier in this chapter. This procedure is very similar to the so-called FOR loop from other languages. Because we learned in Chapter 10 how to add features to Scheme, it would be nice to add actual FOR loops to Mini-Scheme. To illustrate what we mean, consider the following use of the procedure `from-to-do`:

```
(from-to-do 2 (* 3 4)
            (lambda (n) (display (* 2 n))))
```

With FOR loops, we could instead write:

```
(for n = 2 to (* 3 4) do (display (* 2 n)))
```

This exercise will work through the details of adding FOR loops to Mini-Scheme.

Let's choose to implement FOR loops using a new AST constructor `make-for-ast`. The skeleton for `make-for-ast`, with the important code left out, is as follows:

```
(define make-for-ast
  (lambda (var start-ast stop-ast body-ast)
    (define the-ast
      (lambda (message)
        (cond ((equal? message 'evaluate-in)
               (lambda (global-environment)



                        code for evaluate-in            ))



              ((equal? message 'substitute-for)
               (lambda (value name)



                        code for substitute-for         ))



              (else (error "unknown operation on a for AST"
                           message)))))
    the-ast))
```

a. Write the pattern/action that needs to be added to `micro-scheme-parsing-p/a-list` for FOR loops.

b. Add the code for evaluate-in. (*Hint:* You can use the procedure `from-to-do`.)

c. Add the code for substitute-for-in.

▷ **Exercise 12.31**

Imagine the following game: You are given a path that consists of white and black squares. The exact configuration of white and black squares varies with the game but might for example look as follows:

You start on the leftmost square (which we'll call square 0), and your goal is to move off the right end of the path in the least number of moves. However, the rules stipulate that

- If you are on a white square, you can move either 1 or 2 squares to the right.
- If you are on a black square, you can move either 1 or 4 squares to the right.

How can we determine, for a given path, the least number of moves we need? One way to compute this number is to write a procedure `fewest-moves` that takes a path and a position on the path and computes the minimum number of moves from that position. Thus, to determine the minimum number of moves for the preceding path, we would evaluate:

```
(fewest-moves (vector 'white 'black 'white 'white 'white
                      'black 'white 'white 'black 'white
                      'black 'white 'white 'black 'black
                      'white 'white 'white)
          0)
```

Note that we pass the path as a vector as well as the current square (in this case 0). Here is one way to implement `fewest-moves`:

```
(define fewest-moves
  (lambda (path i) ; path is a vector
                   ; i is the position within path
    (cond ((>= i (vector-length path)) ; right of path
           0)
          ((equal? (vector-ref path i) 'white)
           (+ 1 (min (fewest-moves path (+ i 1))
                     (fewest-moves path (+ i 2)))))
          (else
           (+ 1 (min (fewest-moves path (+ i 1))
                     (fewest-moves path (+ i 4))))))))
```

a. Write a memoized version of `fewest-moves`.
b. Write a dynamic programming version of `fewest-moves`. Be sure to remember that the simplest subproblems, in the sense of being closest to the base case, do *not* correspond to smaller values of the argument *i* in this problem.
c. Modify `fewest-moves`, and your memoized and/or dynamic programming version of it, to produce a list of moves rather than just the number of moves that are necessary.

▷ **Exercise 12.32**

The `ps` procedure that follows calculates how many ways we can parenthesize an *n*-operand expression. For example, (ps 4) evaluates to 5 because there are five ways to parenthesize a four-operand expression: $a - (b - (c - d))$, $a - ((b - c) - d)$, $(a - b) - (c - d)$, $(a - (b - c)) - d$, and $((a - b) - c) - d$.

```
(define from-to-add
  (lambda (start end f)
    (if (> start end)
        0
        (+ (f start)
           (from-to-add (+ start 1) end f)))))

(define ps
  (lambda (n)
    (cond ((= n 1) 1)
          ((= n 2) 1)
          (else
           (from-to-add 1 (- n 1)
                        (lambda (k)
                          (* (ps k) (ps (- n k)))))))))
```

a. Write a memoized version of **ps**.

b. Write a dynamic programming version of **ps**.

▷ **Exercise 12.33**

The function $h(n)$ is defined for nonnegative integers n as follows:

$$h(n) = \begin{cases} 1 & \text{if } n < 2 \\ h(n-1) + h(n-2) & \text{if } n > 2 \text{ and } n \text{ is odd} \\ h(n-1) + h(n/2) & \text{if } n \geq 2 \text{ and } n \text{ is even} \end{cases}$$

a. Write a dynamic programming procedure for efficiently calculating $h(n)$.

b. Is it possible to modify the procedure so that it stores all the values it needs in a vector of fixed size, as **walk-count** can be modified to store the values it needs in a two-element vector? (A vector of "fixed size" is one with a size that does not depend on the parameter, n.) Justify your answer.

▷ **Exercise 12.34**

The following **best** procedure determines the best score that is possible on the following puzzle. You are given a list of positive integers. Let's say the first one is k.

You can either claim *k* points for yourself and then skip over *k* more numbers after the *k*, or you can just skip over the *k* itself without claiming any points. These options repeat until the numbers are all gone. When skipping over the next *k* numbers, if there aren't *k* left, you just stop. For example, given the list

```
(2 1 3 1 4 2)
```

your best bet is to first claim 2 points, which means you have to skip over the first 1 and the 3, then pass up the opportunity to take the second 1, so that you can take the 4, which then causes you to skip the final 2. Your total score in this case is 6; had you played less skillfully, you could have gotten a lower score. The **best** procedure returns the best score possible, so (**best** '(2 1 3 1 4 2)) would return 6.

```
(define best
  (lambda (l)
    (if (null? l)
        0
        (let ((k (car l))
              (rest (cdr l)))
          (max (best rest)
               (+ k (best (skip-of k rest))))))))

(define skip-of
  (lambda (n l)   ;skip first n elements of l
    (if (or (= n 0) (null? l))   ;l can be shorter than n
        l
        (skip-of (- n 1) (cdr l)))))
```

a. Write a memoized version of **best**.

b. Write a dynamic programming version of **best**.

Chapter Inventory

Vocabulary

exponential growth	binomial coefficients
Fibonacci numbers	knapsack problem
memoization	Stirling numbers of the second kind
dynamic programming	FOR loops

Slogans

Much computation, little variety sign

Abstract Data Types

two-dimensional tables
chocolates
boxes

changes
collections (of changes)
solutions (line breaking)

New Predefined Scheme Names

`vector-fill!`

Scheme Names Defined in This Chapter

```
walk-count
memoized-walk-count
walk-count-subproblem
ensure-in-table!
store-into-table!
dp-walk-count
from-to-do
dp-walk-count-2
choose
make-table
table-ref
table-set!
table-height
table-width
table-fill!
display-table
memoized-choose
make-chocolate
chocolate-filling
chocolate-covering
chocolate-weight
chocolate-desirability
make-empty-box
box-chocolates
box-weight
box-desirability
add-chocolate-to-box
better-box
```

```
shirks-chocolates-rated-by-max
pick-chocolates
memoized-pick-chocolates
dp-choose
changes
dp-changes
make-empty-collection
add-change-to-collection
collection-size
collection-list
string-width
space-width
line-width
line-cost
make-lines
make-solution
breaks
cost
better-solution
best-solution-from-to-of
num-that-fit
format-paragraph
make-for-ast
fewest-moves
from-to-add
ps
best
skip-of
```

Notes

We mentioned briefly that the `changes-dynamic` procedure for computing the minimum number of changes needed to convert one vector of symbols into another has applications in comparing the sequences occuring in biological molecules such as DNA. For a discussion of this application, as well as the application of this algorithm and its relatives to problems in speech processing and other areas, see [46].

The problem of breaking a paragraph into lines in a visually appealing way by minimizing the sum of the cubes of the amount of excess space on each line is a gross simplification of the actual approach used by the TEX program, which was used to format this book. That program uses a dynamic programming algorithm but takes into account not only the amount of excess space on each line but also the possibility of hyphenation and a number of esoteric considerations. For a complete description of the quantity that it minimizes, see [34]. For the program itself, see [33].

CHAPTER THIRTEEN

Object-based Abstractions

13.1 Introduction

In Chapter 6, we emphasized that each abstract data type should have a collection of operations that was appropriate to how the type needed to be used. This same general principle applies even when we consider types of objects that can be modified. Yet up until now, the only modifiable objects we've seen—vectors and two-dimensional tables—have supported only one particular repertoire of operations. You can put a new value into a numerically specified location or get the current value out from a numerically specified location, which reflects the close link between vectors and the numerically addressed memory of machines like SLIM, as we pointed out in Chapter 11. Yet sometimes our programming would benefit from a different set of operations. For example, we might want an operation that retrieves the most recently stored value, independent of the location at which it was stored.

In this chapter, we'll learn how to work with abstract data types that can be modified, like vectors, but that support operations determined by our needs rather than by the nature of the underlying memory. We'll also see how we can think clearly about objects that undergo change, by focusing on invariant properties that are established when the object is first constructed and preserved by each modification of the object. Finally, we'll see some specific commonly used examples of modifiable data structures. In particular, we'll see a stack-like structure that is useful when evaluating arithmetic expressions, a queue structure that is useful for managing waiting lists fairly, and a tree structure that can be used to efficiently store and retrieve information, such as the collection of movies owned by a video store that constantly acquires new releases. In fact, you'll apply the structure to exactly this problem in the application section at the end of the chapter.

13.2   Arithmetic Expressions Revisited

Recall that we wrote a procedure called `evaluate` in Section 8.3 that computes the value of standard arithmetic expressions that are fully parenthesized. For example, you might have the following interaction:

```
(evaluate '((3 + 4) * (9 - (2 * 3))))
21
```

On the other hand, `evaluate` would be unable to cope with an expression such as

```
'((3 + 4) * 9 - 2 * 3)
```

even though it is a perfectly valid arithmetic expression whose value is 57. Attempting to evaluate the latter expression results in an error because `evaluate` only handles expressions that are numbers or three-element lists. Furthermore, the three-element lists must have a left operand, an operator, and a right operand, in that order. Because the operands had to be expressions of the same form, evaluation was accomplished by recursively applying the value of the operator to the values of the two operands.

We would like to extend our `evaluate` procedure so that it can handle more general arithmetic expressions, such as the preceding one. What makes this difficult is specifying which operands a given operator should operate on. For example, consider the following two expressions:

```
'(3 - 4 + 5)
```

```
'(3 - 4 * 5)
```

In the first case, the - operates on 3 and 4, whereas in the second case, the - operates on 3 and the result of 4 * 5. Why? Because the * operator has *higher precedence* than the + does. Normally, when you have an expression with more than one operator in it, you do the operations with higher precedence first and then do the others, where the precedence convention with the four operators + - * / is that there are two levels, one for * and / and another for + and -, and the first level is higher than the second. If you have an expression with two consecutive operators with the same precedence (for instance, '(10 - 3 - 2)), you do those operations working from left to right.

There is some flexibility in these rules; for instance in evaluating an expression such as '(2 + 5 + 5), many people would do the second addition first. However, we can always do our operations in a left-to-right order *as long as* we always remember that when we have two consecutive operators and one has higher precedence, we do that one first. Here is an example of figuring out the value of an expression using this approach:

$$3 + \underbrace{2 * 4} - 40/5$$
$$\underbrace{3 + 8} - 40/5$$
$$11 - \underbrace{40/5}$$
$$\underbrace{11 - 8}$$
$$3$$

We can therefore view the general evaluation process as a sequence of *reductions*, where each reduction consists of a single operation on two numbers. In the example above, we did four of these reductions.

If we look at expressions with parentheses, such as $3 * (2 + 4)$, we can use a similar process involving reductions. We would reduce $2 + 4$ to 6, yielding $3 * (6)$. Then we could reduce the parenthesized (6) to a plain 6, yielding $3 * 6$, which we would reduce to 18. We'll put off parenthesized expressions for later in this section and stick with unparenthesized expressions for now. However, in both cases the key action is the reduction.

This viewpoint allows us to come up with a method for evaluating unparenthesized expressions from left to right, *provided* we can maintain a little bit of memory. The basic idea is to scan the expression from left to right and do a reduction once we know it should be done. How do we know when to reduce? Consider the example of $3 + 2 * 4 - 40/5$. Having scanned through $3 + 2$, we need to check the next symbol to determine whether to reduce $3 + 2$. Seeing that the next symbol is an operator of higher precedence, we scan further, eventually reaching $3 + 2 * 4$. Because the next symbol is an operator of equal or lower precedence, we determine that a reduction is in order and replace the scanned portion with $3 + 8$. This continues through the remainder of the list, reducing until we have a single number.

What sort of storage mechanism do we need? First note that the basic data being manipulated consists of the numbers and operators in the expression. In a sense, numbers and operators are the "words" from which our expressions are formed. We will adopt the common computer science convention of referring to these basic words as *tokens*. Thus, "scanning down the expression" means `cdr`-ing down the list of tokens. As we scan, we'll keep a collection of already scanned (or reduced) tokens. Each time we scan a new token, we either *shift* it onto the collection of already scanned (or reduced) tokens, or we perform a *reduction* on that latter collection. This collection of already scanned or reduced tokens is precisely the memory storage mechanism we need.

What operations must we perform on this collection? Well, we either *shift* something onto it, or we *reduce* the three most recently scanned tokens by performing the operation. In either case, we need to access the most recently scanned tokens.

Figuratively, we can view this collection of scanned or reduced tokens as a *stack* of tokens, where we access the stack from the top (i.e., the most recently scanned or reduced token). Shifting a token means putting it on top of the stack; reducing means removing the top three items from the stack, performing the operation, and putting the resulting value back on top of the stack.

Actually, there are two other actions we might need to do besides shifting and reducing:

- If we have successfully finished evaluating an expression, we should *accept* it and return the top item on the stack as the value.
- If we encounter an *error*, we should report it and stop the processing altogether.

So we have a total of four possible actions during the course of our processing: shift, reduce, accept, and error. Each of these actions can be easily accomplished, provided we can access the top items on the stack of processed tokens.

One question remains before we can view this as a full-blown algorithm: Given our current state (the stack of processed tokens and the newly scanned token), which of the four actions do we take? The key point here is that we can determine the action with only knowledge of the top two elements on the stack and the next scanned token (or knowledge that we have already reached the end of the expression). To illustrate this, consider the table in Figure 13.1, which describes the sequence of actions taken in order to reduce the expression $3 + 2 * 4 - 40/5$. Note that we have added a special "terminating" symbol $ at the bottom of the expression stack and the end of the

expression stack	rest of expression	next action
$	3 + 2 * 4 - 40 / 5 $	shift
$ 3	+ 2 * 4 - 40 / 5 $	shift
$ 3 +	2 * 4 - 40 / 5 $	shift
$ 3 + 2	* 4 - 40 / 5 $	shift
$ 3 + 2 *	4 - 40 / 5 $	shift
$ 3 + 2 * 4	- 40 / 5 $	reduce
$ 3 + 8	- 40 / 5 $	reduce
$ 11	- 40 / 5 $	shift
$ 11 -	40 / 5 $	shift
$ 11 - 40	/ 5 $	shift
$ 11 - 40 /	5 $	shift
$ 11 - 40 / 5	$	reduce
$ 11 - 8	$	reduce
$ 3	$	accept

Figure 13.1   Evaluation of $3 + 2 * 4 - 40/5$

stack	next token		
top	$	op	num
$	error	error	shift
op	error	error	shift
num	reduce or accept	shift or reduce	error

Figure 13.2   Action table for unparenthesized expressions

expression. Strictly speaking, this symbol is not really needed; after all, we could easily test to see whether the expression stack or the rest of the expression is empty. However, having a symbol that indicates these conditions will be helpful when we finally get around to writing the code because we will then always be testing tokens to determine our action.

Although the example in Figure 13.1 gives some notion of how to determine the next action, we need to be more precise. We increase the precision in Figure 13.2, where we give a table that *nearly* specifies which action to take, given the top of the stack and the next scanned token. In this table the row headings refer to the top of the expression stack, the column headings refer to the next token, *op* refers to any of the four operators, and *num* refers to any number. Therefore, if the top of the expression stack is an operator and the next token is a number, we should surely shift; however, if the next token is an operator, we take the error action because no legal expression can have two consecutive operators.

▶ **Exercise 13.1**

Explain why each of the five error conditions in the table in Figure 13.2 is in fact an error. In each case, give an example of an expression that has the given error, clearly marking where the error occurs.

We said that the table *nearly* specifies the action, because in two cases we need more information:

- If the top of the stack is a number and the next token is $, we accept if the token below the top of the stack is $ (because the expression is then fully reduced), and otherwise we reduce.

- If the top of the stack is a number and the next token is an operator, we shift if the token below the top of the stack is either not an operator or else is an operator of lower precedence than the next token, and otherwise we reduce (this is our evaluation rule).

In both cases, we need only one more piece of information: the token below the top of the stack. This explains our statement that to determine the next action, we at most need to know the top two elements on the stack and the next scanned token.

▶ Exercise 13.2

Work through the steps in evaluating $30 - 7 * 3 - 1$. We recommend that you do this using index cards, at least the first time, to get more of a feel for what is going on. If you want to document your work, you can then do the evaluation a second time in tabular form, using the format shown in Figure 13.1.

To do the evaluation using index cards, you'll use two piles, one for the stack and the other for the remaining input (that is, the two piles of cards correspond to the first two columns in Figure 13.1). The pile that represents the remaining input should start out with eight cards in it, with 30 on the top, then $-$, 7, $*$, 3, $-$, 1, and finally $ on the bottom. The other pile, representing the stack, should start out with just a $ card. You'll also need a few blank cards for when you do reductions.

At each step, you should look at the top cards from the two piles and use those to locate the proper row and column in the action table of Figure 13.2. If the action table entry is one of the two with "or" in it, you'll need to peek down at the second card in the stack and use the rules specified above to determine the correct action.

If the action is shift, you just move the top card from the remaining-input pile to the stack. If the action is reduce, you take the top three cards off the stack, do the computation, write the answer on a blank card, and put that onto the stack. (Be sure to get the order right: The card that was on top of the stack is the right operand, whereas the one that was three deep is the left operand.) If the action is accept, the top card on the stack tells you the answer. If the action is error, you must have done something wrong because the expression we started with, $30 - 7 * 3 - 1$, was well formed.

Having pretty much taken care of unparenthesized expressions (except for writing the code), let's now consider expressions that include parentheses, for example the expression $(3 + 2) * 4 - 40/5$. First off, this means we must add new tokens (words) to our expression vocabulary, namely, left and right parentheses. However, this leads to a bit of a problem, because parentheses are not legal symbols in Scheme; after all, they are used to delimit Scheme lists. We will get around this problem by using strings instead of lists to pass our expressions to `evaluate`. Thus, we would compute the value of the example expression by evaluating the expression

```
(evaluate "(3+2)*4-40/5")
```

Rather than getting bogged down with details involving strings and characters, we describe a procedure called **tokenize** in the sidebar Strings and Characters, later in the chapter. It converts a string to the list of tokens it represents. To illustrate how the procedure **tokenize** works, suppose you have the following interaction:

```
(tokenize "(3+2)*4-40/5")
(lparen 3 + 2 rparen * 4 - 40 / 5 $)
```

The return value of **tokenize** is a list consisting of numbers and symbols, where the special symbols **lparen** and **rparen** represent left parentheses and right parentheses, respectively, and the terminating symbol **$** is at the end of the list.

So how do we extend our algorithm to parenthesized expressions? If we want to continue with our left-to-right approach, once we encounter a parenthesized subexpression, we need to fully reduce it to the number it represents before passing beyond it. Figure 13.3 illustrates how the shift/reduce algorithm might work by evaluating the expression $(3 + 2) * 4 - 40/5$. In a sense, a right parenthesis acts much like the $ symbol, forcing reductions until the subexpression has been fully

expression stack	rest of expression	next action
$	(3 + 2) * 4 − 40 / 5 $	shift
$ (	3 + 2) * 4 − 40 / 5 $	shift
$ (3	+ 2) * 4 − 40 / 5 $	shift
$ (3 +	2) * 4 − 40 / 5 $	shift
$ (3 + 2	) * 4 − 40 / 5 $	reduce
$ (5	) * 4 − 40 / 5 $	shift
$ (5)	* 4 − 40 / 5 $	reduce
$ 5	* 4 − 40 / 5 $	shift
$ 5 *	4 − 40 / 5 $	shift
$ 5 * 4	− 40 / 5 $	reduce
$ 20	− 40 / 5 $	shift
$ 20 −	40 / 5 $	shift
$ 20 − 40	/ 5 $	shift
$ 20 − 40 /	5 $	shift
$ 20 − 40 / 5	$	reduce
$ 20 − 8	$	reduce
$ 12	$	accept

Figure 13.3   Evaluation of $(3 + 2) * 4 − 40/5$

reduced. When that has been accomplished, the right parenthesis is then pushed onto the stack, and the stack is reduced by replacing the parenthesized number with the single number.

Why do we shift a right parenthesis onto the stack, only to immediately throw it away? We are adopting the viewpoint that things get simplified by reduction alone, which occurs at the top of the stack. In our extended algorithm we allow another form of reduction besides performing an arithmetic operation: A parenthesized expression enclosing a number is reduced to the number itself, stripping away the parentheses; this is the reduction that changes the (5) on line 7 to the 5 on line 8 in Figure 13.3. A consequence of this viewpoint is that we must ensure that when the right parenthesis is finally pushed onto the stack, the matching parentheses enclose a simple number, not a more complex expression. This explains why a right parenthesis acts like the $ symbol when it is the next token: It must force a full reduction of the expression on top of the stack back to the matching left parenthesis.

As with unparenthesized expressions, this algorithm is made *nearly* precise by giving a table that explains what to do, given the top of the stack and the next token in the expression. We do this in Figure 13.4, which extends the action table of Figure 13.2 to include left and right parentheses.

Mismatched parentheses are detected by two of the error cases in the num row of the table, that is, when the stack top is a number. If the next token is $ and a left parenthesis lies below the number, we have the kind of error that the input string "(3" exemplifies. If, on the other hand, the next token is a right parenthesis and a $ lies below the number on the stack, we have an error like "3)".

stack top	next token $	op	num	(	)
$	error	error	shift	shift	error
op	error	error	shift	shift	error
num	reduce, accept, or error	shift or reduce	error	error	shift, reduce, or error
(	error	error	shift	shift	error
)	reduce	reduce	error	error	reduce

Figure 13.4   Action table for general expressions

Many of the more complicated parenthesization mismatches reduce to one of the above two cases. For example, in the expression

(3 + 3 * 5)) + 56

the underscored right parenthesis is erroneous, because it has no matching left parenthesis. How can we detect this? Well, in the course of processing the expression up to, but not including, the erroneous right parenthesis, the expression will be reduced to

18) + 56

Because the expression on the top of the stack, 18, is fully reduced, the error is detected by the fact that the token below the top of the stack is a $ rather than a left parenthesis matching the underscored right parenthesis.

▶ **Exercise 13.3**

Explain, using examples, the eight additional error conditions in the table in Figure 13.4, beyond those explained in the foregoing and in Exercise 13.1.

▶ **Exercise 13.4**

Let's consider some of the regularities in this extended table.

a. Why are the columns headed by num and (identical?
b. Why are the rows headed by $ and (identical?
c. Why are these latter rows identical to the row headed by op?

All that remains to make the algorithm precise is to complete our explanation of the additional ambiguous entry in the table, namely, when the top of the stack is a number and the next token is a right parenthesis. Because we showed in the preceding how to detect an error in this situation, we need only explain how to distinguish a shift from a reduce. As we said, we must reduce if the top of the stack is a simple arithmetic expression (i.e., an operator and two numeric operands), because we only want to shift the right parenthesis when the parenthesized expression has been fully reduced. This situation can be detected by checking to see whether the token below the top of the stack is an operator or a left parenthesis. If it is an operator, we should reduce, whereas if it is a left parenthesis, we should shift the right parenthesis onto the stack.

> **Exercise 13.5**

Work through the evaluation of $30 - 7 * (3 - 1)$ using the same technique as in Exercise 13.2.

To finally code up this algorithm, we need to clearly specify the abstract data type *Stack*. As the term is commonly used, a stack allows you to access its top element and to add or delete an item at the top (these latter two operations are generally called *push* and *pop*, respectively). However, we could use something slightly more powerful for our program because we will need to access items below the top as well. For this reason, we are going to use an ADT that we call an *RA-stack* (for Random Access stack), which allows access to all of its elements, while still limiting addition and deletion to the top. Using Scheme notation, we specify the operations of random access stacks as follows:

```
(make-ra-stack)
  ;; returns a newly created empty stack.

(empty-ra-stack? ra-stack)
  ;; returns #t if ra-stack is empty, otherwise #f.

(height ra-stack)
  ;; returns the height (i.e., number of elements) in ra-stack.

(top-minus ra-stack offset)
  ;; returns the element which is offset items below the top of
  ;; ra-stack, provided 0 <= offset < (height ra-stack).
  ;; In particular, (top-minus ra-stack 0) returns the top of
  ;; ra-stack, provided ra-stack is non-empty.

(pop! ra-stack)
  ;; removes the top element of ra-stack, provided ra-stack is
  ;; non-empty.
  ;; The return value is the modified ra-stack.

(push! ra-stack item)
  ;; pushes item onto the top of ra-stack.
  ;; The return value is the modified ra-stack.
```

The two operators **pop!** and **push!** are of particular interest because they cause the stack parameter **ra-stack** to change (mutate); in this respect, they are similar to **vector-set!**. Because the ADT RA-stack allows mutation, it is called a *mutable* *data type*. Another way to say this is that RA-stacks are *objects* rather than *values*. Mutable data types are very useful for modeling phenomena that change in time; in our case, the expression stack changes as the evaluator works.

Turning finally to our version of `evaluate`, most of the work is done by the internally defined procedure `process`, which scans down the expression in the manner described above. The list of as-of-yet-unscanned tokens is maintained through the parameter `rest-of-expr`. `Process` is initialized by first using a `let` to define an empty stack `expr-stack`, then pushing the special token `$` onto `expr-stack`, and finally calling `process` with the tokenization of the input string. Here is the code:

```
(define evaluate
  (lambda (expression-string)
    (let ((expr-stack (make-ra-stack)))
      (define process
        (lambda (rest-of-expr)
          (let ((next-token (car rest-of-expr)))
            (cond ((accept? expr-stack next-token)
                   (top-minus expr-stack 0))
                  ((reduce? expr-stack next-token)
                   (reduce! expr-stack)
                   (process rest-of-expr))
                  ((shift? expr-stack next-token)
                   (push! expr-stack next-token)
                   (process (cdr rest-of-expr)))
                  (else   ; error
                   (error "EVALUATE: syntax error"
                          expr-stack rest-of-expr))))))
      (push! expr-stack '$)
      (process (tokenize expression-string)))))
```

Note that the determination of the next action is offloaded to three predicate procedures `reduce?`, `accept?`, and `shift?`. Similarly, the reduce action has been spun off to the procedure `reduce!`.

The three predicate procedures simply implement the action table in Figure 13.4:

```
(define accept?
  (lambda (expr-stack next-token)
    (if (and (number? (top-minus expr-stack 0))
             (equal? next-token '$))
        (equal? (top-minus expr-stack 1) '$)
        #f)))
```

```
(define reduce?
  (lambda (expr-stack next-token)
    (let ((stack-top (top-minus expr-stack 0)))
      (cond ((number? stack-top)
               (let ((stack-second (top-minus expr-stack 1)))
                 (cond ((equal? next-token '$)
                        (operator? stack-second))
                       ((operator? next-token)
                        (and (operator? stack-second)
                             (not (lower-precedence?
                                    stack-second
                                    next-token))))
                       ((equal? next-token 'rparen)
                        (operator? stack-second))
                       (else #f))))
            ((equal? stack-top 'rparen)
             (or (equal? next-token '$)
                 (operator? next-token)
                 (equal? next-token 'rparen)))
            (else #f)))))

(define shift?
  (lambda (expr-stack next-token)
    (let ((stack-top (top-minus expr-stack 0)))
      (cond ((or (operator? stack-top)
                 (member stack-top '($ lparen)))
             (or (number? next-token)
                 (equal? next-token 'lparen)))
            ((number? stack-top)
             (let ((stack-second (top-minus expr-stack 1)))
               (cond ((operator? next-token)
                      (or (not (operator? stack-second))
                          (lower-precedence? stack-second
                                             next-token)))
                     ((equal? next-token 'rparen)
                      (equal? stack-second 'lparen))
                     (else #f))))
            (else #f)))))
```

The procedure **reduce!** has two branches, corresponding to whether we are
"unparenthesizing" a parenthesized number or performing an arithmetic operation.

```
(define reduce!
  (lambda (expr-stack)
    (cond ((equal? (top-minus expr-stack 0) 'rparen)
           (let ((value (top-minus expr-stack 1)))
             (pop! expr-stack)  ; remove rparen
             (pop! expr-stack)  ; remove the value
             (pop! expr-stack)  ; remove lparen
             (push! expr-stack value)))
          (else ; a simple arithmetic operation
           (let ((left-operand  (top-minus expr-stack 2))
                 (operator       (top-minus expr-stack 1))
                 (right-operand (top-minus expr-stack 0)))
             (pop! expr-stack)  ; remove the right operand
             (pop! expr-stack)  ; remove the operator
             (pop! expr-stack)  ; remove the left operand
             (push! expr-stack
                    ((look-up-value operator)
                     left-operand
                     right-operand)))))))
```

Finally, the procedure `look-up-value` was written in Section 8.3. The remaining auxiliary routines can be implemented as follows:

```
(define operator?
  (lambda (token)
    (member token '(+ - * /))))

(define lower-precedence?
  (lambda (op-1 op-2)
    (and (member op-1 '(+ -))
         (member op-2 '(* /)))))
```

13.3 RA-Stack Implementations and Representation Invariants

We now address the task of implementing RA-stacks. As with all ADTs, we have great freedom in choosing how we represent them and implement their operators; our only real constraint is that RA-stacks must behave as they are supposed to behave. A secondary, though still important, consideration is that they operate efficiently, both in terms of time and memory consumption.

In addition to the RA-stack precedures previously listed, we add one more, `display-ra-stack`, which displays an RA-stack from bottom to top. We can easily

Strings and Characters

Up until this chapter, we only used strings as output arguments in procedures like `display` and `error`. However, the procedure `tokenize` needs to access the contents of a string and construct a list of tokens from it. Therefore, we need to know more about the built-in *String* data type and the operations it supports. We give here a brief overview of strings and the related data type *Character*; much more information is given in the R^4RS Scheme standard, which is available from the web site for this book.

Characters are basic Scheme objects that represent textual characters, such as letters and digits. They are denoted in Scheme by preceding them with `#\`, so `#\a` denotes the character *a*. Certain characters have names; for example the "space" character is written `#\space`. The following procedure determines whether `char` is an arithmetic operator:

```
(define operator-char?
  (lambda (char)
    (member char '(#\+ #\- #\* #\/))))
```

Although strings and vectors are distinct types, strings are essentially vectors that contain characters. Most vector procedures (e.g., `make-vector`, `vector-length`, `vector-ref`, and `vector-set!`) have string equivalents (`make-string`, `string-length`, `string-ref`, and `string-set!`). Also, there are some useful conversion procedures such as `string->number`, which takes a numeric string and converts it to a number it represents, and `string->symbol`, which converts a string to the corresponding symbol.

Given this brief overview of strings and characters, we now present the procedure `tokenize`. By way of explanation, the internal procedure `iter` accumulates the list of tokens from `input-string` in reverse order in the parameter `acc-list`. When `iter` completes, it returns this reverse-order list of tokens. We cons a `$` on the front and reverse the result; therefore, the result is the tokens in correct order and with `$` at the end, as was our desire.

The procedure `iter` processes `input-string` character by character, keeping track of the current position with the parameter `i`, and the "previous state" with the parameter `prev-state`. This state variable tells what type of character we just read, and it is used if we need to process a group of characters together (such as a numeric substring) or are moving to a new token (as would be indicated by a having read a space).

(Continued)

▷ Strings and Characters (Continued)

```scheme
(define tokenize
  (lambda (input-string)
    (define iter
      (lambda (i prev-state acc-lst)
        (if (= i (string-length input-string))
            acc-lst
            (let ((next-char (string-ref input-string i)))
              (cond ((equal? next-char #\space)
                     (iter (+ i 1) 'read-space
                           acc-lst))
                    ((char-numeric? next-char) ;next-char is a digit
                     (if (equal? prev-state 'read-numeric)
                         ;; continue constructing the number, digit
                         ;; by digit, by adding the current digit
                         ;; to 10 times the amount read so far
                         (iter (+ i 1) 'read-numeric
                               (cons (+ (* 10 (car acc-lst))
                                        (digit->number next-char))
                                     (cdr acc-lst)))
                         (iter (+ i 1) 'read-numeric
                               (cons (digit->number next-char)
                                     acc-lst))))
                    ((operator-char? next-char)
                     (iter (+ i 1) 'read-operator
                           (cons (string->symbol
                                  (make-string 1 next-char))
                                 acc-lst)))
                    ((equal? next-char #\()
                     (iter (+ i 1) 'read-lparen
                           (cons 'lparen
                                 acc-lst)))
                    ((equal? next-char #\))
                     (iter (+ i 1) 'read-rparen
                           (cons 'rparen
                                 acc-lst)))
                    (else
                     (error "illegal character in input"
                            next-char)))))))
    (reverse (cons '$ (iter 0 'start '())))))

(define digit->number
  (lambda (digit-char)
    (string->number (string digit-char))))
```

implement it in terms of the other operators:

```
(define display-ra-stack
  (lambda (ra-stack)
    (define display-from
      (lambda (offset)
        (cond ((= offset 0)
               (display (top-minus ra-stack 0))
               'done)
              (else
               (display (top-minus ra-stack offset))
               (display " ")
               (display-from (- offset 1))))))
    (if (empty-ra-stack? ra-stack)
        (display "empty-stack")
        (display-from (- (height ra-stack) 1)))))
```

One advantage of writing `display-ra-stack` in terms of the other operators is that we can then use it to help determine whether the other operators are correctly implemented.

How do we ensure that RA-stacks behave as they should? We must first clearly specify how they are *supposed* to behave. Our description of RA-stacks has so far been very informal, relying on some mental image of a stack, say, as a stack of cafeteria trays, and our ADT operations were supposed to conform to this imagined stack. We can make the specification of RA-stacks more formal by writing equations that specify how the RA-stack operations should work together, much as we did in Section 6.3 for the game-state ADT. For example, here are some equations that describe how `push!` and `pop!` work together with `top-minus`:

$$\texttt{(top-minus (push! }\textit{ra-stack item}\texttt{) 0)} = \textit{item}$$

If $1 \leq i \leq$ (`height` *ra-stack*) and $k = i - 1$,

$$\texttt{(top-minus (push! }\textit{ra-stack item}\texttt{) }i\texttt{)} = \texttt{(top-minus }\textit{ra-stack k}\texttt{)}$$

If $0 \leq i <$ (`height` *ra-stack*) $- 1$ and $k = i + 1$,

$$\texttt{(top-minus (pop! }\textit{ra-stack}\texttt{) }i\texttt{)} = \texttt{(top-minus }\textit{ra-stack k}\texttt{)}$$

▷ **Exercise 13.6**

Ideally we should give a set of equations that, taken together, fully specifies RA-stacks; such a complete set would be called an *axiomatic system* for RA-stacks. Rather than getting into whether we have such a complete set (or, in fact, precisely what "complete" means), let's instead generate some additional equations for RA-stacks. Keep in mind that an equation needn't be between two numerical quantities; it can also state that two boolean values are equal.

a. Write equations that explain how `push!` and `pop!` work together with `height`.

b. Write an equation that explains how `empty-ra-stack?` and `height` are related.

c. Write an equation that explains how `empty-ra-stack?` and `make-ra-stack` are related.

▶ **Exercise 13.7**

The two sides of each of the preceding equations are equivalent in the sense that they produce the same value but not in the sense of also having the same effect. We can make improved versions where the effects as well as the values are identical; for example, if $0 \leq i <$ (height *ra-stack*) $- 1$ and $k = i + 1$,

```
(top-minus (pop! ra-stack) i)

   ≡

(let ((value (top-minus ra-stack k)))
  (pop! ra-stack)
  value)
```

a. Rewrite the other two given equations in this style.

b. Rewrite your equations from Exercise 13.6a in this form.

The previous equations will help guide our implementation. But before we get around to actually writing code, we must first consider how RA-stacks will be represented. By this we mean how a given RA-stack should look in terms of more basic Scheme data objects. In order to come up with a representation, let's first consider what specific needs RA-stacks require from their representation. First and foremost is the need for mutability; and because we only know how to mutate vectors, we will therefore represent an RA-stack with one or more vectors. A secondary consideration is that because we do this mutation at the top of the stack, it would be nice to be able to do so without having to change things elsewhere. Finally, we want to be able to access all elements of the stack efficiently.

Our first representation uses two vectors, one with two cells and the other with a large (though fixed) number of cells. The idea is to use the second vector to store the elements of the stack, starting with the bottom element, and let the first vector maintain the height of the stack as well as a reference to the second vector. Figure 13.5 gives a pictorial representation of the stack 5 2 9 1, where 1 is top

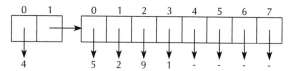

Figure 13.5   Representation of the stack 5 2 9 1, where 1 is top element

element. In this picture, the second vector has eight cells, with the values in the last four cells being immaterial for the stack in question.

The advantage of this representation is that the RA-stack operations are easy to implement, because they involve straightforward vector index computations. For example, the index of the position where the next element should be added is precisely the stack's height, so pushing an element onto the stack involves placing it there and then incrementing the stack's height by 1. Popping an element is accomplished in a similar manner. Accessing an element in a stack is done through a fairly simple index calculation.

Note that this representation imposes an upper limit on the size of the stack, namely, the number of cells in the second vector. We can reflect this restriction by having the following alternative constructor:

```
(make-ra-stack-with-at-most max-num)
  ;; returns an empty stack that can't grow beyond max-num items
```

We can then implement `make-ra-stack` as follows:

```
(define make-ra-stack
  (lambda ()
    (make-ra-stack-with-at-most 8)))
```

The maximum stack size of 8 was somewhat arbitrarily chosen. It is sufficient for most expressions you are likely to encounter when using stacks in the algorithm from the previous section. However, it is insufficient in general because an expression can have arbitrarily many subexpressions, as illustrated by the following example:

```
(1+(2+(3+(4+(5+(6+(7+(8+9))))))))
```

▶ Exercise 13.8

Let's consider the potential size of the expression stack during the course of processing an expression.

a. What is the maximum size of the expression stack during the processing of the preceding expression?

b. What is the maximum size of the expression stack during the processing of an unparenthesized expression?

Let's now work through this implementation scheme. The constructor `make-ra-stack-with-at-most` is straightforward, given the representation described in Figure 13.5. We first create two vectors, called `header` and `cells`, then appropriately initialize the values in `header`, and finally return `header` as the desired empty RA-stack.

```
(define make-ra-stack-with-at-most
  (lambda (max-height)
    (let ((header (make-vector 2))
          (cells (make-vector max-height)))
      (vector-set! header 0 0)     ; header[0] = height = 0
      (vector-set! header 1 cells) ; header[1] = cells
      header)))
```

Note that we used the notation `header[0]` to signify the element in position 0 of the vector `header`. This is *not* allowable Scheme syntax; it is simply an abbreviation we will use in comments and elsewhere when describing the contents of a vector.

Given this construction, the two procedures `height` and `empty-ra-stack?` are also straightforward:

```
(define height
  (lambda (ra-stack)
    (vector-ref ra-stack 0)))

(define empty-ra-stack?
  (lambda (ra-stack)
    (= 0 (height ra-stack))))
```

Note that we've defined `empty-ra-stack?` using `height` rather than directly in terms of `vector-ref`. In general, it makes the implementation of a mutable data type easier to write, read, understand, and modify if arbitrary numerical vector positions needed for `vector-ref` and `vector-set!` are confined to a limited number of procedures. For this reason, we'll also define an "unadvertised" selector, `cells`, which is intended to be used only internally within the implementation of RA-stacks:

```
(define cells   ; use only within the ADT implementation
  (lambda (ra-stack)
    (vector-ref ra-stack 1)))
```

The other operators are more complicated, because we need to do some index computations. For example, consider the operator top-minus, which is supposed to return the element *offset* positions from the top of *ra-stack*. How do we calculate the index of the desired element? Well, we claimed in the foregoing that the index of the position where the next element should be added is precisely the stack's height. If we could count on this, we could then conclude that the top of the stack would be in position *height(ra-stack)* − 1. Therefore, the element *offset* positions from the top would be in position

$$height(\text{ra-stack}) - 1 - offset = height(\text{ra-stack}) - (offset + 1)$$

This information helps us come up with the following implementation of top-minus, which includes some error-checking:

```
(define top-minus
  (lambda (ra-stack offset)
    (cond ((< offset 0)
           (error "TOP-MINUS: offset < 0" offset))
          ((>= offset (height ra-stack))
           (error "TOP-MINUS: offset too large for stack"
                  offset (height ra-stack)))
          (else
           (vector-ref (cells ra-stack)
                       (- (height ra-stack)
                          (+ offset 1)))))))
```

The foregoing reasoning relied on certain assumptions about the representation we are using for RA-stacks, namely, that the index of the position where the next element should be added is the height, which is stored in *ra-stack*[0], and that the stack elements are stored in order from bottom to top starting at *cells*[0], where *cells* = *ra-stack*[1]. How can we rely on these assumptions? The answer is that *we* must maintain them as *representation invariants*; representation invariants are important enough that we give the following definition:

Representation invariant: A *representation invariant* is a property of the representation of an ADT that is valid for all legally formed and maintained instances of the ADT. In other words, if an instance of the ADT was legally formed via one of the ADT's constructors, and was only altered by legal calls to its mutators, the property is guaranteed to be valid.

By *legal*, we mean that the arguments to the constructors or mutators satisfy all of the stipulated or implied preconditions. For example, the *max-height* argument in `make-ra-stack-with-at-most` must be nonnegative.

What are the representation invariants for RA-stacks? Here is one that describes more formally the structure we are relying on from our representation:

> **RA-stack representation invariant (representation 1):** Let *height* = *ra-stack*[0] and *cells* = *ra-stack*[1]. The elements of *ra-stack*, listed from the bottom of the stack to its top, are in *cells*[0], *cells*[1], ..., *cells*[*height* − 1].

In particular, this invariant implies that the element of the stack that is *offset* elements from the top is stored in *cells*[*height* − (*offset* + 1)], the fact we used in our implementation of `top-minus`.

The key point in the definition is that *we* must ensure through our implementation that the representation invariant is valid for any legally formed and maintained instance of an RA-stack. How can we do this? Well, note that any such instance was first formed by an ADT constructor and then was operated on a finite number of times by certain of the ADT selectors and mutators. Because the selectors do not change the instance, the only changes come from the finite sequence of mutations. We can inductively prove the validity of the invariant if we show that

- The invariant is valid for the value returned by a legal call to an RA-stack constructor.
- If the property is valid for an RA-stack before it is passed in a legal call to an RA-stack mutator, it is also valid after the call.

The first condition corresponds to the base case of an induction proof, whereas the second condition corresponds to the inductive step.

Consider first the base case. Note that the invariant is true for the return value for the RA-stack constructor `make-ra-stack-with-at-most` (and therefore also for `make-ra-stack`): After all, there is no i such that $0 \le i < height$ because $height = 0$. We say that the invariant is *vacuously* true in this case.

How about the inductive step in the proof of the invariant? Clearly we can't prove it yet because we have not yet written the two mutators `pop!` and `push!`. On the other hand, we can use our need to prove the inductive step to guide our implementation of the two mutators. Take for example `pop!`. The only thing we need to do in order to remove the top element of the stack while maintaining the invariant is to decrease *ra-stack*[0] (the height) by 1. After all, the remaining elements of the stack will still be in the required order and will still start at location 0 in the *cells* vector, so the invariant will remain valid assuming it had been valid when `pop!` was called. Therefore, we deduce the following implementation for `pop!`:

```
(define pop!
  (lambda (ra-stack)
    (if (empty-ra-stack? ra-stack)
        (error "POP!: attempted pop from an empty stack")
        (begin
          (set-height! ra-stack
                       (- (height ra-stack) 1))
          ra-stack))))

(define set-height!   ; use only within the ADT implementation
  (lambda (ra-stack new-height)
    (vector-set! ra-stack 0 new-height)))
```

Finally, consider push!. Again, the invariant will remain valid if we put the new item in the position with index *height(ra-stack)*. (Recall that the existing elements stop in the location before that one.) After doing the appropriate vector-set! to put it there, all we need to do is increase the value of of the height by 1. Hence:

```
(define push!
  (lambda (ra-stack item)
    (if (<= (vector-length (cells ra-stack))
            (height ra-stack))
        (error "PUSH!: attempted push onto a full stack")
        (begin
          (vector-set! (cells ra-stack)
                       (height ra-stack)
                       item)
          (set-height! ra-stack
                       (+ (height ra-stack) 1))
          ra-stack))))
```

That completes our first implementation of RA-stacks. The main advantage of this implementation is its efficiency: Each operator uses only a small, fixed number of operations. However, there is a definite disadvantage: The stack has a limited size.

▶ Exercise 13.9

One way to overcome this size limitation is to increase the size of the vector holding the stack elements whenever that is necessary, which means rewriting the error clause of the if expression in push!. For example, you could create a vector of twice the size of the current cells vector, copy the old stack elements into the

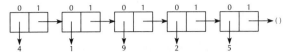

Figure 13.6   Representation of the stack 5 2 9 1, where 1 is top element

new vector, set the new vector as the stack's `cells` vector, and carry on from there. Rewrite `push!` to implement this strategy.

Our second representation of stacks (not counting the one in Exercise 13.9) uses a varying number of two-element vectors. It contains one vector for each element in the stack, plus an additional vector (the *header*) that contains the stack's height and a pointer to the first of the other vectors. Each of the other vectors contains a stack element and a reference to the next vector. In effect, we are implementing something very similar to Scheme lists. Figure 13.6 gives a pictorial representation of the stack 5 2 9 1, where 1 is top element. Notice that the stack is listed from top to bottom, which is the opposite of the first representation. We do this to have easy access to the top of the stack: otherwise we would have to, in effect, "cdr" to the end of the stack in order to add or delete elements. You'll notice in Figure 13.6 that the last two-element vector has the empty list, (), in position 1, which plays the same role as in normal Scheme lists. Because the stack's height is explicitly recorded, this end-marker isn't strictly necessary, but it does make debugging and reasoning easier.

Before starting this implementation, we should try to come up with an invariant that describes our representation. But even before working on the invariant, we have a higher priority: coming up with some terminology so that we can conveniently talk about our representation. We will call the two-element vectors *nodes*, and a *linked list* of nodes such as in Figure 13.6 a *node-list*.

Rather than continuing to talk concretely about the nodes as two-element vectors with "element 0" and "element 1," it would be better if we treated nodes as an abstract data type with the two selectors `node-element` and `node-rest`. That way you don't need to keep straight the 0s and 1s, and we also have the flexibility to later switch to a nonvector representation. For now, the implementation of nodes is as follows:

```
(define make-node
  (lambda (element rest)
    (let ((node (make-vector 2)))
      (vector-set! node 0 element)
      (vector-set! node 1 rest)
      node)))
```

```
(define node-element
  (lambda (node)
    (vector-ref node 0)))

(define node-rest
  (lambda (node)
    (vector-ref node 1)))
```

When we say that an object is a linked list of nodes, or a node-list, we mean that it obeys the following representation invariant:

Node-list representation invariant: A node-list is always represented in one of two ways:

1. As the empty list, (), in which case we say the list is of length 0, or contains 0 nodes.
2. As a node that has as its **node-rest** component a node-list of length $n - 1$, where n is a positive integer; in this case we say that the original node represents a node-list of length n, or contains n nodes.

All node-lists must be assigned a unique well-defined length by the above rules; this forbids cycles such as .

Because our new representation of RA-stacks is as node-lists, we'll be able to take advantage of the preceding invariant for node-lists but will also have the responsibility for maintaining that invariant. However, not just any node-list is a valid representation of an RA-stack, so there is an additional representation invariant specific to RA-stacks in addition to the generic node-list invariant above:

RA-stack representation invariant (representation 2): Let *height* be the **node-element** component of *ra-stack*. Then *ra-stack* is a node-list containing *height* + 1 nodes. Furthermore, the elements of the RA-stack, listed from top to bottom, are the **node-element** components of the nodes in the node-list given by the **node-rest** component of *ra-stack* (that is, the node-list starting with the second node in *ra-stack*).

This invariant already indicates to us how we should implement the operators **make-ra-stack** and **height**. (Note that we no longer have any reason to implement **make-ra-stack-with-at-most**, and **empty-ra-stack?** can remain unchanged, because it is defined in terms of **height**.)

```
(define make-ra-stack
  (lambda ()
    (make-node 0 '()))) ; height 0, no other nodes

(define height
  (lambda (ra-stack)
    (node-element ra-stack)))
```

Given their similarity, it would be very useful if we could mimic some of the functionality of Scheme lists in our node-lists. One such list-like procedure we will use later is `nodes-down`, which is roughly like cdring *n* times down a node-list. Thus, if `ra-stack` is the node-list in Figure 13.6, `(nodes-down 0 ra-stack)` would be `ra-stack` itself, whereas `(nodes-down 2 ra-stack)` would be the node-list starting with the node containing 9.

```
(define nodes-down
  (lambda (n node-list)
    (if (= n 0)
        node-list
        (nodes-down (- n 1) (node-rest node-list)))))
```

This procedure makes `top-minus` quite easy to write, given the invariant describing our current representation:

```
(define top-minus
  (lambda (ra-stack offset)
    (cond ((< offset 0)
           (error "TOP-MINUS: offset < 0" offset))
          ((>= offset (height ra-stack))
           (error "TOP-MINUS: offset too large for stack"
                  offset (height ra-stack)))
          (else
           (node-element (nodes-down (+ offset 1) ra-stack))))))
```

To maintain the invariant in `pop!`, we need to somehow remove the second node in the node-list (because that is where the top element of the stack is contained) and also decrease the stack's height by 1. Both of these tasks involve updating a node, so we'll need the following two mutator procedures for our abstract data type of nodes:

```
(define node-set-element!
  (lambda (node new-element)
    (vector-set! node 0 new-element)))
```

```
(define node-set-rest!
  (lambda (node new-rest)
    (vector-set! node 1 new-rest)))
```

Given a node that represents an RA-stack, the `node-element` component is the height of the stack, so decreasing the height by 1 will be done using `node-set-element!`:

```
(node-set-element! ra-stack (- (height ra-stack) 1))
```

Similarly, the RA-stack's `node-rest` component is what needs updating to reflect the removal of the node containing the top stack element; it should now have as its contents a node-list of all the elements on the stack after the `pop!` (i.e., all except the one that was on top). This node-list can be found using `nodes-down` to skip over the header node and the node containing the top element:

```
(node-set-rest! ra-stack (nodes-down ra-stack 2))
```

Putting these two steps together (with a little error-checking), we get the following:

```
(define pop!
  (lambda (ra-stack)
    (if (empty-ra-stack? ra-stack)
        (error "POP!: attempted pop from an empty stack")
        (begin (node-set-element! ra-stack (- (height ra-stack) 1))
               (node-set-rest! ra-stack (nodes-down 2 ra-stack))
               ra-stack)))))
```

Finally, `push!` requires us to first insert a new node containing the new element between the first two nodes of the old stack and then to increase the height by 1. Figure 13.7 illustrates how this would work when pushing 6 onto the stack in Figure 13.6.

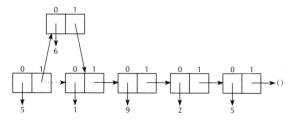

Figure 13.7   Effect of pushing 6 onto the stack from the previous figure

```
(define push!
  (lambda (ra-stack item)
    (let ((new-node (make-node item (node-rest ra-stack))))
      (node-set-rest! ra-stack new-node)
      (node-set-element! ra-stack (+ (height ra-stack) 1))
      ra-stack)))
```

This code completes our second implementation of RA-stacks. It has the advantage of imposing no growth restrictions on RA-stacks. Furthermore, with the exception of `top-minus`, all of the operators are efficient in that they only require a small, fixed number of operations. On the other hand, the procedure `top-minus` has linear complexity, measured in terms of `offset`. In the application from the previous section, this is unimportant, because the largest value of `offset` we used was 2.

Before we leave the linked-list representation entirely, we can make one other interesting observation. The node-lists we have been using are extremely similar to normal Scheme lists; wouldn't it be nice if they really could be lists? That is, we would like to use pairs (of the kind `cons` creates) rather than two-element vectors as the representation of the abstract data type of nodes. The constructor and selectors are no problem—`cons`, `car`, and `cdr` correspond naturally to `make-node`, `node-element`, and `node-rest`. The only problem is with the mutators. But, Scheme has mutators for pairs too—a secret we've been hiding thus far. They are called `set-car!` and `set-cdr!`, and they allow us to reimplement nodes as follows:

```
(define make-node cons)
(define node-element car)
(define node-rest cdr)
(define node-set-element! set-car!)
(define node-set-rest! set-cdr!)
```

With these definitions in place, the RA-stack procedures will work as before, except now the node-lists will be ordinary lists made out of `cons` pairs. The pictures would lose the "0" and "1" labels over the boxes, which were our way of distinguishing two-element vectors from pairs.

13.4　Queues

Stacks have the property that the last item pushed onto the stack is the first one popped off; for this reason, they are also known as *LIFO* structures, for *last in first out*. Sometimes we'd rather store information in a *first in first out*, or *FIFO* fashion. This typically arises from fairness considerations. For example, imagine storing the names of the students waiting to get into a popular course. If a space opens up, we'd like to retrieve the name of the student who has been waiting the longest.

The traditional name for a data structure that works in this way is a *queue* (which is pronounced like the letter Q). In this section we'll look at queues as another example of how representation invariants can guide us in implementing a mutable data type. As with RA-stacks, we'll look at two different styles of representation. In one, we store the elements in consecutive positions within a vector. In the other, we store each element in a separate node, with the nodes linked together into a list.

We'll start by giving a list of operations for the queue ADT:

```
(make-queue)
   ;; returns a newly created empty queue.

(empty-queue? queue)
   ;; returns #t if queue is empty, otherwise #f.

(head queue)
   ;; returns the element which is at the  head of queue,
   ;; that is, the element that has been waiting the longest,
   ;; provided queue is nonempty.

(dequeue! queue)
   ;; removes the head of queue, provided queue is
   ;; nonempty. The return value is the modified queue.

(enqueue! queue item)
   ;; inserts item at the  tail of queue, that is, as the most
   ;; recent arrival. The return value is the modified queue.
```

The two mutators are pronounced like the letters DQ and NQ.

Now consider representing queues like our first representation of RA-stacks. In that representation, we stored the items in consecutive positions of a "cells" vector and used a two-element "header" vector to store the number of items in the RA-stack and the cells vector. If we used this same format for queues, and also maintained the representation invariant that the head of the queue is in cell number 0 and the remaining elements follow in consecutive cells, we might wind up with a picture like Figure 13.8 for a queue that had 5 enqueued, then 2, then 9, and finally 1.

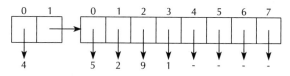

Figure 13.8   Initial, suboptimal, idea for how to represent the queue 5 2 9 1, where 5 is the oldest element (head) and 1 is the newest (tail)

In this representation for queues, all the operations except `dequeue!` would be relatively straightforward. However, because `dequeue!` is supposed to remove the 5 from the head of the queue, in this representation it would be necessary to shift the remaining elements all down by one position. For this reason, the representation isn't a good one. The basic problem is that maintaining the representation invariant is too expensive, given that the elements of the queue should start at position 0 in the cells vector.

One way to cope with an expensive-to-maintain representation invariant is to redesign the representation to be more flexible so that we don't have as constraining of an invariant to maintain. In particular, we'd like to have the flexibility to start the queue at any point in the cells vector rather than always at position 0. That way when a `dequeue!` operation is done, we wouldn't have to shift the remaining elements down. In order to support this flexibility, we'll extend the header vector to now contain three pieces of information. It will still contain the number of elements in the queue and the cells vector. However, it will also contain the position number within the cells vector that the queue's head is at. For example, we could now `dequeue!` the element 5 from the queue 5 2 9 1 as shown in Figure 13.9, changing from having four elements starting in position 0 to having three elements starting in position 1.

Suppose, having dequeued 5 from our example queue, we now were to enqueue some additional elements. Because the cells vector in the figure has four unused cells after the one containing 1, we could insert four more items without any problem. What about adding a fifth item, bringing the total length of the queue to eight? It should be possible to store an eight-element queue in an eight-element cells vector. The trick is to consider the queue's storage as "wrapping around" to the beginning of the vector. Because the queue starts in position 1 within the cells vector, it can continue to positions 2, 3, 4, 5, 6, 7, and then 0, in that order. Similarly, if we dequeued the 2, we would then have freed up space to enqueue one more item, and the queue would now go from position 2 to 3, 4, 5, 6, 7, 0, and 1. This wrapping around of positions can be expressed using modular arithmetic. We can write the representation invariant as follows:

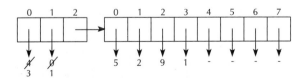

Figure 13.9   Improved idea for how to represent the queue 5 2 9 1, where 5 is the oldest element (head) and 1 is the newest (tail); the indicated changes correspond to using `dequeue!` to remove the 5, changing the queue to 2 9 1

Queue representation invariant (representation 1): Let *queuelength* = *queue*[0], *start* = *queue*[1], and *cells* = *queue*[2]. Let *cellslength* = (vector-length *cells*). The following restrictions are all met:

- $0 \leq$ *queuelength* $\leq$ *cellslength*

- $0 \leq$ *start* $<$ *cellslength*

- There are *queuelength* elements in *queue*. For each *i* in the range $0 \leq i <$ *queuelength*, the element that is *i* elements after the head of *queue* is stored in *cells*[(*start* + *i*) mod *cellslength*].

We can use this representation invariant to guide us in writing the operations as follows:

```
(define queue-length ; use only within the ADT implementation
  (lambda (queue)
    (vector-ref queue 0)))

(define set-queue-length! ; use only within the ADT implementation
  (lambda (queue new-length)
    (vector-set! queue 0 new-length)))

(define queue-start ;use only within the ADT implementation
  (lambda (queue)
    (vector-ref queue 1)))

(define set-queue-start! ; use only within the ADT implementation
  (lambda (queue new-start)
    (vector-set! queue 1 new-start)))

(define queue-cells ; use only within the ADT implementation
  (lambda (queue)
    (vector-ref queue 2)))

(define set-queue-cells! ; use only within the ADT implementation
  (lambda (queue new-cells)
    (vector-set! queue 2 new-cells)))
```

```
(define make-queue
  (lambda ()
    (let ((cells (make-vector 8)) ; 8 is arbitrary
          (header (make-vector 3)))
      (set-queue-length! header 0)
      (set-queue-start! header 0) ; arbitrary start
      (set-queue-cells! header cells)
      header)))



(define empty-queue?
  (lambda (queue)
    (= (queue-length queue) 0)))



(define head
  (lambda (queue)
    (if (empty-queue? queue)
        (error "attempt to take head of an empty queue")
        (vector-ref (queue-cells queue)
                    (queue-start queue)))))



(define enqueue!
  (lambda (queue new-item)
    (let ((length (queue-length queue))
          (start (queue-start queue))
          (cells (queue-cells queue)))
      (if (= length (vector-length cells))
          (begin
            (enlarge-queue! queue)
            (enqueue! queue new-item))
          (begin
            (vector-set! cells
                         (remainder (+ start length)
                                    (vector-length cells))
                         new-item)
            (set-queue-length! queue (+ length 1))
            queue)))))
```

```
(define enlarge-queue! ;use only within the ADT implementation
  (lambda (queue)
    (let ((length (queue-length queue))
          (start (queue-start queue))
          (cells (queue-cells queue)))
      (let ((cells-length (vector-length cells)))
        (let ((new-cells (make-vector (* 2 cells-length))))
          (from-to-do
           0 (- length 1)
           (lambda (i)
             (vector-set! new-cells i
                          (vector-ref cells
                                      (remainder (+ start i)
                                                 cells-length)))))
          (set-queue-start! queue 0)
          (set-queue-cells! queue new-cells)
          queue)))))
```

▶ **Exercise 13.10**

The `enlarge-queue!` procedure is used when the cells vector is full. It makes a new cells vector twice as large and copies the queue's elements into it. It copies the elements into positions starting at the beginning of the new cells vector and correspondingly sets the queue's start to be 0. Explain why the queue's elements can't just be copied into the same positions within the new vector that they occupied in the old vector.

▶ **Exercise 13.11**

We've left out `dequeue!`. Write it. If the queue is empty, you should signal an error. Be sure to maintain the representation invariant by adjusting the start of the queue appropriately. You can't just add 1 to it because you have to keep it in the proper range, $0 \leq start < cellslength$.

Now let's turn our attention to designing an alternative queue representation using a node list. We'll store each element of the queue in one node of the node list, in some order; we still have to decide whether it should be head to tail or tail to head. Recall that node lists are inherently asymmetrical: One end of the node list is the beginning, from which one can start cdring down the list. Queues need to be operated on at both ends because enqueuing happens at the tail end, and dequeuing happens at the head end. Thus, to support both operations efficiently, we'll need

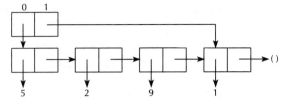

Figure 13.10   Representation of the queue 5 2 9 1 as a header vector that contains the first and last nodes of a node list

some quick way to get directly to the last node in the node list, without cdring down to it starting from the first node. This is true no matter which order we pick; the order just determines which operation's efficiency is at stake. The easiest way to have quick access to both ends of the node list is by using a header vector that directly contains both the first and the last node of the node list. That is, we would have a situation like that shown in Figure 13.10.

If you consider what it would take to maintain the representation invariant, you can figure out which end of the node list should be the queue's head and which should be the queue's tail. Remember that nodes will get added at the queue's tail and removed at its head. So, we have to consider how easily we can update the picture shown in Figure 13.10 under the two options:

- If the beginning of the node list is the head of the queue, we can dequeue by simply adjusting the header vector to point at the next node instead. We can enqueue by adding a new node after the current last node (found using the header vector) and adjusting the header vector to reflect this new last node.
- If the beginning of the node list is the tail of the queue, enqueuing would still be easy because we can tack a new node onto the front of the node list and adjust the header vector to make it the new starting node. However, dequeuing is another matter. There is no efficient way to get to the second to last node, which should now become the last node.

Having considered these options, we see that it is superior to consider the start of the node list the head of the queue. That is, in Figure 13.10, 5 is the head element of the queue. Having made this decision, we should formalize it in a representation invariant.

Exercise 13.12

Write the representation invariant for this second representation for queues. Be sure to specify what the two elements of the header vector should be when the queue is empty.

> **Exercise 13.13**

Now write the queue ADT procedures based on this new representation invariant. Be sure that you maintain the invariant. For example, when you enqueue, you will need not only to make use of the header's information about which node is last but also to update that information.

13.5 Binary Search Trees Revisited

One common problem in computer programming is maintaining large amounts of data in a manner that allows the individual records in the data to be retrieved efficiently. For example, states maintain driver's license information, schools maintain student records, dictionaries maintain definitions, card catalogs maintain book records, and Joe Franksen's video store (Section 8.1) maintains its video records. A data structure that holds this information should allow efficient construction, retrieval, and maintenance.

When we considered this problem in Section 8.1, we investigated binary search trees as such a storage mechanism. (Recall that binary search trees are binary trees where each node has a value that is greater than those in its left subtree and less than those in its right subtree.) Binary search trees have the potential for very efficient data retrieval. Specifically, we showed that searching for an element in such a tree takes $O(h)$ time, where h is the height of the tree. We also showed that the minimum height for a binary tree with n nodes is exactly $\lfloor \log_2(n) \rfloor$ (where $\lfloor \log_2(n) \rfloor$ is the largest integer $\leq \log_2(n)$). Thus, searching for an element in a minimum-height tree would take $O(\log(n))$ time. We even wrote a procedure `optimize-bstree` in Exercise 8.13 on page 224 that produced a minimum-height binary search tree containing the same nodes as a given binary search tree.

Unfortunately, the methods developed in Sections 8.1 and 8.2 did not adequately address the problem of maintenance, by which we mean adding and deleting records when necessary. In particular, the `insert` procedure in Exercise 8.6 on page 220 did not keep the height of the tree as small as possible, and calling the `optimize-bstree` procedure after each insertion would prove time-consuming. What should we do? Well, various strategies have been devised for maintaining binary search trees so that their height is $O(\log(n))$, which will suffice to allow us to write retrieval, insertion, and deletion procedures that have time complexity $O(\log(n))$. We describe one such strategy here, one using *red-black trees*.

Red-black trees are a special subclass of binary search trees. That is, they obey an additional, more restrictive, representation invariant above and beyond the structural invariant that all binary trees satisfy and the ordering invariants that all binary search trees satisfy. Every node in a red-black tree has an additional field, its *color*, which is either red or black. This includes also the "empty nodes" at the bottom of the tree, which we treat as the leaves of the tree. The representation invariant is that the following three conditions hold must hold, in addition to the binary search condition:

- Each leaf (empty) node is black.
- The number of black nodes along a path from the root node to any of the leaf nodes is the same as for any of the other leaves.
- No red node has a red parent.

Figure 13.11 gives an example of a red-black tree containing numbers (the only type of red-black trees we will consider in this section).

We need to show that the height of a red-black tree with n nonempty nodes is $O(\log(n))$. Let h denote the height of our tree. When we say that this tree has height h, we mean that the deepest of the empty nodes is at depth h. For example, in Figure 13.11 the deepest empty node is at depth 5, so the tree has height 5. How about the shallowest empty node? The tree in that figure has its shallowest empty node at depth 3; we will use the name d for the depth of the shallowest empty node. Because d is the depth of the shallowest empty node, all the nodes at depth $d - 1$ must be nonempty. There are 2^{d-1} of these; thus, the number of nonempty nodes, n, is at least this big, and we have $n \geq 2^{d-1}$. Taking the log of both sides we have $\log_2(n) \geq d - 1$, or $\log_2(n) + 1 \geq d$, so we know that d can be no bigger than $\log_2(n) + 1$. When $n \geq 2$, this means that $d \leq 2\log_2(n)$.

This is all well and good for the shallowest empty node, at depth d, but what about the deepest, at depth h? The red-black properties come to our rescue here: There are an equal number of black nodes on any path down from the root to a leaf, and at worst every other node on such a path can be red, because red nodes cannot

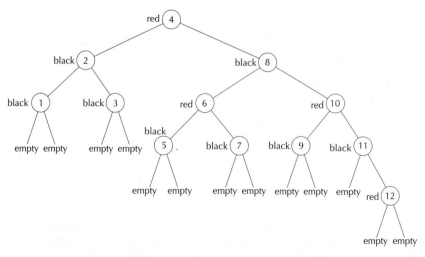

Figure 13.11   A red-black tree containing numbers

have red parents. Thus, the deepest empty node can be at most twice as deep as the shallowest (which would happen if there were no red nodes at all on the path to the shallowest empty node and every other node was red on the path to the deepest empty node). Therefore we have $h \leq 2d$ and hence $h \leq 4\log_2(n)$ for $n \geq 2$. From the foregoing we conclude that h, and therefore also the complexity of retrieval, is $O(\log(n))$ in red-black trees.

We next turn to the insertion algorithm for red-black trees. As a mutator of red-black trees, `red-black-insert!` will take a number and a red-black tree and then insert the number into the tree in a manner that maintains the binary search and red-black invariants. We would naturally want the complexity of `red-black-insert!` to be $O(\log(n))$ as well. But before actually describing the insertion algorithm, we give an equivalent definition of red-black trees that will prove to be better suited for both describing and implementing the algorithm.

According to the new definition, a red-black tree is a binary search tree where every node has an additional field, its *rank*, that is a nonnegative integer. (The rank is in place of the color, not in addition to it.) Again, this definition includes also the "empty nodes" at the bottom of the tree. Furthermore, the following three conditions must hold (in addition to the binary search condition):

■ Each leaf (empty) node has rank 0 and each parent of a leaf has rank 1.
■ *rank(node)* ≤ *rank(parent(node))* ≤ *rank(node)* + 1, provided *node* has a parent.
■ *rank(node)* < *rank(parent(parent(node)))*, provided *node* has a grandparent

Briefly, the latter two conditions say that the rank can either stay the same or increase by 1 when going to a node's parent, but it can't stay the same through all three of the node, its parent, and its grandparent. Figure 13.12 gives the example from Figure 13.11 according to this new definition of red-black trees.

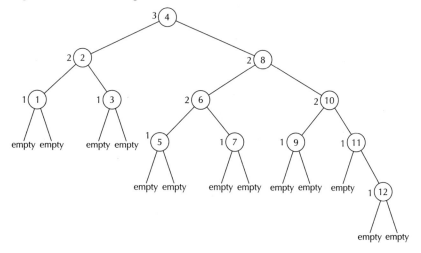

Figure 13.12 Previous red-black tree recast according to new definition

Why are these two definitions of red-black trees equivalent? If you have a red-black tree according to the second definition, color a node black if its rank is different from its parent, and otherwise color it red. (The root node must be black if either of its children are red, but otherwise it can be either red or black.) Because leaves have rank 0 and their parents have rank 1, all leaf nodes are black. Furthermore, the ranks along any path from the root to a leaf will decrease k times, where k is the rank of the root, and each decrease corresponds to a black node; hence, the number of black nodes is the same going to any leaf. Finally, the prohibition against three consecutive generations sharing a rank implies that the parent of a red node is necessarily black.

> ### Exercise 13.14

If you have a red-black tree according to the first definition, you can define the rank of a node to be the number of black nodes encountered along any path from the node down to any descendant leaf (not counting the node itself). Explain why the foregoing results in a red-black tree according to the second definition.

We finally turn to the algorithm for insertion into a red-black tree. The idea is to use the binary search condition to move down the tree until we find a leaf (empty) node where the new item can be inserted while maintaining the binary search condition. We then insert the item, giving it rank 1 and two new rank 0 empty children. Thus far, the insertion is much as for binary search trees. However, the additional red-black invariants may have become violated. Therefore, before calling the red-black tree insertion complete, we repair the damage by performing a sequence of simple "rebalancings" that progress upward until the invariants have been restored, possibly moving as far up the tree as the root node. Just as the number of steps going down the tree was $O(\log(n))$, so too the number of rebalancing steps moving back up the tree is also $O(\log(n))$.

What operations can we do at a given node and how do we determine which one to do in order to rebalance at a given node? The point is that after we have done the binary search insert, only the third of the red-black conditions might fail (the prohibition against three consecutive equal-rank generations), and if it does fail, it will only do so at the newly inserted node. Our strategy will be to move this failure upward in the tree until it finally disappears.

This condition can fail in exactly four ways, each of which is illustrated in Figure 13.13. (The triangles in this diagram correspond to possibly empty subtrees, and the letter k corresponds to a rank). We therefore need rebalancing procedures that will deal with each of these four cases. If we consider the first of these cases, we see that it can be broken down into the two subcases illustrated in Figure 13.14. In the first of these, our only choice is to increase the rank of the grandparent by 1 and continue upward from there. We call the process of increasing a node's rank by one *promotion*.

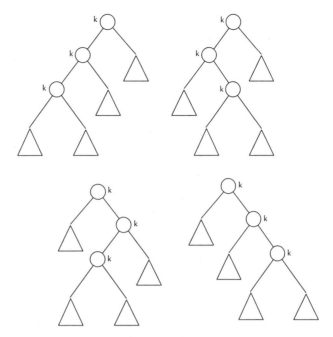

Figure 13.13   Four ways to fail the third red-black condition

The second subcase is more difficult because promoting the grandparent would cause it to have a rank that is 2 larger than the rank of its right child, thereby violating the second red-black condition. We therefore need some operation that will "move things around" slightly. Two such operations, called *right rotation* and *left rotation*, are illustrated in Figure 13.15. Notice that the nodes in the two trees in Figure 13.15 satisfy the following condition (where b and d denote the values at the two displayed nodes, and A, C, and E represent values at any node in their respective subtrees):

$$A < b < C < d < E$$

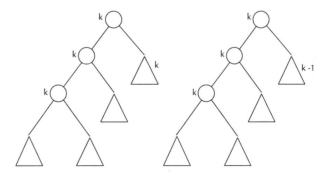

Figure 13.14   Two subcases for failing the third red-black condition

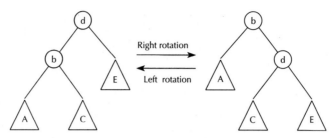

Figure 13.15   Right and left rotation

This condition means that the binary search condition is maintained under both left and right rotation. Figure 13.16 illustrates how right rotation applied to the second tree in Figure 13.14 completely fixes the red-black failure.

What about the other possible red-black failures illustrated in Figure 13.13? Each of these again has a subcase where grandparent promotion applies; we will focus here only on the second subcase of each case, where we can't promote the grandparent. The last case shown in Figure 13.13, which is the mirror image of the first, can be fixed by left rotation. The other cases appear more complicated but can be solved by a couple of rotations. For example, the way to fix the second case is illustrated in Figure 13.17.

As an example of how insertion into a red-black tree works, consider starting with an empty tree and inserting the numbers 1, 2, 3, and 4 in that order. This is illustrated in Figure 13.18. Inserting the 1 puts the value of 1 at the root node, with a rank of 1. Because this node has no grandparent, there is no potential for it to have the same rank as its grandparent, and hence there is no failure of the red-black invariant. Therefore, no rebalancing action is necessary. Now we insert the 2; because 2 is greater than 1, it goes in as the right child of the root, again with rank 1. (Remember, all insertions are at rank 1.) Again, this node has no grandparent, so there can be no problem. Next we insert 3; because it is greater than both 2 and 1, it goes in as the right child of the 2 node, as usual with rank 1. Now we have three

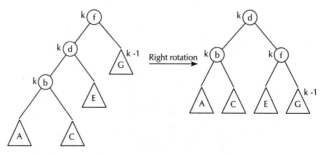

Figure 13.16   Using right rotation to fix case 1, subcase 2

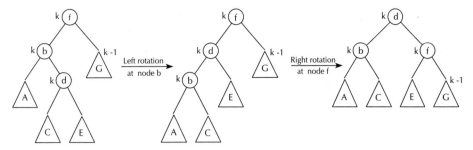

Figure 13.17   Using left and right rotations to fix case 2

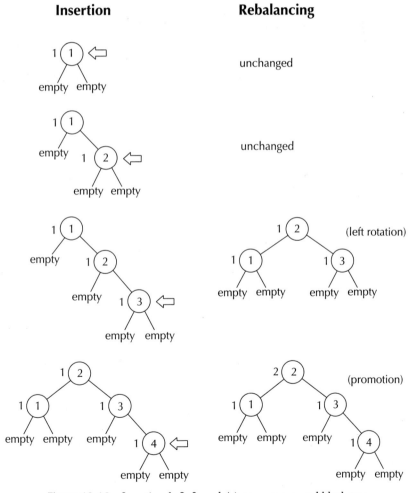

Figure 13.18   Inserting 1, 2, 3, and 4 into an empty red-black tree

nodes in a row all of rank 1: the newly inserted 3, the 2 that is its parent, and the 1 that is its grandparent. This is a violation of the invariant. Because the new node's uncle doesn't share the rank of 1 (it is an empty tree, with rank 0), it isn't permissible to promote the grandparent to rank 2. Instead we do a left rotation at the new node's grandparent, resulting in the node with value 2 now being the root, with the 1 on its left and the 3 on its right. All three of these nodes retain their ranks, (i.e., all are still rank 1). Now the 4 is inserted, and it goes to the right of the 3, with rank 1. Again we have an invariant violation, because three generations in a row share the rank 1: the new 4, its parent 3, and its grandparent 2. However, this time the uncle (the node with value 1) also is of rank 1, so we simply promote the grandparent to rank 2. Because this node is the root of the tree, it doesn't itself have a grandparent, so we can't possibly have introduced a new invariant violation in fixing the old one. Thus, we are done.

We can work through another example, in which the course of events is slightly different. Suppose we again start with an empty tree, but this time insert 12, 1, 4, and 3 in that order, as illustrated in Figure 13.19. The 12 becomes the root and the 1 becomes its left child. Both nodes have rank 1, and no rebalancing is necessary, because neither has a grandparent. Now we insert the 4; because it is smaller than 12 but bigger than 1, it goes to the right of the 1, with rank 1. This action leads to a three-generation chain of rank 1, so we have an invariant violation. Again the uncle is an empty tree of rank 0, so promotion isn't an option. Instead we can first do a left rotation at the parent (the node containing 1) and then a right rotation at the grandparent (the node containing 12). The net result is that the node with value 4 is now the root, with 1 on its left and 12 on its right. All three are still of rank 1. Now when 3 is inserted, it goes to the right of the 1 node, and the resulting invariant violation can be fixed simply by promoting the root node (the new node's grandparent) to rank 2.

We can summarize the rebalancing process as shown in Figure 13.20. Notice that we have two basic kinds of rebalancing, depending on whether the node's uncle shares its rank (which is also shared by the grandparent, or we'd have no problem). If the uncle has the same rank, we promote the grandparent; otherwise we rotate. We mentioned earlier that in the case where we rotate, promotion wouldn't work because it would leave the grandparent with a rank 2 greater than the uncle. In the case where we promote, rotation would just shift the problem from one side of the tree to the other rather than making any headway on solving it. (To see this, consider Figure 13.16, but with G relabeled to be of rank k.) Thus, we never really have any choice—one situation needs promotion and the other needs rotation.

▶ Exercise 13.15

Insert the following numbers one by one into the red-black tree shown in Figure 13.12. After each one is inserted, do the appropriate rotation(s) and/or promo-

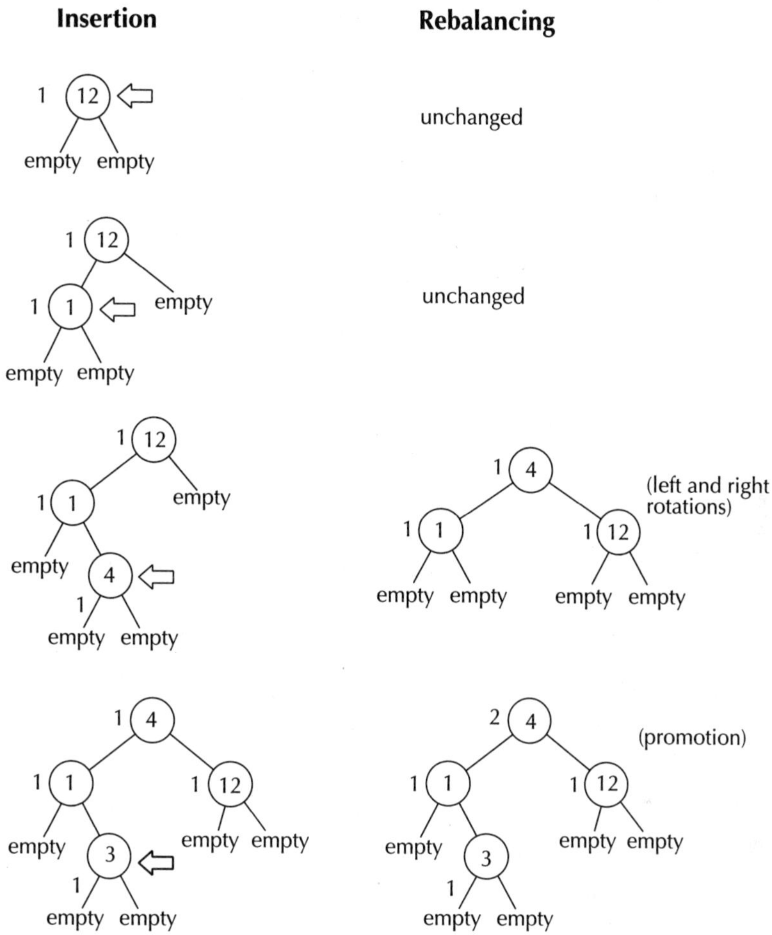

Insertion   **Rebalancing**

Figure 13.19   Inserting 12, 1, 4, and 3 into an empty red-black tree

tion(s) (if any), as previously described. Remember that after you do a promotion, you need to check to see whether it introduced a new invariant violation, necessitating further action.

a. 13

b. 14

c. −10

d. −5

e. 15

f. 16

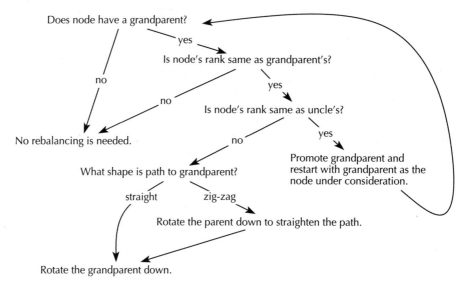

Figure 13.20   A summary of how to rebalance a red-black tree, starting from an inserted node.

Armed with this background, we now turn to the actual implementation of red-black trees. As indicated in the foregoing, we will make the simplifying assumption that the values in our red-black trees are numbers, inserted according to their numeric value. (The final section in this chapter will consider how red-black trees can be extended to more general data, such as movie databases.) Furthermore, we will allow multiple copies of an element to be inserted into the tree. Therefore, our basic operators for red-black trees are as follows:

```
(make-red-black-tree)
  ;; returns a newly created empty red-black tree.
```

```
(red-black-in? item rb-tree)
  ;; returns #t if item is in rb-tree, otherwise #f.
```

```
(red-black-insert! item rb-tree)
  ;; inserts item into rb-tree, maintaining red-black invariants.
  ;; If item is already in rb-tree, another copy of item
  ;; is inserted.
```

Note that we implement **red-black-in?** instead of an operation to do a lookup and return what is found. (We could call such an operation **red-black-retrieve**.) The two procedures are very similar, and retrieval makes little sense for pure numeric trees. We will consider how to convert **red-black-in?** into **red-black-retrieve**

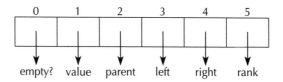

Figure 13.21   Representation of ranked binary trees

in the last section of this chapter. Furthermore, for simplicity, we have decided to not implement deletion.

We have noted that red-black trees are a special class of binary search trees, which in turn are a special class of binary trees. This suggests a "layered" strategy for implementing red-black trees: First we implement ranked binary trees, which are simply mutable binary trees where every node has a rank and where we can access a node's parent as well as its left and right subtrees. None of the binary search or rank conditions hold for these trees; they are just the low-level stratum on which we will construct binary search and red-black trees. On top of this layer we build binary search trees, and on top of that layer we build red-black trees.

So we first turn to the implementation of ranked binary trees. Conceptually, we are extending the binary trees of Chapter 8 by allowing mutation as well as access to a node's parent and rank. In particular, we need something to mutate, so an empty tree cannot simply be the empty list; it should have the same structure as nonempty trees. Figure 13.21 describes the representation we will use for ranked binary trees as six-element vectors, where the names at the end of the arrows indicate the meanings of the various cells.

Figure 13.22 gives an implementation for ranked binary trees in terms of this representation. The code is fairly straightforward because most of what we do involves the selection and mutation of the various attributes of ranked binary trees. The mutators take care to maintain the simple representation invariants that apply to all binary trees. For example, it is impossible using these mutators to set the value without marking the tree as nonempty, and (even more importantly) if *node*1 is made a child of *node*2, *node*2 is automatically made the parent of *node*1. Note, however, that not all cells in a vector need to be set; for example, the first cell being #t indicates that the tree is empty, so we don't care about the values in cells 1, 3, and 4 (the value, the left-subtree, and the right-subtree, respectively). Also note that we use #f in cell 2 (the parent cell) to indicate that the node has no parent (i.e., that we are at the root node of the tree). This is a subtle difference from the binary trees of Chapter 8, because there we had no absolute notion of root: Each node was the root of its own subtree. Here we consider the root node to be the "top-most" node in the tree, that is, the node you get to by following up the parent links as far as possible. We therefore include a selector **root?**, which determines whether we are at the root node of the tree.

```
(define make-empty-ranked-btree
  (lambda ()
    (let ((tree (make-vector 6)))
      (vector-set! tree 0 #t) ; empty-tree? = true
      (vector-set! tree 2 #f) ; has no parent
      (vector-set! tree 5 0)  ; rank = 0
      tree)))
```

```
(define empty-tree?
  (lambda (tree)
    (vector-ref tree 0)))
```

```
(define set-empty! ;makes tree empty
  (lambda (tree)
    (vector-set! tree 0 #t)))
```

```
(define value
  (lambda (tree)
    (vector-ref tree 1)))
```

```
(define set-value!
  (lambda (tree item)
    (vector-set! tree 0 #f) ;not empty
    (vector-set! tree 1 item)))
```

```
(define parent
  (lambda (tree)
    (vector-ref tree 2)))
```

```
(define root?
  (lambda (tree)
    (not (vector-ref tree 2))))
```

```
(define left-subtree
  (lambda (tree)
    (vector-ref tree 3)))
```

```
(define set-left-subtree!
  (lambda (tree new-subtree)
    (vector-set! new-subtree 2 tree) ;parent
    (vector-set! tree 3 new-subtree)))
```

```
(define right-subtree
  (lambda (tree)
    (vector-ref tree 4)))
```

```
(define set-right-subtree!
  (lambda (tree new-subtree)
    (vector-set! new-subtree 2 tree) ;parent
    (vector-set! tree 4 new-subtree)))
```

```
(define rank
  (lambda (tree)
    (vector-ref tree 5)))
```

```
(define set-rank!
  (lambda (tree rank)
    (vector-set! tree 5 rank)))
```

Figure 13.22   Basic operators for ranked binary trees

Although the procedures in Figure 13.22 give a complete implementation of ranked binary trees, there are certain procedures that will prove useful later when we use ranked binary trees to implement binary search trees and red-black trees. In particular, the insertion algorithm in red-black trees requires us to know where we are in the tree (for example, is the current node the left or right child of its parent?) and also to move around easily (for example, to the current node's sibling). The following two procedures accomplish these tasks (note that we use the built-in

Scheme predicate eq?, which tests whether its two arguments actually are the same
Scheme object):

```
(define which-subtree
  (lambda (tree)
    ;; Returns the symbol left if tree is left-subtree of its
    ;; parent and the symbol right if it is the right-subtree
    (cond ((root? tree)
            (error "WHICH-SUBTREE called at root of tree."))
          ((eq? tree (left-subtree (parent tree)))
           'left)
          (else 'right)))))

(define sibling
  (lambda (tree)
    (cond ((root? tree)
            (error "SIBLING called at root of tree."))
          ((equal? (which-subtree tree) 'left)
           (right-subtree (parent tree)))
          (else
           (left-subtree (parent tree)))))))
```

▶ Exercise 13.16

Write display-ranked-btree so that it produces output such as that shown in Figure 13.23 when given the tree shown in that figure. Each line of output corresponds
to one node; the indentation level indicates the depth of the node in the tree, and
the value (or emptiness) and rank are shown explicitly. Each node is followed by its
left-subtree descendants and then its right-subtree descendants.

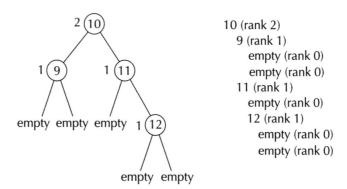

Figure 13.23   An example of display-ranked-btree

We next turn to the implementation of binary search trees. As with red-black trees, we will make the simplifying assumption that the values in our trees are numbers, and we will allow multiple copies of an element to be inserted into the tree. Therefore, our basic operators for binary search trees are as follows:

```
(make-binary-search-tree)
  ;; returns a newly created empty binary search tree.

(binary-search-in? item bs-tree)
  ;; returns #t if item is in bs-tree, otherwise #f.

(binary-search-insert! item bs-tree)
  ;; inserts item into bs-tree, maintaining the binary search
  ;; invariant. If item is already in bs-tree, another
  ;; copy of item is inserted.
```

Again, for simplicity, we will not implement deletion.

The first two operators are easy because we will define an empty binary search tree to be an empty ranked binary tree, and `binary-search-in?` can be implemented the same way as the procedure `in?` was in Chapter 8:

```
(define make-binary-search-tree make-empty-ranked-btree)


(define binary-search-in?
  (lambda (item bs-tree)
    (cond ((empty-tree? bs-tree)
           #f)
          ((= item (value bs-tree))
           #t)
          ((< item (value bs-tree))
           (binary-search-in? item (left-subtree bs-tree)))
          (else
           (binary-search-in? item (right-subtree bs-tree))))))
```

To insert something into a binary search tree, we must first find the point where it should be inserted. In other words, we move down the tree, using the tree's order condition (i.e., exploiting the representation invariant), until we finally arrive at the (empty) leaf node where the item should go. Because we are allowing multiple copies of an item to be inserted, we need to decide in which direction to go if we encounter the item while moving downward. Our choice is to move rightward if the item is encountered; that way, the new node will occur "later" in the tree.

We determine the point at which the item should be inserted through a procedure `insertion-point`, thereby simplifying the code for `binary-search-insert!`:

```
(define insertion-point
  (lambda (item bs-tree)
    ;; This procedure finds the point at which item should be
    ;; inserted in bs-tree. In other words, it finds the empty
    ;; leaf node where it should be inserted so that the
    ;; binary search condition still holds after it is inserted.
    ;; If item is already in bs-tree, then the insertion
    ;; point will be found by searching to the right so that
    ;; the new copy will occur "later" in bs-tree.
    (cond ((empty-tree? bs-tree) bs-tree)
          ((< item (value bs-tree))
           (insertion-point item (left-subtree bs-tree)))
          (else
           (insertion-point item (right-subtree bs-tree))))))
```

```
(define binary-search-insert!
  (lambda (item bs-tree)
    ;; This procedure will insert item into bs-tree at a leaf
    ;; (using the procedure insertion-point), maintaining
    ;; the binary search condition on bs-tree. The return value
    ;; is the subtree that has item at its root.
    ;; If item occurs in bs-tree, another copy of item
    ;; is inserted into bs-tree
    (let ((insertion-tree (insertion-point item bs-tree)))
      (set-value! insertion-tree item)
      (set-left-subtree! insertion-tree
                         (make-binary-search-tree))
      (set-right-subtree! insertion-tree
                          (make-binary-search-tree))
      insertion-tree)))
```

A couple of remarks need to be made about `binary-search-insert!`. First, we have specified its return value, the newly inserted node (rather than the `bs-tree` itself, for example), because our red-black insertion procedure will need to readjust the tree starting at the insertion point, and it would be handy to know where that insertion point is.

The second remark is a warning. Nonempty binary trees, as we have implemented them, are examples of *cyclic* structures, meaning that it is possible to move around the nodes in the tree, eventually returning to the starting node. An example would be simply going from the root node to one of its children and then back again through the parent link. This might seem innocuous enough, and in fact this cyclicality is important for our needs. However, this property could be disastrous if we allow the read-eval-print loop to display a tree. After all, to print out a node would require that its children be printed out, which in turn requires that the children's parent be printed out, thereby leading to an infinite loop. The moral of this story is never to let the read-eval-print loop display a cyclic structure. In our case, we can use the procedure `display-ranked-btree` from Exercise 13.16.

We finally turn to the implementation of the red-black tree operations listed earlier. Two of these operations are trivial, because red-black trees are a special class of binary search trees:

```
(define make-red-black-tree make-binary-search-tree)

(define red-black-in? binary-search-in?)
```

That leaves only `red-black-insert!` yet to be implemented. As we said in the foregoing, our strategy will be to first use `binary-search-insert!` to insert the node and then to use promotion, right rotation, and left rotation to rebalance the tree, starting at the newly inserted node and progressing upward. Hence we must implement these three operations before going on to `red-black-insert!`. Of these three, promotion is the easiest:

```
(define promote!
  (lambda (node)
    (set-rank! node (+ (rank node) 1))))
```

To implement `rotate-left!` and `rotate-right!`, we need to move things around in the tree. We choose to do this through two more elementary procedures. The first one, `exchange-values!`, takes two nonempty nodes and exchanges their respective values, as illustrated in Figure 13.24. We can implement `exchange-values!` as follows:

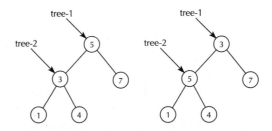

Figure 13.24   Effect of (exchange-values! tree-1 tree-2)

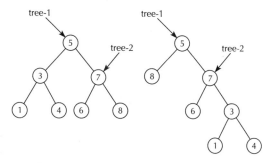

Figure 13.25   Effect of (exchange-left-with-right! tree-1 tree-2)

```
(define exchange-values!
  (lambda (node-1 node-2)
    (let ((value-1 (value node-1)))
      (set-value! node-1 (value node-2))
      (set-value! node-2 value-1))))
```

The other procedure, exchange-left-with-right!, takes two nonempty trees and exchanges the left subtree of the first with the right subtree of the second, as illustrated in Figure 13.25. In particular, (exchange-left-with-right! tree tree) "flips" the two children of tree.

```
(define exchange-left-with-right!
  (lambda (tree-1 tree-2)
    (let ((left (left-subtree tree-1))
          (right (right-subtree tree-2)))
      (set-left-subtree! tree-1 right)
      (set-right-subtree! tree-2 left))))
```

The two rotation procedures become fairly straightforward using exchange-values! and exchange-left-with-right!. For example, Figure 13.26 illustrates how rotate-left! can be accomplished through a sequence of exchanges. The corresponding code for rotate-left! (and by analogy, for rotate-right!) follows:

```
(define rotate-left!
  (lambda (bs-tree)
    (exchange-left-with-right! bs-tree
                               (right-subtree bs-tree))
    (exchange-left-with-right! (right-subtree bs-tree)
                               (right-subtree bs-tree))
```

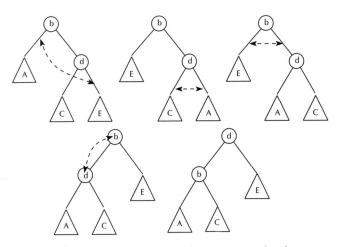

Figure 13.26 Left rotation through a sequence of exchanges

```
(exchange-left-with-right! bs-tree
                           bs-tree)
(exchange-values! bs-tree (left-subtree bs-tree))
'done))

(define rotate-right!
  (lambda (bs-tree)
    (exchange-left-with-right! (left-subtree bs-tree)
                               bs-tree)
    (exchange-left-with-right! (left-subtree bs-tree)
                               (left-subtree bs-tree))
    (exchange-left-with-right! bs-tree
                               bs-tree)
    (exchange-values! bs-tree (right-subtree bs-tree))
    'done))
```

▶ **Exercise 13.17**

Other sequences of exchanges also exist that will accomplish left rotation. Map one of them out analogously to Figure 13.26 and then write the corresponding alternate definition for `rotate-left!`.

We finally arrive at the procedure `red-black-insert!`, which is now accomplished fairly easily using the tools we have developed:

```scheme
(define red-black-insert!
  (lambda (item red-black-tree)
    (define rebalance!
      (lambda (node)
        (cond ((root? node)
               'done)
              ((root? (parent node))
               'done)
              ((< (rank node) (rank (parent (parent node))))
               'done)
              ((= (rank node) (rank (sibling (parent node))))
               (promote! (parent (parent node)))
               (rebalance! (parent (parent node))))
              (else
               (let ((path-from-grandparent
                      (list (which-subtree (parent node))
                            (which-subtree node))))
                 (cond ((equal? path-from-grandparent '(left left))
                        (rotate-right! (parent (parent node))))
                       ((equal? path-from-grandparent '(left right))
                        (rotate-left! (parent node))
                        (rotate-right! (parent (parent node))))
                       ((equal? path-from-grandparent '(right left))
                        (rotate-right! (parent node))
                        (rotate-left! (parent (parent node))))
                       (else ; '(right right)
                        (rotate-left! (parent (parent node)))))))))))
    (let ((insertion-node (binary-search-insert! item
                                                 red-black-tree)))
      (set-rank! insertion-node 1)
      (rebalance! insertion-node))
    'done))
```

Notice that each of the three kinds of trees we layered on top of one another—ranked binary trees, binary search trees, and red-black trees—had mutators that took care to maintain the appropriate invariant. At the ranked binary tree level, the mutators ensured that *node*1 couldn't become a child of *node*2 without *node*2 becoming the parent of *node*1, thus maintaining an important structural invariant. At the binary search tree level, the insertion procedure made sure to maintain the ordering invariant that the `binary-search-in?` procedure relied upon for correct operation. And at the red-black tree level, the `red-black-insert!` procedure maintained the additional invariant properties needed to guarantee $O(\log(n))$ time operation.

13.6　An Application: Dictionaries

To make the exposition clearer in Section 13.5, we restricted the red-black trees to storing numbers rather than more complex records. Some more interesting (and typical) examples of how red-black trees can be applied once the restriction to numbers is lifted were cited at the beginning of that section: databases consisting of driver's license information or student records, dictionaries containing definitions, card catalogs containing book records, or the movie database in Joe Franksen's video store (Section 8.1). In this section we will modify the red-black trees to accommodate the construction of, retrieval from, and maintenance of Joe's movie database.

In each of the cited examples, something is used to look up the records: for drivers' licenses, perhaps the license number; for student records, perhaps the student's name; for dictionaries, the word being defined; etc. In some cases, there might be more than one thing that we could use for looking up: For example, we might look up a movie record either by its title or by its director. The aspect of the record we use for retrieval is called the *key*. Thus, we retrieve a *record* from a *database* by its *key*. Several records may share the same key, in which case retrieval using that key should obtain all those records.

We will use the term *dictionary* as a general term to refer to a mutable data type that stores records and allows retrieval by key, even if the keys aren't words and the records aren't definitions. How can we use keys to organize and retrieve data? Can we be more specific about how we operate on keys? Well, we need to be able to *extract* the key from any given record, and we need to be able to *compare* two different keys to see which one is larger or if they are equal. We will call the procedure that gets the key from the record the *key-extractor*. For example, if we were keying on the movie's title, then the movie ADT selector `movie-title` would be the key-extractor. On the other hand, we will call the procedure that compares two key values the *key-comparator*.

How should we compare two key values? Of course that depends on what the keys are, but we must give a specification of the general form of the comparison procedures. Keeping in mind that keys can compare in three ways (<, =, or >), we will specify that the key-comparator should take two key arguments and return one of the symbols <, =, or > according to whether the first key is less than, equal to, or greater than the second key. For example, if our keys were strings, then we could use the built-in Scheme procedures `string<?` and `string=?` to implement `string-comparator`:

```
(define string-comparator
  (lambda (string-1 string-2)
    (cond ((string<? string-1 string-2) '<)
          ((string=? string-1 string-2) '=)
          (else '>))))
```

In summary, a key-extractor takes a data record and returns a key, whereas a key-comparator takes two keys and returns one of the symbols <, =, and >.

Exercise 13.18

Scheme has a built-in procedure `symbol->string` that takes a symbol and returns the corresponding string. Use `symbol->string` and `string-comparator` to write the procedure `symbol-comparator`, that compares two Scheme symbols. Thus, you should have the following interaction:

```
(symbol-comparator 'erick 'karl)
<

(symbol-comparator 'barbara 'Barbara)
=
```

Note that `symbol-comparator` returned = in the latter case because in Scheme the two expressions `'barbara` and `'Barbara` evaluate to the exact same symbol. (The name of that symbol, returned by `symbol->string`, can be either `"barbara"` or `"BARBARA"`, depending on the particular Scheme implementation.)

Exercise 13.19

Use `symbol-comparator` to write `symbol-list-comparator`, which takes two lists of symbols and returns the appropriate comparison symbol. You should have the following interaction:

```
(symbol-list-comparator '(karl wesley)
                        '(karl knight))
>

(symbol-list-comparator '(abba dabba)
                        '(abba dabba doo))
<
```

We will make it the responsibility of the dictionary to store the key-extractor and key-comparator in addition to the underlying database, which allows the dictionary to make use of comparisons between keys in organizing the database. For example, we will create two dictionaries in this section: one that allows us to retrieve movie records by title and the other one by director. Although they will share the same underlying data, it will be organized in two different ways.

Following are the basic operators for dictionaries:

```
(make-dictionary key-comparator key-extractor)
  ;; returns a newly created empty dictionary with given
  ;; key-comparator and key-extractor

(dictionary-retrieve key dictionary)
  ;; returns the list of all items in dictionary matching key

(dictionary-insert! item dictionary)
  ;; inserts item into dictionary, allowing multiple copies
```

Note that as in the last section, we will not implement deletion.

Because we are going to layer dictionaries on red-black trees, which are in turn layered on binary search trees, we need to next extend binary search trees so that they operate on keys. We will not have binary search trees nor red-black trees store the key-extractor and key-comparator; that will be additional information stored by dictionaries. As a result, the constructors `make-binary-search-tree` and `make-red-black-tree` will remain unmodified. Instead, we will have to modify the other operators so that they will take two additional arguments, the key-comparator and key-extractor.

▶ Exercise 13.20

Modify the procedure `insertion-point` so that a call of the form

```
(insertion-point item bs-tree
                  key-comparator key-extractor)
```

will find the appropriate empty leaf node where the `item` should be inserted.

▶ Exercise 13.21

Modify the procedure `binary-search-insert!` so that a call of the form

```
(binary-search-insert! item bs-tree
                        key-comparator key-extractor)
```

will properly insert `item` into `bs-tree`.

During the course of modifying binary search trees and red-black trees to operate on keys, you will need to test that the procedures work correctly. You can do this using data from the movie database, `our-movie-database` in Section 7.6, which is included in the software on the web site for this book. You could then do the following calls to create a new binary search tree `bs-tree` and insert two elements into it (note that we wrap the calls to `binary-search-insert!` inside a `begin` expression that ends with `'done`, because otherwise the read-eval-print loop would have problems displaying the cyclic structure returned by `binary-search-insert!`):

```
(define bs-tree (make-binary-search-tree))

(begin (binary-search-insert! (make-movie '(amarcord)
                                          '(federico fellini)
                                          1974
                                          '((magali noel)
                                            (bruno zanin)
                                            (pupella maggio)
                                            (armando drancia)))
                              bs-tree
                              symbol-list-comparator
                              movie-title)
       'done)

(begin (binary-search-insert! (make-movie '(the big easy)
                                          '(jim mcbride)
                                          1987
                                          '((dennis quaid)
                                            (ellen barkin)
                                            (ned beatty)
                                            (lisa jane persky)
                                            (john goodman)
                                            (charles ludlam)))
                              bs-tree
                              symbol-list-comparator
                              movie-title)
       'done)
```

> ### Exercise 13.22

In the course of testing your procedures, you will often need to display the trees you are manipulating. You could use the procedure `display-ranked-btree` from Exercise 13.16. Unfortunately, that procedure would display each entire movie record, which would make examining the output difficult.

Make a variant of the procedure `display-ranked-btree` called `display-ranked-btree-by` that takes an additional argument, a selector operating on records. For each nonempty node of the tree, the selector is used to obtain what should be displayed. For example, you should get the following output given that you had defined **bs-tree** as above:

```
(display-ranked-btree-by bs-tree movie-title)
(amarcord) (rank 0)
  empty (rank 0)
  (the big easy) (rank 0)
    empty (rank 0)
    empty (rank 0)
```

Exercise 13.23

Using **binary-search-in?** as a model, write the procedure **binary-search-retrieve**, that will additionally take a key-comparator and key-extractor, and will return a list of all the records matching the key. Thus, you should have the following interaction using the previously defined **bs-tree**:

```
(binary-search-retrieve '(the big easy)
                        bs-tree
                        symbol-list-comparator
                        movie-title)
(((the big easy) (jim mcbride) 1987 ((dennis quaid)
(ellen barkin) (ned beatty) (lisa jane persky) (john goodman)
(charles ludlam))))
```

For efficiency you should use the "onto" parameter idea introduced in Section 8.1, rather than using **append**.

We next need to extend red-black trees so that they operate on keys. Two of the operators remain the same because they are lifted directly from binary search trees:

```
(define make-red-black-tree make-binary-search-tree)
```

```
(define red-black-retrieve binary-search-retrieve)
```

Exercise 13.24

Modify **red-black-insert!** so that it additionally takes a key-comparator and a key-extractor as arguments. Thus, you can construct and put one element into a red-black tree as follows:

```
(define rb-tree (make-red-black-tree))

(red-black-insert! (make-movie '(amarcord)
                               '(federico fellini)
                               1974
                               '((magali noel)
                                 (bruno zamin)
                                 (pupella maggio)
                                 (armando drancia)))
                   rb-tree
                   symbol-list-comparator
                   movie-title)
```

We are finally at the point where we can implement dictionaries. Because we require that a dictionary keeps track of its key-comparator and key-extractor, we start the implementation of dictionaries as follows:

```
(define make-dictionary
  (lambda (key-comparator key-extractor)
    (vector key-comparator
            key-extractor
            (make-red-black-tree))))

(define key-comparator
  (lambda (dictionary)
    (vector-ref dictionary 0)))

(define key-extractor
  (lambda (dictionary)
    (vector-ref dictionary 1)))

(define red-black-tree
  (lambda (dictionary)
    (vector-ref dictionary 2)))
```

Note that the three selectors are for internal usage by dictionaries. A person using dictionaries would use the operators `make-dictionary`, `dictionary-insert!`, and `dictionary-retrieve`. Thus, we would create our desired movie dictionaries as follows (though they don't yet contain the data):

```
(define our-movies-by-title
  (make-dictionary symbol-list-comparator movie-title))
```

```
(define our-movies-by-director
  (make-dictionary symbol-list-comparator movie-director))
```

Exercise 13.25

Implement the procedure `dictionary-insert!`.

Exercise 13.26

Implement the procedure `dictionary-retrieve`.

Exercise 13.27

Scheme has a built-in procedure `for-each` that takes a procedure and a list and applies the procedure to each element of the list. For-each is very similar to `map`, except that it is done for effect, not for its return value. Thus, you would have the following interaction:

```
(for-each (lambda (n)
            (newline)
            (display (* n n)))
          '(1 2 3 4))
1
4
9
16
```

(In this example, all the output is produced by explicit `newline` and `display` invocations. If you try this evaluation, you'll probably also see a value returned by the `for-each` procedure itself, but the Scheme standard leaves that value unspecified.) Use `for-each` to insert the data from `our-movie-database` appropriately into our two dictionaries `our-movies-by-title` and `our-movies-by-director`.

Review Problems

Exercise 13.28

Suppose we want to add the factorial operation, indicated by a postfix !, to the shift/reduce evaluator of Section 13.2. That is, because 4! = 24, we should have (`evaluate "2*4!"`) produce 48 and (`evaluate "(2*2)!"`) produce 24. Notice (from the first example) that ! has higher precedence even than * and /, so to apply the factorial operation to anything other than a single number or another factorial, you need parentheses. We'll now have a new kind of reduction. If the top item on the stack is a ! and a number is below it, we can reduce by popping the two of them off and pushing the factorial on. Extend Figure 13.4 with an extra column and an extra row, each labeled with !. Fill in each of the new blank cells in this row and column with shift, reduce, or error as appropriate; you should detect all errors as early as possible.

Exercise 13.29

Suppose we changed our first representation of RA-stacks so that the stack's elements are stored at the end of the *cells* vector, with the bottom element of the stack in the last element of the vector. For example, a representation of the stack 5 2 9 1, where 1 is the top element, could look like the following:

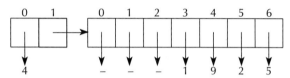

Of the procedures `make-ra-stack-with-at-most`, `height`, `top-minus`, `pop!`, and `push!`, which ones would need changing (relative to the versions from Section 13.3's representation 1) and which wouldn't? Justify your answer.

Exercise 13.30

Reimplement the abstract data type for movies in a mutable version that supports all the same operations (the `make-movie` constructor and such selectors as `movie-title`) and also the following additional operations: `check-movie-out-to!`, `check-movie-in!`, and `movie-status`. Initially, a newly created movie should be considered checked in. The `check-movie-out-to!` operation can only be done on a movie that is currently checked in; otherwise an error is signaled. Conversely, only a movie that is currently checked out can be checked in, or `check-movie-in!` will signal an error. The `check-movie-out-to!` procedure takes a person's name as a second argument and records that information in the movie object. The `movie-status` procedure returns the name of the person to whom the movie is checked out, if it is checked out, or `#f` if it is checked in.

Exercise 13.31

In Chapter 1 we emphasized that the `quarter-turn-right` procedure didn't really rotate an image a quarter turn to the right in the sense of changing the image; a new image was created instead, looking like the original image would have had it been turned.

Now we have the ability to make objects that can really be turned in the sense of themselves changing. Define a mutable abstract data type *turnable image* with a constructor `make-turnable-image` that takes a normal image as its argument, a mutator `quarter-turn-right!` that updates the turnable image, and selector `get-image` that returns a normal image showing the current status of the turnable image.

Write three versions, and make sure they all work indistinguishably. They should use the following approaches:

a. The object contains just a normal image. The turn mutator replaces this image with a new one reflecting the turn. The selector returns it.

b. The object contains both a normal image and a turn count in the range 0 to 3. The turn mutator leaves the image unchanged and instead updates the turn count. The selector uses the turn count and image in order to produce the properly turned image to return.

c. The object contains both a normal image and a turn count in the range 0 to 3, as in part b. The mutator acts as in part b, updating the turn count. However, the selector is different. It not only uses the turn count and image to calculate the turned image to return, but it also then stores that turned image into the object and sets the turn count to 0.

▷ **Exercise 13.32**

Recall that in Chapter 6 we wrote a two-pile Nim game that used a game-state ADT. We implemented the ADT in various different ways, including using `cons`-pairs. Suppose we wanted to model game states, but *with mutation*. In other words, we will implement the following constructor, selector, and mutator:

```
(make-game-state n m)
   ;; returns a game state with n coins in the first
   ;; pile and m coins in the second pile

(size-of-pile game-state p)
   ;; returns an integer equal to the number of coins
   ;; in the p-th pile of the game-state (p = 1 or 2)

(remove-coins-from-pile! game-state n p)
   ;; changes game-state so that there are n fewer
   ;; coins in pile p (p = 1 or 2). The return value of
   ;; remove-coins-from-pile! is unspecified.
```

Note that `remove-coins-from-pile!` actually alters `game-state` so that pile *p* has *n* fewer coins.

Implement this mutable game state ADT using vectors.

▷ **Exercise 13.33**

The three procedures below are the constructor, mutator, and selector for a new kind of object, the widget. Describe in English how widgets behave, from the standpoint of someone using these three procedures but not knowing what is going on inside them or how the widgets are being represented. That is, your explanation shouldn't talk about vectors or vector positions at all but instead should talk about how widget insertion and retrieval relate. If some insertions and retrievals are done, how could you predict what each retrieval was going to retrieve? Once you've provided this outsider's perspective, provide a justification of it in terms of the internal behavior of the procedures. That is, explain how it is that the vector operations these procedures do result in the previously stated external behavior.

```
(define make-widget
  (lambda ()
    (let ((widget (make-vector 3)))
      (vector-set! widget 0 'empty)
      (vector-set! widget 1 'empty)
      (vector-set! widget 2 0)
      widget)))

(define insert-into-widget!
  (lambda (widget value)
    (let ((place (vector-ref widget 2)))
      (vector-set! widget place value)
      (vector-set! widget 2 (remainder (+ place 1) 2))
      'done)))

(define retrieve-from-widget
  (lambda (widget)
    (vector-ref widget (vector-ref widget 2)))))
```

▷ **Exercise 13.34**

In Chapter 10 we turned Micro-Scheme into Mini-Scheme by introducing definitions and used global environments to hold the name/value associations resulting from those definitions.

Unfortunately, there was a serious modularity problem. Only the `read-eval-print-loop` ever added an association to the global environment, and only the evaluation of name ASTs ever looked a name up in the global environment. Yet the global environments needed to be passed around throughout the rest of the program, in particular through all the other kinds of ASTs.

Now that we know how to define mutable data types, we can implement Mini-Scheme much more cleanly. We can start with Micro-Scheme and change only the two communicating partners (`read-eval-print-loop` and the name ASTs), leaving the rest unchanged, because the communication can now be done through an object with state.

In particular, suppose we do the following definitions:

```
(define make-read-eval-print-loop-state
  (lambda ()
    (make-vector 1)))

(define set-global-environment!
  (lambda (repl-state new-global-env)
    (vector-set! repl-state 0 new-global-env)))

(define get-global-environment
  (lambda (repl-state)
    (vector-ref repl-state 0)))

(define repl-state (make-read-eval-print-loop-state))
```

At this point, the `read-eval-print-loop` can take charge of setting the global environment into the `repl-state`, and the name ASTs can get the current global environment back out from there.

As a starting point, you should use all the code from the Micro-Scheme implementation except `read-eval-print-loop`, as well as the four preceding definitions and the following procedures from Chapter 10's Mini-Scheme implementation: `read-eval-print-loop`, `definition?`, `definition-name`, `definition-expression`, `look-up-value-in`, `make-initial-global-environment`, and `extend-global-environment-with-naming`.

a. Modify `make-name-ast` so the name ASTs use `look-up-value-in` rather than `look-up-value`. They should get the global environment from the `repl-state`.

b. Modify the Mini-Scheme `read-eval-print-loop` so that it uses `evaluate` rather than `evaluate-in` and so that at the top of the `loop` it sets the `global-environment` into the `repl-state`.

▷ **Exercise 13.35**

Insert the following numbers in order into an initially empty red-black tree, rebalancing after each insertion. Show the tree after each insertion, but before the rebalancing, and again after each rebalancing. You must show the rank of each node as well as the value stored in it but may omit the empty leaf nodes from your diagrams if you prefer. The numbers are 5, 1, −5, 0, −2, and −1.

Chapter Inventory

Vocabulary

precedence	cycle
reduce	last in first out (LIFO)
token	first in first out (FIFO)
shift	rank
accept	promotion
mutable data type	right rotation
object	left rotation
value	cyclic
axiomatic system	key
representation invariant	record
legal	database
vacuous	key-extractor
header	key-comparator
linked list	

Abstract Data Types

RA-stacks	ranked binary trees
nodes	dictionaries
node-lists	turnable images
queues	mutable game states
binary search trees	widgets
red-black trees	read-eval-print-loop states

New Predefined Scheme Names

`make-string`	`char-numeric?`
`string-length`	`string`
`string-ref`	`set-car!`
`string-set!`	`set-cdr!`
`string->number`	`eq?`
`string->symbol`	`string<?`

```
string=?                              for-each
symbol->string
```

New Scheme Syntax

character constants (#\)

Scheme Names Defined in This Chapter

```
tokenize                    set-queue-cells!
make-ra-stack               enlarge-queue!
empty-ra-stack?             red-black-insert!
height                      make-red-black-tree
top-minus                   red-black-in?
pop!                        root?
push!                       which-subtree
reduce?                     make-empty-ranked-btree
accept?                     empty-tree?
shift?                      set-empty!
reduce!                     value
operator?                   set-value!
lower-precedence?           parent
operator-char?              left-subtree
digit->number               set-left-subtree!
display-ra-stack            right-subtree
make-ra-stack-with-at-most  set-right-subtree!
cells                       rank
set-height!                 set-rank!
make-node                   sibling
node-element                display-ranked-btree
node-rest                   make-binary-search-tree
nodes-down                  binary-search-in?
node-set-element!           binary-search-insert!
node-set-rest!              insertion-point
make-queue                  promote
empty-queue?                rotate-left!
head                        rotate-right!
dequeue!                    exchange-values!
enqueue!                    exchange-left-with-right!
queue-length                string-comparator
set-queue-length!           symbol-comparator
queue-start                 symbol-list-comparator
queue-cells                 make-dictionary
```

dictionary-retrieve
dictionary-insert!
bs-tree
display-ranked-btree-by
binary-search-retrieve
red-black-retrieve
rb-tree
key-comparator
key-extractor
red-black-tree
our-movies-by-title
our-movies-by-director
check-movie-out-to!

check-movie-in!
movie-status
make-turnable-image
quarter-turn-right!
get-image
remove-coins-from-pile!
make-widget
insert-into-widget!
retrieve-from-widget
make-read-eval-print-loop-state
set-global-environment!
get-global-environment
repl-state

Sidebars

Strings and Characters

Notes

Our treatment of red-black trees is patterned rather closely on Tarjan's [50], so that would be one place to turn for guidance on the deletion operation, which we've omitted. However, it is quite dense reading; for a more lengthy treatment, you could turn to an algorithms and data structures textbook, such as Cormen, Leiserson, and Rivest [14].

CHAPTER FOURTEEN

Object-oriented Programming

14.1 Introduction

In this chapter we will primarily be concerned with mixing together two ideas we've already presented: generic operations (from Chapter 9) and object-based abstractions (from Chapter 13). This combination, in which abstract data types with state can have diverse implementations that are operated on through a uniform interface, is the core of the cluster of ideas known as *object-oriented programming*.

Although there is general agreement on these two core concepts, and although there is considerable enthusiasm for object-oriented programming, there is no general consensus on the remainder of the ideas in the cluster—which are essential or inessential, central or peripheral. Nonetheless, we'll cover a few of the more common "extras." The most significant is that rather than clearly distinguishing abstract data types from their implementation, the two are fused together into a single notion of a *class* and organized into a single *class hierarchy* in which the hierarchichal class relationship can represent the sharing of interface between abstract types, the provision of an abstract type's interface by a concrete implementation, or even the sharing of common portions of concrete implementations.

Rather than go into further detail here about object-oriented programming, we'll do so in the next section in the context of a specific example application program. After that, we'll explore some extensions and variations in a separate section and then peek behind the scenes to see how the object-oriented programming system we presume in the earlier sections can be efficiently implemented. Finally, we'll give you a chance to apply the object-oriented programming techniques imaginatively by building your own world in an adventure game.

14.2   An Object-oriented Program

To illustrate object-oriented programming, we'll look at a program for an on-line clothing catalog company. Ideally, users (or customers) would browse through pictures of the various items of clothing, selecting those they wanted. To keep things simple, we'll initially only offer oxford-cloth shirts and chino pants. As the customers browse, they fill in an order form, which is essentially a list of items. They do this by adding items to the list and inputting the specifics of those items, such as size and color. Customers can also, at any time, decide to see what's on their list, get the total price of all their items, delete an item from the list, or revise the specifics of an item on their list. When they are finished, if our system were real, they would pay for their order and, in due time, the items would be sent to them.

To illustrate the ideas of object-oriented programming, our program will concentrate on the items of clothing and on the order form, or list. Because our emphasis is not on the user interface, we'll stick with a style of interaction that is simple to program but not likely to win many customers. Similarly, in place of payment and shipping, we'll simply provide a mechanism for exiting the program.

We can use the preceding description to get started on an *object-oriented design*. First, we can look through this description for important nouns; these serve as clues regarding what classes of objects we'll need. These nouns are items of clothing and a list of items. Thus, we will tentatively assume that we have a class called *item* and a class called *item-list*. We also mentioned two specific kinds of items of clothing, which suggests having *oxford-shirt* and *chinos* classes. There are some other nouns that are less clear-cut. For example, the description mentions "prices," both for individual items and for the total. Should there be a class for prices, or should they simply be numbers? There is no one right answer to this question. For now, we'll use numbers for the prices. However, if there are a variety of interesting things to do with prices, we might want to reconsider this decision.

The next thing we need to do is identify the operations that we'll need to perform on objects of each class. Again, we can get some guidance from our description of the program by looking carefully both at what is explicitly said (for example, that items can be deleted from the list) and what is implicit (for example, to calculate a total price, it must be possible to find the price of each item). This combination will give us an initial list of operations. As we look in more detail at how each operation can be implemented, and as we give more careful consideration to how the operations are used to produce the overall user-visible behavior of the program, we may come up with some additions to our "wish lists."

Let's start by considering the item-list class. What do we need to be able to do to an item-list? The following operations come from the program's description; in each case we've italicized one or more words to serve as the name of the operation:

- *Add* a specified item to the list
- *Display* the list for the user
- Find the *total price* of the items on the list
- *Delete* a specified item from the list
- Allow the user to *choose* an item from the list (to delete or revise)

Once we started to program with these operations, we'd quickly discover we had a problem if the user decides to choose an item from an empty item list. The best way to handle this is to not even present choosing as an option when the list is empty; for the program to do that, it needs to be able to tell if the list is empty. Thus we are forced to add an *empty?* predicate to our catalog of operations.

The item class is somewhat simpler; the operations that appear (at least implicitly) in the program's description are as follows:

- Allow the user to *input specifics* (such as size and color) for an item
- *Display* the description and price of an item to the user
- Allow the user to *revise specifics* (such as size and color) for an item
- Find the *price* of the item

In the introduction to the chapter we indicated that one of the principal ideas in object-oriented programming is the use of generic operations to allow a uniform interface to diverse implementations of an abstract data type. How does this idea fit into shopping for clothing? The key observation is that although the two kinds of clothing in our catalog (oxford-cloth shirts and chinos) have some properties in common, there are considerable differences between them. For example, if you called a catalog company and asked for the price of any item, you would get an answer, but if you ordered a pair of chinos with a sleeve length of 32, the operator would be pretty puzzled. In our program, we'll use *subclasses* of the item class to represent different kinds of clothing. For example, the oxford-shirt class will be a subclass of the item class. Any oxford-cloth shirt is an item of clothing, or, in object-oriented jargon, an object that is an instance of the oxford-shirt class is also implicitly an instance of the item class. That way the oxford-shirt object will support all the operations of the item class, such as finding its price. However, because it is not simply an instance of the item class, but also of the oxford-shirt subclass, it can support additional operations, such as finding the sleeve length, as well.

Now that we have a rough idea of what classes we'll need, let's take a look at some common object-oriented jargon. We start with the word *class*. When we speak generally of items of clothing, we're really talking about the abstract idea of such an item rather than a particular item or items. In object-oriented jargon, this idea makes "item" an example of a class. A class is an abstract grouping of objects that are similar to each other; the fundamental commonality between the objects of a class is that they all can be operated on in the same way. For example, we can find the price of any item in the same way and display the description of any item in the same way, although the results are likely to be different for different items. Just as a set can be a subset of another set, a class can be a *subclass* of a more general *superclass,* Thus, the oxford-shirt class is a subclass of the item class, and the item class is the superclass of the oxford-shirt class. We also say that the oxford-shirt class is *derived* from the *base class* item. The *ancestry* of a class consists of all the classes it is derived from, whether directly or indirectly. We choose to define a class's ancestry as including the class itself, as well as the class's superclass, the superclass's superclass, etc. In our example, the ancestry of the oxford-shirt class consists of the oxford-shirt class, the item class, and the object class. The object class is the ultimate ancestor of all classes in our system. This organization of our program's world into classes that are subclasses and superclasses is called the *class hierarchy*. We can represent this class hierarchy as a tree, with the object class at the root:

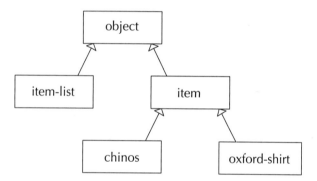

This diagram is our first example of a class diagram in a standard notation known as the *Unified Modeling Language,* or *UML.* This notation also provides means for expressing many other aspects of object-oriented design, not just the class hierarchy. We'll gradually explain more and more of the notation, as the need arises. (Even so, we'll only see the tip of the iceberg.)

The oxford-shirt class is really an abstract notion; when we talk about a particular oxford cloth shirt, this particular concrete shirt is a specific example of the general class. In object-oriented jargon, we say that a particular object is an *instance* of a class. So, for example, if the first item we wanted to order was a blue oxford-cloth shirt with a 32-inch sleeve length and a 16-inch neck size, this particular shirt would be an instance of the oxford-shirt class. One very important principle in object-oriented programming is that a particular object is an instance of all of the ancestor classes of the class it belongs to, which means that our blue oxford-cloth shirt is not only an instance of the oxford-shirt class but also an instance of the item class and an instance of the object class.

The UML class diagram can show information about the individual instances as well as about the overall classes. Our first diagram showed only the hierarchical relationship among the classes. However, an important relationship also exists between instances of the item-list class and instances of the item class. Each item-list is associated with arbitrarily many items. From the item-list, we can find the items. We can add this association to our diagram as follows:

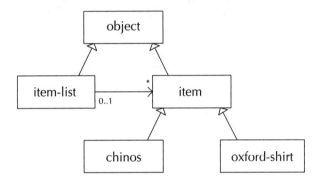

The line between item-list and item represents the association. You can tell it is an association rather than a subclass/superclass relationship because it doesn't have the triangular arrowhead. Instead, it has an arrowhead formed out of two lines. This arrowhead points to the item class, which tells us that from the item-list, we can find the items. If each item also could tell us what item-list it belonged to, we'd have an arrowhead on the other end of the association as well. There is some additional information near the two ends of the association. An asterisk (*) is on the end pointing at the item class. This is a special UML notation indicating that each item-list can have any number of items. If every item-list had to have exactly five items, the number 5 would appear in place of the asterisk. If each item-list was constrained to have somewhere between three and seven items, the notation would be 3..7, and if the requirement was any number from 2 on up, the notation would be 2..*. These notations are called *multiplicities*. On the other end of the association, we see the multiplicity 0..1. As we just indicated, this notation is the UML way of indicating the range from 0 to 1. In other words, each item is associated either with no item-list or with one item-list.

This multiplicity of 0..1 documents a design decision we made. At the moment we only foresee having one item-list for the customer's choices. But what if we changed the program so that there could be multiple customers, each with an individual item-list? We'd still want each item to be on at most one list. Even though an item object is actually just a description of the clothing, and not the real cloth garment, sharing would be a bad idea because we earlier decided that the item class supported an operation for revising the specifics (such as size and color). If two customers had the same item on their item-lists, and one of them changed the size or color, the other customer would be surprised to see the same change. Therefore, we insist that each item appear on at most one item-list. Allowing an item to be on no list at all doesn't seem to do any harm and may come in handy as we explore the little "world" we are constructing, so we left this option open. Another designer might well have chosen to insist that each item be on an item-list, by using a multiplicity of 1 where we used 0..1. This illustrates one of the nice features of putting the associations on the UML diagrams, complete with their multiplicities: it forces us to think about these design decisions.

We've stressed that classes are abstract notions, whereas the objects that are in-stances of the classes are concrete. However, our object-oriented programming system is designed in such a way that each class has a concrete *class object* to represent it. For example, the oxford-shirt class has an object called `oxford-shirt-class` that represents it. These class objects are themselves instances of a class, namely, the class class. The class class is a class that is used just for the concrete representations of classes. For example, not only `oxford-shirt-class` but also `object-class`, `item-class`, `item-list-class`, `chinos-class`, and even `class-class` are all instances of the class class. If we add this class to our hierarchy, the full diagram looks as follows:

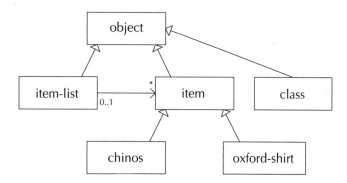

Each instance of a class contains certain pieces of information, stored in *instance variables*. Each instance of that class has the same assortment of instance variables: for example, every oxford shirt has a color, a neck size, a sleeve length, and a price. However, the specific values of those instance variables are stored independently in each instance—each shirt gets to have its own color, size, and price. Moreover, the instance variables are *state variables* that can change over time—if the customer remembers having put on a few pounds, the size of the chinos ordered can be changed.

Because an instance of one class is also an instance of all the ancestor classes, it will have the instance variables of each of these classes. For example, every item has a price, and so if the first thing on the item-list is an item, it has a price. The fact that it is not just a plain item, but rather an oxford-cloth shirt, is irrelevant. (However, oxford-cloth shirts can and do have some additional instance variables, beyond those that all items have.) The way we describe this situation is by saying that a class's instance variables are *inherited* by its subclasses. The oxford-shirt class gets its price instance variable by inheritance from the item class.

Objects do more than just store information, however. They can also perform operations. For example, an item can display its description and an item-list can add another item to itself. The operations are traditionally known as *methods*. We speak of general *method names*, such as `item/display`, which is the name used to make any item display itself, no matter how it chooses to do so. (We include the class name in the method name.) These method names are inherited by subclasses, so any item, even if it is an oxford-cloth shirt, can be operated on using `item/display`. However, the specific *method implementation* that gets used may or may not be inherited; in the case of oxford-cloth shirts and displaying, the implementation gets *overridden* with an oxford-shirt-specific way of displaying. If the method implementation is not overridden, the superclass's implementation is inherited. For example, oxford-cloth shirts report their price exactly the same way as plain items do because this method's implementation is inherited.

Now, having completed our jargon lesson, and having earlier sketched out the classes we need and their interfaces, we turn our attention to how the classes can be implemented. We'll use an object-oriented programming system that allows us to write object-oriented programs in Scheme. (A later section addresses how the object-oriented programming system itself is implemented.) This object-oriented programming system is available from the web site for this book.

The first thing we need to do is to implement the three classes we previously described. We start by defining the item-list class, using a procedure called `define-class`:

```
(define-class
  'item-list     ; the class is named item-list
  object-class   ; it has the object-class as its superclass
  '(item-vector  ; it has instance variables named item-vector
    num-items)   ;   and num-items
  '(add          ; and methods with these names
    display
    total-price
    delete
    choose
    empty?))
```

Most of the preceding arguments to `define-class` follow directly from our earlier discussion of the class and its interface. In particular, the method names come from our "wish list" of operations, and the superclass is `object-class` because we had no more specific superclass in mind. The only genuinely new revelation is the instance variables. As you might guess from their names, we are choosing to use a vector to hold the items, and to allow us to leave some extra unused space in the vector, we use another instance variable to explicitly record the number of items. That way we can make the vector big enough to accommodate some addition of items; if it still turns out to be too small, we can replace it with a larger one.

The `define-class` procedure is an abbreviation for a long list of other definitions. For example, by defining the item-list class as shown, we have defined `item-list-class` to be the actual class object (representing the class) but have also defined `make-item-list` to be the constructor, `item-list?` to be a predicate that tests whether an object is an item-list or not, etc. (We'll have more to say about constructors and predicates later.) Thus, you should not be surprised when we use names that you haven't seen explicitly defined. For example, we'll use `make-item-list` without ever saying (`define make-item-list` ...). The definition was provided by `define-class`.

Next we need to implement the methods. For an example of how this implementation is done, let's first look at the simplest one, `empty?`, which only needs to check whether there are 0 items:

```
(class/set-method!
 item-list-class 'empty?
 (lambda (this)
   (= (item-list/get-num-items this) 0)))
```

Not only does this implementation of the `empty?` method illustrate how `class/set-method!` is used to provide method implementations, it also provides an example of how the value of an instance variable is retrieved. The `item-list/get-num-items` procedure can be applied to any instance of the item-list class to retrieve the current value of its `num-items` instance variable; we call it a *getter* procedure. The particular item-list it is applied to in the foregoing is the one passed in to the `empty?` method as that method's one argument, called `this`. Every method must have at least one argument, the object to operate on. No matter what other arguments a particular method might need, its first argument must be this object. (Here it was the only argument.) By convention this first argument is called `this` because it is "this object." (Another popular convention is to call it `self` because from the object's perspective it is "myself." We'll stick with `this`.) To summarize in the anthropomorphic language that is commonly used by object-oriented programmers, an item-list answers the question of whether it is empty by getting its own number of items and checking to see whether that equals 0.

The `num-items` instance variable will clearly need to be incremented in the `add` method and decremented in the `delete` method. A more subtle question is how it gets set to 0 in the first place. The most logical time to do this would be when the item-list is first created. Our object-oriented system lets us create an item-list as follows:

```
(define example-item-list (make-item-list))
```

What happens when we create this item-list is that a new instance of the item-list class is created and then a special object-class method, called `init`, is automatically invoked on this newly created object. The normal implementation of the `init` method, provided in the object class, does nothing interesting. However, it can be overridden like any other method. Thus we can arrange for `num-items` to start at zero by providing a suitable `init` method in the item-list class.

The item-list class's `init` method should set the `num-items` instance variable using that instance variable's *setter* procedure, which is called `item-list/set-num-items!`. We'll also have it set the `item-vector` to a 10-element vector initially because 10 seems like a large enough number that many customers will stay within it, but it is still a small enough number to not waste a great deal of the computer's memory. (Remember, if a particular customer wants to order more than 10 items, we can always switch to a bigger vector because `item-vector` is a state variable that can change.) Putting these two together, we get the following:

```
(class/set-method!
 item-list-class 'init
 (lambda (this)
   (item-list/set-item-vector! this (make-vector 10))
   (item-list/set-num-items! this 0)))
```

To see this `init` method in action, we can now do the above definition of `example-item-list`, which invokes `make-item-list` and gives a name to the result. Now we can check that it really behaved as expected:

```
(item-list/get-num-items example-item-list)
0
(item-list/empty? example-item-list)
#t
```

Another useful way to see that the item-list was constructed as expected is by using the `object/describe` method, which is provided by our object-oriented programming system for the sake of debugging and exploration:

```
(object/describe example-item-list)
```

An instance of the class item-list
with the following instance variable values:
    num-items: 0
    item-vector: [a 10 element vector]
    class: [an object of class class]

You can see from the preceding that the `num-items` and `item-vector` instance variables are as expected. You can also see that there is a third instance variable called `class`; every object has one of these. It records the most specific class this object is an instance of, which plays an important role in the underlying implementation of the object-oriented programming system. Until we examine that implementation in Section 14.4, you can safely ignore this instance variable.

Incidentally, we sometimes call procedures like `make-item-list` *instantiators* rather than constructors because the way they construct objects is by making instances of classes. From the object's viewpoint it is a constructor, whereas from the class's viewpoint, it is an instantiator. We say that `make-item-list` is `item-list-class`'s instantiator.

We now can continue implementing the methods of `item-list-class` one by one, starting with `add`, which adds an item to the list. It needs to check to see whether there is still room in the vector for the additional item. If not, the vector needs to be replaced with a bigger one, and then the addition can continue. Otherwise, the item can be inserted into the vector and the `num-items` counter increased by 1. For now let's leave out the details of how we upgrade to a bigger vector; a comment indicates where this upgrade will need to go:

```
(class/set-method!
 item-list-class 'add
 (lambda (this item)
    (let ((num-items (item-list/get-num-items this))
          (item-vector (item-list/get-item-vector this)))
       (if (= num-items (vector-length item-vector))
           (begin ; some code (yet to be determined) goes here to
                  ; replace the vector with a bigger one somehow
             (item-list/add this item))
           (begin (vector-set! item-vector num-items item)
                  (item-list/set-num-items! this (+ num-items 1))
                  'added)))))
```

▷ **Exercise 14.1**

Suppose that we forgot to replace the comment with the actual code to upgrade to a bigger vector and therefore used the method exactly as shown. Under what circumstances would users not notice our mistake? When they did notice our mistake, what would the symptoms be? Explain.

Rather than complicate the above method with the details of "growing" into a bigger vector, a better option is to use procedural abstraction to advantage: We concern ourselves here with *what* we want done (growing) and elsewhere with *how* that should be accomplished. That is, here we simply invoke a `grow` procedure and elsewhere define what that procedure does. In the object-oriented programming context, this `grow` procedure actually needs to be a method of the item-list class. Thus, in addition to all the methods from our original wish-list, which constitute the " public interface" of the class, we'll have an additional `grow` method that is for " private" internal use. The `define-class` needs to be revised to show the one additional method name; we'll also put some comments in to distinguish the two categories of methods:

```
(define-class
  'item-list
  object-class
  '(item-vector
  num-items)
  '(
    ;; intended for public consumption:
    add
    display
    total-price
    delete
    choose
    empty?
    ;; intended for private, internal use:
    grow
    ))
```

Having added this method name, we can now replace the comment in our `add` method with real Scheme code:

```
(class/set-method!
 item-list-class 'add
 (lambda (this item)
```

```
(let ((num-items (item-list/get-num-items this))
      (item-vector (item-list/get-item-vector this)))
  (if (= num-items (vector-length item-vector))
      (begin (item-list/grow this)
             (item-list/add this item))
      (begin (vector-set! item-vector num-items item)
             (item-list/set-num-items! this (+ num-items 1))
             'added)))))
```

Now we no longer have the worry that we might forget to replace the comment. Of course, we could forget to implement the **grow** method; if that happens, we'll get an "unimplemented method" error message when growth first becomes necessary, which at least points us right to the problem.

The **grow** method itself can be written quite straightforwardly, particularly if we allow ourself the use of a **vector-copy!** procedure for copying the contents of the old vector into the new, larger vector.

▶ Exercise 14.2

The **vector-copy!** procedure takes two vectors as its arguments. The second vector must be at least as long as the first. The **vector-copy!** procedure copies each element of the first vector into the corresponding position in the second vector. Write this procedure.

▶ Exercise 14.3

Now write the **grow** method for **item-list-class**. It should make a new vector that is twice as long as the current **item-vector**. It should then copy the contents of the old vector into the new one. Finally, it should set the **item-vector** instance variable to be the new vector.

One method commonly invokes another method on the same object, as the **add** method did with the **grow** method. By the same token, a method will often also invoke some methods on other, related objects. For example, to display an item-list, each item in the list needs to be displayed:

```
(class/set-method!
 item-list-class 'display
 (lambda (this)
   (let ((num-items (item-list/get-num-items this))
         (item-vector (item-list/get-item-vector this)))
     ;;(continued)
```

```
    (from-to-do
     0 (- num-items 1)
     (lambda (index)
        (display (+ index 1))
        (display ") ")
        (item/display (vector-ref item-vector index))
        (newline))))
   (display "Total: ")
   (display-price (item-list/total-price this))
   (newline)
   'displayed))
```

As you can see, when `item-list/display` is applied to an item-list, it winds up applying `item/display` to each of the items stored in its vector. Of course, it does some other things as well, namely, decorating each item's display with an item number in front, such as 1), separating the items with newlines, and adding a display of the total price at the end. We assume that there is a procedure `display-price` that can take a numerical price and suitably display it; for example, in the United States there would be a dollar sign at the front and a decimal point before the last two digits.

Exercise 14.4

Write this (United States) `display-price` procedure. Assume that prices are represented within the program as an integer number of cents, such as 1950 for 19 dollars and 50 cents. You can use `quotient` and `remainder` to calculate the number of dollars and remaining cents. (Representing monetary amounts as an integer number of cents is a common practice in business programs because it can eliminate round-off errors. For example, adding together 100 one-cent items should yield an exact dollar, whereas adding 100 copies of .01 together on our computer yields 1.0000000000000007, due to the inexact way in which .01 is represented in the computer.)

Exercise 14.5

Write the `total-price` method for the `item-list` class; you can use `item/price` to get the price of each item.

To delete an item from an item list, we need to decrement the `num-items` instance variable. If the item wasn't the last one in the list, the items after it should be shifted one position closer to the beginning of the vector, to close up the gap.

> ### Exercise 14.6

Write the `delete` method for the `item-list` class in this way. It should take the item to delete as an argument (after the `this` argument) and search the vector to find it, using `eq?` to compare the specified item with each one in the vector. It is an error if the item is not in the item-list.

There is one very subtle problem with a `delete` method that works as we just described. As the simplest illustration, consider starting with a new, empty item-list, inserting a single item into it, and then deleting it again. When the item is inserted into the item-list, position 0 in the vector will be set to the item and `num-items` will be increased to 1. When the item is deleted, `num-items` is decreased to 0 and the vector is left unchanged. Thus, position 0 of the vector still holds the item. From a logical standpoint, this doesn't matter because it will never be accessed; only the first `num-items` elements of the vector ever get looked at. However, the underlying Scheme system won't have any way of knowing this, so it will keep the item around just in case it is accessed, even though it never will be. If the item is not accessible in any way other than through the vector, its needless appearance in the vector will be all that prevents the Scheme system from reusing (*garbage collecting*) the portion of the computer's memory that the item occupies. Thus, although the program will work correctly, it may wind up using more memory than it needs to, or even unnecessarily running out of memory, because deleted items are still in the `item-vector`.

> ### Exercise 14.7

Fix this problem by modifying your `delete` method so that after shifting the items down in the vector to fill the gap, it uses `vector-set!` to store the symbol `empty` (or any other arbitrary value) into the newly unused vector location. This vector location is the one that prior to the deletion held the last item.

At this point, the only method that remains to be implemented for the `item-list` class is the `choose` method, which will get us for the first time into the user interface of this program because we need to provide the user with some way of choosing an item from the list. As a rather crude approach to the user interface, we'll display the whole item-list (using `item-list/display`) and then ask the user to select an item. Because the items are numbered consecutively from 1 by the display method, we can input the user's choice as an integer in the range from 1 to the number of items. Notice that we've got a tight coupling between the `display` method and the `choose` method; this coupling may not be good for the long-term maintainability of our program, particularly if we don't explicitly document it in the requirements for the display method. At any rate, our **choose** method is as follows; we use an input-integer-in-range procedure, which we'll need to write later.

```
(class/set-method!
 item-list-class 'choose
 (lambda (this)
   (if (item-list/empty? this)
       (error "Can't choose an item when there aren't any.")
       (begin
         (display "Which item?")
         (newline)
         (item-list/display this)
         (vector-ref (item-list/get-item-vector this)
                     (- (input-integer-in-range
                          1 (item-list/get-num-items this))
                        1)))))))
```

The input-integer-in-range procedure simply needs to display a prompt, read an input from the user, and if it isn't appropriate, complain and try again:

```
(define input-integer-in-range
  (lambda (min max)
    (display "(enter ")
    (display min)
    (display "-")
    (display max)
    (display ")")
    (newline)
    (let ((input (read)))
      (cond ((not (integer? input))
             (display "input must be an integer and wasn't")
             (newline)
             (input-integer-in-range min max))
            ((or (< input min)
                 (> input max))
             (display "input out of range")
             (newline)
             (input-integer-in-range min max))
            (else
             input)))))
```

At this point we're done implementing the item-list class (although we'll look at variations on it in the next section), and we can move on to our other principal class, item. The only piece of information we can be sure is associated with any item is its price—not all items have distinguishing colors or sizes, for example. Thus we'll put a single instance variable, `price`, in the item class, leaving the rest (color, size, ...) for more specialized subclasses. Recalling our earlier wish list of method names for the item class, we get the following definition:

```
(define-class
  'item
  object-class
  '(price)
  '(
    ;; intended for public consumption:
    price
    display
    input-specifics
    revise-specifics))
```

One decision we'll have to make is how an item's price gets set in the first place. A straightforward possibility is to have it supplied to the `make-item` constructor as an argument, as in

```
(define example-item (make-item 1950)) ; 1950 cents = $19.50
```

Our object-oriented programming system handles constructor arguments such as this one by passing them as additional arguments to the `init` method, after the `this` argument. Thus the item class needs an `init` method that accepts the price as its second argument:

```
(class/set-method!
 item-class 'init
 (lambda (this price)
   (item/set-price! this price)))
```

Most of the remaining methods for the item class are easy. The `price` method needs only to get the value of the price instance variable and return it, the `display` method needs only to display the price (because there is no other information), and the `input-specifics` method doesn't need to do anything at all because there are no "specifics" (such as color or size) to get.

> **Exercise 14.8**

Write these three methods.

> **Exercise 14.9**

Play around with the item and item-list classes. Make some items with various prices and add them to and delete them from an item-list. Display the items and the item-list, redisplaying the item-list after each addition or deletion. Also use `object/describe` to look at the items and at how the item-list evolves. Make sure the item-list successfully outgrows its original vector.

The only remaining method for the item class is `revise-specifics`. At first glance, it would appear that we should simply make this a do-nothing method, like `input-specifics`, because plain items have no specifics. However, there is another, better alternative. We can write a `revise-specifics` method that does nothing except invoke the `input-specifics` method. For a plain item, this will of course still do nothing. For an instance of some subclass of item, such as oxford-shirt, if the `revise-specifics` method isn't overriden, the one from the item class will be used, but it will wind up invoking the subclass's more specialized `input-specifics` method, and all the specifics of color, size, etc., will wind up being input. Finally, if some subclass wishes to override not only `input-specifics` but also `revise-specifics`, it can provide a more sophisticated means of revision that allows some specifics to be left unchanged and others revised, rather than requiring them to all be input over again.

> **Exercise 14.10**

Write the `revise-specifics` method for the item class.

To demonstrate more concretely our point about `revise-specifics`, consider the following example:

```
(define-class
  'special-item
  item-class
  '()
  '())
```

```
(class/set-method!
 special-item-class 'input-specifics
 (lambda (this)
   (newline)
   (display " *** doing special input ***")
   (newline)))

(define a-normal-item (make-item 1950))

(define a-special-item (make-special-item 1000000))

(item/input-specifics a-normal-item)

(item/input-specifics a-special-item)

 *** doing special input ***

(item/revise-specifics a-normal-item)

(item/revise-specifics a-special-item)

 *** doing special input ***
```

As you can see, although we only provided a specialized version of the **input-specifics** method, both **item/input-specifics** and **item/ revise-specifics** now behave differently for the normal item than for the special item. (For the normal item, both are silent, whereas for the special item, both print out the message "doing special input.") This is an important consequence of using generic operations: When one operation invokes another, making a specialized version of the called one effectively specializes the behavior of the calling one as well.

Speaking of specialized subclasses of **item-class**, we should get around to creating one. Oxford-cloth shirts have colors, neck sizes, and sleeve lengths, in addition to the inherited instance variables (**price** from **item-class** and **class** from **object-class**). There is also one other, less obvious, instance variable that we need to add, one to indicate whether the specifics have been input yet or not. That way, if the item is displayed before the specifics have been input, a less detailed description can be produced. For this purpose we'll use a boolean-valued instance variable called **specified-yet**. There are no additional method names beyond those inherited from **item-class**, so the definition is as follows:

```
(define-class
  'oxford-shirt
  item-class
  '(color
    neck
```

```
    sleeve
    specified-yet)
  '(
    ))
```

We'll set up the `init` method so that we can use `make-oxford-shirt` as shown below:

```
(define an-oxford-shirt (make-oxford-shirt))

(item/price an-oxford-shirt)
1950

(oxford-shirt/get-specified-yet an-oxford-shirt)
#f
```

As you can see, we didn't need to specify any arguments to the `make-oxford-shirt` constructor, and we wound up with a price of 1950 and the `specified-yet` instance variable set to `#f`. The question is, how shall we arrange for this result? The most obvious possibility, but not the best, would simply be to have the `init` method set both the `price` instance variable and the `specified-yet` instance variable:

```
(class/set-method!
 oxford-shirt-class 'init
 (lambda (this)
   (item/set-price! this 1950)
   (oxford-shirt/set-specified-yet! this #f)))
```

The problem with this method implementation is that although it works, it contains a nearly verbatim copy of what `item-class`'s version of the `init` method does, which could result in a maintainability problem. Right now all `item-class`'s `init` does is to set the `price` instance variable, but what if we changed it to do more? Would we remember to also make the additions in `oxford-shirt-class`'s `init`? The program would be more maintainable if rather than repeating what `item-class`'s `init` does, we could simply invoke that `init` method and let it do whatever it needs to do. At first, you might think that the following will do that:

```
(class/set-method!
 oxford-shirt-class 'init
 (lambda (this)
   (item/init this 1950)
   (oxford-shirt/set-specified-yet! this #f)))
```

The problem is that when `item/init` is applied to an object, the class of the object determines which implementation of the `init` method is used, just like with any other method invocation. Thus, when it is applied to an instance of the oxford-shirt class, as here, we would wind up using the `init` method from `oxford-shirt-class`. As such, this `init` method is simply reinvoking itself, resulting in an infinite recursion. (Actually, it isn't even an error-free infinite recursion because the recursive call passes in two arguments, but this `init` method only accepts one.)

What we need is to say "please ignore the fact that this object is more than just a plain item; I still want you to invoke the plain item `init` method." In our object-oriented programming system, we can do this by using `item^init` instead of `item/init`:

```
(class/set-method!
 oxford-shirt-class 'init
 (lambda (this)
   (item^init this 1950)
   (oxford-shirt/set-specified-yet! this #f)))
```

This use of `^` rather than `/` is a general feature of our object-oriented programming system. It always means to use the method implementation corresponding to the class that explicitly appears before the `^`, rather than using the method implementation corresponding to the class of the object being operated on. For example, returning to the earlier example of the special-item class, if we were to say `(item^input-specifics a-special-item)`, we wouldn't get the special message we get from `(item/input-specifics a-special-item)` because we are asking to have the method invoked that would be used were the special item just a plain item.

The `^` feature is not nearly as commonly used as normal method invocation; the primary use for it is to allow a method (such as the `init` method above) to invoke the method of the same name from the superclass. In particular, normally every `init` method will invoke the superclass's `init` method in this way; therefore each ancestor class winds up with a chance to do its own initialization.

▶ **Exercise 14.11**

The two `init` methods we previously showed for `item-list-class` and `item-class` violated this guideline. Neither of them gave the superclass's `init` a chance. Luckily, the superclass (`object-class`) doesn't currently do anything in its `init` method. However it would be wiser not to count on that. Revise these two `init` methods so that their first step invokes the superclass's `init` method.

This feature of having a method invoke the like-named method from the super-class provides an intermediate point between the extremes of either inheriting the superclass's method unchanged or totally overriding it with a new method implementation. Instead, an overriding implementation can be provided that *augments* the superclass's implementation by invoking it and also doing some extra work. For example, consider the `display` method. The implementation in `item-class` already does some useful work, namely, displaying the price of the item. If there were ever any additional information that all items had, presumably this `display` method would show it as well. So, when we write a `display` method for the oxford-shirt class, it should add on to that base behavior by taking care of displaying the information specific to that subclass and then using `item^display` as well:

```
(class/set-method!
 oxford-shirt-class 'display
 (lambda (this)
   (if (oxford-shirt/get-specified-yet this)
       (begin
         (display (oxford-shirt/get-color this))
         (display " Oxford-cloth shirt, size ")
         (display (oxford-shirt/get-neck this))
         (display "/")
         (display (oxford-shirt/get-sleeve this))
         (display "; "))
       (display "Oxford-cloth shirt; "))
   (item^display this)))
```

> ### Exercise 14.12

Suppose you do the following:

```
(let ((item-list (make-item-list)))
  (item-list/add item-list (make-item 100))
  (item-list/add item-list (make-oxford-shirt))
  (item-list/add item-list (make-item 200))
  (item-list/add item-list (make-item 300))
  (item-list/add item-list (make-oxford-shirt))
  (item-list/display item-list))
```

What output do you get from this example? Explain why.

The only method we still need to implement for the oxford-shirt class is the `input-specifics` method. (We could also optionally add a `revise-specifics` method.) Our `input-specifics` follows. Notice that it not only sets the instance variables corresponding to the shirt's color and size but also sets the `specified-yet` instance variable to `#t`. To get input from the user, it makes use of the `input-integer-in-range` procedure we saw earlier, as well as an `input-selection` procedure that allows the user to select one of a collection of values, which in this case are colors.

```
(class/set-method!
 oxford-shirt-class 'input-specifics
 (lambda (this)
   (display "What color?")
   (newline)
   (oxford-shirt/set-color!
    this (input-selection '("Ecru" "Pink" "Blue" "Maize" "White")))
   (display "What neck size? ")
   (oxford-shirt/set-neck! this (input-integer-in-range 15 18))
   (display "What sleeve length? ")
   (oxford-shirt/set-sleeve! this (input-integer-in-range 32 37))
   (oxford-shirt/set-specified-yet! this #t)
   'inputted))
```

A simple approach to implementing `input-selection` is to print out each of the choices with a number in front of it and then use `input-integer-in-range` to allow the user to select one. The procedure can then return the element in the list of choices that corresponds to the integer the user entered:

```
(define input-selection
  (lambda (choices)
    (define display-loop
      (lambda (number choices)
        (if (null? choices)
            'done
            (begin
              (display " ")
              (display number)
              (display ") ")
              (display (car choices))
              (newline)
              (display-loop (+ number 1) (cdr choices))))))
    (display-loop 1 choices)
    (list-ref choices
              (- (input-integer-in-range 1 (length choices))
                 1))))
```

At this point we've seen enough of how the classes work that we can turn our attention to the overall program that uses these classes. We call this program compu-duds:

```
(define compu-duds
  (lambda ()
    (let ((item-list (make-item-list)))
      (define loop
        (lambda ()
          (newline)
          (display "What would you like to do?")
          (newline)
          (display " 1) Exit this program.")
          (newline)
          (display " 2) Add an item to your selections.")
          (newline)
          (display " 3) List the items you have selected.")
          (newline)
          (display
            " 4) See the total price of the items you selected.")
          (newline)
          (let ((option
                  (if (item-list/empty? item-list)
                      (input-integer-in-range 1 4)
                      (begin
                        (display
                          " 5) Delete one of your selections.")
                        (newline)
                        (display
                          " 6) Revise specifics of a selected item.")
                        (newline)
                        (input-integer-in-range 1 6)))))
            (newline)
            (cond ((= option 2)
                   (let ((item (input-item)))
                     (item-list/add item-list item)
                     (item/input-specifics item)))
                  ((= option 3)
                   (item-list/display item-list))
                  ((= option 4)
                   (display-price (item-list/total-price item-list))
                   (newline))
                  ;;(continued)
```

```
        ((= option 5)
         (item-list/delete item-list
                           (item-list/choose item-list)))
        ((= option 6)
         (item/revise-specifics
          (item-list/choose item-list))))
      (if (not (= option 1))
          (loop))))) ;end of the loop procedure
    (loop)))) ;this starts the loop
```

As you can see, nothing thus far has embodied any knowledge of what kinds of clothing our on-line clothing store has to offer. That knowledge is used by the input-item procedure, which allows the user to select an item to add. Here is a simple version:

```
(define input-item
  (lambda ()
    (display "What would you like?")
    (newline)
    (display " 1) Chinos")
    (newline)
    (display " 2) Oxford-cloth shirt")
    (newline)
    (if (= (input-integer-in-range 1 2) 1)
        (make-chinos)
        (make-oxford-shirt)))))
```

Although our on-line clothing store offers two kinds of clothing, chinos and oxford-cloth shirts, we've only implemented a class for the shirts. We need to implement a class for chinos in a similar manner so that the rest of the program will work. The definitions of chinos-class and its init, display, and input-specifics methods follow, completing our compu-duds program. However, although the program will now be complete, the next section investigates extensions to and variations on this program.

```
(define-class
  'chinos
  item-class
  '(color
    size   ; waist, in inches
    inseam ; also in inches
    cuffed ; #t = cuffed, #f = hemmed
```

```
              specified-yet)
        '(
          ))


(class/set-method!
 chinos-class 'init
 (lambda (this)
    (item^init this 3300) ; chinos are priced at $33.00
    (chinos/set-specified-yet! this #f)))


(class/set-method!
 chinos-class 'display
 (lambda (this)
    (if (chinos/get-specified-yet this)
        (begin
          (display (chinos/get-color this))
          (display " chinos, size ")
          (display (chinos/get-size this))
          (display ", ")
          (display
           (if (chinos/get-cuffed this)
               "cuffed"
               "hemmed"))
          (display " to ")
          (display (chinos/get-inseam this))
          (display " inches; "))
        (display "Chinos; "))
    (item^display this)))


(class/set-method!
 chinos-class 'input-specifics
 (lambda (this)
    (display "What color?")
    (newline)
    (chinos/set-color! this
                       (input-selection
                        '("Charcoal" "Khaki" "Blue")))
    (display "What waist size? ")
    (chinos/set-size! this (input-integer-in-range 30 44))
    (display "Hemmed or cuffed?")
    (newline)
    (display " 1) Hemmed")
```

```
(newline)
(display " 2) Cuffed")
(newline)
(chinos/set-cuffed! this (= (input-integer-in-range 1 2) 2))
(display "What inseam length? ")
(chinos/set-inseam! this (input-integer-in-range
                          29
                          (if (chinos/get-cuffed this)
                              34
                              36)))
(chinos/set-specified-yet! this #t)
'inputted))
```

> ## Exercise 14.13

Explain the role served by each conditional expression (i.e., if or cond) appearing in chinos-class's methods.

14.3 Extensions and Variations

In this section we'll look at some of the many possible extensions to the compu-duds program from the last section. Because many of these extensions and variations will involve extending the class hierarchy or modifying existing classes, we first look at a couple additional tools our object-oriented programming system provides for helping to keep track of these modifications.

The first of these tools is that at any point you can see the complete class hierarchy by using show-class-hierarchy, as follows:

```
(show-class-hierarchy)

object
    item-list
    item
        chinos
        oxford-shirt
    class
```

In this case, we see that the object class (which is the "root" of the class hierarchy) has three subclasses: item-list, item, and class. (We'll learn more about the class class, which is used for representing classes, in the next section.) The item class in turn has the chinos and oxford-shirt subclasses. By using show-class-hierarchy as you add various new classes or reorganize the existing classes, you'll have an easier time keeping track of what you've done so far. It is also a useful tool if you need to work with someone else's program, in that it provides an overview.

Another useful tool for keeping track of your work as you modify existing classes and create new ones is `object/describe`. We've already seen how `object/describe` can be used to examine the state of a normal object, showing each of its instance variables. However, `object/describe` is also useful when applied to the special class objects, such as `chinos-class`. This is because there is an overriding `describe` method in the class class, which results in a special form of description just for classes. Here is an example:

`(object/describe chinos-class)`

```
The class chinos has the following ancestry:
    object
    item
    chinos
and the following immediate subclasses:
and the following instance variables (including inherited ones):
    specified-yet (new)
    cuffed (new)
    inseam (new)
    size (new)
    color (new)
    price (from item)
    class (from object)
and the following method names (including inherited ones):
    revise-specifics (name from item, implementation from item)
    input-specifics (name from item, new implementation)
    display (name from item, new implementation)
    price (name from item, implementation from item)
    init (name from object, new implementation)
    describe (name from object, implementation from object)
```

As you can see, this output provides a good overview of the status of the class, which could help you keep track of your work as you modify and create classes.

Before we start in on the actual extensions and variations, one final comment is worth making; it is a warning regarding the ordering restrictions that our object-oriented programming system imposes. When a class is defined, the superclass must already have been defined. When a method is set, the class needs to already have been defined. When an object is created, the class it is an instance of must already exist. (However, the methods don't need to have been set yet.) If you redefine a class, you'll need to redefine all the classes descended from it, reset all the methods in those various redefined classes, and remake any instances of those classes. Otherwise, you wind up with the subclasses still being subclasses of the old superclass, the methods existing only in the old class, and the objects still being instances of the old class. If you just reevaluate a `class/set-method!`, on the other hand, no problems result; all instances of the class and any descendant classes that inherit the implementation will immediately get the new version.

Now let's explore some variations and extensions of the `compu-duds` program. The first variation doesn't use any of the fancier features of object-oriented programming but rather takes advantage of data abstraction (i.e., the separation between a class's interface and its implementation). Consider the `total-price` method within the item-list class. As it stands now, it loops through all the items, adding up their prices. If the total price is repeatedly queried, this adding up would be wastefully repeated. Instead, the item-list could keep track of the total price as it added and deleted items and simply return the current total when queried.

▶ **Exercise 14.14**

Modify the definition of the item-list class and of its `add`, `delete`, and `total-price` methods in order to keep and use a running total price in this way. Without changing any other part of the `compu-duds` program, it should work just the same as before, except with regard to efficiency.

Next let's look at adding new subclasses of `item-class`. The existing two subclasses allow you to dress like two-thirds of this book's authors, who are frequently seen wearing oxford-cloth shirts and chinos. But perhaps, like most of our students, you have other tastes in clothing.

▶ **Exercise 14.15**

Add one or more additional kinds of items to `compu-duds` so that it more closely reflects your own taste in clothing.

▶ **Exercise 14.16**

If you added other kinds of pants than chinos, or other kinds of shirts than Oxford shirts, you may have discovered some commonality between your new classes and the existing classes. Reorganize the class hierarchy so there are subclasses of `item-class` for pants and shirts, with the chinos now being a subclass of `pants-class` and Oxford shirts positioned under shirts. Place your own kinds of pants and shirts under the more general classes as well, and figure out what commonality you can centralize.

> **Exercise 14.17**

How about adding yet another level of hierarchy between `shirt-class` or `pants-class` and the specific kinds of pants and shirts? What classes of an intermediate degree of specialization might you include?

In addition to using subclassing to reflect real-world concerns, such as additional kinds of clothing, we can also use it purely for the program's internal purposes. For example, consider the sizing of the vector in the item-list class. Right now, it grows (by doubling in size) whenever addition of an item requires it to, but it never shrinks, no matter how many items are deleted. For many applications, this is a reasonable design decision. However, if you want to be particularly thrifty with the computer's memory, it might be desirable to have a kind of item-list that shrank as deletions occured. Thus we'll define a subclass of `item-list-class` for thrifty-item-lists that is indistinguishable in terms of what operations it provides and how they outwardly behave but that shrinks down to a smaller vector when appropriate.

As a brief side trip, not particularly related to object-oriented programming, consider what "when appropriate" should mean: When should the vector shrink? At first you might think that because we double the vector's size when it overflows, we should cut the vector's size in half when it becomes only half-full. The problem with this approach is that if the customer happens to repeatedly add, then delete, then add, then delete, etc., we might wind up moving to a new size of vector on every single operation. For example, if we start with a 10-element vector and the customer after adding 10 items adds an eleventh, we move to a 20-element vector. The customer then deletes an item, leaving the 20-element vector only half-full, so we move back to a 10-element vector. The eleventh item is added again, leading us back to a 20-element vector, etc.

A way around this oscillation between neighboring sizes is to demand that the vector get even emptier than half-empty before we shrink down to a vector half the size. For example, we can shrink to a vector half the size when a deletion results in the vector being one-third full or less. However, the vector should never shrink below its original size of 10.

> **Exercise 14.18**

Make a thrifty-item-list subclass of `item-list-class` that behaves in this way. By simply changing the `compu-duds` procedure to use `make-thrifty-item-list` in place of `make-item-list`, you should be able to switch to this new kind of item list. In particular, the rest of the program, which thinks it is operating on an item-list, will still be right because a thrifty-item-list is an item-list. Be sure not only to check that the program still works but also to use `object/describe` to make sure the vector size is growing and shrinking appropriately.

As we've remarked before, one of the most central features of object-oriented programming is its use of generic operations to allow instances of various subclasses of a class to be uniformly operated upon, even if the resulting behavior varies. For example, this allows chinos to be displayed differently from Oxford shirts, even though `item/display` is done to both. As a consequence of this, we rarely need predicates to test whether an object is an instance of a particular class because we can generally get appropriate behavior for each class without needing conditionals that say "if this item is an Oxford shirt, display it this way, whereas if it is a pair of chinos, display it this other way." Nonetheless, there are occasionally circumstances for which class predicates are useful, and so our object-oriented programming system provides them. Each class defined using `define-class` automatically gets a predicate with a name formed by adding a question mark to the end of the class name, such as `chinos?`. The most common situation in which these predicates are useful is when sifting a particular kind of object back out of a mixed collection.

> ### Exercise 14.19

Add to the `compu-duds` program a feature that lets the user change in a single step the waist size of all the items selected that are chinos (and hence have a waist size). If in Exercises 14.15 and 14.16 you added other kinds of pants and introduced a general pants class, your new feature should change the waist size of all pants, rather than merely of all chinos.

Another feature of object-oriented programming that we haven't explicitly illustrated before now is that a class can be useful even without implementations for all its methods, if we don't intend to ever instantiate the class but rather use it only as a framework for subclasses that are instantiated and that provide the missing method implementations. In this case the class is called an *abstract class*. The `compu-duds` program very nearly contained an example of an abstract class, in that the item class really has no reason ever to be instantiated to form "plain items," other than for the sake of some of our pedagogic examples; in the program itself, only specific subclasses of item ever get instantiated. So, for example, we could have left out `item-class`'s implementation of the `input-specifics` method. With that omission, the program would have been unaffected, but we would no longer have the option of "plain items." In other words, the item class would have become abstract.

The idea of an abstract class can be taken to the fullest extent, often termed a *pure abstract class*, if the class provides only the names (and presumably specifications) for methods, without providing any method implementations or instance variables. In this case the class is serving as a true abstract data type, that is, just an interface specification, with its subclasses providing the implementations. For example, there is only a relatively minor amount of implementation sharing between the different kinds of item; they share the `price` instance variable and method, and the `display` method for showing the price, which gets augmented in the more specific `display` methods. Because this implementation sharing is so minor, it might make more sense to eliminate it altogether, leaving the item class purely abstract. As a negative consequence, some repetition would occur among the various subclasses, but as a positive consequence, the subclasses would be free to implement the formerly shared methods in other, perhaps simpler, ways. For example, the `price` method could simply return a constant price rather than having to get the value of a `price` instance variable.

Exercise 14.20

Another common use for pure abstract classes is to make explicit an interface that can be implemented using two or more different data structures. For example, we implemented the abstract interface of the item-list class using a vector but could instead have used a true list representation, in the sense of `cons`, `car`, `cdr`, `null?`, and `set-cdr!`. Change the class item-list to be purely abstract, with two subclasses called item-list-as-vector and item-list-as-list that provide these two implementations. You will have to change `compu-duds` to use one of the `make-item-list-as-`... constructors in place of `make-item-list`.

Finally, we'll conclude this section on extensions and variations with two loose ends left from the preceding section.

Exercise 14.21

We mentioned that the `revise-specifics` method could be overridden to allow more selective revision, rather than requiring the user to input all the specifics over again. Illustrate this possibility.

Exercise 14.22

We mentioned the possibility of using a class for prices. Presumably it would be most convenient if the constructor would take the number of dollars and the number of cents as two arguments, and if we had methods for displaying the price and for adding another price to the price. Design a class with this interface. Consider two possible implementations: one that stores the dollars and cents separately and one that stores them combined into a total number of cents, such as we've used previously. Explain the trade-offs between these implementations, and implement whichever of them you decide is on the whole preferable, or both if you think they should coexist. Test your price class in isolation, and then change the `compu-duds` program to use it.

14.4   Implementing an Object-oriented Programming System

In this section, we'll show how the object-oriented programming system used in the preceding sections can be implemented. The object-oriented programming system is a relatively large and complex piece of software, so we'll explain it incrementally in bite-sized chunks, each occupying a subsection. First we'll provide an overview of the system, and then we'll show how instance variables are represented and their getters and setters implemented. Next we'll show how instantiators (constructors) are implemented, then methods, and then predicates. Once we have explained all these features of classes, we'll show how classes themselves are constructed. In the last two subsections we pull it all together. We make extensive use of vectors to provide a reasonably efficient implementation of object-oriented programming, which is similar to some implementations used for object-oriented languages such as Java. If you'd rather accept object-oriented programming as a "black box" technology instead of looking behind the scenes, this section can be skipped without any loss of continuity.

Throughout this explanation we'll use the object-oriented programming system as our technology for describing itself. We'll assume first that we have constructed, somehow, the object class and the class class and we'll use them to explain what `define-class` does. As we do this, we'll see that `define-class` invokes several methods from the class class and the object class; we'll show how each of these methods is implemented. There is an inherent circularity in what we're doing; after all, how can we make a class for representations of classes before we have such a class to represent itself with? In the penultimate subsection, we show how to use *bootstrapping* to get around this circularity, and in the last subsection, we pull the last (superficial) layer of mystery aside by explaining how `define-class` abbreviates many normal definitions.

Overview

Before we delve into the implementation of the object-oriented programming system, we should make clear what needs implementing. One of the primary interfaces we've been using in the preceding sections is `define-class`; however, `define-class` is really just a convenient abbreviation, not the fundamentals of what we need to implement. In particular, evaluating a definition like

```
(define-class
  'widget
  object-class
  '(size)
  '(activate))
```

is really just a shorthand for evaluating the following sequence of definitions:

```
(define widget-class (make-class 'widget
                                 object-class
                                 '(size)
                                 '(activate)))

(define widget? (class/predicate widget-class))

(define make-widget (class/instantiator widget-class))

(define widget/get-size (class/getter widget-class 'size))

(define widget/set-size! (class/setter widget-class 'size))

(define widget/get-class (class/getter widget-class 'class))

(define widget/set-class! (class/setter widget-class 'class))

(define widget/activate (class/method widget-class 'activate))

(define widget^activate
  (class/non-overridable-method widget-class 'activate))

(define widget/init (class/method widget-class 'init))

(define widget^init
  (class/non-overridable-method widget-class 'init))

(define widget/describe (class/method widget-class 'describe))

(define widget^describe
  (class/non-overridable-method widget-class 'describe))
```

In the ensuing subsections we'll see how each of these pieces works; for example, in looking at instance variables, we'll see how `class/getter` produces the getter for `widget-class`'s `size` instance variable, which winds up being called `widget/get-size`. The machinery we will describe is housed in two fundamental classes: *object* and *class*.

As we've remarked before, the object class is the root of the class hierarchy and so is inherited from, directly or indirectly, by every class. It has one instance variable, `class`, that is used to indicate which class the object belongs to. We can indicate this fact, that each object knows which class it is an instance of, in a UML class diagram as follows:

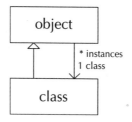

Notice that there are two relationships between these fundamental classes. Each class object is an object, so we have a subclass/superclass relationship between the class class and the object class. However, each object is also associated with one particular class, the class it is a direct instance of, so we have an association arrow as well. The arrowhead is only on one end, indicating that the object knows its class, but the class doesn't know its instances. Next to the multiplicities, we've given a name to each role in this association to help clarify the meaning of the association. In particular, we show not just that each class object is associated with arbitrarily many objects but also what those objects are: the instances of the class. Similarly, the one class object associated with an arbitrary object is that object's class.

When we earlier expanded the `define-class` to show what it was a shorthand for, you could see that the widget class winds up with a getter and setter for the inherited instance variable named `class` as well as for its own `size` instance variable. This example illustrates a general pattern: Every class has getters and setters for all its instance variables, whether inherited or newly added, and similarly for methods. The object class also has two methods, which are inherited by all classes, namely `init` and `describe`. We've already seen the special role that the `init` method plays when a class is instantiated to construct a new object; we've also seen the use of the `describe` method for debugging and exploration. As you can see from the preceding definitions, the widget class winds up with these two methods and its own `activate` method. Each method also has a non-overridable version, which is given a name with a ˆ in it, such as `widgetˆinit`.

The class class is used for representations of classes. For example, `widget-class` is an instance of the class class. These objects of the class class store the information that is shared by the entire class, such as the names of the instance variables and methods. Each class object (i.e., each instance of the class class) is made using `make-class`. Once the class object is made, we use methods of the class class, such as `class/getter`, to obtain the procedures to use with that class.

Instance Variables

Each object is represented simply as a vector containing its instance variable values. To continue our running example, consider the widget class. Each widget has two instance variables: `class` and `size`. Therefore, each widget will be represented as a two-element vector. The vector will contain the widget's `class` instance variable at position 0 and its `size` at position 1. Given this representation, it is easy to see what getters and setters need to do. For example, if we wanted to produce `widget/get-size` and `widget/set-size!` by hand, the definitions would look like this:

```
(define widget/get-size
  (lambda (object)
    (vector-ref object 1)))

(define widget/set-size!
  (lambda (object value)
    (vector-set! object 1 value)))
```

One important aspect of object-oriented programming is that a class's operations (including getters and setters) can be used on any instance of that class *including* instances of subclasses, sub-subclasses, etc. To do this, we will impose a very simple constraint on the layout of the instance variables within the vector: The superclass's instance variables have to come first, in the same order as in the superclass. The newly added instance variables come afterward, at the end of the vector. That is why the `class` instance variable is at position 0 and the `size` instance variable at position 1: The `class` instance variable is inherited from the object class and hence had to come first.

As an example of where this approach would pay off, consider defining a subclass of the widget class, perhaps called colorful-widget. It could have additional instance variables, such as color, that would be stored in vector positions from 2 onward. However, just like any other widget, the size would be stored in position 1. Thus we can use the above `widget/get-size` on any widget, without needing to know whether or not it is a colorful-widget or any other more specialized variety.

Of course, we don't really want to write each getter and setter by hand; instead we want to use `class/setter` and `class/getter` to do it for us. That way, instead of defining `widget/get-size` using `vector-ref` and 1 as in the foregoing, we could just do

```
(define widget/get-size (class/getter widget-class 'size))
```

We have `class/getter` find the correct vector position and then use it to produce the specific getter procedure for us. We'll do that as follows:

```
(class/set-method!
 class-class 'getter
 (lambda (this instvar-name)
```

```
(let ((index (class/ivar-position this instvar-name)))
  (lambda (object)
    (vector-ref object index)))))
```

Notice that we are using object-oriented programming to build the object-oriented programming system itself. In particular, `getter` is a method we are providing for the class class. It in turn uses another method from the class class, `class/ivar-position`, that is in charge of figuring out which vector position each instance variable goes in. For example, it is `class/ivar-position` that figures out that the `size` of a widget should go at position 1. We'll put off defining `class/ivar-position` until after we've seen how classes are created by `make-class`.

The preceding definition would work, so long as nobody ever applied a getter to an object that wasn't of the right class. However, if someone applied `widget/get-size` to an object that wasn't a widget, that person would get whatever instance variable happened to be stored in position 1—perhaps the account number of a bank account or the name associated with an employee record. To catch similar mistakes, we'd prefer that `widget/get-size` were actually defined more like the following:

```
(define widget/get-size
  (lambda (object)
    (if (widget? object)
        (vector-ref object 1)
        (error "Getter applied to object not of correct class:"
               'size 'widget))))
```

To have `class/getter` make such an improved getter for us, it is actually defined as follows:

```
(class/set-method!
 class-class 'getter
 (lambda (this instvar-name)
   (let ((index (class/ivar-position this instvar-name))
         (ok? (class/predicate this)))
     (lambda (object)
       (if (ok? object)
           (vector-ref object index)
           (error
            "Getter applied to object not of correct class:"
            instvar-name (class/get-name this)))))))
```

The definition of `class/setter` is completely analogous, just using `vector-set!` instead of `vector-ref`:

```
(class/set-method!
 class-class 'setter
 (lambda (this instvar-name)
   (let ((index (class/ivar-position this instvar-name))
         (ok? (class/predicate this)))
     (lambda (object value)
       (if (ok? object)
           (begin
             (vector-set! object index value)
             'set-done)
           (error
             "Setter applied to object not of correct class:"
             instvar-name (class/get-name this)))))))
```

To summarize the most important points from this subsection:

1. Each object is represented as a vector storing the instance variable values.
2. The superclass's instance variables come first, in the same order as in the superclass.
3. Aside from error-checking, all a getter or setter does is a single `vector-ref` or `vector-set!`.

Instantiators

As we saw in the preceding subsection, each object is represented as a vector. Thus to a first approximation, we could write the widget class's instantiator as follows:

```
(define make-widget
  (lambda ()
    (make-vector 2)))
```

However, two details are omitted here. First, if the new object is to truly be a widget, its `class` instance variable needs to be set to the `widget-class`. Second, we need to give the `init` method an opportunity to initialize the newly created widget. Thus, a better second attempt at `make-widget` would be as follows:

```
(define make-widget
  (lambda ()
    (let ((instance (make-vector 2)))
      (object/set-class! instance widget-class)
      (object/init instance)
      instance)))
```

At this point, had we stuck with the non-error-checking design for setters in which they only did a `vector-set!`, the `make-widget` procedure would work. But with error-checking setters, `object/set-class!` will first use `object?` to verify that it is really being passed an object (i.e., an instance of the object class). Unfortunately, until the class is set, there is no way this test can succeed. So, our next version of `make-widget` is as follows:

```
(define make-widget
  (lambda ()
    (let ((instance (make-vector 2)))
      (unchecked-object/set-class! instance widget-class)
      (object/init instance)
      instance)))
```

The `unchecked-object/set-class!` procedure that this version uses is like our first, crude `widget/set-size!` procedure. It can be written by hand and simply sets vector location 0.

One final issue is worth addressing before we turn to automating the production of class instantiators. Thus far we have assumed that `make-widget` takes no arguments. But what if, in reality, we want to use it like `(make-widget 1000)`? In this case, the `make-widget` procedure would have to accept the argument and pass it in to `object/init` (after the instance) because, as we've seen in our prior object-oriented programming, the `init` method actually processes any arguments to the instantiator. Rather that adding a single argument in this way, we'll allow any number of arguments to be passed to the instantiator and from there to the `init` method, using the special unparenthesized lambda-parameter notation (Section 10.3) and `apply`:

```
(define make-widget
  (lambda init-args
    (let ((instance (make-vector 2)))
      (unchecked-object/set-class! instance widget-class)
      (apply object/init (cons instance init-args))
      instance)))
```

Now all that remains is to automate the production of such instantiator procedures using `class/instantiator`. We'll assume that the class can find out how many instance variables it has using `class/get-num-ivars`. With this assumption, we can write

```
(class/set-method!
 class-class 'instantiator
 (lambda (this)
   (let ((num-ivars (class/get-num-ivars this)))
     (lambda init-args
       (let ((instance (make-vector num-ivars)))
         (unchecked-object/set-class! instance this)
         (apply object/init (cons instance init-args))
         instance)))))
```

At this point, we've clarified how two features of classes work—instance variables, with their getters and setters, and instantiators, for creating objects that are instances of a class. Of course, we've added some additional items to our agenda—`class/ivar-position` and `class/get-num-ivars` now need explaining too. For now, we'll put these off and continue working through the features we originally identified—methods, predicates, and class creation. Along the way, we're sure to discover yet more supporting machinery we need, and before we can declare ourselves finished, we'll need to have implemented not only the "official interface" methods, like `class/instantiator`, but also the "behind the scenes" methods, like `class/ivar-position`. This process of working from the external interface of a class inward to the supporting mechanisms is a common occurrence in object-oriented programming, no less so when the class we are programming is the class of classes.

Methods

Although at this point we know how to make instances of a class and how to get and set the instance variables contained within those instances, we're still missing one of the most fundamental ingredients of object-oriented programming: methods.

For efficient access, methods can be stored in vectors, just like instance variables are; the primary difference is that one vector of methods is shared by an entire class, whereas the instance variables are unique to each instance. Given a class, we can get its method vector using `class/get-method-vector`. Then we simply need to retrieve the particular method from the vector using `vector-ref` and apply it. Putting it all together, here is an example of how `widget/activate` might be written by hand:

```
(define widget/activate
  (lambda (object)
    (let ((method (vector-ref (class/get-method-vector
                                (object/get-class object))
                              2)))
      (method object))))
```

Notice that we get the method from the method vector of the object's class. That way, if the object wasn't a plain widget, but rather some special kind of widget such as our hypothetical colorful-widget, we'd get the colorful-widget class's `activate` method, which might do something special. This approach contrasts with `widget^activate`, which always gets the method from the `widget-class`'s method vector, even if the particular object turns out to be a colorful-widget:

```
(define widget^activate
  (let ((method-vector (class/get-method-vector widget-class)))
    (lambda (object)
      (let ((method (vector-ref method-vector 2)))
        (method object)))))
```

We wait until `widget^activate` is used to retrieve the method from the method vector so that the method can be changed using `class/set-method!`, which we'll see shortly.

We are making an assumption that underlies our ability to use `widget/activate` on any kind of widget, even special widgets like colorful widgets. Namely, we rely on all subclasses of `widget-class` to still use position 2 of the method vectors to store their `activate` methods. In other words, just as with instance variables, the methods whose names are inherited from the superclass need to be at the beginning of the method vector, in the same order as in the superclass; methods whose names are newly introduced come afterward. This explains how we knew that the `activate` method would be in position 2 of the method vectors: positions 0 and 1 would be occupied by the `init` and `describe` methods because those method names are inherited from `widget-class`'s superclass, `object-class`.

At this point, we've shown how methods can be written by hand. We still need to show how that process can be automated, and we still need to make a few refinements. Also, we'll need to show how methods are installed into the method vectors using `class/set-method!`. Before proceeding with these topics, however, we should point out that procedures such as the one named `widget/activate` aren't the *real* methods but act as though they were. When you apply `widget/activate` to a widget, it retrieves the real method from the method vector and applies the real method to the widget. Thus, the net effect is just as if the real method had been applied in the first place. For this reason we call `widget/activate` a *virtual method*.

▶ **Exercise 14.23**

How many `vector-ref`s are done between the time when the virtual method `widget/activate` is invoked and the time when the real method gets applied? Explain. Be sure to count those done by procedures that `widget/activate` uses. You may omit any that are used only for error-checking, however.

Our first refinement will be to allow the `activate` method to take any number of additional arguments, rather than just the widget being activated. In the following procedure, `args` is a name for a list of all the additional arguments after the widget being activated:

```
(define widget/activate
  (lambda (object . args)
    (let ((method (vector-ref (class/get-method-vector
                                (object/get-class object))
                              2)))
      (apply method (cons object args)))))
```

Next we'll get rid of the explicit number 2 and instead use `class/method-position` to find it for us:

```
(define widget/activate
  (let ((index (class/method-position widget-class 'activate)))
    (lambda (object . args)
      (let ((method (vector-ref (class/get-method-vector
                                  (object/get-class object))
                                index)))
        (apply method (cons object args))))))
```

Now it is time for you to do some of the work.

▶ **Exercise 14.24**

As a third refinement to `widget/activate`, make it check that it really is being applied to a widget and signal an error if not, much as with `widget/get-size`.

▶ **Exercise 14.25**

Rewrite `widget^activate` so it too benefits from these three refinements. That is, it should accept additional arguments, use `class/method-position` rather than the number 2, and verify that it is being applied to a widget.

▶ **Exercise 14.26**

Automate the production of virtual methods like `widget/activate` and `widget^activate` by writing the `class/method` and `class/non-overridable-method` methods as procedure factories. For an example, you could look at `class/getter`.

At this point we can retrieve and use methods, but we haven't seen how they get into method vectors in the first place. If you've been following carefully, you might well think it could be done as follows:

```
(class/set-method!
 class-class
 'set-method!
 (lambda (this method-name method)
   (vector-set! (class/get-method-vector this)
                (class/method-position this method-name)
                method)))
```

This code is very nearly right. Before making the few refinements it needs, we should point out that it brings us face-to-face with the bootstrapping problem that we'll have to solve eventually. We used **class/set-method!** to install into the **class-class** its **set-method!** method—in other words, we used **class/set-method!** to install itself. (This circularity is like trying to pull yourself up by your bootstraps, hence the description of the problem as being a bootstrapping problem.) Clearly this circularity will need to be addressed.

However, for now we'll leave the circularity unaddressed and instead clean up a detail. Namely, if we're putting the activate method into the widget class's method vector, and the widget class has subclasses like colorful-widget, and those subclasses don't have their own overriding methods, the same method that is being installed into the widget class's method vector should be installed into the subclasses' method vectors as well. That's how method implementations (as opposed to just method names) get inherited. In fact, the same method might get installed into the method vectors of sub-subclasses, sub-sub-subclasses, etc. Any class descended from **widget-class** will get this method, unless an overriding method intervenes.

Installing method implementation in descendant classes requires several forms of support. Most fundamentally, each class will need to know its subclasses. We'll assume that we can get a list of the subclasses of a class using **class/get-subclasses**. When we look at how classes are created by **make-class**, we'll see how the list of subclasses is kept up to date. For the time being, we'll record the availability of this information in our UML class diagram:

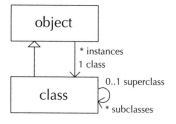

{super/subclass associations form a tree with object-class as the root—the only class with no superclass}

This class diagram illustrates another feature of the UML notation, namely, the ability to express a *constraint* that an association must satisfy. The constraint is written next to the association in curly braces. Here we've recorded the fact that the subclass relationship forms a tree. Starting from `object-class` and going to its subclasses, then their subclasses, etc., we should reach every class eventually, without ever reaching the same class a second time.

Another form of support we'll need is some way to keep track of whether a descendant class has its own overriding implementation of the method and hence shouldn't inherit the superclass's. Therefore, we'll give each class a second vector. In addition to the `method-vector`, there will be a `method-set?-vector` containing boolean values: True means the method has been directly set and hence shouldn't be inherited in, whereas false means that the superclass's implementation is the only one available. Using these, and a higher-order procedure for traversing the tree of descendant classes, we arrive at the following:

```
(class/set-method!
 class-class
 'set-method!
 (lambda (this method-name method)
   (let ((index (class/method-position this method-name)))
     (vector-set! (class/get-method-vector this)
                  index
                  method)
     (vector-set! (class/get-method-set?-vector this)
                  index
                  #t)
     (apply-below this
                  (lambda (class)
                    (vector-set! (class/get-method-vector class)
                                 index
                                 method))
                  (lambda (class)
                    (not (vector-ref (class/get-method-set?-vector
                                      class)
                                     index)))))))
   method-name))

(define apply-below
  (lambda (class proc apply-to?)
    (for-each (lambda (subclass)
                (if (apply-to? subclass)
```

```
(begin (proc subclass)
       (apply-below subclass proc apply-to?))))
(class/get-subclasses class))))
```

Predicates

We need to design our class predicates so that, for example, `widget?` returns `#t` not only when applied to a plain widget that is directly an instance of `widget-class` but also when applied to a colorful widget that is an instance of some descendant class of `widget-class`. Thus it will not suffice to simply check to see if the object's class is equal to `widget-class`.

One straightforward solution would be to get the object's class, check for equality with `widget-class`, and if unequal retrieve the class's superclass and check again, iterating up the class hierarchy until an ancestor equal to `widget-class` is found or the top of the class hierarchy is reached. This approach would work, but it would be our first operation in the whole object-oriented programming system that wasn't accomplished with some small fixed number of vector accesses. Instead, the deeper the inheritance hierarchy, the slower the predicates would be. This is intolerably inefficient if we are going to use the predicates on a precautionary basis before each method invocation or instance variable access. Even if predicates were used more sparingly, we should design them to take a constant number of steps, absent any reason to the contrary.

For this design, we'll focus on each class's ancestry (i.e., the sequence of classes starting with `object-class` and working down the hierarchy to the class in question). We'll call `object-class` the "level 0 ancestor," the subclass of `object-class` that is an ancestor of the class in question its "level 1 ancestor," etc. In this terminology, the `widget?` predicate should return `#t` for any object whose class has `widget-class` as its level 1 ancestor. To test this condition efficiently, we simply store the ancestry as a vector, use `vector-ref` to retrieve element 1, and test to see whether it is equal to `widget-class`:

```
(define widget?
  (lambda (object)
    (let ((ancestry (class/get-ancestry (object/get-class object))))
      (and (> (vector-length ancestry) 1)
           (eq? (vector-ref ancestry 1)
                widget-class)))))
```

Of course, we still need to ensure that the ancestry vectors really exist in each class—we'll address that when we turn to the construction of classes. For now, let's update our UML class diagram, as a reminder of this important design decision:

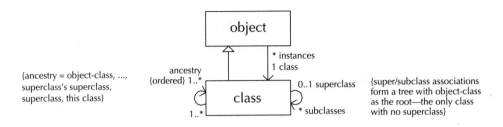

The diagram shows a new notation, the special constraint {ordered}. This notation means that rather than each class being associated with an unordered set of one or more ancestors, it has an ordered list of one or more ancestors—one specific ancestor comes first, etc. We've also used the constraint notation to indicate what the ancestors need to be. The first ancestor (level 0) needs to be object-class, and the last ancestor needs to be the class whose ancestry this is. Immediately preceding that comes the superclass, and before that comes the superclass's superclass. The implication is that the ancestry needs to be consistent with the superclass/subclass association between classes.

The design of the widget? predicate just given has two flaws. First, it invokes object/get-class and class/get-ancestry, which as precautions invoke object? and class?, respectively. However, assuming that object? and class? follow the same design as widget?, they will in turn invoke object/get-class and class/get-ancestry. So, we'll wind up with an infinite recursion. The second flaw in widget?'s design is that no provision is made for the possibility that it might be applied to a value that is not an object at all, as in (widget? 3).

> ## Exercise 14.27

Write out the object? predicate that corresponds to the above widget? predicate. Now trace out the details of the infinite recursion that occurs when it is used.

To provide some measure of foolproofing against predicates being applied to nonobjects, we can test a number of additional consistency conditions. If all of these consistency conditions hold, we can be relatively certain that we have a genuine object and can test the original two conditions: that the ancestry vector is long enough and that it has the widget-class as its element at position 1 (i.e., as the level 1 ancestor). The following version of widget? embodies the additional consistency checks to guard against nonobjects, although it still has the infinite recursion problem:

```
(define widget?
  (let ((level (- (vector-length (class/get-ancestry widget-class))
                  1))
        (min-length (class/get-num-ivars widget-class))
        (min-class-length (class/get-num-ivars class-class)))
    (lambda (object)
      (and (vector? object)
           (>= (vector-length object) min-length)
           (let ((class (object/get-class object)))
             (and (vector? class)
                  (>= (vector-length class) min-class-length)
                  (let ((a (class/get-ancestry class))
                        (size (class/get-num-ivars class)))
                    (and (number? size)
                         (= size (vector-length object))
                         (vector? a)
                         (eq? (vector-ref a
                                          (- (vector-length a) 1))
                              class)
                         (> (vector-length a) level)
                         (eq? (vector-ref a level)
                              widget-class)))))))))
```

> ### Exercise 14.28

Write out an English description of what each of the consistency checks is.

> ### Exercise 14.29

Recall that the infinite recursion is due to the predicate using getters that themselves use predicates to do precautionary checking. The last time we had a problem caused by precautionary checking in the normal getter or setter procedures was in `make-widget` in the Instantiators subsection. Solve the infinite recursion problem using the same approach as we used there.

> ### Exercise 14.30

Using your `widget?` predicate as a starting point, write the `class/predicate` method, which acts as a procedure factory for generating such predicate procedures.

Making Classes

Classes are themselves instances of the class class, made using `make-class`. To see what needs to be done to make a class, let's review the instance variables that we have come to assume each class has: `name`, `subclasses`, `num-ivars`, `method-vector`, `method-set?-vector`, and `ancestry`. In addition, we've assumed the availability of the `ivar-position` and `method-position` methods.

To support `ivar-position` and `method-position`, we'll equip each class with a table showing which vector position each instance variable is stored in and another table showing which vector position each method is stored in. We'll store each table as simply a list of lists; for example, the list `((class 0) (size 1))` would be used to show that `class` is in position 0 and `size` in position 1. Because these tables *associate* a position with each name, they are conventionally called *association lists* or simply *alists*. We'll add two more instance variables to our above list of instance variables the class class needs: `ivar-alist` and `method-alist`. These will hold the two association lists. For convenience we'll also add a `num-methods` instance variable, paralleling `num-ivars`.

At this point, we can show a full definition for `class-class`:

```
(define class-class
  (make-class 'class          ; name
              object-class    ; superclass
              '(name          ; instance variables
                subclasses
                num-ivars
                ivar-alist
                num-methods
                method-alist
                method-vector
                method-set?-vector
                ancestry)
              '(instantiator ; methods
                predicate
                getter
                setter
                method
                non-overridable-method
                set-method!
                ivar-position
                method-position)))
```

Of course, this again raises the bootstrapping issue of circularity: We just used `make-class`, which makes an instance of the class class, to specify what the class

class is. We'll resolve this problem in the next subsection, which is devoted to bootstrapping. For now, we at least have a human-readable description of the class class.

The `make-class` procedure is simply the instantiator for the class class, obtained using `class/instantiator`. As such, all it does is create an appropriately sized vector, install `class-class` into element 0 of that vector, and then invoke the `init` method to do all the real work. We can already sketch out most of what the `init` method will need to do, simply by initializing each of the instance variables:

```
(class/set-method!
 class-class 'init
 (lambda (this class-name superclass instvar-names method-names)
   (object^init this)
   ;; some code should go here to check that none of the new
   ;; instvar-names or method-names are already in use in the
   ;; superclass -- and if any are, to signal an error
   (class/set-name! this class-name)
   (class/set-subclasses! this '())
   (class/set-subclasses! superclass
                          (cons this
                                (class/get-subclasses superclass)))
   (class/set-num-ivars! this (+ (class/get-num-ivars superclass)
                                 (length instvar-names)))
   (class/set-ivar-alist! this
                          ;; some code needs to go here to
                          ;; assign the positions for the instance
                          ;; variables
                          )
   (class/set-method-alist! this
                            ;; some code needs to go here to
                            ;; assign the positions for the methods
                            )
   (let ((num-methods (+ (class/get-num-methods superclass)
                         (length method-names))))
     (class/set-num-methods! this num-methods)
     (let ((method-vector (make-vector num-methods)))
       (class/set-method-vector! this method-vector)
       (vector-copy! (class/get-method-vector superclass)
                     method-vector)
       ;;(continued)
```

```
        (for-each (lambda (method-name)
                    (vector-set! method-vector
                                 (class/method-position this
                                                        method-name)
                      (lambda (object . args)
                        (error "Unimplemented method"
                               method-name))))
                  method-names))
      (let ((method-set?-vector (make-vector num-methods)))
        (class/set-method-set?-vector! this method-set?-vector)
        (vector-fill! method-set?-vector #f)))
    (let ((ancestry (make-vector (+ (vector-length
                                      (class/get-ancestry superclass))
                                    1))))
      (class/set-ancestry! this ancestry)
      (vector-copy! (class/get-ancestry superclass) ancestry)
      (vector-set! ancestry
                   (- (vector-length ancestry) 1)
                   this))))
```

The above outline of `class-class`'s `init` method has two "holes" that need to be filled in with code that computes alists, assigning positions for the instance variables and methods. Recall that all the superclass's instance variable or method names need to be assigned the same positions as in the superclass, with the new names assigned larger position numbers. Thus, a simple approach is to cons new name/position associations onto the front of the superclass's alists, starting with the superclass's number of instance variables or methods as the next available position number. The following procedure handles this process of building onto an existing alist:

```
(define alist-from-onto
  (lambda (names num alist)
    (if (null? names)
        alist
        (alist-from-onto (cdr names)
                         (+ num 1)
                         (cons (list (car names)
                                     num)
                               alist)))))
```

Using this procedure, the two pieces of code we need to fill into the holes are as follows:

```
(alist-from-onto instvar-names
                 (class/get-num-ivars superclass)
                 (class/get-ivar-alist superclass))
```

and

```
(alist-from-onto method-names
                 (class/get-num-methods superclass)
                 (class/get-method-alist superclass))
```

With these filled in, the `init` method will now work; however, it won't provide the user with any error message if they pick a name for an instance variable or method that is already in use from one of the ancestor classes. To provide this error-checking, we need to check to see if any element of `instvar-names` or `method-names` appears in the corresponding alist of the superclass. To check to see if a particular name appears in the alist, we can use the built-in procedure `assq`, which searches the alist for a particular name and returns the first pair that has that name as its car or returns `#f` if the name isn't found. For example,

```
(assq 'size '((class 0) (size 1)))
(size 1)

(assq 'color '((class 0) (size 1)))
#f
```

This procedure makes checking for erroneously reused names fairly straightforward.

▶ Exercise 14.31

Write the error-checking (and reporting) code.

The only remaining features of the class class we need to implement are the `ivar-position` and `method-position` methods. These methods can also be straightforwardly written using `assq`:

```
(class/set-method!
 class-class 'ivar-position
 (lambda (this ivar-name)
   (let ((lookup (assq ivar-name (class/get-ivar-alist this))))
     (if lookup
         (cadr lookup)
         (error "instance variable name not present in class"
                ivar-name (class/get-name this))))))
```

```
(class/set-method!
 class-class 'method-position
 (lambda (this method-name)
   (let ((lookup (assq method-name (class/get-method-alist this))))
     (if lookup
         (cadr lookup)
         (error "method name not present in class"
                method-name (class/get-name this))))))
```

The class class's `init` method in turn invokes the object class's `init` method, using `object^init`. This is just another example of our general practice of having each class's `init` give the superclass's `init` a chance to do any initializing it needs to. As it happens, there is no initializing to do in the object class, so we simply write a place holder:

```
(class/set-method!
 object-class 'init
 (lambda (this) 'done))
```

The next two subsections address the bootstrapping problem and the question of how the `define-class` abbreviation is expanded. Other than these issues, all we have omitted from our description of the object-oriented programming system are the features used for debugging and exploration: the object class's `describe` method, the class class's overriding `describe` method, and the `show-class-hierarchy` procedure. The material above, showing how classes and objects are structured, provides the information you would need to write these debugging tools.

Exercise 14.32

Either write the debugging tools, or write English explanations of our definitions of them, which you can find in the complete version of the object-oriented programming system that is on the web site for this book.

Bootstrapping

Having thus far ignored the circularities inherent in using the object-oriented programming system to implement itself, we now are faced with the following problems:

1. The `class-class` can't possibly be made using `make-class` because what `make-class` does is to instantiate `class-class`.

2. The `object-class` can't be made using `make-class` either. Not only does the same circularity issue apply (because `make-class` would be trying to create `object-class` by instantiating one of its subclasses, `class-class`), but in addition `object-class` has no superclass.

3. Many of the getters, setters, and methods of `object-class` and `class-class` can't be obtained in the usual way, using `class/getter`, `class/setter`, and `class/method`, because of circularity problems. For example, `class/method` clearly can't be used to get the `method` method of the `class-class`, because that would mean it was being used to get itself.

   The simplest approach to the problem of creating `class-class` is simply to build it "by hand" as a 10-element vector (because there are 10 instance variables) with the appropriate contents:

```
(define class-class
  (vector 'class-class-goes-here
          'class ; name
          '()    ; subclasses
          10     ; num-ivars
          '((class 0)        ; ivar-alist (These position numbers must
            (name 1)         ; be matched by the actual positioning
            (subclasses 2)   ; of the items in this class-class vector
            (num-ivars 3)    ; as well as the ones in the object-class
            (ivar-alist 4)   ; vector below.)
            (num-methods  5)
            (method-alist 6)
            (method-vector 7)
            (method-set?-vector 8)
            (ancestry 9))
          11       ; num-methods
          '((init 0) ; method-alist
            (describe 1)
            (instantiator 2)
            (predicate 3)
            (getter 4)
            (setter 5)
            (method 6)
            (non-overridable-method 7)
            (set-method! 8)
            (ivar-position 9)
            (method-position 10))
          ;;(continued)
```

```
(make-vector 11)    ; method-vector
(make-vector 11)    ; method-set?-vector
(make-vector 2)))   ; ancestry
```

Of the 10 positions in this vector, one of them needed to be temporarily filled in with a place holder rather than the real value: Position 0 is supposed to be the class of which the object is an instance, but in the case of `class-class`, it is an instance of itself. Thus, we put the placeholder `'class-class-goes-here` in the preceding and now can fix it:

```
(unchecked-object/set-class! class-class class-class)
```

At this point, the `class-class` has been constructed, but the vectors it contains—its `method-vector`, `method-set?-vector`, and `ancestry`—still need to be filled in. We'll take care of that later.

The `object-class` can be constructed analogously:

```
(define object-class
   (vector class-class          ; class
           'object              ; name
           (list class-class)   ; subclasses
           1                    ; num-ivars
           '((class 0))         ; ivar-alist
           2                    ; num-methods
           '((init 0)           ; method-alist
             (describe 1))
           (make-vector 2)      ; method-vector
           (make-vector 2)      ; method-set?-vector
           (make-vector 1)))    ; ancestry
```

Now we can move on to the getters and setters. For these, we'll write quick-and-dirty versions of those actually needed during the bootstrapping process, and then once the bootstrapping is over, we can (re)define them all the normal way, using `class/getter` and `class/setter`. That will fill in all the ones we skipped over because they weren't needed for bootstrapping, and moreover it will replace all our quick-and-dirty versions (i.e., ones without error-checking) with the normal versions with error-checking. For example, to fill in the above two classes' ancestry vectors, we need `class/get-ancestry`, so we'll define it as follows:

```
(define class/get-ancestry (lambda (obj) (vector-ref obj 9)))
```

Note that the number 9 needs to match the position given in the instance variable alist that is part of `class-class`. The other getters and setters we need can be defined similarly.

Once these are in place, we can fill in some missing details in the classes to show that no methods have been set yet and to show the correct ancestries:

```
(vector-fill! (class/get-method-set?-vector object-class) #f)

(vector-fill! (class/get-method-set?-vector class-class) #f)

(vector-set! (class/get-ancestry object-class)
             0
             object-class)

(let ((a (class/get-ancestry class-class)))
  (vector-set! a 0 object-class)
  (vector-set! a 1 class-class))
```

Once the two fundamental classes are constructed and the necessary getters and setters are jury-rigged, we can set to work defining the various methods. However, we again run into some circularity problems. For example, we can't very well use `class/set-method!` to install itself, can we? Well, we actually can, if we do it carefully, as follows:

```
(define class/method-position ; temporary real, later replaced
  (lambda (this method-name)   ; with virtual
    (let ((lookup (assq method-name
                        (class/get-method-alist this))))
      (if lookup
          (cadr lookup)
          (error "method name not present in class"
                 method-name (class/get-name this))))))

(define class/set-method! ; temporary real, later replaced
  (lambda (this method-name method)            ; with virtual
    (let ((index (class/method-position this method-name)))
      (vector-set! (class/get-method-vector this)
                   index
                   method)
      (vector-set! (class/get-method-set?-vector this)
                   index
                   #t)
      ;;(continued)
```

```
            (apply-below this
                       (lambda (class)
                         (vector-set! (class/get-method-vector class)
                                      index
                                      method))
                       (lambda (class)
                         (not (vector-ref
                               (class/get-method-set?-vector class)
                               index)))))
         method-name))

(class/set-method! class-class 'method-position
                   class/method-position)

(class/set-method! class-class 'set-method!
                   class/set-method!)

; similarly for other methods, including class/method

(define class/method-position
  (class/method class-class 'method-position))

(define class/set-method!
  (class/method class-class 'set-method!))

; and so forth
```

You'll notice that the name `class/set-method!` is temporarily defined to be the specific real method rather than the virtual method. If we had any subclasses of `class-class` during the bootstrapping process, this definition would be a problem, but we don't. Once the bootstrapping is complete, we redefine `class/set-method!` to be the virtual method, which is obtained in the usual way.

The three preceding techniques are all it takes to get the object-oriented programming system off the ground: hand construction of the `class-class` and `object-class` vectors, hand construction of temporary versions of some getters and setters, and temporary definition of method names such as `class/set-method!` and `class/method` to be the real methods rather than the virtual ones. If you want to see all the details, such as exactly which getters and setters need to be provided by hand, you can look at the full implementation of the object-oriented programming system, which is on the web site for this book. (Or, you could work it out for yourself.)

Define-Class

At this point we have a working object-oriented programming system but not one that is very pleasant to use because for each class we need to first make the class using `make-class`, then get its instantiator using `class/instantiator`, then its predicate using `class/predicate`, and then all its getters and setters and methods.

The solution, which we employed in our earlier object-oriented programming, is to use `define-class` as an abbreviation for this tedious list of definitions. Although this is just a superficial abbreviation of many definitions by one definition, it is worth understanding, and so in this subsection we'll look at the mechanism that is used.

We can implement `define-class` using a two-step process: First the definitions for the class are computed, and then those definitions are evaluated "globally," that is, as though they had been typed in:

```
(define define-class
  (lambda (class-name superclass instvar-names method-names)
    (eval-globally
     (class-definitions
      class-name superclass instvar-names method-names))))
```

This code still leaves the problems of writing `class-definitions`, which produces the long list of definitions for a class, and `eval-globally`, which makes those definitions take effect.

To write `class-definitions`, we'll need some way of "gluing together" symbols so that we can take a class name, such as `widget` and glue `make-` onto the front to make the instantiator name `make-widget` or glue a `?` onto the end to make the predicate name `widget?` or glue `/` and the method name `activate` onto the end to make the name `widget/activate`, etc. We can write a procedure to do this gluing together, which we'll call `symbol-append`. Here are some examples of `symbol-append` in use:

```
(symbol-append 'make- 'widget)
```
make-widget

```
(symbol-append 'widget '/ 'activate)
```
widget/activate

We can write `symbol-append` in terms of some built-in procedures: `symbol->string`, for converting the symbols to strings; `string-append`, for gluing the strings together; and `string->symbol` for converting the result back into a symbol. Here is the definition:

```
(define symbol-append
  (lambda symbols
    (string->symbol
      (apply string-append
             (map symbol->string symbols)))))
```

Now that we have this tool in hand, writing **class-definitions** is simply a large amount of relatively boring list-construction code. As an example of one little piece of it, consider the following definition:

```
(define class-predicate-definition
  (lambda (class-name)
    (list 'define (symbol-append class-name '?)
          (list 'class/predicate
                (symbol-append class-name '-class)))))
```

If we apply that procedure to the class name **widget**, we get the definition that would need to be evaluated in order to define **widget?**:

```
(class-predicate-definition 'widget)
(define widget? (class/predicate widget-class))
```

All the definitions that the **define-class** is abbreviating can be produced similarly. The various definitions can then be packaged together by wrapping them in a list starting with **begin**, as in

```
(begin
  (define widget-class ...)
  (define make-widget ...)
  (define widget? ...)
  ...)
```

If you want to see the full, tedious code for generating the necessary definitions as lists, you can find it in the full version of the object-oriented programming system that is on the web site for this book. However, the previous sample should suffice to indicate the general mechanism by which **class-definitions** works.

Now that the definitions have been produced as a list structure, the remaining problem is how to make the Scheme system process those definitions; this is the job of **eval-globally**. Most Scheme systems have an **eval-globally** procedure already built in, but typically it is under a different name. For example, it might just be called **eval**, in which case all you need to do is (**define eval-globally eval**). However, the R[4]RS standard for Scheme doesn't specify any version of this procedure at all. Therefore, the system-independent version of our software takes a somewhat more roundabout approach, but one that works in nearly any

Scheme system. Namely, `eval-globally` writes the definitions out to a file called `evaltemp.scm` and then does (`load "evaltemp.scm"`) to load the file in. Because the R⁴RS standard specifies both the mechanisms necessary for writing to a file and for loading a file in, the only problem that may arise is with the choice of the filename.

As before, if you are interested in the details, we invite you to look at the definition of `eval-globally` in the full version of the object-oriented programming system that we distribute. (The web site also has versions that have been tailored to specific Scheme systems.)

14.5   An Application: Adventures in the Imaginary Land of Gack

Although object-oriented programming is now used for developing every imaginable kind of software, its historical roots are in the development of *simulation* systems, in which the software's objects are used to model the interactions between the real-world objects being simulated. Simulations are used for many practical purposes, such as studying the effectiveness of emergency preparedness plans without needing a real emergency. However, this category of software has also begotten a derivative category with no more practical purpose than having fun: *adventure games*. In an adventure game, the simulation is of a fantasy world and the characters inhabiting it. Typically the player of the game controls one character, and the others are automated. As fun as adventure games can be to play, they are nowhere near as fun to play as they are to construct because in their construction you can exercise unbounded creativity. In this section we'll give you the opportunity to exercise your own creativity in constructing a simulated world for an adventure game, using object-oriented programming as the underlying technology.

We obtained the idea of using an adventure game to illustrate object-oriented programming from Harold Abelson and Gerald Jay Sussman, who together with their colleagues at MIT developed an adventure game in Scheme for use in their course, Structure and Interpretation of Computer Programs. Their game was designed to have places and characters that would be familiar to their students at MIT, and our game started its life simply as an attempt to relocate to places and characters that would be more familiar to our own students. Since then it has evolved, both in terms of the underlying technology and, to a lesser extent, the game, to become increasingly dissimilar from the MIT game. We nonetheless owe a great debt to Abelson, Sussman, and the rest of the MIT team because the game is still recognizably theirs at heart. We use it here with their permission. We would also like to encourage others to engage in the same sort of "localization" we did; rather than just adding on to the base set of locations and characters we provide, how about completely replacing them with ones more familiar to you or more to your own imaginative taste?

Our game, which we call Adventures in the Imaginary Land of Gack, has three major components. The most important of these is a hierarchy of classes for representing people, places, and things. Subclassing is used to achieve many of the special effects of the game, for example, special kinds of automated people who behave differently than normal automated people do. The second component of the game is the particular world, the Land of Gack, which is produced simply by creating specific instances of the various classes, such as a specific automated person named Max, and establishing the relationships between them, such as positioning Max in the offices. The third and final component of the game is a user interface, which allows the player to interact with the game; this component is based on the pattern/action idea that we first introduced in the movie query system.

In contrast to most of the prior chapters' application sections, in which we've chosen to jointly develop an application program with our readers by alternating between portions we supply and exercises for the readers, in this section we present a complete version of the adventure game and then call upon you to extend it in whatever directions suit your fancy (after studying our version, which includes playing it, of course). We provide some suggestions, but they are just starting points.

The class hierarchy portion of our game can be seen in overview most easily by loading it in and then evaluating (**show-class-hierarchy**). If you do this, you'll see the following output:

```
object
    registry
    named-object
        thing
            scroll
        place
        person
            auto-person
                wizard
                witch
    class
```

We can also draw a UML class diagram of this hierarchy, as in Figure 14.1. As you can see, there are two "top-level" classes in the game: registry and named-object. The named-object class clearly plays an important role in that its subclasses are used for representing all the things, places, and persons in the simulated Land of Gack. What these have in common is that they have names. You can also see that we've provided a specialized kind of person, the auto-person, for the characters that are controlled by the program rather than by the player. These characters can all act, although some of them act differently than others. In particular, there are wizards and witches with distinctive behavior patterns. Similarly there could be things or places that behave in supernormal ways. We've left most of those possibilities unexplored (leaving them for you) but provide a simple illustration with a special kind of thing, scrolls that can be read.

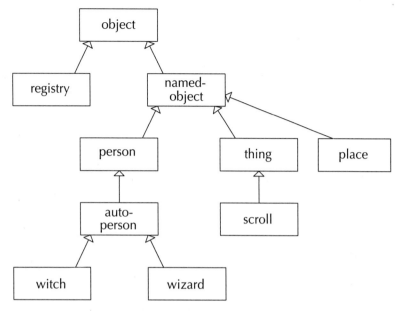

Figure 14.1   The class hierarchy for the Land of Gack

We'll return to the named-object class and its various descendants in more detail shortly, but first we should explain the one other class, the registry class. This class is used to create a single object that serves as a central registry of all the auto-persons who are roaming the Land. To preserve this property, whenever an auto-person is created, the `auto-person/init` method registers it with the registry. When an auto-person becomes no longer free to act (because a witch turned the auto-person into a frog—more on that later), the auto-person is removed from the registry. The registry is used to give all the automated characters a chance to act after each action taken by the player. This makes important use of the generic operations inherent in object-oriented programming. The registry goes down its list of auto-persons applying `auto-person/maybe-act` to each of them in a uniform way, without needing to know or care that some might be witches or wizards. Yet the appropriate kind of action is triggered in each case.

Before we continue with our description of the registry class, we really should take a moment to update our UML class diagram with the new association we have identified between the registry class and the auto-person class. While we're at it, we'll give you a sneak preview (or overview) of the remaining associations by putting them in Figure 14.2 as well. You should be able to look over the diagram and make some sense of it. For example, you can see that there is a bidirectional association between the person and thing classes, whereby each person knows the things that are its possessions, and conversely each thing knows its owner, if any. Each person also knows its place, and the place knows its contents. One new notation is used

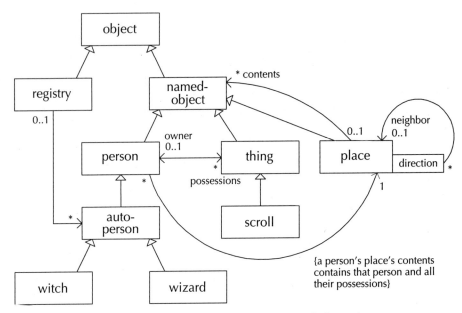

Figure 14.2   The Land of Gack class diagram, including associations

for the neighbor relationship between places. A box labeled "direction" is on the side of the place class, with an arrow back to the place class. This notation means that starting from a particular place object, and given a particular direction, we can then get to the neighboring place in that direction—except that there might not be any neighbor in that direction, a contingency we are warned of by the multiplicity of 0..1.

Having seen the overview diagram, we can look at the individual classes in more detail. To start with, let's return to the registry class. We'll give the registry methods for adding and removing an auto-person, a method for triggering all the auto-persons, and finally a method for repeatedly triggering all the auto-persons, with the repetition count specified by an argument. This last method, **trigger-times**, provides a convenient way for the game to provide variable difficulty levels because it allows for a faster-paced game in which each auto-person gets multiple opportunities to act after each action of the player. The code is as follows:

```
(define-class
  'registry
  object-class
  '(list)
  '(add
    remove
    trigger
    trigger-times))
```

```
(class/set-method!
 registry-class 'init
 (lambda (this)
   (object^init this)
   (registry/set-list! this '())))

(class/set-method!
 registry-class 'add
 (lambda (this person)
   (registry/set-list! this
                        (cons person
                              (registry/get-list this)))))

(class/set-method!
 registry-class 'remove
 (lambda (this person)
   (registry/set-list! this
                        (delq person
                              (registry/get-list this)))))

(class/set-method!
 registry-class 'trigger
 (lambda (this)
   (for-each auto-person/maybe-act
             (registry/get-list this))))

(class/set-method!
 registry-class 'trigger-times
 (lambda (this n)
   (if (> n 0)
       (begin (registry/trigger this)
              (registry/trigger-times this (- n 1)))
       'done)))
```

The **remove** method relies on a procedure called `delq`. This procedure takes an object and a list and returns a new list that looks like the old one with all occurrences of the object removed from it. We can define `delq` as follows:

```
(define delq
  (lambda (item list)
    (filter (lambda (x)
              (not (eq? x item)))
            list)))
```

Now we can move on to the named-object class and its descendants, which are used to model persons, places, and things from the Land of Gack. These objects use instance variables to keep track of their relationships; for example, a person has a list of the things it possesses. Because each thing also has an instance variable recording the person who owns it, this portion of the game also provides a good reinforcement of the importance of representation invariants as always-preserved *consistency conditions*. Clearly one invariant property must be that the person objects' possession lists and the things' owner instance variables remain in agreement; whenever the owner of a thing is changed, the thing must be removed from one person's list of possessions and added to the other's. Similar considerations apply elsewhere in the design as well. For example, each person object knows what place the person is in, and each place knows what persons (and things) are in it.

We maintain these consistency constraints by identifying one of the partners in each relationship as being "in charge." In particular, we will designate persons as being in charge of the things they own and places they are in. Therefore when a person takes or loses a thing, it will tell the thing to change its owner, and when a person moves from place to place, it will tell the places to update their lists of contents. The reverse arrangement would have also been possible, in which (for example) when a thing changed its owner, it told the persons involved to update their lists of possessions. However, having decided which object is in charge, we simply need to initiate all changes through that object, leaving it to update the subordinate partner object.

The named-object class itself is quite simple because it captures only the notion that the object has a name, which can potentially be changed:

```
(define-class
  'named-object
  object-class
  '(name)
  '(name
    change-name))

(class/set-method!
 named-object-class 'init
 (lambda (this name)
   (object^init this)
   (named-object/set-name! this name)))

(class/set-method!
 named-object-class 'name
 (lambda (this)
   (named-object/get-name this)))
```

```
(class/set-method!
 named-object-class 'change-name
 (lambda (this new-name)
   (named-object/set-name! this new-name)))
```

Of the subclasses of `named-object-class`, the simplest is the class for things because all that distinguishes a plain thing (other than its name) is who owns it. The owner is normally a person object but can also be the symbol `no-one`, in which case the `owned?` predicate returns false. Initially a thing is owned by no one, but it can become owned by a person or become unowned again:

```
(define-class
   'thing
   named-object-class
   '(owner)
   '(owned?
     owner
     become-unowned
     become-owned-by))

(class/set-method!
 thing-class 'init
 (lambda (this name)
   (named-object^init this name)
   (thing/set-owner! this 'no-one)))

(class/set-method!
 thing-class 'owned?
 (lambda (this)
   (not (equal? (thing/owner this)
                'no-one))))

(class/set-method!
 thing-class 'owner
 (lambda (this)
   (thing/get-owner this)))

(class/set-method!
 thing-class 'become-unowned
 (lambda (this)
   (thing/set-owner! this 'no-one)))
```

```
(class/set-method!
 thing-class 'become-owned-by
 (lambda (this person)
   (thing/set-owner! this person)))
```

A scroll is simply a thing that can be read. (Its name is the title of the scroll.) A normal scroll is pretty boring to read, but we are including scrolls in the game primarily so that you can add subclasses that behave more interestingly when read. Here is the scroll class:

```
(define-class
  'scroll
  thing-class
  '()
  '(be-read))

(class/set-method!
 scroll-class 'init
 (lambda (this title)
   (thing^init this title)))

(class/set-method!
 scroll-class 'be-read
 (lambda (this)
   (let ((owner (scroll/owner this))
         (title (scroll/name this)))
     (if (scroll/owned? this)
         (person/say owner
                     (list "I have read" title))
         (display-message (list "No one has" title))))))
```

As you can see, although normal scrolls may not do anything very exciting when read, even the little that they do accomplish requires some moderately interesting machinery. In particular, we have a good example of an object's method invoking a method on a related object—the scroll asks its owner to say that he or she has read the scroll. That way, if some people have unusual ways of speaking, when they read a scroll, they will report having done so in their own peculiar way. Because only a scroll's owner is allowed to read it, we report any attempt to read an unowned scroll. This reporting is done using a **display-message** procedure that takes a list of items (such as strings or symbols) to display; it is defined as follows:

```
(define display-message
  (lambda (list-of-stuff)
    (newline)
    (for-each (lambda (s) (display s) (display " "))
              list-of-stuff)))
```

The place class represents the places in the Land of Gack, or "rooms" as they are frequently called by adventure gamers, whether they are actually rooms or not. Each place has a list of contents, which are the things and persons that are at the place, and has the ability to gain or lose such an item (when they arrive or leave). Each place also has a `neighbor-map`, which is a list of pairs used as an association list, associating each exit direction with the neighboring place in that direction. For example, if a pair in the list has the symbol `up` as its car, the cdr is the place object that one would arrive at by going up. This information regarding the spatial connections between places can be accessed via a number of different methods. The `exits` method simply returns the list of valid direction symbols (such as `up`). The `neighbors` method, in contrast, supplies a list of the actual neighboring places. Finally, one can determine which neighbor is in a particular direction using `neighbor-towards` or add a new neighbor in a particular direction using `add-new-neighbor`. The class and its methods are as follows:

```
(define-class
  'place
  named-object-class
  '(neighbor-map ; pairs: car = direction, cdr = neighbor
    contents)     ; people and things
  '(exits
    neighbors
    neighbor-towards
    add-new-neighbor
    gain
    lose
    contents))

(class/set-method!
 place-class 'init
 (lambda (this name)
   (named-object^init this name)
   (place/set-neighbor-map! this '())
   (place/set-contents! this '())))
```

```
(class/set-method!
 place-class 'exits
 (lambda (this)
   (map car (place/get-neighbor-map this))))

(class/set-method!
 place-class 'neighbors
 (lambda (this)
   (map cdr (place/get-neighbor-map this))))

(class/set-method!
 place-class 'neighbor-towards
 (lambda (this direction)
   (let ((p (assq direction
                  (place/get-neighbor-map this))))
     (if (not p)
         #f
         (cdr p)))))

(class/set-method!
 place-class 'add-new-neighbor
 (lambda (this direction new-neighbor)
   (let ((neighbor-map (place/get-neighbor-map this)))
     (if (assq direction neighbor-map)
         (display-message
          (list "there is already a neighbor"
                direction
                "from"
                (place/name this)))
         (place/set-neighbor-map! this
                                  (cons (cons direction
                                              new-neighbor)
                                        neighbor-map))))))

(class/set-method!
 place-class 'gain
 (lambda (this new-item)
   (let ((contents (place/contents this)))
     (if (memq new-item contents)
         (display-message
          (list (named-object/name new-item)
                ;;(continued)
```

```
                            "is already at"
                            (place/name this)))
                  (place/set-contents! this
                                  (cons new-item contents))))))))

(class/set-method!
 place-class 'lose
 (lambda (this item)
   (let ((contents (place/contents this)))
     (if (not (memq item contents))
         (display-message
          (list (named-object/name item)
                "is not at"
                (place/name this)))
         (place/set-contents! this
                         (delq item contents)))))))

(class/set-method!
 place-class 'contents
 (lambda (this)
   (place/get-contents this)))
```

The most interesting of the various kinds of named objects are the persons. They
have a variety of methods intended for internal use within the game but also methods
that, in effect, are directly used by the human player of the game. Strictly speaking,
these are used by the user interface component of the game. For example, when
the player types in to the user interface the command (go north), the effect is the
same as if the user had evaluated the expression (person/go player 'north),
although actually the user interface evaluated it on the user's behalf.

The person class and its methods follow. The methods make use of a utility
procedure that we define afterward, verbalize-list, which turns a list of items into
a spoken form by inserting "and" between consecutive words and using a specified
replacement if there are no items. In reading the methods below, remember that the
person class is "in charge" of its reciprocal relationships with things and places and
hence needs to keep those up to date. The code is as follows:

```
(define-class
  'person
  named-object-class
  '(place
    possessions)
  ;;(continued)
```

```
'(say
  look-around
  list-possessions
  read
  have-fit
  move-to
  go
  take
  lose
  place
  possessions
  greet
  other-people-at-same-place))

(class/set-method!
 person-class 'init
 (lambda (this name place)
   (named-object^init this name)
   (person/set-place! this place)
   (person/set-possessions! this '())
   (place/gain place this)))

(class/set-method!
 person-class 'say
 (lambda (this list-of-stuff)
   (let ((name (person/name this))
         (place (person/place this)))
     (let ((place-name (place/name place)))
       (display-message
        (append (list "At" place-name ":" name "says --")
                list-of-stuff))))))

(class/set-method!
 person-class 'look-around
 (lambda (this)
   (let ((place (person/place this)))
     (let ((other-items
             (map named-object/name
                  (delq this
                        (place/contents place))))
           (exits (place/exits place)))
       ;;(continued)
```

```
              (person/say this
                         (append '("I see")
                                 (verbalize-list other-items "nothing")
                                 '("and can go")
                                 (verbalize-list exits "nowhere")))))))

(class/set-method!
 person-class 'list-possessions
 (lambda (this)
   (let ((stuff (map thing/name
                     (person/possessions this))))
     (person/say
      this
      (append '("I have")
              (verbalize-list stuff "nothing"))))))

(class/set-method!
 person-class 'read
 (lambda (this scroll)
   (if (eq? this (scroll/owner scroll))
       (scroll/be-read scroll)
       (display-message
        (list (person/name this)
              "does not have"
              (scroll/name scroll))))))

(class/set-method!
 person-class 'have-fit
 (lambda (this)
   (person/say this '("Yaaaah! I am upset!"))))

(class/set-method!
 person-class 'move-to
 (lambda (this new-place)
   (let ((name (person/name this))
         (old-place (person/place this))
         (possessions (person/possessions this)))
     (display-message
      (list name "moves from" (place/name old-place)
            "to" (place/name new-place)))
     (place/lose old-place this)
     ;;(continued)
```

```
                (place/gain new-place this)
                (for-each (lambda (p)
                            (place/lose old-place p)
                            (place/gain new-place p))
                          possessions)
                (person/set-place! this new-place)
                (person/greet this
                            (person/other-people-at-same-place this)))))

(class/set-method!
 person-class 'go
 (lambda (this direction)
   (let ((old-place (person/place this)))
     (let ((new-place (place/neighbor-towards
                        old-place
                        direction)))
       (if new-place
           (person/move-to this new-place)
           (display-message
            (list "you cannot go" direction "from"
                  (place/name old-place))))))))

(class/set-method!
 person-class 'take
 (lambda (this thing)
   (if (eq? this (thing/owner thing))
       (display-message
        (list (person/name this) "already has" (thing/name thing)))
       (begin
         (if (thing/owned? thing)
             (let ((owner (thing/owner thing)))
               (person/lose owner thing)
               (person/have-fit owner))
             'unowned)
         (thing/become-owned-by thing this)
         (person/set-possessions!
          this
          (cons thing (person/possessions this)))
         (person/say
          this
          (list "I take" (thing/name thing)))))))
```

```scheme
(class/set-method!
 person-class 'lose
 (lambda (this thing)
   (if (not (eq? this (thing/owner thing)))
       (display-message (list (person/name this) "doesn't have"
                              (thing/name thing)))
       (begin
         (thing/become-unowned thing)
         (person/set-possessions!
          this
          (delq thing (person/possessions this)))
         (person/say
          this
          (list "I lose" (thing/name thing)))))))

(class/set-method!
 person-class 'place
 (lambda (this)
   (person/get-place this)))

(class/set-method!
 person-class 'possessions
 (lambda (this)
   (person/get-possessions this)))

(class/set-method!
 person-class 'greet
 (lambda (this people)
   (if (not (null? people))
       (person/say this
                   (cons "Hi"
                         (verbalize-list
                          (map person/name people)
                          "no one")))
       'no-one-to-greet)))

(class/set-method!
 person-class 'other-people-at-same-place
 (lambda (this)
   (delq this
         (filter person?
                 (place/contents (person/place this))))))
```

The `verbalize-list` utility procedure used by the `person` class is as follows:

```
(define verbalize-list
  (lambda (items none-word)
    (define loop
      (lambda (items)
        (if (null? (cdr items))
            items
            (cons (car items)
                  (cons "and"
                        (loop (cdr items)))))))
    (if (null? items)
        (list none-word)
        (loop items))))
```

The player of the game controls a normal person, but all the remaining characters are automatically triggered by the registry and so are instances—at least indirectly—of the auto-person class. What distinguishes the auto-person class is that it has a method `maybe-act` for use by the registry. Each auto-person has some frequency with which it acts that is controlled using a threshold to which its "restlessness" has to rise before it acts. Each time the `maybe-act` method is invoked, it checks to see if the threshold has been reached, and if not, increases the restlessness by 1. When the restlessness reaches the threshold, the `maybe-act` method in turn invokes the `act` method, to trigger the automated person's behavior, and then resets the restlessness to zero. Normal auto-persons `act` by moving to a randomly chosen adjoining room, but there are subclasses that have more interesting `act` methods. The auto-person class and its methods are given below; note that the auto-person is in charge of its relationship with the registry.

```
(define-class
  'auto-person
  person-class
  '(threshold
    restlessness)
  '(maybe-act
    act))
```

```
(class/set-method!
 auto-person-class 'init
 (lambda (this name place threshold)
   (person^init this name place)
   ;;(continued)
```

```
(auto-person/set-threshold! this threshold)
(auto-person/set-restlessness! this 0)
(registry/add registry this)))

(class/set-method!
 auto-person-class 'maybe-act
 (lambda (this)
   (let ((threshold (auto-person/get-threshold this))
         (restlessness (auto-person/get-restlessness this)))
     (if (< restlessness threshold)
         (auto-person/set-restlessness! this
                                        (+ 1 restlessness))
         (begin (auto-person/act this)
                (auto-person/set-restlessness! this 0))))))

(class/set-method!
 auto-person-class 'act
 (lambda (this)
   (let ((new-place (random-element
                      (place/neighbors
                       (auto-person/place this)))))
     (if new-place
         (auto-person/move-to this new-place)))))

(define random-element
  (lambda (list)
    (if (null? list)
        #f
        (list-ref list (random (length list))))))
```

We've provided two subclasses of the **auto-person-class** with more interesting act methods. The witch class has the special behavior that when there is someone else in the room with the witch when she acts, she curses the person. (Otherwise she acts just like any other auto-person.) The wizard, on the other hand, is basically a scroll collector. The two classes, with their methods, follow:

```
(define-class
  'witch
  auto-person-class
  '()
  '(curse))
```

```scheme
(class/set-method!
 witch-class 'act
 (lambda (this)
   (let ((victim (random-element
                   (witch/other-people-at-same-place this))))
     (if victim
         (witch/curse this victim)
         (auto-person^act this)))))

(class/set-method!
 witch-class 'curse
 (lambda (this person)
   (let ((person-name (person/name person)))
     (person/say this
                 (list
                   "Hah hah hah, I'm going to turn you into a frog"
                   person-name))
     (turn-into-frog person)
     (person/say this
                 (list "Hee hee" person-name
                       "looks better in green!")))))

(define turn-into-frog
  (lambda (person)
    (for-each (lambda (item) (person/lose person item))
              (person/possessions person))
    (person/say person '("Ribbitt!"))
    (person/move-to person pond)
    (registry/remove registry person)))

(define-class
  'wizard
  auto-person-class
  '()
  '())

(class/set-method!
 wizard-class 'act
 (lambda (this)
   (let ((place (wizard/place this)))
     (let ((scrolls (filter scroll?
                            (place/contents place))))
```

```
(if (and (not (null? scrolls))
         (not (eq? place chamber-of-wizards)))
    (begin
      (wizard/take this (car scrolls))
      (wizard/move-to this chamber-of-wizards)
      (wizard/lose this (car scrolls)))
    (auto-person^act this))))))
```

At this point we have the entire class hierarchy for the Land of Gack—or rather, the entire class hierarchy, as far as we've developed it for you. After you've played (and become bored with) the existing game, you'll be expected to invent new kinds of characters, new and magical scrolls and other kinds of things, and maybe even enchanted places that behave in unusual ways.

The next major component of the game, you will recall, is simply the "setting of the stage": in other words, the establishment of the specific individuals, places, and things that constitute the Land of Gack. For example, this is where we decide that the Land of Gack has (initially) only a single witch, named Barbara:

```
;; The "registry" is an object that keeps track of all
;; the auto-person objects that need to be given an
;; opportunity to act.

(define registry (make-registry))

;; Here we define the places in the imaginary world of Gack

(define food-service (make-place 'food-service))
(define PO (make-place 'PO))
(define alumni-hall (make-place 'alumni-hall))
(define chamber-of-wizards (make-place 'chamber-of-wizards))
(define library (make-place 'library))
(define good-ship-olin (make-place 'good-ship-olin))
(define lounge (make-place 'lounge))
(define computer-lab (make-place 'computer-lab))
(define offices (make-place 'offices))
(define dormitory (make-place 'dormitory))
(define pond (make-place 'pond))

;; One-way paths connect individual places in the world.

(place/add-new-neighbor food-service 'down PO)
(place/add-new-neighbor PO 'south alumni-hall)
```

```scheme
(place/add-new-neighbor alumni-hall 'north food-service)
(place/add-new-neighbor alumni-hall 'east chamber-of-wizards)
(place/add-new-neighbor alumni-hall 'west library)
(place/add-new-neighbor chamber-of-wizards 'west alumni-hall)
(place/add-new-neighbor chamber-of-wizards 'south dormitory)
(place/add-new-neighbor dormitory 'north chamber-of-wizards)
(place/add-new-neighbor dormitory 'west good-ship-olin)
(place/add-new-neighbor library 'east alumni-hall)
(place/add-new-neighbor library 'south good-ship-olin)
(place/add-new-neighbor good-ship-olin 'north library)
(place/add-new-neighbor good-ship-olin 'east dormitory)
(place/add-new-neighbor good-ship-olin 'up lounge)
(place/add-new-neighbor lounge 'west computer-lab)
(place/add-new-neighbor lounge 'south offices)
(place/add-new-neighbor computer-lab 'east lounge)
(place/add-new-neighbor offices 'north lounge)

;; We define persons as follows:

;; We've chosen to define max-the-person rather than
;; redefining max, which is predefined in Scheme to
;; be a procedure for finding the largest of its numeric
;; arguments.
(define max-the-person
  (make-auto-person 'max offices 2))

(define karl
  (make-auto-person 'karl computer-lab 4))

(define barbara
  (make-witch 'barbara offices 3))

(define elvee
  (make-wizard 'elvee chamber-of-wizards 1))

(define player
  (make-person 'player dormitory))

;; and now we'll strew some scrolls around:

(define scroll-of-enlightenment
  (make-scroll 'scroll-of-enlightenment))
(place/gain library scroll-of-enlightenment)
```

```
(for-each (lambda (title)
            (place/gain library
                        (make-scroll title)))
          '(crime-and-punishment war-and-peace
                                 iliad
                                 collected-works-of-rilke))

(define unix-programmers-manual
  (make-scroll 'unix-programmers-manual))
(place/gain computer-lab unix-programmers-manual)

(define next-users-reference
  (make-scroll 'next-users-reference))
(place/gain computer-lab next-users-reference)
```

Finally, we need a user interface for the game so that the player can say things like
(go north) instead of (person/go player 'north), as you would have to do to
play from the normal read-eval-print loop. The user interface also makes the game
more fun by triggering the registry after each move to give the automated persons
a chance to do their things. The user interface is entered via the `play` procedure,
by simply evaluating (play). This procedure is based on the pattern/action-list idea
we've seen in earlier chapters. Each command you can execute has a particular
pattern. For example, the pattern for commands like (go north) and (go up) is
(go _).

One additional kind of pattern has been added, beyond those described in Chapter 7. A pattern can contain not only symbols and wild cards but also predicate
procedures. For example, the pattern for commands for taking things is made using
the expression (list 'take thing?), which makes a pattern rather like (take _),
except that the word after `take` is restricted to be the name of a thing that is in the
place where the player is. The requirement that the object satisfies the predicate (as
well as has the right name and is nearby) prevents you from committing kidnaping
by saying (take max), because Max is not a thing. A similar pattern, made using
(list 'read scroll?), ensures that you can only read scrolls, not other kinds of
things or people. These predicate wild cards also behave specially once it has been
determined that the pattern matches, and the action procedure is being applied. For
example, suppose you are in the library with the `scroll-of-enlightenment` and
you say (take scroll-of-enlightenment). The pattern matches, because the
scroll is a thing, has the right name, and is in the same place as the player. Now
the action procedure is applied. However, rather than being applied to the name
`scroll-of-enlightenment`, the way it would if the pattern were (take _), the
action procedure is instead applied to the scroll object itself.

The code for the user interface is as follows:

```
(define difficulty 1)

(define play
  (lambda ()
    (define loop
      (lambda ()
        (newline)
        (let ((user-input (read)))
          (if (equal? user-input '(quit))
              'done
              (begin
                (respond-to-using user-input gack-p/a-list)
                (loop))))))
    (newline)
    (display "Enter your name, using one word only, please.")
    (newline)
    (person/change-name player (read))
    (display-message
     (list "OK," (person/name player)
           "enter your commands one by one"
           "as scheme lists; to get help enter (help)."))
    (loop)))


(define gack-p/a-list
  (list (make-pattern/action '(help)
                             (lambda ()
                               (newline)
                               (display "Possibilities:")
                               (newline)
                               (for-each (lambda (command)
                                           (display " ")
                                           (display command)
                                           (newline))
                                         '((help)
                                           (quit)
                                           (drop thing)
                                           (lose thing)
                                           (take thing)
                                           ;;(continued)
```

```
                                        (go direction)
                                        (read scroll)
                                        (inventory)
                                        (list possessions)
                                        (look)
                                        (look around)
                                        (say ...)))
                              (newline)))
(make-pattern/action (list '(drop lose) thing?)
                     (lambda (verb thing)
                       (person/lose player thing)
                       (registry/trigger-times
                        registry difficulty)))
(make-pattern/action (list 'take thing?)
                     (lambda (thing)
                       (person/take player thing)
                       (registry/trigger-times
                        registry difficulty)))
(make-pattern/action '(go _)
                     (lambda (direction)
                       (person/go player direction)
                       (registry/trigger-times
                        registry difficulty)))
(make-pattern/action (list 'read scroll?)
                     (lambda (scroll)
                       (person/read player scroll)
                       (registry/trigger-times
                        registry difficulty)))
(make-pattern/action '(inventory)
                     (lambda ()
                       (person/list-possessions player)
                       (registry/trigger-times
                        registry difficulty)))
(make-pattern/action '(list possessions)
                     (lambda ()
                       (person/list-possessions player)
                       (registry/trigger-times
                        registry difficulty)))
(make-pattern/action '(look)
                     (lambda ()
                       (person/look-around player)))
;;(continued)
```

```
                    (make-pattern/action '(look around)
                                (lambda ()
                                  (person/look-around player)))
              (make-pattern/action '(say ...)
                                (lambda (stuff)
                                  (person/say player stuff)
                                  (registry/trigger-times
                                   registry difficulty)))))

(define respond-to-using
  (lambda (command p/a-list)
    (cond ((null? p/a-list)
           (display-message '("I don't understand.")))
          ((matches? (pattern (car p/a-list)) command)
           (apply (action (car p/a-list))
                  (substitutions-in-to-match
                   (pattern (car p/a-list))
                   command)))
          (else (respond-to-using command (cdr p/a-list))))))

;; The versions of matches? and substitutions-in-to-match
;; given below not only are after doing various chapter 7
;; exercises, but moreover have an additional feature that a
;; predicate can be used as one of the components of a pattern,
;; in which case it means that at that position in the command,
;; a symbol is needed that is the name of an item in the player's
;; place that satisfies the predicate.

(define matches?
  (lambda (pattern question)
    (cond ((null? pattern)  (null? question))
          ((not (pair? question)) #f)
          ((equal? (car pattern) '_)
           (matches? (cdr pattern) (cdr question)))
          ((list? (car pattern))
           (if (member (car question) (car pattern))
               (matches? (cdr pattern)
                         (cdr question))
               #f))
          ((equal? (car pattern) '...) #t)
          ;;(continued)
```

```
         ((equal? (car pattern) (car question))
          (matches? (cdr pattern)
                    (cdr question)))
         ((procedure? (car pattern))
          (let ((object (object-with-name (car question))))
            (if (and object
                     ((car pattern) object))
                (matches? (cdr pattern)
                          (cdr question))
                #f)))
         (else #f)))))

(define substitutions-in-to-match
  (lambda (pattern question)
    (cond ((null? pattern)
           (if (null? question)
               '()
               (error
                "substitutions-in-to-match without a match")))
          ((not (pair? question))
           (error "substitutions-in-to-match without a match"))
          ((equal? (car pattern) '_)
           (cons (car question)
                 (substitutions-in-to-match (cdr pattern)
                                            (cdr question))))
          ((list? (car pattern))
           (if (member (car question) (car pattern))
               (cons (car question)
                     (substitutions-in-to-match (cdr pattern)
                                                (cdr question)))
               (error
                "substitutions-in-to-match without a match")))
          ((equal? (car pattern) '...) (list question))
          ((equal? (car pattern) (car question))
           (substitutions-in-to-match (cdr pattern)
                                      (cdr question)))
          ;;(continued)
```

```
              ((procedure? (car pattern))
               (let ((object (object-with-name (car question))))
                 (if (and object
                          ((car pattern) object))
                     (cons object
                           (substitutions-in-to-match
                             (cdr pattern) (cdr question)))
                     (error
                       "substitutions-in-to-match without a match"))))
              (else (error
                      "substitutions-in-to-match without a match")))))

  (define object-with-name
    (lambda (name)
      (let ((objects (filter (lambda (obj)
                               (equal? (named-object/name obj)
                                       name))
                             (place/contents
                               (person/place player)))))
        (if (or (null? objects)
                (not (null? (cdr objects))))
            #f
            (car objects)))))
```

Now it is time for you to take charge of the game.

Exercise 14.33

First you'll need to familiarize yourself with the game. Load it and try playing the following simple game, using the (play) procedure. Try to get from the dormitory to the computer lab without getting turned into a frog along the way. To make it more challenging, try to get to the lab possessing the scroll of enlightenment. If you want, you can make the other characters move several times after each move of yours (rather than just once) by redefining difficulty to be some number larger than 1. Be sure to get familiar with the game's other features too.

Exercise 14.34

Modify the Land of Gack so that there is a new scroll, called late-lab-report, in the dormitory. Now you can play the game with a new goal: Pick up the late-lab-report, go catch up with max, wherever he may have wandered to, and try to give `max` the report even though it's late. You'll need to add some additional mechanisms to the person class and the interface's pattern/action list to be able to use a command like (`give max late-lab-report`) or (`give late-lab-report to max`). Verify that at the end the lab report thinks `max` is its owner, `max` thinks the lab report is one of his possessions, and `player` no longer thinks the lab report is one of its possessions.

■ **Exercise 14.35**

Of course, you can make the game much more interesting by adding additional twists. Implement some that interest you. We give a list of suggestions below but feel free to come up with some of your own. Be sure to describe in English whatever new ideas you introduce.

- Add chocolate as a kind of thing. It should be able to `be-eaten`. When a chocolate is eaten, the owner loses it and it is gone from the place where the owner is located. You can optionally add cute sound effects or make a wrapper or some crumbs appear at the place. Make some chocolates appear at `food-service`.
- Modify the person class so people have an `eat` method that causes a chocolate they own to be eaten, much like the `read` method.
- Now that we have chocolates, we can modify the witch class to reflect a little-known property of witches: They can be bought off with chocolates. Change the `act` method so that if Barbara's victim has any chocolates, Barbara will take and eat one rather than turning the victim into a frog. Only victims who possess no chocolates will become frogs. This makes the game more interesting in that you have to decide whether to take the extra time to make a detour to food service for chocolates or go for speed but risk being caught unprepared by Barbara.
- If you want to make the game harder yet, you can make it difficult to hoard protective chocolates by creating a troll who wanders around eating chocolates. Perhaps you should change Max from being a normal person to being the troll—it was probably just the fact that he wrote this section that kept him from being cast as a troll in the first place.
- Introduce magic scrolls into the game as an abstract subclass of `scroll-class` that has a limited number of "charges" (let's say n) and when read the first n times invokes its `do-magic` method. Define one or more specific kinds of magic scrolls as subclasses of the magic-scroll class with interesting `do-magic` methods; for example, you might make a `scroll-of-teleportation`.
- It makes the game rather easy if the title of a magic scroll tells what it does. You could add a feature so that initially the `name` method of any magic scroll just returns `a-mysterious-scroll`, but when you read the scroll the first time the name changes to the actual title. This feature is particularly effective if you

include scrolls with undesirable effects as well as desirable ones. Of course, you could counter by including a scroll-of-identification that can be used to decode the titles.

▪ Currently Elvee, the wizard, always takes the first scroll at a place. Because some scrolls are more valuable than others, this action can make the game boring. Change the definition of the wizard class so wizards choose a scroll to take at random.

▪ Feel free to add you own interesting kinds of people, places and things.

Review Problems

▷ **Exercise 14.36**

If you apply `object/describe` to most objects, you'll see the instance variables that constitute the object. On the other hand, if you apply `object/describe` to a class object (such as `item-class`), you'll instead see a description of the class that the object represents, with detailed information such as the ancestor class from which it inherits each inherited instance variable, method name, or method implementation. How can you get a description of a class object that shows the actual instance variables of the class object? (For example, the description should make the `method-set?-vector` instance variable visible.)

▷ **Exercise 14.37**

a. Write a procedure that returns a list of all the classes currently in existence. (It should return the actual class objects, not the names of the classes.) *Hint:* See the definition of `show-class-hierarchy` and also the material on tree traversal in Chapter 8.

b. Write a predicate procedure that tests whether a given class has a given method name.

c. Write a procedure, using the previous two, that returns a list of the class names for all those classes in existence that have a given method name.

▷ **Exercise 14.38**

In Section 13.5, we built a layered collection of data types: `ranked-binary-trees`, `binary-search-trees`, and `red-black-trees`. This layering is suggestive of object-oriented programming's class hierarchy; we can imagine having `ranked-binary-tree` as a base class, with `binary-search-tree` derived from it as a subclass, and `red-black tree` derived further as a subclass of binary search tree.

On closer examination, no reason exists to have *ranked* binary trees as the base. After all, the notion of rank only becomes relevant when we build the red-black tree abstraction. In Section 13.5, we had to include the ranks from the beginning because only the procedures for operating on the trees changed from layer to layer; the data representation stayed the same. Now with object-oriented programming, we can add a new instance variable in a subclass rather than just adding new procedures (methods).

Reimplement red-black trees in the object-oriented programming system. Start with a base class that is just plain binary trees, without ranks. Then build the binary search tree class as a subclass. Finally, implement red-black trees as a subclass of binary search trees, which is where you'll add the rank instance variable.

Exercise 14.39

When a method is overridden in a subclass, the new implementation should comply with whatever the external specification of the method is so that users are not surprised. For example, it would not be appropriate for a kind of item (in the compu-duds example) to implement the `display` method by switching to a new randomly selected color rather than by actually displaying the item's description and price. On the other hand, the specification will no doubt have some flexibility in it; for example, we haven't pinned down exactly what sort of "description" should be displayed because if we were too precise about that, there would be no room to accommodate different kinds of subclasses.

One interesting point is that depending which of several potential specifications the designer chooses to articulate for a particular class and its methods, the exact same subclass of that class might be either "in compliance" or "out of compliance" with the specification, even though the specifications might all be reasonable for the original class.

Give a concrete illustration of this phenomenon by defining a class and its subclass and giving two reasonable specifications for the superclass, one of which leads to the subclass being compliant and the other of which doesn't. Also, write up some thoughts on the subject of how a software designer should anticipate and cope with this phenomenon.

Exercise 14.40

Suppose you wanted to change the Land of Gack so that it was possible to ask people to introduce themselves; that is, you could do the following:

```
(person/introduce-self barbara)
```

or

```
(person/introduce-self max-the-person)
```

or

```
(person/introduce-self elvee)
```

Whoever you ask to introduce themselves would then say

Hello, I'm barbara.
I'm known to be fond of chocolate and turning people into frogs.
Pleased to meet you.

or

Hello, I'm max.
Pleased to meet you.

or

Hello, I'm elvee.
I've got this problem with scrolls.
Pleased to meet you.

Note that the first and last lines are similar for all people, but what comes in between (if anything) is particular to the given subclass of **person-class**. How would you arrange for this dialogue in a way that takes full advantage of the class hierarchy? Illustrate with sample code.

▷ Exercise 14.41

In Exercise 14.34, you added to the Land of Gack the ability to give a scroll to someone else. There the intent was to give the late lab report to Max. However, you probably made the mechanism general enough that you could also give a scroll to the wizard, Elvee. If you do this, you may later see Elvee (when he acts) trying to take a scroll that he already has, which results in a message reporting this oddity. Explain how this occurs and what can be done to eliminate this behavior.

▷ Exercise 14.42

When a person says something in the Land of Gack, it is "heard" only by the player, in that whatever is said gets displayed. It would be more interesting if other objects within the Land of Gack itself could also hear—and potentially respond to—what was said. That way you could have characters who behaved differently if you said "please," magic portals that opened when you said "open sesame," etc.

a. Add a method called `named-object/hear` that takes two arguments: the person speaking and what was said. Put an implementation in the `named-object-class` that does nothing because ordinary objects ignore what they hear.

b. Change the `person/say` method so that it invokes the `named-object/hear` method of each object in the place where the person is speaking.

c. Now have fun introducing special classes of object that respond to what they hear.

▷ **Exercise 14.43**

Write a procedure `instance-of?` that can be used to test whether a particular object is an instance of a particular class. Examples of its use follow:

```
(instance-of? barbara witch-class)
#t

(instance-of? barbara person-class)
#t

(instance-of? barbara place-class)
#f

(instance-of? lounge place-class)
#t
```

Chapter Inventory

Vocabulary

object-oriented programming	multiplicity
class	class object
class hierarchy	instance variable
object-oriented design	inherit
subclass	method
superclass	method name
object	method implementation
instance	override
derived class	getter
base class	this or self
ancestry	setter
Unified Modeling Language (UML)	instantiator
class diagram	public
association	private

garbage collection
augment (the superclass's method)
abstract class
pure abstract class
bootstrapping
role (in a UML association)
virtual method

constraint (on a UML association)
association list
alist
simulation
adventure game
consistency condition

Classes

```
item-class
item-list-class
oxford-shirt-class
chinos-class
object-class
class-class
special-item-class
pants-class
thrifty-item-list-class
item-list-as-vector-class
item-list-as-list-class
registry-class
```

```
named-object-class
thing-class
place-class
person-class
auto-person-class
wizard-class
witch-class
scroll-class
chocolate-class
troll-class
magic-scroll-class
```

New Predefined Scheme Names

```
assq
string-append
load
```

Methods

```
item-list/add
item-list/display
item-list/total-price
item-list/delete
item-list/choose
item-list/empty?
item/input-specifics
item/display
item/revise-specifics
item/price
class/set-method!
object/init
item-list/init
object/describe
```

```
item-list/grow
item/init
special-item/input-specifics
oxford-shirt/init
oxford-shirt/display
oxford-shirt/input-specifics
chinos/init
chinos/display
chinos/input-specifics
class/predicate
class/instantiator
class/getter
class/setter
class/method
```

```
class/non-overridable-method        place/gain
class/ivar-position                 place/lose
class/method-position               place/contents
auto-person/init                    person/init
auto-person/maybe-act               person/say
registry/init                       person/look-around
registry/add                        person/list-possessions
registry/remove                     person/read
registry/trigger                    person/have-fit
registry/trigger-times              person/move-to
named-object/init                   person/go
named-object/name                   person/take
named-object/change-name            person/lose
thing/owned?                        person/place
thing/init                          person/possessions
thing/owner                         person/greet
thing/become-unowned                person/other-people-at-same-place
thing/become-owned-by               auto-person/act
scroll/init                         witch/act
scroll/be-read                      witch/curse
place/exits                         wizard/act
place/neighbors                     chocolate/be-eaten
place/neighbor-towards              person/eat
place/add-new-neighbor              magic-scroll/do-magic
place/init                          magic-scroll/name
```

Objects From the Land of Gack

```
registry                            pond
food-service                        max-the-person
PO                                  karl
alumni-hall                         barbara
chamber-of-wizards                  elvee
library                             player
good-ship-olin                      scroll-of-enlightenment
lounge                              unix-programmers-manual
computer-lab                        next-users-reference
offices                             late-lab-report
dormitory
```

Other Scheme Names Defined in This Chapter

define-class	eval-globally
vector-copy!	symbol-append
display-price	class-predicate-definition
input-integer-in-range	delq
input-selection	display-message
compu-duds	verbalize-list
input-item	turn-into-frog
show-class-hierarchy	play
unchecked-object/set-class!	difficulty
apply-below	gack-p/a-list
alist-from-onto	respond-to-using
class-definitions	object-with-name

Notes

One version of the MIT adventure game we based ours on was published in [1].

We touched only briefly on the design of object-oriented software, emphasizing the search for nouns in the problem statement as potential classes of objects and verbs and implicit operations as potential methods. Books such as those of Rumbaugh [44] and Booch [7] provide a much more extensive treatment of these issues of analyzing a problem, modeling it in terms of objects, and designing the software. Another important approach, complementing the finding of "natural objects" in the problem specification, is the recognition of common patterns of object creation and behavior; an excellent source-book for this approach is *Design Patterns*, by Gamma, Helm, Johnson, and Vlissides [21].

In addition to these general topics of design, you may want to read up on the concrete realization of object-oriented software in currently popular object-oriented programming languages. At the time we are writing this book, the greatest enthusiasm centers around the Java programming language. The next chapter contains a quick introduction to Java, and the notes at the end of that chapter provide some suggestions for further reading.

At the time of our writing, the only definitive source for information on UML is the web site, http://www.rational.com/uml/; documentation published on paper is still forthcoming. There is, however, an introductory overview book by Fowler [18].

The techniques we used to implement the object-oriented programming system are typical of those used for implementing such systems. Most of these techniques have been used for decades. Surprisingly, however, one of them was published as recently as 1991. That was the year when the technique we use for the class predicates, based on ancestry vectors, was described by Norman Cohen [13].

Java, Applets, and Concurrency

15.1 Introduction

In this chapter, we'll turn our attention from Scheme to another programming language, Java. Scheme has served us well, providing a simple context for learning many important computing concepts. However, now it is advantageous to look at another language, for the following reasons:

- We want to emphasize the continuity of concepts between what we've done in the rest of the book and the programming you are likely to do after leaving us.

- Although the big concepts carry over, there are some variations at a more superficial level, and it will help you if we point those out.

- We have a couple new concepts we consider it important to introduce that would not be easy or natural to introduce in Scheme. In particular, we are going to move away from programs that sequentially do one thing at a time to programs that divide their attention between multiple activities.

In the next section, we'll provide a basic introduction to the Java programming language by taking a program you are familiar with—the compu-duds program from the previous chapter—and rewriting it in Java. We'll show how the same object-oriented programming concepts are realized in a different notation.

After completing our crash course in how object-oriented programming maps into Java, we'll turn our attention to a new class of programs: those that present the user with a graphical interface and respond to the user's manipulation of interface elements, such as clicking on buttons. In particular, we'll look at *applets*, which are programs with graphical user interfaces that are intended to be embedded into World Wide Web documents.

Finally, we'll use Java applets as the setting in which to introduce the most conceptually significant material, *concurrency*. A concurrent system is one in which multiple activities go on at once. We'll show how to develop programs that can divide their attention between multiple activities. Most importantly, we'll show how the concept of representation invariant, which we've emphasized in prior chapters, gains renewed importance as the key to preventing unwanted interactions between concurrent activities. The chapter concludes with an opportunity for you to apply concurrent programming techniques to a simulation applet.

15.2 Java

The Java programming language is heavily biased toward the object-oriented style of programming we introduced in the previous chapter. All programming is organized into classes: Every single procedure you write in a Java program must be associated with some class, unlike in Scheme, where in addition to classes' methods, we also had "normal" procedures that floated free from the class hierarchy. In Java, even a procedure that just squared a number would have to be part of a class.

Another big difference between Java and Scheme is that we'll need to explicitly declare what *type* of object or value each name is a name for. For example, in the compu-duds program, we'll have to explicitly state that the argument to the add method of the item-list class is an item, that the choose method returns an item, and that the item-vector is a vector that holds items (no big surprise). On the one hand, this is sort of a nuisance because you have to type in all sorts of *declarations* that don't do any of the program's real work but instead just state what type of objects are being manipulated. On the other hand, the presence of these declarations provides a number of advantages:

- The declarations allow the automatic detection of many common programming errors. By now you surely have applied a Scheme procedure to the wrong kind of argument. If the faulty argument gets passed around untouched for a while before any operation is performed on it that causes symptoms to arise, you can have quite a debugging puzzle. If the symptoms only arise in some infrequently executed part of your program, matters are worse. In Java, by contrast, you can get immediate feedback regarding any place in your program where a type mismatch occurs.

- The declarations provide useful information to readers of your program. For example, does the item-list class's delete method expect to be told which item to delete or which numerical position it should delete the item from? One look at the type declaration for the parameter answers this question.

■ The declarations can actually contribute to the brevity of your program by allowing method names to be abbreviated. In Scheme, every time you operated on an item, you needed to specify that it was an item, by using method names like `item/price` or `item/display`. In Java, you declare once and for all that it is an item and then can operate on it with method names like `price` or `display`.

These two areas are broad differences between Java and Scheme: types must be declared, and the entire program must be organized into classes. However, smaller differences also exist, particularly at the superficial level of what the notation looks like. A few of these are purely arbitrary, reflecting the different background and taste of the languages' designers or intended audience. Most, however, can be accounted for in terms of a desire for succinctness: Java is a much more terse notation than Scheme and allows lots of optional shorthands that can make it even terser. For an example, consider what a method of the item-list class does to get the current value of the `num-items` instance variable stored in `this` item-list (i.e., the one the method is operating on). In Scheme we wrote (`item-list/get-num-items this`). In Java, the "longhand" option would be `this.numItems`, and the shorthand that is normally used is just `numItems`, because if you don't specify what object an instance variable should be fetched from, it is assumed to be `this`.

We renamed the instance variable from `num-items` to `numItems` because arithmetic operators in Java are written between their operands, so `num-items` would mean `num` minus `items`. Because the hyphen means subtraction—and no spaces are required around it—we are forced to separate words some other way. The Java convention is to use capitalization of the first letter of each new word within the name. (For class names, even the first word is conventionally capitalized, for example, `ItemList`, whereas for other names the first word is left lowercase, as in `numItems` or `displayPrice`.)

Enough general comments about Java; the time has come for an example program. We'll do a straightforward translation of the compu-duds (or CompuDuds) program into Java, sticking close to the Scheme original so you have a basis for comparison. To refresh your memory, here is the class hierarchy from the Scheme version:

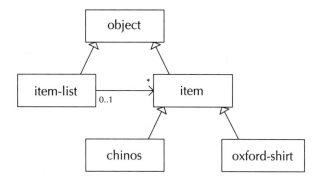

The variant of this class hierarchy we will implement in Java includes two changes:

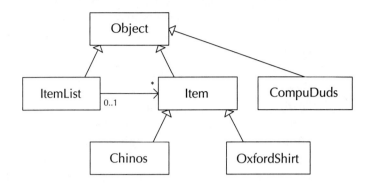

The first change concerns the Java naming convention described in the previous paragraph (e.g., `ItemList` instead of `item-list`). The second change is the addition to our hierarchy of the class called `CompuDuds`. We need this class as a place to put the "normal" procedures that in Scheme floated free from the class hierarchy. One of those procedures was the main `compu-duds` procedure that was the program itself; in Java, this procedure is renamed to be the `main` method of the `CompuDuds` class, because the Java system assumes that the program to run is the `main` method of the specified class.

Because of its relative simplicity, we will start our description of the CompuDuds program with the `Item` class, followed in short order by its subclasses `OxfordShirt` and `Chinos`, after which we will look at the `ItemList` and `CompuDuds` classes. Because the code is so extensive, and there are so many new language features you will be learning, we will divide the remainder of this section into subsections corresponding to each of these classes.

Item Class

Recall that the `Item` class maintained the price of each item and otherwise existed mainly as a base for its subclasses. Here is the full Java implementation of `Item`, which must be in a file named `Item.java`:

```
public class Item extends Object {

  private int price;

  public Item(int initialPrice){
    price = initialPrice;
  }
```

```
  public int price(){
    return price;
  }

  public void display(){
    CompuDuds.displayPrice(price);
  }

  public void inputSpecifics(){
  }

  public void reviseSpecifics(){
    inputSpecifics();
  }
}
```

To understand the meaning of this notation, recall that in Scheme we first used `define-class` to provide some basic information about the class: its name, superclass, instance variable names, and method names. We then added the method implementations one by one, using `class/set-method!`. In Java, by contrast, we provide the method implementations in the same chunk of code with the rest of the information about the class. This notation is as though in Scheme all the calls to `class/set-method!` were stuck in as extra arguments to `define-class`. The overall form is therefore as follows:

```
public class Item extends Object {
  // all the instance variables and methods go in here
}
```

The first line states that the Item class has the `Object` class as its superclass. Actually, we can leave "`extends Object`" out because Java assumes the superclass is `Object` if you don't specify otherwise. The keyword `public` indicates that this class can be freely used from anywhere within the overall program. For simplicity, we'll stick exclusively to `public` classes, although in large programs it can be helpful to delimit the visibility of some classes, as a complexity control measure. Each `public` class needs to be defined in a file named after the class; for example, we stated earlier that the definition of the Item class must be in `Item.java`. Because all our classes will be `public`, each will need to be put in its own individual file.

We've taken this early opportunity to show what a comment looks like in Java; the line

```
  // all the instance variables and methods go in here
```

is a comment, because anything from `//` to the end of the line is ignored by the Java system, much like Scheme comments that extend from `;` to the end of the line. Java also offers comments that extend from `/*` to `*/`, even if the `*/` is on a subsequent line, such as this example:

```
/* all the instance variables and methods go
   in here  */
```

The instance variables and methods in a class's definition can be listed in any order between the outer curly braces. We could list all the instance variables and then all the methods or vice versa or mix them up. In the examples we give, we'll follow the convention of first listing the instance variables and then the methods.

The class `Item` has a single instance variable, named `price`, that is declared in the line

```
private int price;
```

Notice that `price` is flagged `private`. This means that no code outside the class can get or set it: The only access is through this class's methods. If you look back over the code in the previous chapter, you'll see that we've always used instance variables that way. Doing so makes the program as a whole much more resilient to changes in individual classes.

In addition to the instance variable's name, we also included one other piece of information, between the `private` keyword and the name, namely, what *type* of value the instance variable will hold. (We warned you that such declarations were coming.) In particular, we've declared that the `price` instance variable will always hold an integer (called an `int` in Java).

Consider next how the five methods for class `Item` are written in Java. The first of these, which is named `Item`, has a special role—it is used to initialize a new instance of the `Item` class when that instance is constructed, which is analogous to the Scheme version's `init` method. In Java, instead of being called `init`, it is given the same name as the class. Also, in Java terminology it isn't strictly speaking a method but rather a *constructor*. In Scheme, we used the same word, *constructor*, to instead refer to the `make-item` procedure. Recall that in Scheme we could construct an item with the following code:

```
(define example-item (make-item 1950))   ; 1950 cents = $19.50
```

The corresponding Java code would be

```
Item exampleItem = new Item(1950);
```

This statement declares `exampleItem` to be a variable of type `Item` and assigns it the value returned by the *class instance creation expression*, `new Item(1950)`. Because of the parenthesized 1950, the newly created Item is initialized by the constructor applied to 1950. We define the constructor Item by

```java
public Item(int initialPrice){
   price = initialPrice;
}
```

This code introduces several features of Java. As you can see, this constructor is public, in other words, available for use from outside the class. In parentheses after the constructor name is the list of parameters; if there were more than one, they would be seperated by commas. The this parameter is not listed. Thus, Item takes a parameter named initialPrice, which is of type int. The reason Java omits the this parameter is not because it doesn't exist but rather because every constructor and method necessarily has it, so for conciseness it isn't explicitly mentioned. Next comes the body of the constructor, surrounded by braces. The single statement within the body illustrates the use of the equal sign as a setter: The instance variable to the left of the equal sign is being set to the value indicated on the right. Thus, the price instance variable is set to the desired initial price. This assignment statement ends with a semicolon.

Consider next the price method:

```java
public int price(){
   return price;
}
```

The int between the public and price() says that price is a method that returns an integer value. Notice that we need to explicitly say that the value should be returned, unlike in Scheme. The empty parentheses are because this method takes no arguments, other than the implicit this.

Before describing the remaining methods in the Item class, consider the following code, which illustrates how the price method could be invoked:

```java
int itsPrice = exampleItem.price();
```

This statement (which assumes that exampleItem was declared as before) declares a new variable of type int and assigns it the value returned by invoking the price method on exampleItem, namely, 1950. The pair of parentheses after the method name contains all the arguments other than which object the method is being invoked on; that special argument (exampleItem) appears before the method name, separated by a dot. Because it is so common for methods to invoke other methods on the same object (i.e., on this), Java allows the shorthand form in which you just write price() instead of this.price().

Returning to the remaining methods in the `Item` class, consider next `display`, which illustrates how to call a method that is not associated with any particular object:

```
public void display(){
  CompuDuds.displayPrice(price);
}
```

First note that the word `void`, appearing before the method name, is in the position where normally we would specify what kind of value this method returns. What it means is that no value at all is returned: The method is invoked solely for its effect. This use of `void` contrasts with the way we declared the `Item` constructor. Constructors have no return type specifier at all, not even `void`, whereas methods must have a return type specifier, whether `void` or a real type like `int`.

The interesting feature of `display`'s invocation of `displayPrice` is that `CompuDuds` isn't an object; it is a class. As descibed, we normally put an object before the dot to show which object the method should be invoked on. However, the `displayPrice` procedure isn't really an object's method at all; it is just a normal procedure. As we mentioned earlier, even normal procedures in Java need to be grouped into classes; in Java terminology, they are called *class methods* as opposed to *instance methods*. We've given the `CompuDuds` class the responsibility of holding all the utility procedures for our program, like this one for showing a price as dollars and cents. To access such a procedure, we just write the class name before the dot.

This leaves the final two methods in the `Item` class, which are fairly straightforward:

```
public void inputSpecifics(){
}

public void reviseSpecifics(){
  inputSpecifics();
}
```

We don't have much new to say about these two procedures, other than to point out that `inputSpecifics()` has an empty body and therefore does nothing. Otherwise, these two procedures are direct translations of their Scheme counterparts.

OxfordShirt Class

The `OxfordShirt` class extends a superclass other than `Object`, namely, `Item`. Following is the portion of its implementation dealing with its instance variables and constructor. Take a particularly close look at the line involving **super** that we've flagged with a comment; we'll have more to say about it presently:

```
public class OxfordShirt extends Item {

  private String color;
  private int neck;
  private int sleeve;
  private boolean specifiedYet;


  public OxfordShirt(){
    super(1950);  // <-- allow Item class to initialize the price
    specifiedYet = false;
  }

  // Methods display() and inputSpecifics() go here;
  //  we will show them later.
}
```

First note that two new Java types are used for the instance variables: String and boolean. These types have pretty much the same meaning as in Scheme.

The line we flagged invokes the constructor from the superclass (i.e., the Item class). In the Scheme version, the init method for the oxford-shirt class invoked the init from the item class as follows:

```
(item^init this 1950)
```

Here in Java, the analogue is super(1950).

The display() method in OxfordShirt introduces a number of new features:

```
public void display(){
  if(specifiedYet){
    System.out.print(color);
    System.out.print(" Oxford shirt, size ");
    System.out.print(neck);
    System.out.print("/");
    System.out.print(sleeve);
    System.out.print("; ");
  } else {
    System.out.print("Oxford shirt; ");
  }
  super.display();  // <-- now do displaying the Item way
}
```

First note that `display()` uses the `if...else` construct to choose between two forms of output. Also, the code contains a number of instances of the expression `System.out.print(...)`. These produce output for the user to see, analogously to Scheme's `display` procedure. Similarly, `System.out.println(...)` will produce output and then start a new line. In particular, `System.out.println()` has the same effect as Scheme's `newline` procedure. Actually, `print` and `println` are methods that can be used to cause output to be produced elsewhere as well (like into a file), and `System.out` is the object we invoke those methods on when we want the output to go to the normal place, typically the user's display screen.

Regarding the statement flagged with a comment in the preceding code, recall that the Scheme version of the `oxford-shirt` class's `display` method ended by invoking the `item` class's `display` as follows:

```
(item^display this)
```

In Java, the `display` method from the superclass is invoked as `super.display()`.

Finally, consider the `inputSpecifics()` method in the `OxfordShirt` class:

```java
public void inputSpecifics(){
  System.out.println("What color?");
  String[] colors = {"Ecru", "Pink", "Blue", "Maize", "White"};
  color = CompuDuds.inputSelection(colors);
  System.out.print("What neck size? ");
  neck = CompuDuds.inputIntegerInRange(15, 18);
  System.out.print("What sleeve length? ");
  sleeve = CompuDuds.inputIntegerInRange(32, 37);
  specifiedYet = true;
}
```

Note first that the actual input is offloaded to the two utility procedures, `inputSelection` and `inputIntegerInRange`, just like in the Scheme version. We'll provide their definitions when we get to the `CompuDuds` class.

We need to explain a number of new Java features that are implicit in the following line:

```java
String[] colors = {"Ecru", "Pink", "Blue", "Maize", "White"};
```

This is Java shorthand for the following code, which is what we will actually explain:

```java
String[] colors = new String[5];
colors[0] = "Ecru";
colors[1] = "Pink";
```

```
colors[2] = "Blue";
colors[3] = "Maize";
colors[4] = "White";
```

The first line declares `colors` to be a temporary local variable; that is, rather than being a permanent instance variable of the object, it is a name that can only be used from its declaration to the end of the curly braces. The variable `colors` is declared to have the type `String[]`, which means that `colors` is an *array* (Java's word for vector) that can hold `Strings`. (The brackets indicates that it is an array, whereas the name before the brackets indicates what type of object the array holds.) The expression `new String[5]` is analogous to Scheme's `(make-vector 5)` except that the array can only hold `Strings`. Because of the equal sign, the newly made array becomes the value of `colors`.

The remainder of the code illustrates how array elements are set in Java. For example, the Java code

```
colors[2] = "Blue";
```

is directly analogous to the Scheme code

```
(vector-set! colors 2 "Blue")
```

Just as in Scheme, array elements in Java are numbered from 0, not 1.

Finally, note that the shorthand form involving {"Ecru", "Pink", "Blue", "Maize", "White"} has the big advantage of leaving the counting to the computer.

Chinos Class

The `Chinos` class is so similar to the `OxfordShirt` class that we won't bother showing it all here; the full version is on the web site for this book. The only really novel issue arises in the `inputSpecifics` method, at the point where the Scheme version does the following:

```
(chinos/set-inseam! this (input-integer-in-range
                          29
                          (if (chinos/get-cuffed this)
                              34
                              36)))
```

This code sets the `inseam` instance variable to a value chosen from a range that always has 29 as its minimum value but can extend to a maximum of either 34 or 36 depending on whether the chinos are to be cuffed or not. We've seen that Java also has an `if` construct; however, it can't be used in this fashion. The reason is that Java, unlike Scheme, distinguishes between *expressions*, which calculate values, and *statements*, which command the computer to carry out some action. An `if`, in Java, is a conditional statement that selects between two alternative actions to carry out, not a conditional expression that can select between alternative values. For example, we used `if` in the `OxfordShirt` class's `display` method to select which of two forms of output to produce, but we can't use it here to choose between 34 and 36. We'll see that there are two options for dealing with this in Java.

The most common approach taken by Java programmers is simply to reformulate the task in such a way that a conditional statement becomes appropriate. For example, they would write

```
if(cuffed){
   inseam = CompuDuds.inputIntegerInRange(29, 34);
} else {
   inseam = CompuDuds.inputIntegerInRange(29, 36);
}
```

The disadvantage, of course, is that the part that doesn't vary winds up repeated.

An alternative is to stick with a conditional expression, as we had in the Scheme version. It turns out that Java *does* have conditional expressions; they just aren't called `if`. Here is how the code would look written this way:

```
inseam = CompuDuds.inputIntegerInRange(29, cuffed ? 34 : 36);
```

As you can see, the conditional expression has a peculiar syntax; you state the controlling boolean expression (here `cuffed`), then a question mark, the alternative to use if the condition is true, a colon, and the other alternative. Because this syntax is rather idiosyncratic, many Java programmers avoid it. However, it does solve the problem of allowing control to be exerted only over that which needs to vary.

ItemList Class

Following is an abbreviated version of `ItemList`'s implementation, giving complete code only for its instance variables, its constructor, and the method `empty`:

```
public class ItemList extends Object {

  private Item[] itemVector;
  private int numItems;
```

```
public ItemList(){
  itemVector = new Item[10];
  numItems = 0;
}

public boolean empty(){
  return numItems == 0;
}

/* Code will be given later for the following methods:
 *
 *    public void display()
 *    public int totalPrice()
 *    public void add(Item item)
 *    private void grow()
 *    public void delete(Item item)
 *    public Item choose()
 */
}
```

Note the double equal sign in empty, which checks for equality just like a single equal sign does in Scheme. We have to have a separate notation for equality checking because the single equal sign is used in Java for assigning new values to variables.

The ItemList class's display method needs to loop through all the individual items, displaying them one by one using the Item class's display method. In Scheme we used the from-to-do procedure to loop through the positions the items occupy in the item vector; in Java, the equivalent is the for loop:

```
public void display(){
  for(int index = 0; index < numItems; index = index + 1){
    System.out.print(index + 1);
    System.out.print(") ");
    itemVector[index].display();
    System.out.println();
  }
  System.out.print("Total: ");
  CompuDuds.displayPrice(totalPrice());
  System.out.println();
}
```

The for loop is controlled by the parenthesized code immediately following the keyword for, which consists of three parts separated by two semicolons. The first part is an initializer, which is evaluated once before everything else is evaluated. In our case we declare and initialize the integer variable `index`, used for counting through the positions. It is a temporary local variable that can be used up to the curly brace ending the `for` loop's body. The second part of the loop control, `index < numItems`, specifies how long the loop should continue: so long as the index hasn't run past the part of the array that is actually in use. Finally, before the body of the loop we specify how `index` should be changed each time, by setting it to the old value plus 1. Note that this setting is actually done *after each execution* of the loop body, even though it is written before. (For example, the first time the body is executed, `index` is 0, because it hasn't yet been incremented to 1.)

The line

```
itemVector[index].display();
```

is the equivalent of the Scheme

```
(item/display (vector-ref item-vector index))
```

In other words, the brackets are being used here to indicate that an element is to be fetched from the array, like Scheme's `vector-ref` operation. We saw earlier that if the brackets are used to the left of an equal sign, they corresponded instead to `vector-set!`, and after `new`, they indicated the size of an array being created, analogous to `make-vector`. One of the prices of concision is that the same symbols get pressed into service for multiple roles. Once you become familiar with the language, you should have no problem telling from context what role a particular pair of brackets is serving.

The method for computing the total price of the items doesn't introduce any new Java features, but it does give another example of a `for` loop:

```
public int totalPrice(){
  int sum = 0;
  for(int i = 0; i < numItems; i = i + 1){
    sum = sum + itemVector[i].price();
  }
  return sum;
}
```

Because there is nothing new in this method, maybe it is time to introduce a couple extra Java shorthands that you'll frequently see used. You'll notice that there are two places where a variable is set to a new value found by adding the old value to something: `i` gets 1 added to it, and `sum` gets a price added to it. This pattern shows up frequently enough to have a shorthand; using it we can write

```java
public int totalPrice(){
  int sum = 0;
  for(int i = 0; i < numItems; i += 1){
    sum += itemVector[i].price();
  }
  return sum;
}
```

Because incrementing a variable by 1 is so common, you can get one step more terse and instead of writing i += 1, write i++.

The add method is a fairly straightforward translation of the Scheme version into Java:

```java
public void add(Item item){
  if(numItems == itemVector.length){
    grow();
    add(item);
  } else {
    itemVector[numItems] = item;
    numItems++;
  }
}
```

The only novel aspect concerns how one finds the length of a array in Java: Although the notation is different (the dot and then length), what it does is the same as Scheme's vector-length.

The grow method is also a fairly straightforward translation of the corresponding Scheme method:

```java
private void grow(){
  Item[] newItemVector = new Item[itemVector.length * 2];
  for(int i = 0; i < itemVector.length; i++){
    newItemVector[i] = itemVector[i];
  }
  itemVector = newItemVector;
}
```

Note that grow is declared private, because it is only used internally within the Item class.

In the delete method, we'll use not only the ++ shorthand but also the analogous -- shorthand, which decrements a variable by 1:

```
public void delete(Item item){
  for(int i = 0; i < numItems; i++){
    if(itemVector[i] == item){
      for(int j = i + 1; j < numItems; j++){
        itemVector[j - 1] = itemVector[j];
      }
      itemVector[numItems - 1] = null;
      numItems--;
      return;
    }
  }
  System.err.println
    ("Error: ItemList delete done with Item not in list.");
  System.exit(1);
}
```

When this method finds the item that is to be deleted, it slides all the items after it in the array down by one position. Then it puts a special `null` value into the newly vacated array position. The `null` value is used as a placeholder when an array element or variable does not refer to any object at all. Once the array has been updated in this manner, and the `numItems` is decremented, the method immediately `returns`, without continuing to search further for the item (because it has already found and deleted it). Notice that because this method isn't supposed to return any value, we have no expression between the keyword `return` and the semicolon. Rather than specifying a value to return, the `return` statement is serving only to terminate the method without further execution.

If the loop instead *does* run to completion, because the item is not found, an error message is printed out and the program exits. The error message is printed on `System.err`, which is just like `System.out`, except that even if the user asks for normal output to go somewhere other than the display screen (for example, to go into another program for further processing), the output produced on `System.err` will still be displayed on the screen. The `println` method is being used here both to print the message and to start a new line afterward. The call to `System.exit` causes the program to stop; by convention a value of 0 is passed to indicate a normal termination, whereas nonzero values (like 1) are used to indicate that something went wrong.

The remaining method from the `ItemList` class, `choose`, doesn't introduce any new features of Java:

```
public Item choose(){
  if(empty()){
    System.err.println("Error: choose done on empty ItemList.");
```

```
    System.exit(1);
  }
  System.out.println("Which item?");
  display();
  return
    itemVector[CompuDuds.inputIntegerInRange(1, numItems) - 1];
}
```

CompuDuds Class

At this point, we've covered all of the classes that existed in the Scheme version of compu-duds, but the Java version still has one class left, the CompuDuds class that we are using to collect together all the utility procedures, like displayPrice and inputIntegerInRange. This class will also provide the main program itself, which repeatedly lets the user choose what to do next.

The CompuDuds class is a rather strange class in that there will never be any objects that are instances of it—not even by way of subclasses. So, there will be no instance variables, no constructor called CompuDuds, and no methods in the normal sense. Instead the class will contain nothing but class methods, which are really just normal procedures. Each class method is flagged as such with the keyword static. Here's how the class starts out:

```
public class CompuDuds {

  public static void displayPrice(int totalCents){
    int dollars = totalCents / 100;
    int remainingCents = totalCents % 100;
    System.out.print("$");
    System.out.print(dollars);
    if(remainingCents < 10){
      System.out.print(".0");
    } else {
      System.out.print(".");
    }
    System.out.print(remainingCents);
  }

  // more class methods go here
}
```

As you can see, the static keyword is used to signal that displayPrice is a class method; when it is invoked, it isn't going to be associated with any object—there will be no implicit **this** argument. The other novelties occur in the first two lines of the body: the use of the slash and percent-sign characters to find the quotient and remainder when **totalCents** is divided by 100. In Java, the rule is that if a slash has an integer on both sides, it represents the quotient operation. (By contrast, in Scheme, a slash would produce a fractional answer, and so we use an explicit **quotient** procedure.) The percent sign indicates remainder; the rationale is that it visually resembles the slash, to remind you that they go together.

The **CompuDuds** class is the main class for the program—the one you tell the Java system you want to run. (How you tell the Java system that depends what sort of system you have.) When you say that you want to start up the program associated with the **CompuDuds** class, what the Java system does is run the procedure named **main** in that class; here it is:

```java
public static void main(String[] commandLineArgs){
  ItemList itemList = new ItemList();
  while(true){ // infinite loop terminated by program exiting
    System.out.println();
    System.out.println("What would you like to do?");
    System.out.println(" 1) Exit this program.");
    System.out.println(" 2) Add an item to your selections.");
    System.out.println(" 3) List the items you have selected.");
    System.out.println
      (" 4) See the total price of the items you selected.");
    int option;
    if(itemList.empty()){
      option = inputIntegerInRange(1, 4);
    } else {
      System.out.println(" 5) Delete one of your selections.");
      System.out.println
        (" 6) Revise specifics of a selected item.");
      option = inputIntegerInRange(1, 6);
    }
    if(option == 1){
      System.exit(0);
    } else if(option == 2){
      Item item = inputItem();
      itemList.add(item);
      item.inputSpecifics();
    } else if(option == 3){
      itemList.display();
    } else if(option == 4){
      displayPrice(itemList.totalPrice());
```

```
        System.out.println();
      } else if(option == 5){
        itemList.delete(itemList.choose());
      } else if(option == 6){
        itemList.choose().reviseSpecifics();
      }
    }
  }
```

The most interesting parts of this procedure are actually in the first three lines:

```
public static void main(String[] commandLineArgs){
  ItemList itemList = new ItemList();
  while(true){ // infinite loop terminated by program exiting
```

As you can see, the **main** procedure (which constitutes the actual program itself) needs to accept an argument that is an array of **Strings**. This is used because in some systems you can start a program up with arguments provided to the program as a whole—with *command-line arguments*. We'll ignore these entirely but need to have the declaration there to keep the Java system happy. The second line shows how a new object is created as an instance of a class; the **new ItemList()** is the analog of Scheme's (make-item-list). Finally, we have a new kind of loop, the **while** loop. This loop is just a stripped down version of the **for** loop that doesn't have a variable to initialize before the loop or to step from one iteration of the loop to the next. Instead, all that remains is the test condition that determines whether the loop should continue. (Of course, the loop body remains as well.) In this case, our test expression is the boolean constant **true**, the Java analog of Scheme's **#t**. That means the loop will always keep looping—at least until **System.exit** causes the whole program to stop.

By the way, notice that where the **main** procedure invokes other procedures contained within the **CompuDuds** class, it doesn't need to explicitly put the **CompuDuds** class name and a dot before the procedure name; for example, it can say **inputIntegerInRange(1, 4)** rather than **CompuDuds.input IntegerInRange(1, 4)**. This is a shorthand, just like omitting the prefix **this** when one method invokes another on the same object.

To reinforce the notion of how objects are created, here is the **inputItem** procedure, which is used by **main**:

```
private static Item inputItem(){
  System.out.println("What would you like?");
  System.out.println(" 1) Chinos");
  System.out.println(" 2) Oxford shirt");
```

```
    if(inputIntegerInRange(1, 2) == 1){
      return new Chinos();
    } else{
      return new OxfordShirt();
    }
  }
```

As you can see, this code creates either a new instance of the `Chinos` class or a new instance of the `OxfordShirt` class. Either one gets returned; notice that the procedure is declared as returning an `Item`, and sure enough, it does return an `Item`—of some kind. The empty parentheses after the class name occur because no arguments are being passed to the class's constructor. For an example where this case wouldn't be true, consider creating a plain `Item` with a price of $19.50, such as our earlier `exampleItem`; you would write `new Item(1950)`.

There are only two procedures left in the `CompuDuds` class: `inputInteger InRange` and `inputSelection`. The latter is rather straightforwardly written in terms of the former, so we'll skip it here; you can get it from the web site for this book. The `inputIntegerInRange` procedure, on the other hand, is quite interesting. Not only does it show how input is done, it also shows the handling of *exceptions* (i.e., unusual circumstances). In this case, two kinds of exceptions could occur: Something could go wrong while reading the input (such as the computer noticing that the keyboard is unplugged) and something could go wrong while trying to convert the input into a number (such as the input not being composed of digits). The following procedure has handlers for both of these exceptions:

```
public static int inputIntegerInRange(int min, int max){
  System.out.print("(enter ");
  System.out.print(min);
  System.out.print("-");
  System.out.print(max);
  System.out.println(")");
  String inputAsString = null;
  try{
    inputAsString = reader.readLine();
  } catch(java.io.IOException e){
    System.err.print("Problem reading input: ");
    System.err.println(e);
    System.exit(1);
  }
  if(inputAsString == null){ // this means end of file on input
    System.exit(0);  // handle as a normal program termination
  }
```

```
    int inputAsInt;
    try{
      inputAsInt = Integer.parseInt(inputAsString);
    } catch(NumberFormatException e){
      System.err.println("input must be an integer and wasn't");
      return inputIntegerInRange(min, max);
    }
    if(inputAsInt < min || inputAsInt > max){
      System.err.println("input out of range");
      return inputIntegerInRange(min, max);
    } else{
      return inputAsInt;
    }
  }
```

As we said, there are two places where we need to be prepared for exceptional things to go wrong (the input itself and the conversion of the input to an integer). Each of these is handled with a `try` and `catch` construct. The code between the `try` and the `catch` is where the exception might originate, and the code after the `catch` is what deals with it if it does occur. Each `catch` specifies what kind of exception it is prepared to catch; our first one catches `java.io.IOExceptions`, and the second one catches `NumberFormatExceptions`. Either way, we provide a name for the exception that is caught; that is what the `e` is. This `e` is like a parameter to a procedure; a particular exception object has been caught, and we give it a name so that we can refer to it in the code that handles it. In fact, it is literally an object; in our second example, it is an instance of the class `NumberFormatException`. We don't do anything with that exception object, but in the first exception handler, we print the `java.io.IOException` object itself out as part of our error message.

Another generally useful feature is the double vertical bar to indicate "or" in the following line:

```
    if(inputAsInt < min || inputAsInt > max){
```

If the input is either too small or too big, we want to deal with it as out of range. One fine point is that the second condition is only tested if the first one isn't true, which means you can safely write code like

```
    if(diplomacySucceeds() || goingToWarSucceeds()){
```

and know that you won't even try going to war if diplomacy succeeds. An analogous situation occurs with `&&`, which is used for "and." For example, you can write

```
    if(diplomacyFails() && goingToWarFails()){
```

The second condition is only tested if the first one is true—if the first is false (diplomacy didn't fail), we already know that they aren't both true (diplomacy and going to war didn't both fail).

One detail we glossed over in the `inputIntegerInRange` method was the `reader` that the `readLine` method is invoked on, to get a line of input as a `String`. What is this `reader`? It is defined by the following component of the `CompuDuds` class:

```
private static java.io.BufferedReader reader =
  new java.io.BufferedReader
   (new java.io.InputStreamReader(System.in));
```

This example looks like a `private` instance variable, except that it has a `static` keyword, which means there is a single variable shared by the whole class rather than one per instance. (Remember, the `CompuDuds` class has no instances, so that wouldn't make much sense.) This variable called `reader` is declared to be of the class `java.io.BufferedReader` and is initialized by a big long mess that constructs a `java.io.BufferedReader`. To tell you the full story would get into grungy details of input that you can probably afford to ignore, because most Java programs don't interact this way; instead they use graphical user interfaces, such as we'll consider in the next section. If you ever need to know more about what a `java.io.BufferedReader` really is, plenty of good documentation is available—see the end-of-chapter notes for references.

Now that we've translated CompuDuds into Java, you can try it out and can try your hand at adding various enhancements (just like you did in Scheme in the prior chapter).

Exercise 15.1

Find out how to run Java programs on your computer system, and try out the CompuDuds program as it comes from the web site for this book. It is important to try out the program unmodified first so that you can work out any kinks in the mechanics of running a Java program.

Exercise 15.2

Change the `ItemList` class so that it keeps a running total price as `Item`s are added and `delete`d and then just returns that from the `totalPrice` method, rather than looping through adding up all the prices. Check that the program still works.

> **Exercise 15.3**

Add some more subclasses of `Item`, reflecting your own taste in clothing. Change `inputItem` so that these additional choices are available to the user, and check that your changes work correctly.

> **Exercise 15.4**

Assuming the CompuDuds program is being operated by sales personnel, rather than directly by the customer, it might be desirable to provide a means of applying a discount.

a. Add a method to the `Item` class that marks down the price by 10 percent. Be forewarned that you can't legally say

```
price = .9 * price;
```

because multiplying by .9 results in something that isn't an `int` and hence can't be stored into `price`. Instead you can multiply by 9 and then take the quotient upon division by 10.

b. Use your new `Item` method to add a method to the `ItemList` class that marks down the price of all the `Items` by 10 percent.

If you've done Exercise 15.2, in which you changed the `ItemList` class to maintain a running total price, you'll have a problem with simply discounting each `Item` by 10 percent and discounting the accumulated total price by 10 percent. If you do so, under some circumstances you'll wind up with a total price that doesn't match the sum of the individual prices, due to roundoff. The solution is to recompute the total price whenever a discount is applied.

c. Finally, add a new option to the main CompuDuds user interface that discounts everything that has been selected by 10 percent.

15.3   Event-Driven Graphical User Interfaces in Applets

The CompuDuds program interacts with its user in a very old-fashioned style, characterized by two primary features:

▪ All input and output is textual: the user and the program both type lines of text instead of the user pointing at visual information that the program shows.

▪ The program is in charge of the interaction. The user is reduced to answering the questions the program asks rather than taking charge and directly manipulating the program.

This textual, program-directed style of interaction made sense in its original histor-ical context, roughly the early 1960s. Among other things, the typical computer user didn't have access to any hardware that supported graphical interaction: Sending the computer a line of text and receiving a line of text in response was the best that most could hope for. (Many users had to settle for *batch processing*, which involved send-ing enough textual input for the entire running of the program and then receiving back a printout of the entire output rather than being able to incrementally give and take.)

However, times have changed, and today users typically have computers that allow for a tightly coupled graphical interaction, in which the user takes charge and directly manipulates the program's interface by pushing buttons, sliding sliders, checking checkboxes, typing into fields, etc. The role of the program is no longer to step through a fixed sequence of questions and answers but rather to perform two basic functions:

- Present a collection of objects to the user.
- Respond to whatever manipulations of those objects the user performs.

In this section, we'll see how such programs are written. They are called *event-driven graphical user interface* (GUI—pronounced gooey) programs because they not only present a GUI but moreover are driven by outside events, such as the user clicking on a button.

In particular, we'll look at applets, which are event-driven GUI programs that are designed to be components of documents on the World Wide Web rather than standing alone. Instead of running lots of separate programs, users run a single web browser program, which lets them view and interact with lots of different kinds of multimedia hypertext documents. Those documents contain all the usual kinds of content, like words, tables, and pictures, and also interactive content in the form of applets.

Object-oriented programming turns out to play a critical role in event-driven GUI programs, both from our perspective as programmers of individual applets and also from the perspective of the programmers of the overall web browsers that our applets run inside of.

From our own perspective, we will be able to write our programs reasonably simply and easily because there is a large "library" of prewritten classes for such interaction components as buttons and checkboxes. Thus we can just create appro-priate instances of these classes, without worrying about the details of how they work inside.

From the perspective of the programmers of the main browser program, the key fact is that all these individual component classes, like `Button` and `Checkbox`, are actually subclasses of a general `Component` class. Any `Component` knows how to draw itself. Any `Component` knows how to respond to a mouse button being pressed while the mouse is pointing into that `Component`'s area. Thus the browser doesn't have to concern itself with the many different kinds of interaction mechanisms. It can just uniformly treat the whole applet as a bunch of `Components`. It asks each `Component` to draw itself on the screen without knowing or caring that they do so in varying ways. When a mouse button is pressed, it notifies the appropriate `Component`, without caring that a `TextField` might treat this action entirely differently from a `Button`—they are both still `Components`.

Our first example applet is shown in Figure 15.1. It is a simulation of the sliding 15-tile puzzle. The real puzzle has 15 numbered tiles that can slide around inside a frame that has room for 16 tiles, so there is always one empty position. After sliding the tiles around for a while to scramble them, the goal is to get them back into their original arrangement, in numerical order with the blank space in the lower right corner. Our applet simulates the puzzle with a grid of 16 buttons, of which 15 are labeled with the numbers 1 through 15, and the remaining one has a blank label, representing the empty position. If the user clicks on a numbered button that is in the same row or column as the blank one, that means he or she wants to slide the tile clicked on, pushing along with it any others that intervene between it and the empty position. We simulate this action by copying the numeric labels over from each button to its neighbor. We also set the clicked-on button's label to an empty string, because it becomes the newly empty one.

To program this puzzle, we will adopt the object-oriented perspective and view the program as a collection of interacting objects. Some of the objects have visible representations on the screen when our applet is running. These are the objects that are instances of the subclasses of `Component`. The `Component` class, like many others that we'll use, is found in the *Abstract Window Toolkit* (AWT), a GUI-specific portion of Java's rich hierarchy of library classes. The `Components` in our applet are as follows:

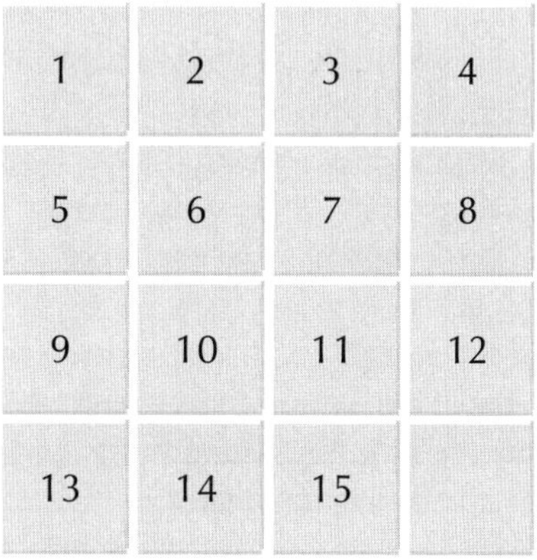

Figure 15.1   The sliding 15-tile puzzle applet

- There are 16 instances of the class **Button**, which is an AWT class derived from **Component**. Each **Button** has a label (empty in one case) and can respond to being pushed.
- One object represents the applet as a whole, containing the grid of **Buttons**. This object is an instance of a class we'll define, called **Puzzle**. The **Puzzle** class is a subclass of an AWT class called **Applet**, used for all applets. As the class hierarchy in Figure 15.2 shows, the **Applet** class is indirectly descended from **Component** because an **Applet** is visibly present on the screen. More specifically, because an **Applet** can contain other **Components** (like our **Buttons**), the **Applet** class is descended from a subclass of **Component** called **Container**, which is an AWT class providing the ability to contain subcomponents.

In addition to the objects mentioned above, our applet has some others that operate behind the scenes:

- Our **Puzzle**, like any **Container**, needs a layout manager to specify how the subcomponents should be laid out on the screen. Because our subcomponents are the **Buttons**, which we want to form a 4 × 4 grid, we'll use a **GridLayout** as

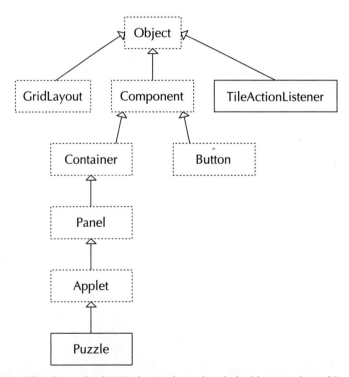

Figure 15.2   Class hierarchy for 15-tile puzzle applet (dashed boxes indicate library classes)

the layout manager. The `GridLayout` class is also provided for us as part of the AWT because this grid is a commonly desired layout.

■ Each of our 16 `Button`s needs to cause some response when it is pushed, rather than just being displayed on the screen. The `Button` class lets us tailor the response by giving each `Button` a companion object to notify when the `Button` is pushed. That companion object is in charge of providing the appropriate response. We'll define a class, `TileActionListener`, for these companion objects and make 16 `TileActionListener`s, one per `Button`.

The portion of the class hierarchy used in this applet is shown in Figure 15.2. Note that we mark library classes with dashed boxes, and those we will write ourselves with solid boxes. Of the library classes, all except the fundamental `Object` class are from the AWT. (Actually, the `Applet` class is technically not in the AWT but rather is in a package of its own that builds on top of the AWT. For many purposes it is convenient to treat it as part of the AWT, as we do.)

Now, let's go directly to the portion of the `Puzzle.java` file that deals with the initial construction and layout of the `Puzzle` object:

```
import java.awt.*;

public class Puzzle extends java.applet.Applet {

  private int size = 4;           // how many buttons wide and high
  private Button[][] buttons;
  private int blankRow, blankCol;  // position of the blank space

  public void init(){
    setLayout(new GridLayout(size, size));
    buttons = new Button[size][size];
    int buttonCount = 0;
    for(int row = 0; row < size; row++){
      for(int col = 0; col < size; col++){
        Button b = new Button();
        buttons[row][col] = b;
        b.addActionListener(new TileActionListener
                            (this, row, col));
        buttonCount++;
        b.setLabel("" + buttonCount);
        add(b);
      }
    }
    blankRow = size - 1;
    blankCol = size - 1;
```

```
        buttons[blankRow][blankCol].setLabel("");
    }

    /* Code will be given later for the following method:
     *
     *     public void pushTile(int row, int col)
     *
     */
}
```

This code includes a number of new Java features that bear explaining, one of which is the `import` line at the top of the file. This line allows us to use shortened names for the library classes we'll be using. For example, we'll be able to use the short name `Button` rather than the full name, which is `java.awt.Button`.

A more significant difference between the Puzzle class and our earlier Java classes is the apparent nonexistence of a constructor for the `Puzzle` class and the use of the `init` method, which seems to hearken back to our Scheme version of object-oriented programming. Regarding the apparent nonexistence of a constructor, `Puzzle` is in fact using a *default constructor*, which does nothing except invoke the `Applet` constructor. Java writes this do-nothing-extra constructor for us as a shorthand if we don't provide any constructor explicitly. Although the `Puzzle` constructor might seem the natural place to initialize the instance variables for the `Puzzle` class, standard practice dictates that applet initialization be accomplished by overriding the `Applet` class's `init` method. This standard practice derives from the special nature of applets, namely, that they are intended to run inside other programs, most notably in web browsers. In particular, because the browser is in charge of the applet's run-time environment, it needs to set up two-way communications between itself and the applet when it creates the applet. The two-way communication is necessary so that the browser and applet can react in tandem to various events that might occur (such as resizing), as well as to allow the applet access to information it might need (such as the location of image or audio files).

To deal with this two-way communication, the designers of Java have set up a protocol for programmers to follow when writing applets. The only aspect of this protocol that bears on us now concerns the roles of the applet constructor and the `init` method. Specifically, when the browser creates an applet, it first invokes applet's constructor, next sets up the two-way communication between itself and the applet, and then invokes the applet's `init` method. Because the applet's initialization often involves certain aspects of its run-time environment, which requires the two-way communications to have already been established, the standard practice is to wait until the `init` method to do the applet-specific initialization. This is the model we have followed.

A third new feature in the code is the double set of brackets we use for the two-dimensional array of buttons. Actually `buttons` is strictly speaking just a normal one-dimensional array, each element of which is itself another one-dimensional array, which in turn holds `Button`s. This is the same as what we've done in Scheme, where we represented two-dimensional tables as vectors of vectors. However, Java has a handy shorthand; we can say

```
buttons = new Button[size][size];
```

to create the entire structure, consisting in this case of five arrays: four arrays to hold `Button`s and then one "outer" array that contains the four others.

As you can see, we use nested `for` loops to loop over all the columns of all the rows. For each position, we create a new `Button` (temporarily called `b`), store `b` at the appropriate position in the `buttons` array, invoke two methods on `b` to configure it appropriately (`addActionListener` and `setLabel`), and finally `add b` itself to the applet. Let's look more closely at the actual statements in this code.

First, recall that applets are types of `Container`s, so named because they can contain other components such as buttons. Components are added to a container by `Container`'s `add` method. Precisely how these components are arranged in the container is controlled by the container's layout manager, which is specified by `Container`'s `setLayout` method. In our case, we have specified the layout as a 4×4 grid. The `GridLayout` object places the components in the grid from left to right, top to bottom, in the order they are added.

Adding the action listener is how we specify what response should occur when the user clicks on the `Button`. If we omitted that line, the applet would still display the same 4×4 grid of buttons, but we couldn't scramble their labels and then get them back into order; the puzzle would stay permanently in its solved state. We'll say more about the action listener later.

The button's label is set by the `setLabel` method from the `Button` class. The argument to this method is a `String` specifying the new label. For example, at the end we label the bottom right `Button` with an empty string so that it will be blank. How about the rest of the labeling, done inside the nested `for` loops? This takes a bit more explaining. We have a numerical variable, `buttonCount`, which records how many buttons have been created so far. We need to convert that numerical value into the corresponding string of digits, which in the first case is the string `"1"`. This conversion is done by a very strange Java idiom, namely, adding the number onto the empty string: `"" + buttonCount`. This idiom works because of the combination of two facts:

- For `String`s, the plus sign indicates sticking the two `String`s together (like Scheme's `string-append`) rather than numerical addition.

- If the plus sign only has a String on one side, whatever is on the other side gets converted to a String first, so that it can be appended.

Thus we are asking for the numerical buttonCount to be implicitly converted into a String and then tacked onto the end of an empty String. As roundabout as this may seem, it is in practice a quick and easy idiom to type.

At this point we have finished with the initial presentation of the applet and merely have to make it responsive to the user's pushing on its buttons. Recall that this responsiveness is provided by using the addActionListener method on each Button to give it its own TileActionListener. The idea is that the Button notifies the action listener whenever it is pushed. Notice that when we construct the TileActionListener, we specify what Puzzle it is a part of (by passing in this) as well as what row and column its Button is in. Here is the code for the TileActionListener class:

```java
import java.awt.event.*;

public class TileActionListener implements ActionListener {

    private Puzzle puz;
    private int row, col;

    public TileActionListener(Puzzle p, int r, int c){
        puz = p;
        row = r;
        col = c;
    }

    public void actionPerformed(ActionEvent evt){
        puz.pushTile(row, col);
    }
}
```

As you can see, TileActionListener isn't a very big class. It stores the Puzzle and row and column position in instance variables, and when it is told by the Button that an action has been performed (namely, the user pushed the Button), the actionPerformed method simply invokes the Puzzle's pushTile method, passing in the row and column numbers. Thus the real work of shifting all the labels over by one is done in the Puzzle class's pushTile method.

Although the core of what this TileActionListener class does is quite straightforward, it has a couple oddities in the first few lines. A minor one is that this class has a different import, to get short names for the ActionListener and ActionEvent classes. A more interesting one is that TileActionListener

implements ActionListener—notice the **implements** keyword where we previously have seen **extends**. The reason for this difference is that **ActionListener** isn't strictly speaking a class, it is an *interface*. Interfaces are extremely close relatives of classes, with two differences:

- An interface must be purely abstract. That is, it can only provide a declaration of the method names and types. It can't provide any method implementations or any instance variables to provide a representation. All implementation details are confined to the classes that implement the interface.
- A class can implement as many interfaces as you like, even though it can only extend one superclass.

We won't define any interfaces, so the only place you'll see them is when we **implement** an interface provided by the standard library, like **ActionListener**. We should point out, however, that **LayoutManager** is also an interface; the AWT provides several implementations of this interface, including **GridLayout**. We can add the two interfaces, **ActionListener** and **LayoutManager**, to our UML class diagram as shown in Figure 15.3. The interfaces are labeled as such, and

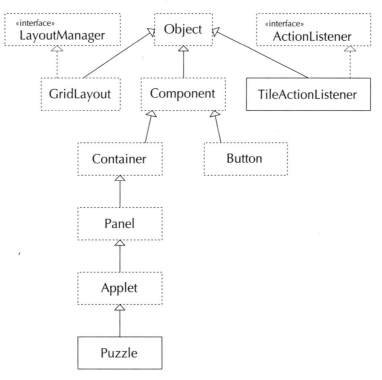

Figure 15.3 The puzzle class hierarchy with interfaces added; dashed boxes still indicate library classes or interfaces, but the dashed arrows are part of the UML notation.

a dashed arrow with a triangular arrowhead is used to connect the specific class (`TileActionListener` or `GridLayout`) to the general interface that it implements.

Now that we have the interfaces in our diagram, we can also add some associations, as shown in Figure 15.4, that will help clarify the relationships between the `Puzzle`, the `Buttons`, and the `TileActionListeners`. The `Puzzle` keeps track of the 16 `Buttons` so that it can manipulate their labels. Each `Button` is associated with one `TileActionListener`, which is specific to that `Button`. Each of the 16 `TileActionListeners` knows about the `Puzzle`, so that the `TileActionListener`'s `actionPerformed` method can invoke the `Puzzle`'s `pushTile`, as we have seen. So far, the associations are much as we've seen in other programs. But, we have one key new annotation, namely the `:ActionListener` near the arrow from the `Button` class to the `TileActionListener` class. This annotation is our way of showing that the `Button` only makes use of the `ActionListener` interface, not any of the specifics of the `TileActionListener` class. This point is essential because it allows the `Button` class to be general enough to work with other kinds of `ActionListeners` as well.

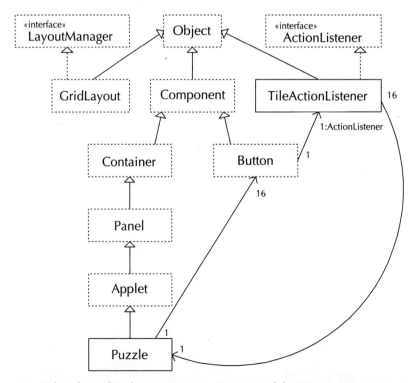

Figure 15.4 The relationships between `Puzzle`, `Button`, and the `TileActionListener` implementation of the `ActionListener` interface

All that is left now is the `pushTile` method in the `Puzzle` class, which takes care of the mechanics of shifting the `Button`s' labels. To do so, it will use not only the `setLabel` method of the `Button` class, which we saw previously, but also the converse `getLabel` method. The code loops through the affected positions, getting the label from one `Button` and setting it into the neighboring `Button`. If the tile being pushed is in the same row as the blank space, the tiles need shifting to the right or left, whereas if the tile being pushed is in the same column as the blank space, the tiles need shifting down or up. If neither row nor column matches, no shifting happens:

```java
public void pushTile(int row, int col){
  if(row == blankRow){
    for( ; blankCol < col; blankCol++){
      buttons[blankRow][blankCol].setLabel
        (buttons[blankRow][blankCol+1].getLabel());
    }

    for( ; blankCol > col; blankCol--){
      buttons[blankRow][blankCol].setLabel
        (buttons[blankRow][blankCol-1].getLabel());
    }
  } else if(col == blankCol){
    for( ; blankRow < row; blankRow++){
      buttons[blankRow][blankCol].setLabel
        (buttons[blankRow+1][blankCol].getLabel());
    }
    for( ; blankRow > row; blankRow--){
      buttons[blankRow][blankCol].setLabel
        (buttons[blankRow-1][blankCol].getLabel());
    }
  }
  buttons[blankRow][blankCol].setLabel("");
}
```

The correctness of the above code critically depends on a feature of `for` loops that we haven't stressed previously. If the test condition isn't true to start with, the loop's body will be executed zero times. That is, the test is done before each iteration of the loop, even the first one.

▷ Exercise 15.5

Explain in more detail how this assures correctness. In particular, answer the following questions:

a. Suppose both the row and the column are equal to the blank position. What will happen?

b. Suppose the row is equal, but the column number of the blank square is less than that which is clicked on, which means that the first `for` loop's body will be executed at least once. When that first loop finishes, how do you know that the second `for` loop's body won't also be executed?

The applet itself is now complete; however, in order to view it, we need a *World Wide Web* document that contains it. This document gets written in a special *HyperText Markup Language*, known as HTML. It can contain headings, normal text, etc., as well as a special indication of where the applet should go. We won't delve into HTML here, because this information is widely available and peripheral to our topic. However, the following HTML file would be adequate to show our puzzle applet:

```
<!DOCTYPE HTML PUBLIC "-//W3C//DTD HTML 3.2//EN">
<html>
<head>
<title>Puzzle (original)</title>
</head>
<body>
<h1>Puzzle (original version)</h1>
<applet code="Puzzle" width=150 height=150>
</applet>
</body>
</html>
```

The specifics of how you can get your web browser to access this file and the applet that it contains depend on what sort of computer system you are using. You should be able to get the necessary information from the documentation for your web browser and Java system or from a local expert.

We'll now consider some variations on this applet. The first two just add new features to the puzzle, but one actually changes it to be an entirely different puzzle. We'll also look at some additional variants in the next section, using concurrency.

For our first variant, let's consider adding an "Initialize" button above the grid of tiles, which restores the labels to their starting configuration. That way frustrated users can get a fresh start. To reprogram `Puzzle` to accomplish this task, we will spin off the task of labeling the tiles in their initial state to a method called `initializeTiles`.

More significantly, to make the applet look as shown in Figure 15.5, we need to change our applet's configuration a bit. Rather than consisting of the 16 tile buttons, we'll view the applet as containing a thin control panel along the top and then a big

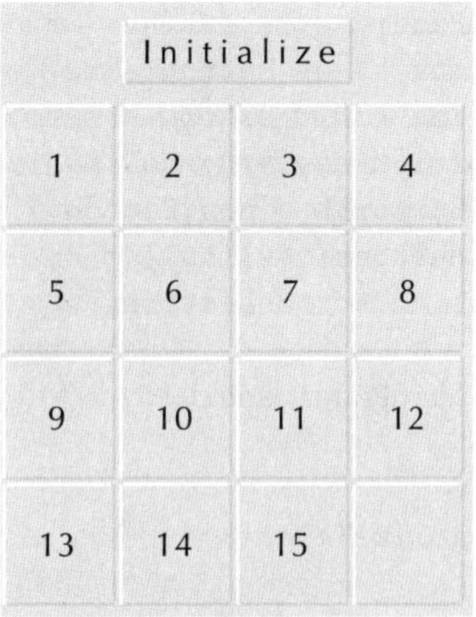

Figure 15.5   The puzzle applet with the Initialize button added

main panel on the bottom. (As noted in Figure 15.2, **Panel** is the intermediary class between **Container** and **Applet**; it is the most basic **Container** subclass.) The main panel, in turn, will contain the 16 tiles. The control panel, for now, will have only the "Initialize" button. This change is confined to the **init** method, because that is where the various pieces are put together. Here is the new version:

```
import java.awt.*;

public class Puzzle extends java.applet.Applet {

   private int size = 4;           // how many buttons wide and high
   private Button[][] buttons;
   private int blankRow, blankCol;  // position of the blank space

   public void init(){
     setLayout(new BorderLayout());
     Panel controlPanel = new Panel();
     add(controlPanel, "North");
     Panel mainPanel = new Panel();
     add(mainPanel, "Center");

     Button initializeButton = new Button("Initialize");
     initializeButton.addActionListener
       (new InitializeActionListener(this));
     controlPanel.add(initializeButton);
```

```
        mainPanel.setLayout(new GridLayout(size, size));
        buttons = new Button[size][size];
        for(int row = 0; row < size; row++){
          for(int col = 0; col < size; col++){
            Button b = new Button();
            buttons[row][col] = b;
            b.addActionListener(new TileActionListener
                              (this, row, col));
            mainPanel.add(b);
          }
        }
        initializeTiles();
    }

    public void initializeTiles(){
        int buttonCount = 0;
        for(int row = 0; row < size; row++){
          for(int col = 0; col < size; col++){
            buttonCount++;
            buttons[row][col].setLabel("" + buttonCount);
          }
        }
        blankRow = size - 1;
        blankCol = size - 1;
        buttons[blankRow][blankCol].setLabel("");
    }

    /*
     *  Code for pushTile(int row, int col) is unchanged
     */
}
```

As you can see, the applet itself no longer has a `GridLayout`—that has been moved to the `mainPanel`. Instead, the overall layout is now what is called a `BorderLayout`, which is what lets us add the `controlPanel` with a specification that it should form the `"North"` border. We could also, if we wanted, provide borders on the other three sides; we don't, though. The `mainPanel` gets added as the `"Center"` component, which simply means it takes up the remainder of the applet's space.

We still need to write the `InitializeActionListener` class, but it is no big deal at all:

```
import java.awt.event.*;

public class InitializeActionListener implements ActionListener {

  private Puzzle puz;

  public InitializeActionListener(Puzzle p){
    puz = p;
  }

  public void actionPerformed(ActionEvent evt){
    puz.initializeTiles();
  }
}
```

We made a design decision to call `initializeTiles` from `init`, rather than leaving `init` as it was, performing essentially identical actions to what is in the new `initializeTiles` method. We can describe this decision as having chosen *separating out* over *copying out*. This decision involved a trade-off of short-term versus long-term quality considerations:

- Copying the code out while leaving the existing `init` code unchanged would mean not changing that which was already working—and hence (in the short term) would run less risk of breaking it.
- Separating the code out (as we did) makes it more obvious to a reader that `initializeTiles` necessarily is putting the tiles back into the same configuration as `init` puts them in. There is less risk that this equality would be broken if the code is later changed.

Said another way, short-term quality considerations argue for minimizing changes to working code, whereas long-term quality is improved by making those changes necessary to enforce the following dictum:

The sameness principle: Coincidental sameness should be indicated by duplication; necessary sameness should be indicated by sharing.

▶ Exercise 15.6

We should have followed this principle elsewhere in the book but didn't always.

a. Find other examples of where we have adhered to the sameness principle.
b. Find an example of where we have strayed from the principle, and show how to modify our code so as to bring it into compliance.

Exercise 15.7

The sameness principle can be violated in two ways: Code that is coincidentally the same can be shared, and code that is necessarily the same can be duplicated. Compare the dangers inherent in these two forms of violation.

If we want to add additional features, we can just **add** more items to the `controlPanel`. For example, it would be nice if we had a "Randomize" button next to the "Initialize" one, for people who don't want to do their own scrambling of the tiles. We'll write a `randomizeTiles` method for the `Puzzle` class and then leave you to add the appropriate `ActionListener` class and `Button`. One aside: When we add a new `Button` to the `controlPanel`, we said it would go next to the "Initialize" one. Why? Well, that has to do with the `controlPanel`'s layout. But if you look at the preceding `Puzzle` constructor, you'll see we didn't set a layout for the `controlPanel`, just for the applet itself and the `mainPanel`. The solution to this mystery is that each `Panel` when constructed starts out with a default layout, called `FlowLayout`. For the other two panels, we had to change to a different layout, but for the `controlPanel` the default was just what we wanted. It puts a little space between the constituents (for example, between the "Initialize" and "Randomize" buttons) and then centers the whole group.

We have two basic approaches to how the `randomizeTiles` method could work. One would be to literally randomize the 16 labels, by selecting any of the 16 to be on the first tile, then any of the remaining 15 to go on the next tile, etc. A different approach would be to simply randomly shove the tiles around for a while, using `pushTile`, until we were satisfied that they were adequately scrambled. The big problem with the first approach is that you can get into configurations that can't be solved. To see this in a simpler setting, consider what might happen in a 2×2 sliding tile puzzle, which has three numbered tiles. It shouldn't take much playing around to convince you that the configuration shown in Figure 15.6 can't be solved because the tiles can only be cycled. Keep in mind that for the puzzle to be solved, the blank space needs to be in the lower right corner—it doesn't suffice for the numbers to be

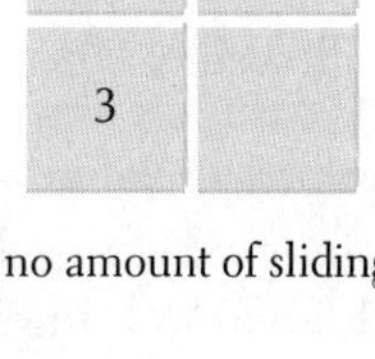

Figure 15.6   From this configuration, no amount of sliding the tiles will put the numbers in order with the blank in the lower right.

in order. A similar but more complicated argument can be made to show that half the configurations in the 15-tile puzzle are also unsolvable.

We therefore make the design decision to write `randomizeTiles` so that it randomly slides tiles around, which can be accomplished by the following code:

```
public void pushRandomTile(){
  int row = (int) (Math.random() * size);
  int col = (int) (Math.random() * size);
  pushTile(row, col);
}


public void randomizeTiles(){
  for(int i = 0; i < 100; i++){
    pushRandomTile();
  }
}
```

The lines that pick the random row and random column need some explanation. The procedure `Math.random` generates a random fraction between 0 and 1; multiplying that by `size` (i.e., 4) and then truncating the result to an `int` gives us a random integer from 0 through 3. The notation `(int)` is called a *cast* and converts the number to an `int` by throwing away its fractional part. Other than that magic, the only question you are likely to have is Why 100? The answer is that it seemed like a reasonable number: big enough to do a pretty good job of scrambling but not so large as to take a long time. You can change it if you want to make a different trade-off. At any rate, to see how long it does take on your computer, you'll need to provide a button to activate it.

Exercise 15.8

Provide a "Randomize" button, by doing the following:

a. Write a `RandomizeActionListener` class, similar to `InitializeAction Listener`, but which invokes the `randomizeTiles` method.

b. Add a "Randomize" `Button` to the `controlPanel` with a `RandomizeAction Listener`.

We'll see a rather different applet in the application section at the end of the chapter. For now, let's stick close to home and do another puzzle that involves a square grid of `Buttons`. The physical version of this puzzle is played with a square grid of pennies, initially all head side up. At each move you can flip any penny over, but then you also have to flip over the four neighboring ones (not counting the diagonal neighbors). If the penny you flip is on an edge of the grid, so that it is missing a neighbor, or in a corner, where it misses two neighbors, you just flip the neighbors that it does have. As with the sliding tile puzzle, the goal is to do a bunch of moves to scramble the grid up and then try to get back to the starting position. If you want to make the puzzle relatively easy, you might want to change `size` from 4 to 3; if you like challenge, you might up it to 6.

▶ Exercise 15.9

Change the puzzle applet to this new puzzle, by doing the following:

a. Get rid of the `blankRow` and `blankCol` instance variables, and in their place add two new instance variables of type `String`, called `heads` and `tails`, each set equal to an appropriate string. The strings you choose needn't have any resemblance to coins, and it is best if the two are visually very distinct, for example, `heads = "Flip!"` and `tails = ""`.

b. Change the `initializeTiles` method to set the label of all the buttons to `heads`.

c. Add a new method, `flip`, which takes a `Button` as an argument and changes its label. If the current label is `heads`, it should change to `tails` and vice versa.

d. Change the `pushTile` method to `flip` the `Button` in the pushed position and also `flip` each of its four neighbors, provided that they exist.

15.4　Concurrency

In the introduction to this chapter, we defined a concurrent system as one in which multiple activities go on at once, but we didn't say anything about why anyone would want to build such a system. You might think that the answer is to get a computation done faster, by doing multiple subproblems simultaneously. This goal can indeed be a motivation for concurrency, but it is not the most important one in practice. To start with, most "concurrent" computer programs don't truly carry out their multiple activities at the same time; instead, the computer switches its attention back and forth between the activities, so as to give the impression of doing them simultaneously. Truly concurrent computation would require the computer hardware to have multiple processors; although some systems have this feature, many don't. On a single-processor computer, all the activities necessarily have to take turns being carried out by the single processor. At any rate, concurrency has far more fundamental importance than just as a way to (maybe) gain speed, because the world in which the computer is embedded is concurrent:

▪ The user is sitting in front of the computer thinking all the time the computer is computing. Maybe the user decides some other computation is more interesting before the computer is done with the one it is working on.

▪ Computers today communicate via *networking* with other computers. A *client* computer may well want to do other computations while waiting for a response from a *server* computer. A server, in turn, may well want to process requests it receives from clients, even if it is already busy doing work of its own or handling other clients' earlier requests.

In other words, the primary motivation for concurrent programming is because a computer needs to interact with outside entities—humans and other computers—that are operating concurrently with it.

In this section we'll see how to write a concurrent program and some of the interesting issues that arise from interactions between the concurrently executing parts of the program. To illustrate our points, we'll use some further variations on the sliding 15-tile puzzle applet from the previous section. The basic premise is that the puzzle isn't challenging enough for some users, so we're going to add a new twist, which requires the user to stay alert. Namely, the computer will occasionally slide the tiles on its own, without the user doing anything. We call this the "poltergeist" feature because it resembles having a mischievous invisible spirit (i.e., a poltergeist) who is playing with your puzzle and thereby with your mind.

In broad outline, it seems relatively obvious how to program a poltergeist into the puzzle. We'll just add a third button to the control panel after the "Initialize" and "Randomize" buttons, with some appropriate label (maybe "Mess with me"), and an action listener that when the button is pushed goes into an infinite loop, and each time around the loop it pushes a random tile.

The one big problem with this plan is that when the user pushes a button and the action listener is notified, the user interface goes dead until the action listener's `actionPerformed` method has finished responding. Depending on how fast your computer is, you may have noticed this phenomenon with the "Randomize" button. If not, you could try the experiment of increasing how many random pushes it does from 100 to some larger number, say 500. You should be able to notice that no additional button pushes get responded to until all the random sliding around is done. Thus a button that didn't loop 100 or 500 times, but instead looped forever, would never let the user push any tiles. That defeats the whole point of the poltergeist—the point is to have it sliding tiles *while* the user slides them too.

Thus, we need the program to be concurrent: One part of the program should loop forever, sliding tiles randomly, and another part of the program should continue to respond to user interaction. Rather than speaking of "parts" of the program, which is rather vague, we'll use the standard word: *threads*. One thread will do the random pushing, while the original main thread of the program continues handling the user's actions. Thus our applet will now be *multithreaded*.

Rather than attempting a precise definition of threads, let us instead suggest that you think of them as independently executing strands of computations that can be braided together to form a concurrent program. This description implies a different model of computation from the one presented in Chapter 11, where the computer followed a single strand of execution determined by a program's SLIM instructions. In our new multithreaded case, you can still follow linearly along any one strand and see the instructions one after another in their expected sequence. However, if you look not at the one strand but at the entire braid, you'll see the instructions from the various strands mingled together. If you are wondering how the computer can mingle different instruction sequences this way, we congratulate you. You should indeed be wondering that. We'd like to answer the question, and for our own students, we do—but in a later course. We unfortunately don't have the time or space here.

From our perspective, however, it is enough to note that the Java language requires a specific model of concurrency from its implementations. To be more specific, Java implementations must support the class `Thread`, which allows the creation and simultaneous execution of concurrent threads of computation. As you will soon see, even though the operations involving threads are designed and specified well in Java, the very nature of concurrency gives rise to new and interesting problems not encountered in single-threaded applications. The Java language specification gives the implementation considerable flexibility with regard to how it mingles the threads of execution—different implementations might take the same strands and braid them together in different ways. This flexibility will be one of the reasons why we'll need to marshal our intellectual tools so that we can keep things simple rather than succumbing to potential for complexity.

We create our poltergeist by defining a subclass of `Thread`. This subclass is called `Poltergeist Thread`. The only `Thread` method we need to override is `run`, which tells what the thread does when it executes. Here then is our definition of the class `PoltergeistThread`:

```
public class PoltergeistThread extends Thread {

   private Puzzle puz;

   public PoltergeistThread(Puzzle p){
     puz = p;
   }

   public void run(){
     try{
       while(true){
         Thread.sleep(1000); // 1000 milliseconds = 1 second
```

```
                puz.pushRandomTile();
            }
        } catch(InterruptedException e){
            // If the thread is forcibly interrupted while sleeping,
            // an exception gets thrown that is caught here. However,
            // we can't really do anything, except stop running.
        }
    }
}
```

The one part we hadn't warned you about in advance is that rather than just madly looping away at full speed, pushing random tiles as fast as it can, the poltergeist instead sleeps for 1 second between each random push. This is important; otherwise the user still wouldn't have any real chance to do anything. Therefore, we've programmed in a 1-second delay using `sleep`, a static method in the `Thread` class. The only nuisance with using `sleep` is that it can throw an `InterruptedException`, so we have to be prepared to `catch` it. This exception gets thrown if some other thread invokes an operation that interrupts this thread's sleep. That never happens in our program, but we're still required to prepare for the eventuality. This requirement that we include a `catch` arises because the `run` method's declaration doesn't list any exceptions that might be thrown out of it, which the Java system interprets as a claim that none will be. It therefore requires us to back this claim up by catching any exceptions that might be thrown by other procedures that `run` calls, such as the `InterruptedException` that `Thread.sleep` can throw.

Here is the `PoltergeistActionListener` class, which responds to a push of the poltergeist button by creating a new `PoltergeistThread` object and telling it to `start` running:

```
import java.awt.event.*;

public class PoltergeistActionListener implements ActionListener {

    private Puzzle puz;

    public PoltergeistActionListener(Puzzle p){
        puz = p;
    }

    public void actionPerformed(ActionEvent evt){
        new PoltergeistThread(puz).start();
    }
}
```

Note that the `actionPerformed` method creates a new `PoltergeistThread` object and then calls the `start` method on the newly created object. This point is where the concurrency happens: The `start` method immediately returns, so the main thread can go on its way, processing other button presses from the user. However, although the `start` method has returned, the new `PoltergeistThread` is now off and running separately.

Assuming you add the appropriate `Button` to the `controlPanel`, you now have an applet that can (if the user chooses) go into poltergeist mode, where the tiles slide around on their own sporadically. The only problem is, the program is a bit buggy. We'll spend much of the rest of this section explaining the bug and what can be done about it.

▶ **Exercise 15.10**

Even a buggy program is worth trying out. Add a `Button` to the `ControlPanel` for firing up a poltergeist, and try it out.

Recall that different Java implementations can braid the same strands of a multithreaded program together in different ways. Therefore, we can't be sure what behavior you observed when you ran the program. The chances are good that it behaved properly, which may leave you wondering why we called the program buggy. The problem is: What happens if just as the poltergeist is sliding a tile, the user chooses to push a button too? Normally one or the other will get there first and be already done with the sliding before the other one starts. In this case, all is well. But if by an amazingly unlucky coincidence of timing, one starts sliding a tile *while* the other is still doing so, interesting things happen. Our main focus in this section will be on how you can design a program so that timing-related bugs like this one can't possibly occur, rather than merely being unlikely. However, because it is worthwhile to have some appreciation of the kind of misbehaviors we need to prevent, we'll first take some time to look at how we can provoke the program to misbehave.

We have two ways to experimentally find out some of the kinds of interesting behavior that can occur. One is to click the poltergeist button and then click away on the other buttons a lot of times until you get lucky and hit the timing just right. (Or maybe we should say until you get unlucky and hit the timing just wrong.) The problem with this approach is that you might get a repetitive strain injury of your mouse finger before you succeeded. So, we'll let you in on the other approach, which exploits a special feature of the program: You can have more than one poltergeist. If you think about it, clicking on the poltergeist button creates a new `PoltergeistThread` and `starts` it running. Nothing checks to see whether there already is one running. So, if you click the button again, you get a second `PoltergeistThread`, concurrent with the first one and the user. A few clicks later you can have half a dozen poltergeists, all sliding away at random. Now you just sit back, relax, and wait for something interesting to happen when two of the poltergeists happens to slide a tile at the same time.

When we tried this experiment, the first interesting thing that happened was that the number of blank tiles gradually started going up. (Initially there was just one, of course.) Occasionally, though much less frequently, the same number appeared on more than one tile. After a while there were just a few numbered tiles left and mostly blanks. The final interesting thing, which happened after most of the tiles were blank, was that we got error messages from the Java system telling us that some of the array references being done in `pushTile` were out of bounds. In other words, one of the array indices (row or column) was less than 0 or greater than 3.

Looking at the code, it appears at first that none of these problems should occur. For example, consider the following argument for why our array references should never be out of bounds: The row and column being pushed on are necessarily always in the range from 0 to 3. The blank row and blank column should also always be in this range, because they are initially, and the blank spot only moves from where it is one position at a time toward the tile being pushed, until it reaches that position. Therefore, because it starts at a legal position, and moves one space at a time to another legal position, it will always be in a legal position, and all the array accesses will always be in bound—except that they aren't.

The flaw in our reasoning is where we said that the blank position only moved one space at a time, stopping at the destination position. Suppose two threads both push the tile that is immediately to the right of the blank spot. Both check and find that the blank column is less than the destination column. Then both increment the blank column. Now the blank column has increased by 2—shooting right past where it was supposed to go.

This kind of anomaly, where two threads interact in an undesirable fashion when the timing is just wrong, is known as a *race*. Such errors can occur when two independent threads are accessing the same data (in our case, the instance variables in the `Puzzle` object itself) and at least one of them is modifying it. We should point out that our explanation of how the array reference errors might occur is just one possible scenario. The Java language specification provides sufficient freedom in how the threads are intermingled that lots of other possibilities exist as well.

▶ **Exercise 15.11**

Having given a plausible explanation for the out-of-bound array references, let's consider the other two bugs we found:

a. Explain how two threads could interact in a manner that would result in two blank tiles.

b. Explain how two threads could interact in a manner that would result in two tiles with the same number.

As you can see, even detecting a race can be difficult; trying to understand them can be downright perplexing. Therefore, one of our main goals in this section will be to show you a way to avoid having to reason about races, by ensuring that they can't occur. It is incredibly important to make sure that the races *can't* occur because you can never rely on experimentally checking that they *don't* occur. Because a race by definition depends on the timing being just wrong, you could test your program any number of times, never observe any misbehavior, and still have a user run into the problem.

This occurence is not just a theoretical possibility: Real programs have race bugs, and real users have encountered them, sometimes with consequences that have literally been fatal. For example, there was a race bug in the software used to control a medical radiation-therapy machine called the Therac 25. This machine had two modes of operation: one in which a low-energy beam directly shined on the patient, and one in which the beam energy was radically increased, but a metal target was put between the beam source and the patient so that the patient received only the weaker secondary radiation thrown off by the metal when struck by the beam. The only problem was that if a very quick-typing therapist set the machine to one mode, and then went back very quickly and changed it to the other mode, the machine could wind up with the beam on its high power setting, but the metal not in the way. This caused horrifying, and sometimes fatal, damage to several patients; the descriptions are too gruesome to repeat. The problem causing this was a race condition between two concurrent threads; it only showed up for the very fastest typists and only if they happened to carry out a particular action (rapidly changing the operating mode). Because of this, it not only wasn't found in initial testing, but it also showed up so sporadically in actual use that the service personnel failed to track the problem down and allowed the machine to continue causing (occasional) harm.

Not every concurrent system has the potential to kill, but many can at least cause serious financial costs if they fail unexpectedly in service. Therefore, it is important to have some way to avoid race conditions, rather than just hoping for the best. Luckily we've already taught you the key to designing race-free concurrent systems: representation invariants.

Recall that a representation invariant of a class is some property that is established by the class's constructor and preserved by all of the class's mutators, so all of the class's operations can count on the property being true (by induction). For example, if we ignore the concurrency muddle for the moment, the `Puzzle` class has the following representation invariant:

Puzzle representation invariant: Any instance of the `Puzzle` class will obey the following constraints at the time each method is invoked:

- $0 \leq$ `blankRow` $<$ `size`.
- $0 \leq$ `blankCol` $<$ `size`.
- The `Button` stored in `buttons[blankRow][blankCol]` has the empty string as its label.
- The remaining `size`$^2 - 1$ `Buttons` are labeled with the numerals from 1 to `size`$^2 - 1$ in some order.

The whole point of having such a representation invariant is that it frees us from having to reason about what specific mutations are done in what order because we have an inductive guarantee that holds over *all* sequences of mutations.

This ability to know what is true over all sequences, so that we don't have to consider each individual sequence, is exactly what we need to deal with concurrency. Consider, for example, a simple program with two threads, each of which performs two mutations. The first thread does mutations *a* and then *b*, whereas the second thread does A and then B. Then even this very simple concurrent system has six possible interleaved sequences in which the mutations might occur: *abAB*, *aAbB*, *aABb*, *AabB*, *AaBb*, and *ABab*. Would you really want to check that each of these six orders leaves the program working? And if six hasn't reached your pain threshold, consider what happens as the number of threads or mutations per thread grows much beyond two. So clearly, it is a big win to be able to show that the program is correct under any ordering, without considering each one individually.

However, having representation invariants that we can inductively rely on to be true after any sequence of mutator operations only helps us if we have some way of knowing that the program's execution *is* some sequence of mutator operations. In the case of the `Puzzle` applet, the two mutator operations that are in charge of maintaining the invariants are `pushTile` and `initializeTiles`. Therefore, we need some way of knowing that the Java system will invoke those operations in some sequential fashion, rather than jumbling together parts of one invocation with parts of another. The reason why individual parts of the mutators can't be jumbled is that they don't preserve the invariant; for example, even if the invariant holds before executing `blankCol++`, it won't hold afterward. So, what we need to do is identify for the Java system the invariant-preserving units that it needs to treat as indivisible (i.e, that it is not allowed to intermingle).

Java provides the ability to mark certain methods as indivisible in this sense, using the modifying keyword `synchronized`. Because `initializeTiles` and `pushTile` are the two `Puzzle` mutators that preserve the invariant (if left uninterrupted), we use the following code to mark them as `synchronized`:

```
public synchronized void initializeTiles(){
  // body same as before
}
```

```
public synchronized void pushTile(int row, int col){
  // body same as before
}
```

With these keywords in place, the Java system won't let any thread start into one of these methods if another thread is in the midst of one of them on the same `Puzzle`. Instead, it waits until the other thread has left its `synchronized` method. One way to envision this is that each object has a special room with a *lock* on the door. It is a rule that `synchronized` methods may only be performed in that room, with the door locked. This rule forces all threads that want to perform `synchronized` methods to take turns.

In the `Puzzle` class, the only methods that directly rely on the representation invariant are the two mutator operations that are also responsible for preserving the invariant. Some other programs, however, have classes with methods that rely on the invariant but play no active role in preserving it, because they perform no mutation. (They just observe the object's state but don't modify it.) These methods need to be `synchronized`, too, to ensure that they only observe the object's state after some sequence of complete mutator operations has been performed rather than in the middle of one of the mutator operations.

As you can see, freedom from races is the result of teamwork between the programmer and the Java system: The programmer uses a representation invariant to ensure that all is well so long as `synchronized` methods are never executing simultaneously in different threads, and the Java system plays its part by respecting those `synchronized` annotations.

▷ Exercise 15.12

Consider the `itemVector` in the `ItemList` class, in the Java version of CompuDuds. Although each position in that array can hold an `Item`, it is not necessarily true that they all do. For example, when the array is initially created by the line

```
itemVector = new Item[10];
```

10 different positions can each hold an `Item`, but none of them yet does. (Instead, each holds the special `null` value.) Similarly, when we do a `delete` operation, the vacated position has the special `null` value stored into it, which isn't an `Item`. Thus, when we retrieve an element from the array, as in the line

```
itemVector[index].display();
```

we have in principle the possibility that the retrieved value might not be an `Item` but instead might be the `null` value from when the array was created or from when a `delete` was done. If so, we would get an error when we tried to invoke the `display` method on that non-`Item`.

a. Write a paragraph or two explaining how the design of the `ItemList` class ensures that this will never happen, given that CompuDuds is a single-threaded program.

b. Write a paragraph explaining why the reasoning would break down if an `ItemList` were used from more than one thread and briefly stating what should be done about it.

Having seen how to keep one thread from stepping on another thread's toes, we'll now turn to another important concurrency topic: how one thread can wait for an action in another thread.

Nested Calls to Synchronized Methods and Deadlock

You might wonder what happens if one `synchronized` method invokes another one. In terms of our analogy, a thread that is currently inside a locked room is trying to do another operation that requires being inside a locked room.

In Java, if the second method is on the same object, we have no problem at all. The thread is already inside that object's locked room and so can go ahead with the nested `synchronized` method. Moreover, when it is done with that inner method, it doesn't make the blunder of unlocking the door and leaving the room. Instead, it waits until the outer `synchronized` method is done before unlocking.

How about if the inner `synchronized` operation is on a different object? Our physical analogy of locked rooms starts to break down here. The thread manages to stay inside its current locked room while waiting for the other room to become available. Then without unlocking the room it is in, it locks the new room and is (somehow) simultaneously in two locked rooms.

There is a real pitfall here for unwary programmers. Suppose one thread is inside the locked room for object *A*, while another is inside the locked room for object *B*. Now the first thread tries to invoke a `synchronized` method on *B*, and the second thread tries to invoke a `synchronized` method on *A*. Each thread waits for the other room to become available. But because each is waiting with its own room locked, neither room ever will become available—the two will simply wait for each other forever. This situation, in which threads cyclically wait for one another, is known as *deadlock*.

Suppose we want to change our applet so that rather than having a button that causes a poltergeist to come into existence, it has a checkbox that we can use to turn the poltergeist on or off. A checkbox is a GUI element that switches between an on state and an off state each time you click on it. On some systems, it looks like a box that is empty for off and has a checkmark or X in it for on. On other systems it is a square that has shadows that make it look like it is sticking out for off and recessed in for on.

One way to implement this would be to handle turning the poltergeist on just the same way as we previously handled the button presses (create a thread and start it running) and handle turning the poltergeist off by somehow killing off the thread. Then the next time the checkbox was clicked to turn the poltergeist back on, a new thread would be created, etc.

However, there is another, more interesting, alternative. We can have a single `PoltergeistThread` that starts running at the beginning and is never killed off (at least, not until the whole applet is terminated). However, the poltergeist can be in a dormant state, where it just waits for the checkbox to turn it on. Then it starts doing its usual random pushing of tiles, until such time as the checkbox is clicked again. Then it goes back into the dormant state, once more waiting to be turned on.

To implement this design, we'll give the `PoltergeistThread` three more methods. Two will be `public` methods used by the user interface to exert control: `enable` and `disable`. The `disable` method puts the thread into its dormant state, where it doesn't do any random pushes, and the `enable` state wakes it back up. Finally, we'll add a `private` method called `waitUntilEnabled` that can be used by the thread's main loop to do the actual waiting; here is that main loop:

```
public void run(){
  try{
    while(true){
      Thread.sleep(1000); // 1000 milliseconds = 1 second
      waitUntilEnabled();
      puz.pushRandomTile();
    }
  } catch(InterruptedException e){
    // If the thread is forcibly interrupted while sleeping,
    // an exception gets thrown that is caught here. However,
    // we can't really do anything, except stop running.
  }
}
```

As you can see, we made just one change from the previous version. Each time around the loop it performs `waitUntilEnabled` before pushing a random tile. If the thread is currently enabled, this call will immediately return and the tile will be pushed. If the thread is disabled, on the other hand, the `waitUntilEnabled` method won't return until after the `enable` method has been called by the user interface.

Now we have to see how the three new methods are written. We'll add a new instance variable to the `PoltergeistThread` class:

```
private boolean enabled;
```

The two controlling methods can just set this variable appropriately:

```
public void enable(){
  enabled = true;
}

public void disable(){
  enabled = false;
}
```

Now comes the tricky part: waiting for the `enabled` variable to be set to true. One simple approach (but not a terribly good one) is to simply go into a loop, checking each time around the loop to see if the variable is true yet. To avoid hogging the computer's time too much, we can sleep for a fraction of a second between each check:

```
private void waitUntilEnabled() throws InterruptedException {
  while(!enabled){
    Thread.sleep(100);
  }
}
```

We have two new Java language features in this method. One is the use of the exclamation point to indicate "not." That is, the loop continues so long as the poltergeist is "not enabled," in other words, so long as the `enabled` variable has the value `false`. The other new feature is the phrase "`throws InterruptedException`." You'll recall that the `Thread.sleep` procedure can throw this particular exception. In the `run` method, we handled that by use of a `try` and `catch` construct. Here, however, we have made a different choice. Rather than catching the exception, we've allowed it to continue on out of the `waitUntilEnabled` method so that it can be caught in the caller. Here that makes sense because the caller is `run`, and `run` is in a much better position to do something sensible about being interrupted while waiting. To indicate that an exception of this kind may now emerge from the `waitUntilEnabled` procedure, we need to include the `throws` declaration.

The preceding approach, in which waiting is accomplished by nervously glancing at the controlling variable every fraction of a second, is known as *busy waiting*. We chose, rather arbitrarily, to wait 100 milliseconds (one tenth of a second) between each check. If this time is made too short, the computer will be bogged down doing nothing but checking over and over. If the time is made too long, on the other hand, the program will be very sluggish in responding to changes. In this particular program, the situation isn't unbearable because only one thread is ever waiting, as opposed to lots of threads each checking over and over, and also a bit of sluggishness isn't such a bad thing for a poltergeist that only acts sporadically anyway. In general, however, busy waiting is a terrible way for a thread to wait for some relevant change to occur. (There is also a subtle problem with our specific implementation of busy waiting. Because doing busy waiting at all is a bad idea, we'll describe the subtle problem in the end-of-chapter notes section and move on here to a better alternative.)

So, we need another approach to waiting. What we would really like is to put the thread to sleep not for some predetermined period but rather until the situation changes. How will we know when the situation has changed? It changes when the `enable` method is invoked by the user interface. Therefore, we can have the `enable` method explicitly provide a "wake up call" for the poltergeist thread. Java provides a pair of methods for providing this "wait until awakened" and "wake up" functionality: `wait` and `notify`. Using them, we can change our code as follows:

```
// Warning: these two routines don't work, see below for why.
private void waitUntilEnabled() throws InterruptedException {
  while(!enabled){
    wait();
  }
}

public void enable(){
  enabled = true;
  notify();
}
```

As the comment warned you, these methods still aren't quite right. However, they do show the essence of what is needed. The `waitUntilEnabled` method simply uses `wait` where it previously used `Thread.sleep`, and the `enable` method uses `notify` to wake the waiting thread back up.

The problem with the preceding code is that it has a race bug. Suppose the poltergeist thread invokes `waitUntilEnabled` and finds that currently `enabled` is `false`. Therefore, it is going to `wait`. However, in the instant in between when the `while` loop checked the `enabled` flag and when the `wait` is executed, the user clicks the checkbox, turning it on. This invokes the `enable` method. The `enable` method sets the enabled variable to true and executes notify. The notify method finds that there currently isn't any waiting thread to wake up, so it returns without having done anything. Then, just after notify has failed to find a waiter to wake up, the poltergeist thread resumes executing, calls wait, and goes to sleep. Now the thread is nominally enabled but is sleeping.

This problem can be solved the same way as other races, by using the synchronized keyword. In fact, the Java system will force you to do so by signaling an error if you forget. In addition to the enable and waitUntilEnabled methods, you should add the synchronized keyword to disable, because that is another method that accesses the shared state. (The details of why disable should be synchronized are explained in the end-of-chapter notes.) Thus our correct version using wait and notify is as follows:

```
public synchronized void enable(){
   enabled = true;
   notify();
}


public synchronized void disable(){
   enabled = false;
}


private synchronized void waitUntilEnabled()
      throws InterruptedException {
   while(!enabled){
      wait();
   }
}
```

You might have this question: The waitUntilEnabled method is synchronized, so in our metaphor it goes into the lockable room, locks the door, and then if the enabled variable is false, it waits. If it waits with the room locked, how can the enable method get in to change enabled to true? The answer is that the lock is temporarily unlocked while waiting using wait and is relocked before wait returns.

This need to relock the lock before returning from wait also explains why we need a while loop around the wait, rather than just an if. A brief period occurs where the lock is unlocked, between when enable leaves and when wait relocks it before continuing. Conceivably disable could slip in during this window of opportunity and change enabled back to false. If so, when wait does (later) get the lock and resumes execution, the while loop will discover this and wait again.

Do we now have a working puzzle applet with a checkbox for turning a poltergeist on and off? If you've stayed awake yourself, you may realize that we're still missing something: the checkbox itself, and the associated listener that actually calls the `enable` and `disable` methods. In the `Puzzle` constructor, we can add the following lines (right after the Initialize and Randomize buttons):

```
PoltergeistThread thread = new PoltergeistThread(this);
thread.disable(); // just to emphasize that it starts disabled
thread.start();
Checkbox poltergeistCheckbox = new Checkbox("Poltergeist");
poltergeistCheckbox.addItemListener
  (new PoltergeistItemListener(thread));
controlPanel.add(poltergeistCheckbox);
```

As you can see, `Checkboxes` don't have `ActionListeners`; they have `Item Listeners`, which is a rather fine distinction that the Java system makes. A `Button` can be "acted upon," with each action independent from any previous ones, whereas a `Checkbox` is an "item" that can "change state" from "selected" to "deselected" or vice versa. `Checkboxes` are initially deselected.

In practical terms, this distinction means that we need to write the `Poltergeist ItemListener` class as follows:

```
import java.awt.event.*;

public class PoltergeistItemListener implements ItemListener {

  private PoltergeistThread thread;

  public PoltergeistItemListener(PoltergeistThread t){
    thread = t;
  }

  public void itemStateChanged(ItemEvent evt){
    if(evt.getStateChange() == ItemEvent.SELECTED){
      thread.enable();
    } else {
      thread.disable();
    }
  }
}
```

The `ItemEvent` that is passed in to `itemStateChanged` tells us information about the state-change that occurred; in particular, we can tell whether it was a change to selectedness (being turned on) or deselectedness (being turned off) as shown in the preceding code.

Before we leave the puzzle applet entirely, we can make one other improvement to it. Right now if you are viewing this applet in a web browser and have the poltergeist turned on, and then you tell the browser to switch to viewing some other web page, the poltergeist will keep right on sliding tiles, even if you can't see the applet. If you then tell the browser to go back to the page with the applet on it, you'll find that the tiles have moved around in your absence. This is probably not what most users would want. To fix this, we can `disable` the `PoltergeistThread` when the user stops viewing the applet. We can know when to do this because the browser will invoke the `stop` method of an applet whenever it stops showing that applet. The default implementation of this method, inherited from the `java.applet.Applet` class, doesn't do anything. We can override it with a version that puts our thread on hold:

```
public void stop(){
    thread.disable();
}
```

We'll also need to change where we declare `thread`. At the moment it is a temporary local variable inside the `Puzzle` constructor; we'll need to change it to be an instance variable instead.

When the user goes back to looking at the applet, we need to set the poltergeist going again. The browser invokes another method to notify the applet that it is once again being viewed; not surprisingly, it is called `start`. At first you might think it could just do `thread.enable()`. However, that would turn the poltergeist "back" on even if it hadn't been on in the first place. To solve this problem, we can check the current state of the checkbox and only re-enable the thread if the checkbox is in the on state:

```
public void start(){
    if(poltergeistCheckbox.getState()){
        thread.enable();
    }
}
```

Because this code uses the `poltergeistCheckbox` variable, we'll again need to move that declaration so as to turn it into an instance variable. Notice that the `Checkbox` class has a `getState` method that returns `true` or `false` to indicate whether the box is currently in the on or off state, respectively.

Finally, we can add a `destroy` method to the `Puzzle` class, which gets called by the browser when the applet is being completely evicted, as opposed to just temporarily ceasing to be viewed. What we'll do in that case is to entirely kill off the poltergeist thread so that it doesn't keep running when there is no longer an applet for it to mess with. We can kill off the thread using the `Thread` class's `stop` method:

```
public void destroy(){
  thread.stop();
}
```

Exercise 15.13

Another possibility, rather than forcibly killing off the poltergeist thread, would be to politely ask it to stop running. We could change the main loop in the `run` method from `while(true)` to `while(!terminated)`, with a boolean instance variable called `terminated`. We would initialize `terminated` to `false` and set it to `true` in a new `terminate` method we could add to the `PoltergeistThread` class. Then the `Puzzle` class's `destroy` method could call `terminate` instead of `stop`. Implement this approach. Here's the tricky part: Make sure it works even if the poltergeist is disabled at the time it is terminated.

15.5   An Application: Simulating Compound Interest

Imagine that you have just started work for a small company that produces Java applets for use in education. One of the company's applets is used to illustrate how compound interest works; it is shown in Figure 15.7. This applet simulates the passage of years at a rate of 1 year per second, displaying information in the scrolling area that occupies the main portion of the applet. The figure is just a snapshot, showing what it looked like after 22 simulated years had passed, but keep in mind that it keeps getting updated. Meanwhile the top "control panel" portion of the applet has three controls. One is a checkbox labeled "Run" that can be used to pause the simulation or resume it. (The applet actually starts in the paused state; the box was clicked on 22 seconds prior to the snapshot in the figure.) The other two controls allow the initial amount of money and the interest rate to be changed. If the user changes either of these, the output area is cleared and the simulation is reset to year 0. The applet is included on the web site for this book, so you can try it out.

Like many junior programmers, you have been assigned to fix bugs in the company's existing programs, rather than writing a new program from scratch. Occasionally you may get to add a new feature.

The boss, Mr. Wright, comes to you with an interesting problem concerning the compound-interest simulation applet. Although it generally seems to work properly,

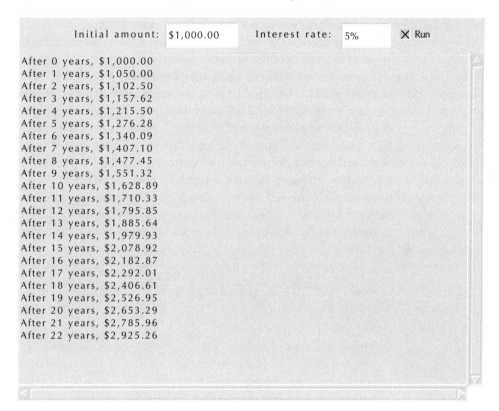

Figure 15.7   Compound interest simulation applet

a few customers have reported seeing it occasionally produce bizarre behavior, which they have never managed to replicate. The common thread is that after changing one of the values (initial amount or interest rate) while the simulation was running, the customers report seeing output on the screen that was clearly wrong or was missing some years. Your boss normally wouldn't care that a few customers were claiming to occasionally see strange things, but it happens that some of them are very important clients that the company is trying to make a good impression on, and right now the reliability of the program is in question. The boss tells you your job is to get to the bottom of the matter and restore the company's reputation for rock-solid quality.

Because you have had the benefit of learning from a textbook that introduced concurrent programming, you immediately blurt out to the boss that you are sure— without even looking at the code—that you know what the problem is. Obviously the applet must have two threads, one to simulate the passage of years and one to respond to the user interface (much like in the puzzle with the poltergeist). Clearly the boneheaded programmer who preceded you at the company didn't bother to put "synchronized" where it was needed, and so there is a race condition that causes problems when the user makes a change just at the instant a year is being simulated. You say that you can fix the problem in a few minutes by just sticking "synchronized" in front of some methods.

The boss is not thrilled, which may be partially an emotional response, given that you just called his teenaged son a bonehead. However, mostly it is just good, cautious business sense. Right now, the program appears to work when tested. When you add the synchronized keywords, it still will appear to work when tested. How can the boss confidently tell the VIP clients that you definitely have gotten to the bottom of the matter and solved their mysterious problem? How can he know that your explanation accounts for their symptoms when the symptoms aren't even showing up in testing in the first place? How can he be sure the symptoms won't keep showing up for the client?

Because of the questions, you agree on a more careful plan of work:

1. You will examine the code and come up with a few specific race scenarios that would exhibit the kind of behavior the clients have mentioned. That is, you'll map out exactly what order things would have to happen in to make the symptoms show up.

2. Then you'll rig the applet so that these race conditions can be made to repeatably happen, rather than just once in a blue moon, to show your boss that they are real. You'll do this by introducing extra time-delay sleeps at the critical points so that rather than having to change one of the values at just exactly the wrong moment, you'll have a much bigger window of opportunity.

3. Then you'll put the synchronized keywords in that you are convinced will solve the problem.

4. Finally, you'll show that even with the extra time delays that you put in to make the races easy to trigger, the symptoms no longer show up in your fixed version.

If your theory is correct, the problem is definitely localized within the CompoundingThread class, which provides the guts of the simulation; the other classes just provide the user interface and seem quite innocent. From your perspective, all you need to know about them is how they relate to the CompoundingThread class:

■ The main applet class, Compounder, provides two methods for managing the scrolling output area: outputLine (for adding an additional line of output) and clearOutput (for clearing the area).

■ The user interface calls two methods from the CompoundingThread class, setInitial Amount and setInterestRate, to convey this information in and also uses enable and disable methods, much like the poltergeist's.

Here is the code for the class in question:

```
public class CompoundingThread extends Thread {

  private boolean enabled;
  private double initial, current, multiplier;
  private int year;
  private Compounder c;
  private java.text.NumberFormat fmt;

  // Invariant:
  //    (1) current = initial * (multiplier raised to the
  //        year power)
  //    (2) year also specifies how many lines of output c has
  //        gotten since it was last cleared, corresponding to
  //        years from 0 up through year-1.


  public CompoundingThread(Compounder comp){
    c = comp;
    fmt = java.text.NumberFormat.getCurrencyInstance();
  }

  synchronized private void waitUntilEnabled()
      throws InterruptedException {
    while(!enabled){
      wait();
    }
  }

  synchronized public void disable(){
    enabled = false;
  }

  synchronized public void enable(){
    enabled = true;
    notify();
  }

  public void run(){
    try{
      while(true){
```

```
            Thread.sleep(1000);
            waitUntilEnabled();
            doYear();
          }
      } catch(InterruptedException e){
        // ignore, but stop running
      }
    }

    private void doYear(){
      c.outputLine("After " + year + " years, " +fmt.format(current));
      year++;
      current *= multiplier;
    }

    public void setInitialAmount(double amount){
      initial = amount;
      initialize();
    }

    public void setInterestRate(double rate){
      // note that a rate of 5% (e.g.) would be .05, *not* 5
      multiplier = 1 + rate;
      initialize();
    }

    private void initialize(){
      current = initial;
      year = 0;
      c.clearOutput();
    }
}
```

We have a few new Java features in this code, as usual. Perhaps the most significant is that it uses numbers that aren't integers—this is what the type "double" is for. For example, unlike the CompuDuds program, which stored $19.50 as 1950 (the number of cents), the compound interest applet stores it as 19.5. In order to multiply the current amount of money by the multiplier (which might, for example, be 1.05 if the interest rate was 5 percent), the doYear method uses *=. This operator is analogous to +=, in that it uses the old value to compute the new one; here it does so by multiplication. Finally, this code uses a fancy library class, java.text.NumberFormat, to format the current amount of money for the output line. For example, if current is

19.5, the expression `fmt.format(current)` would evaluate to the string `"$19.50"`. Not only does this expression take care of details like making sure there are two digits after the decimal point, it also has an additional big win: It automatically adjusts to other currencies that are used elsewhere in the world. (For more details, look up the documentation for this library class.)

Exercise 15.14

As an important preparation for figuring out the race conditions, you need to understand the class's invariant. Assume for the moment that there is no concurrency, and write out explanations of how the invariant is preserved by each of the three methods `doYear`, `setInitialAmount`, and `setInterestRate`.

Exercise 15.15

Now come up with at least three different specific misbehaviors that could result from a race between `doYear` and one of the other methods. Explain exactly what order the events would have to occur in. For example, you might say that right between the user interface thread setting the year to 0 and clearing the output, the simulation thread might slip in and do a complete invocation of `doYear`. Also, explain for each scenario what the user would see. Try to come up with at least three scenarios with different symptoms from one another.

Exercise 15.16

Now make each of your misbehaviors happen. Rather than developing the knack of getting the timing just perfect, you should use `Thread.sleep` to open up a big window of opportunity. For example, if you put a several-second sleep between setting the year to 0 and clearing the output, it is a sure thing that at least one `doYear` will slip into that gap. (Provided, of course, that the simulation is enabled to run, rather than being paused in the disabled state.)

Exercise 15.17

Now add the `synchronized` keyword to the appropriate methods, and verify that the misbehaviors have all gone away, even when you use `Thread.sleep` to give them ample opportunity to show up.

Your boss is sufficiently impressed with your work to let you add a new feature customers have been requesting. Many people aren't as interested in answering questions like If I invest $1000 now, how much will I have when I retire? as they are in questions like If I invest $1000 each year from now until I retire, how much will I have? So, you are to add a feature to the program so that it has *two* fields for monetary input: the initial amount and the additional amount to add each year.

Of course, this gets you into the user-interface part of the program, which you've been able to ignore until now. The most relevant portions are the `InitialAmountField` class and the part of the `Compounder` class that creates the initial amount field. You'll be able to add the new field just by following that example because it is another currency amount field.

The part of the `Compounder` class's constructor that creates the initial amount field and adds it to the control panel is as follows:

```
controlPanel.add(new Label("Initial amount:", Label.RIGHT));
controlPanel.add(new InitialAmountField(1000.00, compThread));
```

The first line adds a `Label`, which is just a fixed chunk of text. The argument `Label.RIGHT` indicates that it should be positioned to the far right end of the space it occupies, which looks correct given that it ends with a colon and is followed by the field in which the amount is entered. The `InitialAmountField` itself follows. The first argument to its constructor is the value the field should start out with (`1000.00`), pending any modification by the user, while the second argument, `compThread`, is the `CompoundingThread` that should receive `setInitialAmount` notifications.

Here's the `InitialAmountField` class:

```
public class InitialAmountField extends FormattedField {

    private CompoundingThread compThread;

    public InitialAmountField(double initialValue,
                              CompoundingThread ct){
        super(10, java.text.NumberFormat.getCurrencyInstance());
        compThread = ct;
        Double value = new Double(initialValue);
        setValue(value);
        valueEntered(value);
    }

    public void valueEntered(Object value){
        compThread.setInitialAmount(((Number) value).doubleValue());
    }
}
```

This little class contains some fairly tricky stuff, and although you don't really need to understand it to make another one just like it, we don't want to pass up an opportunity for explanation.

The superclass, `FormattedField`, handles the general problem of being a text-entry field that has some specified special format—in this case, the format of a currency amount. Its constructor needs to be told how wide a field is desired and what format should be used; those are the two arguments in

```
super(10, java.text.NumberFormat.getCurrencyInstance());
```

The format object that is passed in as the second argument here formats numbers as currency amounts, but in general it can specify formats for all sorts of things—for example, dates as well as numbers. Therefore, the interface of the `FormattedField` class needs to be very general. In particular, its `setValue` method takes an arbitrary `Object` as an argument, so as not to be limited to numbers. The only problem is that the `initialValue`, which is a `double`, isn't an `Object`. Any instance of any class is an `Object`, because all classes are descended from `Object`. However, `double` isn't a class (nor are `int`, `boolean`, or the other basic numeric and character types). So, we need to make an `Object` that holds the `double` inside, which is what the `Double` class is for. We make a `Double` called `value` that holds the `initialValue`, and we pass that `Double` object into `setValue`.

When the user types a new value into the field, the `FormattedField` class responds by invoking the `valueEntered` method to process this newly entered value. We do the same thing with the initial value so that it gets handled the same way. Again, because `FormattedField` needs to work for all kinds of data, it passes an `Object` to `valueEntered`. Our `valueEntered` method needs to recover the actual `double` value from that `Object`. The first thing we do is to declare that we know the `Object` must be a `Number`. (The `Number` class is the superclass of `Double`. It has other subclasses that similarly hold other kinds of numbers.) We make this declaration with the notation `(Number)`, which is another *cast*, much like the `(int)` we saw earlier. Then we invoke the `Number`'s `doubleValue` method to retrieve the actual value as a `double` and finally notify the `CompoundingThread` by invoking its `setInitialAmount` method.

Exercise 15.18

Add a new labeled field for the annual contribution, and arrange for it to get passed to the `CompoundingThread`. Modify the `CompoundingThread` so that it incorporates this additional amount each year.

Review Problems

▷ **Exercise 15.19**

Suppose we add one more method to the `ItemList` class, in the Java version of the CompuDuds program. The method follows, with the nondescriptive name `mystery`:

```java
public class ItemList extends Object {

  ... all the existing stuff goes here ...

  public Item mystery(){
    Item soFar = itemVector[0];
    for(int i = 1; i < numItems; i = i + 1){
      if(itemVector[i].price() > soFar.price()){
        soFar = itemVector[i];
      }
    }
    return soFar;
  }
}
```

a. Under what conditions can the `mystery` method be legally invoked to retrieve an `Item`?

b. Describe as precisely as you can what the `mystery` method returns, while retaining an "outsider's" perspective. That is, your description should focus on what the method returns and not how it finds it. Your description should not be in terms of the representation of an `ItemList` (for example, it should not mention the `itemVector`); instead, your description should use terminology that is understandable to someone who is using the `ItemList` class but has not seen the code for it.

c. Give three examples of options that could be added to the user interface that would make use of the `mystery` method. You don't need to show the code, just list what the option would do. It is okay if their usefulness is questionable. You can use existing methods in addition to the new `mystery` method but shouldn't assume any other new methods are added.

▷ **Exercise 15.20**

Modify the `ItemList` class so that when a deletion leaves the `itemVector` less than one-third full, a new `itemVector` half as big is created. However, the `itemVector` should never be made any smaller than its original size, 10. See Exercise 14.18 and the text preceding that exercise for more information on this technique.

Chapter Inventory

Vocabulary

applet	default constructor
concurrency	interface
type	World Wide Web
declaration	HyperText Markup Language (HTML)
class method	cast
instance method	networking
array	client
expression	server
statement	thread
command-line argument	multithreaded
exception	race
batch processing	lock
event-driven graphical user interface (GUI)	deadlock
	busy waiting
Abstract Window Toolkit (AWT)	

Slogans

The sameness principle

Java syntax

`public`	`...?...:...`
`extends`	`==`
`//`	`for`
`/*...*/`	`+=`
`private`	`++`
`int`	`length`
`new`	`--`
`this`	`null`
`=`	`static`
`return`	`/`
`void`	`%`
`super`	`while`
`boolean`	`true`
`if...else...`	`try...catch...`
`[]`	`||`

`&&`	`synchronized`
`import`	`!`
+ for string concatenation	`false`
and conversion	`throws`
`implements`	`double`
(*type*)	`*=`

Library Classes and Interfaces

Note that these all are listed with their full name, even though many were used with shortened names. For example, we used `String` rather than the full name `java.lang.String`. The short form is available without needing an `import` directive for those classes that are in the `java.lang` package.

`java.lang.String`	`java.awt.event.ActionListener`
`java.lang.System`	`java.awt.event.ActionEvent`
`java.io.IOException`	`java.awt.Panel`
`java.lang.NumberFormatException`	`java.awt.BorderLayout`
`java.io.BufferedReader`	`java.awt.FlowLayout`
`java.io.InputStreamReader`	`java.lang.Math`
`java.awt.Button`	`java.lang.Thread`
`java.awt.Checkbox`	`java.lang.InterruptedException`
`java.awt.Component`	`java.awt.event.ItemListener`
`java.awt.TextField`	`java.awt.event.ItemEvent`
`java.applet.Applet`	`java.text.NumberFormat`
`java.awt.Container`	`java.awt.Label`
`java.awt.LayoutManager`	`java.lang.Double`
`java.awt.GridLayout`	`java.lang.Number`

Nonlibrary Classes

`Item`	`RandomizeActionListener`
`OxfordShirt`	`PoltergeistThread`
`Chinos`	`PoltergeistActionListener`
`ItemList`	`PoltergeistItemListener`
`CompuDuds`	`CompoundingThread`
`Puzzle`	`Compounder`
`TileActionListener`	`InitialAmountField`
`InitializeActionListener`	`FormattedField`

Library Methods

print (in java.io.PrintStream)
println (in java.io.PrintStream)
readLine
    (in java.io.BufferedReader)
add (in java.awt.Container)
setLayout (in java.awt.Container)
setLabel (in java.awt.Button)
addActionListener
    (in java.awt.Button)
getLabel (in java.awt.Button)
random (in java.lang.Math)

sleep (in java.lang.Thread)
start (in java.lang.Thread)
wait (in java.lang.Object)
notify (in java.lang.Object)
getStateChange
    (in java.awt.event.ItemEvent)
getState (in java.awt.Checkbox)
stop (in java.lang.Thread)
format (in java.text.NumberFormat)
doubleValue (in java.lang.Number)

Nonlibrary Methods

price (in Item)
display (in Item, OxfordShirt,
    Chinos, and ItemList)
inputSpecifics (in Item,
    OxfordShirt, and Chinos)
reviseSpecifics (in Item)
empty (in ItemList)
totalPrice (in ItemList)
add (in ItemList)
choose (in ItemList)
displayPrice (in CompuDuds)
main (in CompuDuds)
inputItem (in CompuDuds)
inputIntegerInRange (in CompuDuds)
inputSelection (in CompuDuds)
init (in Puzzle)
actionPerformed
    (in TileActionListener,
    InitializeActionListener, and
    PoltergeistActionListener)
initializeTiles (in Puzzle)
randomizeTiles (in Puzzle)
flip (in Puzzle)
run (in PoltergeistThread

    and CompoundingThread)
enable (in PoltergeistThread
    and CompoundingThread)
disable (in PoltergeistThread
    and CompoundingThread)
waitUntilEnabled
    (in PoltergeistThread
    and CompoundingThread)
itemStateChanged
    (in PoltergeistItemListener)
stop (in Puzzle and Compounder)
start (in Puzzle and Compounder)
destroy (in Puzzle and Compounder)
terminate (in PoltergeistThread)
outputLine (in Compounder)
clearOutput (in Compounder)
setInitialAmount
    (in CompoundingThread)
setInterestRate
    (in CompoundingThread)
setValue (in FormattedField)
valueEntered (in FormattedField,
    InitialAmountField,
    and InterestRateField)

Sidebars

Nested Calls to Synchronized Methods and Deadlock

Notes

We mentioned that our implementation of busy waiting (Section 15.4) was flawed. The problem is as follows. The Java language specification says that in the absence of `synchronized` constructs, an arbitrarily long delay can occur between when one thread changes a variable and when that change is apparent to other threads. (This permission to delay the news allows more efficient implementations, especially on multiprocessor systems.) The consequence of this specification is that when the main user interface thread sets the `enabled` variable to `true`, there is no guarantee when, if ever, the busy-waiting poltergeist thread will see it as having become `true`. The only way to fix this problem is to use `synchronized`, which guarantees that all variables' values are updated. But the non-busy-waiting version, using `wait` and `notify`, is superior in any case. The same issue explains why in the `wait`/`notify` version the `disable` method needs to be `synchronized`—otherwise the poltergeist thread might never get word of a disablement.

Our discussion of developing graphical user interfaces (GUIs) in Java has been in the context of applets. However, we should point out that nearly everything we said is equally applicable to developing stand-alone Java application programs.

One important source for Java documentation is Sun's Java web site, `http://java.sun.com`. The AWT library classes we used for applets are also documented in a book by Chan and Lee [11], and the language specification is a book by Gosling, Joy, and Steele [23]. Some less definitive but more tutorial sources are the books by Arnold and Gosling [5], Horstmann and Cornell [27], and Campione and Walrath [9].

Leveson and Turner [35] provide a good summary of the Therac-25's problems. They make the point that far more was wrong than just the race bugs we chose to highlight. The software development methodology was badly flawed, the hardware was missing safety interlocks on the theory that the software provided adequate safety assurances, and the procedures for following up on trouble reports were inadequate.

Nonstandard Extensions to Scheme

We presume the existence of the following predefined procedures, which are not part of the R[4]RS standard for Scheme:

(error *string value*...) Signals an error to the user in some form. The *string* should be a description of the error. There can be any number of *values*, and they are also displayed to the user to further describe what went wrong.

(filled-triangle x_0 y_0 x_1 y_1 x_2 y_2) Produces a standard-sized square image containing a filled-in triangle with vertices (x_0, y_0), (x_1, y_1), and (x_2, y_2). The coordinate system for the vertices ranges from $(-1, -1)$ in the lower left corner of the image to $(1, 1)$ in the upper right corner.

(invert *image*) Produces a new image of the same size as *image* and with the same contents as *image* except that black and white are reversed.

(line x_0 y_0 x_1 y_1) Produces a standard-sized square image containing a line segment from (x_0, y_0) to (x_1, y_1). The coordinate system and size are the same as for filled-triangle.

(overlay *image$_1$* *image$_2$*) Produces a new image with the same size as *image$_1$* and *image$_2$*, which must have the same width and height as each other. The contents of the new image is formed by combining the contents of the two existing images, much as though two transparencies were laid together.

(quarter-turn-right *image*) Produces a new image with the contents of *image* turned 90 degrees clockwise. The width of the new image is the same as *image*'s height, and the height of the new image is the same as *image*'s width.

(`random` *n*) Produces a nonnegative integer, chosen in a pseudo-random fashion from the range from 0 up to but not including *n*. The argument *n* must be an exact positive integer. The *n* possible values are returned equally frequently over the long run.

(`stack` *image₁* *image₂*) Produces a new image by stacking the contents of *image₁* on top of the contents of *image₂*. The width of *image₁* must equal the width of *image₂*, which becomes the width of the resulting image. The height of the resulting image is the sum of the heights of *image₁* and *image₂*.

In addition to presuming the above non-R⁴RS procedures, we make use of several features specified in the R⁴RS as being "inessential." In other words, these are features that the standard describes but does not require all implementations to provide. We list below the inessential features we use, with some comments on how common it is for an implementation to omit each feature and what impact such an omission would have on using this book:

internal definitions The R⁴RS permits an implementation to not support nested definitions inside the body of a lambda expression or let expression. Such an implementation would be awkward to use with this book, because we use internal definitions freely. However, such implementations are very rare.

disjointness of #f and () The R⁴RS allows a single value to be used as both false and the empty list. It is relatively common for Scheme implementations to make this choice. All our examples will work in such implementations, with the minor exception that wherever we show `#f` in the output, () will be displayed instead. (In input, `#f` should still be used.)

exact rationals Not every implementation needs to support exact rational numbers. This area is the one that is likely to cause the most trouble because relatively many implementations have opted out of exact rationals and we use them moderately freely in the early chapters. The book can be used with such an implementation, however, provided you are willing to work around a few difficulties as you encounter them. For example, in most systems that only have inexact "floating point" numbers, you will not be able to get an approximation to the golden ratio that is good to one part in 10^{79} and will get an infinitely looping process if you try. However, simply using a more tolerant tolerance will solve this problem.

the procedures `sqrt`, `expt`, `denominator`, `list-tail`, `vector-fill!`, **and** `with-output-to-file` These predefined procedures are all labeled "inessential" by the R⁴RS. Nearly all implementations include `sqrt` and `expt`, so they are unlikely to present a problem. The `denominator` procedure is used only in approximating the golden ratio; it is only likely to be missing in implementations that don't have exact rationals, and in such a case, the exercise could simply be omitted. We define `list-tail` and `vector-fill!` in the text, so it wouldn't matter if they weren't predefined. On the rare system that doesn't support `with-output-to-file`, the examples using it can be rewritten to use the essential procedure `call-with-output-file`.

Bibliography

[1] Harold Abelson, Gerald J. Sussman, and friends. *Computer Exercises to Accompany Structure and Interpretation of Computer Programs*. New York: McGraw-Hill, 1988.

[2] Harold Abelson and Gerald Jay Sussman. *Structure and Interpretation of Computer Programs*. Cambridge, MA: The MIT Press and New York: McGraw-Hill, 2nd edition, 1996.

[3] Alfred V. Aho and Jeffrey D. Ullman. *Foundations of Computer Science*. New York: Computer Science Press, 1992.

[4] Ronald E. Anderson, Deborah G. Johnson, Donald Gotterbarn, and Judith Perville. Using the new ACM code of ethics in decision making. *Communications of the ACM*, 36(2):98–107, February 1993.

[5] Ken Arnold and James Gosling. *The Java Programming Language*. Reading, MA: Addison-Wesley, 2nd edition, 1998.

[6] Henk Barendregt. The impact of the lambda calculus in logic and computer science. *The Bulletin of Symbolic Logic*, 3(2):181–215, June 1997.

[7] Grady Booch. *Object-oriented Analysis and Design with Applications*. Menlo Park, CA: Benjamin/Cummings, 2nd edition, 1994.

[8] Charles L. Bouton. Nim, a game with a complete mathematical theory. *The Annals of Mathematics*, 3:35–39, 1901. Series 2.

[9] Mary Campione and Kathy Walrath. *The Java Tutorial: Object-Oriented Programming for the Internet*. Reading, MA: Addison-Wesley, 2nd edition, 1998.

649

[10] Canadian Broadcasting Company. Quirks and quarks. Radio program, December 19, 1992. Included chocolate bar puzzle posed by Dr. Ian Stewart of the Mathematics Institute, University of Warwick, United Kingdom.

[11] Patrick Chan and Rosanna Lee. *The Java Class Libraries*, volume 2. Reading, MA: Addison-Wesley, 2nd edition, 1998.

[12] Alonzo Church. *The Calculi of Lambda-conversion*. Princeton, NJ: Princeton University Press, 1941.

[13] Norman H. Cohen. Type-extension type tests can be performed in constant time. ACM *Transactions on Programming Languages and Systems*, 13(4):626–629, October 1991.

[14] Thomas H. Cormen, Charles E. Leiserson, and Ronald L. Rivest. *Introduction to Algorithms*. Cambridge, MA: The MIT Press and New York: McGraw-Hill, 1990.

[15] Philip J. Davis. *The Lore of Large Numbers*. New York: Random House, 1961.

[16] Paul Fahn. Answers to frequently asked questions about today's cryptography. Part #999-100002-100-000-000, RSA Laboratories, 100 Marine Parkway, Redwood City, CA 94065, September 1992. Version 1.0, draft 1e.

[17] Association for Computing Machinery. ACM code of ethics and professional conduct. *Communications of the ACM*, 36(2):99–105, February 1993.

[18] Martin Fowler and Kendall Scott. *UML Distilled*. Reading, MA: Addison-Wesley, 1997.

[19] Joseph A. Gallian. Assigning driver's license numbers. *Mathematics Magazine*, 64(1):13–22, February 1991.

[20] Joseph A. Gallian and Steven Winters. Modular arithmetic in the marketplace. *The American Mathematical Monthly*, 95(6):548–551, 1988.

[21] Erich Gamma, Richard Helm, Ralph Johnson, and John Vlissides. *Design Patterns: Elements of Reusable Object-Oriented Software*. Reading, MA: Addison-Wesley, 1995.

[22] Martin Gardner. *The 2nd Scientific American Book of Mathematical Puzzles and Diversions*. New York: Simon and Schuster, 1961.

[23] James Gosling, Bill Joy, and Guy Steele. *The Java Language Specification*. Reading, MA: Addison-Wesley, 1996.

[24] David Grogan and Claudia Staniford. Uncle Sam's birthday greeting to some California teens has the government licking its wounds. *People Weekly*, 22:42, 47, September 3, 1984.

[25] G. H. Hardy and E. M. Wright. *An Introduction to the Theory of Numbers*. New York: Oxford University Press, 5th edition, 1980.

[26] Andrew Hodges. *Alan Turing: The Enigma*. New York: Simon and Schuster, 1983.

[27] Cay S. Horstmann and Gary Cornell. *Core Java 1.1: Fundamentals*, volume 1. Englewood Cliffs, NJ: Prentice-Hall, 1997.

[28] Flavius Josephus. *Josephus*. Cambridge, MA: Harvard University Press, 1956. With an English translation by H. St. J. Thackeray in nine volumes.

[29] Flavius Josephus. *The Jewish War*. Baltimore, MD: Penguin Books, 1967. Translated with an introduction by G. A. Williamson.

[30] Gerry Kane and Joe Heinrich. *MIPS RISC Architecture*. Englewood Cliffs, NJ: Prentice-Hall, 1992.

[31] Donald E. Knuth. *Sorting and Searching*, volume 3 of *The Art of Computer Programming*. Reading, MA: Addison-Wesley, 2nd edition, 1998.

[32] D[onald] E. Knuth. *Surreal Numbers*. Reading, MA: Addison-Wesley, 1974.

[33] Donald E. Knuth. *TeX: The Program*. Reading, MA: Addison-Wesley, 1986.

[34] Donald E. Knuth. *The TeXbook*. Reading, MA: Addison-Wesley, 1986.

[35] Nancy G. Leveson and Clark S. Turner. An Investigation of the Therac-25 Accidents. *Computer*, 26(7): 17–41, July 1993.

[36] Benoit B. Mandelbrot. *Fractals: Form, Chance & Dimension*. New York: W. H. Freeman, 1977.

[37] Benoit B. Mandelbrot. *The Fractal Geometry of Nature*. New York: W. H. Freeman, 1982.

[38] S. Brent Morris. *Magic Tricks, Card Shuffling and Dynamic Memories*. Washington, DC: The Mathematical Association of America, 1998.

[39] David A. Patterson and John L. Hennessy. *Computer Organization and Design: The Hardware/Software Interface*. San Francisco, CA: Morgan Kaufmann, 2nd edition, 1998.

[40] George Polya. *How to Solve It: A New Aspect of Mathematical Method*. Princeton, NJ: Princeton University Press, 2nd edition, 1971.

[41] Paulo Ribenboim. *The New Book of Prime Number Records*. New York: Springer-Verlag, 3rd edition, 1996.

[42] Irma von Starkloff Rombauer and Marion Rombauer Becker. *Joy of Cooking*. Indianapolis, IN: Bobbs-Merill Company, Inc., 1975.

[43] Helen Whitson Rose. *Quick-and-Easy Strip Quilting*. New York: Dover Publications, 1989.

[44] James Rumbaugh et al. *Object-oriented Modeling and Design*. Englewood Cliffs, NJ: Prentice-Hall, 1991.

[45] Steve Russell. First versions of LISP, March 1996. Posted on alt.folklore.computers newsgroup; archived with related messages at URL `http://wwwis.cs.utwente.nl:8080/~faase/Ha/CAR_CDR.txt`.

[46] David Sankoff and Joseph B. Kruskal. *Time Warps, String Edits, and Macromolecules: The Theory and Practice of Sequence Comparison*. Reading, MA: Addison-Wesley, 1983.

[47] John R. Searle. Minds, brains, and programs. In John Haugeland, editor, *Mind Design*, pages 282–306. Cambridge, MA: MIT Press, 1981. Reprinted from *The Behavioral and Brain Sciences*, Vol. 3 (1980), pp. 417–424.

[48] John R. Searle. *The Rediscovery of the Mind*. Cambridge, MA: MIT Press, 1992.

[49] Ravi Sethi. *Programming Languages: Concepts and Constructs*. Reading, MA: Addison-Wesley, 1989.

[50] Robert E. Tarjan. *Data Structures and Network Algorithms*. Philadelphia, PA: Society for Industrial and Applied Mathematics, 1983.

[51] A. M. Turing. On computable numbers, with an application to the Entscheidungsproblem. *Proceedings, London Mathematical Society*, 2(42):230–265, 1936. See also number 43, pages 544–546.

[52] A. M. Turing. Computing machinery and intelligence. In Douglas Hostadter and Daniel Dennett, editors, *The Mind's I*, pages 54–67. Basic Books, 1981. Reprinted from *Mind*, Vol. 59 (1950), pp. 433–460.

[53] Alfred North Whitehead and Bertrand Russell. *Principia Mathematica*. Cambridge, England: Cambridge University Press, 2nd edition, 1925–1927.

Index

!, 627
#\, 433
#f, 13, 646
#t, 13
$, 423
%, 594
&&, 597
', 138, 170
(type), 615, 639
*, 7
*=, 636
+, 6, 605
++, 591
+=, 590
-, 7, 35
--, 591
/, 7, 594
/*...*/, 582
//, 582
;, 30
<, 12
<=, 13
=, 13, 138, 201, 583
==, 589
>, 13
>=, 13
?:, 588
[], 438, 587, 590, 605
^, 505, 519
||, 597
15-tile puzzle, 601

abstract class, 515
abstract class, pure, 515, 516
abstract data type, 134
abstract syntax tree, 291
Abstract Window Toolkit, 601
⟨abstraction⟩, 282, 283
accept, 423
accept?, 430
accuracy, 225
ACM, 225, 242
act, auto-person/, 558, 559
act, witch/, 560, 569
act, wizard/, 560
action, 192, 279
action, 195
ActionEvent, 606
ActionListener, 606
actionPerformed, 606, 612, 619
actors, 254, 257
add, 341, 591, 605
add, item-list/, 488, 495, 496, 513
add, registry/, 547
add-change-to-collection, 405
add-chocolate-to-box, 394
add-new-neighbor, place/, 551, 552
add-one, 124
add-to-end, 180
add-to-set, 275
addActionListener, 606
address, 335, 336
address register, 338

ADT, 134
adventure game, 543, 576
algorithm, 76
alist, 532
`alist-from-onto`, 534
`all-are`, 208, 287
`allocate-registers`, 347
ALU, 337
`alumni-hall`, 561
ancestry, 489, 529
and, 597
`and`, 68
`announce-winner`, 138, 143, 144
`answer-by-pattern`, 193–194
append, 218
`Applet`, 602
applet, 578, 600, 604, 610
application, 6, 291
⟨application⟩, 282
apply, 6
`apply`, 194, 300
`apply-all`, 205
`apply-below`, 528, 529
`approximate-golden-ratio`, 63, 64
architecture, 334
`area`, 274
argument, 7
argument, command-line, 595
arithmetic expression, 284, 290
arithmetic if, 325
arithmetic logical unit, 337
arithmetic sequence, 248
`ark-volume`, 7
array, 587, 590, 591, 605, 624
artificial intelligence, 116, 202–204
assembler, 341
assembly language, 341
association, 490
Association for Computing Machinery, 225,
　　242
association list, 532
associative, 87
`assq`, 535
AST, 291
AST, pictorial version, 291
asymptotic outlook, 76
atomic, 623–625, 629, 633, 637, 644
atomic data, 133
atomic expression, 227

augment, 506
`auto-person-class`, 544, 545, 558
`auto-person/act`, 558, 559
`auto-person/init`, 545, 558
`auto-person/maybe-act`, 545, 558, 559
automata theory, 286
AWT, 601
axiomatic system, 435

Backus-Naur Form, Extended, 278, 280
`barbara`, 562
base case (of a procedure), 25
base case (of a proof), 30
base case imperative, 25
base class, 489
basic block, 15
`basic-image-size`, 264
basis (of a fractal), 95
batch processing, 600
`be-eaten`, `chocolate/`, 569
`be-read`, `scroll/`, 550
`become-owned-by`, `thing/`, 550
`become-unowned`, `thing/`, 549
`best`, 416
`best-solution-from-to-of`, 410
`better-box`, 395
`better-solution`, 409
binary operator, 227
binary search, 213, 216
binary search tree, 214, 453, 463, 466, 474
binary tree, 221
binary tree, ranked, 463
`binary-search-in?`, 466, 476
`binary-search-insert!`, 466–468, 474
`binary-search-retrieve`, 476
⟨binding⟩, 284
binomial coefficient, 104, 388, 399
biology, molecular, 399
bit, 341, 342
`bitw-bb`, 41
`blank-line-at`, 321
Blowing in the Wind, 40, 42, 47
BNF, 280
body, 8
`book?`, 256
boolean, 12
⟨boolean⟩, 282
`boolean`, 585
bootstrapping, 517, 527, 532, 536

BorderLayout, 612
bound, 301
box (of chocolates), 394
box and pointer diagram, 155, 171
box-chocolates, 394
box-desirability, 394
box-weight, 394
bracket, 587, 590, 605
breaks, 409, 411
bs-tree, 475
BufferedReader, java.io., 598
bug, 31
busy waiting, 628, 643
Button, 600, 602

c-curve, 96, 108
c-curve, 97
cadddr, 188
caddr, 188
cadr, 188
candy-temperature, 12
car, 150, 151, 169
cast, 615, 639
catalog item, 244, 254, 276
catch, 597
categorize-by-first-label, 238, 239
cd?, 256
cdr, 150, 151, 169
cdr down, 173, 175
cells, 438
center-x, 274
center-y, 274
chamber-of-wizards, 561
change, 405
change-name, named-object/, 549
changes, 401, 402
changes-dynamic, 419
character, 433
character constant, 433
character string, 139, 141
check-isbn, 122
check-movie-in!, 479
check-movie-out-to!, 479
Checkbox, 600, 626, 630, 631
checkerboard, 42
child, 221
Chinese room argument, 203
Chinos, 587
chinos-class, 487, 509, 513

chinos/display, 509
chinos/init, 509
chinos/input-specifics, 509
chocolate, 135, 156, 160, 166, 168, 232–233,
    393–395, 400, 412, 569
chocolate caramel, 12
chocolate-class, 569
chocolate-covering, 394
chocolate-desirability, 394
chocolate-filling, 394
chocolate-weight, 394
chocolate/be-eaten, 569
choose, 388, 592
choose, item-list/, 488, 499, 500
class, 254, 486, 488
class constructor, 495, 501
class diagram, 489–491, 518, 527, 529, 544,
    545, 580, 602, 607, 608
class hierarchy, 254, 486, 489, 511
class instance variable, 495, 518, 522
class method, 584, 593
class object, 491
class predicate, 529
class, abstract, 515
class, pure abstract, 515, 516
class-class, 518, 519, 532, 536, 537
class-definitions, 541, 542
class-predicate-definition, 542
class/describe, 512
class/getter, 517, 518, 520, 521
class/init, 533
class/instantiator, 517, 523
class/ivar-position, 521, 532, 535
class/method, 517, 526
class/method-position, 526, 532, 536
class/non-overridable-method, 517,
    526
class/predicate, 517, 531
class/set-method!, 493, 513, 527, 528,
    539
class/setter, 517, 520, 521
clause (of a cond), 35
clearOutput, 634
client, 617
closest-power, 70
coherence, 644
coin, fake, 102
collection (of changes), 405
collection-list, 405

collection-size, 405
combinations, 104
command-line argument, 595
comment, 30
common interface, 244, 253
commonality, 253
commutative, 87
company, 254
compiler, 348
complete tree, 222
Component, 600, 601
compose, 123
composition, 123
compound data, 133
Compounder, 634, 638
CompoundingThread, 634, 638, 639
compu-duds, 508, 511
CompuDuds, 593
computational process, 3
computer core, 335
computer science, 3, 116
computer-lab, 561
computer-move, 138, 140, 142, 144, 156,
    157, 159
concurrency, 578, 616, 617
cond, 35, 284
⟨conditional⟩, 282
conditional expression, 588
conditional jump, 345
confidentiality, 226
cons, 150, 151, 155, 169
cons up, 171, 175
consistency condition, 548
⟨constant⟩, 282, 283
constant?, 227
constraint, 528
constructor, 134, 582
constructor, class, 495, 501
constructor, default, 604
Container, 602
contents, 255
contents, place/, 553
continuation address, 354
continuation register, 354
continued fraction, 63, 73
contradiction, proof by, 115
control signal, 339
control unit, 337
corner-bb, 16

cost, 409
count-combos, 185–186, 398
couple, 206
coupling, 499
course, 162
creator, 254, 256
creators, 261
cube, 119
current instruction, 338
current instruction address, 339
curse, witch/, 560
cycle, 443
cyclic, 467
cylinder-volume, 10

d-curve, 98
data abstraction, 134, 143, 243
data memory, 335
data type, mutable, 430
data-abstraction principle, 149
data-abstraction principle, strong, 150
database, 188, 472
database, 255, 259
date, 244
⟨datum⟩, 282
deadlock, 625
debug, 31
debunk-halts?, 115
declaration, 582
decoder, instruction, 339
default constructor, 604
define-class, 492, 493, 517, 541
definition, 7
definition, global, 304
definition, internal, 59, 646
definition, nested, 59, 646
definition, top-level, 304
definition-expression, 305
definition-name?, 305
definition?, 305
degree, 229
delete, 591
delete, item-list/, 488, 499, 513
delq, 547
denominator, 64, 646
depth, 221, 454
dequeue!, 447, 451
derived class, 489
describe, class/, 512

describe, object/, 494, 512, 519, 536, 570
design patterns, 576
destination register, 338
destroy, 632
diagonalization proof, 115, 129
dictionary, 472–474, 477
dictionary-insert!, 474, 478
dictionary-retrieve, 474, 478
difficulty, 564
digest function, 84
⟨digit⟩, 281
digit->number, 434
digital signature, 83
Direct Memory Access, 336
disable, 626, 627, 629, 631, 634, 644
disclosure, 225
display, 140, 141, 580, 585, 589
display, chinos/, 509
display, item-list/, 488, 497, 498
display, item/, 488, 498, 501
display, oxford-shirt/, 506
display-game-state, 140, 152
display-histogram, 365, 366
display-item, 254
display-message, 550
display-phone-numbers, 234, 235
display-price, 498
display-ra-stack, 432
display-ranked-btree, 465, 468, 475
display-ranked-btree-by, 475
display-table, 391
display-times, 313
displayPrice, 593
distance, 61, 164
distributive, 87
div, 341
divide and conquer, 213
divides?, 59, 60
DMA, 336
do-grade-histogram, 364
do-instruction-in-model, 368, 370
do-magic, magic-scroll/, 569
document management, 399
dollar sign, 423
dormitory, 561
dot-product, 162
Double, 639
double, 118, 636
double equal sign, 589

double quote, 139
doubleValue, 639
dp-changes, 403, 405
dp-choose, 400
dp-walk-count, 386
dp-walk-count-2, 387
dragon curve, 98
draw-filled-triangle-on, 263
draw-line-on, 263
draw-on, 263
drawing medium, 262, 265, 271
dynamic programming, 383, 386, 399
dynamic programming, comparison to memoization, 406

eat, person/, 569
EBNF, expressiveness of, 285–286
edit distance, 400, 419
element-of-set?, 275
else, 35, 586
elvee, 562
empty, 588
empty list, 168, 170, 646
empty-labels?, 237
empty-queue?, 447, 449
empty-ra-stack?, 429, 436, 438
empty-sequence, 249
empty-sequence?, 245, 247
empty-tree?, 216, 464
empty-trie?, 231
empty?, item-list/, 488, 493
enable, 626–629, 631, 634
Encapsulated PostScript, 271
enlarge-queue!, 449
enqueue!, 447, 449
ensure-in-table, 384
environment, global, 304
EPS, 271
eq?, 465
equal sign, 583
equal sign, double, 589
equal?, 138, 179
error, 202
error, 139, 257, 645
error checking, 142, 257
ethics, 5, 225, 242
eval, 542
eval-globally, 541–543
evaltemp.scm, 543

evaluate, 227, 290, 295, 421, 425, 430
evaluate-additional-in-at, 322
evaluate-in, 306, 311
evaluate-in-at, 313, 314, 316, 322
evaluation, 5, 279, 290
even-part, 183–184
even?, 13
event-driven, 600
exact rationals, 646
exception, 596
exchange-left-with-right!, 469
exchange-values!, 468
exclamation point, 363, 627
execute, 335
exit, 592
exit?, 192
exits, place/, 551, 552
expand, 208
explode-symbol, 236
exponent, 28, 342
exponent-of-in, 147
exponential growth, 381
expression, 5, 588
⟨expression⟩, 282
expression tree, 227, 284, 289, 290
expression, arithmetic, 284
expressiveness of EBNF, 285–286
expt, 28, 646
extend-global-environment-with-
    naming, 306
Extended Backus-Naur Form, 278, 280
extends, 581

factorial, 23
factorial, 24–26, 36, 48, 72, 120
factorial-product, 49, 50, 55
factorial-sum1, 99
factorial-sum2, 99
factorial2, 37
fake coin, 102
fall through, 345
falling factorial power, 71
false, 627
family-name-last, 256
Fermat number, 57, 73
fermat-number, 57
fewest-moves, 415
Fibonacci number, 382
FIFO, 446

15-tile puzzle, 601
filled-triangle, 18, 645
filter, 175, 189, 238
first in first out, 446
first-elements-of, 176
first-label, 237
first-perfect-after, 60, 61
flip, 616
floating point, 342
⌊⌋ (floor), 223
flow chart, 349
FlowLayout, 614
food-service, 561
for, 589, 609
FOR loop, 413
for-each, 478
formal language, 286
format, 637
format-paragraph, 412
format-paragraph, 411
FormattedField, 639
formatting paragraphs, 406, 419
fractal, 95, 108
free, 301
from-to-add, 416
from-to-do, 387
function-sum, 204
functional, 362

Gack, Land of, 561
gain, place/, 552
game state, 136, 145, 147–149, 151, 152, 157
game state, mutable, 480
game, adventure, 543, 576
game-state-<, 163
game-state-<=, 163
game-state-=, 163
game-state->, 163
garbage collection, 499
gcd, 353
generic operation, 243, 488, 515
get-global-environment, 482
get-image, 480
get-mem, 367, 370
get-pc, 367, 370
get-reg, 367, 370
getLabel, 609
getState, 631
getStateChange, 631

getter, 493, 519, 520
getter, class/, 517, 518, 520, 521
global definition, 304
global environment, 304
go, person/, 556
gold-num, 86
golden ratio, 62, 74
good-ship-olin, 561
grammar, 280
graphical user interface, 600
greet, person/, 557
GridLayout, 602, 607
grow, 591
grow, item-list/, 496, 497
GUI, 600

Hailperin, Karl, 184, 186, 187, 398
half-turn, 16
halt, 343
halt!, 367, 370
halted?, 367, 370
halting problem, 114
halts-on?, 126
Harvard architecture, 338
have-fit, person/, 555
head, 168
head, 245, 247, 447, 449
header, 442
height, 222, 454
height, 263, 429, 436, 438, 443
higher-order procedure, 111, 118
HTML, 610
human-move, 138, 142, 144, 157
HyperText Markup Language, 610

if, 12–13, 586, 588
if, arithmetic, 325
image, 262
image, turnable, 480
image->eps, 272
image-of-digit, 46
image-of-number, 46
imperative, 362
implements, 606
import, 604
improve, 64
improvement, iterative, 61
in-order, 219
in-order?, 178

in?, 216, 224, 466
increasing-on-integer-range?, 125
indentation, 7
induction, 30, 440
induction hypothesis, 30
inductive step, 30
infinite sequence, 276
infinity, 276
infix, 227, 284
information process, 3
inherit, 492, 527
init, 603, 604, 611
init, auto-person/, 545, 558
init, chinos/, 509
init, class/, 533
init, item-list/, 494, 505
init, item/, 501, 504, 505
init, named-object/, 548
init, object/, 494, 501, 519, 522, 536
init, oxford-shirt/, 504, 505
init, person/, 554
init, place/, 551
init, registry/, 547
init, scroll/, 550
init, thing/, 549
InitialAmountField, 638
InitializeActionListener, 612
initializeTiles, 610, 611, 623
inorder, 219, 224, 225
input, 142
input device, 335
input-integer-in-range, 500
input-integer-in-range, 500
input-item, 509
input-selection, 507
input-specifics, chinos/, 509
input-specifics, item/, 488, 501, 515
input-specifics, oxford-shirt/, 507
input-specifics, special-item/, 502
inputIntegerInRange, 596
inputItem, 595
inputSelection, 596
inputSpecifics, 580, 586, 587
insert, 220, 453
insert-into-widget!, 481
insertion-point, 467, 474
instance, 489
instance method, 584
instance variable, 491, 493, 494, 519

instantiator, 495, 522
`instantiator, class/`, 517, 523
instruction, 334
instruction decoder, 339
instruction memory, 338
instruction set, 334
`int`, 582
`integer-in-range-where-smallest`,
124
`integers-from-to`, 171
integrity, 225
intelligence, artificial, 116, 202–204
intentionality, 203
interface, 243, 244, 607
interface, common, 244, 253
`interleave`, 176
internal definition, 59, 646
internal node, 221, 290
interpreter, 348
`InterruptedException`, 619, 627
interval, 161
invariant, 54, 73
invariant, representation, 439, 440, 622–624
inventor's paradox, 50, 73
`invert`, 42, 645
`IOException, java.io.`, 597
`Item`, 580
`item-class`, 487, 488, 501, 515, 516
`item-list-as-list-class`, 516
`item-list-as-vector-class`, 516
`item-list-class`, 487, 488, 492, 496,
513, 514, 516
`item-list/add`, 488, 495, 496, 513
`item-list/choose`, 488, 499, 500
`item-list/delete`, 488, 499, 513
`item-list/display`, 488, 497, 498
`item-list/empty?`, 488, 493
`item-list/grow`, 496, 497
`item-list/init`, 494, 505
`item-list/total-price`, 488, 498, 513
`item/display`, 488, 498, 501
`item/init`, 501, 504, 505
`item/input-specifics`, 488, 501, 515
`item/price`, 488, 498, 501, 516
`item/revise-specifics`, 488, 502, 516
`ItemEvent`, 631
`ItemList`, 588
`ItemListener`, 630
`itemStateChanged`, 630, 631

iteration, 48, 349
iterative improvement, 61
`ivar-position, class/`, 521, 532, 535

`j`, 345
Java, 576, 578
`java.io.BufferedReader`, 598
`java.io.IOException`, 597
`java.text.NumberFormat`, 636
`jeqz`, 345
Josephus, 65
jump, 339
jump target address, 339

`karl`, 562
key, 472
key-comparator, 472–474
`key-comparator`, 477
key-extractor, 472–474
`key-extractor`, 477
keyword, 280, 283
`keyword?`, 283
knapsack problem, 393
Knight, Erick, 184, 186, 187, 398

`Label`, 638
label, 346
`labeled-value`, 236
`labeled-values->trie`, 238, 239
`labels`, 236
`ladder-height`, 19
lambda expression, 8, 302, 309
Land of Gack, 561
language, formal, 286
language, object-oriented, 247
`larger`, 206
`largest-element-of-vector`, 367
`largest-odd-divisor`, 69
`last`, 205
last in first out, 446
`late-lab-report`, 568
`LayoutManager`, 602, 605, 607
`ld`, 341
leaf, 215, 221, 290
leak, memory, 499
left rotation, 457, 468
`left-operand`, 227
`left-subtree`, 216, 464
`length`, 172, 249, 591

length (of a path), 221
length-of-c-curve, 98, 108
let, 61, 284, 303
letter->number, 236
level, subproblem nesting, 313, 315
li, 343
library, 561
LIFO, 446
line, 97, 645
line breaking, 406, 419
line-cost, 408
line-width, 407
linear recursion, 25
linearization, 362
linked list, 443
list, 167–169
list, 169
list-<, 174
list->bstree, 220, 224, 225
list->sequence, 248–251
list->tagged-list, 255
list-by-key, 218, 219
list-of-length->sequence, 250
list-of-lists, 179
list-possessions, person/, 555
list-ref, 174
list-tail, 176, 646
list?, 198
lists-compare?, 174
⟨literal⟩, 282, 283
load, 341
load, 543
load immediate, 343
load-and-run, 368
location, 333
lock, 624, 625
logarithm, 82
look-around, person/, 554
look-up-phone-number, 233, 235
look-up-value, 227, 297, 299, 325
look-up-value-in, 306, 309
look-up-with-menu, 233, 234
loop, 349
loop-forever, 114
lose, person/, 557
lose, place/, 553
lounge, 561
lower-endpoint, 161
lower-precedence?, 432

machine language, 340
machine model, 367, 369
magic-scroll-class, 569
magic-scroll/do-magic, 569
magic-scroll/name, 569
main, 594
maintainability, 499, 504
make-x, *see* x-class and x/init
make-3D-vector, 162
make-abstraction-ast, 301, 307
make-add-inst, 368, 371
make-application-ast, 300, 308, 312, 314, 315
make-arithmetic-if-ast, 326
make-averaged-procedure, 126
make-binary-search-tree, 466
make-chocolate, 394
make-circle, 274
make-class, 517, 532, 533
make-conditional-ast, 299, 307, 324
make-constant, 227
make-constant-ast, 299, 306
make-couple, 206
make-dictionary, 474, 477
make-div-inst, 368, 371
make-empty-box, 394
make-empty-collection, 405
make-empty-ranked-btree, 464
make-empty-tree, 215
make-empty-trie, 231, 239
make-exponentiater, 119
make-expr, 227
make-filled-triangle, 263, 264, 266
make-for-ast, 414
make-function-with-exception, 123
make-game-state, 137, 145, 147–149, 151–153
make-game-state-comparator, 163
make-generator, 126
make-halt-inst, 368, 371
make-initial-global-environment, 306, 309, 311
make-interval, 161
make-jeqz-inst, 368, 371
make-jump-inst, 368, 371
make-labeled-value, 236
make-line, 263–265
make-lines, 409, 411
make-list-combiner, 209

make-list-scaler, 207
make-load-immediate-inst, 368, 371
make-load-inst, 368, 371
make-machine-model, 367, 369
make-mini-scheme-version-of, 310, 315
make-mirrored-image, 270
make-move-instruction, 156
make-movie, 188
make-mul-inst, 368, 371
make-multiplier, 118
make-name-ast, 297, 306, 482
make-node, 442
make-nonempty-tree, 215
make-nonempty-trie, 231, 232, 239
make-overlaid-image, 266
make-pattern/action, 195
make-person, 232
make-point, 163, 263
make-procedure, 301, 302, 309, 315
make-queue, 447, 449
make-quo-inst, 368, 371
make-ra-stack, 429, 436, 437, 443
make-ra-stack-with-at-most, 437, 438
make-read-eval-print-loop-state, 482
make-read-inst, 368, 371
make-red-black-tree, 462, 468, 476
make-rem-inst, 368, 371
make-repeated-version-of, 119
make-scaled, 124
make-scaled-image, 270
make-schedule-item, 162
make-seq-inst, 368, 371
make-sge-inst, 368, 371
make-sgt-inst, 368, 371
make-sle-inst, 368, 371
make-slt-inst, 368, 371
make-sne-inst, 368, 371
make-solution, 409
make-square, 274
make-store-inst, 368, 371
make-string, 433
make-sub-inst, 368, 371
make-table, 258, 260, 391, 392
make-transformed-medium, 268
make-turnable-image, 480
make-turned-image, 269
make-type, 258
make-uncons-ast, 327
make-vector, 363

make-verifier, 121
make-widget, 481
make-write-inst, 368, 371
make-*x*, *see* *x*-class and *x*/init
mantissa, 342
map, 178, 179, 239
map-2, 207
matches?, 193, 196, 198, 199, 287
Math, 615
mathematical induction, 30
max-the-person, 562
maximum-bar-size, 366
maybe-act, auto-person/, 545, 558, 559
medium, drawing, 262, 265, 271
mem-size, 369
member, 190, 192, 198
memoization, 383, 388
memoization, comparison to dynamic
    programming, 406
memoized-choose, 392
memoized-pick-chocolates, 397
memoized-walk-count, 384, 385
memory, 333, 336
memory leak, 499
mental state, 204
menu, 233, 235
merge, 183
merge sort, 78, 80, 82, 83, 107, 182–184
merge-sort, 182
merging, 79
message, 246
message digest, 84
message passing, 246, 247, 276
method, 492, 519, 524
method implementation, 492
method name, 492
method, class, 584, 593
method, class/, 517, 526
method, instance, 584
method, virtual, 525
method-position, class/, 526, 532, 536
Micro-Scheme, 278, 289
micro-scheme-parsing-p/a-list, 295
micro-scheme-syntax-ok?-p/a-list,
    288
mid-point, 161
min, 103, 402
min-x-of-c-curve, 103
Mini-Scheme, 279, 304, 481

minimum, 217
MIPS, 378
mod*, 88
mod+, 88
mod-, 88
mod-expt, 90, 91, 93, 94, 111
modular arithmetic, 85, 87
modularity, 313
module, 367
modulus, 85, 87
modulus, 86
molecular biology, 399
move instruction, 156, 157
move-to, person/, 555
movie, 188, 479
movie, 259
movie query system, 287
movie-actor, 188
movie-director, 188
movie-p/a-list, 195, 199
movie-status, 479
movie-title, 188
movie-year-made, 188
movie?, 256, 257, 261
movies-directed-by, 190
movies-made-in-year, 189
movies-satisfying, 190
movies-with-actor, 190
much computation, little variety sign, 383,
    390
mul, 341
multi-threaded, 617
multiple representations, 244
multiple-shuffle, 177
multiplicity, 490
multiply, 36
multiply-by!, 375
mutable data type, 430
mutable game state, 480
mutator, 369
mutual recursion, 184, 288
mystery, 112, 124

name, 6
⟨name⟩, 282
name, 232
name, magic-scroll/, 569
name, named-object/, 548
name->labels, 236, 237

name?, 283
named-object-class, 544, 548
named-object/change-name, 549
named-object/init, 548
named-object/name, 548
natural language interface, 191
natural language query system, 188
neighbor-towards, place/, 551,
    552
neighbors, place/, 551, 552
nested definition, 59, 646
nesting level, subproblem, 313, 315
networking, 617
new, 582, 587, 595
new-procedure, 126
newline, 140, 141
next-game-state, 157, 159
next-users-reference, 563
Nim, 135, 166
Nim, three-pile, 153
node, 215, 221, 442
node-element, 442
node-list, 442, 443
node-rest, 442
node-set-element!, 444
node-set-rest!, 444
nodes-down, 444
noise word, 199
non-overridable-method, class/, 517,
    526
nonterminal, 281
not, 627
not, 68
notify, 628, 629
nova-bb, 16, 18
null, 592, 624
null?, 168
num-6s, 113
num-digits, 39, 113
num-digits-in-satisfying,
    112–113
num-odd-digits, 113
Number, 639
number, 5
⟨number⟩, 282
number system, 87
number-in-trie, 235
number-of-nodes, 217
number?, 202, 282

NumberFormat, java.text., 636
NumberFormatException, 597

O (big oh), 213, 242
object, 430
object-class, 489, 518, 537, 538
object-oriented analysis, 576
object-oriented design, 487, 571, 576
object-oriented language, 247
object-oriented modeling, 576
object-oriented programming, 254, 486, 517, 543
object-with-name, 568
object/describe, 494, 512, 519, 536, 570
object/init, 494, 501, 519, 522, 536
odd-part, 183–184
odd?, 13
offices, 561
one-layer data structure principle, 217
one-layer thinking, 32
one-layer thinking maxim, 32
opcode, 341
operand, 291
operand specifier, 341
operate, 259
operating system, 334
operation code, 341
operation table, 258, 259
operational definition of intelligence, 117
operational stance, 149
operator, 291
operator, 227
operator-char?, 433
operator?, 432
optimize-bstree, 224, 453
or, 597
or, 68
order of growth, 81
ordered tree, 229
other-people-at-same-place, person/, 557
our-movie-database, 188, 189, 475, 478
our-movies-by-director, 478
our-movies-by-title, 478
output, 140
output device, 335
outputLine, 634
over?, 138, 143, 144
overlay, 18, 645

override, 492
owned?, thing/, 549
owner, thing/, 549
oxford-shirt-class, 487, 503, 513
oxford-shirt/display, 506
oxford-shirt/init, 504, 505
oxford-shirt/input-specifics, 507
OxfordShirt, 584

pair, 150
pair, nested, 153
pair?, 275
palindrome, 179–182
palindrome, 182
Panel, 611
pants-class, 513, 514
paragraph breaking, 406, 419
parameter, 9
parameter list, 8
parent, 221
parent, 464
parenthesize, 416
parse, 290, 293, 313
parsing, 290
path length, 221
pattern, 192, 194, 279
pattern, 195
pattern/action pair, 192, 195, 287
patterns, design, 576
PC, 339
percent-sign, 594
perfect number, 58, 73, 114
perfect shuffle, 175–178
perfect?, 58
permutation, 23
person, 232
person-class, 544, 545, 548, 553
person/eat, 569
person/go, 556
person/greet, 557
person/have-fit, 555
person/init, 554
person/list-possessions, 555
person/look-around, 554
person/lose, 557
person/move-to, 555
person/other-people-at-same-place, 557
person/place, 557

person/possessions, 557
person/read, 555
person/say, 554
person/take, 556
personal information, 225, 226
phone-number, 232
phone-trie, 232, 233
pick-chocolates, 396
pinwheel, 17
pixel, 263
place, person/, 557
place-class, 544–546, 548, 551
place/add-new-neighbor, 551, 552
place/contents, 553
place/exits, 551, 552
place/gain, 552
place/init, 551
place/lose, 553
place/neighbor-towards, 551, 552
place/neighbors, 551, 552
play, 563, 564
play-with-turns, 138, 139, 141, 144, 159, 161
player, 562
PMSE, 280
PO, 561
point, 163
poltergeist, 617
PoltergeistActionListener, 619
PoltergeistItemListener, 630
PoltergeistThread, 618, 626, 630–632
pond, 561
pop, 359, 429
pop!, 429, 435, 436, 440, 444, 445
porting, 134
position, 174
positional tree, 229
positive-integer-upto-where-smallest, 127
possessions, person/, 557
post-order traversal, 284
postfix, 229, 284, 290
postorder, 228
post-order, 220, 228
PostScript, Encapsulated, 271
potential Micro-Scheme expression, 280
power, 28, 55, 71, 111
power-product, 55, 56, 351
pre-order, 219

precedence, 421, 425
predicate, 12
predicate, class, 529
predicate, class/, 517, 531
prefix, 227, 284, 290
preorder, 218
preorder, 218, 219
preorder-onto, 219
presents-on-day, 43
presents-through-day, 44
price, 580
price, item/, 488, 498, 501, 516
prime number, 57, 73
primitive procedure, 15
print, 586
println, 586
privacy, 225
private, 496
private, 582
procedural parameter, 110, 142
procedural representation, 148, 149
procedural result, 118
procedure, 6, 8
procedure?, 275
process, 3
processing, batch, 600
processor, 335
product, 72
production, 280
professional conduct, 225, 242
program, 4, 334
program counter, 339
programming language, 4
promote, 468
promotion, 456, 468
prompt, 142, 144
proof by contradiction, 115
proof by diagonalization, 115, 129
proof by reduction, 118
ps, 416
pseudo-random, 160
public, 496
public, 581, 583
pure abstract class, 515, 516
push, 359, 429
push!, 429, 435, 436, 441, 445
pushTile, 609, 623
Puzzle, 602, 603, 622, 631
puzzle, 15-tile, 601

puzzle1, 14
puzzle2, 14

quarter-turn-left, 16
quarter-turn-right, 16, 645
quarter-turn-right!, 480
query system, 188, 191
query-loop, 191, 192
queue, 447
queue-cells, 449
queue-length, 449
queue-start, 449
quilt, 40
quo, 341
quot, 34, 35
⟨quotation⟩, 282, 283
quote, 138, 170
quote, 283
quotient, 34

RA-stack, 429, 432, 443
race, 621, 622, 624, 628, 629, 633, 637
RAM, 333
random, 159, 615, 646
Random Access Memory, 333
random-mix-of, 160
RandomizeActionListener, 615
randomizeTiles, 614, 615
rank, 455
rank, 464
ranked binary tree, 463
rational approximation, 73
rb-tree, 476
rcross-bb, 16
read, 142, 282, 343
read, person/, 555
read-eval-print loop, 278
read-eval-print-loop, 289, 304, 315, 482
read-eval-print-loop state, 482
readLine, 598
rebalancing, 456–460
record, 472
recurrence relation, 222
recursion, 22, 168
recursion strategy, 23
recursive procedure, 54, 304, 329
recursive process, 25, 357
red-black tree, 453, 455, 456, 462, 463, 472, 474, 485

red-black-in?, 462, 468
red-black-insert!, 455, 462, 468, 471
red-black-retrieve, 476
red-black-tree, 477
reduce, 422, 427
reduce!, 430, 431
reduce?, 430
reduction, proof by, 118
reg-bank-size, 369
register, 337
registry, 561
registry-class, 544–546, 558
registry/add, 547
registry/init, 547
registry/remove, 547
registry/trigger, 547
registry/trigger-times, 547
rem, 341
remainder, 39
remove, registry/, 547
remove-coins-from-pile, 137, 145, 146, 152, 157
remove-coins-from-pile!, 481
repeat, 208
repeatedly-square, 57, 119
Repeating Crosses, 15–17, 21
repl-state, 482
representation, 134, 149, 150, 186
representation invariant, 439, 440, 548, 622–624
representations, multiple, 244
respond-to-using, 566
responsibility, 5
retention, 226
retrieve-from-widget, 481
return, 583, 592
return address, 378
return-seven, 114
reverse, 180–182
Reverse Polish notation, 284
revise-specifics, item/, 488, 502, 516
reviseSpecifics, 580
revision control, 400
right rotation, 457, 468
right-half, 161
right-operand, 227
right-subtree, 216, 464
RISC, 378

role, 519
room, 162
root, 214
root, 216
root-values, 231
root?, 463, 464
rotate-left!, 468, 469
rotate-right!, 468, 469
rotation, left, 457, 468
rotation, right, 457, 468
round, 12
RPN, 284
RSA cryptosystem, 107
run, 335
run, 618, 626
run length encoding, 208

sameness principle, 613
say, person/, 554
schedule item, 162
Scheme, 4
scroll-class, 544, 550
scroll-of-enlightenment, 562
scroll/be-read, 550
scroll/init, 550
Searle, John, 203, 204
selection sort, 77, 80
selector, 134, 369
self, 493
self-similarity, 95
self-similarity strategy, 24
self-verifying number, 120, 129
semantic error, 280
semicolon, 30
separation of concerns, 313
seq, 341
seq-from-to, 250
sequence, 245
sequence comparison, 400, 419
sequence, arithmetic, 248
sequence, infinite, 276
sequence->list, 248
sequence-append, 251, 252
sequence-cons, 251, 252
sequence-from-to, 246, 248, 250
sequence-from-to-with, 248
sequence-length, 245, 247, 249, 252
sequence-map, 251, 252
sequence-ref, 250–252

sequence-with-from-by, 248, 249
server, 617
set-car!, 446
set-cdr!, 446
set-empty!, 464
set-global-environment!, 482
set-height!, 441
set-left-subtree!, 464
set-mem!, 367, 370
set-method!, class/, 493, 513, 527, 528, 539
set-pc!, 367, 370
set-queue-cells!, 449
set-queue-length!, 449
set-queue-start!, 449
set-rank!, 464
set-reg!, 367, 370
set-right-subtree!, 464
set-value!, 464
setInitialAmount, 634, 638, 639
setInterestRate, 634
setLabel, 605
setLayout, 605
setter, 519, 520
setter, class/, 517, 520, 521
setValue, 639
sevens, 179, 204
sge, 341
sgt, 341
shared-memory multiprocessor, 336
shift, 422
shift!, 374
shift?, 430
shirks-chocolates-rated-by-max, 395
shirt-class, 513, 514
show, 265
show-class-hierarchy, 511, 536
shuffle, 177
shuffle-number, 178
sibling, 465
side-by-side, 16
Sierpinski's gasket, 95
sierpinskis-gasket, 99
signature, 86
signing-exponent, 89
simple-strategy, 158
simulation, 543
size-of-pile, 137, 145, 147–149, 151–154
skip-of, 417

slash, 594
sle, 341
sleep, 619, 637
sliding 15-tile puzzle, 601
SLIM, 334
slt, 341
smaller, 206
Smalltalk, 247
sne, 341
solution (line breaking), 409
sort, 225
sorted-list->min-height-bstree, 224
source register, 338
SP, 359
space-width, 407
special-item-class, 502
special-item/input-specifics, 502
sqrt, 6, 646
square, 9, 28, 33, 119
square-sum, 205
st, 341
stack, 359, 423, 429
stack, 16, 646
stack discipline, 359
stack pointer, 359
stack-copies-of, 40, 54, 111
start, 619, 620, 631
state, 362
state oriented, 362
state variable, 491
state, read-eval-print-loop, 482
statement, 588
static, 593
Stirling number of the second kind, 413
stop, 631, 632
store, 341
store-into-table, 385
stored program computer, 334
strategy, 156, 158, 166
strictly ordered, 214
String, 585
string, 433
⟨string⟩, 282
string, 434
string->number, 433
string->symbol, 433, 541
string-append, 541
string-comparator, 472

string-length, 433
string-ref, 433
string-set!, 433
string-width, 407
string<?, 472
string=?, 472
strip-one-label, 237
strong data-abstraction principle, 150
sub, 341
sub1-each, 207
subclass, 488, 489, 514
subproblem nesting level, 313, 315
substitute-for-in, 295
substitution, 301
substitution model, 10–12, 295
substitutions-in-to-match, 193, 196, 197, 199, 201, 287
subtract-the-first, 37
subtree, 214
subtrie, 230
subtrie-with-label, 231, 232
subtries, 232
successor-of-in-or, 239
sum, 173
sum-integers-from-to, 38
sum-of-cubes, 38, 120
sum-of-digits, 121, 375
sum-of-divisors, 58, 60
sum-of-first, 36, 120
sum-of-powers, 38
sum-of-squares, 38, 120
summarize-image, 274
super, 584–586
Super-Lean Instruction Machine, 334
superclass, 489
survives?, 66, 68
symbol, 138
symbol->string, 473, 541
symbol-append, 541
symbol-comparator, 473
symbol-list-comparator, 473
symbol?, 282
synchronized, 623–625, 629, 633, 637, 644
syntactic category, 280
syntax, 279
syntax, superficial, 291
syntax-ok?, 287
System, 586, 592

table, two-dimensional, 390, 391, 412
table-fill!, 391
table-find, 259, 260
table-height, 391, 392
table-ref, 391, 392
table-set!, 391, 392
table-width, 391, 392
tag, type, 255, 258, 259
tagged-datum, 255
tagged-movies, 255
tail, 168
tail, 245, 247
take, person/, 556
take-all-of-first-nonempty, 159
take-one-from-random-pile, 159
target address, 339
tax, 12
terminal, 281
terminate, 632
termination, 30, 31, 114
test, 12
test-bb, 16, 18
TextField, 601
the-only-element-in, 197
Therac 25, 622
Θ (big theta), 81, 107
thing-class, 544, 545, 548, 549
thing/become-owned-by, 550
thing/become-unowned, 549
thing/init, 549
thing/owned?, 549
thing/owner, 549
this, 493, 583
Thread, 618
thread, 617
three-dimensional vector, 162
thrifty-item-list-class, 514
throws, 627
TileActionListener, 603, 606
time, 162
title, 254, 256, 259
titles-of-movies-satisfying, 190
together-copies-of, 110–112
token, 422
tokenize, 426, 433, 434
tolerance, 64
top-level definition, 304
top-minus, 429, 435, 439, 444
total-price, item-list/, 488, 498, 513

total-size, 143, 152
totalPrice, 590
transform-point, 265
traversal, post-order, 284
tree recursion, 83, 95
tree traversal, 218–220
tree, binary, 221
tree, binary search, 214, 453, 463, 466, 474
tree, complete, 222
tree, expression, 227, 284
tree, ordered, 229
tree, positional, 229
tree, ranked binary, 463
tree, red-black, 453, 455, 456, 462, 463, 472,
    474, 485
tri-block, 104
triangle, 99
trie, 230, 242
trigger, registry/, 547
trigger-times, registry/, 547
triple, 118
troll-class, 569
true, 595
truth value, 12
try, 597
Turing machine, 116
Turing test, 117, 203
Turing, Alan, 116–117, 128, 203, 204
turkey-servings, 13
turn-into-frog, 560
turnable image, 480
two-dimensional table, 390, 391, 412
two-factorials, 354
two-part list viewpoint, 168
type, 258, 582
type, 255
type checking, 157, 158
type tag, 255, 258, 259
type-name, 258
type-operation-table, 258

UML, 489–491, 518, 527, 529, 544, 545,
    580, 602, 607, 608
unchecked-object/set-class!, 523
uncomputable, 114, 118
unconditional jump, 345
uncons, 326
Unified Modeling Language, 489–491, 518,
    527, 529, 544, 545, 580, 602, 607, 608

union-set, 275
universality principle, 278
unix-programmers-manual, 563
unparse, 312, 313
upper-endpoint, 161
user interface, 563

vacuous, 440
value, 5, 430
value, 236, 464
value oriented, 362
value->labeled-value, 237
valueEntered, 639
values->trie, 235, 238
values-in-trie, 235
values-with-first-label, 238
vector, 333, 363
vector, three-dimensional, 162
vector-copy!, 497
vector-fill!, 385, 646
vector-length, 363
vector-ref, 363
vector-set!, 363
verbalize-list, 553, 558
verification function, 84
verify, 85
version control, 400
virtual method, 525
void, 584

wait, 628, 629
waiting, busy, 628, 643
waitUntilEnabled, 626–629

walk-count, 380, 383
walk-count-subproblem, 384
ways-to-factor, 100
ways-to-factor-using-no-smaller-than, 100
Web, World Wide, 610
Whacky Gator, 184–186, 398
which-subtree, 465
while, 595
widget, 481
width, 263
wild card, 195
witch-class, 544, 559, 569
witch/act, 560, 569
witch/curse, 560
with, 303
with-output-to-file, 272, 646
wizard-class, 544, 559, 560, 570
wizard/act, 560
word, 342
word size, 342
World Wide Web, 610
write, 290, 343
write-with-at, 321

x-coord, 162, 163, 263

y-coord, 162, 163, 263
year-made, 254

z-coord, 162
zero-out-vector!, 365